D0472618

Baedeker's
GERMANY

A SPECTRUM BOOK

PRENTICE-HALL, Inc., Englewood Cliffs, New Jersey 07632

Cover picture: Neuschwanstein Castle in the Allgäu

143 colour photographs
75 maps and plans
1 large road map

Text:
Rosemarie Arnold (history)
Walter R. Arnold (music)
Rudolf Rautenstrauch (Germany from A to Z)
Gerald Sawade (climate)
Christine Wessely (art)

Editorial work:
Baedeker Stuttgart
English language: Alec Court

Cartography:
Huber & Oberländer, Munich

Design and layout:
Creativ+Druck (Kolb), Stuttgart

Conception and general direction:
Dr Peter Baumgarten,
Baedeker Stuttgart

English translation:
James Hogarth

© Baedeker Stuttgart
Original German edition

© The Automobile Association
United Kingdom and Ireland

© Jarrold and Sons Ltd
English Language edition Worldwide

Licensed user:
Mairs Geographischer Verlag GmbH & Co.,
Ostfildern-Kemnat bei Stuttgart

Reproductions:
Gölz Repro-Service GmbH,
Ludwigsburg

The name *Baedeker* is a registered trademark

Source of illustrations:

Most of the colour photographs were provided by local, municipal, district, regional and provincial tourist information offices and by resort management authorities. Others:

Deutsche Presse-Agentur, GmbH (dpa), Frankfurt/Main (cover picture, pp. 45, 49).
Zentrale Farbbild Agentur GmbH (ZEFA), Düsseldorf (pp. 50, 51, 93, 102, 103, 124, 263, 264).
Bildarchiv Hans Huber KG, Garmisch-Partenkirchen (pp. 7, 72, 119, 132, 280).
Photo Hartmann, Badenweiler (pp. 24, 84).
Herrmann & Kraemer, Garmisch-Partenkirchen (p. 38).
Herzog-August-Bibliothek, Wolfenbüttel (p. 39).
Rainer Gaertner, Bergisch Gladbach (p. 57).
Emil Bauer, Bamberg (p. 71).
Mainauverwaltung (p. 101).
M. Jeiter, Aachen (pp. 90, 244).
Ars Liturgica, Maria Laach (p. 115).
Bernward-Verlag, Hildesheim (p. 152).
Hans-Jürgen Wohlfahrt, Ratzeburg (p. 169).
Toni Schneiders, Lindau/Bodensee (p. 174).
Joachim Kinkelin, Worms (p. 181).
Leonore Ander, Ottobrunn/München (p. 193).
Peter Nahm, Ostfildern (p. 198).
Georg Quedens, Norddorf/Amrum (pp. 203, 204).
Landratsamt Erbach/Odenwald (p. 209).
Nord Consulting GmbH, Weissenhäuser Strand (p. 69).
Ernst Baumann, Bad Reichenhall (p. 219).
Dr Kurt Struve, Westerland/Sylt (p. 241).
W. G. Jöst, Weinheim (p. 261).
Allianz-Archiv (p. 262).
Knab-Verlag, Schonach (p. 299).
Prof. Dr A. Herold, Gerbrunn (p. 304).

How to Use this Guide

The principal towns and areas of tourist interest are described in alphabetical order. The names of other places referred to under these general headings can be found in the very full Index.

Following the tradition established by Karl Baedeker in 1844, features of particular interest and hotels and restaurants of particular quality are distinguished by either one or two asterisks.

The abbreviations used should give no difficulty. In the lists of hotels b.=beds, rest.=restaurant, SB=indoor swimming bath and SP=outdoor swimming pool. Evang., in reference to a church, means that it belongs to one of the Protestant (*evangelisch*) denominations.

In the town plans pedestrian precincts are shown by shading. The names of buildings, etc., are generally given in their German form: the meanings of common topographical terms and elements in place-names can be found by reference to the Glossary on p. 273. In the text English forms are used whenever possible; but some German names would appear clumsy and perhaps meaningless in translation, and some terms (like Schloss and Stiftskirche, to mention only two of the commonest) cannot always be reduced to a single English term. Here again the Glossary will be found helpful.

The symbol ⓘ indicates addresses from which further information can be obtained.

Notes on Measurement

Europe uses the metric system of measurement. Since this is the only system you will encounter in your travels, many of the measurements in this guide are expressed in metric terms. Conversion is easy. Multiply metres by 3·3 to get the approximate dimension in feet. A kilometre (1000 m) is approximately 0·62 mile.
To convert European Centigrade temperatures to Fahrenheit, multiply by 9/5 and add 32°.

In a time of rapid change it is difficult to ensure that all the information given is entirely accurate and up to date and the possibility of error can never be entirely eliminated. Although the publishers can accept no responsibility for inaccuracies and omissions they are always grateful for corrections and suggestions for improvement.

Printed in Great Britain by Jarrold & Sons Ltd, Norwich ★★★★★

0-13-055830-3 : Paperback
0-13-055848-6 : Hard Cover

This guidebook forms part of a completely new series of the world-famous Baedeker Guides to Europe.

Each volume is the result of long and careful preparation and, true to the traditions of Baedeker, is designed in every respect to meet the needs and expectations of the modern traveller.

The name of Baedeker has long been identified in the field of guidebooks with reliable, comprehensive and up-to-date information, prepared by expert writers who work from detailed, first-hand knowledge of the country concerned. Following a tradition that goes back over 150 years to the date when Karl Baedeker published the first of his handbooks for travellers, these guides have been planned to give the tourist all the essential information about the country and its inhabitants: where to go, how to get there and what to see. Baedeker's account of a country was always based on his personal observation and experience during his travels in that country. This tradition of writing a guidebook in the field rather than at an office desk has been maintained by Baedeker ever since.

Lavishly illustrated with superb colour photographs and numerous specially drawn maps and street plans of the major towns, the new Baedeker Guides concentrate on making available to the modern traveller all the information he needs in a format that is both attractive and easy to follow. For every place that appears in the gazetteer, the principal features of architectural, artistic and historic interest are described, as are its main areas of scenic beauty. Selected hotels and restaurants are also included. Features of exceptional merit are indicated by either one or two asterisks.

A special section at the end of each book contains practical information, details of leisure activities and useful addresses. The separate road map will prove an invaluable aid to planning your route and your travel within the country.

Contents

Introduction
to Germany

The Zugspitze group above Garmisch-Partenkirchen

Federal Republic of Germany

Land	Capital	Area (sq. km.)	Population	Land	Capital	Area (sq. km.)	Population
Baden-Württemberg	Stuttgart	35,751	9,288,000	Niedersachsen	Hanover	47,415	7,267,000
Bayern	Munich	70,547	10,959,000	Nordrhein-Westfalen	Düsseldorf	34,069	17,046,000
Bremen		404	691,000	Rheinland-Pfalz	Mainz	19,839	3,641,000
Hamburg		748	1,637,000	Saarland	Saarbrücken	2,568	1,063,000
Hessen	Wiesbaden	21,113	5,612,000	Schleswig-Holstein	Kiel	15,696	2,619,000
West Berlin		480	1,889,000	Federal Republic	Bonn	248,150	59,823,000

After the collapse of Germany at the end of the Second World War the former Reich was split up into the three western zones occupied by United States, British and French forces, the eastern zone occupied by the Soviet Union and the areas under Polish and Soviet administration east of the Oder-Neisse line; the capital, Berlin, was similarly divided by the Allies into four sectors. On 7 September 1949, under the "Basic Law" (Grundgesetz) adopted by an elected constituent assembly, the Parliamentary Council, the western occupation zones became the **Federal Republic of Germany**, whose tourist and other attractions, along with those of West Berlin, are described in this Guide.

The Federal Republic consists of the ten *Länder* or provinces shown on the map opposite – Baden-Württemberg, Bavaria (Bayern), Bremen, Hamburg, Hesse (Hessen), Lower Saxony (Niedersachsen), North Rhineland-Westphalia (Nordrhein-Westfalen), Rhineland-Palatinate (Rheinland-Pfalz), the Saar, Schleswig-Holstein and the two cities of Bremen and Hamburg are divided into *Regierungsbezirke* (regions), the *Bezirke* into *Kreise* (districts).

The Second World War caused enormous destruction, particularly in the large cities but also in many smaller places. Reconstruction went forward with great energy, however, and all war damage has now been made good. Many historic old buildings have been re-erected in their original style, others have been replaced by new buildings. The country's communications, already well developed before the war, have been further improved in the post-war period and now offer visitors abundant scope for exploring its many beauties by whatever means of transport they prefer.

Germany is a tourist country of inexhaustible variety, with an ever-changing pattern of scenery extending from the sea to the mountains, from the lowland regions along the North Sea and Baltic coasts by way of the rolling forest-clad uplands to the Bavarian Alps.
Human habitation in this country takes a similar variety of forms, ranging from the isolated farm-house, the clustered houses of a large village, the frowning medieval castle and the old walled town to the modern industrial city with its carefully planned housing areas. Many small towns have preserved the aspect of past centuries, many cities have brought new life into the old town centres. In the north handsome old brick-built houses bear witness to the wealth of the Hanseatic towns which once ruled the seas. Farther south the old free Imperial cities, princely capitals and episcopal cities have their splendid cathedrals, palaces and town halls to proclaim in the stone language of architectural styles the changes in human attitudes and in economic

importance which time has brought, while great expanses of open country and countless holiday and health resorts offer recreation and relaxation to those seeking relief from the strains and stresses of modern life.

The life of the North German **COASTAL REGIONS** is conditioned by the sea. The sea deposited the material which formed the *Marschen* (salt-marshes, fenland) and consumed the land it had created in wild storm tides which in earlier centuries carved out the Dollart and Jade Bay; it tempted man to embark on its waters and range over the oceans; and sea fishing and sea-borne trade still play the major part in the economy of these regions.

Along the North Sea coast the *tides* raise and lower the water level by between 2 and 3·5 m, and, advancing up the funnel mouths of the Elbe and the Weser, allow seagoing ships to sail some 100 km inland to Hamburg and 70 km to Bremen. In the port of Hamburg the difference between high and low tide is still of the order of 2 m. The wind carries the moisture and the almost frost-free winter temperatures of the sea deep inland, and when it rises into a storm it dominates the scene both at sea and on land.

The flat North Sea coast is protected by dikes, in front of which extends the *Wattenmeer*, an area of shallows ranging in width between 5 and 30 km from which the sea retreats at low tide. Stretches of this are diked to form polders of new fenland.

The ancient coastline is marked by the **North Frisian Islands**, mainly consisting of expanses of sandy soil (*Geest*), on which the wind has piled the sand up into great dunes, and the Halligen, now partly diked, the surviving fragments of a larger area of fenland. The **East Frisian Islands** have extensive beaches and dunes. 70 km off the mouth of the Elbe is **Heligoland**, with its red cliffs towering to a height of 60 m out of the sea.

The *lowlands between the Ems and the Elbe* reach a height of barely 40 m 100 km from the coast, with only the occasional hill. There are numerous shipping canals which carry heavy traffic. North-east of the Elbe the edge of the glaciers moving westward in the last Ice Age left a terminal moraine of boulder clay which now runs across Schleswig-Holstein from north to south-east as a range of hills partly covered with forest. To the west of these hills is a sandy and unproductive expanse of *Geest*, while to the east is a fertile region of boulder clay. Here the ice has gouged out long troughs which now contain lakes or, on the Baltic coast, form long fjord-like inlets (*Förden*) with steep wooded shores which reach deep inland and have led to the establishment of ports.

The landscape pattern is set by the contrasts between the fenlands, the sandy *Geest* and the expanses of marshland. The flat *fenlands* form an almost continuous strip up to 20 km wide along the North Sea coast and the estuaries of the rivers. Dark-coloured clays deposited by the sea and the rivers form a fertile soil which consists mainly of grazing for the black and white cattle. The farmhouses and villages lie along the edge of the *Geest* or on artificial mounds (*Warften* or *Wurten*) which provide protection against storm tides.

The *Geest* is the undulating stretch of land whose green and yellow slopes rise above the fenland. It consists of glacial sands and provides grazing for sheep and arable land, with some areas of thin woodland and fields of grain.

In the low-lying depressions there are large areas of *marshland*, parts of which have been brought into cultivation. Straggling marshland villages extend along the countless canals, used for transporting the peat which is cut here for fuel. The austere beauty of this region was discovered only at the end of the 19th century by the Worpswede school of artists.

The INHABITANTS are cautious and reserved by nature, to the point of seeming almost withdrawn, but holding firmly to their own ways and sticking to their word. The Low German dialect (Plattdeutsch) is used both in conversation and in writing; the distinctive old Frisian language is dying out and is still spoken only in the marsh-ringed Saterland area.

The traditional FARMHOUSES are long single-storey buildings under a high-pitched roof thatched with straw or reeds. The rooms are laid out round the hall (Diele) in a pattern which varies between Lower Saxony and East Friesland, with a parlour (Pesel) which is often very handsomely furnished.

VILLAGE LAYOUT varies from place to place. East of the Weser large irregularly built villages predominate, west of the river separate farms. In the fenland and marshland regions long straggling villages are the normal pattern, in East Holstein small round villages.

Schleswig-Holstein, the most northerly of the *Länder*, is washed by two seas, with its principal coastline facing the Baltic. Here the *Förden* cut deep into the land between ridges of wooded hills, forming excellent natural harbours. Along the flat west coast new land is continually being wrested from the sea by the construction of dikes.

The capital of Schleswig-Holstein, **Kiel**, with the imposing Naval Memorial at Laboe, is also a great sailing centre, notable for the regattas of "Kiel Week". Visitors to the resorts on Kiel and Lübeck Bays should not fail to explore the beautiful scenery of the "*Switzerland of Holstein*", with its lakes and forests.

Lübeck, in medieval times chief town of the powerful Hanse, possesses in its churches, its magnificent town hall, its sturdy Holsten Gate and its fine burghers' houses splendid evidence of its great past and impressive examples of North German brick-built architecture. On the fjord-like Schlei lies the old town of *Schleswig*, whose cathedral contains the great Bordesholm Altar.

From *Flensburg*, Germany's most northerly town, with many fine old buildings, it is well worth making the trip to the charming little town and seaside resort of *Glücksburg*, with one of the finest moated castles in Germany. On the west coast there are the towns of *Meldorf*, with the "Cathedral of Dithmarschen", *Heide* and *Husum*, Theodor Storm's "grey town by the sea".

The **North Sea islands** lie in a wide arc off the coasts of Schleswig-Holstein (the North Frisian Islands) and East Friesland (the East Frisian Islands). The fashionable island of *Sylt*, linked with the mainland by a railway causeway, Föhr and Amrum, Norderney and Borkum, the Halligen and numerous smaller dune-fringed islands are filled with life and activity by the holidaymakers who flock there in summer. There are pleasant boat trips to *Heligoland*, Germany's only rocky offshore island, which has recovered from its heavy wartime destruction and become a popular seaside resort.

The Hanseatic towns of Hamburg and Bremen are the leading German commercial ports handling overseas trade. **Hamburg**, Germany's "gateway to the world", more than 100 km from the North Sea, fascinates visitors not only with its port installations and the shipping on the Elbe, but also with its elegant townscape round the Alster basin, its imposing business houses, its carefully restored old districts and its great range of cultural activities. From here excursions can be made to the *Altes Land* with its springtime profusion of blossom, the fertile Vierlande, the Saxon Forest, with Bismarck's tomb at Friedrichsruh, and the Lüneburg Heath.

Bremen, whose overseas trade is handled mainly by *Bremerhaven,* still preserves the aspect of a dignified old Hanseatic town. In front of the beautiful Town Hall stands the famous statue of Roland, a medieval symbol of the city's independent legal status and market rights.

The **NORTH-WEST GERMAN LOW-LANDS** were covered during the Ice Age with massive deposits of boulder clay. They consist of three very different parts – the coastal region, the Lüneburg Heath and the area of heath and moorland between the Weser and the Ems to the west.

Taken in its widest sense, the name of Lüneburg Heath applies to the ridge of *Geest* which extends between the lower Elbe and the valley of the Aller and the Weser. The real **Lüneburg Heath**, however – an infertile expanse of *Geest* with great stretches of heather and juniper bushes and areas of beautiful deciduous and coniferous forests – lies west of the town of Lüneburg from which it takes its name. The best impression of

The beach on the East Frisian island of Spiekeroog

this rather sombre landscape in its natural state is to be found in the nature reserves round the Wilseder Berg (169 m: the highest point in the Heath, with splendid wide-ranging views), at Hermann Löns's grave near Fallingbostel and in the Südheide round Hermannsburg.

The ECONOMY of the Heath has changed in recent years. Much of it has been brought into agricultural use, and to the traditional sheep- and cattle-farming, now practised on a much smaller scale, have been added bee-keeping and the rearing of carp and trout. Industry and the holiday and weekend tourist trade are now increasing in importance and large parts of the Heath are used as military training areas.

The eastern part of the Lüneburg Heath is occupied by the **Wendland** area, which consists partly of fertile fenland and partly of sandy hills like *Göhrde* (noted for its mushrooms) and **Drawehn**.

To the south-west of the Heath is the lower *Aller-Weser valley* with its fertile river fens. Among particular tourist attractions in this area are the beautiful bird park at Walsrode and the large "Safari Park" at Hodenhagen with its African big game.

On the edge of the Heath, well worth a visit, are the old salt-working and trading town of **Lüneburg**, with fine old brick buildings which bear witness to its Hanseatic days, and the former Ducal residence of **Celle** with its many-gabled Schloss and its old town of half-timbered houses.

To the west of the Lüneburg Heath, between the Weser and the Ems, is a great expanse of heath and moorland, a flat landscape varied only by low hills of *Geest* like the *Dammer Berge* and the ridge of the Hohe Geest. Once a fifth of this area was covered with marshland, but much of it has now been brought into cultivation. There are two different types of country here – the "low marshes" (*Niedermoore*), with stretches of stagnant water like the *Steinhuder Meer* and the *Dümmer* which are slowly drying out round the edges, and the "high bogs" (*Hochmoore*), on which sphagnum moss establishes itself on beds of sand, absorbs great quantities of water and extends in all directions. Most of the marshland in North-West Germany is of this latter type. The marshland landscape is bleak and featureless. In the drier parts there are frequently a few isolated birch-trees as well as heather; in the low-lying areas an occasional windmill relieves the monotony of the scene. A particularly fine stretch of the Heath is to be seen round *Ahlhorn*.

The INHABITANTS are of Low German stock. They are of stolid disposition, good judges of their own capacity and reluctant to undertake anything they cannot be sure of achieving, but persistent in carrying through what they do undertake.

This independence of mind is reflected in the FARMHOUSES of Lower Saxony with their thatched straw roofs and their surrounding clumps of oak-trees. Everything is under one roof, with the living quarters and farm offices set round the central *Diele*. West of the Weser the isolated farmhouse predominates, east of the river the large irregular village. The Wendland area has small round villages, huddled together for protection; the fenlands have long single-street villages.

The old TRADITIONAL COSTUMES have practically disappeared except in Bückeburg, where the farmers' wives still go to market in their black winged caps, red skirts and brightly coloured bodices.

In **Lower Saxony**, the lowland region between the Elbe and the Ems which extends from the coast to the verge of the uplands, the larger towns have also much to attract the tourist.

Hanover, capital of the *Land* of Lower Saxony, is an entirely modern city, as a result mainly of its boldly conceived reconstruction after severe war damage. The famous Herrenhausen gardens recall its great days as a princely capital.

Two towns used to vie with one another in their wealth of well-preserved late Gothic and Renaissance half-timbered buildings and Romanesque and Gothic churches – the old Ducal residence of **Braunschweig** (Brunswick), the town of Henry the Lion, with consummate examples of Romanesque architecture in its Cathedral, Gothic in the Town Hall in its old town and Renaissance in its Gewandhaus, and **Hildesheim**, where Romanesque church art achieved a flowering hardly equalled anywhere else in Germany. They are still well worth a visit, since most of their important buildings have been preserved or restored.

The **HARZ AND ITS BORDERLAND** lie along the north-western edge of the German coastal uplands, made up of both sedimentary (sandstone and limestone) and igneous rocks (granite and basalt) which were folded in a north-west to south-east direction, eroded into an undulating plateau and finally carved up by rivers into a number of separate groups of hills.

The **Northern Harz Borderland** is an area of great geological interest. Here the folded and eroded hills lie deep under the surface, overlaid by deposits of salt left by the ancient Permian sea and massive beds of rock belonging to the following Mesozoic era, like the extensive reserves of iron ore in the *Salzgitter* industrial area. Between the troughs of arable land extend wooded ridges of harder rock like the Lappwald, the Elm and the Asse. At *Helmstedt*, on the frontier with the German Democratic Republic, is a large field of lignite.

The **Harz** thrusts out like a bastion from the northern edge of the central uplands into the lowlands. It is made up of slates, greywackes and limestones which have been penetrated and altered by volcanic rocks (granites, porphyry). In the *West Harz* (Upper Harz) the old eroded landscape has survived as a gently undulating residual plateau at heights of between 600 and 700 m not much broken up by valleys. Above this rise a few flat-topped hills and ridges of harder rock, the highest points in the range, reaching 1142 m in the *Brocken* (within the GDR). The fringes of the hills are deeply indented by valleys, some of which have impressive rock formations and sheer cliff faces.

Apart from mining and tourism the economy of the region depends mainly on forestry, since two-thirds of the Harz is covered with forest. Important also are cattle-rearing (the brown Harz breed) and dairying (Harz cheese).

MINING of silver, copper, lead, zinc and iron was at one time of major importance in the economy of the Harz. As early as 968 a large lode of silver was discovered on the Rammelsberg near Goslar, and from about 990 this was properly worked. By the 16th century mining had spread to more than 30 places in the western Harz, and this period saw the establishment of the seven free mining towns of Grund, Wildemann, Lautenthal, Clausthal, Zellerfeld, St Andreasberg and Altenau as well as other mining places. After a period of decline during the Thirty Years War mining made fresh strides in the early 18th century, and in 1775 a School of Mining (later a Mining Academy; now the University of Technology) was founded in Clausthal. In the 19th century the mines of the Upper Harz began to be worked out, and nowadays only the Rammelsberg and the Bad Grund area are of any importance.

In addition to the large irregular villages found in narrow valleys the straggling one-street village is common in the Harz. The farmhouses follow the pattern of the Franconian half-timbered house: in this well-wooded region timber construction was the norm.

With its range of scenic beauty concentrated within a small area and the old-world towns on its borders, the **Harz** offers particular attractions to the inhabitants of the large cities of north-western Germany. Only the western part lies within the Federal Republic; the Eastern Harz, with the Brocken, is in the German Democratic Republic. Visitors who go to *Braunlage, Hahnenklee* or *St.*

Andreasberg for the mountain air or to such resorts as *Bad Harzburg, Bad Lauterberg* and *Bad Sachsa* have an opportunity also of visiting the beautiful little towns on the fringes of the Harz – **Goslar** with its numerous interesting old buildings, including the Kaiserpfalz, the largest Romanesque palace in Germany, or *Herzberg* and *Osterode* on the south-western edge of the range. The western part of the scenically beautiful Harz-Hochstrasse (Harz Ridgeway) leads to the hill town of *Clausthal-Zellerfeld*, the little climatic resort of *Wildemann* and the attractive *Bad Grund.*

Of the numerous river valleys of the Harz the rocky *Oker valley*, with the Oker dam, is the most beautiful. And from Braunlage there is an attractive tour through the beautiful *Oder valley* to the Oder dam, framed in wooded hills, and on from there to Herzberg.

West of the Harz, to the north of a line from Herzberg to Holzminden, is the **Leinebergland**, a region of varied scenery mainly given up to agriculture, centred on the interesting town of *Einbeck*. To the west of the lower Leine is round Hils basin, enclosed by three hills – the sandstone massif of Hils, Ith with its picturesque limestone crags, and Külf. This has on its north side the *Osterwald*, a range of hard white sandstone hills in the Weserbergland, and to the north-west the broad *Deister* ridge with its coal-mines. To the west of this are the *Bückeberge*, which also contain coal, and to the south of both Deister and the Bückeberge is *Süntel*, the beginning of the long chain of Weser hills, the northern ridge of which, the Weser-Wiehengebirge, peters out in the lowlands near Bramsche, north-west of Osnabrück. To the east of the River Leine rise the limestone uplands of the *Sieben Berge*, covered with deciduous forest, and north of this is the Hildesheim Forest, with the town of *Hildesheim* on its northern edge.

South of the Herzberg-Holzminden line is the southern Hanover plateau, a region of Bunter sandstone and Muschelkalk limestone, horizontally bedded, extending to the Weser. Within a bend on the upper Leine lies the gently rolling *Unteres Eichsfeld*, an agricultural area at a height of some 300 m. To the north of this the *Göttingen Forest*, with the university town of **Göttingen**, extends above the fertile valley of the middle Leine; farther west are the wooded hills of the Solling and Bramwald.

At Münden the **Weser valley** turns north, forming the eastern boundary of Westphalia. At the *Porta Westfalica* near the cathedral city of *Minden* it passes through the northern ranges of hills into the open lowlands. The picturesque winding valley, with its wooded slopes rising to 300 m above the valley bottom, has a unifying character which is reflected in the ancient little towns and monastic houses (the most important of which is the former Benedictine abbey of Corvey) and in the architectural forms of the so-called "Weser Renaissance" style. The Weser valley is also the country of such legendary characters as the Pied Piper of *Hamelin*, Eisenbart the wonder doctor of *Münden* and the mendacious Baron Münchhausen of *Bodenwerder*, and of the 19th century novelist Wilhelm Raabe of *Eschershausen*.

WESERBERGLAND extends round the east and north-east sides of the Münster lowlands. At its eastern end is Velmerstot (468 m), the highest peak in the **Teutoburg Forest**, whose wooded ridges extend north-west for over 100 km to peter out in the lowlands of the Ems valley. On the east side of these ridges, with the pleasant old residence town of *Detmold* − starting point of a visit to the Hermannsdenkmal and the *Externsteine* − and the old linen-weaving town of *Bielefeld*, begins a hilly region which, under various names, extends east beyond the Weser. The southern part of this region is of varied character, partly forest and partly arable land; its northern edge, under the name of Wiehengebirge, runs west from the Weser at Minden to taper away in the plain north-west of the old episcopal and Hanseatic city of **Osnabrück**. This hilly region contains numerous spas, among them *Bad Pyrmont, Bad Salzuflen* and *Bad Oeynhausen*.

MÜNSTERLAND, lying within the *Land* of **North Rhineland-Westphalia**, extends south-east between the Teutoburg Forest and the Sauerland in a wide expanse of lowlands. This level region, interspersed only by a few groups of low hills, is a country of fertile soil, mainly devoted to agriculture, which has given Westphalia such delicacies as its pumpernickel bread, its hams, its Münsterland *Korn* (corn brandy) and its *Steinhäger* (juniper brandy). The farmers live in imposing houses, which have often belonged to the same family for centuries.

Many old moated castles (Nordkirchen, Raesfeld, Gemen, etc.) and manor-houses belonging to noble families have been preserved. Among them is Haus Hülshoff, birthplace of the poetess Annette von Droste-Hülshoff (1797− 1848).

In the western Münsterland there are patches of marshland and heath; in the eastern part, north of the old episcopal city of *Paderborn*, is the *Senne*, formerly an area of wind-blown sand.

In the middle lies the episcopal city of **Münster**, chief town of the Münsterland and an important traffic junction This old provincial capital shows itself to be a centre of spiritual life by the number of its churches, and the Baroque town houses of the local nobility reflect an atmosphere of gracious living.

Soest is an architectural gem, with its well-preserved and unspoiled old town and its beautiful old churches.

The 272 km long *Dortmund-Ems Canal* provides a navigable waterway from the industrial region to the port of Emden.

The unity of the Westphalian landscape results from the strong sense of community felt by its PEOPLE, without the backing of any political unity as a state. The Westphalians are the descendants of the old western Saxons and speak a Low German dialect. The *Rheinfranken* (Rhineland Franconians) who live in the south-west belong to the Central German linguistic zone. The Westphalians are naturally cautious, straightforward and reliable, strong-willed and persistent, combining a contemplative turn of mind with a racy and often robust sense of humour.

SAUERLAND (actually "south land", the southern part of Westphalia) occupies the most northerly part of the Rhenish Uplands. The predominant rocks are slates and greywackes, with occasional occurrences of Devonian limestones containing remarkable caves like the Attahöhle and the Dechenhöhle. The landscape pattern of the eastern Sauerland is set by the **Rothaargebirge** with its low round-topped hills, reaching their highest point in the Kahler Asten (841 m) near Winterberg. To the west the land falls, half of it forest-covered, broken up by picturesque winding valleys, the largest of which are the Ruhr valley in the north and the Sieg valley in the south. The most westerly ridges of hills, historically belonging to the Rhineland, are known as the **Bergisches Land**. The water power of the rivers, used at an early stage for industrial purposes, is now harnessed by numerous dams, which have added a new element to the beauty of the scenery. The Sauerland with its wooded countryside is a popular playground (Arnsberg, Brilon, Winterberg) in both summer and winter, particularly with the inhabitants of the industrial area.

Westphalia and the Lower Rhineland occupy the area between the Weser (from Münden to Minden) in the east and the Dutch frontier in the west. They lie partly in the North German lowlands, with their great expanses of arable land and their stretches of marshland and heath, partly in the uplands, with their wooded hills and picturesque well-watered valleys, and partly in the wide valley of the mighty Rhine. In sharp contrast to these landscapes of tranquil charm with their ancient little towns is the industrial region of Rhineland-Westphalia, which within a relatively small space in the west central part of the area overlies all three of these natural landscapes and forces its own imprint on them.

The **RHINELAND-WESTPHALIAN INDUSTRIAL REGION**, for long one of the largest concentrations of industry in Europe, extends over the south-western edge of the Münsterland, the north-

western part of the Sauerland and the adjoining Rhine valley almost to the Dutch frontier. In the centre of the region is a landscape of urban type covering some thousands of square kilometres, within which there is room not only for mighty industrial complexes, houses for a population of some millions and a dense network of busy traffic routes but also for a surprising amount of natural scenery.

The basis for the large-scale development of industry was provided by the availability of COAL as a source of energy. At first the coal was worked by opencast methods in the seams which outcropped in the Ruhr valley; then from the 18th century onwards the seams had to be followed northward at ever greater depths. From the middle of the 19th century, with large mining companies increasingly dominating the industry, output rose rapidly. Fierce competition and economic crises led to amalgamations which produced very large industrial concerns.

The IRON AND STEEL INDUSTRY was closely bound up with coal. Smelting with coal began in 1784, and about 1830 the seams of black-band ironstone between the coal measures began to be worked. From the end of the 1860s iron-ore from the Lahn, Sieg and Dill region was also used; from 1878 it was brought in from Lorraine; until increasing demand eventually led to the import of ore from many different countries. The output of the iron- and steelworks is processed by countless firms, ranging from heavy industry to small hardware producers. Other industries less directly dependent on the mines and steelworks

Air view of the Biggesee

include the textile industry based in Wuppertal and west of the Rhine, and the chemical industry for which, nevertheless, coal is an important raw material. For several decades coal production has been declining. There are plans to increase the use of coal in transporting energy (heating plants).

The towns of the industrial region, having developed rapidly in relatively recent times, present an almost entirely modern aspect; but they do not now consist solely of blast-furnaces, pithead gear and factory chimneys.

Essen, centre of the Ruhr coalfield, has one of the oldest churches in Germany, and **Dortmund** possesses not only one of Europe's largest sports halls, the Westfalenhalle, but a number of medieval buildings.

Düsseldorf, capital of the *Land* of North Rhineland-Westphalia, a city of fashion and of art, holds out many attractions to the visitor.

Duisburg has the largest inland port in Europe. *Wuppertal* is famous for its overhead railway.

The **LOWER RHINELANDS** are a down-faulted basin between the Belgian and Dutch frontier and the north-western edge of the Rhenish Uplands, a gently undulating region of loess soils on which wheat and sugar-beet are grown. The pattern of habitation is based mainly on villages and towns of some size. In the western part of the region is the important coal and industrial area round Aachen. **Aachen** itself, the most westerly city in the Federal Republic, is notable not only for its Cathedral, the most important surviving Carolingian building in Germany, but also as a spa and congress centre.

In the northern half of the basin of the Lower Rhine is that part of the Rhineland-Westphalian industrial region which lies on the left bank of the river, with coal-mines at *Homberg* and *Moers* and a varied range of industry, notably the textile industry of *Krefeld* and *Mönchengladbach.*

The **Lower Rhine** in the strict sense is the continuation of the Lower Rhinelands to the north-west and the Münsterland to the south-west. It is an area of sandy soil and coniferous forest; only the immediate river valley has fertile water-meadows. Habitation takes the form of individual farmsteads and small and ancient towns like *Xanten*, the Roman Colonia Ulpia Traiana and the home of Siegfried, the hero of Germanic legend.

The *Land of* **HESSE** extends from the Rhine in the west to the frontier of the German Democratic Republic (Thuringia) in the east and from the Neckar valley at Heidelberg in the south to the Weser bend at Bad Karlshafen in the north. It is a region of very varied character falling within the central upland region of Germany. The close juxtaposition of barren and largely forest-covered uplands and fertile depressions gives the country an intimate and attractive character which is also reflected in the varied patterns of life and culture of its inhabitants.

The **Hessian Uplands** were by no means discovered by the modern tourist trade. From time immemorial the Hessian Depression, lying between the Rhenish Uplands and the hills round the Fulda and Werra valleys, has been a major traffic route between North Germany and the Upper Rhine, and it was largely on account of this that during the Middle Ages the territorial rivalries of the ruling princes focused on this region. In our own day Hesse, apart from the higher areas of forest-covered hills, makes a major contribution to the German economy.

The western part of Hesse is occupied by the Taunus and Westerwald hills, which form part of the Rhenish Uplands. After being upfolded at an early stage of geological history in a south-westerly and north-easterly direction, these hills were then eroded into a rolling plateau area. The main ridge of the **Taunus**, a range of isolated hills of grey and white quartzites with a steep scarp on the south side, rears above the Rhine-Main plain, reaching its highest point in the Grosser Feldberg (881 m). To the north the hills slope gradually down, forming a plateau which is slashed by numerous tributaries of the Lahn. North of the Lahn the Taunus runs into the **Westerwald**, a rolling plateau mainly composed of Palaeozoic slates with a few rounded basaltic hills rising to a slightly greater height. This region, bounded on the north by the industrialised *Sieg valley* and on the south by the *Lahn valley*, which is particularly attractive between Limburg and Bad Ems, has an average height of between 300 and 600 m and reaches its highest point in the Fuchskaute (657 m). The western part has extensive stretches of forest; the eastern part is sparsely wooded and has a fairly raw climate. In the *Kannenbäckerland* to the south-west the rich deposits of clay gave rise to a notable pottery industry. The Westerwald is a region of small agricutural holdings, with the working of basalt, clay and lignite also making their contribution to the subsistence of the population (who are not all of Hessian origin). In the north-east the Westerwald merges into the Rothaargebirge, within the Sauerland district of Westphalia, while its most easterly hills jut out into the *Wittgensteiner Land* and *Upland* areas.

Between the Rothaargebirge with its northern foothills and the Hessian Depression are the *Burgwald*, the *Kellerwald*, the *Wildungen Hills* and the *Waldeck Uplands*, an abundantly forested region which offers little scope for agriculture. The valleys are deeply indented, a feature which made possible the construction of the large *Eder Valley Dam*.

To the east of the Taunus, separated from it by the Hessian Depression, rears up the almost isolated **Vogelsberg**, whose conical form betrays the former volcano. This is a remote hill-farming region, with a fertile but thin and stony soil. The austere and solitary landscape has a certain charm, particularly in the Oberwald area. The highest peaks are the *Taufstein* (772 m) and *Hoherodskopf* (767 m).

From the Vogelsberg a ridge of high ground runs east to the **Rhön**, an upland region of very distinctive scenery, composed of a sharply articulated massif of Bunter sandstone to which volcanic flows of basalt have given rounded summit forms. The Rhön forms the ancient boundary between Hesse and Franconia; its highest peak, the *Wasserkuppe* (950 m), a favourite resort of gliding enthusiasts, lies in Hessian territory. The High Rhön (Hochrhön), with its sombre coniferous forests and great expanses of mountain pasture, is one of the remotest of Germany's upland regions.

To the north the Vorderrhön runs into the *Seulingswald*. Farther north still is the **Meissnerland**, with the most varied scenery in Hesse. Its central features are the legendary *Hoher Meissner* (750 m), a steeply scarped tabular hill of basalt, *Knüll*, north of the Vogelsberg, and the *Habichtswald* west of Kassel. The northern part of the area is occupied by the *Kaufunger Wald*, which, like the *Reinhardswald* to the north-west beyond the Fulda, is a continuation of the Bunter sandstone plateau of southern Hanover.

The most important parts of Hesse from the economic point of view are the fertile valleys and basins through which the main traffic routes run. The *Lahn* and the *Fulda* are the most important rivers whose catchment areas lie entirely within Hesse. At Hannoversch Münden the Fulda joins with the Werra, whose valley forms the north-eastern boundary of the *Land*, to form the Weser. The Fulda's best known tributary is the Eder, with one of the largest dams in Europe. The Eder in turn has as one of its tributaries the Schwalm, which flows through one of the most fertile regions in Hesse.

The **Hessian Depression**, which extends from Frankfurt am Main to Bad Karlshafen on the Weser, is a chain of low-lying basins and river valleys, whose warm and sheltered situation makes them one of Hesse's principal agricultural regions. The southern part of the depression is occupied by the *Wetterau*, a particularly fertile area between the Taunus and the Vogelsberg, with Bad Nauheim on its eastern slopes. To the north of this is the Lahn valley between Giessen and Marburg. Thereafter the depression becomes gradually narrower and bears north-east into the Schwalm valley, which it follows into the Fulda valley and the rich agricultural area round Kassel, and continues between the Reinhardswald and the Habichtswald to reach the Weser valley at Bad Karlshafen. Frankfurt am Main and Kassel are the principal centres of economic life and communications in Northern and Southern Hesse respectively.

Hesse shows wide variations in population density, the north being much more thinly populated than the south. The difference is due to the very different economic structure of the two regions. In the north, which is basically agricultural, more than half the POPULATION live in little towns or villages of under 2000 inhabitants, while in the highly industrialised south more than a third of the population live in towns of between 20,000 and 100,000 inhabitants. Since the last war, however, the rural population has been considerably increased by the influx of people who had lost their homes in other parts of Germany.

The old-established inhabitants show a strong attachment to their native soil and great steadfastness of character. They cling to old ways and old ideas, they are cautious and thrifty, sometimes rather dour and reserved. The admixture of Franconian blood, however, has brought a lighter touch, and the people of Southern Hesse tend to be of cheerful disposition.

Many old traditions and local COSTUMES have been preserved in Hesse. In the Schwalm area the country folk still wear the traditional costumes as their everyday dress, and beautiful old costumes are still sometimes to be seen in the Schlitz, Vogelsberg and Waldeck areas.

Physical Zones

The territory of the Federal Republic of Germany is made up of five different physical zones. In the north and north-west are the extensive **North German Lowlands**, bounded on the south by the **Central German Uplands**.

South Germany is divided into the **South German Uplands** and the **Alpine Foreland**, above which, in the extreme south-east, rear the **Bavarian Alps**.

The normal SETTLEMENT PATTERN in Hesse is the large irregular village, with the isolated farmhouse and the small hamlet in the hill regions with a poorer climate. The predominant house type, particularly in Southern Hesse, is the Franconian (Central German) farmstead, in which the two-storey dwelling-house with its trim half-timbered gable, the barn and the stall or stable are built round a central courtyard entered through a gateway. In Northern Hesse the Low German house type was formerly normal but has now become rare. The many small and medium-sized towns in Hesse, with their charming half-timbered buildings, are laid out on a regular plan, often with a wide main street which serves as market-place.

Hesse is an old farming region in which large areas are still predominantly agricultural. Something like a fifth of the population gain their subsistence from AGRICULTURE, with a predominance of small holdings. In the basins and valleys intensive arable farming is practised; grassland and pasture are found mainly in the hills. Forestry also plays an important part in the economy, a third of Hesse being wooded. Most of the INDUSTRY is concentrated in the Rhine-Main plain, the Kassel basin, the district of Hersfeld and the Lahn-Dill area, but there are also industrial establishments in many rural areas. Roughly half the population is employed in industry and craft production. The main industrial centres are Frankfurt am Main, Wiesbaden, Kassel, Fulda, Offenbach and Hanau, whose metal-working industry, engineering, optical works, leather goods and jewellery have an international reputation.
The most important MINERALS in Hesse are iron-ore (Lahn-Dill area), potash (Werra valley) and lignite (Hessian Depression). There are also numerous mineral springs (e.g. Selters).

The scenery of Hesse is characterised by the constant alternation of wide river valleys, fertile depressions and small ranges of round-topped hills.

Kassel, once the seat of the Elector of Hesse, is notable particularly for its excellent art collections and the avant-garde "Documenta" exhibition, the magnificent park of Schloss Wilhelmshöhe and, a few kilometres away, the delightful Rococo palace of Wilhelmsthal.

On the way south is the Baroque city of **Fulda**, which also has one of the few surviving Carolingian churches in Germany.
In the Lahn valley there are the university town of **Marburg**, in which visitors should not fail to walk up through the charming old-world lanes from St Elizabeth's Church to the old castle of the Margraves, and *Limburg* with its imposing Cathedral, seeming to grow out of the rock above the Lahn valley on which it stands. Here too are the spas of *Bad Ems* and *Nassau*, *Balduinstein* and *Diez* with their castles.

Frankfurt am Main, a city rich in tradition and long noted for its trade fairs, is the most important commercial city and centre of communications in the Federal Republic. The town centre suffered heavy destruction during the last war, but the Cathedral survived and several historic buildings around the Römerberg were reconstructed, as was the house in which Goethe was born. A number of modern tower blocks now punctuate the skyline. Among its other tourist attractions the Städel collection of pictures, the Senckenberg Natural History Museum and the well-known Zoo rank high. Within easy reach of the city are the forests of the Taunus, with such old-established resorts as *Bad Nauheim, Bad Homburg vor der Höhe* (near which is the *Saalburg*, the reconstruction of a Roman fort on the Limes), *Bad Soden, Bad Schwalbach* and the capital of the *Land* of Hesse, **Wiesbaden**, lying at the gates of the Rheingau.

One of Europe's great tourist attractions has long been the **RHINE VALLEY**, a cheerful wine-growing region which combines scenic beauty with architectural masterpieces and a historic past.
The area where the Rhine forces its way through the **Rhenish Uplands** is of great geological interest. At Mainz the natural wall formed by the hills of the Rheingau forces the river to turn west, but beyond Bingen, in what is known as the "Bingen hole" (Binger Loch), it breaks its way through the hills and resumes its northward course. The conflict between the river and the hard rock of its bed has produced a gorge-like valley with irregularities of gradient which create hazards for shipping. The depth of the river at this point is due to the upthrust of the local rock, which in the early Tertiary period had lain at a lower level, making it necessary for the Rhine to cut its way through this rock in successive stages when it rose as a result of upthrusts during the later Tertiary. The result of this process can be clearly seen in the raised terraces of river-borne rock debris on the banks of the Rhine.
Farther downstream the Rhine encounters softer rock, in particular slate, which allow the valley to open out. It narrows again at certain points where harder greywackes occur, for example at the legendary *Loreley Rock* and at St. Goar. In the more open parts of the valley deposits of loess have provided fertile soil for the development of thriving towns and villages, vineyards and fruit orchards. All this, combined with the castles perched

above the steeply scarped banks and the occasional islands, creates an ever-changing landscape pattern.

Below Koblenz, where the Moselle flows into the Rhine, the valley opens out into the little *Neuwied basin*, formed by a downfaulting of the slates in Tertiary times, with subsequent infilling by river-borne deposits and flows of volcanic rock. The towns on this stretch of the Rhine have developed active industries (blast furnaces, iron and steel works), while the hinterland on the left bank, together with the *Maifeld* which forms a transition to the Eifel, is the great potato-growing area of the Rhineland.

Shortly before the river enters the Lower Rhine plain it passes on the right an outlier of the Westerwald, the **Siebengebirge** (460 m), which takes its name from the seven hills, mainly composed of volcanic debris, which here form a shapely group. It provides a magnificent terminus to the Middle Rhine, with the most northerly of the Rhine vineyards growing on its flanks.

Beyond Bonn we enter the third section of the Rhine's course, the **Lower Rhinelands**, a gently undulating region resulting from the downfaulting of a range of hills. Only in the area south of Cologne is there more variety in the topographical pattern. The deposits of lignite in this region, laid down in the middle Tertiary period to a depth of over 100 m and covered with only a thin layer of earth, so that they can be worked by opencast methods, are the largest so far discovered anywhere in the world. On this stretch of the Rhine have developed a number of important towns which have played major roles in the cultural and economic life of Germany – Bonn, Cologne, Neuss, Düsseldorf and Duisburg, where the real Lower Rhine begins.

At **Mainz**, capital of the *Land* of **Rhineland-Palatinate**, the Rhine passenger services start, offering a pleasant way of seeing Germany's most beautiful river. Mainz Cathedral ranks with those of Worms and Speyer among the finest achievements of Romanesque architecture. Along the banks of the river lie the wine towns of the sunny Rheingau, the steep rock faces lining the passage through the Rhenish Upland hills, castles, ruins and picturesque little townships. Many celebrated beauty spots tempt the tourist to linger – *Rüdesheim* in the shadow of the Niederwald memorial

commemorating the establishment of the German Empire, *Bingen, Assmannshausen, Bacharach, Kaub* with the Pfalz in the middle of the Rhine, *St. Goar* and *St. Goarshausen* with the Loreley Rock, *Boppard* or *Braubach* with the Marksburg, and above all **Koblenz** with the "Deutsches Eck" and the fortress of Ehrenbreitstein.

Farther downstream are the old-world little town of *Andernach*, the Siebengebirge, from the tops of which the view extends to the very doors of Cologne Cathedral, on the opposite bank Bonn's embassy quarter of *Bad Godesberg*, and finally **Bonn** itself – university city, birthplace of Beethoven and now also capital and political centre of the Federal Republic.

In the old Hanseatic city of **Cologne**, which suffered heavy damage in the last war but has risen from the ashes and rubble as a fine new modern town, visitors are still most immediately impressed by the majestic bulk of its Gothic Cathedral; but after seeing this they will discover within the wide semicircle of the old town a number of important Romanesque churches and museums containing masterpieces of art and relics of the city's Roman past.

In the lateral valleys opening off the Rhine and the neighbouring upland regions the pattern of life and landscape is quieter, less spoiled by the 20th century. The Rhine's most famous tributary is the beautiful **MOSELLE**, which was given its name by the Romans (Mosella, the little Maas or Meuse). It rises in the southern Vosges and flows into the Rhine at Koblenz after a course of more than 500 km.

The most attractive part of the Moselle is between **Trier**, the oldest German town, with the most important remains of Roman buildings north of the Alps, and Koblenz. After passing through the Trier basin the river begins its winding course through the Rhenish Uplands between the Hunsrück and the Moselle Hills, outliers of the Eifel. The ever-changing scenery is given additional attraction, particularly between *Bernkastel* and *Cochem*, by numbers of old castles on the slopes above the river and in side valleys and by a series of old-world little towns and wine villages. The development of towns of any size was prevented by the river's meandering course and the narrowness of the valley; but this had the great benefit of leaving the Moselle to its more contemplative way of life, in contrast to the busy activity of the Rhine valley. Large-scale river regulation works, however, have now made possible the development of an active shipping traffic. And still, as in Roman times, the sun warms the slaty soil which produces the long-famed wine of the Moselle.

The Moselle valley is caught between two ranges of hills, the Eifel and the Hunsrück. The **Eifel** – the eastern part of the Ardennes – was formerly one of the remotest and most inaccessible parts of Germany but is now served by a considerable network of excellent roads. This austere and lonely region of wooded uplands and winding valleys, suitable only for forestry and cattle-rearing, nevertheless has a special charm of its own. In geological terms the Eifel is a range of residual hills some 70 km long by 30 km across, with an average height of some 600 m, in which numerous volcanoes erupted in Tertiary and Pleistocene times. The flows of lava from these volcanoes can still be recognised in the present-day landscape, particularly round the Nürburg

Ring, the world-famous racing circuit, and in the neighbourhood of Daun and Manderscheid. The *Maare*, so characteristic of the Eifel, are funnel-shaped volcanic craters, now mostly containing small lakes. A typical example is the *Laacher See*, 52 m deep, which is surrounded by over 40 volcanic vents and four extinct volcanoes.

In the north-western Eifel there are a number of beautiful artificial lakes formed by dams across the valleys, like the *Schwammenauel Dam* on the River Rur.

To the north of the Eifel is the **Ahr valley**, which offers great attractions in its beautiful scenery, its fragrant wine and the medicinal springs of *Bad Neuenahr*.

South of the Eifel, bounded by the Rhine, the Moselle, the lower course of the Saar and the Nahe, is the **Hunsrück**, the most southerly part of the Rhenish Uplands on the left bank of the Rhine. This upland region lies between 400 and 500 m, traversed by a long ridge of quartzite hills reaching their highest point in the *Erbeskopf* (816 m). The undulating plateau has been cleared of much of its forest cover

The Zell bend in the middle Moselle valley

and has many small settlements; the hills are one of the largest areas of forest in Germany, mainly beautiful deciduous forest. The excellently engineered *Hunsrück-Höhenstrasse* (Hunsrück Ridgeway) runs through the whole length of the range.

The **Nahe valley** offers the visitor its picturesque old towns, in particular *Bad Kreuznach* and *Idar-Oberstein*, with its jewellery and precious-stone workshops and its rock church.

The most beautiful part of the **Palatinate**, which lies between the Nahe and the Rhine, is the *Palatinate Forest* (most of it now protected as a nature reserve), the western part of which is also known as the Haardt. There are numerous castles on the steep eastern face of the hills.

The road through the Palatinate Forest by way of Frederick Barbarossa's city of **Kaiserslautern** with its three-towered Stiftskirche, or the road up the Nahe valley from Bingen lead into the industrial **SAAR**. The capital of the *Land*, **Saarbrücken**, is a lively town with a number of handsome buildings, and the surrounding area contains not only coal-mines and factories but much natural beauty as well.

The **UPPER RHINE PLAIN**, a depression between 30 and 40 km wide, was created by faulting in the Oligocene period. It is bounded on the east by the Black Forest, the Kraichgau and the Odenwald, on the west by the Vosges, the Haardt and the uplands of the northern Palatinate. The underlying rock which outcrops on the borders of the plain is overlaid in the plain itself by Pleistocene deposits of loess, which form a fertile soil for the growing of fruit and vines.

On the Upper Rhine the hills with the vineyards and orchards on their slopes draw back and give place to a fertile plain. From the former Hessian Grand-Ducal capital of **Darmstadt**, a great artistic centre, the **Bergstrasse** – where spring first comes to Germany – runs along the foot of the Odenwald by way of the picturesque little towns of *Zwingenberg*, at the foot of Melibokus, *Bensheim*, *Heppenheim* and *Weinheim* to the famous old university town of **Heidelberg**, with its incomparably beautiful ruined castle. From here attractive trips can be made to the towns in the lower Neckar valley, the industrial city of **Mannheim** with its 18th century grid

plan and Baroque palace or *Schwetzingen* with its beautiful palace gardens. On the left bank of the Rhine are the Imperial cities of *Speyer* and *Worms* with their Romanesque cathedrals. From Worms trips can be made on the Nibelungenstrasse to Miltenberg and Wertheim on the Main, or on the Deutsche Weinstrasse into the Palatinate with its numerous old castles.

The **BLACK FOREST** has a north–south length of some 160 km from Pforzheim to Lörrach, with a breadth of some 20 km in the north and 60 km in the south. With its dark forest-clad hills, its hilltop meadows and its valleys watered by abundant mountain streams, it is of all German upland regions the one which offers the richest variety of scenery both grandiose and charming.

On the west side, rising some 800 m above the Upper Rhine plain, the Black Forest presents a steep scarp, slashed by valleys well supplied with water by the rain-bringing west winds, and some of them narrow and gorge-like. The highest points are also in the west.

To the east the hills slope down more gently, with broader valleys and flatter ridges, to the upper Neckar and Danube valleys, both of which are some 250 m higher than the Rhine plain.

The main ridge of the Black Forest is an undulating plateau, with round-topped hills rising to a somewhat greater height. The plateau is broken up by numerous valleys, so that it does not form a continuous ridge but is irregularly shaped, with the watershed following a rather tortuous course. Between Freudenstadt and Offenburg the Kinzig valley cuts right across the whole of the Black Forest.

The **Northern Black Forest** (above the Kinzig valley) is made up of broad ridges of Bunter sandstone, and almost two-thirds of its area are covered with forest. The settlements are strung out along the deep valleys, many of them still showing the pattern of the linear villages of the early medieval period of forest clearance. Only in modern times have roads been built along the high ground. Attractive features of the landscape are the little mountain lakes like the Mummelsee and Wildsee nestling in hollows gouged out by glaciers, particularly round the highest peak in the Northern Black Forest, *Hornisgrinde* (1166 m), along the slopes of which passes the Schwarzwald-Hochstrasse (Black Forest Ridgeway) on its way from Baden-Baden to Freudenstadt.

The **Central Black Forest**, which may be defined as lying between the Kinzig valley and the Höllental road, is – like the Southern Black Forest – mainly composed of granites and gneisses, with frequent intrusions of

Permian porphyries. On the west side downfaulted beds of younger rock form foothills, like the Bunter sandstone hills north of Emmendingen. To the east horizontally bedded Bunter sandstones and limestones (Muschelkalk) form a fringe of lesser scenic attraction, which along with the exposed but fertile *Baar* plateau runs into the Swabian Jura.

The lower parts of the valleys in the Central Black Forest are wide and favourable to settlement. Higher up there is usually a steeper stretch, cut deeply into the rock, which may form beautiful waterfalls as at Triberg. In a wider section of the valley above this there may be fields and meadows reclaimed from the forests which cover the plateau. The highest peak in the Central Black Forest is *Kandel* (1241 m), between the Elz, Simonswald and Glotter valleys.

The **Southern Black Forest**, with the most impressive scenery, is dominated by the 1493 m high *Feldberg*. From here a ridge runs west to *Belchen* (1414 m), the most beautifully shaped hill in the Black Forest, and *Blauen* (1165 m), the hill projecting farthest into the Rhine plain. Round the Feldberg deeply indented valleys radiate in all directions: the Höllental, the Wiesental, the Albtal and the Gutachtal or Wutachtal, whose beauty is enhanced by lakes like the *Titisee*, *Schluchsee* and *Feldsee*, occupying depressions carved out by Ice Age glaciers. In this region forests cover barely half the total area, and villages and fields reach up to greater heights (Blasiwald, 1190 m). The mountain meadows on the summits provide good pasturage, and on the Feldberg and Belchen are used for summer grazing in a manner reminiscent of Alpine dairy-farming methods.

To the east of Lörrach extends the Dinkelberg plateau, an area of downfaulted Muschelkalk with some karstic formations. Between the Wutach and the Rhine is a tabular hill of Jurassic date, *Randen* (926 m), which forms a bridge between the Swabian and Swiss Jura, with its southern half actually in Switzerland. From Randen there is a road through the striking scenery of the *Hegau*, with its volcanic cones, to Lake Constance, Germany's largest lake.

The POPULATION of the Black Forest has its ancestry not only in the Celts and the Romans, but also in the Swabians, the Alemanni and the Franks, and even today shows great diversity. The Celtic element is most evident in the heart of the uplands. North of the River Murg the Frankish strain can be detected. The bulk of the population, however, is of Swabian and Alemannic stock.

The LANGUAGE of the ordinary people is predominantly the Alemannic dialect, merging into Swabian in the east and Franconian in the north. The picturesque traditional COSTUMES are usually now seen only in the remoter parts of the region, and then only on special occasions. Formerly each valley had its own distinctive costume, even the colours of which were different. At the Shrovetide carnival interesting costumes and sometimes artificial masks can still be seen.

The typical Black Forest HOUSE TYPE is a version of the Alpine house, found south of the Kinzig valley: a timber-built house on stone foundations with numerous small windows, which seeks protection against the long winter, with its abundant snow, by bringing the living quarters and farmstead together under a single overhanging roof covered with shingles or thatch (though the latter is becoming increasingly rare). Often a gallery – usually decked with flowers – runs round the upper storey.

Iron-mining once played an important part in the ECONOMY of the Black Forest, but this has now almost completely disappeared. Its decline in the 16th century turned the people of the Black Forest towards agriculture. On account of the altitude, however, there is little arable farming, and the predominant activity is cattle-rearing, using the mountain pastures above the tree-line for summer grazing. Fruit-growing is also of importance, mainly in the valleys to the west. The types of fruit most commonly grown are cherries (which produce the famous Black Forest liqueur, kirsch) and plums (the Bühl area being famous for its early plums).

A major contribution to the economy is made by forestry and woodworking. Formerly the finest trunks were floated down the Rhine to Holland; but after the coming of the railways the floating of logs down the Black Forest rivers (the Kinzig, the Nagold, the Enz) gradually died out. The old small-scale crafts of the Black Forest like glass-making, charcoal-burning and pitch-making have likewise disappeared, giving place to large sawmills and woodworking plants.

The industry of the region developed out of a widespread cottage industry, which to some extent still exists. The famous Black Forest CLOCK-MAKING industry, introduced about the middle of the 17th century, was originally a craft solely for woodcarvers, but by about 1750 the wheels were also being made from brass. The best-known clock factories are at Schramberg and Villingen-Schwenningen. The manufacture of musical boxes and radio and television sets has developed alongside this industry.

Trossingen is famous for its mouth-organs and accordions. Other local crafts are brush-making and straw-plaiting. There is also some textile industry (particularly ribbon-making), mainly in the Wiesental. In recent years there has been some development of hydroelectric power. The most notable hydroelectric stations are on the Murg at Forbach and on the Schluchsee.

The Black Forest must be one of Europe's upland regions with the greatest flow of visitors, attracted by its romantic valleys with their rushing mountain streams, the relaxing air of its dark coniferous forests, the wide views to be had from its hilltops and mountain pastures.

The series of beautiful towns round its fringes which serve as gateways into the Black Forest begins with **Karlsruhe**, former capital of Baden, with its fan-shaped pattern of streets radiating from the Margrave's palace and its richly stocked museums. Then come *Rastatt* at the entrance to the Murg valley, with another handsome palace, and the magnificently situated resort of **Baden-Baden**, already some way into the hills, with its old-established casino and its racecourse in nearby Iffezheim. Baden-Baden is the

Traditional Black Forest costumes

starting point of the Schwarzwald-Hochstrasse (Black Forest Ridgeway), the popular tourist route which runs along the ridge, past a series of hotels and other establishments offering health-giving relaxation in the mountain air as well as beautiful views, to the *Kniebis* plateau, a favourite winter sports area.

Farther south is the university town of **Freiburg im Breisgau**, with a Minster which has perhaps the most perfect of Gothic spires.

Among the many spas and health resorts in the Black Forest only a few can be mentioned – *Freudenstadt*, *Herrenalb*, *Triberg*, *Titisee-Neustadt* and *Wildbad* in the heart of the forest, *Bad Krozingen*, the elegant *Badenweiler* and the rising resort of *Bad Bellingen* on the western edge of the Southern Black Forest.

Among particularly beautiful valleys are the *Höllental* near Freiburg, the *Murg valley* at Forbach and the *Gutach valley* at Triberg; among hills offering particularly fine views are the Badener Höhe, Hornisgrinde, Kandel, Feldberg, Belchen, Blauen and Hohe Möhr.

The south-western termination of the Black Forest is the **Markgräfler Land**, a hilly region noted for its wine. Even better vineyards are to be found on the volcanic *Kaiserstuhl*.

The great attraction of **SWABIA** for visitors lies in the diversity of its scenery, the alternation of hills and valleys, forests and fields, orchards and vineyards. To the attentive eye, however, these changing scenes fall into a logical sequence of natural landscapes reflecting, perhaps more clearly than anywhere else in Germany, the constitution and structure of the soil. Entering Swabia from the

Upper Rhine plain or travelling south-east from the lower Main valley, we pass from older into ever younger geological formations, climbing up a series of great steps in the scarplands of South Germany.

In the **Odenwald**, which along with the Black Forest forms the western boundary of these scarplands, the underlying granites and gneisses are still exposed on the west side of the hills. This region, broken up by a dense network of valleys into a landscape of round-topped hills and covered with a patchwork of forests, fields and villages, contrasts with the extensive eastern part in which the coherence of the old residual hills has been preserved in spite of the deeply indented valleys. The thin soils of the reddish-brown Bunter sandstone, unsuitable for arable farming, are covered with magnificent beech forests. The Neckar flows through the southern tip of the Odenwald in a deeply slashed valley, its romantic charm scarcely affected by its development into a major waterway. On the steep tree-clad slopes of the valley stand a chain of beautiful old castles and ruins in warm red Bunter sandstone, first among them the proud ruins of Heidelberg Castle.

The *Unterland* of Baden-Württemberg, or **Neckarland**, consisting mainly of Muschelkalk and Keuper (middle and upper Triassic) formations, which lies immediately south-east of the Odenwald, is the old heartland of Swabia, rich in historical associations and monuments of art and architecture. Starting from its south-western corner between the Black Forest and the Swabian Alb, it broadens out towards the north-east and merges imperceptibly into the expanses of Lower Franconia. The extensive Muschelkalk plains are fertile arable land, with their covering of loess and their mild climate in the rain-shadow of the hills to the west. It is a bright and smiling landscape, with trim villages set among apple-orchards (cider). The valleys of the Neckar and its tributaries (Enz, Kocher, Jagst) and of the Tauber form sharp angular indentations which divide up the land into a series of *gaus* – to the west of the Neckar the *Oberes Gäu*, the *Strohgäu*, the *Zabergäu* and the *Kraichgau*, which provides a passage from the Upper Rhine into Swabia through the wide gap between the Odenwald and the Black Forest; to the east the *Hohenlohe plain*, the *Bauland* and the *Taubergrund*.

Wherever the eye travels to the south or

east from these plains it encounters the dark forest-covered slopes of the Keuper (middle Triassic) hills. The resistant beds of middle Keuper rock everywhere form sharp "steps" in the landscape. In contrast to the continuous scarp of the Jurassic hills farther south the Keuper scarp in **Württemberg** is much broken up, projecting here, retreating there, and thus giving the Unterland its varied landscape pattern. The Keuper hills are carved up by the intervening valleys into narrow tubular formations, buttresses and ridges. As in the Bunter sandstone region, almost the whole area is occupied by forests. Only in those areas where the fertile Lias (Triassic) is found, as in the *Filder* area south of Stuttgart and in the Alb foreland, does open arable farming develop. In earlier times the Keuper hills, being so much broken up, had no name applying to the whole range; more recently the term *Swabian Forest* has come into use, but the various separate parts are still known by their own names. Thus to the south-west, between Stuttgart and Tübingen, is the old ducal hunting reserve of *Schönbuch*; to the east of the Neckar are the *Schurwald* and *Welzheimer Wald* and, projecting far to the north-west, the *Löwensteiner Berge*, the *Mainhardter Wald* and the *Waldenburger Berge*; and beyond these the *Ellwanger Berge* form a transition to the Frankenhöhe range in which the Keuper scarp turns northward into Franconia. Far to the west are two Keuper outposts in the Kraichgau, the *Heuchelberg* and *Stromberg*.

However diverse these landscape patterns may be, they nevertheless have many features in common, reflecting the Swabian traditions of peasant farming and small holdings of land. Characteristic features of the landscape are the orchards on the gently rolling hills and the vineyards on the slopes of the valleys. Everywhere picturesque old towns bear witness to the vicissitudes of a long past – one time capitals of petty principalities like Weikersheim, Waldenburg, Öhringen and Löwenstein; former free Imperial cities like Wimpfen, Heilbronn, Schwäbisch Hall, Schwäbisch Gmünd, Esslingen and Weil der Stadt; Stuttgart, capital of the *Land*, situated on the boundary between the Gäue and the Keuper hills, which has developed into the cultural and economic centre of South-West Germany. The Unterland has a varied range of industries, covering almost every type of industrial activity with the exception of heavy industry, which provides an appropriate balance to the region's agriculture and a safeguard against the effects of economic crises.

The boundary of the Unterland and its most striking feature is formed by the impressive escarpment of the **Swabian Alb**. Here the geological structure is reflected with particular clarity in the landscape pattern. Out of the Lias plains of the Lower Jurassic in the foreland area gently rolling slopes of Middle Jurassic rock, traversed only at some points by a preliminary scarp, climb 200–300 m to the Albtrauf, the rim of the escarpment, composed of resistant Upper Jurassic limestones. From a distance the escarpment appears to be a continuous wall, which seems particularly massive when seen against the light of the midday sun; but on a closer approach the hill face, covered with beech forests, breaks down into a number of separate buttresses of varying width separated by short but deeply indented valleys. Evidence of the scarp which once extended farther to the north-west is provided by isolated outliers like the *Hohenstaufen* and *Hohenzollern*, the ancestral homes of two great Imperial dynasties. The busy life of the Unterland swirls up against the escarpment, in front of which lie a whole series of active little towns like Hechingen, Tübingen, Reutlingen, Nürtingen, Kirchheim unter Teck, Göppingen, Schwäbisch Gmünd and Aalen.

In sharp contrast to the mild and smiling fruit-growing district below is the bleak and austere plateau of the Swabian Alb, which slopes down gradually in a gently undulating plain, covered with arable fields and pastureland but with little forest and little water, to the Danube and the Alpine Foreland. The permeable limestone shows many karstic features – dry valleys, caves and swallow-holes, seepage from rivers (the Danube) and underground watercourses which surface again as abundant springs like the Blautopf at Blaubeuren.

The few large villages lie widely separated from one another, mostly in the valley bottoms; their long-standing shortage of water was made good only by large-scale water-supply works in the last quarter of the 19th century. From a height of some 700 m in the north-east the Swabian Alb rises gradually to 1000 m in the south-west, reaching its greatest height in the Lemberg, on the Heuberg plateau.

Between Tuttlingen and Sigmaringen the *Danube* cuts its way through the Alb plateau in an impressive rocky gorge.

In **Upper Swabia**, part of the Alpine Foreland falling within Württemberg, the scenery changes once again. The wide plain is covered by sediments deposited by a shallow sea of the Tertiary period, debris left by the Alpine glaciers, which thrust far out into the Foreland during the Ice Age, and boulders and sand deposited by the rivers. In the northern part of Upper Swabia these deposits have produced a fairly uniform surface pattern, but there is greater diversity in the southern part. Here the recent terminal moraine landscape has been preserved almost unchanged – round-topped hills covered by dark stretches of dark forest extending in wide arcs or in contorted patterns, small lakes or bogs filling depressions, intricately winding valleys and narrow gullies. Scattered over this unruly and apparently random landscape are isolated farmhouses, the normal pattern of settlement in this area. Stock-rearing begins to predominate over arable farming in many parts of the area.

From Upper Swabia, whose scenic beauties and treasures of art may tempt the visitor to linger, the road runs south to Lake Constance, the "Swabian sea". The smiling and fertile landscape of Swabia is here given additional attraction by the atmosphere of the South and the views of the majestic mountains.

Stuttgart, capital of the *Land* of Baden-Württemberg, is one of Germany's most beautifully situated cities. From the basin in which the town lies, its houses climb up the surrounding slopes, still partly clad with vineyards, to the fringe of villas along the wooded rim of the hills, with the well-known Television Tower (the first of its kind), and reach out into the industrial and port areas on the Neckar.

Among the other beautiful and interesting towns in Württemberg only a selection can be mentioned: **Heilbronn**, with its legendary heroine Käthchen and its fine St Kilian's Church; the picturesque little farming township of Besigheim, preserved intact; the 18th century princely capital of *Ludwigsburg*, with the largest of the palaces built in Germany on the model of Versailles; the nearby *Marbach*, Schiller's birthplace, with the interesting National Schiller Museum; the little country town of Markgröningen with its

fine old half-timbered town hall; up the Neckar valley the old Imperial city of **Esslingen** with its beautiful Gothic churches and the university town of **Tübingen**, picturesque straggling up the hillside above the river; the old salt town of *Schwäbisch Hall* on the Kocher, with its fine market square and, just outside the town, the fortified monastery of Comburg; in the Hohenlohe district the tiny princely capitals of Langenburg, Neuenstein and Öhringen; in the Rems valley the half-timbered town of Schorndorf and the former free Imperial city of *Schwäbisch Gmünd*, with two important churches; **Ulm** on the Danube, with the spire of its Minster soaring above the old town; on the Upper Swabian plateau Biberach and the many-towered *Ravensburg, Steinhausen*, with the "most beautiful village church in the world", and *Weingarten* monastery. Along the escarpment of the Swabian Alb are the Hohenstaufen, once the seat of the great family whose name it bears; Teck with its ruined castle; the delightfully situated little town of *Bad Urach*; the massive ruins of Hohenneuffen; the romantic Schloss Lichtenstein; and the proud castle of *Hohenzollern*. In the rocky upper reaches of the *Danube valley* is the Benedictine abbey of Beuron, with many old castle in the surrounding area.

The hospitable resorts on the shores of **LAKE CONSTANCE**, Germany's largest lake, have long attracted visitors, with their vineyards and orchards, their bathing beaches and their view across the great expanse of the lake, dotted with sailing boats, to the jagged blue line of the Alps: the frontier town of **Konstanz**, from which excursions can be made to the flower island of *Mainau* and the vegetable-growing island of *Reichenau* with its beautiful Romanesque churches; the old town of *Überlingen*; *Meersburg*, picturesquely climbing up the hill to its old castle; **Friedrichshafen**, home of the Zeppelin; the island town of **Lindau**. Within easy reach of the lake is the *Hegau*, with the Hohentwiel and other conical hills which were once volcanoes.

The geologically interesting **FRANCONIAN SCARPLAND** owes its origin to the erosional work of rivers over many millions of years. It consists of interbedded Triassic and Jurassic rocks of varying hardness which were given a slight eastward tilt in the middle Tertiary period during the uplifting of the Upper Rhine area and the downfaulting which produced the Rhine rift valley. Thereafter the action of the Rhine river-system in the west and the Danube in the east carved prominent scarps from the hard rocks. During this process erosion was most active in the areas of greatest upthrust, and the Rhine moved its point of entry steadily farther east. Travelling from west to east, we pass from older to ever younger rocks. This clearly marked rhythm gives the scenery of Franconia an attractive diversity and great tourist charm.

The most westerly of the Franconian scarps is the **Spessart**, which is bounded on the south by the rectangular course of the Main and on the north by the rivers Kinzig and Sinn. It is mainly composed of sandstone, which abuts on the basement rock in the Vorderer Spessart to the west. The tabular sandstone is of little use for agriculture but is covered with extensive beech forests which attract large numbers of town-dwellers in quest of recreation. The sandstone also makes an admirable building stone whose beautiful flesh-coloured tones contribute to the beauty of the Franconian towns. The Spessart sandstone formations continue beyond the Sinn into the southern **Rhön**, to the north of which, in Hesse, rises the Hochrhön, covered with basaltic lava from Tertiary volcanoes.

A completely different picture from the Spessart and the Rhön, with their relatively sparse population, is presented by the limestone scarp of the **Franconian Plateau**, immediately east of the Main rectangle and along the Franconian Saale, which abuts on the Bunter sandstone scarp, with a less sharply defined edge. This area of loess and clay – with the *Marktheidenfelder Gau* in the west, the *Grabfeld* in the north, the *Gerolzhofener Gau* in the east, the *Ochsenfurter Gau* in the south-east and the *Würzburger Gau* in the centre – is fertile agricultural land. The villages are ringed by large orchards, and excellent wines grow on the limestone slopes of the Main valley and in the Steigerwald area on the edge of the scarp. The economic and cultural centre of the plateau is Würzburg, once residence of

View from Überlingen across Lake Constance to the Swiss Alps

the Prince-Bishops, with its magnificent architecture and sculpture.

To the east of the Franconian Plateau is another prominent scarp forming the **Franconian Terrace**, composed of sandstones of the middle Keuper period, which begins in the north with the *Hassberge*, continues south of the broad Main valley in the *Steigerwald*, and then beyond the Windsheim "bay" by way of the *Frankenhöhe* to the Keuper scarp of the Swabian Forest. On the Frankenhöhe the sandstone cover is dissected into a series of separate tabular formations; in the Steigerwald there are still intact areas of some size; and in the Hassberge the sandstone survives substantially unbroken as a ridge projecting towards the Grabfeld.

The Franconian Terrace, mostly forested and broken up by broad valleys, slopes down very gradually and merges into the **Middle Franconian Basin**, drained by the Regnitz-Redwitz. Here again arable land predominates over forest, though not to the same extent as on the plateau. Among the main agricultural areas are the *Bamberger Gau* (fruit-growing) and the noted hop-growing district of Rednitz in the *Rangau*, south of Nuremberg. Only on the sandy soils round Nuremberg are there areas of woodland interspersed with heath. Bee-keeping which has been practised here for many centuries provides the basis for the manufacture of the well-known Nuremberg gingerbread, while the local timber long provided the raw material for the equally well-known Nuremberg toy industry. The Middle Franconian Basin is the most populous part of Franconia, with the former free Imperial city of Nuremberg as its natural centre.

The most easterly, and with a relative height of some 250 m the most pronounced, of the scarps is the **Franconian Jura** or *Franconian Alb*, with light-coloured limestone cliffs of Upper Jurassic date, visible from afar, rearing up above a narrow lower scarp of the Middle Jurassic. With an altitude of some 600 m, the Franconian Alb, and particularly the area known as the *"Franconian Switzerland"* in its northern part, has all the characteristics of a karstic landscape – large-scale clefting and leaching away of the carbonate limestone, with the formation of caves and swallow-holes, underground watercourses and dry valleys on the surface – giving it some of

the most attractive scenery in the whole of the Alb. That this scarp formerly extended farther west is shown by a number of outlying hills like the Hesselberg (689 m), north of the Ries, and the Hahnenkamm (644 m), at the point where the River Altmühl enters the Jura. In the picturesque gorge of the Altmühl to the south the famous limestone flags of *Solnhofen* are worked.

West of this is the **Ries** round Nördlingen, a circular basin formed by the impact of a large meteorite on the boundary between the Franconian and the Swabian Jura. To the north-east the Franconian Switzerland gives place along the line of several fault scarps to the relatively fertile *Upper Main Uplands*, built up from rocks of Triassic and Jurassic date, with the former Margravial residences of Bayreuth and Kulmbach as its principal towns.

Beyond this, in the extreme north-eastern corner of Bavaria, is the *Franconian Forest*, dissected by the river system of the Rodach and the White Main and displaced below the Upper Main Uplands by several faults. This plateau covered with coniferous forest forms a bridge between the Thuringian Forest (German Democratic Republic) and the East Bavarian border hills to the south-east. The Carboniferous slate worked in numerous quarries makes a valuable contribution to the economy of this unproductive forest land.

Along the southern edge of the Alb flows the **Danube** (*Donau*), whose valley opens out several times into wide flood plains and areas of marshland, now brought into cultivation, like the *Donauried* at Dillingen, now meadowland, and the boggy *Donaumoos* at Ingolstadt. Only to the east of Donauwörth, in the Neuburg narrows, do the hard Jurassic limestones come closer to the river.

South of the Danube extends the **Swabian-Bavarian Plateau**. The northern part of this is a fertile upland region of Tertiary marls and sands, to which the *Holledau* or Hallertau hop-growing district belongs. In the western part, between the rivers Lech and Iller, is a zone of Ice Age river debris with stretches of pine forest, heathland and bog. To the north of Munich are the *Dachau* and *Erding Bogs*; to the south the area merges into the hilly Alpine Foreland.

The old-established POPULATION consists predominantly of Franconians (Franks), who are of Central German stock and have been settled in the Main area since the 5th century. They are noted for their intellectual flexibility, sober energy and enterprise, and are less attached to the soil than the steady Old Bavarians of Upper German stock. After the Second World War many Germans who had lost their homes (for example in Czechoslovakia) settled in Franconia.

In the south the area occupied by Swabians extends as far east as the River Lech and takes in the old Imperial city of Augsburg.

Lower Franconia, like Swabia, is mainly of Roman Catholic faith; in Central and Upper Franconia Protestantism is predominant.

TRADITIONS are still preserved in many old customs, in local pageant plays (Rothenburg, Dinkelsbühl, etc.) and to some extent in local costumes, particularly in the Ochsenfurt area, in the Regnitz basin round Forchheim (Effeltrich) and in the Ries round Nördlingen.

The usual HOUSING PATTERN is the old Germanic type of large irregular village; only on the Franconian Terrace and in the Franconian Jura are separate farms and small hamlets commonly found. The Franconian or Central German type of farmhouse extends as far as the Franconian Jura. In this the trim half-timbered gable of the two-storey dwelling house faces on to the street, with the barn and animal stalls forming part of the same building, all set round a rectangular courtyard entered through a gateway.

The numerous small and medium-sized towns with their charming half-timbered houses are regularly laid out, often with a broad main street which serves as a market square.

In the AGRICULTURE of Franconia small and medium-sized holdings predominate. Almost two-thirds of the land is cultivated, mostly with corn. The production of hops is vital to the brewing trade, and the major part of the Bavarian crop comes from the Holledau (Hallertau) area. Other important hop-growing areas are the Rezat valley (Spalt) and between Nuremberg and Bamberg, where hops of good quality have been cultivated since the 14th century. In the lower Regnitz basin, round Bamberg, tobacco is grown, while the Main valley produces fruit and excellent wine.

A considerable development of INDUSTRY and CRAFTS has taken place in Franconia. It has a number of major industrial centres in Nuremberg, Fürth, Erlangen, Augsburg and Schweinfurt, whose machinery works, ball-bearings and toys have an international reputation. In the Franconian Forest between Hof and Bayreuth a varied range of textile industries has developed out of the old Upper Franconian hand-weaving trade.

Franconia has no MINERALS apart from the Solnhofen slate worked in the Altmühl valley. It has, however, numerous mineral springs.

In **FRANCONIA**, the most northerly part of the Free State of Bavaria, the scarped landscape of Württemberg continues, but here the plains are more extensive, the edges of the scarps smoother, the hills lower. A number of handsome towns punctuate the winding course of the Main in Lower Franconia – *Aschaffenburg* with its four-towered Schloss, *Miltenberg* with its half-timbered buildings, *Wertheim* with its massive ruined castle, the walls and gates of Kitzingen, Iphofen and Ochsenfurt.

Fine architecture, but on a larger and more sumptuous scale, is to be found in the university town of **Würzburg**, which receives its particular architectural stamp from the Baroque buildings erected by the Prince-Bishops. The famous Residenz has been restored after partial destruction during the war, and the fortress on the Marienberg still lords it over the old city as it has for so long. In *Veitshöchheim*, a short distance away, is the little pleasure palace of the Prince-Bishops with its famous Rococo gardens.

In Upper Franconia is the old Imperial and episcopal city of **Bamberg**, with its Cathedral and its magnificent sculpture as its main tourist attractions but with many other masterpieces of architecture as well. **Bayreuth** attracts music-lovers from all over the world with its Wagner associations and its Wagner festival.

Coburg, Kronach and *Kulmbach* have preserved their massive medieval fortifications. Magnificent buildings of a very different kind are the sumptuous Baroque churches of *Banz* and **Vierzehnheiligen** in the Main valley.

In Central Franconia three little towns which have barely grown beyond their medieval bounds have preserved almost intact the scale and pattern of life in the Middle Ages: **Rothenburg**, the most famous of the three, situated on the steep slopes of the Tauber valley; **Dinkelsbühl**, on a level plateau, smaller than Rothenburg but of equal quality; and *Nördlingen* within its almost precisely circular ring of walls in the wide Ries basin.

Among the cities of Franconia, however, pride of place must go to **Nuremberg**, whose old town, dominated by its imperial castle, has preserved something of the aspect of a free Imperial city of the Middle Ages. The National Germanic Museum displays treasures of art and culture from Germany's past, and Nuremberg also has an interesting Transport Museum.

Between Franconia and Bohemia extends a region of more austere character which seems almost out of place amid the smiling and varied landscapes of southern Germany – a tract of secluded forest land which offers a refuge from the stresses of modern life in surroundings of unspoiled natural beauty. The western slopes and foreland of the hills on the Bavarian-Bohemian frontier form a natural unit and a continuous stretch of tourist country, but they are divided up by administrative boundaries, so that most of the Fichtelgebirge falls within Upper Franconia, the Bavarian Forest with its foreland extending across the Danube to the south belongs to Lower Bavaria, and the Upper Palatinate – the central core of the area – stretches from the plateau of the Franconian Alb by way of the Naab depression to the East Bavarian border hills.

The Franconian Alb turns its face, with its steep and furrowed brow, towards Franconia: to the rear it slopes imperceptibly down to the east and south-east, falling from 600 to 500 m in a plateau of limestones and dolomites of Upper Jurassic date, merges on its northern flank, roughly between Bayreuth and Schwandorf, into the Naab depression and at the bend on the Danube at Regensburg dips under the Tertiary uplands of the Bavarian plateau. The rolling and inhospitable Jurassic plateau has a covering of short grass over much of its area, with some stretches of forest. Cultivated fields and pastureland are found only at certain places, particularly in the valleys, where the barren limestone has a covering of clay.

The finest scenery of this region is to be found in the sharply indented river valleys – the *Pegnitz* valley at Hersbruck (the Hersbruck Alb), the *Altmühl* valley between Beilngries and Kelheim and the *Danube* valley at Weltenburg.

There are no towns of any size apart from *Amberg*, formerly the chief town of the **Upper Palatinate**. The large towns lie outside the hills: Nuremberg in the western foreland, Regensburg at the south-east corner, where the Alb, the Bavarian Forest and the Alpine Foreland meet.

The central feature of the Upper Palatinate is the **Naab valley**, a depression of moderate depth between the Franconian Alb and the East Bavarian border hills. The geological substructure in this area is complex. Little is to be seen on the surface, since all earlier formations have been overlaid by the gently undulating surface of Tertiary deposits. The underlying rocks can, however, be detected in vegetation and crop patterns – the impermeable Tertiary clays being revealed by the countless ponds, Upper Triassic and Cretaceous sandstones by the forests, hills of New Red Sandstone by arable fields. The River Naab, formed by the junction of the Fichtelnaab coming from the Fichtelgebirge and the Waldnaab coming from the Upper Palatinate Forest, flows down at a moderate gradient through a valley which varies in width – now narrow, now opening out to form a basin – to join the Danube above Regensburg. *Weiden* and *Schwandorf*, both situated in wide basins, are important as traffic junctions and market towns as well as for the production of ceramics. Characteristic features of this area, once a major traffic route between Central Germany and Czechoslovakia, are the numerous castles, many of them watching over ancient little towns.

The Upper Palatinate and Lower Bavaria are decisively terminated by the East Bavarian border hills, which extend south-east from the Fichtelgebirge into Austria for a distance of some 300 km. Here the underlying gneisses and granites form rounded ridges and wide plateaux which have been broken up by longitudinal valleys and wide pass-like transverse valleys. The residual hills, thrust upwards and sideways, present steep escarpments to the south-west and fall away more gently to the north-east to merge into the Bohemian plateaux in Czechoslovakia. Although the character of this long range of hills changes several times and each part has, very properly, its own particular name, the whole range nevertheless has an overall unity. These lonely expanses of forest are an impressive sight when seen from one of the peaks.

The **Fichtelgebirge**, although at the northern end of the East Bavarian border hills, does not properly form part of the range. The Saale, the Eger, the Main and the Naab all rise in these hills. The meeting of two differently aligned ranges of hills (the Thuringian Forest, running from north-west to south-east, the Erzgebirge running from north-east to south-west – both in the German Democratic Republic) led to the upthrusting of horsts almost at right angles to one another and gave the Fichtelgebirge a horseshoe-shaped form. Above a gently undulating residual plateau forest-covered granite ridges rear up to a height of some 300 m, reaching the 1000 m mark in the Schneeberg and Ochsenkopf. The extensive spruce forests, beautiful river valleys, tumbles of boulders and weathered granite crags hold great attractions for visitors. The area within the horseshoe is mainly arable land and pasture, but also has active industries (china, woodworking, textiles). The chief town of the Fichtelgebirge is the centrally situated *Wunsiedel*, but the largest place is the porcelain town, *Selb*, which – like *Weiden* in the Upper Palatinate – has large factories producing fine china, domestic china and industrial ceramics. Since there are wide gaps between the ridges of hills, the Fichtelgebirge presents no great obstacles to traffic: only the west side falls steeply down into the valley basin in which lies Bayreuth, a town attractive to large numbers of visitors not only for its Wagner festival but also as a convenient point from which to explore the hills.

Grafenau, in the Bavarian Forest

The broad Tirschenreuth plateau, glittering with numerous little lakes, forms a transition between the Fichtelgebirge and the **Upper Palatinate Forest**, which extends for a distance of some 90 km to the Furth Depression. It consists of a series of graduated residual ridges whose flat gneiss summits rarely rise higher than 900 m. Large-scale clearance has removed more of the forest cover here than in other parts of the border hills, but the thin soil and harsh climate yield only a modest subsistence to the sparse population who live from agriculture – though forestry work, glass-blowing and the china industry to some extent make up for this. For the visitor there are old-world little towns and imposing ruined castles to be discovered in this lonely and out-of-the-way region.

The *Furth Depression* (470 m), the old gateway between Bohemia and Bavaria, is a 15 km wide gap in the East Bavarian border hills, traversed by the little River Chamb, which rises on the Bohemian side.

The **BAVARIAN FOREST** is the last, the highest and the most impressive part of the East Bavarian border hills. It begins above the Furth Depression and is bounded on the north-west by the rivers Chamb and Regen and on the south-west by the Danube valley, extending southeast to the Linz basin in Austria and merging on the north into the Bohemian Forest in Czechoslovakia.

Here too the underlying rocks are gneiss and granite, and here too the hills are broken up by longitudinal valleys with individual hills presenting steeply scarped slopes to the south-west. From extensive level areas of drift emerge broad step-like formations in which the rivers have carved out narrow gorges since the further upthrust of the hills. Evidence of these tectonic processes is given by the *Pfahl*, a long quartz dyke which can be clearly recognised only at those points where it has been exposed by erosion and has resisted the effects of weathering longer than the softer neighbouring stones. It marks the boundary between the two principal ranges in the Bavarian Forest, the Vorderer Wald and the Hinterer Wald.

The **Vorderer Wald** (Einödsriegel, 1126 m) is a rolling residual plateau which rises above the Danube depression in two stages of 500 and 700 m; it is also known as the *Donaugebirge* or Danube Hills. Above these two stages the summit region attains 1000 m, broken up into smaller ranges of hills by the numerous gorges carved out by rivers flowing down to the Danube. The very varied scenery of the western part of the range – a mingling of forests, meadows and arable fields, round-topped hills and valleys – is dotted with small hamlets and isolated farms.

The **Hinterer Wald** is also made up of a number of ranges of hills extending from north-west to south-east – the *Hoher Bogen* (1081 m), south of the Furth Depression; the Künisches Gebirge (*Osser*, 1293 m); the ridge from the Kaitersberg (1134 m) to the *Grosser Arber* (1457 m), the highest peak in the whole of the range; the massif of *Rachel* (1452 m) and *Lusen* (1371 m), within the Bavarian Forest National Park; and the

Dreisesselgebirge, with the *Dreisessel* (1312 m) and *Plöckenstein* (1378 m). The massive ridges and steep flanks of the whole Hinterer Wald have a continuous cover of magnificent natural forest, much of it with the aspect of unspoiled primeval woodland. On the northern and eastern slopes, just below the summit region, dark-surfaced lakes in glacier-hewn hollows bear witness to the action of the ice, here on a relatively small scale. Over the broad summit ridges extend areas of moorland or (above the tree-line) hill pastures with dark clumps of dwarf pines, with, here and there, weathered granite crags or tumbles of boulders. Human settlement is confined to some longitudinal valleys (Kötzting, Viechtach, Zwiesel) and to the lower levels below the main summit ridge where clearance has produced sizeable gaps in the forest cover, particularly round Grafenau and Freyung and along the "Goldener Steig" ("Golden Path") leading into Bohemia. Given the harsh climate and the thin soil, agriculture produces only modest yields of rye, oats and potatoes. Since there are no minerals the only other sources of income for the local people – some of whom still live in simple timber houses – are to be found in exploiting the resources of the forest and, more recently, in the tourist trade.

East Bavaria, now more easily accessible on the beautiful Ostmarkstrasse ("Eastern Marches Highway"), offers visitors attractive forest walks, quiet holiday resorts and excellent facilities for winter sports. In the Fichtelgebirge there are, in addition to its chief town of Wunsiedel with its labyrinth of rocks in the Luisenburg (open-air theatre), such attractive spots as *Bad Berneck*, *Bischofsgrün*, *Warmensteinach* and *Alexandersbad*. In *Waldsassen* the church and library of the former Cistercian monastery are well worth a visit.

The particular beauty of the Bavarian Forest lies in its stretches of unspoiled natural forest. At the foot of the much-visited "king of the forest", Arber, are *Bodenmais* and *Bayerisch Eisenstein*. Other popular resorts are *Zwiesel*, at the foot of Rachel, and *Haidmühle*, from which there is a motor road up the Dreisessel.

Scenery of quite a different kind is to be found to the south of the Bavarian Forest in the Danube depression and the Tertiary

hills of **LOWER BAVARIA**. The valley of the Danube between Regensburg and Vilshofen, here some 30 km wide, was the original area of settlement of the Bajuwari after their movement westward out of Bohemia. The villages lie close to one another in this region amid fertile fields of wheat, barley and sugar-beet. The market town for the agricultural produce is *Straubing*. The city of **Regensburg**, at the western end of the depression, enjoys a particularly favourable situation and has had a correspondingly successful development.

The Tertiary uplands, falling gently away into the Danube depression, are broken up into long ridges of hills by numerous rivers (the Laaber, the Isar, the Vils, the Rott) and their tributaries, producing a landscape which is basically uniform but offers an attractive variety of detail. Along the larger rivers lie the market villages and a few towns, of which only Landshut rose to major importance as residence of the Dukes of Lower Bavaria. The rural population live in small hamlets or individual farms scattered about in the upland countryside. The main crop is wheat; the Holledau (Hallertau) district to the west is noted for its hops.

On the southern edge of the hills are the two venerable old episcopal towns of Regensburg and Passau, on the *Danube*. Arriving in **Regensburg**, the visitor has an impressive view over the river of the old stone bridge and the twin spires of the Cathedral. In the neighbourhood, recalling great men and great events of the past, are *Walhalla*, the "German Temple of Fame", and the *Hall of Liberation* above Kelheim, which is the starting point of an attractive excursion up the Altmühl valley with its castles and country houses.

Passau, "the town of three rivers", with its old fortress of Oberhaus and its newly established university, is notable for the beauty of its situation on a narrow tongue of land between the Inn and the Danube, which here is joined by a third river, the Ilz.

The **ALPINE FORELAND** reached its present form only as a result of glacial action during the Ice Age. The glaciers surged out of all the large valleys from the Iller to the Salzach and spread out over the foreland area in great carpets of ice, carrying with them the rubble they had scoured off the mountains and depositing it along their edges in the form of moraines. The basins gouged out by the arms of the glaciers are now filled by lakes (Ammersee, Starnberger See, Chiemsee) or bogs, or have been drained by rivers. At the end of the glacial period the edge of the ice might pause for a considerable period during its retreat or make a minor advance, thus creating smaller basins on the edge of the mountains like the Tegernsee, the Kochelsee or the Walchensee.

Thus the Alpine Foreland is by no means a featureless plain. The varied land-forms, the alternation of forests, rivers and lakes and the snug little towns and villages with their onion-domed churches combine to produce a very attractive landscape pattern with a distinctive character.

Among the towns in the Bavarian Alpine Foreland pride of place must go to the Fugger city of **Augsburg**, still presenting the very image of proud and far-seeing civic consciousness with its Gothic churches, Renaissance buildings and beautiful fountains, and *Ingolstadt*, former residence of the Dukes of Bavaria, with its many fine religious and secular buildings. But there are also a host of smaller towns with much to offer the visitor – *Wasserburg* on the Inn and *Burghausen* on the Salzach with their characteristic southern architecture; *Altötting* with its pilgrimage chapel; the former Ducal residence of *Landshut*, with its brick-built churches and Burg Trausnitz; the towns of *Landsberg am Lech, Memmingen* and *Kempten* in Bavarian Swabia.

Then there are the monasteries and pilgrimage churches, often in out-of-the-way places, like *Ottobeuren* and *Ettal*, the **Wieskirche** and many more, which offer all the splendours of South German Baroque.

Facilities for water sports of all kinds are provided by the shimmering waters of the *Starnberger See*, the *Ammersee* and the *Chiemsee*, with its sumptuous royal palace of Herrenchiemsee.

The major attractions of Southern Bavaria are Munich and the Alps.

Munich, capital of the Free State of Bavaria, has long been a magnet for visitors from all over the world, drawn by the manifold cultural delights and the friendly atmosphere of this city of art and *joie de vivre*. It is also an ideal base from which to explore the magnificent mountain world of Upper Bavaria.

In the **BAVARIAN ALPS** the oldest and most resistant rocks (Triassic limestones of Wetterstein and Dachstein type) lie in the south, where they form the highest peaks, the *Zugspitze* (2963 m) and the *Watzmann* (2714 m). To the north of these jagged limestone mountains are less rugged sandstone hills like the Zwiesel at Bad Tölz. When the primeval sea developed into a fresh-water bog in the middle Tertiary period the molasse was deposited in the form of conglomerates (nagelfluh), clays and coal. West of the Iller these rocks form such hills as the Stuiben; farther east only foothills in the plain like the Auerberg and the Hoher Peissenberg.

In the **Allgäu Alps** the hard limestone forms only the topmost peaks, so that the valleys are wider and have less steeply sloping sides than farther east.

In the *Central Bavarian Alps* the alternation of hard and soft layers led to regular folding and the development of longitudinal valleys and ridges running from east to west.

In the **Berchtesgaden Alps** the Dachstein limestones, up to 2000 m thick, resisted folding, so that massifs like the Reiter Alpe and the Untersberg were left standing as we see them today. The solubility of the limestone in water, however, led to the creation of karstic forms, with pavements of clefts and ridges, swallow-holes and larger cavities (for example in the Steinernes Meer).

In general, variations in height are the result of mountain folding movements; the formation of the valleys, on the other hand, was the work of running water, the carrying power of which is amply demonstrated by the debris deposited on many valley bottoms. The detailed shaping of the landscape, however, was due to the action of ice. Local glaciers carved out of the rounded mountain forms steep and rugged peaks like the pyramids of the Watzmann and the Schönfeldspitze in the Steinernes Meer, and gouged out of the flanks of the summit ridges recesses or depressions (*Kare*) which now contain small mountain lakes or have developed into large rounded valley-heads (for example at the Obersee above the Königssee). From the Central Alps came great flows of ice which filled up the valleys on the edge of the hills to a height of 1500 m above sea level and scoured them out (for example the Loisach valley at Garmisch and the Isar valley at Mittenwald). This also gave rise to the steep valley sides,

Ramsau in the Berchtesgadener Land

their lower slopes covered with rock debris, above which is the flatter region of Alpine meadows.

The POPULATION of this region in the early centuries of our era consisted of Romanised Celts, who were known to the Germanic peoples as "Welschen" ("foreigners") – a term which is still found in a number of place-names (e.g. the Walchensee). The permanent settlement by Germanic tribes began at the end of the great migration period. From the end of the 5th century onwards parts of various tribes, mainly coming from Bohemia (Bojoarii or Bajuwari), moved into the region between the Bavarian Forest and the Alps and consolidated their position to become the Bavarians. About the middle of the 6th century the Swabians, coming from western Germany, reached the River Lech, which marks the approximate boundary between Swabian place-names ending in -ingen and Bavarian names ending in -ing.

The fact that the Ducal territory of Bavaria was never split during the Middle Ages into so many small principalities as the neighbouring region of Swabia was no doubt due partly to the quieter and steadier disposition of the Bavarians as compared with the more volatile Swabians and partly to the greater unity of the landscape pattern in Upper Bavaria as compared with the patchwork of different landscape forms in South-West Germany. This developed the Bavarians' feeling of racial solidarity at an earlier stage than that of the Swabians and created a strong sense of their own separate identity. While in Swabia almost all the numerous towns were at one stage free Imperial cities, in Bavaria most of the towns – which were in any case fewer in number – were subject to the authority of the Duke. Old Bavaria (i.e. the old ducal possessions before the accession of new territories in

the early 19th century) preserved more strongly than other regions the sturdy individuality of a land of peasant farmers.

Traditional COSTUMES are still worn to a greater extent in Upper Bavaria than elsewhere in Germany, and even in Munich have not been entirely displaced by modern dress. The characteristic features of men's dress are leather shorts, a cloth waistcoat with silver buttons, a jacket of heavy woollen material (Loden) with stag-horn buttons and a green hat with a chamois beard or other hunting trophy, while the women wear a black bodice laced with silver and a kerchief or tucker on the bosom; there are, however, many local variations.

FOLK ART, too, is still vigorously alive, interacting fruitfully with the artistic life of Munich. Among its characteristic manifestations are the painted biers used in funerals, the memorial tablets set up at the scene of an accident, the decorated domestic utensils and the painted house-fronts. Oberammergau is noted for its woodcarving; Berchtesgaden for its wooden caskets; while Mittenwald has been famed for more than two centuries for its violin-making.

The Bavarian attachment to the heritage of the past has preserved many TRADITIONAL CUSTOMS. Old Bavaria is a land of religious processions, with its various "St George's rides" and "St Leonard's cavalcades" and its Corpus Christi processions. In autumn there is the "Almabtrieb", when the cattle, gaily decorated, are driven down from their mountain pastures. At weddings the decorated "Kammerwagen" containing the bride's trousseau is often to be seen. And everywhere the visitor will encounter the Bavarian folk songs and dances, with the traditional zither accompaniment. In this field a special place is occupied by the yodelled songs and "Schnaderhüpferl", a four-lined verse, often in a satirical vein, which may be improvised on the spot. The "Schuhplattler" dance represents a lover's wooing. There are, too, a variety of dramatic performances, like the famous Oberammergau Passion Play, which carries on the tradition of the medieval mystery, and the plays performed at the peasant theatres of Tegernsee and Schliersee and the folk theatre of Kiefersfelden.

The typical DOMESTIC ARCHITECTURE in the mountains is the so-called "Alpine house", which has a flat roof weighted with stones and incorporates the cow-stalls on the ground floor. In the Alpine Foreland the houses have more steeply pitched roofs and the dwelling house and farmstead buildings are separate, often laid out round a rectangular courtyard. The towns on the Inn and Salzach have distinctive Italian-style houses with straight-ended roofs and arcades. The HOUSING PATTERN shows a predominance of separate farms, particularly in the morainic zone in the Foreland. The villages tend to avoid the lowest part of the valley bottoms, which are exposed to flooding and in winter are cold and misty. In the mountains the favoured sites are the upper edge of the valley bottom and the detrital cones of lateral streams; in the Foreland the morainic hills and the middle terraces.

The **Bavarian Alps** achieve their effect by their great variety of land-forms and scenery. The *Allgäu Alps* are given their specific character by their steep mountain meadows and beautifully shaped peaks, while the *Wettersteingebirge* has its sheer rock faces and Germany's highest mountain, the Zugspitze, now accessible even to the non-climber through its mountain railways. Farther east the gentle contours of the *Tegernsee Hills* are juxtaposed with the mighty limestone massifs of the *Berchtesgaden Alps* (Alpine National Park).
Among the host of climatic, holiday and winter sports resorts three are outstanding – **Garmisch-Partenkirchen** with its mountain railways and winter sports facilities; **Berchtesgaden** with the proud *Watzmann* and picturesque *Königssee*, one of the high spots of the German Alps; and **Oberstdorf** with its magnificent panorama of mountains. In addition there are *Füssen*, with the royal castles of *Hohenschwangau* and *Neuschwanstein* a short distance away; *Oberammergau* with its Passion Play; *Ettal* with its famous Benedictine abbey and the nearby *Schloss Linderhof*; **Mittenwald**, the beautiful little town of violin-makers; *Bayrischzell* with its excellent skiing; the health resorts of *Bad Tölz, Bad Wiessee* and *Bad Reichenhall*; and the little towns of *Kochel, Walchensee, Tegernsee* and *Schliersee* on the shores of romantic mountain lakes. The magnificent German Alpine Highway from Lindau to Berchtesgaden links all these places.

The former German capital of **BERLIN**, devastated during the Second World War and thereafter split into a western and an eastern part, has nevertheless shown astonishing vitality as the focal point of international political differences and is still Germany's largest city, with more to attract the visitor than ever before. The divided city lies within the territory of the German Democratic Republic and is most easily reached by air; but getting to Berlin by rail or road is now also relatively trouble-free. In spite of its isolated situation West Berlin is a cosmopolitan world city pulsating with life, with great industrial potential, richly endowed with cultural institutions and events and with an abundance of modern buildings. Nor should visitors omit a trip into *East Berlin* (the museums on the Museum Island, the Alexanderplatz, the Television Tower, "Unter den Linden", etc.).

Climate

The Federal Republic of Germany lies within the temperate climatic zone of Central Europe, but has the benefit, compared with other countries in the same latitude, of the moderating influence of the Gulf Stream. The country's climatic pattern shows a gradual transition from the more oceanic type found in the north-west, with mild winters and only moderately warm summers, to the more continental east and south, with greater seasonal variations. The increase in temperature towards the south, at the rate of $\frac{1}{3}$ °C ($\frac{3}{5}$ °F) for each degree of latitude, is more than balanced by the usually greater altitudes in South Germany. Only in the wide Upper Rhine plain and its larger lateral valleys does the influence of the more southerly latitude come fully into play, and it is here that the highest annual mean temperatures are recorded. But the weather of Central Europe remains unpredictable because of its situation between the depression over Iceland to the north-west (with the prevailing north-west winds bringing rain), the anticyclone over the Azores to the south-west (with a considerable northward displacement in summer), which is responsible for good weather, and the area of high pressure which lies almost continuously over Russia, particularly in winter, and the continual movement of these areas.

There are considerable variations in **temperature** depending on the predominance of one or other of these factors. The most markedly oceanic pattern of temperatures in the Federal Republic is found in Heligoland (alt. 41 m (135 ft); mean annual temp. 8·4 °C (47 °F), Jan. 1·8° (35°), July 15·5° (60°)). The temperature range of 13·7° (57°) between the coldest and the warmest month is characteristic of this balanced climate. An example of the climate of the North German plain, already showing a more continental pattern, is provided by Helmstadt (alt. 139 m (459 ft); annual 8·4 °C (47 °F), Jan. −1° (30°), July 16·3° (61°), range 17·3° (63°)). Still more continental is Berlin (alt. 42 m (139 ft); annual 8·8 °C (48 °F), Jan. −1° (30°), July 17° (63°), range 18·7° (66°)). The highest annual and the highest July temperatures among the larger towns are found in Ludwigshafen in the Upper Rhine valley (10·5° (51°) and 19 °C (66 °F); Jan. 1·7° (35°), range 17·3° (63°)), the highest January temperature in Cologne (2·5 °C (37 °F); annual 10·2° (50°), July 18° (64°), range 15·5° (60°)). Places at higher altitudes in the upland regions of Central Germany and in South Germany show a drop of about $\frac{1}{2}$ °C ($\frac{9}{10}$ °F) in mean annual temperature for every 100 m (330 ft) (fall in winter 0·3–0·5 °C (0·54–0·6 °F), in summer 0·5–0·7° (0·6–0·61°)). An example of a climate of more oceanic type in South Germany is Stuttgart (alt. 267 m (881 ft): annual 10 °C (50 °F), Jan. 1·5° (34°), July 16·5° (61°), range 16·5° (61°)), and of a more continental climate Munich (alt. 529 m (1745 ft): annual 7·4 °C (45 °F), Jan. 2·6° (36°), July 16·5° (61°), range 19·1° (66°)). The summits of the mountains, which are under stronger oceanic influence on account of the prevailing west winds, show annual temperature fluctuations comparable to those found on the North Sea coast: thus the Zugspitze (2962 m (9775 ft): annual −5 °C (23 °F), Jan. −11·7° (11°), July 2° (35°)) has the same temperature range as Heligoland, 13·7° (56°). A good indication of relative temperatures is given by the first appearance of apple-blossom, which marks the beginning of spring. In the Upper Rhine valley between Basle and Freiburg this falls between 10 and 20 April, in the Neckar valley north of Stuttgart, the lower Main valley and the Middle and Lower Rhine valley between 25 and 30 April, in the inner Black Forest, the Swabian Alb and the higher part of the

Sauerland not until 20–31 May. The lowest recorded temperatures on Heligoland are −15·6 °C (4 °F), in Hamburg −21·1° (−6°), at Freiburg im Breisgau −21·7° (−7°), at Stuttgart −25° (−13°), at Münsingen in the Swabian Alb −31° (−23°), and on the Zugspitze −36·6° (−33°).

The level of **precipitation** in the North German plain increases slightly with increasing distance from the sea: Emden 738 mm (29 in.) annually, Hamburg 712 mm (28 in.), Hanover 644 mm (25 in.), Helmstedt 613 mm (24 in.), Berlin 527 mm (20 in.). In general the amount of rainfall at a particular place depends on its height above sea level and above all on its situation in relation to the rain-bringing west winds. Thus the Rhine valley, lying between upland regions, has a markedly low rainfall − Cologne 660 mm (25 in.), Mainz 515 mm (20 in.), Karlsruhe 672 mm (26 in.). But even here there are differences between the windward and leeward sides of the valley − Mannheim (leeward) 528 mm (20 in.), Heidelberg (windward) 718 mm (28 in.). In the upland regions too there are often considerable differences between neighbouring places: for example, in the Black Forest, Calw/Nagold (350 m (1155 ft)) 738 mm (29 in.), Freudenstadt (728 m (2402 ft)) 1471 mm (58 in.), Kniebis (904 m (2983 ft)) 1679 mm (66 in.), Feldberg (1494 m (4930 ft)) 1929 mm (76 in.). In southern Bavaria the decisive factor is the situation of a place in relation to the Alps: Regensburg (343 m (1131 ft)) 591 mm (23 in.), Landshut (400 m (1320 ft)) 698 mm (27 in.), Munich (529 m (1745 ft)) 866 mm (35 in.), Trostberg (493 m (1626 ft)) 1065 mm (42 in.), Lechbruck (732 m (2415 ft)) 1204 mm (47 in.), Ettal (884 m (2917 ft)) 1509 mm (59 in.), Urfeld on the Walchensee (857 m (2828 ft)) 1812 mm (71 in.), Untersberg (1663 m (5787 ft)) 1912 mm (75 in.), Wendelstein (1727 m (5700 ft)) 2869 mm (113 in.). At still greater altitudes the level of precipitation begins to decline again: Zugspitze (2962 m (9774 ft)) 1350 mm (53 in.) (with over 5 m (16 ft) of snow in some winters). Rain falls throughout the year, generally with a distinct maximum in July, less rain in June and August and a minimum in February (or in some places March). Examples: Cologne (alt. 56 m (184 ft)), average annual rainfall 660 mm (26 in.), min. in February 42 mm (1½ in.), max. in July 77 mm (3 in.); Stuttgart (267 m (881 ft)), annual 673 mm (26 in.), min. in February 34 mm (1 in.), max. in June 84 mm (3 in.). In the North Sea area rain falls more often in autumn and winter (with frequent fog and strong winds) but more abundantly in summer (max. in August); the spring is sunny. On the islands of Heligoland and Sylt October is the rainiest month. On many hills in the upland regions rainfall reaches its maximum in winter: Kahler Asten (848 m (2798 ft)), annual 1438 mm (56 in.), min. in May 95 mm (3 in.), max. in December and January, both 150 mm (6 in.); Feldberg in the Black Forest (1494 m (4930 ft)), annual 1929 mm (76 in.), min. in April 135 mm (5 in.), max. in December 185 mm (7 in.). It occasionally happens, with heavy and continuous rain, that the average figure for a whole month or even more falls within a period of 24 hours, sometimes leading to catastrophic floods: thus in South-West Germany at the end of May 1978 up to 100 mm (4 in.) of rain fell in a single day. Climatic phenomena which occur in particular conditions are the "climatic reversal" which takes place in winter under the influence of an anticyclone when the peaks, bathed in sunshine, may be anything up to 10 °C (50 °F) warmer than the valleys and basins below, lying in a "cold patch" and shrouded in mist, and the *Föhn*, a warm dry wind which blows down from the Alps into South Bavaria and Upper Swabia in spring and melts the snow (increase in temperature of 1° for every 100 m (330 ft)).

Sunshine

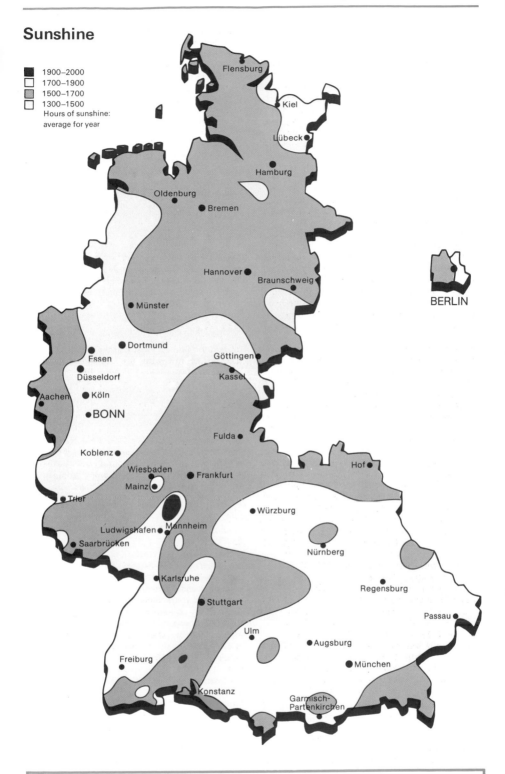

Legend:
- 1900–2000
- 1700–1900
- 1500–1700
- 1300–1500

Hours of sunshine: average for year

Map labels: Flensburg, Kiel, Lübeck, Hamburg, Oldenburg, Bremen, Hannover, Braunschweig, Münster, BERLIN, Dortmund, Essen, Göttingen, Düsseldorf, Kassel, Aachen, Köln, BONN, Fulda, Koblenz, Hof, Wiesbaden, Frankfurt, Mainz, Trier, Würzburg, Ludwigshafen, Mannheim, Saarbrücken, Nürnberg, Karlsruhe, Regensburg, Stuttgart, Passau, Ulm, Augsburg, Freiburg, München, Konstanz, Garmisch-Partenkirchen

The map shows zones and smaller pockets with approximately the same number of hours of sunshine over the year.

It can be seen that the most favoured areas are the northern end of the Upper Rhine rift valley and a small pocket in the southern part of the Swabian Alb.

History

Prehistoric period. – During the *Palaeolithic period* (*c.* 600000–10000 B.C.) men live in large groups, gaining their subsistence by hunting, food-gathering and fishing, fashioning implements and weapons from stone, wood or bone and dwelling in tents, huts or caves.

500000–150000   The oldest known human remains on German soil are the lower jaws of *Homo heidelbergensis* found at Mauer, near Heidelberg, the skull found at Steinheim an der Murr and the skeleton of "Neanderthal man" from the Neander valley near Düsseldorf.

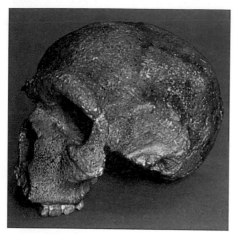

The Steinheim skull

8000–1800   Transition towards the establishment of settlements, log-built houses, pile-dwellings (on Lake Constance), and towards agriculture and stock-rearing; beginnings of trade and inter-communication; "Hunengräber" (megalithic tombs) on Lüneburg Heath.

1800–750   *Bronze Age* in Central Europe; the most highly prized materials are bronze, amber and gold. Tumulus tombs.

Around 1000   Beginning of *Iron Age* in Europe.

800–400   First Central European culture (La Tène) developed by the **Celts** (at first in southern Germany, then extensive migrations in Europe); construction of hill forts (e.g. the Heuneburg, near Sigmaringen).

800–70   The **Germanic peoples** thrust into Celtic territory from Schleswig-Holstein, advancing to the Oder and Rhine and into southern Germany.

Around 58 B.C.   In a succession of military campaigns the **Romans** make the Rhine the north-eastern frontier of the Roman Empire. First accounts of Germany in Caesar's "Gallic War". Romanisation of the left bank of the Rhine.

After 40 B.C.   Construction of forts at Cologne, Trier, Koblenz, Mainz, etc., to secure the Rhine frontier.

A.D. 9   A Roman army led by *Varus* is defeated by the Cheruscan leader *Arminius* in the Teutoburg Forest. Germany as far as the Rhine and the Danube is freed.

From A.D. 90   Construction of the LIMES, 550 km long defensive line from the Rhine to the Danube designed to check German advances over the frontier, and of numerous forts (at Wiesbaden, Augsburg, Regensburg, Passau, etc.).

From 200   Emergence of a number of large West Germanic tribes – Alemanni, Franks, Chatti, Bajuvari, Saxons, Frisians, Thuringians, Langobardi.

Around 260   The Germans break through the Limes and the Danube frontier.

From the great migrations to the end of the Carolingian Empire (300–918). – The period of the great *migrations*, which change the whole map of Europe, begins with the advance of the Huns into Europe (*c.* 375). the Eastern Germanic peoples destroy the Western Roman Empire (476), but the states they found do not last. The Western Germans move into the territory of the Roman Empire without losing contact with their own ancestral lands. The mingling between Germanic traditions and the Christian Church (which also embodies the cultural traditions of antiquity) gives rise to the pattern of life of the medieval West.

481–511   By unifying the **Franks** and conquering Gaul the Merovingian king *Chlodwig* (Clovis) becomes the founder of the Frankish kingdom. Strengthening of the common feeling between Germans and Romans.

496   The Franks defeat the Alemanni, accept the Catholic faith and so gain the support of the Church.

From 600   Christianisation of the Germans by Iro-Scottish monks; foundation of monasteries at Würzburg, Regensburg, Reichenau, etc.

From 720   Missionary activity in the Merovingian kingdom by the Anglo-Saxon monk *Boniface*; foundation of monasteries at Fritzlar, Fulda, etc.; establishment of bishoprics by Papal authority

751   *Pippin* (Pépin), controller of the palace under the Merovingian king, himself assumes the title of king and is anointed by the Church. The Frankish kings now set up as protectors of the Pope, and begin to take an interest in Italian affairs.

772–814   **Charlemagne** extends the Carolingian empire into Northern Italy and the territory of all the West Germanic peoples (the Saxons and Bajuvari or Bavarians).

800   Charlemagne's authority in Western Europe is confirmed by his coronation as Emperor in Rome; re-establishment of the Roman Empire. The Frankish empire is subdivided into counties, and its frontiers are protected by border Marches. The Imperial strongholds (*Kaiserpfalzen*) at Aachen, Ingelheim, Worms, Nijmegen, etc., become economic and cultural centres. The "Carolingian Renaissance": revival of Greek and Roman culture, promotion of education and scholarship.

The German Empire in the Middle Ages, down to the Reformation (*c.* 919–1517). – In the *struggle* which now begins *between the Pope and the Emperor*, between the supreme spiritual and the supreme secular power, the Emperor is compelled to give way; but at the same time the foundations of ecclesiastical authority are undermined, since the Popes bring about a secularisation of the Church.

843–880   Successive partitions of the Carolingian empire; the German Empire develops out of the East Frankish kingdom.

919–936   The Germanic peoples (Franks, Saxons, Swabians and Bavarians) are united under Duke *Henry* of Saxony, who takes the title of king. The term Kingdom (Empire) of the Germans ("Regnum Teutonicorum") is applied for the first time to the East Frankish kingdom.

936–973 *Otto the Great*, crowned king at Aachen in 936, strengthens the royal authority by appointing bishops and abbots as Princes of the Kingdom (*Reichsfürsten*); establishment of a national church (*Reichskirche*).

951 Otto wins the Langobardic (Lombard) crown by marrying the widowed queen *Adelheid*.

955 Decisive victory over the Hungarians at Lechfeld, near Augsburg; Submission of the Slavs between the Elbe and the Oder.

962 Otto I is crowned Emperor in Rome; strong influence on the Papacy. *First flowering of German culture*, with women playing a large part (Otto's mother Mathilde, Adelheid, his daughter-in-law Theophano, Rosthwitha of Gandersheim, etc.); monasteries as cultural centres; flowering of Romanesque architecture (Mainz, Speyer, Hildesheim, etc.).

Around 1000 Revival of monasticism and founding of new monasteries, daughter houses of Cluny (the principal foundation in Germany being at Hirsau in the Black Forest).

1033 The kingdom of Burgundy is united with the German Empire.

1039–1056 During the reign of *Henry III* Germany supports the Cluniac reform of the Church: the Peace of God, prohibition of simony (the purchase of clerical offices) and of the marriage of priests. Imperial authority over the Pope reaches its peak. Construction of Imperial stronghold (*Pfalz*) at Goslar.

From 1075 The *investiture dispute* between *Henry IV* and Pope *Gregory VII* over appointments to ecclesiastical offices.

1077 Henry IV submits to the Pope at Canossa.

1122 Temporary reconciliation between *Henry V* and the Pope in the Concordat of Worms. Consequences of the investiture dispute: weakening of the Ottonian Reichskirche, strengthening of the secular princes in Germany.

1096–1291 The *Crusades*. Establishment of knightly religious orders (Templars, Knights of St John, Teutonic Order). Emergence of a European nobility with common aims and ideals, expressed particularly in the ideas of chivalry. Cultural and commercial exchanges with the East.

1152–1190 Emperor *Frederick I* **Barbarossa**, of the Staufen dynasty. An accommodation is reached with the rival Guelf party by the grant of the Duchy of Bavaria to *Henry the Lion*. Austria becomes a separate Duchy. Return to the Italian policies of the Ottonian emperors and their successors the Salians. Resumption of German colonisation in the East.

1177 Reconciliation between the Emperor and the Pope in Venice.

1180 Henry the Lion is outlawed; Bavaria is given to *Otto von Wittelsbach* (founder of a dynasty which was to rule in Bavaria until 1918) and Saxony is divided. Setback for the colonisation movement in the East.

1184–1186 The Staufen Empire under Barbarossa reaches its peak in the "Reichsfest" (Imperial celebrations) held at Mainz and the marriage of his son Henry in Milan to the Norman princess Constance of Sicily. The power of the feudal lords is undermined by the appointment of "ministerials" (unfree servants of the Emperor) as officials.

Flowering of chivalry (practices of knighthood, courtly love, courtly life in castles) and of epic poetry and the Minnesang ("Nibelungenlied", Wolfram von Eschenbach, Gottfried von Strassburg, Hartmann von der Aue, Walther von der Vogelweide).

1212–1250 *Frederick II* establishes a modern, professionally administered state in Sicily. Grant of extensive sovereign powers to ecclesiastical and secular princes, leading to the rise of independent territorial states. The struggle with the Papacy saps the Empire's strength. Fall of the Staufen dynasty after Frederick II's death, followed by an interregnum when there is no Emperor.

1250–1450 Gothic cathedrals built at Freiburg, Marburg, Strassburg, Cologne, etc.

From 1100 Foundation of new towns round Imperial strongholds, castles, bishops' palaces and monasteries. The towns begin to establish municipal rights and liberties, while the rural population remain in a state of serfdom. Strict control of markets. The towns are ruled by patricians (merchants carrying on long-distance trade); the craftsmen form *guilds*, governed by strict rules, which seek to obtain control of the towns. Intensification of long-distance trade with the East and the North; the trading towns come together in the **Hanse** (Hanseatic League), under the leadership of Lübeck; action against pirates. Decline of the Hanse in the 15th century.
Colonisation movement in the East: German settlers (peasants, townspeople, the Teutonic Order) move into the thinly populated Slav territories east of the Oder (Bohemia, Silesia, Pomerania, Poland), establishing towns and villages governed by German law.

Between 1220 and 1235 *Eike von Repgau* composes the "Sachsenspiegel" ("Mirror of the Saxons"), the oldest German law-book of the Middle Ages (first in Latin, later in Low German).

1226 Conquest and Christianisation of Prussia by the Teutonic Order.

1346–1378 *Charles IV* (of Luxembourg) seeks to restore the royal authority by establishing a strong dynastic power. Policy of expansion in the East.

A page from the "Sachsenspiegel"

Around 1350 The Black Death ravages Europe. Persecution of the Jews, on religious and economic grounds.

1356 The Golden Bull: in future the Emperor is to be chosen by seven Electors (the Archbishops of Mainz, Trier and Cologne, the King of Bohemia, the Count Palatine of the Rhine, the Duke of Saxony and the Margrave of Brandenburg).

1300–1648 The Empire loses territory on all its frontiers (Switzerland, Schleswig-Holstein, West Prussia, the Low Countries).

1493–1519 Reform of the Empire by *Maximilian I*: establishment of Imperial High Court (Reichskammergericht), levying of Imperial taxes, increasing power of the Imperial Diet (Reichstag). The reforms are, however, frustrated by the territorial fragmentation of the Empire.

From 1400 The knightly classes are impoverished by the introduction of mercenary armies and foot-soldiers; the "robber knights" come to the fore.

1300–1500 Foundation of universities at Prague, Vienna, Heidelberg, Cologne, Leipzig and Rostock.

From 1400 The **modern world** comes into being, as a result of far-reaching intellectual, political and economic changes. The beginnings of natural science; *Copernicus* founds modern astronomy. About 1450 Gutenberg invents the art of printing with movable type in Mainz. *Humanism* in Germany: rediscovery of ancient literature, concern with the world and with nature. German humanists: Ulrich von Hutten, Johannes Reuchlin, Jakob Wimpheling, Melanchthon. The *Renaissance*: rebirth of ancient art (architecture and sculpture); discovery of beauty in nature and the individual qualities in human personality. German painters: Albrecht Dürer, Hans Holbein the Younger. Increasing *particularism* of the territorial princes in face of the preponderant power of the Habsburgs. Social discontents of the knights and peasants as a result of the establishment of a money economy. Changes in the art of war with the increasing use of firearms. Economic power of the towns. The beginnings of *capitalism*. Rise of the **Fuggers** through commercial and financial activities; they become financiers to both ecclesiastical and secular rulers.

From the Reformation to the end of the Holy Roman Empire (c. 1517–1815). – The *Reformation* destroys the unity of the Roman Church, while at the same time the increasing power of the state constricts the liberty of the nobility and the townspeople. The system of *absolutism* gradually develops in the territorial states, so that the Emperor's authority is confined to his own dynastic possessions and the German Empire (now known as the "Holy Roman Empire of the German Nation") falls apart into a multiplicity of separate states.

Around 1500 There is much criticism in Germany of abuses in the Church and a desire for reform. Popular piety mingled with superstition.

1517 Beginning of the **Reformation**, when *Luther* nails his 95 "theses" against the abuse of indulgences to the church door in Wittenberg.

1521 Luther is outlawed at the Diet of Worms. The Reformation spreads rapidly, helped by the Emperor Charles V's wars with France and the Turks. Luther's translation of the Bible establishes the basis of modern German.

1522 Luther in conflict with Anabaptists and Iconoclasts. Unsuccessful rising of the discontented Imperial knights (Reichsritter) led by Franz von Sickingen.

1524–1525 *Peasant wars* in Swabia, Franconia (Götz von Berlichingen, Florian Geyer) and Thuringia (Thomas Münzer) against ruling princes and lords; repressed by the territorial princes.

From 1545 Beginning of the *Counter-Reformation* in Germany, the main motive force being provided by the Jesuit order, founded by the Spaniard, Ignatius de Loyola. Central and north-eastern Germany almost wholly Protestant, western and southern Germany predominantly Catholic.

1546–1547 *War of the League of Schmalkalden* between the Emperor Charles V and the Protestants.

1555 Peace of Augsburg: recognition of the Lutheran faith; the religion of a state to be that of its ruler ("Cuius regio, eius religio").

1556 Abdication of Charles V; division of the Habsburg Empire.

1608–1609 Formation of the Protestant Union and the Catholic League.

1618–1648 **Thirty Years War.** Causes: the conflicts between Catholics and Protestants, the efforts by the various states within the Empire to increase their power and the Habsburg Emperor's attempt to achieve the religious and political unity of the Empire. The immediate occasion of the war is the rising of the Protestant nobility of Bohemia against the Emperor ("Defenestration of Prague"), but the conflict is widened into a European war by the intervention of King *Christian IV* of Denmark, the Spaniards, King *Gustavus II Adolphus* of Sweden and France under Cardinal *Richelieu*. Germany becomes the main theatre of war and the scene of the final conflict between France and the Habsburgs for predominance in Europe. Large areas of Germany are laid waste and it loses something like a third of its population; general impoverishment.

1640–1688 Rise of Brandenburg-Prussia under the *Great Elector Frederick William*. Establishment of *absolutism*.

1648 Peace of Westphalia (signed at Münster and Osnabrück): cessions of territory to France and Sweden; the Low Countries and Switzerland are lost to the Empire. Decline of the Imperial power; rise of Brandenburg-Prussia.

1678–1681 *Louis XIV* of France conquers parts of Alsace and Lorraine.

1683 The Turks are defeated outside Vienna by a German and Polish army led by Prince *Eugene of Savoy*. Reconquest of Hungary; German settlement in the Banat. Austria develops under the Habsburgs into a great power.

1688–1697 Louis XIV wages an unsuccessful war in the Palatinate; great devastation (Heidelberg Castle, Speyer, Worms). French language and culture are adopted by the German courts and nobility.

1701 Elector *Frederick of Brandenburg* is crowned "King in Prussia".

1713–1740 Establishment of a highly centralised state by *Frederick William I*, the "Soldier King".

18th century Baroque and Rococo art (Castle, Berlin; Zwinger, Dresden; great musicians – Bach, Händel, Telemann, Haydn, Mozart). The Age of

Enlightenment (belief in progress, tolerance, rights of man). Writers of the German classical period (Herder, Goethe, Schiller).

1740–1748 War of the Austrian Succession: *Maria Theresa* fights for recognition of her succession to the throne. Loss of Silesia to **Frederick II, the Great**, of Prussia (1740–86) in the Silesian Wars and the Seven Years War (1756–63).

1763 Peace of Hubertusburg between Austria, Prussia and Saxony: *Prussia becomes a European great power.* Beginning of the rivalry between Prussia and Austria for the leadership of Germany.

After 1763 Establishment of "enlightened absolutism" in Prussia and Austria (the ruler as "the first servant of the state"), against resistance from the nobility and citizenry. Economic development; legal reforms (abolition of torture, improvement in the status of Jews); first emancipations of the peasants; promotion of education.

1795 Peace of Basle between France and Prussia: left bank of the Rhine ceded to France; Prussia to be neutral. Austria continues the struggle.

1803 Under the "Reichsdeputationshauptschluss" (a resolution of a committee of the Imperial Diet meeting in Regensburg) **Napoleon** abolishes almost all the ecclesiastical and the smaller secular states and most of the free Imperial cities. New medium-sized states established in south-western Germany; expansion of Prussia.

1806 Establishment of the Confederation of the Rhine under Napoleon's protection; dissolution of the Holy Roman Empire. Prussia defeated at Jena and Auerstedt.

1807 Peace of Tilsit: cession of all Prussian possessions west of the Elbe; establishment of the Kingdom of Westphalia under Napoleon's brother *Jérôme.*

1808–1812 Reconstruction and reform in Prussia: regulation of municipal government, liberation of the peasants, freedom to practise trades, emancipation of the Jews, reform of the army (Freiherr vom Stein, Hardenberg, Scharnhorst, Gneisenau).

1813 Beginning of the *Wars of Liberation*, following the destruction of Napoleon's army in Russia (1812). Germany is liberated after the Battle of the Nations at Leipzig. End of the Confederation of the Rhine.

1815 Final defeat of Napoleon at Waterloo by Wellington and Blücher.

1814–1815 **Congress of Vienna** for the regulation of European affairs, under the leadership of Prince *Metternich* (Austria). Political principles: the restoration, legitimacy and solidarity of the rulers for the repression of revolutionary and nationalist ideas. Foundation of the German Confederation (*Bund*) of 39 states (35 ruling princes and 4 free cities) under Austrian leadership, with a Federal Diet (Bundestag) meeting at Frankfurt am Main.

From the Restoration to the First World War (1815–1914). – The history of the 19th century is principally determined by the effects of the French Revolution and the developing *Industrial Revolution*. Liberal and nationalist ideas are fostered by the middle classes (bourgeoisie). The conditions of the bourgeois-capitalist world give rise to the difficulties and discontents of the working classes.

1817 The "Wartburg festival", organised by student organisations; burning of reactionary books.

1819 Karlsbad decrees: introduction of censorship, supervision of universities. "Persecution of the demagogues" (Arndt, Jahn, Görres).

1825 First steamship on the Rhine.

1833 *Gauss* and *Weber* construct the first telegraph.

1834 Establishment of the Zollverein, a customs union between Prussia and most other German states (excluding Austria).

1835 First German railway line, between Nuremberg and Fürth.

1847–1848 *Marx* and *Engels* write the Communist Manifesto (though it does not acquire significance until later).

1848 **March Revolution** in the German states. In May the German National Assembly meets in the Paulskirche in Frankfurt to draw up a national German constitution. – Foundation of the Hamburg-Amerika shipping line (HAPAG).

1849 The 1848 revolution proves abortive: King *Frederick William IV* of Prussia refuses the Imperial crown, the Frankfurt Parliament is dissolved, the ruling princes repress the risings by military force and the German Confederation is re-established.

After 1850 Increased rate of capital formation (joint-stock companies). Rise of the bourgeoisie, economically, politically and socially. Formation of a propertyless proletariat.

1857 Foundation of the Norddeutscher Lloyd shipping line in Bremen.

1862 Prince *Bismarck* becomes chief minister of Prussia.

1864 Prussia and Austria at war with Denmark over Schleswig-Holstein.

1866 *Austro-Prussian War;* Prussian victory at Königgrätz. – *Siemens* constructs the first dynamo.

1867 Establishment of the North German Confederation under the leadership of Prussia; offensive and defensive alliances between Prussia and the South German states. Exclusion of Austria.

1870–1871 *Franco-Prussian War.* After the French defeat at Sedan the cession of Alsace and Lorraine to Germany creates an obstacle to Franco-German understanding.

1871 The **German Empire** is proclaimed in the Palace of Versailles as a federal state (a "Little German" solution).

1872–1878 *"Kulturkampf"* between the state and the Catholic Church in Prussia and the German Empire.

1875 Foundation of the Socialist Workers' Party of Germany (the "Gotha Programme").

1878 Unsuccessful efforts by Bismarck to repress social democracy. Congress of Berlin to secure the maintenance of peace in Europe, with Bismarck as "honest broker".

1879 Dual Alliance of Germany with Austria-Hungary.

1882 Triple Alliance (Germany with Austria-Hungary and Italy).

1883–1889 Introduction of social insurance.

1884–1885 The Emperor *William II* seeks to make Germany a world power ("a place in the sun"); establishment of German colonies in South-West Africa, the Cameroons, Togo, East Africa, etc.

1885   Gottlieb *Daimler* and C. F. *Benz* each construct a petrol engine independently of one another.

1887   "Reinsurance Treaty" between Germany and Russia.

1890   Bismarck is dismissed by William II on account of policy and personal differences.

1893   Rudolf *Diesel* develops the diesel engine.

1895   Opening of the Kiel Canal between the North Sea and the Baltic.

From 1898   Negotiations for an alliance between Germany and Britain break down as a result of Admiral *Tirpitz*'s programme of warship construction. Increasing isolation of Germany.

1900   Promulgation of Code of Civil Law (Bürgerliches Gesetzbuch).

1907   First flight of the dirigible airship built by Graf *Zeppelin* at Friedrichshafen.

From the First World War to the present day (1914–1983). – Imperialist power politics and the determined pursuit of national interests lead to the outbreak in 1914 of the *First World War*, the consequences of which hold the germ of renewed political tensions between the states of Europe. Under the pressure of economic necessity new ideologies come to the fore, particularly in Italy and Germany, and as a result of the reckless policies pursued by the authoritarian powers lead to the *Second World War*, the catastrophic consequences of which bring about even profounder and more far-reaching changes in the world political situation than the first war. The political centre of gravity shifts towards the United States and the Soviet Union, and Europe declines in importance. The unbridgeable differences between the world powers prevent the creation of a new political order and peaceful cooperation between the peoples.

1914–1918   **First World War**. The incident which sparks off the war is the murder of the Austrian heir-apparent and his wife at Sarajevo in Serbia (28 July 1914). The causes are the opposing power policies of the European states, the armaments race, German-British rivalry, the difficulties of the Austro-Hungarian multi-national state, Russia's Balkan policy and over-hasty mobilisations and ultimatums. Germany declares war on Russia on 1 August and on France on 3 August; Britain declares war on Germany on 4 August. – Fighting in Western, Southern and Eastern Europe, in the Near East and the German colonies. In the West a war of position with bloody battles; no decisive victories in the East; the British blockade has crippling effects on Germany's supply of raw materials and foodstuffs.

1917   The United States entry into the war marks a major turning-point.

1918   Peace treaty of Brest-Litovsk between Russia and Germany. – *Revolution in Germany* (9 November); abdication of the Emperor and all German ruling princes; proclamation of a **Republic** by the Social Democrat Philipp *Scheidemann*. Armistice signed at Compiègne (11 November). – Foundation of the German Communist Party (Dec. 1918) and German Workers' Party (Jan. 1919), which became in 1920 the National Socialist German Workers' Party (NSDAP).

28 June 1919   *Treaty of Versailles*. Germany loses Alsace-Lorraine, Eupen-Malmédy, North Schleswig, Posen, West Prussia, the Memel area, Upper Silesia and all its colonies; the Rhineland and Saar

are occupied; limits on the size of the German army (100,000 men) and navy; no German air force; Germany accepts sole responsibility for the war; reparations (amount not stated) to be paid; etc.

11 August 1919   The Weimar Constitution comes into effect, with Friedrich *Ebert* as first President (unitl 1925).

1920   Kapp Putsch and Communist disturbances in Central Germany and the Ruhr.

1922   Treaty of Rapallo between Germany and the Soviet Union: resumption of diplomatic relations.

1923   "Passive resistance" against French occupation of the Ruhr. – *Inflation*; loss of confidence in the democratic regime. – Hitler's Munich putsch; the National Socialist Party is banned (until 1925).

1925   Field-Marshal *Hindenburg* elected President. Locarno Treaty: guarantee of peace with France. – Opening of the German Museum in Munich.

1926   Germany is admitted to the *League of Nations*.

1929   Beginning of the *world economic crisis*.

1930–1932   Government of presidential type by Heinrich *Brüning*. Emergency decrees. Growth of unemployment (over 6 million) and of the radical parties.

30 January 1933   *End of the Weimar Republic*: Hindenburg appoints *Adolf Hitler* Chancellor (Reichskanzler). The Reichstag fire (27 February). Abrogation of basic rights by the "Emergency Decree for the Protection of the People and the State". "Enabling Law" (24 March) giving Hitler's government full legislative power. A centralised totalitarian state is established (dissolution of the *Länder* or provinces of Germany and of all parties and trade unions, no longer based on the rule of law (hostility to religion and the Church, persecution of Jews, liberty of thought abolished, concentration camps established). – In October Germany leaves the League of Nations.

1934   Shooting of *Ernst Röhm*, leaders of the SA (*Sturmabteilungen*, "brown shirts") and political opponents (June). Beginning of the "SS state" (*Schutzstaffeln*, "black shirts").

1935   "Nuremberg race laws" against Jewish citizens (ban on marriage between Germans and Jews; loss of German citizenship). – Universal military service; open rearmament.

1936   German troops march into the demilitarised Rhineland. German-Italian treaty (the "Berlin-Rome axis") in October; Anti-Comintern Pact with Japan (November). – Olympic Games in Munich and Garmisch-Partenkirchen.

1938   The *Anschluss*: Austria is annexed to Germany (March). Munich Agreement: Sudeten German territory in Czechoslovakia is ceded to Germany (September).

1939   Germany takes over the rest of Czechoslovakia as the "Protectorate of Bohemia and Moravia" (March). Military alliance between Germany and Italy (May). Non-Aggression Pact between Germany and the Soviet Union (August).

1939–1945   **Second World War**. "Blitzkrieg" against Poland (1 September 1939).

1940   German occupation of Denmark, Norway, the Netherlands, Belgium, Luxembourg and France; beginning of the Battle of Britain.

1941 German troops in North Africa (February). Conquest of Yugoslavia and Greece (April). German attack on the Soviet Union (June). The United States enters the war (December).

1941–1945 Systematic murder of some 6 million Jews (412 concentration camps); killing of the mentally ill and of political opponents.

1943 Surrender of the German 6th Army at Stalingrad (February). Withdrawal from Russia and North Africa. Devastating air attacks on German cities.

1944 Allied landing in Northern France (June). Unsuccessful attempt on Hitler's life by Count *Stauffenberg* (20 July). Germany occupied by American, British, French and Russian forces.

1945 **Germany surrenders** (beginning of May), and is divided into *four occupation zones* (June). German territory east of the Oder-Neisse line is incorporated in Poland and the Soviet Union (Potsdam conference, August).

1945–1946 Over 11 million Germans are evacuated from the eastern territories. Trials of war criminals at Nuremberg.

1948 Beginning of Marshall Aid to Europe. *Currency reform* in the occupation zones.

1948–1949 The Berlin blockade; division of the city into two. Foundation of the Free University in West Berlin.

1949 *Division of Germany* into the *German Democratic Republic* and the **Federal Republic of Germany**. Temporary Basic Law (*Grundgesetz*). The President is Theodor *Heuss* (Free Democratic Party), the Chancellor Konrad *Adenauer* (Christian Democratic Union). Rapid economic development (the "German economic miracle") in a "social market economy" promoted by Ludwig *Erhard*.

17 June 1953 Rising in the Soviet sector of Berlin and the German Democratic Republic.

1955 The Federal Republic becomes a member of NATO. – Adenauer visits Moscow and secures the release of German prisoners of war and the re-establishment of diplomatic relations with the Soviet Union.

1956 Building up of the German army (Bundeswehr); introduction of universal military service.

1957 Establishment of the European Economic Community and the European Atomic Community.

1958 The Berlin crisis.

1961 The Berlin crisis becomes more acute with the building of the **Berlin Wall** (13 August).

1963 Franco-German treaty of friendship signed in Paris. State visit of US President *Kennedy* to the Federal Republic and West Berlin.

1966 Economic crisis (rising prices); structural crisis in the Ruhr mining industry. – Coalition between the CDU/CSU (Christian Democratic Union/Christian Social Union) and the SPD (Social Democratic Party) under K.-G. *Kiesinger*.

1967 Formation of an extra-parliamentary opposition.

1968 Emergency powers law passed.

1969 "Social-liberal" coalition government under Willy *Brandt*, which pursues a policy of improving relations with the Communist states.

1970 A treaty renouncing the use of force is signed with the Soviet Union in Moscow (August), and an agreement is reached with Poland in Warsaw (December).

1971 Four-power agreement on Berlin.

1972 Summer Olympic Games in Munich.

1973 **Treaty with the German Democratic Republic.** Both states become members of the United Nations.

From 1974 Steep increases in the price of oil lead to a world-wide *energy crisis* and economic *recession*; rise in unemployment. – Political radicalism escalates into **terrorism**. – Various forms of private initiative.

1974 Willy Brandt resigns as a result of the "Guillaume affair" and is succeeded by Helmut *Schmidt*. Fall in the rate of inflation.

1976 Decree banning the employment of political extremists in the public service.

1977 Terrorists murder the Federal Attorney-General, *Buback* (April), and a leading banker, *Ponto* (July). – German commandos free hostages in hijacked plane at Mogadishu (Somalia); kidnapping and murder of the chairman of the German Employers' Federation, *Schleyer*.

1978 Controversial law against terrorism (February). – Long-term economic treaty with the Soviet Union (May). – *Sigmund Jähn* of the German Democratic Republic flies into space in the Soviet space-ship "Soyuz 31", the first German to do so (August).

1979 Discussions and controversies on problems of environmental protection and energy supply (in particular nuclear energy). – Election of *Carstens* (CDU) as new Federal President (23 May). Agreement on scientific and technical cooperation with the People's Republic of China (October, November). Double resolution of NATO (December).

1980 Foundation congress of the "Green Party" in Karlsruhe (13 January). In the election to the Bundestag the coalition of SPD and FDP maintains its majority. Schmidt is re-elected Federal Chancellor (5 November).

1981 Discussion on the stationing of new US atomic weapons in Europe. – From October protests against the extension of the west runway of Frankfurt Airport.

1982 Economic stagnation. Rapid rise in unemployment. – NATO summit in Bonn (10 June). The coalition government of SPD and FDP breaks up after differences on economic and political questions. *Kohl* (CDU) is elected by parliament as the provisional federal chancellor (1 October). On a vote of confidence proposed by Kohl, the CDU and CSU abstain and the SPD faction votes against (17 December).

1983 Federal President Carstens dissolves the Bundestag and orders new elections (7 January). As a result of the election (6 March) a coalition of DEU/CSU and FDP is formed. Kohl is once again chancellor; the Green Party enters the Bundestag. – Meeting of the European Community Heads of State in Stuttgart (June). – Protests at the proposed stationing of American middle-range weapons in Europe (autumn).

Art

This section is essentially concerned with the territory of the Federal Republic of Germany. It must be remembered, however, that intellectual and artistic developments took place within the larger framework of the whole German language area.

Germanic art is mainly represented by examples of applied art. In the earliest period these consist of ornaments shaped out of stone and bone; later, when the skill of metal-working was acquired, items of adornment (fibulas, etc.) were produced. The basic form of ornament was the circle, no doubt a symbol for the solar disc. In the BRONZE AGE the abstract geometric forms which originally served as decoration develop into lively patterns of running spirals and scrolls. In the 1st century A.D., with improved technical skills, the repertoire of design becomes richer, and under the influence of other peoples (Celts, Scythians) the first animal decoration appears. During the MIGRATION PERIOD animal motifs come to predominate, and the intricate bands of ornament and complex interlace patterns are frequently worked into the shape of animal bodies, the heads being identifiable only by their staring eyes. These fabulous beasts give the ornament a grotesque and spectral air.
Little sculptured work of any size has been preserved, and what there is dates only from the Migration period. Here again animal figures are predominant; anthropomorphic figures are presumably always divinities, like the pair of figures from Braak, near Eutin. In the predominantly pagan art of the Scandinavian VIKINGS the Germanic animal and demon figures live on into the 12th century; and indeed they are also found in the decoration of the Romanesque churches of the medieval period.

The Roman Limes with its 1000 watchtowers and 100 forts, which was begun in A.D. 83 in the time of Domitian and began to fall into disrepair towards the end of the 3rd century, leaving remains scattered across South Germany between the Rhine and the Danube, was an indication that the Romans had been unable to subdue the Germanic peoples. Nevertheless there are abundant remains of the ROMAN PERIOD (small sculpture, glass and pottery, remains of buildings) to be seen within the areas of Germany which were incorporated in the Roman Empire: an outstanding example is the Porta Nigra in Trier, the north gate, erected after A.D.316, of the fortifications of the Roman town.

The encounter with antiquity, so fruitful for the development of art, took place in Germany only during the "Carolingian Renaissance" of the 8th and 9th centuries. **Carolingian** (*West Frankish*) **art** was able to develop after the centre of gravity of the western world moved under the Carolingian rulers to the Paris-Metz-Aachen area. The process of Christianisation was carried through on the basis of the universality of the Roman Church. Charlemagne built his churches as a conscious expression of Germanic (i.e. Frankish) and Roman power. Odo of Metz erected the Palatine Chapel in Aachen (796–804) on the model of the Byzantine imperial church of San Vitale in Ravenna (built in 552 after the collapse of the Ostrogothic empire); and with this church Charlemagne sought to legitimise himself as successor to the Byzantine Emperors and to Constantine the Great. The octagonal form reflects the conception of the number eight as a symbol of Heaven. Another building of this period which has survived is the gatehouse of the Benedictine monastery of Lorsch (consecrated 774), also founded by Charlemagne. Otherwise the art of this period is represented mainly by small sculpture, carved ivory panels from the bindings of books, mostly harking back to the Christian art of late antiquity. The illumination of books shows very divergent stylistic trends, sometimes following late antique, Syrian or Byzantine models (e.g. the manuscripts of Abbess Ada's Gospel Books in Trier). In view of the absence of any Germanic pictorial art the first representations and symbolic images associated with the new Christian religion show astonishing creative power.

The **Romanesque period** (1000–1300) marks the beginning of an independent German art, associated with the consolidation of political power under the OTTONIANS. The churches which were now built adopted the form of the Roman basilica, with a rhythmic articulation of the interior and a clear disposition of the external masses. Two buildings of the Ottonian period in Lower Saxony are the Stiftskirche at Gernrode (GDR), begun in 961, and St Michael's Church (1001–36) in Hildesheim, where there was much building activity under Bishop Bernward. At the beginning of the Romanesque period a new feeling for reality appears. Examples of this can be found in the ivory work of the Master of Echternach (binding of the Echternach Codex, c. 990: now in the National Germanic Museum in Nuremberg) and in the bronze "St Bernward's Door" in Hildesheim Cathedral (1050). Other masterpieces of plastic art dating from this period are the arresting wooden crucifix in Cologne Cathedral (c. 970) and the "Golden Virgin" in the treasury of Essen Münster (c. 1000). The goldsmith's art reached incomparable heights (Otto I's imperial crown of 962, now in the Secular Treasury in Vienna). – One of the great centres of Ottonian book illumination was on the island of Reichenau in Lake Constance; among the books produced here were Otto II's Gospel Book and Henry II's Pericopes (both now in the Bavarian State Library in Munich) and the Bamberg Apocalypse (Municipal Library, Bamberg). There were also important painting schools in the monasteries of Trier, Echternach, Cologne, Fulda, Hildesheim and Regensburg. On the island of Reichenau there are also wall paintings of the Ottonian period.

The period of the SALIANS is represented by the ruined Stiftskirche in Limburg an der Haardt, founded by Conrad II in 1025. Speyer Cathedral, begun about 1025, became about 1100 the first basilican church to be completely vaulted. As in almost all the large Romanesque cathedrals in Germany, there is a massive crypt under the choir.
Trier Cathedral offers another example of the magnificent architectural tradition of the Holy Roman Empire. The last of the great imperial cathedrals of the Rhineland and the second to be completely vaulted is Mainz Cathedral, which, with its trefoil sanctuary, represents the supreme achievement of Romanesque architecture in Germany at a time when the great Gothic cathedrals were being built in France (end of 12th to mid 13th century). – Like Speyer and Mainz Cathedrals, the monastery church of Maria Laach also had vaulted roofs, while the rigorously planned churches of the Hirsau architectural school (ruined Stiftskirche at Paulinzella, GDR, and others), influenced as it was by the Cluniac reform, held to the flat roof, like most of the Cluniac churches.

Mainz Cathedral

During the Salian period representational forms settled into hieratic severity: e.g. Bishop Imad's "Madonna Enthroned" (1058) in Paderborn Cathedral treasury, a work of almost Byzantine rigidity; the carving on the doorway of St Emmeram's in Regensburg; the ascetic bronze Christ of Werden (c. 1060) and the squarer figure of Minden (c. 1070); the brass of Rudolf of Swabia in Merseburg Cathedral in the GDR (after 1080); and the reliefs on the wooden door of St. Maria im Kapitol in Cologne (c. 1050), which with all their crudeness are of great expressive force, combining Byzantine traditions with simple spirituality. – The stained glass in Augsburg Cathedral (c. 1100) shows the Salian figural style in its fully established form. In book illumination we find it particularly in the work of the Echternach school.

In the STAUFEN period the cathedrals of Bamberg, Worms and Mainz (renovated in the reign of Henry IV) received their final form, combining monumentality with magnificence. The complex articulation of the exterior now achieved its finest consummation, as in the abbey church of Maria Laach (before 1220).

In spite of the gradual penetration of the Gothic style the buildings of the Staufen period long remained within the Romanesque tradition. This can be seen most clearly in the royal strongholds (*Pfalzen*), like those at Wimpfen, Gelnhausen and Nuremberg, which were now built at all places of political importance in the Empire, since the German Emperors did not rule from any permanent residence. Much monastic building of the period is also still Romanesque, like the Herrenrefektorium at Maulbronn (1225: other parts Gothic).

Sculpture enjoyed a great flowering in the Staufen period. Still in purely Romanesque style are the Brunswick Lion (1160), the choir screen in St Michael's Church in Hildesheim (c. 1180) and Henry the Lion's tomb in Brunswick Cathedral (c. 1230). The Master of the Golden Doorway in Freiberg Cathedral (GDR), however, must have known French doorways with figure decoration. The outstanding achievements of the school of sculpture which developed out of the chivalrous spirit of the Staufen period into a classical nobility of form are to be found in Strasbourg Cathedral, Bamberg Cathedral (the Prince's Door, the "Bamberg Horseman") and Naumburg Cathedral in the GDR (figures of the founders, Crucifixion). The masters who created these works had worked on the French cathedrals. In the field of painting the outstanding work of the Staufen period includes the important series of frescoes in the monastery church of Prüfening, near Regensburg, the Double Chapel at Schwarzrheindorf and the painted wooden ceiling of St Michael's in Hildesheim (end of 12th century). A fine example of the book illumination of the period is the Evangelistary from Speyer Cathedral (c. 1170: now in the Baden Provincial Library in Karlsruhe).

While Romanesque art was slowly dying out in Germany the Gothic style was already in full flower in France. The new influences, however, were assimilated only hesitantly, at first mainly in the form of decorative elements or particular structural features which when combined with traditional Romanesque spatial conceptions produced charming buildings in ROMANESQUE-GOTHIC TRANSITIONAL STYLE, like the Cathedral of Limburg an der Lahn (after 1215) and St Elizabeth's Church in Marburg (after 1236).

Gothic (1300–1500). – In Magdeburg Cathedral (GDR), begun in 1209, the pattern of the French cathedrals was followed for the first time. Cologne Cathedral (begun 1284 but not completed until 1842–80) followed the model of Amiens. The HIGH GOTHIC period in Germany is represented by Freiburg Minster with its openwork spire (begun after 1311), Regensburg Cathedral (spires built 1859–69), Ulm Minster (part of it not completed until 1844–90) and St Mary's Church in Lübeck (brick-built Gothic) – all still on the traditional basilican plan.

Of more significance for the future, however, was the new type of hall-church which originated in Westphalia, sometimes classified as a specifically GERMAN GOTHIC. It is found in the 13th century in Paderborn and Minden Cathedrals; an example belonging to the High Gothic period is the Wiesenkirche in Soest. The hall-church became the preferred type in the late Gothic period (14th and 15th centuries), one of Germany's greatest periods of artistic flowering, which coincided, particularly in South Germany, with a time of eager building activity – exemplified by St Martin's Church in Landshut (begun 1387) and the two supremely beautiful hall-churches of St Lawrence in Nuremberg (1439–72) and St George in Dinkelsbühl (1448–89). In place of the twin-towered façade of the basilican church the hall-church usually preferred a façade with a single tower, in a style varying from place to place: Schwäbisch Gmünd (after 1351), Freiburg im Breisgau (tower of Minster, 1300–50), Nuremberg (St Sebaldus, Frauenkirche).

Few secular buildings of the Gothic period have come down to us unaltered. Among those which have are the town halls of Gelnhausen, Lübeck, Aachen and Münster, usually serving also as courthouses, trading establishments and banqueting halls. Graduated or stepped gables are commonly found. Alongside building in stone, the 15th century saw a rich development of half-timbered building. Out of the technique of building in brick, used from the 12th century onwards, which had originally been brought to North Germany from Lombardy, there developed the style known as BRICK-BUILT GOTHIC (*Backsteingothik*) which became particularly characteristic of North Germany (Holstentor and St Mary's Church in Lübeck).

The aspect of a medieval town is well known to us from old representations: a place of anything up to 30,000 inhabitants enclosed within a circuit of strong walls, often supplemented by towers. With the increasing economic strength of the citizens the town hall became the centre of the town's administration; and imposing guild houses and fine half-timbered buildings with oriel windows and decorated gables still bear witness to the prosperity and artistic sense of the burghers of the late Middle Ages.

While in the field of sculpture the classical works of the Staufen period are still in the Romanesque-Gothic transitional style, the first purely Gothic forms (after the figures on the west doorway of Strasbourg Cathedral) appear in the figures on the pillars in Cologne Cathedral (c. 1310). In the second half of the 14th century a new realism emerges in place of the previous immaterialised representations, and in South Germany the type of the "beautiful Madonna" appears (c. 1400). In the LATE GOTHIC period, from the middle of the 15th century onwards, the names of many individual masters are known to us: Nikolaus Gerhaert of Leyen, Jörg Syrlin (choir-stalls, Ulm, 1469–74), Gregor Erhart (high altar, Blaubeuren, 1494), Adam Krafft (tabernacle in St Lawrence's, Nuremberg, 1496), Tilman Riemenschneider (splendid carved altars in Würzburg, Rothenburg ob der Tauber, Bamberg, etc.) and Veit Stoss (1450–1533).

In the early 16th century sculpture developed a highly wrought style which has been called "Late Gothic Baroque", as in the work of the master known only by his initials, H.L. (high altar, Breisach, 1526). During this period, too, Peter Vischer and his sons were working in bronze in Nuremberg (tomb of St Sebaldus in St Sebaldus's Church, 1519), beginning in the Gothic style but in his maturest works aiming at a noble and harmonious expression in the clear forms of the Italian Renaissance.
Towards the middle of the 16th century a decline in creative power began to show itself, and during the following period of the Renaissance few great works were produced. There were, however, a number of charming smaller pieces, like the work of the Nuremberg goldsmith W. Jamnitzer.

Gothic painting is displayed in the beautiful stained glass with which the numerous windows in the walls of the Gothic cathedrals were now filled, creating a semi-darkness of almost mystical effect in the interior (Frauenkirche, Munich). A new creation of the Gothic period was panel painting, at first used only in the panels of winged altars. The devotional images (*Andachtsbilder*), an iconographical innovation found from the early 14th century onwards, give expression to profound religious feeling. The COLOGNE SCHOOL OF PAINTERS, whose work is notable for its deep fervour, used a new painting technique and began to introduce landscape backgrounds in place of the gold ground which had been normal. The advance to the greater freedom of the panel painting, now frequently on secular themes, took place in the 15th century: Stefan Lochner's "Altar der Stadtpatrone" (Altar of the patrons of the town; c. 1445), incorrectly known as the "Dombild"; in Cologne Cathedral. Konrad Witz's "St Christopher" (Museum of Art, Basle), the "Paradise Garden" of a Middle Rhineland master (c. 1410: Städel Art Institute, Frankfurt am Main), the "Annunciation" by the Master of the Life of Mary (c. 1460: Alte Pinakothek, Munich), Martin Schongauer's "Madonna in the Rose-Garden" (1473: at present in the Dominican Church, Colmar).

The **Renaissance** came into being in Italy as the visible expression of a new approach to life and a revival of ancient forms. Germany, without any classical tradition, was slower to break away from the Middle Ages, and the new spirit sought expression in the further development of the artistic sensibility of the later medieval period. Nevertheless the Reformation and the increasing power of the burghers on the one hand and the princes on the other inevitably broke down the old political and religious certainties.
There are few purely Renaissance buildings in Germany, mostly the work of travelling Italian architects. The great bulk of the buildings now erected were the work of native architects, still using Gothic forms (steeply pitched roofs, stepped gables), like the Knochenhauerhaus in Hildesheim (1529: destroyed 1944). As in the Gothic period, the main building activity was in the towns. The technique of half-timbered construction which had been popular in the Gothic period was developed further within the greater freedom of Renaissance forms (Celle, Höxter, Goslar, Hamelin, Hildesheim). In South Germany Rothenburg ob der Tauber is a celebrated example of a German Renaissance town (with some notable Gothic buildings as well). The town halls became particularly splendid through the combination of native architectural concepts with Italian decorative forms (Lübeck; Bremen, re-

built 1608; Lüneburg; Paderborn). With Augsburg Town Hall, the greatest secular building of the Renaissance in Germany, Elias Holl cast aside all reminiscences of Gothic and brought the "Augsburg Renaissance" to its full perfection (1615–20).

In the field of church building, which was now slowly beginning to revive, the most interesting work was perhaps the Jesuit St Michael's Church in Munich (1583–97), an imposing example of late 16th century German architectural skill in the organisation of space, but already showing Mannerist, early Baroque influences from the Gesù in Rome.
In this period, too, there was a great upsurge in the building of castles and palaces. Here Italian influence makes itself more strongly felt than in the buildings erected in towns: Heidelberg Castle (Ottheinrichsbau 1556–59, Friedrichsbau 1601), Residence of the Dukes of Bavaria in Landshut, Old Residence in Munich.

In painting the encounter with the Italian Renaissance, beginning in the 16th century, led to a great flowering of German painting and graphic art. Matthias Grünewald (more correctly Mathis Gothart) still clings to medieval forms, as to some extent do the painters of the South German DANUBE SCHOOL, who seek to achieve an intimate fusion of landscape and figures. Nature is not regarded merely as a background of secondary importance: it is a dramatic setting for the figures, which are usually quite small. The leading master of the Danube school was Albrecht Altdorfer of Regensburg ("Alexander's Victory", "Danube Landscape"). The Upper Franconian painter Lukas Cranach the Elder is also counted as a member of this school, at least in his early works ("Rest on the Flight").
The great master of German painting, however, was Albrecht **Dürer** of Nuremberg (1471–1528), who was also a master of drawing and the woodcut. Widely travelled and familiar with Italian and Dutch painting, he attained the highest mastery as a portraitist. Perhaps his most impressive work is the representation of the four Apostles which he painted for Nuremberg Town Hall – a work of monumental expressiveness which shows a characteristically German mingling of idealism and down-to-earth realism. – Hans Holbein the Younger, of Augsburg, was a leading master of the Reformation period, a great portraitist who worked in Basle and at the English court ("Henry VIII").

The development of **Baroque** art was severely hampered in the first half of the 17th century by the Thirty Years War and the Peasant Wars. From the middle of the century Italian architects flocked into Germany (A. Barelli and E. Zuccalli, Theatinerkirche, Munich, c. 1665); but it was not until the end of the century that German architecture achieved European standing, thanks to the work of great architects like J. B. Fischer von Erlach and Lukas von Hildebrandt in Austria and South Germany who brought the full splendour of Baroque to Germany. Influences from France now also began to make themselves felt, continuing with increasing force until the Wars of Liberation.
Among notable religious buildings of the Baroque period are Johann Michael Fischer's Benedictine church at Ottobeuren (1748–66) and Balthasar Neumann's pilgrimage church of Vierzehnheiligen (after 1743), with its interesting combination of nave and central altar. Neumann also created secular buildings of incomparably harmonious spatial effect, like the Residenz in Würzburg (c. 1740) with its magnificently vaulted staircase hall and ceiling painting by Tiepolo. The Palace of Versailles became the model for many German palaces (Mannheim).
The building activity of the rising Prussian state now brought Berlin to the fore as an artistic centre. Here the leading part was played by Andreas Schlüter: sculpture on the Arsenal, equestrian statue of the Great Elector (1700: now in the courtyard of Charlottenburg Palace), rebuilding and extension of the Palace (pulled down after 1945). Schlüter sought to express the heroic ideal of classicism, with a display of solidity and magnificence – tending towards the ponderous – designed to reflect the royal power and dignity.
In its further development into **Rococo** the Baroque stylistic canon was transmuted into a gayer and lighter mode, often falling into the over-elaborate and whimsical. Stuccoed walls and ceilings, a confusing riot of decoration and playful prettiness characterise the interior of the Amalienburg, in the park of Nymphenburg Palace near Munich, rebuilt in

The Rococo palace of Amalienburg, Munich

1755–57 by François Cuvilliés, who was also responsible for the Residenztheater in Munich (1751–53). Other important Rococo palaces are Ansbach Palace (c. 1740) and Sanssouci in Potsdam (GDR), built for Frederick the Great by Georg Wenzeslaus von Knobelsdorff (1745–47: "Friderician Rococo"). In Bavaria the late Baroque and Rococo periods saw the erection of numerous churches, like the monastery church of Weltenburg (after 1717), St John of Nepomuk in Munich (1733 onwards), the church at Zwiefalten and Dominikus Zimmermann's churches at Steinhausen and the Wies.

The gardens of the Baroque and Rococo periods were modelled on the work of André Le Nôtre and the park he created at Versailles. The park was now designed as a fit setting for the splendour of the palace. Among the principal German gardens of the Baroque period are Herrenhausen (Hanover), Nymphenburg (Munich), Schleissheim and Wilhelmshöhe (Kassel).

Among Baroque sculptors of the 17th century was J. Glesker ("Crucifixion" in Bamberg Cathedral, 1648–53). In the 18th century the leading figure was Andreas Schlüter, among a large number of other masters who included E. Bendel in Augsburg, P. Egell in Mannheim and Egid Quirin Asam – who also worked as an architect along with his brother Cosmas Damian (e.g. churches at Rohr, after 1717, and Weltenburg, c. 1725). Rococo sculpture flourished particularly in Bavaria, with such artists as Johann Baptist Straub and Ignaz Günther (both in Munich), Christian Wenzinger in Freiburg and Franz Anton Bustelli, who worked for the Nymphenburg porcelain manufactory in Munich.

The **neo-classical** period in Germany was influenced by the writings of Johann Joachim Winckelmann and his concept of the "noble simplicity and tranquil grandeur" of the art of classical antiquity. The absolutism of the late Baroque period and the courtly Rococo art both fell victim to the French Revolution, and with the 19th century the age of the middle classes began.
In Berlin Carl Gotthard Langhans built the Brandenburg Gate (1791) in a strictly observed neo-Doric style. The purest manifestation of the neo-classical style, however, is to be found in the work of Friedrich Schinkel (Neue Wache, 1816; Schauspielhaus, 1818; Old Museum, 1822–28). – The Munich neo-classical school was rather warmer in character. Karl von Fischer built the Hoftheater and the Prinze-Karl-Palais, Josef von Herigoien the gateway of the Old Botanic Garden. Leo von Klenze (1784–1864), Ludwig I's architect, built the Residenz in Max-Joseph-Platz and the Walhalla near Regensburg, and was also a masterly designer of imposing streets and squares (Odeonsplatz, Königsplatz, Ludwigstrasse). The Romantic architect Friedrich von Gärtner used a great variety of architectural styles of the past in his completion of Ludwigstrasse.

The leading sculptors of the neo-classical period were Johann Gottfried Schadow and Christian Rauch ("Queen Luise", 1817). Among the sculptors working in Ludwig I's Munich was Ludwig Schwanthaler.

After this preoccupation with the art of antiquity the **Romantic** period looked back to the (German) Middle Ages and the Romanesque and Gothic styles. Friedrich Weinbrenner built the Basilica in Karlsruhe (1814), Georg Ziebland St Boniface's Church in Munich (1835–50). – The Romantic park rebelled against the unnaturalness of the Baroque park, in which even nature had been made subject to the will of the absolutist ruler, and German landscape gardeners took over from England the concept of the garden as an artificial wilderness, a landscape without regularity or symmetry (Schwetzingen palace gardens, Englischer Garten in Munich).

The painting of the Romantic period, which – stimulated by the patriotic enthusiasm of the Wars of Liberation – created works in which ideals and sensibility prevailed, is of higher quality than the work of the neo-classical artists. Classical mythology was now displaced by German heroic legends and fairy-tales, and the beauties of German landscape were discovered. The most gifted painter of the period was Caspar David Friedrich; others were Philipp Otto Runge and the group of NAZARENES led by Friedrich Overbeck, who treated Biblical themes in the manner of the old masters. Ludwig Richter is noted for his illustrations to fairy-tales, the painter and poet Carl Spitzweg for his lovingly transfigured anecdotal pictures of life in the Biedermeier period.

In Adolf Menzel a new spirit of REALISM appears, looking forward to the 20th century. Wilhelm Leibl depicts scenes of ordinary life in Bavaria, and Hans Thoma does the same for the Black Forest. Anselm Feuerbach represents the neoclassical ideal of culture (*Bildung*) of the 19th century. The name of Hans von Marées also merits mention.

The theory known as **Historicism**, which practically dominated the architecture of the second half of the 19th century, reduced the imitation of styles to a rapid and eclectic sequence of decorative forms, often totally devoid of content. It is seen at its most characteristic in the building activity of Ludwig II in Bavaria (Herrenchiemsee, Linderhof, Neuschwanstein) and in the numerous pompous buildings of the GRÜNDER PERIOD, the commercial boom of the early 1870s.

Meanwhile in painting an entirely new style, strongly influenced by France, had come to the fore in the form of **Impressionism**, in which impressions of light and colour predominate over the actual subject depicted. Its principal representatives in Germany were Max Liebermann, Max Slevogt and Lovis Corinth, who is already close to Expressionism.

Around the turn of the century the **Jugendstil** (Art Nouveau) began to assert its dominance in all fields of art. Architects had now learned to handle the technical possibilities of new building materials like steel, glass and concrete and had developed structural principles appropriate to these materials. The architecture of the period is exemplified by Alfred

Lamp in Jugendstil

Messel's department store, Wertheim's, in Berlin (1897–1904), August Endell's Haus Elvira in Munich (1899) and the large complex of the artists' colony on the Mathildenhöhe in Darmstadt (1899).

Jugendstil painting and graphic art shows a strong leaning towards symbolism; formally it depends largely on clear ornamentally patterned lines. Applied art and book decoration reach a high standard.

Expressionism developed out of the BRÜCKE ("Bridge") group founded in 1905, the members of which included Ernst Ludwig Kirchner, Karl Schmidt-Rotluff, Erich Heckel and for a time Emil Nolde (real name Hansen). These artists sought to carry the expression of the artistic experience to the highest pitch. Another important group, founded in Munich in 1911, was known as the BLAUER REITER ("Blue Rider"); its most prominent members were the Russian painter Wassily Kandinsky, Franz Marc and Paul Klee. This group leaned towards a rather romantic and lyrical representation of subjects which were often of a dream-like character; out of their work developed the later school of abstract painting.

The DADAISTS sought in their arbitrary montages to destroy all rational artistic structure and to elimate causality. At the same time other notable artists – Käthe Kollwitz, George Grosz, Otto Dix – practised REALISM.

In the early 20th century sculpture turned

to follow new formal laws calling for classical purity of line (G. Kolbe, A. Gaul). Expressionism made possible a new intensity of creative force (Wilhelm Lehmbruck, Ernst Barlach).

The WERKBUND, founded in 1907, set itself the task of renewing the artistic crafts. In Henry van de Velde's Theatre at the Werkbund Exhibition in Cologne (1914) the move towards **Neue Sachlichkeit** ("New Objectivity") found its most powerful and most forward-looking expression. The BAUHAUS, founded by Walter Gropius in 1919 and dissolved in 1934, sought to achieve the union of all the arts and crafts in architecture; it also influenced painting (L. Feininger, O. Schlemmer). Other great architects of the period in addition to Gropius were Hans Bernhard Scharoun and Ludwig Mies van der Rohe.

During the National Socialist "Third Reich" art and architecture were mainly conceived as forms of propaganda – a constriction from which only industrial building was able to escape.

After the Second World War great changes took place in the field of art. The avant-garde artists who had emigrated from Germany to Paris in the thirties mostly made their way to the United States when Paris was occupied by German forces and remained there after 1945, giving fresh impulses to American artistic life.

In the second half of this century, as in the first, no generally accepted style has developed, but a whole range of new trends have emerged. Joseph Albers, once associated with the Bauhaus, is now in the United States working on the theory of colour, while in Paris the half-French Hans Hartung paints elegant "movement trails". The vigorous coloured woodcuts of Helmut Andreas Paul Grieshaber, originally bearing the stamp of Expressionism, now claim allegiance to REPRESENTATIONAL MODERNISM.

The painters of the post-war period also include exponents of the various contemporary international styles – ABSTRACT EXPRESSIONISM or Tachism (the "Frankfurt Quadriga" of K. O. Goetz, O. Greis, H. Kreitz and B. Schultze), SURREALISM (whose great master, Max Ernst, transposes the processes of psychoanalysis into art) and REPRESENTATIONAL EXPRESSIONISM.

The artists of the **present day** prefer a completely abstract form of creation, which frequently seeks to transcend or break down the traditional boundaries between sculpture and painting, or indeed, by resorting to acoustic and kinetic effects, to abolish altogether the accepted

Philharmonic Hall, Berlin

frontiers of the arts. The DOKUMENTA exhibition in Kassel tries to present these latest developments to the public. –

Basing himself on the artistic principles laid down by Vasarély, the "object-maker" Heinz Mack transposes the optical contrasts of a plane surface into three-dimensional form and into "objects" (for example the play of reflections in the brilliant Sahara sun, as seen on television). A representative of a number of closely associated trends – HAPPENING, ENVIRONMENT, PROCESS ART and FUNK ART – is Joseph Beuys. In an extension of BODY ART into the field of human actions, Ha Schult's "Aktion 20,000 km" involved driving 20 times to and from Munich and Hamburg. From these examples it can be seen that artists are steadily attempting to move from the concept of art as something to be collected or to be observed to the concept of art as something to be experienced.

As a reaction to this development the end of the 1970s saw a return to painting in the traditional sense. The representatives of this movement – principally younger artists from the cities (West Berlin, Hamburg, Cologne) – employed dazzling colours and painted pictures with a strong sense of movement, partly in imitation of expressionist subjects and styles, so that they came to be called "violent painters" or "the new wild ones". Representatives of this movement include Rainer Fetting, Helmut Middendorf, Werner Büttner, Albert Oehlen, Hans Peter Adamski and Peter Bömmels.

In the field of architecture and town planning it has been possible in only a few places (e.g. in Hanover) to plan the rebuilding necessary after the destructions of the war on a far-seeing long-term basis, though there have been many fine individual buildings (theatres, schools, churches). The new BRUTALISM developed by disciples of the later Bauhaus school has had long-lasting influence on contemporary architecture.

Attempts to grapple effectively with the problem of bringing fresh life to the traffic-strangled inner cities have been made only since the 1960s. Considerable efforts are, however, being made in many places to rehabilitate run-down areas in towns and to preserve and protect buildings of historical and artistic value.

Music

We have, of course, no evidence about primitive society or the early feudal period, but it is reasonable to suppose that the Germanic peoples used music for magical purposes, as an accompaniment to work and an incitement to martial vigour (cf. the lurs, the long horns found by archaeologists). The musical culture of the Middle Ages was strongly influenced by the Roman Catholic Church and the German imperial court. The earliest manuscripts date from between 1200 and 1500 ("Carmina Burana", 13th century; Glogau or Berlin Song-Book, *c.* 1470, etc.). From the 11th century onwards courtly poets, modelling themselves on the French troubadours, developed the MINNESANG (minne-song or love-song), whose leading practitioners were *Walther von der Vogelweide* (*c.* 1170–1230), *Reinmar von Hagenau* (before 1210) and *Neidhart von Reuenthal* (*c.* 1240). – In the 15th and 16th centuries the MEISTER-GESANG (master-song), the beginnings of which date back to the 13th century, reached its highest perfection in the guilds of master craftsmen. Its best known exponents were *Michel Behaim* (1416–74) and *Hans Sachs* (1494–1576).

With the rise of the burghers and the social conflicts within the feudal order there was a great flowering of PART-SONG in Germany (songs, motets, masses). The hymns of the Reformed Church, fostered by *Martin Luther* (1483–1546), achieved greater importance in the chorale and developed into cantatas and Passions. The first independent instrumental music to emerge, in the 15th century, was ORGAN MUSIC, with *Adam of Fulda* (*c.* 1445–1505), *Hans Leo Hassler* (1564–1612), *Michael Praetorius* (1571–1621) and others. – The principal instrument for DOMESTIC MUSIC became the lute, for which *Hans Judenkünig* (*c.* 1450–1526) and others wrote music. Various independent instrumental forms now evolved – fantasias, variations, sonatas, concertos.

The Thirty Years War interrupted this development, and the court orchestras and choirs were among the casualties of the war. The outstanding musical figure of the 17th century was *Heinrich* **Schütz** (1585–1672), who wrote psalms, polyphonal motets, spiritual concertos and choral Passions, combining influences from Italy with the German tradition and acting as organiser of musical life in Germany.

After the Thirty Years War there was a musical revival in which the re-established choirs, town orchestras, the "Collegia Musica" of students and burghers and opera-houses played an important part. After 1660 OPERA began to develop, at first often with Italian composers and singers at the larger courts (Vienna, Munich, Dresden). A central rôle in the emergence of the early German opera was played by Hamburg (opera-house opened in 1678). The leading operatic composers of this period were *Johann Siegmund Kusser*, *Reinhard Keiser* and *Georg Philipp* **Telemann** (1681–1767).

Johann Sebastian **Bach** (1685–1750: "St Matthew Passion", Brandenburg Concertos) and *Georg Friedrich* **Händel** (1685–1759:"Messiah","Julius Caesar", "Xerxes") gave CHAMBER MUSIC, solo music and also the cantata, the Passion, the oratorio and the opera an entirely new depth of expression. – Under the influence of pre-Revolutionary France there was carried through from 1740 onwards a considerable and sometimes radical simplification of the forms of musical expression. Between 1757 and 1778 there was an active circle of composers at the court of Karl Theodor of the Palatinate, the "Mannheim School", including *Johann Stamitz, Franz Xaver Richter* and *Christian Cannabich*. The early "Viennese School", with *Matthias Georg Monn*, J. S. Bach's two sons *Carl Philipp Emanuel Bach* (1714–88) and *Johann Christian Bach* (1735–82) and the theatrical composer *Johann Adam Hiller* (1728–1804), shows the same trends. NEW MUSICAL forms like the symphony, the quartet, the quintet, the piano sonata and the singspiel were now developed.

Christoph Willibald **Gluck** (1714–87: "Alceste", "Iphigenie auf Tauris") carried through in his late works a reform of the opera which had already been begun in Italy, making the music subordinate to the text and developing the form out of the content.

Joseph **Haydn** (1732–1809) and *Wolfgang Amadeus* **Mozart** (1756–91) gave the symphony, the concerto with a solo instrument, the string quartet and the piano sonata their classical form. Mozart's operas ("The Marriage of Figaro", "Don Giovanni", "The Magic Flute") are high points in the MUSICAL THEATRE of the 18th century. The ideas of the French Revolution left their imprint on the ideas and the creative work of *Ludwig van* **Beethoven** (1770–1827); in his opera "Fidelio" and his 9th Symphony he gives expression to man's striving for freedom and humanity. With the music of the ROMANTIC PERIOD Germany achieved a new cultural flowering. In his opera "Der Freischütz" *Carl Maria von Weber* broke free from foreign influences. Other notable composers of the period were *Louis Sphor, Heinrich Marschner* and *Otto Nicolai. Albert Lortzing* devoted himself mainly to the SINGSPIEL ("Zar und Zimmermann", "Der Wildschütz").

The German LIED was created by *Franz Schubert* (1797–1828), with his cycles "Die Winterreise" and "Die schöne Müllerin", and his works provided the basis for all the composers of lieder of the 19th and 20th centuries (Robert Schumann, Johannes Brahms, Hugo Wolf, Hans Pfitzner, Richard Strauss, Arnold Schönberg, Anton von Webern).

Richard **Wagner** (1813–83) brought the German Romantic opera to its highest pitch of achievement. His "total works of art" (*Gesamtkunstwerke*) represent a new operatic form whose musical sonorities point the way towards realism ("Lohengrin", "Tristan and Isolde", "The Mastersingers of Nürnberg", "The Ring of the Nibelung", "Parsifal", etc.: annual Wagner Festival in Bayreuth). He had a direct successor in *Richard* **Strauss** (1864–1949: "Salome", "Der Rosenkavalier", "Capriccio", etc.).

The INSTRUMENTAL MUSIC of the first half of the 19th century – *Felix Mendelssohn-Bartholdy* (1809–47), *Robert Schumann* (1810–56) – mainly follows the classical model. A gradual dissolution of the sonata form was brought about principally by *Franz Liszt* (1811–86), *Anton Bruckner* (1824–96) and *Johannes Brahms* (1833–97).

The generation which included *Gustav Mahler* (1860–1911), *Hans Pfitzner* (1869–1949), *Richard Strauss* and *Max Reger* (1873–1916) already showed in their work the transition towards contemporary music.

In the 19th century the distinction between SERIOUS MUSIC and LIGHT MUSIC made its appearance. The tradition established by *Jacques Offenbach* (1819–80: "Orpheus in the Underworld", "Paris Life") was followed by *Josef Lanner, Johann Strauss* (father and son), *Franz von Suppé* and others. – In Berlin around 1900 *Paul Lincke* and *Walter Kollo* wrote music on an even more popular level for vaudeville and revues.

Arnold **Schönberg** (1874–1951), striving to achieve greater objectivity in music, devised the system of TWELVE-TONE MUSIC (dodecaphony) and thus opened up new paths of musical development. His leading disciples were *Alban Berg* (1885–1935) and *Anton von Webern* (1883–1945).

Paul **Hindemith** (1895–1963), with his opera "Mathis der Maler", turned back towards more traditional forms. – *Kurt Weill* (1900–50) sought to adapt light music to serve the purposes of social criticism ("Die Dreigroschenoper"). – The work of *Carl Orff* (1895–1982), whose scenic oratorio "Carmina Burana" and opera "Die Kluge" achieved an international reputation, is characterised by rhythm and close relation to the text. – Notable operatic composers are *Werner Egk* (b. 1901: "Der Revisor") and *Gottfried von Einem* (b. 1918: "Dantons Tod"). – *Ernst Křenek* (b. 1900), *Hans Jelinek* (b. 1901) and *Karl Amadeus Hartmann* (1905–63) follow the path opened up by Schönberg, as do *Wolfgang Fortner* (b. 1907) and his pupil *Hans Werner Henze* (b. 1926: "Der junge Lord"), who went over to the dodecaphonal system only after the Second World War.

A complete break with tradition is seen in the work of *Karlheinz Stockhausen* (b. 1928), the most consistent practitioner of EXPERIMENTAL AND SERIAL MUSIC. An international forum for contemporary music is provided by the Studio for Electronic Music in Cologne, established in 1951.

Germany from A to Z

Cologne Cathedral

Aachen
(Aix-la-Chapelle)

Land: North Rhineland-Westphalia.
Vehicle registration: AC.
Altitude: 125–410 m. – Population: 245,000.
Post code: D-5100. – Dialling code: 02 41.
ⓘ **Kur- und Verkehrsamt der Stadt Aachen**, Markt 39–41;
tel. 3 34 91 and 47 23 01.
Verkehrsverein Bad Aachen, Bahnhofplatz 4; tel. 3 06 00 and 2 53 12.
Information bureaux at the motorway frontier crossings at Lichtenbusch (Aachen-Süd) and Vetschau (Aachen-Nord).

HOTELS. – *Steigenberger Parkhotel Quellenhof*, Monheimsallee 52, 300 b., thermal SB; *Novotel*, Josef von Görres Str. (Europlatz), 238 b., SP; *Aquis Grana Cityhotel*, Büchel 32, 159 b., SB; *Central*, Römerstr. 5–9, 65 b.; *Royal* (no rest.), Julicher Str. 1, 42 b.; *Buschhausen*, Adenauerallee 215, 140 b., SB, sauna; *Am Marschiertor* (no rest.), Wallstr. 1–7, 78 b.; *Danica* (no rest.), Franzstr. 36–38, 45 b.; *Danmark* (no rest.), Lagerhausstr. 21, 32 b.; etc. – YOUTH HOSTEL: *Colynshof*, Maria-Theresia-Allee 260, 178 b. – CAMPING SITE: Pass-str. 87 (Stadtgarten).

RESTAURANTS. – *Ratskeller*, Markt; *Heidekrug*, Friedrich-Wilhelm-Platz 5–6; *Zum Postwagen*, Krämerstr. 1–2 (a small historic inn, 1657); *Elisenbrunnen*, Friedrich-Wilhelm-Platz 13a; *China-Restaurant*, Kleinmarschierstr. 78; *Zum Schiffgen*, Hühnermarkt 21–23; *Belvedere*, revolving restaurant in observation tower on Lousberg; *Schloss Friesenrath*, Pannekoogweg 46, Aachen-Friesenrath (authentic furniture and setting).

International Casino, Monheimsallee 44 (roulette, baccarat, blackjack: open daily 3 p.m.–2 a.m., Fridays and Saturdays until 3 a.m.).

EVENTS. – Award of the *Charlemagne International Prize* for services to the unification of Europe; presentation of the "Carnival Order"; the Federal Republic's *International Riding, Jumping and Driving Tournament* (CHIO).

Germany's most westerly city, historically one of Europe's most important towns, lies near the Dutch and Belgian frontiers in a forest-ringed basin in the foothills of the Eifel and the Ardennes.

Aachen is an educational centre, with the Rhineland-Westphalian Technical College and other vocational colleges, and an industrial centre widely known for a varied range of products – needles, cloth, glass, machinery, rolling-stock, light-bulbs, television tubes, tyres, umbrellas and chemicals. It is also noted for its honey-cakes (*Printen*). – The hot springs (brine, containing sulphur) of Bad Aachen are particularly effective in the treatment of gout, rheumatism and sciatica.

Aachen is also noted as a centre of equestrian sport. The riding stadium in the district of Soers is the scene of international riding, jumping and driving tournaments, held every year.

HISTORY. – *Aquae Granni*, the hottest springs in Europe (37–75 °C), were already frequented in Roman times for their curative properties. In the Middle Ages Aachen was one of Germany's leading towns, a frequent residence of the Frankish kings, a stronghold much favoured by Charlemagne, and from the time of Otto I (936) to that of Ferdinand I (1531) the place of coronation of 32 German kings and the meeting-place of numerous Imperial Diets and church assemblies. In the 18th and 19th c. it was the "watering-place of kings". During the Second World War the greater part of the town was destroyed, but post-war reconstruction has repaired all the damage, restored important historic buildings and created a modern city.

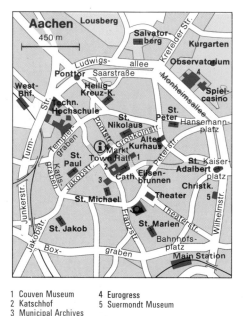

1 Couven Museum
2 Katschhof
3 Municipal Archives
  (Grashaus)
4 Eurogress
5 Suermondt Museum

SIGHTS. – In the MARKTPLATZ stands the **Town Hall**, built *c.* 1350 on the foundations of the Carolingian imperial fortress, with its fine Coronation Hall (frescoes on the life of Charlemagne by A. Rethel). Nearby, in an old burgher's house at Hühnermarkt 17, is the *Couven Museum* (Aachen house interiors from 1740 to about 1840). At Pontstrasse 13 is the *International Newspaper Museum* (first and most recent issues of some 100,000 titles). S of the Town Hall is the *Katschhof*, marking the site of the Carolingian palace courtyard.

The *Cathedral consists of an octagonal central structure built about 800 as Charlemagne's palace church and a

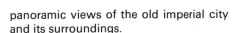

Gothic choir completed in 1414. Under the dome of the octagon is a candelabrum presented by Frederick I Barbarossa; in the gallery is Charlemagne's marble throne; the *"goldenes Haus" containing the Emperor's remains is being restored; valuable *Treasury. Near the Cathedral, where now stands the reproduction of a Roman portico, the remains of Roman baths and temples were brought to light in 1967–68. SW of the Cathedral, in the so-called "Grashaus" (1267: Aachen's first town hall), are the *Municipal Archives*.

In FRIEDRICH- WILHELM- PLATZ is the **Elisenbrunnen**, the emblem of Aachen's role as a spa, with the drinking-well. A few steps away is the Municipal Theatre (1825: opera, operettas, plays). Some 500 m NE of the Elisenbrunnen, in Komphausbadstrasse, is the *Old Kurhaus* (Altes Kurhaus), which now houses the *New Gallery* and *Ludwig Collection* (mainly 20th c. art; special exhibitions).

At the E end of the pedestrian precinct is the KAISERPLATZ, with St Adalbert's Church. A little way S of this is the **Suermondt Museum** (sculpture, paintings). – E of the Hauptbahnhof, in Burg Frankenberg, is the municipal **Heimatmuseum**. – In the N of the town are the **Eurogress** (social centre, meeting and conference centre), the *International Casino Bad Aachen* (new Kurhaus) the Steigenberg Parkhotel Quellenhof and the *Kurpark*. To the W, at the end of the Ludwigsallee, is the frowning *Ponttor* with its barbican (*c.* 1320). From the "Belvedere" revolving tower restaurant on the 340 m high *Lousberg* there are fine panoramic views of the old imperial city and its surroundings.

SURROUNDINGS. – In the SE and S the German-Belgian Nature Park extends across the frontier and into the Eifel.

Ahr Valley

Land: Rhineland- Palatinate.

ⓘ **Fremdenverkehrsverband Rheinland-Pfalz,** Lohrstrasse 103–105, D-5400 Koblenz; tel. (02 61) 3 10 79.

The Ahr valley in the northern Eifel, noted for its wines, is one of the most beautiful of the Rhine's tributary valleys. The river, 89 km long, rises at Blankenheim and flows into the Rhine below Sinzig.

The finest part of the valley is the romantic middle stretch between Altenahr and Bad Neuenahr, where the river forces its way in a winding course between rugged slate crags; particularly impressive is the high rock face known as the *Bunte Kuh* at Walporzheim. The hills are crowned by ruined castles, and their slopes are covered with forests and vineyards. In the narrow valley nestle the wine towns and villages – *Altenahr, Mayschoss, Rech, Dernau, Marienthal, Walporzheim, Bachem, Ahrweiler*. In this area are produced Germany's best red wines, the delectable Spätburgunder, as well as "spritzig" (semi-effervescent) white wines.

WINE has been produced in this most northerly wine-growing region in Germany since Roman times (perhaps since about A.D. 260). The medieval *Ahrweiler*, which was combined with *Bad Neuenahr* (situated under the basalt cone known as the Landskrone, where warm medicinal springs emerge from the volcanic soil) in 1969 and given the status of a town, is a noted centre of the trade in red wine.

Facilities for enjoying the local wines are available to suit every taste. If you want a quiet drink there is the Weinstube St. Peter in Walporzheim; if you prefer a gay and lively atmosphere there is the popular "Lochmühle" at Mayschoss. For hikers there is the 30 km long "red wine trail" which runs through a delightful landscape of vineyards from Lohrsdorf to Altenahr.

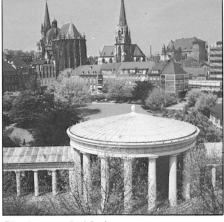

Elisenbrunnen, Bad Aachen

Alfeld

Land: Lower Saxony.
Vehicle registration: ALF.
Altitude: 93 m. – Population: 25,000.
Post code: D-3220. – Dialling code: 0 51 81.
ⓘ **Verkehrsverein**, Ständehausstr. 1;
tel. 70 41.

HOTELS. – *City Hotel*, Leinstr. 14, 33 b.; *Deutsches Haus*, Holzerstr. 25, 27 b. – IN HÖRSUM: *Zur Eule*, Horststr. 45, 45 b., SB.

RESTAURANT. – *Ratskeller*, Markt 1.

Alfeld, situated on the right bank of the Leine at the foot of the Sieben Berge (Seven Hills), is the centre of the Leinebergland (see p. 170). The old town has magnificently preserved its medieval character. It has a number of nurseries noted for the growing of cyclamens and a varied range of industry (paper-making, manufacture of shoe-lasts, metalworking).

HISTORY. – First recorded in 1020 as *Alevellon*, Alfeld received its municipal charter around 1250 from the Bishop of Hildesheim, who had a castle here to defend the ford over the Leine and the important trade route from the Weser valley to Hildesheim. In the Middle Ages the town was a member of the Hanse. It was devastated by a great fire in 1846. Its industrial development began with the completion of the railway line from Hanover to Kassel in 1854.

SIGHTS. – The old town is dominated by the twin towers of the parish church, **St Nicholas's**, a 15th c. Gothic hall-church with lateral aisles (triumphal cross, font, tabernacle). In the churchyard is the *Old Latin School* (1610), with rich figural decoration, which now houses the *Heimatmuseum* (material of local interest). Nearby is the **Shoemakers' Guild House**, an imposing half-timbered building of 1570. The oldest half-timbered house in the town (1490) is at Seminarstrasse 3. – N of the church is the **Town Hall**, built 1584–86, with a picturesque staircase tower. The "Blue Stone", left of the entrance, features in a local legend about the daughter of a burgomaster of Alfeld who was abducted. – There are also many legends associated with the *Lippoldshöhle*, a cave in the depths of the forest 1·5 km SW of the suburb of Brunkensen. It consists of a number of rooms and passages hewn from the rock and originally formed part of a castle belonging to the robber knight Lippold von Rössing (*c.* 1300).

Allgäu

Länder: Bavaria and Baden-Württemberg.
ⓘ **Fremdenverkehrsverband Allgäu/ Bayerisch Schwaben**,
Fuggerstr. 9, D-8900 Augsburg;
tel. (08 21) 3 33 35.

The *Allgäu is an attractive hill and mountain region (molasse ridges and morainic deposits) in the Alpine Foreland which takes in the southern part of Bavarian Swabia between Lake Constance and the Lech valley and extends NW into Württemberg. The high Alpine chain of the Allgäu Alps, part of the Northern Calcareous Alps, forms with its bizarrely shaped peaks the frontier between Bavaria and the Austrian provinces of Vorarlberg and Tirol. The highest point is the Grosser Krottenkopf (2657 m) in Northern Tirol.

The scenery of the Allgäu, with its tiers of steep foothills, magnificent lakes (Grosser and Kleiner Alpsee, Grüntensee, Weissensee, Hopfensee, Forggensee, etc.), quiet ponds and moors, extensive forests, lush mountain meadows and trim mountain villages set against an imposing backdrop

The Attlesee, near Nesselwang, Allgäu

of mountains, is impressively beautiful and attracts large numbers of visitors both during the summer and when it is under snow. Characteristic of the region are the "grass hills", whose steep slopes hold potential danger for hill-walkers (e.g. Höfats, 2258 m). With its high valleys which offer the assurance of good snow and its excellent downhill runs, the Allgäu is a very popular winter sports region.

The Allgäu is noted for its intensive cattle-rearing, the Allgäu breed being famous, and its highly developed dairying industry (milk, butter, cheese), and is also a land of spas and medicinal springs. The well-known Kneipp water cure was first devised in Bad Wörishofen, and is also applied in many other spas and health resorts. There are also mud-baths and various mineral springs. The health-giving effects of sunshine and mountain air draw many visitors to mountain resorts like Oberstdorf and Hindelang-Bad Oberdorf or to other favourable health spas.

Among the principal tourist resorts in the Allgäu are the regional capital of **Kempten** (see p. 162) and the widely known **Oberstdorf** (see p. 208), the starting-point for a visit to the *Kleinwalsertal* in Austria (German customs area); *Sonthofen* and *Immenstadt* in the Iller valley; the health resort of *Hindelang-Bad Oberdorf*, on the Jochstrasse with its numerous bends; *Pfronten*, with its "sun terrace" on the Breitenberg and the Hochalpe skiing area; **Füssen**, with the Forggensee; and **Schwangau**, with the "fairy-tale castles" of *Neuschwanstein* (illustrated on the cover of this Guide) and *Hohenschwangau*. In the western Allgäu are *Oberstaufen* (view of three countries from "Paradise"), *Lindenberg*, centre of the Allgäu hat industry (hat museum), the picturesque little town of **Wangen** (see p. 247), the former free Imperial cities of *Isny* and *Leutkirch*, and, farther N, *Ottobeuren* with its famous Benedictine abbey, *Memmingen*, *Mindelheim*, *Bad Wörishofen*, *Kaufbeuren* and *Marktoberdorf*. Here, too, is the Fugger city of **Augsburg** (see p. 66).

The very rewarding *Deutsche Alpenstrasse (German Alpine Highway) cuts across the mountainous southern part of the Allgäu. Farther N runs a branch of the **Oberschwäbische Barockstrasse** (Upper Swabian Baroque Highway).

Alsfeld

Land: Hesse. – Vehicle registration: VB.
Altitude: 268 m. – Population: 18,000.
Post code: D-6320. – Dialling code: 0 66 31.
ⓘ **Städtisches Verkehrsbüro**, Rittergasse 3–5; tel. 43 00.

HOTELS. – *Krone*, Schellengasse 2, 55 b.; *Klingelhöffer*, Hersfelder Str. 47, 70 b.; *Zum Schwalbennest*, Pfarrwiesenstr. 14, 56 b.; *Zur Erholung*, Grünberger Str. 26, 58 b.

This charming little town on the upper course of the Schwalm between Vogelsberg and Knüll was chosen as European model town for the preservation of the architectural heritage on account of its well-preserved old town (half-timbered houses). Its economic life centres on the textile and woodworking industries. Its favourable situation on the Kassel–Frankfurt am Main motorway makes it a convenient conference centre.

HISTORY. – Alsfeld is first recorded around 1069 as part of the Landgraviate of Thuringia. In 1247 it was incorporated in Hesse, and in the 13th c. it was a member of the League of Rhenish Towns. At the end of the 14th c. it was for a period the residence of Hermann the Learned, Landgrave of Hesse, who promoted the development of the local guilds. It went over to the Reformation at an early stage, and Luther lodged here on his way to and from the Diet of Worms. In 1871 the railway came to Alsfeld, in 1938 a connection to the motorway network.

SIGHTS. – The hub of the old town is the MARKTPLATZ, on the E side of which stands the late Gothic *Town Hall (1512–16) with its pointed-roofed oriel windows, one of the finest half-timbered buildings in W Germany, with a handsome council chamber and court room. On the N side of the square is the *Weinhaus* (1538), stone-built, with a stepped gable; to the left is the *Bückingsches Haus* (end of 16th c.), with a beautiful oriel. On the W

Marktplatz, Alsfeld

side, opposite the Town Hall, is the *Stumpfhaus* (1609), with rich carved and painted decoration. In the S corner of the square is the *Hochzeitshaus* (Wedding House), a handsome Renaissance building (1564–1571) which now houses a museum (history of the town, material of local interest). – In the nearby RITTERGASSE is the half-timbered *Neurathsches Haus* (1688), and adjoining it is the *Minnigerode-Haus*, a stone-built Baroque mansion of 1687 with a flying spiral staircase. – Behind the Town Hall, to the left, at the end of FULDERGASSE (many half-timbered houses), is the **Walpurgiskirche** (St Walburga's: 13th–15th c., with late Gothic wall paintings and fine monuments). At the far end of the street is the *Leonhardsturm* (1386). – In the Rossmarkt is *Trinity Church* (14th c.), with remains of conventional buildings adjoining it.

SURROUNDINGS. – *Schloss Altenburg* (18th c.), with church, on a hill above the Schwalm (2 km S).

Altes Land

Land: Lower Saxony.
ⓘ **Gemeindeverwalting Jork**, D-2155 Jork; tel. (0 41 62) 13 23.
  Tourist Information Hamburg, Bieverhaus at Main Station, D-2000 Hamburg 1; tel. (0 40) 24 12 34 and 32 69 17.

The **Altes Land ("Old Land") on the lower Elbe between Süderelbe and Stade is the richest and most beautiful of the Elbe fenlands (Elbmarschen), 32 km long and 2–7 km wide (area 157 sq. km). It is Germany's most northerly fruit-growing region, at its most enchanting when the cherry-trees are in flower, turning the orchards into a sea of white blossom. This is the time for a walk along the high dikes of the dark fenland rivers or the Elbe, looking down on the fruit-orchards below. Apples, pears and plums are grown as well as cherries. The region was settled and the dikes constructed by Dutch immigrants in the 12th and 13th c. Until 1832 it had its own constitution.*

A striking feature of the Altes Land is its handsome and colourful *farmhouses*, with tiles between the white timber framing and high thatched roofs. The windows are painted in dark colours, the

Typical farmhouse, Altes Land

brackets and corbels are green. The gables are decorated with elegant finials in the form of swans' necks. Here and there can be seen, beyond the bridge over the ditch, a richly carved entrance doorway.

The chief town of the Altes Land is **Jork**, with its experimental fruit-growing station and its brick-built Baroque church. The churches of *Neuenfelde* and *Steinkirchen* have fine organs by Arp-Schnitger. The famous organ-builder had a house in Neuenfelde, and he is buried in the church.

From *Lühe*, a popular place of resort on the Elbe, there is a ferry service to Schulau. Between Lühe, Schulau and St.-Pauli ply the ships of the HADAG company, offering a convenient way of approaching the Altes Land by water.

In the extreme north of the Altes Land lies **Stade**, once a Hanseatic town and Swedish fortress (17th c). The old town with its narrow streets and half-timbered houses, is still surrounded by a moat; by the Alter Hafen is an educational centre with a regional museum.

Altötting

Land: Bavaria. – Vehicle registration: AÖ.
Altitude: 402 m. – Population: 11,000.
Post code: D-8262. – Dialling code: 0 86 71.
ⓘ **Wallfahrts- und Verkehrsverein**, Kapellplatz 2a; tel. 80 68.

HOTELS. – *Gasthof zur Post*, Kapellplatz, 2, 167 b.; sauna; *Schex*, Kapuzinerstr. 11, 100 b.; *Scharnagl*, Neuöttinger Str. 2, 180 b.; *Plankl*, Schlotthammerstr. 4, 125 b.

RESTAURANT. – *Bräu im Moos*, Moos (with beer-garden).

Altötting, situated at the intersection of two main roads, is the most celebrated pilgrimage centre of the Virgin Mary in Bavaria, visited every year by more than 500,000 pilgrims. In the town is the central monastery of the Capuchin order.

HISTORY. – The place is first recorded in 748, the chapel in 877. It became a place of pilgrimage after a local miracle in 1489. The worship of the Virgin of Altötting reached its highest point in the reign of Elector Maximilian I (1598–1654). On 18 November 1980 Pope John Paul II visited the Holy Chapel.

SIGHTS. – The **Holy Chapel** (Heilige Kapelle) in the spacious KAPELLPLATZ is an early Romanesque octagonal structure (originally c. 600). Inside, enclosed in a silver tabernacle (1645), is the famous carved wooden *figure of the Virgin*, now black with soot, known as the "Black Madonna" (c. 1300). Silver urns contain the hearts of 21 Bavarian rulers and of Tilly, the celebrated Imperial general of the Thirty Years War. – On the S side of the square is the **Stiftskirche**, a three-aisled hall-church (c. 1500), with the tombs of King Carloman and Tilly. The *Treasury* is richly endowed with valuable things, among them the *"Golden Horse"* ("Goldenes Rössl"), a masterpiece of late Gothic French court art (c. 1400). – Also of interest is the *Bruder Konrad Church* containing the saint's reliquary and the

The "Golden Horse", Stiftskirche Treasury, Altötting

Panorama, a colossal circular painting of the Crucifixion. A film on the subject of the Madonna and slides are shown in the "Neues Haus".

Amberg

Land: Bavaria. – Vehicle registration: AM.
Altitude: 374 m. – Population: 47,000.
Post code: D-8450. – Dialling code: 0 96 21.
ⓘ **Stadtisches Fremdenverkehrsburo,** Zeughausstr. la; tel. 1 02 31.

HOTELS. – *Heiner Fleischmann*, Wörthstr. 4, 50 b.; *Brunner* (no rest.), Batteriegasse 3, 70 b.; *Gall,* Sulzbacherstr. 89, 40 b.; *Bahnhof-Hotel*, Batteriegasse 2, 65 b.

RESTAURANT. – *Casino*, Schrannenplatz 8 (Old-style German Parlour).

Franconian Jura, nestling in the valley of the Vils, which flows through the old town. The late medieval and Baroque town centre is still enclosed within a ring of walls, with their towers and gates. The line of the old ramparts is now marked by a series of gardens.

HISTORY. – Amberg appears in the records for the first time in 1034, in a charter of Konrad II. In 1269 it was granted in fee to Duke Ludwig the Severe of Bavaria; in 1329 it fell to the sons of Count Palatine Rudolf and was incorporated in the Rhineland Palatinate; and in 1628 it passed to Maximilian I of Bavaria along with the Upper Palatinate. Its favourable situation on the trade route between Nuremberg and Prague and its ironworking industry ensured the town's prosperity until the time of the Thirty Years War. The navigable River Vils played an important part in the transport of iron ore and salt.

SIGHTS. – The hub of the old town within its oval circle of walls is the MARKTPLATZ, with the **Town Hall** (14th–16th c.; Large and Small Council chambers, with handsome coffered wooden ceilings) and the late Gothic *hall church* (St Martin's), the most important Gothic church in the Upper Palatinate after Regensburg Cathedral (built 1421–83; W tower, 91 m high, finished in 1534. Inside is the imposing tomb of Count Palatine Ruprecht Pipan, d. 1397). – Behind the church is the old 13th–14th c. *Castle*, now Heimatmuseum, with material of local interest. – SW of the Marktplatz is the 17th c. *Electoral Palace* (Kurfürstliches Schloss: now local government offices). From the Palace the town wall leads across the Vils, borne on two arches which are known as the

Town Hall, Amberg

"Stadtbrille" (the town's "spectacles"). – In SCHRANNENPLATZ (NW of the old town) is the **Schulkirche** and the Stadttheater (sumptuous Rococo interior) which is built into a former Franciscan church. From the Marktplatz the GEORGENSTRASSE (pedestrian street) leads to the **Maltesergebäude** (a former Jesuit college; fine meeting hall). Behind this is the substantial Gothic *St George's Church* (stucco work by J. B. Zimmermann).

SURROUNDINGS. – *Mariahilf pilgrimage church* (stucco interior decoration by Giovanni Battista Carlone, ceiling painting by Cosmas Damian Asam), on a hill with wide views (3 km NE).

Ammersee

Land: Bavaria.
ⓘ **Verkehrsamt Diessen**, Müllstr 4;
D-8918 Diessen;
tel. (0 88 07) 12 83.

The Ammersee lies 35 km SW of Munich in the Alpine Foreland. It came into existence in the last Ice Age, when a mighty glacier advanced northward from the Loisach valley. Originally the green waters of the lake covered an area almost twice as large as its present surface, but silt deposited by the River Ammer has steadily encroached on its N and S ends.

The lake, surrounded by forest-covered morainic hills, has an area of 47 sq. km (16 km long, 3–6 km wide) and is up to 81 m deep. All round its shores are attractive resorts, linked by boat services on the lake (including one "old-time" boat). Beach lidos offer excellent facilities for bathing, and sailing and rowing enthusiasts are well catered for. There is also good fishing

(whitefish, vendace, zander) and opportunities for cycle tours. In spite of these attractions the Ammersee is less crowded at weekends than the nearby Starnberger See.

Diessen possesses a masterpiece of Bavarian Rococo in the church built for the Augustinian canons by Johann Michael Fischer. At Herrsching is the pilgrimage church of **Andechs**, towering above the Kien valley with its tall "onion-domed" tower; it has ceiling paintings and stucco work by Johann Baptist Zimmermann. The nearby inn offers the visitor good food and drink. Andechs beer has long been famed.

Near *Raisting*, S of Diessen, stands the largest telecommunications station in the world with gigantic parabolic reflectors. On more than 2500 channels for telephone, telex and data traffic, communication via Raisting is maintained with over 50 countries. A satellite receives the transmitted signals and relays them to other stations.

To the S the Ammergebirge and the Benediktenwand form a backdrop to the attractive lake scenery. In clear weather the Zugspitze in the Wettersteingebirge can be seen.

Ansbach

Land: Bavaria. – Vehicle registration: AN.
Altitude: 409 m. – Population: 40,000.
Post code: D-8800. – Dialling code: 09 81.
ⓘ **Stadtisches Verkehrsamt**, Rathaus, Martin-Luther-Platz 1;
tel. 5 12 43.

HOTELS. – *Am Drechselsgarten*, Am Drechselsgarten 1, 76 b.; *Christi* (no rest.), Richard-Wagner-Str. 41, 37 b.; *Der Platengarten*, Promenade 30, 30 b.; *Fantasie*, Eyber Str. 75, 40 b.; *Windmühle*, Rummelsberger Str. 1, 41 b.; *Residenz*, Maximilianstr. 16, 21 b.; *Schwarzer Bock*, Pfarrstr. 31, 20 b.

RESTAURANT. – *Café-Restaurant Orangerie*, in the Hofgarten.

EVENTS. – Annual *Civic Festival* (May/June); every four years *Ansbach Festival* (beginning July); Annual *Rococo Plays* (beginning July); every other year (odd numbered years) *International Ansbach Bach Festival* (end July/beginning August).

Ansbach, in the forest-encircled valley of the Rezat, is the "city of Franconian Rococo" – a designation it owes to its former status as residence of the Margraves of Brandenburg-Ansbach. It is now chief town of the administrative region of Central Franconia and an important communications centre. Its various manufacturing and processing industries supply meat products, electronic goods, artificial materials and paper.

HISTORY. – Ansbach (earlier Onoldsbach) grew up round a Benedictine monastery founded by St

Gumbertus in 748. It is first recorded as a town in 1221. In 1331 it passed by purchase to the Burgrave of Nuremberg; then from 1460 to 1791 it was the residence of the Margraves of Brandenburg-Ansbach. In 1791 Ansbach passed to Prussia, in 1806 to Bavaria.

SIGHTS. – On the edge of the old town, at the end of the Promenade, is the *Margrave's Palace, one of the most important 18th c. palaces in Franconia with 27 state rooms (Great Hall and *Mirror Room in charming early Rococo style; the Gothic Hall houses the Bavarian state collection of Ansbach faience and porcelain). – SE of the palace is the Hofgarten with the 102 m long Orangery (1726–34) and a tablet commemorating the enigmatic foundling Kaspar Hauser who was stabbed to death here in 1833.

In the OLD TOWN are the Church of St Gumbertus (Evang.) in JOHANN-SEBASTIAN-BACH-PLATZ, with the Chapel of the Knights of the Swan (Romanesque crypt and burial-vault of the princes (25 sarcophagi), and the late Gothic St John's Church (Evang.) in MARTIN-LUTHER-PLATZ.

SURROUNDINGS of Ansbach. – 50 km SE in Weissenburg is a Roman museum.

Aschaffenburg

Land: Bavaria. – Vehicle registration: AB.
Altitude: 130 m. – Population: 59,000.
Post code: D-8750. – Dialling code: 0 60 21.
ⓘ Fremdenverkehrsamt und Verkehrsverein, Dalbergstr. 6;
tel. 3 04 26 and 2 37 44.

HOTELS. – *Post, Goldbacher Str. 19, 116 b.; Aschaffenburger Hof, Frohsinnstr. 11, 100 b.; Kolping, Treibgasse 26, 40 b.; Wilder Mann, Fischergasse 1, 80 b.; Mainperle, Weissenburger Str. 42a, 60 b. – YOUTH HOSTEL: Beckerstr. 47.

RESTAURANTS. – Ratskeller, Dalbergstr. 15; Schlossweinstuben, in Schloss Johannisburg.

EVENTS. – Mineral market (April); Aschaffenburg Folk Festival (12 days in June).

Aschaffenburg lies in Lower Franconia on the hilly right bank of the Main, on the edge of the Spessart. The old town is dominated by the massive bulk of the Renaissance palace once occupied by the Electors of Mainz. Aschaffenburg is an important centre of the West German clothing industry and transhipment point for water-borne traffic on the Main.

HISTORY. – Aschaffenburg grew up round a Frankish fortress and, probably around 957, came under the control of the Archbishop of Mainz along with a collegiate house founded in the mid 10th c. It remained attached to Mainz until 1803. It rose to prosperity thanks to its situation at a bridge over the Main and as a tax-collecting point, and was walled in 1122. At the end of the 13th c. it became a residence of the Elector of Mainz in addition to Mainz itself. Between 1803 and 1810 it was capital of the principality of Aschaffenburg newly established for Karl von Dalberg, which was incorporated in Bavaria in 1814. The 19th and 20th c. saw the development of industry in the town.

SIGHTS. – To the W of the old town, on the banks of the Main, is *Schloss Johannisburg, a palace in late Renaissance style erected 1605–14 as residence of the Elector, with the State Picture Gallery, the Elector's State Apart-

Schloss Johannisburg, Aschaffenburg

ments, the *Palace Library* and *Museum*. NW of the palace is the *Schlossgarten*, and beyond this is the *Pompejanum*, a reproduction (erected 1842–49) of the Villa of Castor and Pollux in Pompeii. – Schlossgasse runs SE to the **Stiftskirche of SS. Peter and Alexander* (12th and 13th c.), which contains important works of art (including a "Lamentation" by Matthias Grünewald); Romanesque cloister. The former chapter-house now contains the **Stiftsmuseum** (religious art, collection of china). Opposite the Museum is the modern *Town Hall* (1957), and to the E in Wermbachstr. the *Science Museum*. – Sandgasse leads to *Schöntal Park*, E of the old town, laid out in 1780.

SURROUNDINGS. – **Schönbusch Park**, with a little "pleasure palace" in early neo-classical style (3·5 km SW).

Augsburg

Altitude: 496 m. – Population: 249,000.
Post code: D-8900. – Dialling code: 08 21.
ⓘ **Verkehrsverein**,
   Bahnhofstr. 7; tel. 3 60 26 and 3 60 27.

HOTELS. – **Steigenberger Drei Mohren Hotel*, Maximilianstr. 40, 170 b. (an historic old inn frequented by princes); *Turmhotel Holiday Inn*, Imhofstr. 12, 350 b., SB, solarium, sauna, grill on 35th floor; *Post*, Fuggerstr. 7, 85 b.; *Ost* (no rest.), Fuggerstr. 4–6, 85 b.; *Riegele*, Viktoriastr. 4, 57 b.; *Dom Hotel*, Frauentorstr. 8, 80 b.; *Langer*, Gögginger Str. 39, 55 b.; *Fischertor*, Pfärrle 16, 35 b. – IN AUGSBURG-HAUNSTETTEN: *Gregor*, Landsberger Str. 62, 60 b. – IN AUGSBURG-OBERHAUSEN: *Alpenhof*, Donauwörther Str. 233, 250 b. – YOUTH HOSTEL: Beim Pfaffenkeller 3, 160 b. – CAMPING SITES: *Augusta*

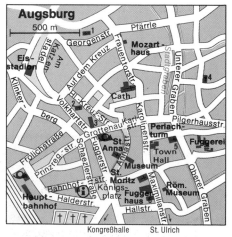

1 St George's Church   3 Municipal Theatre   5 Barfüsserkirche
2 Holy Cross Church   4 St Max's Church   6 Schaezler-Palais

and *Ludwigshof*, a short distance from the Augsburg–Ost motorway exit.

RESTAURANTS. – *Ratskeller*, Rathausplatz 2 (Terrace); *Fuggerkeller*, Maximilianstr. 38 (in the Fuggerhaus); *Arnemann*, Parkrestaurant in the *Agnes Bernauer Stuben*, Ludwigstr. 19; *Ecke-Stuben*, Elias-Holl-Platz (an artists' haunt); *Sieben-Schwaben-Stuben*, Bürgermeister-Fischer-Str. 12 (Swabian specialities); *Fischertor*, Pfärrle 16; *Fuggerei-Stube*, Jakober Str. 26.

WINE-BARS. – *Badische Weinstuben*, in Town Hall; *Bürgermeister*, Maximilianstr. 45; *Sieben Schwaben Klause*, Kleines Katharinengässchen 8.

CAFÉS. – *Bertele*, Philippine-Welser-Str. 4; *Drexl*, Maximilianstr. 18; *Parkcafé*, in Stadtgarten, Gögginger Str. 10; *Eber*, Philippine-Welser-Str. 6.

EVENTS. – *Mozart Summer Festival*, concerts in Schaezler-Palais.

Augsburg, the third largest city in Bavaria (after Munich and Nuremberg), lies N of the Lechfeld at the confluence of the Wertach and the Lech. This ancient and famous Imperial city, home of the great medieval merchant dynasties, the Fuggers and the Welsers, is now the chief town of the administrative region of Bavarian Swabia (Bayersich-Schwaben).
In Roman times Augsburg was connected with Verona by the Via Claudia, and its favourable situation promoted the development of commerce and industry. Its present-day industries include large textile and engineering firms. The city has a very active cultural life, and its new university opened its doors in 1970. Augsburg is served by a motorway, and one of the most popular tourist routes in Germany, the Romantic Highway, runs from the Main valley via Augsburg to Füssen.

HISTORY. – The origin of the town was a Roman military camp established by Drusus in 15 B.C., and in the 1st c. A.D. it became capital of the province of Raetia under the name of *Augusta Vindelicorum*. Soon after 400 Roman rule came to an end. The city had a Christian community and became the seat of a bishop at an early stage. In 955 King Otto I put a stop to the frequent incursions of the Hungarians by his victory in the battle of the Lechfeld. In the 10th c. there is mention in the records of a settlement of merchants with widespread trading connections S of the episcopal town, and in the 11th c. this received a municipal charter. In 1276 Rudolf of Habsburg granted Augsburg the status of a free Imperial city. The rising town was now encircled by walls and towers, and it reached its peak of prosperity in the second half of the 15th and the 16th c. as the principal entrepôt in the trade between S Germany, Italy and the East. The Fuggers and Welsers were now among the wealthiest merchant princes in the world.

Augsburg was the meeting-place of many Imperial diets, and at the Diet of 1530 the Protestant princes put before the Emperor Charles V the "Augsburg Confession", the basic creed of the Lutheran Church. The Thirty Years War brought economic and cultural decline. In 1805 Augsburg lost its status as a free Imperial city, and in 1806 it became part of the new kingdom of Bavaria. With the coming of the industrial age a new period of prosperity began. During the Second World War more than half the city was destroyed. In 1972 the city's area was considerably increased by taking in land from neighbouring communes.

SIGHTS. – In the centre of the city, whose main traffic artery is formed by Karolinenstrasse and Maximilianstrasse, stands the *Town Hall, an imposing Renaissance structure by the municipal architect Elias Holl (1615–20). Nearby are the 78 m high *Perlachturm* (panoramic view) and the *Augustus Fountain* (1589–94). – E of the Town Hall in the Jakobervorstadt is the *Fuggerei*, a little "town within the town" with its own four gates, founded by the Fugger family to provide homes for poor citizens of Augsburg. This is the oldest public housing scheme in the world (1519), and the tenants still pay a rent of only 1 Rhenish guilder (=DM 1.71) for a 2½-roomed house (museum). – From the Town Hall Karolinenstrasse and the Hoher Weg lead to the **Cathedral** (9th–14th c.), with a fine bronze door in the S aisle (35 relief panels, 11th c.). Features of the interior are five windows on the S side of the nave, the oldest figured stained glass in Germany, which may date from before 1100, and altar paintings by Hans Holbein the Elder. – E of the Cathedral in Springergässchen is a house once occupied by *Rudolf Diesel* (1858–1913), inventor of the diesel engine (1892). N of the Cathedral in Frauentorstrasse is the *Mozarthaus*, birthplace of the composer's father Leopold Mozart (memorial museum).

Town Hall, Augsburg

In MAXIMILIANSTRASSE (the beginning of the old Roman road between Germany and Italy), which runs S past the Town Hall, is the Gothic *St Moritz's Church*; in front of it the *Mercury Fountain* (1599). Opposite the church, to the N, is the *Weberhaus* (Weavers' House), one of the many old guild-houses. – To the S is the **Fuggerhaus** (1512–15), the town house of the Princes Fugger von Babenhausen, who in the 15th and 16th c. rose from being apprentice weavers to become the world's richest merchants (Damenhof, 1516; Museum of Science). Beyond this, on the right, is the *Schaezler-*

Palais, a Rococo mansion with a large banqueting hall, the *Municipal Art Collections* ("German Baroque gallery") and the *State Gallery* (early German masters, including Holbein the Elder, Hans Burgkmair the Elder and Dürer). In front of the palace is the *Hercules Fountain*, by Adriaen de Vries (1602). – A short distance E, in the old *Dominican Church* (16th–18th c.), is the *Roman Museum*. – At the far end of Maximilianstrasse is **St Ulrich's Minster** (SS. Ulrich and Afra, 1500: R.C.), which forms an attractive architectural ensemble with the little *St Ulrich's Church* (1458: Evang.). – SE of St Ulrich's Church is the *Rotes Tor* (Red Gate), with a tower by Elias Holl (1622). Adjoining are the water towers, the Hospital of the Holy Ghost (1631), an open-air theatre and the Augsburg Puppenkiste (puppet theatre).

SW of the Town Hall, in Philippine-Welser-Strasse, is the *Maximilian Museum, which offers a vivid picture of the city's historic, artistic and cultural past. Here, too, in Annastrasse, is **St Anna's Church** (14th–17th c.: Evang.; Lutherhöfle – commemorating Luther's visit in 1518), in which is the *funerary chapel of the Fugger family, the first considerable Renaissance work in Germany (1509–12). – S of the Hauptbahnhof, in the **Stadtgarten**, are the **Kongresshalle** (1974: Parkrestaurant) and the *Hotelturm* (117 m). – Since the 1972 Olympic Games Augsburg has possessed a *canoe slalom stadium* on the Hochablass.

Baden-Baden

Land: Baden-Württemberg.
Vehicle registration: BAD.
Altitude: 183 m. – Population: 50,000.
Post code: D-7570. – Dialling code: 0 72 21.
ⓘ **Kur-Direktion** (*Tourist Information*),
Augustaplatz 1;
tel. 27 52 00 and 27 52 01.

HOTELS. – *Brenner's Parkhotel,* Lichtentaler Allee,
168 b., Schwarzwald Grill, SB, sauna, solarium;
Steigenberger Hotel Europaischer Hof, Kaiserallee 2,
210 b.; *Steigenberger Badhotel Badischer Hof,*
Lange Str. 47, 235 b., SB, sauna, solarium; *Quisisana,*
Bismarckstr. 21, 90 b., SP, sauna, solarium; *Holiday
Inn Sporthotel,* Falkenstr. 2, 200 b., SB, sauna,
solarium; *Badhotel zum Hirsch* (no rest.), Hirschstr.
1, 80 b.; *Holland Hotel* (no rest.), Sofienstr. 14, 93 b.;
Atlantic, Lichtentaler Allee, 80 b.; *Müller* (no rest.),
Lange Str. 34, 40 b. – OUTSIDE THE TOWN: *Golfhotel,*
Fremersbergstr. 113, 140 b., SB, sauna, golf course;
Waldhotel Der Selighof, Fremersbergstr. 125, 116 b.,
SB, tennis courts; *Waldhotel Fischkultur,* Gaisbach
91, 60 b.

RESTAURANTS. – *Kurhaus-Restaurant,* Kaiserallee
1; *Stahlbad,* Augustaplatz 2; *L'Auberge,* Gerns-
bacher Str. 10; *Sinner-Eck,* Leopoldsplatz.

WINE-BARS. – *Schloss Neuweier,* in the Neuweier
district, 12 km SW; *Zum Bocksbeutel,* in the Umweg
district, 8 km SW.

CAFÉS. – *König,* Lichtentaler Str. 12; *Löhr,* Augustaplatz; *Dietsch,* Lichtentaler Str. 74. – Several bars and
night-clubs.

International Casino (roulette, baccarat, blackjack:
daily 2 p.m.–2 a.m., Saturdays to 3 a.m.), in the right
wing of the Kurhaus.

EVENTS. – *Grosse Woche* (Festival), in August, with
international horse-races in Iffezheim.

**Baden-Baden, in the Oos basin amid
the western foothills of the Northern Black Forest, within the Upper
Rhine Plain, is a very popular international health resort, thanks to
its favourable situation, its mild
climate and its radioactive brine
springs (68 °C; 800,000 litres daily).
The incorporation of the township
of Steinbach into Baden-Baden has
also made it into a wine-producing
town. The Schwarzwald-Hochstrasse (Black Forest Ridgeway)
skirts the extensive forests within
the municipal boundaries. Baden-
Baden is the headquarters of Süd-
westfunk, the South-Western Radio
and Television Corporation.**

HISTORY. – The healing powers of the local thermal
springs were known to the Romans, and the town's
name, *Aquae Aureliae,* is recorded on Roman
milestones. The Franks built a royal stronghold on the
Schlossberg, and towards the end of the 12th c. the

Racecourse, Iffezheim

Altes Schloss became the seat of the Zähringen family.
The medieval town grew up at the foot of the
Schlossberg. Margrave Christoph I built the Neues
Schloss in 1479, surrounded the town with walls and
in 1507 issued an ordinance regulating the use of the
mineral springs and the lodging of visitors. In 1689 the
town was burned to the ground by the French. In
1771 Baden-Baden passed to Baden-Durlach under a
succession settlement. At the beginning of the 19th c.
it became the summer capital of the Grand Duchy of
Baden-Baden created by Napoleon. The establishment of the Casino (1838) and the *Iffezheim* races
(1858) soon made the developing resort a meeting-
place of the fashionable world and the "summer
capital of Europe". In the 20th c. the town's area has
been expanded by taking in land from neighbouring
communes.

SIGHTS. – The hub of fashionable life in
Baden-Baden is the *Kurgarten,* laid out in
front of the **Kurhaus** built by Weinbrenner in 1821–24 (café-restaurant, Casino,
conducted tours daily 10–12). In the
Kurpark, N of the Kurhaus, is the *Trinkhalle* or Pump Room (frescoes illustrating
Black Forest legends). On the Michaelsberg, above the Trinkhalle to the NW, is
the *Greek-Romanian Chapel,* built by Leo
von Klenze in 1863–66, with the tombs of
the Stourdza boyar family (view). S of the
Kurhaus are the *Little Theatre* and the
Kunsthalle. – Here begins the famous
Lichtentaler Allee, Baden-Baden's
popular promenade, which runs along the
left bank of the Oos to **Lichtental
Cistercian Abbey,** founded in 1245
(Princes' Chapel).

The closely packed OLD TOWN is built on
the slopes of the Schlossberg. Half-way
up is the **Stiftskirche** (R.C.: tomb of
Margrave Ludwig Wilhelm, known as
"Türkenlouis", d. 1707; sandstone crucifix by Nicholas of Leyden, 1467). To the
NE are the thermal springs, which supply

the Friedrichsbad (1869–77). In Römerplatz is the *Convent of the Holy Sepulchre* (17th c.); under the square are the remains of *Roman baths*. To the E are the *Kurmittelhaus* (spa establishment) or "Augustabad" (1966) and the late Gothic *Spitalskirche*; a new spa complex is under construction (completion date mid 1985). – On top of the hill (access road) is the **Neues Schloss** (alt. 212 m), built by Margrave Christoph I in 1479, occasionally used as a residence by the former Grand-Ducal family, with the *Zähringen Museum* (porcelain, etc.: seen by arrangement). In the old stables (Marstall) is a *museum* (history of the town).

SURROUNDINGS. – *Merkur, viewpoint on hill (670 m: cable car), 4 km E. – *Altes Schloss (Hohenbaden, 403 m), once residence of the Margraves of Baden, now a ruin; magnificent views from tower (4·5 km N: access road).

Baltic Coast

Land: Schleswig-Holstein.
(i) **Fremdenverkehrsverband Schleswig-Holstein,**
Niemannsweg 31, D-2300 Kiel;
tel. (04 31) 56 30 27.

The Baltic coastline of the Federal Republic extends for a distance of 383 km from Lübeck-Travemünde to Flensburg. Bights and fjord-like inlets penetrate deeply inland – Lübeck

Bay, the Kieler Förde, Eckernförde Bay, the Schlei and the Flensburger Förde. The Fehmarnsund Bridge links Fehmarn, the Federal Republic's largest island (185 sq. km), with the mainland. In contrast to the treeless fen landscapes of the North Sea coast, much of the Baltic coast is attractively wooded (mostly beech). The Baltic has scarcely any tide.

The principal Baltic bathing resorts are to be found on the shores of LÜBECK BAY: the fashionable *Travemünde* and *Timmendorfer Strand-Niendorf*, *Haffkrug-Scharbeutz*, *Sierksdorf* (with the Hansaland leisure park), the little resorts of *Pelzerhaken* and *Rettin* (belonging to the town of *Neustadt in Holstein*), *Grömitz*, *Kellenhusen* and *Dahme*. Ninety per cent of all visitors to the Baltic coast spend their holidays here.

The island of FEHMARN has a beautiful bathing beach at *Burg-Südstrand.* On the W coast, in and around the *Wallnau* bird reserve, there are a number of fine beaches. Opposite Fehmarn, on the Steinwarder peninsula, is the modern holiday centre of *Heiligenhafen*. Below the steep wooded slopes of the *Hohwacht* coast are other attractive beaches. – *Weissenhäuser Strand* leisure centre.

In the FIRTH OF KIEL are the bathing resorts of *Heikendorf* and *Laboe* (Naval

Weissenhäuser Strand leisure centre on the Hohwachter Bucht

Boating harbour at the Fehmarnsund bridge

Memorial), the modern sailing marina of *Wendtorf*, the Olympic harbour of *Schilk-see* (where the sailing events of the 1972 Summer Olympics were held) and the little neighbouring resort of *Strande*. – In ECKERNFÖRDE BAY are *Schwedeneck* with its sandy beaches at *Dänisch Nienhof* and *Surendorf*, the health resort and harbour town of *Eckernförde* and the modern holiday centre of *Damp 2000*. – Finally there is the resort of *Glücksburg* (with a picturesque *moated castle) on the FLENS-BURGER FÖRDE.

Many resorts have helped to lengthen the season by building indoor baths, often with sea-water and artificial waves.

Among the many places in the region of interest to the tourist are the medieval city of **Lübeck**, once queen of the Hanse; **Kiel**, capital of the *Land* of Schleswig-Holstein; the cathedral city of **Schleswig**; and **Flensburg**, with its churches and town gates. Inland from Lübeck Bay is "**Holstein Switzerland**" (see p. 153), with its hills and lakes.

Bamberg

Land: Bavaria. – Vehicle registration: BA.
Altitude: 231–386 m. – Population: 71,000.
Post code: D-8600. – Dialling code: 09 51.
ⓘ **Städtisches Fremdenverkehrsamt**,
Hauptwachstr. 16;
tel. 2 64 01.

HOTELS. – *Bamberger Hof Bellevue*, Schönleinsplatz 4, 70 b.; *National*, Luitpoldstr. 37, 69 b.; *Barockhotel am Dom* (no rest.), Vorderer Bach 4, 36 b.; *Neukauf*, An der Breitenau 2, 158 b.; *Die Alte Post*, Heiliggrabstr. 1, 75 b.; *Straub* (no rest.), Ludwigstr. 31, 70 b.; *Altenburgblick* (no rest.), Panzerleite 59,

60 b.; *Hospiz* (no rest.), Promenade 3, 60 b.; *Alt Bamberg*, Habergasse 1, 32 b.; *Graupner* (no rest.), Lange Str. 5, 31 b.; *Brudermühle*, Schranne 1, 28 b.; *Weierich*, Lugbank 5, 52 b.; *Wilde Rose*, Kesslerstr. 7, 39 b. – YOUTH HOSTELS: Pödelsdorfer Str. 178, 125 b.; Oberer Leinritt 70, 120 b. – CAMPING SITE: In the district of Bug, 4 km S of town centre.

RESTAURANTS. – *Messerschmitt*, Lange Str. 41 (garden terrace); *Theaterrose*, Schillerplatz 7 (garden terrace); *Böttingerhaus*, Judenstr. 14; *Steinernes Haus*, Lange Str. 8 (fresh-water fish); *Altenburg*, Burghof 1; *Schlenkerla*, Dominikanerstr. 6 (Rauchbier: see below).

WINE-BARS. – *Würzburger Weinstube*, Zinkenwörth 6; *Pizzini*, Obere Sandstr. 17.

CAFÉS. – *Rosengarten*, Neue Residenz (May–Oct.); *Café am Dom*, Ringleinsgasse 2.

EVENTS. – *Organ Concerts* (Cathedral; May/Oct.); *Calderón Festival* (June/July).

Bamberg, the old Frankish imperial and episcopal city, the most important town in Upper Franconia, lies on the western edge of a wide basin in the valley of the Regnitz, here divided into two arms, which flows into the Main 7 km downstream. The oldest part is the episcopal town on the high W bank of the left arm of the river, with the Cathedral and the old Benedictine abbey of Michaelsberg. The borough which grew up from the 12th c. onwards lies on the flat ground between the two arms of the Regnitz. Bamberg has a university. The Bamberg Symphony Orchestra has an international reputation. The town has a river port on the Main-Danube Canal; its industrial zone (principally engineering, textiles and electrical goods) is E of the town. It has numerous breweries; a local speciality is Rauchbier, brewed from smoked malt (to be had in the Schlenkerla restaurant and elsewhere in the town).

HISTORY. – Bamberg is first recorded in 902 as the seat of the Babenberg family (*castrum Babenberch*). The bishopric was established by Emperor Henry II in 1007, and he was also responsible for building the first cathedral (completed 1012). In the 16th c., under Prince-Bishop Georg III Schenk von Limpurg, Bamberg was a great centre of humanism. During the Thirty Years War it sided with the Catholic League. From 1648 to 1802 it had a university. Under Prince-Bishops Franz and Friedrich Carl von Schönborn Bamberg enjoyed a great cultural flowering, and Baroque art flourished in the town. In 1818 the bishopric became an archbishopric. The town suffered little damage during the Second World War. It now receives, along with Lübeck and Regensburg, priority attention from the authorities responsible for the preservation of the country's architectural heritage.

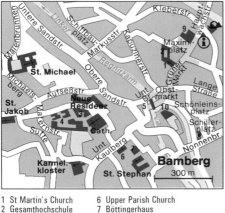

1 St Martin's Church
2 Gesamthochschule
3 Alte Hofhaltung
4 Canons' houses
5 Old Town Hall
6 Upper Parish Church
7 Böttingerhaus
8 E. T. A. Hoffmann House
9 New Town Hall
10 Town Hall II

SIGHTS. – In the old borough between the two arms of the Regnitz, in the long GRÜNER MARKT (the main artery of the town centre), stands the Baroque *St Martin's Church* (1689–91). A little way N, at Fleischstr. 2, near the New Town Hall (1733–36), is the well-stocked *Natural History Museum.* – S of the Grüner Markt by way of the Obstmarkt is the *Obere Brücke* (Upper Bridge: 1453–56), with an attractive view to the right of the fishermen's houses of Klein-Venedig ("Little Venice"). In the middle of the bridge is the *Old Town Hall, built by J. J. M. Küchel 1744–56, which owes its unusual situation to the need to conciliate the interests of the borough and the episcopal town, separated by the river.

In the commanding *DOMPLATZ stands the early 13th c. **Cathedral with its four towers, one of Germany's finest medieval buildings. In the N aisle is the *Fürstentor* (Prince's Door), the principal entrance to the Cathedral, with figures of Apostles and prophets; in the tympanum is a Last Judgment. On the S side of the east choir is the *Adamspforte* (Adam's Door); six statues from this are now in the Diocesan Museum. On the N side of the east choir is the *Marienpforte* or *Gnadenpforte* (Virgin's Door), with the oldest sculpture in the Cathedral (*c.* 1210).

INTERIOR of the Cathedral. – In front of the east choir (Georgenchor) is the *tomb* (by Riemenschneider, 1499–1513) *of Emperor Henry II* (d. 1024) *and his wife Kunigunde* (d. 1039). By the left-hand pillar of the choir is the figure of the famous **Bamberger Reiter** or Bamberg Horseman (*c.* 1240: traditionally identified as King Stephen of Hungary – St Stephen – Henry II's brother-in-law). On the outside of the stone choir screens are *figures of the twelve Apostles and twelve prophets by the Master of the Georgenchor; on

a pillar between the prophets are **Mary and Elizabeth; on the Apostle side are allegorical figures of Church and Synagogue (by the sculptor who carved the Horseman). In the E crypt is the modern sandstone sarcophagus of King Conrad III (d. 1152 in Bamberg), in the west choir (St Peter's Choir) and marble tomb of Pope Clement II (d. 1047), previously Bishop of Bamberg – the only Papal tomb in Germany (*c.* 1235). On the W wall of the S transept is the so-called *altar by Veit Stoss (1520–23). – The *Diocesan Museum in the cathedral chapterhouse contains the rich cathedral Treasury, precious vestments (including Henry II's imperial cloak) and the figures from the Adamspforte.

On the W side of the Domplatz is the *Alte Hofhaltung or Alte Residenz, one of the finest creations of the German Renaissance, built as the bishop's palace 1571–76. It now houses the *Historical Museum* (applied art, etc.). The Calderón Festival is held in the courtyard. – On the N side of the square is the *Neue Residenz (1695–1704), J. L. Dientzenhofer's greatest work, with the Prince-Bishop's residential apartments, the *Altdeutsche Galerie* (Heisterbach altar, works of the 15th–18th c.) and the Staatsbibliothek (temporary special exhibitions). In the courtyard is a beautiful rose-garden with a magnificent view.

On top of the hill, visible from a long way away, is the former Benedictine abbey of *Michaelsberg (1009–1803), with *St Michael's Church* (12th–15th c.). To the N and W of the church are the new abbey buildings erected by J. L. Dientzenhofer (1696–1702) and Balthasar Neumann (1742).

On the Kaulberg in the southern part of the old town is the **Upper Parish Church**, (14th/15th c.), Bamberg's

The Bamberg Horseman

finest Gothic building (14th c.). A little way E is the *Böttingerhaus*, a distinguished Baroque building of 1707–13. Beyond this, on the banks of the Regnitz, is *Concordia*, a handsome Baroque palace of 1716–22. – At Schillerplatz 26, opposite the Municipal Theatre, is the *E. T. A. Hoffmann House*, in which the writer lived from 1809 to 1813. On the SE outskirts of the town, at E.Th.-A.-Hoffmann-Str. 2, is the *Karl May Museum*. To the S in BUG the *Bug Mission Museum* (India, South America).

SURROUNDINGS. – **Altenburg** (3 km SW) on a conical hill (alt. 387 m), with a fine view of Bamberg. – *Schloss Pommersfelden (Weissenstein, 20 km SW), a sumptuous Baroque palace by J. Dientzenhofer (1711–18), with a famous staircase hall and a picture gallery.

Bavarian Alps

Land: Bavaria.
(i) **Fremdenverkehrsverband München-Oberbayern**, Sonnenstr. 10, D-8000 München 2; tel. (0 89) 59 73 47.

The ****Bavarian Alps, with their Alpine foreland, extend south from Munich to the Austrian frontier and from Lake Constance in the W to the neighbourhood of Salzburg in the E. They are part of the Northern Calcareous Alps, behind which, after a zone of slate with rounded landscape forms, the higher Central Alps tower up.**

The mountains reach a height of almost 3000 m in the *Zugspitze;* the main valleys lie between 700 and 1000 m. The foreland consists of a high plateau with numerous lakes, sloping down to the N from some 700 m at the foot of the mountains to some 500 m and slashed by valleys ranging in depth from 50 to 200 m.

The Calcareous Alps are relatively young mountains, having been formed by Tertiary folding roughly 70 million years ago. The deeply indented valleys which separate the mountain masses from one another were carved out by Ice Age glaciers, which also patterned the hilly Alpine foreland with their moraines and deposits of rock debris. The numerous lakes were formed when the ice melted.

The Alps afford endless scope for excursions of all kinds. The Alpine Forelands – which takes in the *Ammergau Alps*, the hills of the attractive *Isarwinkel* between Bad Tölz and Walchensee and the beautiful *Tegernsee Hills* and *Schliersee Hills* – offer magnificent forest walks, easy climbs and rewarding views of the plain and the mountains. On a larger scale are the *Allgäu Alps*, where the retreat of the forests has revealed more clearly the

The Geroldsee (Wagenbrüchsee), with the Karwendel Mountains in the background

variety of form of the mountains, and the limestone masses of the *Berchtesgaden Alps* (National Park), whose plateaux (Untersberg and Steinernes Meer) are a paradise for the hill walker. The most impressive mountain scenery is to be found in the *Wettersteingebirge*, with Germany's highest peak, the Zugspitze (2963 m), and in the wild and rugged *Karwendelgebirge*.

Kleiner Arbersee

ALPINE FAUNA. – The characteristic Alpine animal is the agile *chamois*, with backward-turned horns and a black dorsal stripe on a coat which is reddish brown in summer and dark brown or black in winter. It lives mainly in the upper forest zone, but in summer is found also among the rocks. – The *marmot* has an ash-grey back, turning greyish brown in the middle. When danger threatens it utters shrill alarm calls and disappears into its burrow, in which it also hibernates. – The *blue hare*, which has a greyish-brown to grey summer coat and a white winter coat, lives at altitudes of over 1300 m. Its presence is revealed by its tracks, which are in the shape of a hand. – The *Alpine vole*, with a white tail and a light brownish-grey back, is a good jumper, climber and swimmer, and is almost always found in the neighbourhood of Alpine rhododendrons. – The *golden eagle*, with a wing-span of 2 m and normally a hovering flight, is rare; it nests on high rock ledges. Still rarer is the *griffon vulture*, with a white head, light brown body and black tail. – The yellow-billed *Alpine chough* is found on rocky summits and Alpine meadows. – The *ptarmigan*, with white wings in summer and a completely white plumage in winter, lives gregariously on Alpine meadows above 2000 m. It can be recognised by its low whirring flight.

ALPINE FLORA. – The following are the principal Alpine plants, now protected in view of the danger of extinction to which they are exposed: aconite, anemone, aquilegia, auricula, daffodil, daphne, edelweiss, feather-grass, some ferns (including hart's tongue), yellow foxglove, gentian, globe-flower, hellebore, hepatica, iris, martagon lily, orchis (all species), Alpine pansy, pasque-flower, primrose, Alpine rhododendron, saxifrage, silver thistle, yew. It should be noted that in nature reserves no flowers may be picked, even if they are not normally protected species.

Bavarian Forest

Land: Bavaria.

ⓘ Fremdenverkehrsverband Ostbayern,
Landshuter Str. 13,
D-8400 Regensburg;
tel. (09 41) 5 71 86.

The *Bavarian Forest is the name given to the great forested upland area in E Bavaria; in the S it is bounded by the Danube (from Regensburg to Passau). In the NE it merges into the Bohemian Forest (Czechoslovakia and Austria) and is continued on the other side of the

Furth Depression by the Upper Palatinate Forest. Here, too, the disappearance of forest is causing great problems.

Near the Danube is the *Vorderer Wald*, a rolling upland region at altitudes of up to some 1100 m, in which only the highest parts and the steeper slopes are still wooded. Behind this is the *Hinterer Wald*, the main part of the range, reaching its highest point in the *Arber* (1457 m), near Bayerisch Eisenstein. Other major peaks are *Osser* (1293 m), near Lam; *Rachel* (1452 m) and *Lusen* (1371 m) near Grafenau, in the BAVARIAN FOREST NATIONAL PARK (120 sq. km); and *Dreisessel* (1378 m), in the SE of the range. – Between the Vorderer and Hinterer Wald is the *Pfahl*, a quartz dike between 50 and 100 m wide which has been weathered out of the granite and gneiss and can be followed for a distance of 140 km.

The particular beauty of these hills lies in their natural woodland, described by the 19th c. novelist Adalbert Stifter, which in certain nature reserves (on the Arber, Falkenstein, Dreisessel, etc.) preserves the appearance of primeval forest (beeches, pines, spruces). Below the Arber and Rachel lie solitary mountain lakes formed by Ice Age glaciers.

The people live mainly from timber-felling and woodworking; there is also a considerable glass industry. The tourist trade also contributes to the economy of the area (over a million visitors annually), for the Bavarian Forest is an attractive holiday region and good value for the tourist.

Bayreuth

Land: Bavaria. – Vehicle registration: BT.
Altitude: 342 m. – Population: 70,000.
Post code: D-8580. – Dialling code: 09 21.
ⓘ **Fremdenverkehrsverein,** Luitpoldplatz 9;
tel. 2 20 11.

HOTELS. – *Bayerischer Hof,* Bahnhofstr. 14, 96 b.,
SB, sauna, solarium; *Königshof,* Bahnhofstr. 23, 74 b.,
sauna, solarium; *Goldener Anker,* Opernstr. 6, 42 b.;
Am Hofgarten (no rest.), Lisztstr. 6, 30 b.; *Goldener
Hirsch,* Bahnhofstr. 13, 70 b.; *Kolpinghaus,* Kolping-
str. 5, 52 b.; *Weihenstephan,* Bahnhofstr. 5, 38 b. – IN
SURROUNDING AREA: *Schlosshotel Thiergarten,* 6 km
SE in Bayreuth Thiergarten, 20 b., garden terrace;
Waldhotel Stein, 8 km E in Bayreuth Seulbitz, 86 b.,
SB, SP, sauna. – YOUTH HOSTEL: Universitätsstr. 28.

RESTAURANTS. – *Eule,* Kirchgasse 8; *Wolffenzacher,*
Badstr. 1; *Postei,* Friedrichstr. 15.

CAFÉS. – *Dippold,* Maximilianstr. 69; *Operncafé,*
Opernstr. 16; *Jean Paul Café,* Friedrichstr. 10.

EVENTS. – *Franconian Festival* (June); **Richard
Wagner Festival** (July–Aug.).

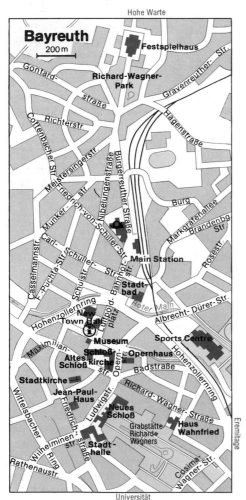

Bayreuth lies in the wide valley of the
Roter Main between the Fichtelgebirge and the "Franconian Switzerland". Its Baroque buildings and
Rococo palaces recall its former
status as residence of a Margrave. It
now has a university, founded in
1975. It is world-famed as a festival
city committed to the operas of
Wagner.

HISTORY. – From 1604 to 1768 Bayreuth was the
residence of the Margrave of Brandenburg-Kulmbach,
and until 1791 of the Margrave of Ansbach. It enjoyed a
great flowering of architecture under Margrave
Frederick (1753–63) and his wife Wilhelmine,
Frederick the Great's favourite sister. In 1874 Wagner
and his wife Cosima settled in Haus Wahnfried. The
Wagner Festival House was built in 1872–76.

SIGHTS: – A short distance SE of the
STERNPLATZ, the hub of the town's life,
stands the *Margravial Opera House,* built
1745–48, with a magnificent *Baroque
interior (Franconian Festival). Nearby in
Münzgasse is the Iwalewa Haus (contemporary art from the third world). – In
Maximilianstrasse is the **Altes Schloss**
(17th c.: destroyed by fire in 1945 but since
rebuilt). In the former *palace church*
(1753–54; R.C.) is the tomb of Margrave
Frederick and his wife Wilhelmine. – To
the SW is the 15th c. *Town Parish Church*
(Evang.), with the burial vault of the
Margraves. – At Friedrichstrasse 5 is the
house in which the Romantic writer *Jean
Paul* (Jean Paul Friedrich Richter,
1763–1825) lived and died. In Ludwigstrasse is the **Neues Schloss,** built
1753–59, with the fine residential apartments of the margraves, several museums
(including the State Picture Gallery, the
Municipal Museum with a collection of
pottery and the "Klingendes Museum")
and the *Wagner Memorial Rooms.* Behind
the palace is the *Hofgarten* (Museum of
Freemasonry; zoo).

At Richard-Wagner-Strasse 48 is
Wagner's **Haus Wahnfried,** built 1873,
now a museum. Behind the house is the
tomb of Wagner and his wife Cosima
(daughter of Franz Liszt). At the corner of
Wahnfriedstrasse and Lisztstrasse is the
house in which *Franz Liszt* (1811–86)
died.

On rising ground N of the town (1 km from
the station) is the **Richard Wagner
Festival House** (1800 seats), built

Berchtesgaden, with the Watzmann

1872–76, home of the Wagner Festival held almost every year in July and August.

SURROUNDINGS. –*Eremitage (5 km E), with the *Altes Schloss* (1715–18) and *Neues Schloss* (1749–53), a beautiful park and fountains.

Berchtesgadener Land

Land: Bavaria.
ⓘ **Fremdenverkehrsverband München–Oberbayern,**
Sonnenstr. 10, D-8000 München 2;
tel. (0 89) 59 73 47.

The *Berchtesgadener Land, once held directly from the Emperor by the Augustinian canons of Berchtesgaden, lies in the SE corner of Bavaria, driving a wedge into Austrian territory. It is enclosed by high Alpine peaks with precipitous rock faces.

The king of these mountains is the *Watzmann* (2713 m), whose east face, a challenge to climbers, drops steeply down to the idyllic *Königssee.* The area round the lake, extending to the Austrian frontier, forms the **Berchtesgaden Alpine National Park.**

On the shores of the lake is the picturesque little pilgrimage church of *St. Bartholomä,* a popular excursion by motorboat from the village of *Königssee,* where

there is a fast bobsleigh run which attracts many enthusiasts. There is a cableway up to the 1874 m high *Jenner.* From **Berchtesgaden,** once centre of the ecclesiastical territory, with the house of the Augustinian canons, and now a very popular holiday resort (weapon museum, open by prior arrangement), a daringly engineered mountain road climbs up by way of the *Obersalzberg* (no private cars beyond this point: mail bus) to the 1885 m high *Kehlstein,* which affords magnificent views. From Obersalzberg visitors can also reach the 9·5 km long *Rossfeld-Ringstrasse,* a beautiful scenic circuit which is used for mountain car races. An unusual experience is offered by a visit to the Berchtesgaden *salt-mine,* on an underground railway which runs for 600 m through the workings. – At the entrance to the Berchtesgadener Land is **Bad Reichenhall** (See p. 219), where 48 brine springs gush out of the ground, including one of the strongest in Europe, with a salt content of 24%.

Bergisches Land

Land: North Rhineland-Westphalia.
ⓘ **Landesverkehrsverband Rheinland,**
Rheinallee 69, D-5300 Bonn 2 (Bad Godesberg);
tel. (02 28) 36 29 21/22.

The Bergisches Land, once the county of Berg, lies between the Ruhr and the Sieg, the Rhine and the

The Aggertal reservoir

Sauerland region, with a landscape patterned by hills, forests, meadows and rivers. In earlier times water power provided the motive force for ironworks and mills, leading to the development of a local small-scale ironworking industry. Many rivers have now been harnessed by the building of dams, which have created a whole series of artifical lakes – among them the Bever, the Neye, the Sengbach and the Wupper Reservoir.

The chief town of the Rhineland-Berg district is *Bergisch Gladbach*, which is noted for its paper-making industry. *Solingen* has long been world-famous for its cutlery. In the vicinity is Schloss Burg with the Bergisch Museum. *Remscheid* is the centre of the tool-making industry, *Wuppertal* of artificial silk manufacture. In the district of Lennep in Remscheid Wilhelm Konrad Röntgen, the discoverer of X-rays, was born in 1845. The town has preserved many handsome slate-roofed houses. The typical local house has black and white half-timbering with green shutters and a slated roof; often the side walls are also clad with slates.

In *Bensberg* is a magnificent palace built by Elector Johann Wilhelm of the Palatinate in 1705–16. Amid the woods and meadows of the Dhünn valley nestles the former Cistercian abbey of *Altenberg*, founded by Adolf von Berg in 1133, with the "Bergischer Dom" (13th–14th c.), a master work of High Gothic which has become the emblem of the Bergisches Land.

Bergstrasse

Länder: Baden-Württemberg and Hesse.
(i) **Landesfremdenverkehrsverband Baden-Württemberg,**
Bussenstr. 23, D-7000 Stuttgart 1;
tel. (07 11) 48 10 45.
Hessischer Fremdenverkehrsverband,
Abraham-Lincoln-Str. 38–42,
D-6200 Wiesbaden;
tel. (0 61 21) 7 37 25.

The Bergstrasse, the Roman "strata montana", runs alongside the rift valley of the Upper Rhine on the western slopes of the Odenwald from Darmstadt to Heidelberg. The region is noted for its mild climate, and in spring – which comes here earlier than in the rest of Germany – it is a sea of blossom. In late March and early April the influx of visitors reaches its peak. In addition to fruit, wine and vegetables the region also produces figs and almonds, and exotic trees grow in the parks.

From the hilltops, crowned by old castles, there are magnificent views. The finest of

Spring blossom on the Bergstrasse (ruins of Windeck Castle)

the hills is *Melibokus* (315 m), near Zwingenberg. In the picturesque little town of *Bensheim* the Bergstrasse cuts across the Nibelungenstrasse. Not far away is *Lorsch* with its Carolingian gatehouse, one of Germany's oldest buildings. The town of *Heppenheim*, dominated by the ruined Starkenburg (11th c.: observatory), has a charming market-place surrounded by half-timbered buildings. The ruins of *Windeck* (12th/13th c.) overlook the old town of *Weinheim*. In the park of Berckheim Castle are rare plants and old cedars. Above the little wine-producing town of *Schriesheim* stands the ruined Strahlen-burg, the name of which recalls the Ritter von Strahl in Kleist's play "Käthchen von Heilbronn".

Gedächtniskirche, Kurfürstendamm

Berlin (West)

Vehicle registration: B (West Berlin). – Access: see p. 268.
Altitude: 35–50 m. – Population: *c.* 2,000,000.
Post code: D-1000. – Dialling code: 0 30.
(i) **Verkehrsamt**, Europa-Center, Berlin 30; tel. 2 12 34 (until mid 1984, then: 2 62 60 31) and 7 82 30 31.

HOTELS. – NEAR THE KURFÜRSTENDAMM AND THE ZOOLOGICAL GARDENS STATION: *Bristol Hotel Kempinski*, Kurfürstendamm 27, Berlin 15, 646 b., SB, sauna, solarium; *Steigenberger*, Berlin, Los Angeles Platz 1, B. 30, 220 b., SB, sauna, Park Restaurant; *Inter-Continental*, Budapester Str. 2, B. 30, 1150 b., SB, sauna, solarium, restaurant "Zum Hugenotten"; *Penta*, Nurnberger Str. 65, B. 30, 850 b., SB, sauna, solarium; *Palace*, in Europa Center, Budapester Str., B. 30, 250 b.; *Ambassador*, Bayreuther Str. 42, B. 30, 198 b., SB, sauna, solarium, Conti Fischstuben; *Schweizerhof*, Budapester Str. 21, B. 30, 876 b., SB, sauna, solarium; *Excelsior*, Hardenbergstr. 14, B. 12, 603 b.; *Berlin*, Kurfurstenstr. 62, B. 30, 426 b., restaurant "Berlin Grill"; *Hamburg*, Landgrafenstr. 4, B. 30, 330 b.; *Alsterhof*, Augsburger Str. 5, B. 30, 250 b., SB, sauna, solarium, restaurant "Alsterstube"; *Sylter Hof*, Kurfurstenstr. 116, B. 30, 220 b.; *Am Zoo*, Kurfurstendamm 25, B. 15, 200 b.; *Savoy*, Fasanenstr. 9, B. 12, 200 b.; *Arosa*, Lietzenburger Str. 79, 175 b., specialty restaurant "Walliser Stuben"; *Savigny* (no rest.), Brandenburgische Str. 21, B. 31, 100 b. – Hotel ship *Spree Berlin*, Hansabrucke, B. 30, 262 b.

IN CHARLOTTENBURG: *Seehof*, Lietzensee Ufer 11, B. 19, 120 b., SB, sauna, solarium, terrace on lake; *Ibis*, Messedamm 10, B. 19, 250 b.; *Am Studio* (no rest.), Kaiserdamm 80, B. 19, 93 b.; *Apartment Hotel Heerstrasse*, Heerstr. 80, B. 19, 70 b., SB, sauna, solarium. – IN DAHLEM: *Apartment Hotel*, Clayallee 150, B. 33, 30 b. – IN GRUNEWALD: *Schlosshotel Gerhus*, Brahmsstr. 4, B. 33, 50 b.; *Belvedere*, Seebergsteig 4, B. 33, 31 b., sauna, solarium. – IN KREUZBERG: *Hervis International* (no rest.), Stresemannstr. 97, B. 61, 118 b.

YOUTH HOSTELS. – *Ernst Reuter*, Hermsdorfer Damm 48, B. 28 (Hermsdorf), 136 b.; *Bayernallee*, Bayernallee, B. 19 (Charlottenburg), 104 b.; *Jugendgästehaus Berlin*, Kluckstr. 3, B. 30 (Tiergarten), 420 b.; *Jugendgästehaus Wannsee*, Kronprinzessinnenweg 27, B. 39 (Wannsee), 264 b. – CAMPING SITES: German Camping Club: *Wannsee*, Neue Kreisstr.; *Kladow*, Krampnitzer Weg 111; *Dreilinden*, near the Control Point Dreilinden; *Haselhorst*, opposite the Havel Island "Eiswerder".

RESTAURANTS. – *Ritz*, Rankestr. 26, B. 30 (dishes from all over the world); *Mampes Gute Stube*, Kurfürstendamm 14, B. 15 (traditional Berlin atmosphere); *Alexander*, Kurfürstendamm 46, B. 15 (international cuisine); *Heinz Holl*, Damaschkestr. 26, B. 31 (frequented by artists); *Hardtke*, Meinekestr. 26, B. 15 (Berlin specialties); *Funkturm-Restaurant*, at height of 55 m, B. 19 (view); *Alt Berliner Schneckenhaus*, Kurfürstendamm 37, B. 15 (traditional Berlin atmosphere); *Puvogels Medaillon*, Pestalozzistr. 8, B. 12; *Alter Krug Dahlem*, Königin-Luise-Str. 52, B. 33 (one of Berlin's oldest village inns); *Wannsee-Terrassen*, Wahnseebadweg, B. 38.

FOREIGN CUISINE: *Tessiner Stuben*, Bleibtreustr. 33, B. 33 (Swiss); *Bacco*, Marburger Str. 5, B. 30 (Italian); *Alt Luxemburg*, Pestalozzistr. 70, B. 12 (French); *Kopenhagen*, Kurfürstendamm 203, B. 15 (Danish); *Zlata Praha*, Meinekestr. 4, B. 15 (Czech).

WINE-BARS. – *Hardy an der Oper*, Zauritzweg 9, B. 12; *Kurpfalz*, Wilmersdorfer Str. 93, B. 12; *Weinkrüger*, Kurfürstendamm 25, B. 15. – BEER-HOUSE: *Schultheiss Bräuhaus*, Kurfürstendamm 220, B. 15.

CAFÉS. – *Kranzler*, Kurfürstendamm 18, B. 15 (long-established reputation); *Café des Westens*, Kurfüstendamm 227, B. 15; *Möhring*, Kurfürstendamm 213, B. 15; *Huthmacher*, Hardenbergstr. 292, B. 12 (concerts); *i-Punkt*, Europa-Center (20th floor: view).

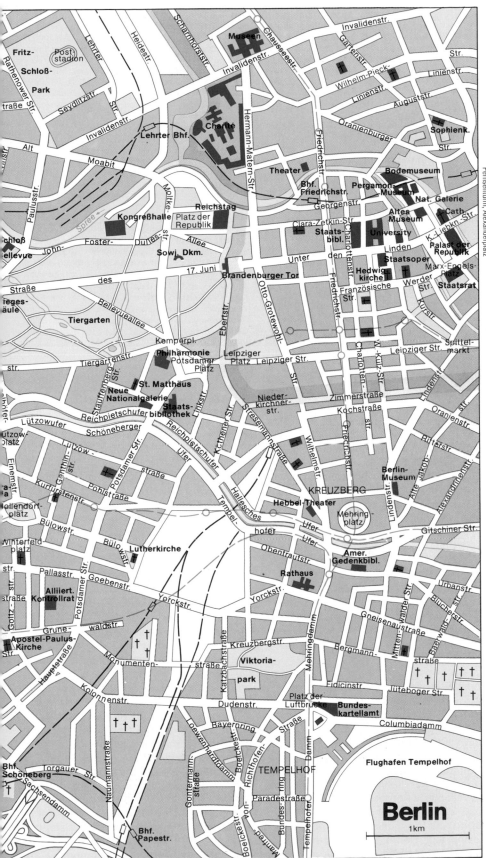

Berlin

1km

EVENTS. – *International Green Week (Jan.); *International Film Festival* (Feb./Mar.); *International Tourism Exchange* (March); *International Radio Exhibition* (alternate years Aug./Sept.); *Berlin Festival Weeks* (Sept.); *German Riding Championships* (Sept., alternate years); *Six Day Race* (Oct.); *Berlin Jazz Days* (Nov.); *Christmas Market* at the Radio Tower (Dec.); *Sporting Press Festival* (Dec.); Federal Horticultural Exhibition in 1985.

Berlin Casino (roulette, baccarat, blackjack, daily 3 p.m.–3 a.m.) in the Europa Center.

CITY TOURS of West and East Berlin.

Berlin, situated on the navigable River Spree, which flows into the Havel at Spandau, is still, in spite of its division, the largest German city, a focal point of political and cultural life and Germany's principal industrial city. Of its total population of 3·3 million, 2·2 million live in West Berlin and 1·1 million in East Berlin. Of its total area of 883 sq. km, 481 sq. km are in West Berlin and 402 sq. km in East Berlin.

West Berlin has all the flair of an international city, pulsating with life. The Berlin Opera and Berlin Philharmonic Orchestra are world-famed. The museums in Dahlem, Charlottenburg and the Tiergarten are of international standing. The Film Festival and Radio Exhibition, the "Green Week" in the Messehallen and the sporting events in the Olympic Stadium bear witness to the vigour and energy of this "island city".

West Berlin has two universities (the Free University and the Technical University) and numerous other higher educational establishments and research institutes (including the Hahn-Meitner Institute of Nuclear Research and five institutes run by the Max Planck Society). It is the seat of both a Protestant (Evangelical) and a Roman Catholic bishop.

The city's economy is still based on its traditional industries – electrical (including Siemens, AEG and IBM), clothing and engineering (including Borsig). Other major industries are chemicals, foodstuffs and printing and publishing. Berlin's traditional role as the scene of important trade fairs has been re-established with the reconstruction of the exhibition halls (63,000 sq. km of roofed accommodation) at the Funkturm. As a fashion centre, too, Berlin has an international reputation for quality and chic.

HISTORY. – Berlin grew out of the two fishing villages of Kölln and Berlin, which amalgamated in 1307. In 1443 Count Frederick II of Hohenzollern began building a permanent castle, and the town became the ruler's residence. After the Thirty Years War it had no more than 5000 inhabitants, but under the purposeful rule of the Great Elector (1610–88) the town and Mark Brandenburg prospered again. Berlin became a well-defended stronghold and was enlarged by the incorporation of the towns of Friedrichswerder and Dorotheenstadt to the W. Under the Great Elector's son Frederick I, first king of Prussia, it received a further accretion in the form of Friedrichstadt. In 1709 all five towns were united to form the capital city and royal residence of Berlin. Under Frederick the Great Berlin became a manufacturing town and Prussia's leading industrial city, and was now embellished with numerous handsome buildings like the Forum Fridericianum. The university founded by Wilhelm von Humboldt in 1810 made the Prussian capital a centre of intellectual life. At the same time the town developed into a major industrial city, and in the second half of the 19th c. it became a focal point of the European railway system and the commercial capital of Germany. In 1871 it became capital of the newly established German Empire. After the First World War a new municipal entity, Greater Berlin (Gross-Berlin), was created by the amalgamation of Berlin with seven adjoining independent towns, 59 rural communes and 27 Gutsbezirke (demesnes not included within communes). Before the outbreak of the Second World War, which cost the city heavy loss of life and enormous destruction of property, Greater Berlin had a population of 4·3 million. In 1945, at the Yalta conference, Berlin was put under four-power administration. Differences of view between the occupation powers led in 1948 (Soviet blockade) to a division of the city, which was aggravated by the construction of the Berlin Wall on 13 August 1961.

SIGHTS. – In the E of the district of CHARLOTTENBURG, in the busy BREITSCHEIDPLATZ, stands the emblem of West Berlin, the ruined tower of the neo-Romanesque *Kaiser-Wilhelm-Gedächtniskirche (Emperor William Memorial Church), built 1891–95. Adjoining it is the new church (1959–61), a flat-roofed octagonal structure designed by Professor Eiermann. To the E is the Europa-Center (1963–65), a shopping and business complex with a 22-storey tower block (86 m: streets of shops, restaurants, planetarium, water-clock, ice-rink, roof swimming pool, casino, etc.). – From this point two of the city's major arteries take off: TAUENTZIENSTRASSE, lined with shops, runs SE to WITTENBERGPLATZ, with the large *Ka-De-We* department store ("Kaufhaus des Westens", the "shopping centre of the West"); to the E, at Kleiststrasse 13, is the Urania building, with the *Transport Museum* and the *Postal Museum*; in NOLLENDORFPLATZ is the Metropol "super-disco". The *Kurfürstendamm, running W for a distance of 3½ km, is a magnet for visitors to Berlin, with its elegant shops, its restaurants and

cafés and its many cinemas and theatres. –
To the N of Breitscheidplatz are the new
Kunsthalle and, in BUDAPESTER STRASSE,
the well-stocked *Zoological Garden*,
with some 10,900 animals (over 1500
species: its lion enclosure, in which the
animals live in conditions of semi-
freedom, is the largest of its kind in the
world) and a famous *Aquarium*.
In the adjoining TIERGARTEN district, to
the N, is the beautiful park of that name. It
is traversed from W to E by the STRASSE
DES 17. JUNI, with the GROSSER STERN, a
roundabout in the middle of which stands
the 67 m high **Victory Column** (Sie-
gessaule), commemorating the campaigns of 1864, 1866 and 1870 (wide
panoramic views from the platform). In
the northern part of the park is the
Bellevue Park, laid out in the English style,
with *Schloss Bellevue* (rebuilt 1959), the
Berlin residence of the President of the
Federal Republic. W of Bellevue Park
extends the **Hansaviertel**, laid out as a
model residential district (1955–57) by
leading international architects (Aalto,
Düttmann, Eiermann, Gropius, Niemeyer),
with interesting examples of modern
church architecture (e.g. the *Kaiser-
Friedrich-Gedächtniskirche* and *St.-
Ansgar-Kirche*). S of Tiergartenstrasse, on
the Herkulesufer, stands the *Bauhaus
Archiv*, built according to plans of Walter
Gropius and opened in 1979. – At the SE
corner of the Tiergarten, off KEMPERPLATZ,
is the **Philharmonie** (by H. Scharoun,
1960–63: photograph, p. 51). A little way

S, at Potsdamer Strasse 50, is the *New
National Gallery* (by Mies van der Rohe,
1965–68: 19th and 20th c. pictures and
sculpture). Opposite it are the new **State
Library** (1978: 3 million volumes) and
the *Ibero-American Institute* (1976). – At
the E end of the Strasse des 17. Juni, on
the left, is the *Soviet Memorial* (1945).
The ***Brandenburg Gate** (1788–91;
new quadriga on top, 1958), inaccessible
since 1961, stands on the boundary
between West and East Berlin. – In the
PLATZ DER REPUBLIK is the former
Reichstag building, built by Paul
Wallot 1884–94 in Italian Renaissance
style (rebuilding completed 1969). To
the W of the Platz der Republik is the
architecturally interesting ***Kongresshalle** (1957). Since the collapse of the
roof in 1981 the building has been
temporarily out of commission.

HARDENBERGSTRASSE runs NW from the
Gedächtniskirche past the **Zoo Station**
to the UNIVERSITY QUARTER, with the
Technical University and the *College of
Art*. At the NE end of Hardenbergstrasse is
the attractively laid out **Ernst-Reuter-
Platz** (fountains), surrounded by high-
rise office blocks. Nearby, at the end of
Bismarckallee, is the *Schiller Theatre*
(1950–51), and to the W of this is the
*Deutsche Oper Berlin (Berlin Opera
House), opened in 1961.

In the heart of the old town of Charlottenburg lies ***Schloss Charlottenburg**,

Schloss Charlottenburg

a long range of 17th and 18th c. buildings dominated by a tall dome (restored). In the grand courtyard is an **equestrian statue of the Great Elector* (Schlüter and Jacobi, 1697–1700). The *historical apartments* are in the central range of buildings (the Nehringbau and Eosander-bau); in the E wing (Knobelsdorff wing) are further historical apartments and the *Museum of Applied Art* (*Guelf Treasure) on the ground floor, and the rooms occupied by Frederick the Great (pictures) and the "Golden Gallery" on the upper floor; in the Langhausbau is the *Museum of Prehistory and Early History.* In the *Schlosspark* is the simple *Mausoleum* of Queen Luise (d. 1810) and her husband King Frederick William III (d. 1840), which also contains the remains of Emperor William I (d. 1888) and his wife the Empress Augusta (d. 1890). The noble marble sculpture is by C. Rauch and E. Encke. In the *Belvedere* in the park is a collection of "Berlin Porcelain" (Royal Porcelain Factory, KPM). – Opposite the palace is the building known as the Stülerbau (1850). In the W part of this is the *West Berlin Collection of Antiquities,* and adjoining this the *Bauhaus Archives.* In the E section, on the other side of Schloss-strasse, is the *Egyptian Department* of the State Museums, with the world-famous painted limestone **bust of Queen Nefertiti (*c.* 1360 B.C.).

In the WESTEND district, which forms part of Charlottenburg, are the **Trade Fair and Exhibition Grounds**, with a range of exhibition halls and pavilions which house all the great Berlin exhibitions and a massive *Congress Centre. Here too is one of Berlin's landmarks, the 138 m high (150 m including the aerial) **Funkturm** (Radio Tower), erected 1924–26 for the Radio Exhibition (restaurant at 55 m, viewing platform at 125 m: lift). At the foot of the tower is the *German Radio Museum.* On the Messedamm is the *International Congress Centre (*ICC*, seating for 20,000). – A short distance away to the SE are the N end of the **Avus** practice driving track, constructed in 1921, and the **Deutschlandhalle**.

NW of Theodor-Heuss-Platz is the *Olympic Stadium, one of Europe's largest and finest sports installations, built in 1936 to the design of Werner March for the 11th Olympic Games. The oval stadium, 300 m long and 230 m across, can take 90,000 spectators. Immediately

NW is the popular **Waldbühne**, an open-air theatre with seating for 25,000. S of the Olympic Stadium, at the Heilsberger Dreieck, is the 17-storey *Corbusierhaus* (1957), a gigantic block of flats which houses a population of 1400.

E of Charlottenburg are the districts of SCHÖNEBERG and STEGLITZ, with busy shopping streets like Schloss-strasse. **Schöneberg Town Hall**, in J.-F.-Kennedy-Platz, is the headquarters of the Mayor of Berlin; in its tower is the *Freedom Bell,* presented by the United States in 1950. – In Steglitz are two striking modern buildings, the *Steglitzer Turm* (with restaurant) in the northern part of Schloss-strasse and the controversial *Steglitzer Kreisel* in the southern part of that street. On Munsterdamm is the Wilhelm Foerster Observatory (Planetarium). A short distance away to the SW is the *Botanic Garden** (42 hectares: Victoria Regia house, tropical houses, mountain flora, botanical museum).

The district of ZEHLENDORF includes DAHLEM, with the Great Hall of the **Free University of Berlin**, various institutes run by the Max Planck Society and the **Dahlem Museum*: picture gallery (world-famous masterpieces, including 26 Rembrandts), sculpture collection, collection of engravings, Museum of Ethnography (rich collection of material from all over the world), Museum of Indian Art, Museum of East Asian Art.

Zehlendorf, with attractive rural housing developments, extends along the shores of the Schlachtensee and Nikolassee to the Havel, which here swells out to form the **Wannsee**, a favourite resort of the people of Berlin. One of the most delightful spots in the Havel region is the 1500 m long *Pfaueninsel, with a castle built in 1794 to resemble a ruin and a beautiful English-style park. – SE of the Wannsee lies the museum village of *Düppel,* a reconstruction of a medieval settlement.

West Berlin's lung is the extensive (3149 hectares) forest area of **Grunewald**, with the *Grunewaldsee, Krummer Lanke, Schlachtensee, Hundekehlensee* and *Teufelssee,* and the *Teufelsberg,* the highest point in West Berlin (115 m), built up after the war from rubble from demolished buildings. Here too is **Jagd-schloss Grunewald**, a hunting lodge which was originally built in Renaissance style in 1542 and received its present form in the 18th c. (hunting museum and collection of pictures).

The most northerly of the Havel lakes is the **Tegeler See** (408 hectares). The neo-classical **Schloss Tegel** was built by Schinkel (1821–23) for Wilhelm von Humboldt; it involved the reconstruction of an earlier hunting lodge (mementoes of the scholar and statesman; Humboldt family tomb in the park).* **Tegel Airport**, with its hexagonal terminal building, replaced the older *Tempelhof* as a civil airport in 1976. In front of Tempelhof airport stands the **Air-Lift Memorial**, commemorating the solidarity of the Western world with Berlin at the time of the Soviet blockade in 1948–49. N of the airport is the Volkspark (People's Park) of **Hasenheide**, with a hill of rubble 69·5 m high.

Bielefeld

Land: North Rhineland-Westphalia. – Vehicle registration: BI.
Altitude: 115 m. – Population: 313,000.
Post code: D-4800. – Dialling code: 05 21.

(i) **Tourist Information,**
Verkehrsverein Bielefeld e. V.,
Am Bahnhof 6;
tel. 17 88 99.

HOTELS. – *Novotel*, Am Johannesberg 5, 238 b., SB; *Brenner Hotel Dieckmann*, O. Brenner Str. 133, 100 b.; *Conta Hotel*, Schelpsheide 19, 90 b., sauna; *Bielefelder Hof*, Am Bahnhof 3, 71 b.; *Waldhotel Brands Busch*, Furtwänglerstr. 52, 70 b.; *Altstadt Hotel*, Ritterstr. 15, 33 b.; *Stadt Bremen* (no rest.), Bahnhofstr. 32, 69 b. – IN GADDERBAUM: *Emmermann's Hotel*, Bodelschwinghstr. 79, 16 b., sauna. – IN DORNBERG: *Hoberger Landhaus*, Schäferdreesch 18, 50 b., SB, sauna, solarium; *Waldhotel Peter auf'm Berge*, Bergstr. 45, 16 b. – IN SENNESTADT: *Miedermeyer*, Paderborner Str. 290, 77 b. – YOUTH HOSTEL: Bielefeld-Sieker, Oetzer Weg 25, 168 b. – CAMPING SITES: Bielefeld-Quelle, Vogelweide 9; Bielefeld-Schröttinghausen, Beckendorfstr./Campingstrasse.

RESTAURANTS. – *Ratskeller*, Niederwall 25; *Löwenhof-Rauchfang*, Niederwall 43; *Haus des Handwerks*, Papenmrkt 11; *China*, Herforder Str. 29 (Chinese specialities). – IN HILLEGOSSEN: *Beograd*, Hillegosser Str. 349 (Yugoslav specialities).

EVENTS. – *British Music Parade* (beginning May: 1985, 1987, etc.); *Linen Weavers' Market* (end May); *Sparrenburg Festival* (end summer holidays); *Bielefeld Wine Market* (beginning Sept.).

Bielefeld, situated where an old trade route passed through the Teutoburg Forest, is the economic and – with its university – also the cultural centre of Eastern Westphalia and Lippe. While half-timbered buildings characterise the centre of the town, the district of Sennestadt to the S, was built as a result of recent planning. For centuries the production and processing of linen was predominant, but today engineering is the principal economic factor. Electronics, vehicle manufacture and food and clothing are of importance. The charitable homes in Bethel, in the building of which Pastor Freidrich von Bodelschwingh played a considerable part, are well known.

HISTORY. – First recorded in 1015, Bielefeld was given its town charter by Count Hermann von Ravensberg in 1214. At the end of the 14th c. it became a member of the Hanse. In 1647 the Ravensberg lands passed to Prussia. Thereafter the Great Elector strengthened the old castle of the Counts of Ravensberg and in 1678 erected a model linen factory. His fostering of the linen trade laid the foundations of the town's later industrial development.

SIGHTS. – The centre of the old town is the ALTE MARKT. On the S side of the square is the *Batig-Haus* (1680), with a beautiful Renaissance gable. Opposite it is the *Theater am alten Markt*. To the W, at the end of Obernstrasse, one of the principal business and shopping streets, is the **Crüwell-Haus** (*c.* 1530), with a magnificent late Gothic stepped gable. N of the Markt is **St Nicholas's Church** or Altstädter Kirche (destroyed in the Second World War but rebuilt). E of the church is the *Linen Weavers' Fountain* (1909).

In Obernstrasse, half concealed, is the late Gothic **Church of St Jodokus** (consecrated 1511: "Black Madonna" of 1220); to the S of the church, at Welle 61, is the *Historical Museum*. In Artur-Ladebeck-Strasse is the **Kunsthalle** (1966–68), with important collections of 20th c. art; in front of it is Rodin's sculpture, "The Thinker".

In Kreuzstrasse are *Spiegels Hof*, a 16th c. nobleman's mansion (now a registry office), with a beautiful cloverleaf gable, and the 14th c. **St Mary's Church** or Neustädter Kirche (fine monuments). Farther S is the **Sparrenburg** (*c.* 1240), the old castle of the Ravensberg family (underground defensive works; 37 m high observation tower), with a castle guesthouse. During the Sparrenburg Festival musical plays on medieval and chivalrous themes are performed. SW of the Sparrenburg are the *Bethel Homes*, founded by Pastor Friedrich von Bodelschwingh (1831–1910).

Kurhaus and Burgberg, Badenweiler

In the NW of the town are the *Farmhouse Museum* (domestic furnishings and equipment, farming implements, costumes), the *Botanic Garden, Olderdissen Animal Park* (850 species), the *Rudolf Oetker Concert Hall* and the *University*.

Black Forest

Land: Baden-Württemberg.

(i) **Fremdenverkehrsverband Schwarzwald,** Bertoldstr. 45, D-7800 Freiburg/Brsg.; tel. (07 61) 3 13 17.

The ****Black Forest (Schwarzwald),** with its dark forest-covered hills perhaps the most visited upland region in Europe, lies in the SW corner of Germany, extending for some 160 km from Pforzheim in the N to Waldshut, on the Upper Rhine, in the S. At the northern end it is some 20 km wide, at the southern end 60 km. On the W side it descends to the fertile Upper Rhine plain in a steep scarp which is slashed by well-watered valleys; to the E it slopes more gently down to the upper Neckar and Danube valleys. The main ridge is broken up by numerous valleys, with the flat-topped sum-

mits, covered with hill pasturage, rising to only a moderate height above it. Deforestation continues.

The **Northern Black Forest** – the part lying N of the Kinzig valley, which cuts through the whole range from Freudenstadt to Offenburg – is made up of broad ridges of Bunter sandstone and reaches its highest point in the *Hornisgrinde* (1166 m), on whose slopes several romantic little lakes like the *Mummelsee* and *Wildsee* nestle in glacier-cut valleys. The main tourist attractions of this region are the *Schwarzwald-Hochstrasse* (Black Forest Ridgeway) which runs through it, affording magnificent views, the splendidly equipped spa of *Baden-Baden*, the valleys of the *Murg* with its interesting hydroelectric installations, the *Alb* with the spa of *Bad Herrenalb*, the *Enz* with its popular resort of *Wildbad* and the *Nagold* with the attractive *Bad Liebenzell* and the picturesque *Hirsau*, and the beautiful forests around *Freudenstadt*.

The **Central Black Forest**, between the Kinzig valley and the Höllental, consists mainly of granite and gneiss, and reaches its highest point in the 1241 m *Kandel*, between the beautiful Simonswald, Elz and Glotter valleys. The area most popular with tourists is the stretch along the Schwarzwaldbahn, centred on *Triberg* with its famous falls. To the E the Central Black Forest runs into the high plateau of the *Baar*, which in turn leads into the Swabian Jura.

The **Southern Schwarzwald**, scenically perhaps the most magnificent part, is dominated by the 1493 m high **Feldberg**, from which a ridge runs W to the beautifully shaped *Belchen* (1414 m) and *Blauen* (1165 m), the peak nearest to the Rhine plain. Among the most striking beauty spots in this region are the two

St. Blasien in the Southern Black Forest

large lakes carved out by glaciers on the slopes of the Feldberg, the *Titisee* and the *Schluchsee*, the valleys which radiate from the Feldberg (particularly the wild and romantic *Höllental*), and the *Wiese* and *Alb* valleys which run down to the Upper Rhine.

There are so many SPAS and HEALTH RESORTS in the Black Forest that only the most important can be mentioned here. In the Northern Black Forest, apart from the long-famed spa resorts of **Baden-Baden** and **Wildbad**, there are **Freudenstadt**, *Bad Herrenalb, Gernsbach, Schönmünzach, Bad Liebenzell, Hirsau, Bad Teinach,* the resorts in the *Rench valley;* in the Central Black Forest there are *Triberg* and the neighbouring resorts of *Schonach* and *Schönwald, Königsfeld, St. Märgen, Glottertal* and the highest brine spa in Europe, *Bad Dürrheim* (700–850 m); and in the Southern Black Forest the *Titisee, Hinterzarten,* the whole area round the *Feldberg, St. Blasien, Menzenschwand, Schönau* and the health resort of **Badenweiler** – all places with considerable attraction.

Popular WINTER SPORTS CENTRES in this oldest skiing area in Germany (the first "snowshoe club" having been founded at Todtnau in 1891) are the *Feldberg* (1493 m) and surrounding area, *Freudenstadt* (740 m), the *Kniebis* plateau (875–1054 m), the hotels on the *Schwarzwald-Hochstrasse* (754–1166 m), *Dobel* (691 m), *Baiersbronn* (584 m), *Triberg* and surrounding area (650–1000 m), *Furtwangen* (870 m), *Neustadt-Titisee* (805 m) and *Lenzkirch* (810 m).

The famous and very popular *Schwarzwald-Hochstrasse* (Black Forest Ridgeway: 654–1166 m) runs from *Baden-Baden* along the top of the ridge, with wide views, passing through magnificent fir forests along the *Hornisgrinde* to the *Kniebis* and on to *Freudenstadt.* There are many hotels along this road.

Bochum

Land: North Rhineland-Westphalia.
Vehicle registration: BO.
Altitude: 104 m. – Population: 425,000.
Post code: D-4630. – Dialling code: 02 34.
ⓘ **Verkehrsverein**, Hauptbahnhof; tel. 1 30 31.
Informationszentrum Ruhr-Bochum, Rathaus; tel. 6 21 39 75.

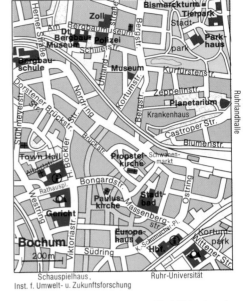

Schauspielhaus,   Ruhr-Universität
Inst. f. Umwelt- u. Zukunftsforschung

HOTELS. – *Novotel,* Stadionring 22, 120 b.; *Arcade,* Universitätsstr. 3, 168 b.; *Savoy* (no rest.), Huestr. 11, 78 b.; *Ostmeier,* Westring 35, 54 h.; *Plaza,* Hellweg 20, 40 b.; *Haus Oekey,* Auf dem Alten Kamp 10, 35 b. – IN GERTHE: *Borgmann,* Lothringer Str. 13, 35 b. – IN STIEPEL: *Wald und Golf Hotel Lottental,* Grimbergstr. 52, 152 b. – IN WATTENSCHEID: *Hotel Restaurant am Südpark,* Höntroper Str. 103, 25 b.

RESTAURANTS. – *Stammhaus Fiege,* Bongardstr. 23; *Stadtpark,* Bergstr. 68; *Bochumer Brauhaus,* Rathausplatz 5; *Mutter Wittig,* Bongardstr. 35; *Asia,* Brüderstr. 2 (Chinese); *Peking,* Viktoriastr. 51 (Chinese). – IN SUNDERN: *Haus Waldesruh,* Papenloh 8 (garden). – IN WATTENSCHEID: *Casa Blanca,* Jung-Stilling-Str. 61.

CAFÉ. – *Döhmann,* Grosse Beckstr. 2.

Bochum, in the heart of the Ruhr, between the rivers Emscher and Ruhr, offers a textbook example of the structural change which is taking place in the economy of this region. This town which owed its rise to coal and steel has no longer a mine and has acquired new industrial and commercial interests: thus in addition to its traditional steel industry it now manufactures cars and radio and television sets. In the scientific and cultural field it has the new Ruhr University (founded 1965), the Institute of Environmental Research and its Theatre (Schauspielhaus). It is also the home of the German Shakespeare Society.

HISTORY. – Bochum originated as a Carolingian imperial stronghold, first recorded in 1041. In 1321 it received a municipal charter from Count Engelbert von der Mark. In 1609, along with the county of Mark, it passed to Brandenburg (later Prussia). With the industrial development of the mid 19th c. it began its rise to prosperity as one of the leading towns in the Ruhr.

Bochum Observatory

SIGHTS. – In the town centre are the *Town Hall* (1931: carillon) and **Propsteikirche** (14th c.: Romanesque shrine of St Perpetua). To the N are the ***German Mining Museum** (am Bergbaumuseum 28: demonstration mine, winding-house) and the *Geological Museum* (Herner Str. 45). On the site of the old Friederika pit (Querenburger Str.) in the S of the town is a *Geological Garden* which gives a clear picture of the local rock structures. – Other features of interest are the **Planetarium** (Castroper Str.), which illustrates the movements of heavenly bodies and the orbits of artificial satellites, the *Museum Bochum* (Kortumstr. 147), the *Schauspielhaus* (Königsallee), the *Ruhrlandhalle* (Stadionring), the *Municipal Park* (observation tower, animal park, aquarium, restaurant) and the *Railway Museum Rhein-Ruhr* in Dahlhausen. – To the SE is the **Ruhr University**, with good *art collections* (museum of antiquities, modern painting). Nearby is the *Botanic Garden*.

SURROUNDINGS. – 10 km SE, in *Stiepel*, is the late Romanesque St Mary's Church (*c.* 1200: frescoes). On the left bank of the Ruhr is the *Haus Kemnade*, a moated house of 1664 (museum of peasant culture, collection of musical instruments). – 7 km S, in Sundern, is ***Bochum Observatory**, with the well-known *Institute of Environmental Research*.

Bonn

Land: North Rhineland-Westphalia.
Vehicle registration: BN.
Altitude: 64 m. – Population: 286,000.
Post code: D-5300. – Dialling code: 02 28.
ⓘ **Werbe- und Verkehrsamt der Stadt Bonn,**
Rathaus Bonn-Bad Godesberg,
Kurfürstenstr. 2–3;
tel. 7 71.
Informationsstelle Bonn,
Cassius-Bastei (opposite Main Station);
tel. 7 74 66/7.

HOTELS. – NEAR MAIN STATION: ***Bristol*, Poppelsdorfer Allee 117, 200 b., Majestic restaurant, SB, sauna, solarium; ***Continental*, Am Hauptbahnhof 1, 60 b., (terrace); *Kurfürstenhof*, Baumschulallee 20, 42 b. – IN TOWN CENTRE: ***ETAP-Hotel Königshof*, Adenauer-Allee 9–11, 152 b., terrace on Rhine; *Beethoven*, Rheingasse 26, 99 b., terrace on Rhine; *Bergischer Hof*, Münsterplatz 23, 43 b.; *Sternhotel*, Markt 8, 120 b.; *Rhineland* (no rest.), Berliner Freiheit 11, 35 b.; *Haus Hofgarten* (no rest.), Fritz-Tillmann-Str. 7, 22 b. – OUTSIDE TOWN CENTRE: ***Steigenberger*, Am Bundeskanzlerplatz, 320 b., Atrium Restaurant, Ambassador Club, SB; ***Am Tulpenfeld*, Heussallee 2–10, 154 b., first-class restaurant, open terrace; ***Schlosspark-Hotel*, Venusbergweg 27, 85 b., SB, sauna, solarium; *Kölner Hof* (no rest.), Kölnstr. 502, 65 b.; *Altes Treppchen*, Endenicher Str. 308, 22 b.; *Casselsruhe*, Venusberg, 19 b. – IN BAD GODESBERG: ***Rheinhotel Dreesen*, Rheinstr. 45, 139 b. (terrace on Rhine, concerts and dancing in summer); ***Insel Hotel*, Theaterplatz 5–7, 99 b.; ***Park Hotel*, Am Kurpark 1, 68 b.; ***Godesburg Hotel*, Auf dem Berg 5, 19 b. (panoramic view); *Rheinland*, Rheinallee 17, 58 b.; *Zum Adler*, Koblenzer Str. 60, 54 b.; *Am Hohenzollernplatz* (no rest.), Plittersdorfer Str. 56, 17 b.; *Zum Löwen*, Von Groote Platz 1, 55 b.; *Schaumburger Hof*, Am Schaumburger Hof 10, 50 b. (terrace on Rhine); *Cäcilienhöhe*, Goldbergweg 17, 19 b.; *Flora* (no rest.), Viktoriastr. 16, 13 b.

YOUTH HOSTELS. – *Hermann-Ehlers-Haus*, Haager Weg 42, Bonn-Venusberg, 276 b.; *Landeshauptmann-Horion-Haus*, Horionstr. 60, Bonn-Bad Godesberg, 90 b.

RESTAURANTS. – ***Petit Poisson*, Wilhelmstr. 23a (French specialties); *Im Bären*, Acherstr. 1–3; *Kupfergrill*, Kölnstr. 45; *Schaarschmidt*, Brüdergasse 14; *Grand Italia*, Bischofsplatz 1 (Italian specialties); *Hongkong*, Brassert-Ufer 1 (Chinese); *Beethovenhalle*, Fritz-Schröder-Ufer; *Bundeshaus-Restaurant*, Görresstr. 5 (terrace on Rhine); *Em Höttche*, Markt 4 (historic restaurant with original interior); *Im Stiefel*, Bonngasse 30 (old German beerhouse and student haunt). – IN BAD GODESBERG: ***St. Michael*, Brunnenallee 26 (authentic specialty restaurant); *Maternus*, Löbestr. 3 (popular meeting-place); *La Redoute*, Kurfürstenallee 1; *Stadthalle*, Koblenzer Str. 80 (open-air terraces).

WINE-BARS. – *Weinkrüger*, Mauspfad 6–10 (historic old wine-bar); *Jacobs*, Friedrichstr. 18. – IN BAD GODESBERG: *Weinhaus Maternus*, Löbestr. 3; *Weinhäuschen am Rhein*, Fährst. 26 (in Mehlem, at ferry); *Zum Ännchen*, Ännchenplatz 1.

CAFÉS. – *Berg Café*, Haager Str. 19; *Dahmen*, Poststr. 2; *Müller Langhardt*, Markt 36; *Rittershaus*, Kaiserstr. 1d; *Bonner Kaffeehaus*, Remigiusplatz 5. – IN BAD GODESBERG: *Linder*, Gotenstr. 1; *Schöner*, Am Frohnhof 7; *Pohl*, Koblenzer Str. 83.

EVENTS. – *Carnival*, with Rose Monday parade; *Bonner Sommer* ("Summer in Bonn"), art exhibitions in the streets and squares (July–Aug.); *Pützchens Markt*, the largest Rhineland market, over 600 years old (September); *International Beethoven Festival* (every three years in April and September: 1986, etc.); *Federal Press Ball* (November).

The capital of the Federal Republic lies on both banks of the Rhine, which here enters the Cologne lowlands after its passage through the

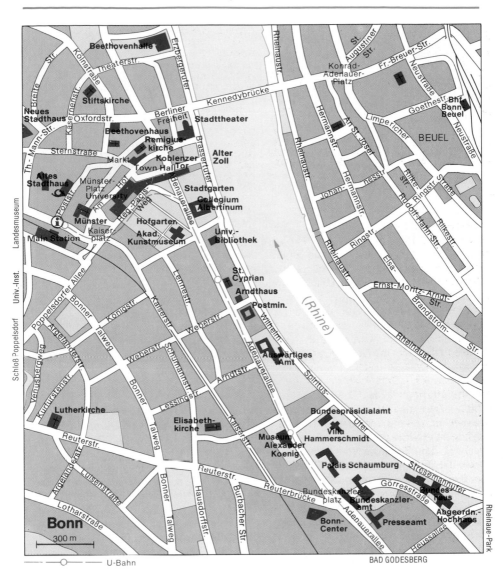

Bonn
300 m

——○—— U-Bahn

BAD GODESBERG

Rhenish Uplands. The pattern of the city's life is set by its old and famous university, the political activity centred on the government buildings round the Adenauer-Allee, its busy commercial life and its attractive setting (particularly on the river side, with its view of the nearby Siebengebirge). Since the incorporation of Beuel and Bad Godesberg into the city it has also possessed a renowned spa resort. Bonn was the birthplace of Beethoven.

HISTORY. – Bonn was one of the earliest Roman forts on the Rhine. From 1238 to 1794 it was the residence of the Archbishops of Cologne. On 10 May 1949 it was selected as the seat of the Federal Goverment.

SIGHTS. – In the centre of the OLD TOWN is the MARKTPLATZ, with the *Town Hall* (1737–38). At Rathausgasse 7 is the *Municipal Art Collection* (20th c. German painting and sculpture). A little way N is the Church of *St Remigius* (13th and 14th c.). At Bonngasse 20 is the *Beethovenhaus*, birthplace of the great composer (1770–1827), now a museum. SW of the Markt, in MÜNSTERPLATZ, is the venerable *Minster (SS. Cassius and Florentinus)*, one of the finest Romanesque churches in the Rhineland (11th–13th c.; E crypt 11th c.); on the S side is an attractive 12th c. cloister. – At the end of Adenauer-Allee is the *Koblenz Gate* in the E wing of the extensive **University** buildings, erected by Enrico Zuccali and Robert de Cotte

Bonn: the government office district from the air

(1697–1725) as the Electoral palace; beyond it is the *Hofgarten*. Along Adenauer-Allee are numerous official and government buildings: at No. 135 the *Villa Hammerschmidt*, official residence of the President of the Federal Republic; at Nos. 139–142 the *Palais Schaumburg* and the *Federal Chancellor's Office* (1975–77); at No. 150 the *Alexander König Zoological Museum* (fine collection of animals, particularly notable for its birds). In BUNDESKANZLERPLATZ is the *Bonn-Center*. To the E, in Görresstrasse, is the parliament building, the **Bundeshaus**, with a rear façade looking on to the Rhine; striking 30-storey tower block, the *Abgeordneten-Hochhaus* ("Langer Eugen" members' offices). Behind it is the *Freizeitpark Rheinaue* (leisure park). – E of the Koblenz Gate, on the Rhine, are the *Stadtgarten* and the ALTER ZOLL (Old Custom House), a former bastion with a celebrated *view of the Rhine and the Siebengebirge. Higher up is a memorial to the patriotic writer and poet *Ernst Moritz Arndt* (1769–1860), whose house at Adenauer-Allee 79, upstream is now a museum. N of the Alter Zoll, at the bridge over the Rhine, is the *Municipal Theatre* (1963–65). Beyond the bridge, on the banks of the Rhine, is the *Beethovenhalle* (1957–59), damaged by fire in 1983. To the SW of the town, at the end of the beautiful Poppelsdorfer Allee, is the

Poppelsdorfer Schloss (1715–30); beyond it is the *Botanic Garden*. SW of the Poppelsdorfer Schloss (20 min.) is the **Kreuzberg** (125 m), with a Franciscan friary and a prominent Baroque church (1627–37; "Sacred Staircase" on E side by Balthasar Neumann, 1746–51). – W of the station is the *Rhineland Museum* (Rheinisches Landesmuseum), with a rich collection of antiquities (Roman and Frankish art), medieval works of art and pictures.

In the district of BAD GODESBERG to the S, where there are numerous diplomatic missions, are the ruins of the *Godesburg* (tower of 1210; hotel), the *Redoute* (a Rococo Electoral palace, now used for splendid state receptions) and the *Deutschherrenkommende*, a former house of the Teutonic Order, now an embassy. – In the SCHWARZ-RHEINDORF district on the right bank of the Rhine is the unique Romanesque *Double Chapel* (12th c.).

SURROUNDINGS. – **Siebengebirge**, with the ruins of *Drachenfels Castle* (20 km SE). – *Schloss Augustusburg*, Brühl (20 km NW), begun by J. C. Schlaun in 1725–28, a gem of Rococo architecture with a famous staircase hall by Balthasar Neumann, now used for government receptions and other state occasions. – Near Brühl is the *Phantasialand Amusement Park* (see p. 99).

Bremen

The Free Hanseatic City of Bremen, a *Land* in its own right.
Vehicle registration: HB.
Altitude: 5 m. – Population: 550,000.
Post code: D-2800. –
Dialling code: 04 21.

ⓘ **Verkehrsverein** (*Tourist Information*) am, Bahnhofsplatz;
tel. 3 63 61.

HOTELS: – *Parkhotel*, Burgerpark, 210 b., garden terrace; *Columbus*, Bahnhofsplatz 5, 160 b.; *Zur Post*, Bahnhofsplatz 11, 340 b., SB, sauna, solarium; *Uberseehotel* (no rest.), Wachstr. 27, 210 b.; *Bremer Hospiz*, Löningstr. 16, 110 b.; *Westfalia*, Lange-marckst 38, 110 b.; *Schaper-Siedenburg*, Bahnhofstr. 7, 100 b.; *Residence*, Hohenlohestr. 42, 60 b., sauna, solarium. – IN HORN: *Landhaus Louisenthal*, Leher Heerstr. 105, 75 b. – IN SCHWACHHAUSEN: *Crest Hotel*, August-Bebel Allee 4, 204 b.; *Munte am Stadtwald*, Am Stadtwald 33, 128 b., SB, sauna, solarium; *Heldt*, Friedhofstr. 41, 67 b. – IN VEGESACK: *Strandlust*, Rohrstr. 11, 38 b. (terrace on the Weser). – YOUTH HOSTELS: *Bremen*, Kalkstr. 6, 177 b.; *Bremen-Blumenthal*, Weserstrand 31, 59 b. – CAMPING SITES: International Camping site *Freie Hansestadt Bremen*, Am Stadtwaldsee 1.

RESTAURANTS. – *Flett*, Bottcherstr. 3; *Schnoor 2*, Schnor 2 (unusual decor); *Beck's In'n Snoor*, Schnoor 34 (Brewery Inn); *Ratskeller*, Am Markt (famous wine-cellar); *Das Kleine Lokal*, Besselstr. 40; *Le Bistro*, Sögestr. 54; *Martini*, Böttcherstr. 2 (grill); *Alt-Bremer Brauhaus Remmer*, Katharinenstr. 32 (local Bremen dishes); *Meierei*, Bürgerpark; *Borg-felder Landhaus*, Warfer Landstr. 73, Bremen-Borgfeld (out of town); *Fährhaus Meyer-Farge*, Berner Fährweg 8, Bremen-Farge (ship-greeting point).

CAFÉS. – *Knigge*, Sögestr. 42; *Jacobs*, Knochen-hauerstr. 4; *Raths-Konditorei*, Am Markt 11; *Sub-tropica*, Vahrer Str. 239, Bremen-Vahr (tropical plants, light music, dancing). – Several dancing places and night-clubs.

Bremen Casino (roulette, blackjack; daily 3 p.m.– 2 a.m., Fri. and Sat. to 3 p.m.), Bottcherstrasse.

EVENTS. – *Bremen Ice-sports* (6 January, with banquet); *Schaffermahlzeit* (traditional banquet, beginning Feb.); *Vegesack Autumn Market* (Sept.); *Bremen Free Market* (held since 1035), on the Bürgerweide (second half of Oct.); *Christmas Market* round the Liebfrauenkirche (Dec.).

The Free Hanseatic City of Bremen on the lower Weser (57 km from Bremerhaven), capital of the *Land* of Bremen, is the second largest sea-port and maritime trading city in the Federal Republic, carrying on a considerable trade in grain, cotton and tobacco. The oldest part of the city, with the Marktplatz Bött-cherstrasse and Schnoor, extends between the hill on which the Cathedral stands and the Weser.

The Neue Vahr district to the E of the city is an influential example of a modern residential and dormitory suburb. Bremen University was founded in 1970. The principal local industries are shipyards, steel-works, an oil refinery, electrical equipment, cars, textiles, coffee-roasting and brewing.

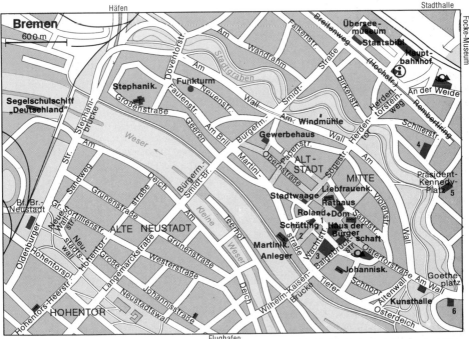

1 Markt   2 Böttcherstrasse   3 Cotton Exchange   4 Central Baths   5 Municipal Archives   6 Theatre, Goetheplatz

Bremen: the Markt, with the Town Hall, Cathedral and House of the Citizens

HISTORY. – The town was made the see of a bishop by Charlemagne in 787, and became an archbishopric in 845. Unaer Archbishop Adalbert (1043–72) Bremen achieved its early prosperity. In 1358 it became a member of the Hanse, and in 1646 a free Imperial city. Bremerhaven was founded by the city's active burgomaster, Smidt, in 1827. Between 1886 and 1895 large-scale works were carried out to regulate the shipping channel and enable seagoing vessels to sail up the Weser to Bremen in safety. Reconstruction after the heavy damage suffered during the Second World War has considerably altered the aspect of the city.

SIGHTS. – In the picturesque MARKT, in front of the Town Hall, stands a celebrated *figure of Roland (1404), 5·4 m high, the emblem of the city's freedom and independent jurisdiction (at present under restoration). – The *Town Hall is a brick-built Gothic structure (1405–10), with a magnificent Renaissance façade added in 1609–12. It has one of the most elegant banqueting and reception halls in Germany, the *Grosse Halle (40 m long, 13 m wide, 8 m high), with a large mural painting (1537) of the "Judgment of Solomon". This is the scene of the annual Schaffermahlzeit, the oldest fraternity meal in the world. On the side nearest the market, adjoining the "Golden Chamber", is a richly carved spiral staircase. – On the E side of the Old Town Hall stands the New Town Hall and on the W side is the entrance to the famous *Ratskeller, noted for its well-stocked wine-cellar; in the Hauff Room are frescoes (1927) by Max Slevogt illustrating Wilhelm Hauff's "Fantasies in the Bremen Ratskeller" (1827). Under the NW tower is a bronze group, "The Bremen Town Musicians" (a donkey, a dog, a cat and a cock – who feature in an old folk tale), by Gerhard Marcks (1953).

The Cathedral (St Peter's: Evang.) dates from the 11th, 13th and 16th c.; the exterior, with the 98 m high towers, was rebuilt 1888–98; the richly decorated Baroque pulpit (1638) was presented by Queen Christina of Sweden; in the "Lead Cellar" are a number of leathery mummified bodies. – Opposite the Cathedral is the modern House of the Citizens (Haus der Bürgerschaft), the Land parliament (1966). To the W is the Schütting (1537–38), the old merchant guild house, occupied since 1849 by the Chamber of Commerce.

Beyond the Schütting is the entrance to the narrow *Böttcherstrasse, which in 1926–30 was transformed from a street of artisans' dwellings into a museum street at the expense of the Bremen coffee-dealer Dr L. Roselius. On the left is the Paula-Becker-Modersohn-Haus, with works by the Worpswede female painter (d. 1907), on the right the Hag-Haus, then on the left the Roselius-Haus (1588: examples of Low German art from Gothic to Baroque), the Haus des Glockenspiels (Carillon House) the Bremen Casino and the Robinson Crusoe House. – Beyond the Cotton Exchange in Wachstrasse is the charming *Schnoorviertel, the haunt of artists and the oldest part of Bremen, with burghers' houses of the 15th to 18th c. and friendly old inns.

SE of the old town, within its ramparts and moat, is the *Kunsthalle, at the Ostertor

(17th c. Dutch painting, early German masters, 19th and 20th c. French and German painting, works of the Worpswede painters' colony). – In the N of the old town, on the W side of the Bahnhofsplatz, is the interesting *Overseas Museum, ethnography, natural history, trade (Pacific, Australia, Asia); exhibition of import and export trade of Bremen. To the NE is the *Bürgerpark* (200 hectares), laid out in the English style in 1866. – In the north-eastern district of SCHWACHHAUSEN, at Schwachhauser Heerstr. 240, is the Focke Museum, the Bremen Provincial Museum of the History of Art and Culture, with Bremen bygones, furniture and domestic equipment, material illustrating the Low German way of life and a shipping section (the Hanseatic "Kogge" or merchant ship). To the E are the large *Rhododendron Park* and the *Botanic Garden*. – Farther SE, in the VAHR district, is the modern residential and dormitory suburb of Neue Vahr (1957–63: c. 32,000 inhabitants).

NW of the old town are Bremen's harbours (15 basins capable of taking seagoing vessels: harbour tours from the Martinianleger at the Wilhelm Kaisen Brücke). The principal harbours are the *Overseas, Europe* and *Neustadt Harbours* (with container terminal), all customs-free harbours.

SURROUNDINGS. – Worpswede (23 km NE), a well-known artists' colony (Vogeler, Modersohn, Mackensen, Hans am Ende, etc.: permanent art exhibitions) on the Teufelsmoor. – Bremerhaven (57 km N), with the *Columbus Quay* for overseas traffic, the Wilhelm Kaisen Container Terminal, the largest in Europe, and the largest *fishing harbour* in Europe (interesting fish auction on weekdays 7–8.30 a.m., North Sea Museum) and the *German Shipping Museum* (a Bremen "Kogge" of 1380, historic ships in the Old Harbour).

Brunswick (Braunschweig)

Land: Lower Saxony. –
Vehicle registration: BS.
Altitude: 80 m. – Population: 260,000.
Post code: D-3300. – Dialling code: 05 31.
ⓘ Städtischer Verkehrsverein,
   Hauptbahnhof and Bohlweg;
   tel. 7 92 37.

HOTELS. – *Mövenpick Hotel*, Packhof, 189 b., SB, sauna, solarium; *Atrium*, Berliner Platz 3, 200 b., sauna; *Deutsches Haus*, Burgplatz 1, 120 b.; *Fürstenhof*, Campestr 12, 62 b., SB, sauna, solarium; *Frühlingshotel*, Bankplatz 7, 90 b.; *Lessinghof*,

Okerstr 13, 74 b.; *Zur Oper* (no rest.), Jasperallee 21/ 22, 65 b.; *Forsthaus*, Hamburger Str. 72, 60 b.; *Lorenz*, Friedrick-Wilhelm-Str. 2, 58 b.; *An der Stadhalle* (no rest.), Leohardstr. 21, 36 b.; *Gästehaus Braur. schweig*, Zuckerbergweg 2, 24 b.; *Eich* (no rest.), Wolfenbütteler Str. 67, 42 b.; *Gästehaus Wartburg* (no rest.), Rennelbergstr. 12, 32 b. – IN BUCHHORST: *Aquarius*, Ebertallee, 44g (on the B1), 71 b., sauna. – CAMPING SITE: in the Burgerpark.

RESTAURANTS. – *Gewandhauskeller*, Altstadtmarkt 1; *Haus zur Hanse*, Güldenstr. 7 (half-timbered house of 1567); *Löwenkrone*, Leonhardplatz; *Das Alte Haus*, Alte Knochenhauerstr. 11 (dates from 1470); *Wolters am Wall*, Fallersleber Str. 35; *Hongkong*, Friedrich-Wilhelm-Str. 30 (Chinese).

WINE-BARS. – *Gewandhaus*, Altstadtmarkt 1; *Zum Fallstaff*, Bohlweg 67/68; *Zum Stillen Winkel*, An der Katharinenkirche 12–15; *Weinkrüger*, Kohlmarkt 10.

CAFÉS. – *Tolle*, Bohlweg 69/70; *Wagner*, Bohlweg 41/42; *Haertle*, Steinweg 22.

The old Guelf town of Brunswick, Lower Saxony's second largest city, lies on the Oker in a fertile plain in the N of the Harz foreland. In the old town a few islands of tradition bear witness to the rich history of the town, which suffered severe destruction in the Second World War. Brunswick's Technical College (now a university) is the oldest in Germany (founded 1745). It also has a College of Art and a number of research institutes and government establishments (e.g. the Federal Physical and Technological Institute). It has a wide range of industry, from the manufacture of machinery and lorries through precision engineering to vegetable canning. The Mittelland Canal runs N of the town.

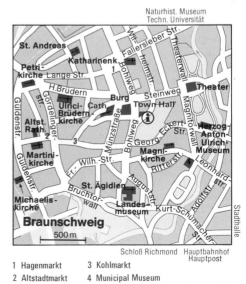

1 Hagenmarkt   3 Kohlmarkt
2 Altstadtmarkt   4 Municipal Museum

HISTORY. – In the 12th c. Brunswick was a favourite residence of Henry the Lion (1129–95), who gave the town its charter. In 1247 it became a member of the Hanse, and thanks to its favourable situation at the crossing of major trade routes developed into an important domestic entrepôt. From 1753 to 1918 it was the residence of the Dukes of Brunswick. During the Second World War the old town centre was almost completely destroyed, and apart from one or two old-world corners Brunswick is now a modern city.

Brunswick: the town centre from the air

SIGHTS. – In the *Burgplatz, in the centre of the town, is the restored **Burg Dankwarderode**, built around 1175 by Henry the Lion (two-storey hall of 1887). In the middle of the castle square is a magnificent bronze *Lion, erected by Henry the Lion in 1166 as a symbol of his power. On the N side of the square is the *Huneborstelsches Haus (1536), now a guildhall, which was re-erected here in 1902.

The Romanesque *Cathedral, the first large vaulted building in Lower Saxony, was built in 1173–95 during the reign of Henry the Lion. In the nave is the *tomb of Henry the Lion and his wife Mathilde (c. 1250), a masterpiece of Saxon late Romanesque carving. In front of the choir, under a brass plate of 1707, are the remains of Emperor Otto IV (d. 1218) and his wife Beatrix. In the choir, which, like the S transept, has Romanesque wall paintings, is a seven-branched candelabrum, 4·5 m high, presented by Henry the Lion. The oldest and historically most important feature of the Cathedral is the *Imerward Crucifix of 1150. – Facing the Cathedral, to the E, is the **Town Hall** (1886–1900, with an extension of 1969).

N of the Burgplatz is the large HAGEN-MARKT, with a fountain commemorating Henry the Lion (1874) and **St Catherine's Church** (12th–14th c.: Evang.; organ of 1980 with parts of the Baroque organ of 1623). A short distance to the W is St Andrew's Church (12th c., rebuilt in Gothic style in 13th and 14th c.). – N of the town centre is the **Technical University**, originally founded in 1745 as the Collegium Carolineum, and nearby the State Natural History Museum.

The ALTSTADTMARKT, SW of the Burgplatz, is the heart of the old trading and Hanseatic city. It developed out of a street market of the 11th and 12th c. On the W side of the square is the **Old Town Hall** (Altstadt-Rathaus), originally a 14th c. banqueting hall, with a two-tier arcade in front. Opposite it is the restored **St Martin's Church** (12th–14th c.: Evang.). On the S side of the square is the medieval Cloth Hall (Gewandhaus: restaurant), also restored, the *E gable of which (1591) is the finest piece of Renaissance architecture in the town. – A short distance SW of the Altstadtmarkt is the little **St Michael's Church** (Evang.), a 14th c. Gothic hall-church originally consecrated in 1157. Nearby are several half-timbered houses of the 15th–17th c.: at Alte Knochenhauerstr. 11 the town's oldest half-timbered front, at Güldenstr. 7 the handsome Haus zur Hanse of 1567.

S of the Burgplatz, round the Gothic church of ST. ÄGIDIEN or St Giles (R.C.: choir 13th c., nave 14th c.), is the picturesque Ottilienteil quarter (half-timbered buildings). Adjoining the church, in the choir (Paulinerchor) of a former Dominican monastery, is the Brunswick Provincial Museum (history, local material).

SE of the Burgplatz is the impressively restored **Magnikirche** (St Magnus's, consecrated 1031: Evang.), with modern sculpture. Behind the church is a picturesque little group of half-timbered buildings. In St Magnus's Cemetery (700 m SE) is the tomb of the writer and philosopher G. E. Lessing (1729–81). On the E side of the cemetery is the **Stadthalle** (1965: restaurant).

On the eastern edge of the town centre, at Museumstr. 1 (beside the Museumspark), is the **Herzog Anton Ulrich Museum** (art and applied art, including Otto IV's imperial robes and Rembrandt's *'Family

Group", *c.* 1668). Some 200 m S (Löwenwall) is the interesting *Municipal Museum* (folk traditions and ethnography, religious art, applied art, furniture and domestic equipment). – In the eastern district of RIDDAGSHAUSEN, on the far side of the Prinz Albrecht Park, is a notable church belonging to a former Cistercian monastery (13th c.). To the N and S lie the nature reserve of Riddagshausen and the protected area of Buchhorst, a region of natural beauty.

Celle

Land: Lower Saxony.
Vehicle registration: CE.
Altitude: 40 m. – Population: 73,000.
Post code: D-3100. – Dialling code: 0 51 41.
ⓘ **Verkehrsverein**, Schlossplatz 13; tel. 2 30 31.

HOTELS. – *Fürstenhof*, Hannoversche Str. 55, 96 b. (restaurant "Endtenfang"), SB, sauna, solarium; *Celler Hof*, Stechbahn 11, 92 b. (restaurant "Heiderose"); *Borchers*, Schuhstr. 52, 37 b.; *Thüringer Hof* (no rest.), Planckstr. 17, 25 b.; *Sattler am Bahnhof*, Bahnhofstr. 46, 42 b.; *Schifferkrug*, Speicherstr. 9, 24 b. – IN ALTENCELLE: *Schaperkrug*, Braunschweiger Heerstr. 85, 58 b. – YOUTH HOSTEL: Weghausstr. 2, Celle-Klein Hehlen, 143 b. – CAMPING SITES: *Silbersee*, Celle-Vorwerk; *Alvern*, Celle-Alvern.

RESTAURANTS. – *Ratskeller*, Rathaus, Am Markt 14; *Städtische Union*, Thaerplatz 1; *Schwarzwaldstube*, Bergstr. 14; *Schweine-Schulze*, Neue Str. 36.

CAFÉS. – *Kiess*, Grosser Plan 16–17; *Kraemer*, Stechbahn 7. – Several bars.

EVENTS. – *Spring Festival* in the Schützenplatz (beginning of April); *Celle Stallion Parade* (last Sunday in Sept. and first Sunday in Oct.); *Oktoberfest* in the Schützenplatz.

The old Ducal town on the Aller, on the southern fringe of the Lüneburg Heath, has preserved its character as a princely residence down to our own day; the rectangular layout of the picturesque *half-timbered streets of the old town is aligned on the palace. Celle is also famous, however, for its Provincial Stud Farm. Its principal industries are the manufacture of television sets, paint, machinery and textiles, and it also has one of the largest orchid nurseries in Europe. Celle has long been a garrison town and still is, with both German and British troops.

HISTORY. – The name *Kellu*, meaning "settlement by a river", first appears in a charter of Otto III's 990; this later became Zelle, Latinised as Celle. In the 12th c. Henry the Lion granted the settlement at the ford on the Aller privileges as a depot for the long-distance trade which was now developing. It received its municipal charter from Otto I of Brunswick. In 1292 Duke Otto the Severe, with the interests of navigation on the river in mind, founded a new town and castle 3 km downstream and moved the inhabitants of the older settlement there. In 1378 Duke Albrecht made Celle capital of the Duchy of Lüneburg, and under its last Duke, Georg Wilhelm, the town enjoyed a great flowering of art. The palace and the town church were rebuilt, the French Garden laid out and the court theatre founded. In 1705 the principality of Lüneburg was amalgamated with the Electorate of Hanover, and in 1711 Celle became the seat of the Higher Appeal Court (later the Provincial Supreme Court) – almost by way of compensation for the loss of its status as a princely capital. In 1735 the Royal Stud Farm was established here. During the period of French occupation Celle became chief town of the *département* of Aller. The old town emerged unscathed from the Second World War.

SIGHTS. – The **Schloss**, built partly in late Gothic style and partly in the Baroque of the second half of the 17th c., was from 1292 to 1866 the residence of the Dukes of Brunswick and Lüneburg. It contains fine state apartments and the oldest court theatre in Germany (1674); the chapel has a splendid Renaissance interior. A short distance N is the *Provincial Supreme Court*. Opposite the Schloss is the **Bomann Museum**, with a rich collection of material on the history of Hanover, including a Lower Saxon farmhouse of 1571.

E of the palace is the **OLD TOWN**, with its picturesque half-timbered streets and

Town Hall, Celle

lanes. Particularly fine is KALANDGASSE, with the old *Latin School.* At the S end of this street is the STECHBAHN, once the scene of knightly tournaments. – In the MARKT is the **Town Church** (14th and 17th c.), with epitaphs and tombstones of the last Dukes of Celle and a princely burial vault (tomb of the Danish Queen Caroline Mathilde, d. 1775). The late Renaissance **Town Hall** was built 1530–81. Among the houses in the old town the *Hoppener-Haus* (1532) at Poststr. 8 and the *Stechinelli-Haus* (17th c.) at Grosser Plan 14 are of particular interest. – S of the old town is the *French Garden*, with a monument to Queen Caroline Mathilde (1784) and the Lower Saxony Institute of Bee Research. – Farther S, on both banks of the Fuhse, is the *Provincial Stud Farm* (Landgestüt), founded in 1735 by the Elector of Hanover who was also George II of Great Britain (breeding of stallions: stallion parades in autumn).

SURROUNDINGS. – *Kloster Wienhausen (10 km SE), a former Cistercian convent (13th–14th c.: now an Evang. house of retreat for women) which possesses some notable art treasures (nuns' choir with 14th c. *wall and vaulting paintings and a *Holy Sepulchre of 1445; famous 14th and 15th c. **tapestries, shown only once a year at Whitsun).

Chiemsee

Land: Bavaria.
(i) **Verkehrsverband Chiemsee**, Rathausstr. 11, D-8210 Prien; tel. (0 80 51) 22 80.

The *Chiemsee, with an area of 82 sq. km, is the largest lake in Bavaria, measuring between 5 and 15 km across and up to 73 m in depth. It fills the middle of a basin carved out by an Ice Age glacier, and once extended southwards as far as Grassau, over an area which has been silted up by deposits from the Tirolean River Ache. In summer the surface of the lake is gay with large numbers of sailing boats.

There are three islands in the lake: the **Herreninsel** (250 hectares, mostly wooded), with *Schloss Herrenchiemsee*, built 1878–85 on the model of Versailles for King Ludwig II of Bavaria (state apartments, including a 98 m long Hall of Mirrors: candlelight concerts on summer

Fraueninsel, Chiemsee

evenings); the *Fraueninsel (8 hectares), with a Benedictine nunnery, set among lime-trees, founded by Duke Tassilo III in the 8th c. (church with late Romanesque wall paintings) and a picturesque little fishing village; and the small uninhabited *Krautinsel*, lying between the other two. From the middle of the lake there is a fine view of the jagged ridge of the Chiemgau Alps, with Kampenwand (1669 m) and Hochfelln (1670 m).

Round the shores of the lake there are many holiday resorts which draw large numbers of visitors. The largest of these is **Prien**, on the W side of the lake, a health resort which also offers the Kneipp water cure; Prien-Stock is the home harbour of the motor boats which ply on the lake. One of the most popular bathing resorts is *Chieming*, on the E side, which has a beach 1 km long.

Coburg

Land: Bavaria. – Vehicle registration: CO. Altitude: 297 m. – Population: 47,000. Post code: D-8630. – Dialling code: 0 95 61.
(i) **Fremdenverkehrsamt**, Rathaus, Herrengasse 4; tel. 9 50 71/2.

HOTELS. – *Stadt Coburg*, Lossaustr. 12, 80 b.; *Goldener Traube*, Viktoriabrunnen 2, 137 b.; *Goldener Anker*, Rosengasse 14, 86 b., SB, sauna, solarium; *Coburger Tor*, Ketschendorfer Str. 22, 32 b. (restaurant "Schaller"); *Haus Blankenburg*, Rosenauer Str. 30, 66 b. – IN NEU-NEERSHOF: *Schloss Neuhof*, Neuhofer Str. 10, 34 b. – YOUTH HOSTEL: *Schloss Ketschendorf*, Parkstr. 2, 130 b.

RESTAURANTS. – *Alt-Coburg*, Steinweg 25; *Loreley*, Herrngasse 14; *Kongresshaus*, Berliner Platz 1; *Ratskeller*, Markt 1.

CAFÉS. – *Schilling*, Mohrenstr 21; *Schubart*, Mohrenstr. 11.

This former Ducal capital lies on the southern slopes of the Thuringian Forest, on the River Itz, a tributary of the Main, with a massive fortress looming over it. Economically the town is known for the manufacture of upholstered furniture, machine tools and car accessories, as well as for ceramics and toys.

HISTORY. – Over the centuries Coburg was linked with a number of different Thuringian territories, but in 1920 passed to Bavaria after a referendum.

SIGHTS. – In the attractive MARKT stand the *Town Hall* (1579) and the former *Regierungsgebäude* (government buildings: now the Town House), a richly decorated late Renaissance structure of 1599. – SE of the Markt is the **Moriz-kirche** (St Maurice's: 14th–16th c.), with the 12 m high tomb of Duke Johann Friedrich II of Saxony (d. 1595). Opposite the church is the *Gymnasium Casimirianum*, in 17th c. Renaissance style, a school founded by Duke Johann Casimir.

On the E edge of the old town is the SCHLOSSPLATZ, with the **Ehrenburg** (formerly the Ducal palace), rebuilt by Schinkel 1816–38, which contains interesting state and private apartments as well as the Coburg Provincial Library. The Baroque *Hofkirche* (palace church) is incorporated in the W wing. – Beyond an arcade which came from the former ballroom building is the beautiful Hofgarten, running up the hill to the castle. Halfway up is the *Natural History Museum*, with a collection of birds.

The castle, *Veste Coburg (464 m), dating mainly from the 16th c. (restored in the 19th and 20th c.), is one of the largest in Germany. In the Fürstenbau are the former residential apartments of the Ducal family: Luther Room, in which the reformer sought refuge during the Diet of Augsburg in 1530; Luther Chapel; *Collections of works of art, weapons and coins. In the S of the town, at the N end of the *Rose Garden*, is the *Kongresshaus* (1962).

SURROUNDINGS. – 8 km W is the recreation centre *Wildpark Schloss Tambach*.

Cologne (Köln)

Land: North Rhineland-Westphalia.
Vehicle registration: K.
Altitude: 36 m. – Population: 1,013,000.
Post code: D-5000. – Dialling code: 02 21.
ⓘ **Verkehrsamt**, Am Dom;
tel. 2 21 33 45.

HOTELS. – *Excelsior Hotel Ernst*, Domplatz, 250 b. (Hansa Room); *Dom Hotel*, Domkloster 2a, 200 b.; *Inter-Continental*, Helenenstr. 14, 580 b., SB, sauna; *Mondial*, Bechergasse 10, 300 b.; *Consul*, Belfortstr. 9, 160 b., SB, sauna; *Senats Hotel*, Unter Goldschmied 9, 100 b.; *Königshof* (no rest.), Richartzstr. 14, 141 b.; *Am Augustinerplatz* (no rest.), Hohe Str. 30, 105 b.; *Coellner Hof*, Hansaring 100, 100 b.; *Haus Lyskirchen*, Filzengraben 26, 83 b.; *Leonet* (no rest.), Rubenstr. 33, 151 b., SB, sauna; *Rheingold*, (no rest.), Engelbertstr. 33, 130 b.; *Ludwig* (no rest.), Brandenburger Str. 24, 100 b.; *Conti-Continental* (no rest.), Brusseler Str. 40, 90 b.; *Kolpinghaus-International*, St Apern Str. 32, 85 b.; *Merian* (no rest.), Allerheiligenstr. 1, 48 b. AT COLOGNE-BONN AIRPORT: *Holiday Inn*, Waldstr. 255, 160 b., SB, sauna. – IN BRAUNSFELD: *Regent*, Melatengürtel 15, 268 b. – IN DEUTZ: *Panorama* (no rest.), Siergburger Str. 33, 45 b. – IN LINDENTHAL: *Crest Hotel*, Durener Str. 287, 200 b.; *Bremer*, Dürener Str. 225, 100 b., SB. – IN PORZ: *Spiegel*, Hermann-Löns-Str. 122, 24 b. – IN RODENKIRCHEN: *Rheinblick*, Uferstr. 20, 28 b. (terrace on Rhine).

YOUTH HOSTELS: Konrad-Adenauer-Ufer 111, 172 b.; Siegesstr. 5a, in Deutz, 338 b.; An der Schanz 14, Riehl, 366 b. – CAMPING SITES: *Fischerhaus Poll*, on banks of Rhine in Poll; *Berger*, on Rhine in Rodenkirchen; *Waldbad*, Peter-Baum Weg, Dünnwald.

RESTAURANTS. – *Bastei*, Konrad-Adenauer-Ufer 80 (view of Rhine); *Opernterrassen*, Offenbachplatz; *Börsen-Restaurant*, Unter Sachsenhausen 10; *Alt-Köln Am Dom*, Trankgasse 7; *Em Krützche*, Am Frankenturm 1; *Gürzenich-Grill*, Martinstr. 2; *Hopp am Hahnentor*, Habsburgerring 20; *Messeturm Restaurant*, Kennedyufer (on Exhibition Complex); *Goldener Pflug*, Olpener Str. 421, Merheim. – FOREIGN CUISINE: *La Poêle d'or*, Komödienstr. 50–52; *Chez Alex*, Mühlengasse 1, *Auberge de la Charrue d'Or*, Habsburger Ring 18, *Sigi's Bistro*, Kleiner Griechenmarkt 23 (all French); *Chalêt Suisse*, Am Hof 20 (Swiss); *Ristorante Grand'Italia*, Hansaring 66, *Ristorante Alfredo*, Tunisstr. 3 (both Italian); *Balkangrill*, Friesenstr. 33; *Peking am Dom*, Marzellenstr. 2, *Tai-Tung*, Hohenzollernring 11 (both Chinese).

WINE-BARS. – *Weinhaus im Wallfisch*, Salzgasse 13; *Weinkruger*, Marsplatz 3–5.

KÖLSCHLOKALE (typical Cologne beer-houses). – *Brauhaus Sion*, Unter Taschenmacher 5–7; *Früh am Dom*, Am Hof 12.

CAFÉS. – *Reichard*, Am Dom (terrace); *Kranzler*, Offenbachplatz; *Eigel*, Brückenstr. 1; *Füllenbach*, Neumarkt 45 (on Ring); *Fassbender*, Mittelstr. 12–14 (in Cologne Bazaar).

EVENTS. –*Carnival*, with various festivities, dances and *Rose Monday procession* (Feb.); *West German Art Fair*, Cologne and Düsseldorf (March); *music*,

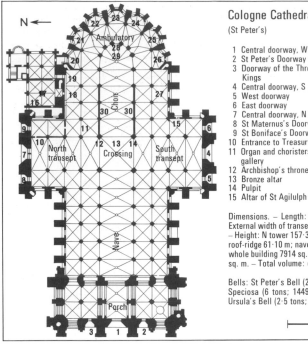

Cologne Cathedral
(St Peter's)

1 Central doorway, W front
2 St Peter's Doorway
3 Doorway of the Three Kings
4 Central doorway, S side
5 West doorway
6 East doorway
7 Central doorway, N front
8 St Maternus's Doorway
9 St Boniface's Doorway
10 Entrance to Treasury
11 Organ and choristers' gallery
12 Archbishop's throne
13 Bronze altar
14 Pulpit
15 Altar of St Agilulph
16 Tabernacle
17 Chapel of the Sacrament
18 Cross Chapel
19 Gero Cross
20 St Engelbert's Chapel
21 St Maternus's Chapel
22 St John's Chapel
23 Axial chapel
24 St Agnes's Chapel
25 St Michael's Chapel
26 St Stephen's Chapel
27 Lady Chapel
28 Reliquary of the Three Kings
29 High altar
30 Choir stalls

Dimensions. – Length: 144·58 m externally, 119 m internally. – External width of transept 86·25 m; internal width of nave 45·19 m. – Height: N tower 157·38 m, S tower 157·31 m; ridge-turret 109 m; roof-ridge 61·10 m; nave (interior) 43·35 m; aisles 19·80 m. – Area: whole building 7914 sq. m; windows c. 10,000 sq. m; roof c. 12,500 sq. m. – Total volume: c. 407,000 cu. m.

Bells: St Peter's Bell (24 tons; 1923); Pretiosa (11·2 tons; 1448); Speciosa (6 tons; 1449); Three Kings' Bell (3·8 tons; 1880); St Ursula's Bell (2·5 tons; 1862).

50 m

---

floor shows and dancing at the Tanzbrunnen, Rheinpark (May–Sept.); *"Müheimer Gottestracht",* Corpus Christi procession on Rhine; *"Rheinwoche" sailing regatta* (beginning of June); *European Grand Prix,* Weidenpesch racecourse (mid Oct.); *Christmas Market,* in the old town. – Numerous industrial, trade and craft fairs.

This old cathedral city on the Rhine is one of the most important traffic junctions and commercial centres in Germany, with world-famed trade fairs and busy shipping traffic (sea-going and on the Rhine). Cologne is the seat of an archbishop, with a university, a sports college and the headquarters of the WDR (West-deutscher Rundfunk) radio and tele-vision corporation, and is noted also for sport (Federal Football League matches; Union races and European Grand Prix on Weidenpesch race-course) and for the Rhineland Carni-val. With its old churches and its Roman remains it is one of the focal points of Western culture.

The development of the city can be traced in its present layout. The outer circle of streets known as the Ring marks the line of the medieval fortifications dating from the Staufen period, while the 10 km long green belt lying farther out represents the Prussian fortifications of a later period.

HISTORY. – Cologne developed out of the Roman colony of *Colonia Claudia Ara Agrippinensis*. From the end of the 5th c. it was incorporated in the kingdom of the Franks, and was made the seat of an archbishopric by Charlemagne. In the Middle Ages it was one of Germany's leading towns, and for a time was, along with Lübeck, the most important member of the Hanse. The foundation stone of the cathedral was laid in 1248, and 1388 saw the establishment of the old university (re-founded in 1919). In the 19th c., as part of the province of the Rhine, the town became Prussian. The Second World War destroyed most of the inner city, now rebuilt in modern style along with the business district round the Hohe Strasse.

SIGHTS. – Not far from the left bank of the Rhine towers Cologne's mighty landmark, the ****Cathedral**, a masterpiece of Gothic architecture and one of Europe's largest cathedrals (photograph, p. 57). Begun in 1248, it was the most ambitious building project of the Middle Ages, but work came to a halt at the beginning of the 16th c., and the cathedral was not completed until 1842–80. Features of the imposing interior (6166 sq. m, with 56 pillars) are the *Reliquary of the Three Kings above the high altar, a masterpiece of the goldsmith's art of the Rhineland (made in the 12th–13th c. to the design of Nicholas of Verdun to house relics brought from Milan); the famous *Adoration of the Kings *c.* 1440 (incorrectly called the "Dombild") in the choir ambulatory; fine early Gothic statuary (14th c.) on the pillars of the choir; the *Gero Cross in the Cross Chapel; and many precious objects in the *Treasury (shrines, Gospel books, vestments, monstrances, reliquaries).

From the S tower (over 500 steps; notable bells) there is a wide*view.

On the S side of the Cathedral is the magnificently laid out **Roman-Germanic Museum**, with the *Dionysus mosaic (2nd c. A.D.), the 15 m high funeral monument of Poblicius (1st c. A.D.), Roman glass, pottery, mosaics and oil lamps, and a harbour street. The Treasury contains Germanic gold jewellery. Nearby is the *Diocesan Museum*.

A short way W, in Wallrafplatz, is the *headquarters of Westdeutscher Rundfunk* (Funkhaus des WDR). Facing it on the S is the **Wallraf-Richartz Museum** (*Ludwig Museum*), with a magnificent gallery of European painting (works by Rembrandt, Manet, Renoir, Leibl, Liebermann, Slevogt; substantial representation of the early Cologne school), a rich collection of engravings and large collections of modern art (it is proposed to move the museums into a new building).

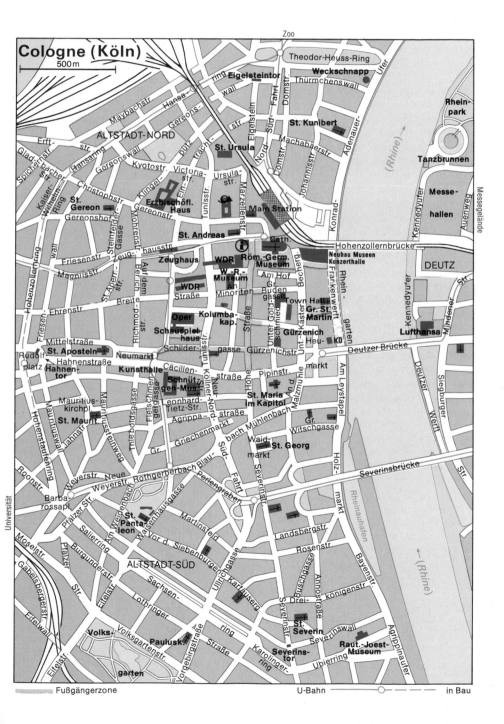

– Still farther S, in Brückenstrasse, is *St Columba's Chapel* (1949–52), which contains a stone figure of the Virgin (*c.* 1460).

W of the Cathedral, in Komödienstrasse, is *St Andrew's Church* (15th c.; remains of St Albertus Magnus in a Roman sarcophagus in the funerary chapel). In the adjoining Zeughausstrasse is the *Regierungsgebäude* (Government Building, 1951–52), opposite which is the rebuilt *Zeughaus* (Arsenal), now housing the *Cologne Municipal Museum* (material on the history of Cologne, large model of the city). At the end of Zeughausstrasse, to the left, is the *Roman Tower* (1st c. A.D.), a relic of the Roman town walls. – A little way N is *St Gereon's Church, the city's most unusual Romanesque church, with a long choir (11th c.) built on to a decagonal domed structure erected in Roman times and enlarged in 1227 (renovated and re-opened in 1979).

S of the Cathedral is the *Old Town Hall* (15th–16th c., rebuilt 1964–72: Hanseatic Chamber). Opposite it is the *New Town Hall* (1954–57), built on the remains of the Roman *praetorium* (museum). To the SW is the **Gürzenich**, Cologne's most important old secular building, erected in 1441–44 as a warehouse and banqueting hall (restored). Farther S is the *Church of St. Maria im Kapitol* (11th–13th c.); the nave (restored) contains two beautifully carved early medieval doors (1050–65); under the choir is a massive *crypt. E in Overstolzenhaus (Rheingasse) is the *Museum of Applied Art*.

Gürzenichstrasse runs W from the Heumarkt into the busy and elegant HOHE STRASSE, the city's principal shopping street (pedestrians only as far as Wallrafplatz). From here SCHILDERGASSE (also a pedestrian precinct) continues W to the NEUMARKT, in which stands the late Romanesque **Church of the Holy Apostles** (11th–13th c., restored). – A little way N is the new **Municipal Theatre**, in modern style (opera-house 1954–56, theatre 1959–62). – SE of the Neumarkt, in St Cecilia's Church, is the *Schnütgen Museum* (*collections of ecclesiastical art). $\frac{3}{4}$ km S of the square is *St Pantaleon's Church* (10th–17th c., restored), with the tomb of the Empress Theophano (d. 991), wife of Otto II.

Round the old town runs a semicircular circuit of "Ring" streets, laid out in front of the former town walls. Of the old fortified town gates there remain the *Eigelsteintorburg* in the N, the *Hahnentorburg* in the W and the *Severinstorburg* in the S. A short distance N of the Severinstor is the well-restored **Church of St Severinus** (11th–15th c.), with an interesting Roman and Frankish cemetery. In the nearby Ubierring is the *Rautenstrauch-Joest Museum* (ethnography). On the western edge of the town is the Museum of East Asian Art.

On the right bank of the Rhine is the district of DEUTZ, linked with the left bank by the *Severinsbrücke* (1959: a road bridge 691 m long), the *Deutzer Brücke* (1948: road bridge), the *Hohenzollernbrücke* opposite the Cathedral (railway and pedestrians) and the *Zoobrücke* (1966: road bridge), almost opposite which is the Rhine cableway. In Deutz are *trade fair and exhibition halls*, a *conference centre* and the beautiful *Rheinpark* ("Tanzbrunnen"; hot mineral baths; chair-lift; restaurant). – The district of MÜLHEIM, to the N, is reached by way of the *Mülheimer Brücke*, a suspension bridge with a span of 315 m, rebuilt 1949–51.

SURROUNDINGS of Cologne. – *Altenberg Cathedral (20 km NE), one of the finest examples of the early Gothic architecture of the Rhineland (1255–1379).

*Schloss Augustusburg, Brühl (15 km S). Built in the 18th c. as the residence of the Archbishop of Cologne, sumptuously decorated and furnished, this is one of the most charming palaces in the transitional style between late Baroque and Rococo (magnificent *staircase by Balthasar Neumann; large park).

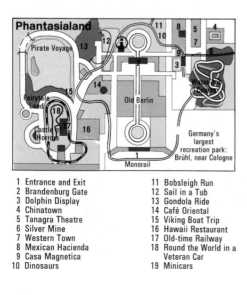

Germany's largest recreation park: Brühl, near Cologne

1 Entrance and Exit
2 Brandenburg Gate
3 Dolphin Display
4 Chinatown
5 Tanagra Theatre
6 Silver Mine
7 Western Town
8 Mexican Hacienda
9 Casa Magnetica
10 Dinosaurs
11 Bobsleigh Run
12 Sail in a Tub
13 Gondola Ride
14 Café Oriental
15 Viking Boat Trip
16 Hawaii Restaurant
17 Old-time Railway
18 Round the World in a Veteran Car
19 Minicars

Near Brühl is the * **Phantasialand Amusement Park**, the largest of the kind in Germany (28 hectares), with model buildings, boat trips, dolphin exhibition and numerous other attractions and entertainments.

Lake Constance (Bodensee)

Länder: Baden-Württemberg and Bavaria. Also bounded by Switzerland and Austria.

ⓘ **Fremdenverkehrsverband Bodensee-Oberschwaben und Internationaler Bodensee-Verkehrsverein,** Schützenstr. 8, D-7750 Konstanz; tel. (0 75 31) 2 22 32.

FACTS AND FIGURES. – Geographical **situation:** Konstanz lat. 47°30' N, 9°10' E, Bregenz lat. 47°30' N, long. 9°44' E.

Mean water level: 395 m.

Area: total 545 sq. km (Obersee and Überlingersee together 480 sq. km, Untersee 65 sq. km).

Greatest length: between Bregenz and Stein am Rhein 76 km (as the crow flies 69 km), between Bregenz and the mouth of the Stockacher Aach 63 km; longest direct line over water, from Hard to near the mouth of the Aach, 60 km.

Greatest width: between Kressbronn and Rohrschach 14·8 km.

Greatest depth: in Obersee (between Fischbach and Uttwil) 252 m, in Überlinger See 147 m, in Untersee 46 m.

Circumference (at half-tide level): total 263 km, of which 168 km (64%) are in Germany (150 km in Baden-Württemberg, 18 km in Bavaria), 69 km (26%) in Switzerland and 26 km (10%) in Austria.

Average **volume of water:** total 48,430 million cu. m (Obersee and Überlinger See together 47,600 million cu. m, Untersee 830 million cu. m).

Tides (at Konstanz tide-gauge): mean high water (end June/beginning July) 440 cm (highest recorded, beginning Sept. 1817, 623 cm); mean low water (end Feb.) 280 cm (lowest recorded this century, end March 1972, 237 cm).

Visibility from surface: annual average *c.* 7·50 m (in Jan. up to 12 m).

Colour of water: in Überlinger See and western Obersee blue-green, becoming increasingly yellowish towards the E as a result of the inflow of muddy water from the Rhine.

The NATIONAL FRONTIERS IN LAKE CONSTANCE between the three border states are largely undemarcated. Only the Untersee has a clearly established boundary line along the middle of the lake under a treaty of 1855 between the Grand Duchy of Baden and the Swiss canton of Thurgau. The Überlinger See, which is bounded on three sides by German territory, falls within the *Land* of Baden-Württemberg as far as a line from Meersburg to Eichhorn (Konstanz). In the Obersee the international boundary is fixed only for the small inlet at Konstanz, roughly along the middle of the Konstanzer Bucht, under an agreement between Baden and Switzerland. For the whole of the rest of the Obersee there is no international agreement defining national areas of sovereignty; but since the end of the First World War there has been fairly general tacit agreement about the frontier lines.

NAMES. – The natural name is the *Rhine Lake* (Rheinsee) – in Latin *Lacus Venetus* (Illyrian) or *Lacus Brigantinus* (in Celtic the "Lake of Bregenz"). In the early Middle Ages: Latin *Lacus Acronius* or *Lacus Moeslus*; in German "Kostnizer See" (=Konstanzer See). Since Carolingian times *Podmensee, Bodmensee, Bodamer See, Bodmer See* and other similar forms (after Bodman Palace). Latinised about 900 in St Gall as *Lacus Podamicus* or *Lacus Potamicus.* Wolfram von Eschenbach writes *Bodemsê* about 1200. The first known evidence for today's usual designation *Bodensee* is in a document of St Gall, dated 1438. Picturesque alternatives: *Swabian Sea* (Schwäbisches Meer, originally Frankish), common since the 16th c., *German Sea* (Teutsches Meer) in the 18th c. In other languages: English – *Lake Constance;* French – *Lac de Constance;* Italian – *Lago di Constanza* (similar names in the other Romance languages): Russian, however, *Bodenskoje Osero.*

*Lake Constance, lying under the northern edge of the Alps, is by far the largest lake in Germany, the third largest lake in Central Europe (after Lake Balaton in Hungary and Lake Geneva) and the second largest of the lakes bordering the Alps. From SE to NW it is divided into the Obersee, extending from Bregenz

Yacht harbour, Unteruhldingen, Lake Constance

Bay to Eichhorn (Konstanz), and the much narrower, shorter and shallower Überlinger See, between the Bodanrück and Linzgau, and the Untersee, separated from the main lake by a strip of land traversed by the Rhine at Konstanz. At its northern end the Untersee splits into the Gnadensee, between the island of Reichenau and the Bodanrück, and the Zeller See, between the Höri and Mettnau peninsulas in Radolfzell Bay.

In each of the three parts of the lake there is an island of some size. Near the E end of the Obersee is the island town of **Lindau**, at the S end of the Überlinger See the island of flowers, **Mainau**, and in the Untersee the vegetable-growing island of Reichenau with its historic and artistic treasures.

The lake offers scenery of striking beauty, with its majestic expanse of water and its fringe of old lakeside towns and attractive villages. Along the S side is an imposing backdrop of wooded hills and, farther away, the Appenzell Alps (Säntis, 2504 m); to the E, beyond the wide valley of the Rhine, the Vorarlberg Alps and above them Rätikon and Schesaplana (2964 m), and, farther E still, the Bregenz Forest (Pfänder, 1064 m) and the Allgäu Alps.

The Upper Swabian foreland to the N of the lake, with the Linzgau to the W, is an upland region with numerous rivers, rising to its highest point at 837 m – a region of scattered villages, woodland, fields and fruit-orchards.

The shores of the Obersee are mainly flat, with a number of large bays, particularly at the delta-mouths of the Rhine, Dornbirner Ach and Bregenzer Ach. The long-settled land round the western end of the lake, patterned by the Bodanrück, the Mettnau and Höri peninsulas and the fjord-like Überlinger See, continues westward without any interruption in the Hegau, which with its boldly shaped hills ranks among the most attractive volcanic landscapes in Germany.

The GEOLOGICAL ORIGIN of the Lake Constance basin can be traced to the mighty force of the Rhine glacier, which here has carved out a deep basin running from SE to NW – unlike the other glacial basins in the German Alpine foreland, which run from S to N. This unusual diagonal orientation is probably to be attributed to tectonic movements. Although the lake basin and the Hegau with its volcanic cones fall within the girdle of recent moraines, they have a distinctive landscape pattern of their own, mostly within the area of the most recent terminal moraines, with only some gently contoured drumlins (mounds of boulder clay aligned in the direction of the ice thrust). Evidence of the transformations wrought by glacial action is provided also by old melt-water channels, moraine lakes like the Mindelsee and the morainic spurs between the small plains at the mouths of the tributary rivers. The lake lies within the great trough of molasse between the Jura and the Alps, which come close to the shores of the lake in the E (Pfänder, 1064 m); to the N it is bounded by a Tertiary ridge, to the S by molasse hills.

Swiss geologists have recently established beyond reasonable doubt that a meteorite fell in this area, probably in the lake basin itself, some 15 million years ago. It is believed to have driven into the earth to a depth of some 2000 m – as is suggested by the fact that limestone fragments were hurled as far afield as the Sittertal, NW of St. Gallen. The fragments were first found in 1945, but their origin could not at first be explained.

Various areas on the shores of the lake, particularly at the mouths of the larger tributary rivers, have been declared landscape or nature reserves in order to maintain them in their relatively unspoiled condition. The most important *nature reserves* are the **Wollmatinger Ried**, where the Rhine flows from the main lake into the Untersee, the SE part of the *Mettnau* peninsula, various sections of the shores of the *Höri* peninsula, the *Mindelsee* and the marshland surrounding it, the mouth of the *Stockacher Aach*, the N shore of the *Bodanrück* round the Marienschlucht and a stretch between Litzelstetten and Wallhausen, the mouth of the *Seefelder Aach* between Seefelden and Unteruhldingen, and the *Eriskircher Ried* between Rohrspitz and Friedrichsspitz (mouth of the Old Rhine).

In these protected areas and in other remote stretches of the lake shores the banks of reeds and sedge provide quiet nesting-places for numerous BIRDS. The species to be found on Lake Constance include coots, ducks, swans, gulls, grey herons, cormorants, great crested grebes, little grebes, terns, red and black kites, curlews, lapwings, plovers, dunlins, reed warblers and great reed warblers.

The most important of the 30 or so species of FISH found in the lake are blue char (the fishermen's "bread-and-butter" catch, a gastronomic specialty), various kinds of whitefish, grayling (mainly in running water), perch, bream, pike (up to 1·40 m long and 20 kg in weight), zander, burbot (succulent liver), sea-trout (up to 15 kg), river-trout (occasionally at river-mouths), char (rare), carp, tench, barbel, gudgeon, sheatfish (up to 2 m long and 60 kg in weight; very rare in Lake Constance itself but found in the inland lakes like the Mindelsee), eel.

The TOURIST TRADE takes a prominent place among the service industries of Lake Constance, its volume having increased very considerably in recent decades. Its great assets are the agreeable climate, the varied natural beauties of the region and its many features of artistic and historical interest, all of which combine to attract crowds of visitors during the summer months, leading to heavy traffic on the roads during the height of the season.

Mainau, the island of flowers: view over the rose-garden towards Konstanz University

Recently, too, the area has become increasingly popular with weekend visitors.

The amount of **accommodation** available has increased considerably, and there are now some 25,000 beds in hotels, pensions, holiday chalets and private houses, together with numbers of camping sites, most of them beautifully situated and well equipped. In many places there are blocks of flats used as holiday or second homes.

Everywhere there are excellent **recreation and leisure facilities** and abundant scope for walking and hiking, sports and games, as well as for relaxing and health-giving holidays.

A particular attraction is the variety of facilities which the lake offers for **water sports**. In order to extend the bathing season a whole range of open-air pools with heating facilities, indoor pools and bathing lidos have been provided. The number of pleasure-boats – mainly sailing boats but also motor boats of ever greater power – is growing steadily, and the numbers of moorings available in the harbours are also increasing. New yacht harbours have been constructed, and others are on the way. The sport of *wind-surfing* which has been introduced into Europe in recent years is particularly popular on Lake Constance. There are also facilities for *water-skiing, diving* (decompression chamber in Überlingen) and *fishing*. For all these activities schools and hire firms are to be found everywhere.

There are numerous **historic buildings**, on which restoration has been carried out, and much excellent work has also been done in cleaning up and improving the towns and villages. The region offers examples of the creative artistic achievement of every period and style, and visitors interested in ART AND ARCHITECTURE may therefore find it helpful to have some notes about the outstanding sights:

The finest examples of **Romanesque** are to be found on the monastery island of Reichenau (Minster, Mittelzell; St George's, Oberzell; SS. Peter and Paul, Niederzell) and in Konstanz (Minster) and Lindau (St Peter's).
Gothic buildings, both religious and secular, are much more plentiful: Konstanz (St Stephen's, Mauritiusrotunde; Council Building); Meersburg (Grethgebäude); Überlingen (Minster); Linda (Diebsturm); Eriskirch (parish church); Radolfzell (Minster); Markdorf (St Nicholas's; Stadtschloss); Salem (monastic church); Ravensburg (St Jodok's; Town Hall, Weighhouse).
Impressive **Renaissance** buildings are the palaces of Heiligenberg and Wolfegg and the town halls of Lindau and Konstanz.

The **early Baroque** period is represented by the Altes Schloss in Meersburg, the palace church in Friedrichshafen and the Ritterschaftshaus in Radolfzell. The outstanding achievements of **High Baroque** and **Rococo** are Weingarten abbey church and the pilgrimage church at Birnau. Other examples are the Neues Schloss in Meersburg, the Imperial Hall in the former Salem monastery, the Neues Schloss in Tettnang, the old monastic church at Weissenau (near Ravensburg), the churches of St Martin at Langenargen and St Mary in Lindau, and the palace and palace church on the island of Mainau.

Modern architecture of the post-war period is well represented by the new university buildings in Konstanz.

BOAT SERVICES on Lake Constance run from mid April to mid October. (Passport or equivalent document required for visits to Switzerland or Austria.) The main routes are as follows (with numerous other intermediate calls, and additional services between some of the intermediate stations): Konstanz–(Mainau)–Meersburg–Friedrichshafen–Lindau–Bregenz; Konstanz–Meersburg–(Mainau)–Überlingen; Überlingen–Ludwigshafen–Bodman; Kreuzlingen–Konstanz–Reichenau–Radolfzell or Schaffhausen; Lindau–Bad Schachen–Wasserburg–Rorschach.

There are **ferry services** (passengers and cars) all year round between Friedrichshafen and Romanshorn and between Konstanz-Staad and Meersburg; the latter runs day and night. There are also local passenger ferries between Allensbach station and Reichenau (Mittelzell) and across the Rhine at Konstanz.

Excursions. – There are numerous excursions of various kinds from the larger towns on the lake during the summer (whole-day or half-day trips, shorter breakfast or coffee trips, evening dancing parties, mystery excursions, special trips for particular events).

Like all shipping on the lake, pleasure boats are subject to the Lake Constance shipping regulations, which every skipper must know.

Sailing on the lake is not for the novice. Although the wind usually blows steadily from either E or W, it is often gusty near the shore. Danger may arise from the storms which blow up suddenly, and attention should be paid to the storm warning lights on the shore.

For **fishing** in the lake or from the shore it is necessary to have both an annual fishing licence and a permit from the appropriate local authority: for information apply to any tourist office, local authority or angling club. Particularly good fishing grounds are Fussach Bay, the Rhine between the Obersee and Untersee and the whole of the Untersee. There is also fishing, subject to local regulations, in the waters round the lake.

Round Lake Constance on foot. – A signposted path (marked by a black arrow encircling a blue dot) runs right round the lake, at varying distances from the shore and varying heights, for a distance of 272 km. Within Germany it frequently coincides with the signposted paths (blue and yellow lozenge) of the Schwarzwaldverein; on the S side of the lake between Konstanz and Bregenz it follows the line of European Long-Distance Path No. 5 (Lake Constance to the Adriatic: white signposts).

Danube Valley

Länder: Baden-Württemberg and Bavaria.

ⓘ **Landesfremdenverkehrsverband Baden-Württemberg,**
Bussenstr. 23, D-7000 Stuttgart 1;
tel. (07 11) 48 10 45.
Fremdenverkehrsverband Allgäu/Bayerisch Schwaben,
Fuggerstr. 9, D-8900 Augsburg;
tel. (08 21) 3 33 35.
Fremdenverkehrsverband Ostbayern,
Landshuterstr 13, D-8400 Regensburg;
tel. (09 41) 5 71 86.

The **Danube, 2840 km long, is Europe's second largest river after the Volga.** Along its course runs an ancient traffic route, followed by the Nibelungs on their way to the court of King Etzel (Attila) and their own destruction. The Romans built forts and settlements on the banks, and in later centuries these were succeeded by monastic houses and princely residences. The present-day tourist can travel down the river in motor-ships from Regensburg to Passau (and on to the Black Sea if he desires), savouring its many attractions.

In the Schlosspark at **Donaueschingen** can be seen the so-called "source of the Danube". Here two little Black Forest rivers, the Brigach and the Breg, combine to form the Danube, the real source river being the Breg. A short distance downstream some of the water seeps away through the permeable limestone and re-emerges 12 km S as the source of the Aach. At *Kloster Beuron* (monastery founded in the 11th c. which fostered

The Donaudurchbruch at Weltenburg

Walhalla, Donaustauf

choral singing, science and the arts: fine Baroque church) the river breaks through the Swabian Alb in numerous bends – one of the first of the major beauty spots on its course.

At *Sigmaringen* the imposing castle of the Hohenzollerns rears above the river. Between Riedlingen and Ehingen can be seen the magnificent Baroque churches of *Zwiefalten* (by Johann Michael Fischer) and *Obermarchtal* (by Michael Thumb, with rich stucco work by Josef Schmuzer). Soon afterwards comes the old cathedral city of **Ulm**. At *Günzburg* is the splendid Frauenkirche (by Dominikus Zimmermann, 1736–41). *Neuburg an der Donau* is a trim little princely capital, set above the river on a high Jurassic crag. **Ingolstadt**, a former residence of the Dukes of Bavaria and university city, is now also a considerable industrial town.

Another scenic high point is at Weltenburg, where the Danube breaks through the Jurassic limestone between steep and bizarrely fashioned rock faces: this is the famous *Donaudurchbruch*. *Weltenburg* has a monastic church built by Cosmas Damian Asam, one of the great masters of the South German Baroque (1717–21). At Kelheim can be seen the *Befreiungshalle* (Hall of Liberation), a circular structure built by King Ludwig I of Bavaria in 1842–63 to commemorate the Wars of Liberation of 1813–15.

At the cathedral city of **Regensburg**, the Roman Castra Regina, the Danube reaches the most northerly point in its course. At Donaustauf is the *Walhalla*, a marble temple modelled on the Par-

thenon, built by Ludwig I in 1830–42 as a German "Temple of Fame".

The river now traverses, with numerous windings, the depression on the S side of the Bavarian Forest. **Straubing** preserves the memory of Agnes Bernauer, daughter of an Augsburg barber, who became the wife of Duke Albrecht II of Bavaria: whereupon his enraged father had her accused of witchcraft and drowned in the Danube.

Metten and *Niederalteich*, near Deggendorf, are old and famous Benedictine abbeys with fine Baroque churches. At the old episcopal city of **Passau** – which Alexander von Humboldt included among the world's seven most beautiful towns – the Inn and the Ilz flow into the Danube, which just E of the town leaves German territory to enter Austria.

Darmstadt

Land: Hesse. – Vehicle registration: DA.
Altitude: 146 m. – Population: 138,000.
Post code: D-6100. – Dialling code: 0 61 51.
ⓘ **Städtisches Verkehrsamt,**
Luisenplatz 5;
tel. 13 20 71.
Tourist-Information, Main Station;
tel. 13 27 82.

HOTELS. – *Maritim*, Rheinstr. 105, 624 b., SB, sauna, solarium; *Weinmichel*, Schleiermacherstr. 10, 100 b. (wine bar); *Prinz Heinrich*, Bleichstr. 48, 85 b.; *Mathildenhöhe* (no rest.), Spessartring 53, 50 b.; *City Hotel* (no rest.), Adelungstr. 44, 73 b.; *Bockshaut*, Kirchstr. 7, 49 b.; *Zum Rosengarten*, Frankfurter Str. 79, 36 b.; *Ernst Ludwig* (no rest.), Ernst Ludwig Str. 14, 30 b. – IN EBERSTADT: *Schweizerhaus*, Mühltalstr. 35, 25 b. – IN KRANICHSTEIN: *Jagdschloss Kranichstein*, 22 b. – YOUTH HOSTEL: Landgraf-Georg-Str. 119.

RESTAURANTS. – *Ratskeller*, Marktplatz 8; *Rustica*, at Main Station; *Datterich-Klause*, Steinackerstr. 2; *Da Marino*, Heinrichstr. 39 (Italian); *Alexis Sorbas*, Adelungstr. 10 (Greek); *China-Restaurant*, Mühlstr. 60.

CAFÉS. – *Bormuth*, Marktplatz 5; *Mathildenhöhe*, in Exhibition Building.

The former capital of the Grand Duchy of Hesse lies on the edge of the Upper Rhine plain amid the foothills of the Odenwald. Here the Bergstrasse comes to an end. In Darmstadt are a Technical University, the organisation for mathematics and data processing, the European operations centre for space research, and the organisation

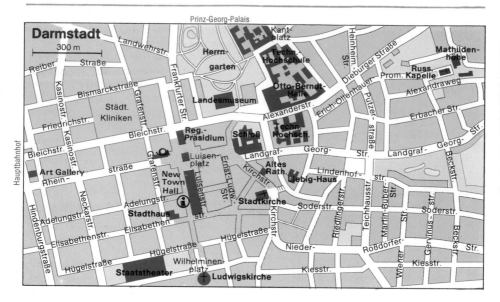

for research into heavy ions, but it is also the headquarters of the German Academy of Language and Writing and the German PEN centre. It is the economic and communications centre of southern Hesse, with considerable chemical and electronics industries.

HISTORY. – In the Middle Ages Darmstadt was the residence of the Counts of Katzenelnbogen. In 1330 it was granted the right to erect fortifications and hold markets. In 1479 it passed to Hesse along with the county of Katzenelnbogen. 1597 saw the establishment of the Landgraviate of Hesse-Darmstadt, which became a Grand Duchy at the end of the 18th c. Under Grand Duke Ludwig I (1790–1830) the town enjoyed a great cultural flowering and the Grand Duchy gained a considerable accession of territory. In 1899 Grand Duke Ernst Ludwig established the artists' colony of Mathildenhöhe. In 1918 the Grand Duchy came to an end. In 1949 Darmstadt became the seat of the German Academy of Language and Writing.

SIGHTS. – The central point of the town is the **Luisenplatz**, with the 33 m high *Ludwig Column*, crowned by a bronze figure of Grand Duke Ludwig I (by Schwanthaler, 1844). On the N side of the square is the former *Kollegiengebäude* (1780), now the *Regierungspräsidium* (district administrative offices). – To the W, in Steubenplatz, is the *Kunsthalle* (1957: temporary exhibitions). – To the S, in Wilhelminenplatz, is the neo-classical *St Ludwig's Church*, modelled on the Pantheon in Rome. – E of Luisenplatz is the **Schloss**, an extensive range of buildings dating from the 16th, 18th and 19th c.; in it are the *Provincial and University Library* and the *Schlossmuseum*.

S of the Schloss are the *White Tower*, a relic of the town's medieval fortifications, the rebuilt *Old Town Hall* (Renaissance, with a staircase tower in front) and the *Town Church* (15th–18th c.: burial vault with tombs of Landgraves of Hesse).

N of the Schloss, in Friedensplatz, is the *Provincial Museum (Landesmuseum)*, with a picture gallery, collections of sculpture and graphic art, a section of applied art and a rich collection of "Jugendstil" art. Behind the Museum, to the N, is the *Herrngarten*, with the burial mound of the "great Landgravine" Henriette Caroline (1721–74). On the E side of the garden is the *Technical University*, on the N side the *Prinz-Georg-Palais* (17th c.), with a valuable collection of porcelain and a Rococo garden.

In the E of the town is the *Mathildenhöhe*, on which Grand Duke Ernst Ludwig established the "artists' colony" in 1899 (Jugendstil houses with studios). In the middle are the *Exhibition Building* (temporary art exhibitions) and the 48 m high *Marriage Tower* (view). Nearby are the *Russian Chapel* and the *Ernst-Ludwig-Haus* (German Academy of Language and Writing).

SURROUNDINGS. – **Jagdschloss Kranichstein** (5 km NE), an impressive Renaissance building with an interesting Hunting Museum. – **Melibokus** (25 km S), a hill 515 m high with fine *views.

Detmold

Land: North Rhineland-Westphalia.
Vehicle registration: DT.
Altitude: 134 m. – Population: 69,000.
Post code: D-4930. – Dialling code: 0 52 31.
ⓘ Städtisches Verkehrsamt,
Rathaus, Lange Strasse;
tel. 7 73 27/8.

HOTELS. – *Detmolder Hof*, Lange Str. 19, 35 b.; *Lippischer Hof*, Hornsche Str. 1, 36 b.; *Gästehaus Am Wall* (no rest.), Wall 8, 20 b., sauna. – IN BERLEBECK: *Kanne*, Paderborner Str. 155, 45 b. – IN HEILIGEN-KIRCHEN: *Friedrichshöhe*, Paderborner Str. 6, 27 b. – IN HIDDESEN: *Römerhof*, Maiweg 37, 40 b.; *Hiddeser Hof*, Friedrick Ebert Str. 86, 30 b. – IN PIVITSHEIDE: *Forellenhof*, Gebr. Meyer Str. 50, 14 b. – IN SCHÖNE-MARK: *Berghof Stork*, Leistruper Wald Str. 100, 12 b. – YOUTH HOSTEL: Schirrmannstr. 49, Detmold Hiddesen, 112 b. – CAMPING SITES: Three sites in Pivitsheide.

RESTAURANTS. – *Alte Muhle*, Allee 32; *Alte Kogge*, Krumme Str. 44; *Schlosswache*, Lange Str. 58.

CAFÉS. – *Wortmann*, Lange Str. 33; *Elbing*, Allee 4; *Grabbe Café*, Unter der Wehme 7.

The old residence and garrison town of the former principality of Lippe-Detmold lies in the valley of the Werre on the northern slopes of the Teutoburg Forest. The picturesque old town still preserves many 16th and 17th c. half-timbered houses.

Residenzschloss, Detmold

Detmold is the chief town of an administrative region (Bezirk), with the North-West German Academy of Music. It is a convenient place from which to visit the Hermannsdenkmal and the Externsteine, a busy tourist centre.

HISTORY. – First recorded in 783 as *Theotmalli*, the scene of a victory by Charlemagne over the Saxons, Detmold received its municipal charter from the Lippe family in the 13th c. There was a castle here in the 14th c., destroyed in 1447. From 1501 to 1918 (with a brief interruption from 1585 to 1613, when Simon VI resided in Schloss Braken near Lemgo), Detmold was the residence of a branch of the House of Lippe.

SIGHTS. – The central feature of the OLD TOWN is the MARKT, with the neo-classical *Town Hall* (1830), the 16th c. *Church of the Redeemer* (Reformed: organ of 1795) and the *Donop Fountain*. To the N is the *Hofgarten* (entrance in Lange Str.), with the **Schloss**, a palace in the style of the Weser Renaissance with four wings, built 1548–57 by Jörg Unkair and Cord Tönnis (round tower of 1470; splendid interior, with valuable Gobelin tapestries and porcelain). Farther N is the *Provincial Theatre* (1914–18). NW of the Hofgarten, on the Ameide, is the **Lippe Provincial Museum** (natural history, ethnography, local material). – W of the Markt, at Unter der Wehme 5, is the birthplace of the poet *Ferdinand Freiligrath* (1810–76). At No. 7 is the house in which the dramatist *Christian Dietrich Grabbe* (1801–36) died.

On the S side of the town, in the beautiful ALLEE, is the *Neues Palais* (1708–18), now occupied by the North-West German Academy of Music, behind which is the beautiful *Palaisgarten*. $\frac{1}{2}$ km S is the ***Westphalian Open-Air Museum**, covering an area of 80 hectares on the Königsberg, with groups of houses from different parts of Westphalia.

SURROUNDINGS. – *Bird park* in the district of Heiligenkirchen (4 km S), with 320 different species. – *Eagle Observatory* in the district of Berlebeck (5 km S), with over 80 birds of prey from many different regions. – ***Hermannsdenkmal** (Hermann's Memorial, 8 km SW), on the 386 m high Grotenburg, erected 1838–75 by Ernst von Bandel to commemorate the battle in the Teutoburg Forest in A.D. 9 in which the Cheruscan chieftain Hermann (Arminius) inflicted a crushing defeat on the Roman army. (Photograph, p. 242) – ***Externsteine** (12 km SE), a group of fissured sandstone rocks, the highest rising to 37·5 m, originally a pagan shrine and later a Christian place of pilgrimage (monumental stone carving, *Descent from the Cross, of *c.* 1120).

Deutsche Weinstrasse ("German Wine Highway")

Land: Rhineland-Palatinate.

(i) Aussenstelle des Fremdenverkehrsverbandes Rheinland-Pfalz, Hindenburgstr. 12, D-6730 Neustadt an der Weinstrasse; tel. (0 63 21) 24 66.

The 83 km long * Deutsche Weinstrasse runs along the E side of the Palatinate Forest (Haardtgebirge) with its many old castles, through one of the largest continuous wine-producing regions in Germany (some 21,000 hectares). It begins at Bockenheim and ends at the Weintor ("Wine Gate") at Schweigen.

Grapes were already cultivated here in Roman times, and in the reign of Charlemagne the Rhineland Palatinate was an important supplier of wine for the Emperor's table and for his coronation. In addition to grapes the mild climate favours the cultivation of peaches, apricots, almonds, figs, sweet chestnuts and lemons. Visitors will find an abundance of hospitable inns and wine-bars, in which the wine is accompanied by the onion pasties of the Palatinate or by "white cheese". Nuts and chestnuts are eaten with the young wine. Another speciality of the Palatinate is Saumagen mit Weinkraut (hog's paunch with cabbage cooked in wine), which is washed down with a glass of fragrant riesling.

The road runs through a long succession of wine towns and villages – Bockenheim at the N end of the Weinstrasse, then Grünstadt, Kallstadt and Bad Dürkheim, whose Wurstmarkt ("Sausage Market") in September is Germany's biggest wine festival. Then come Deidesheim (with the oldest inn in the Palatinate, the "Kanne"), Wachenheim and Gimmeldingen – all familiar names to the connoisseur of wine. Neustadt an der Weinstrasse, dominated by the two towers of its church, is the centre of the Palatinate wine trade. In the nearby Schloss Hambach a great demonstration calling for the unity of Germany was held in 1832.

At Maikammer begins the southern section of the Weinstrasse, the chief town of which is the garden city of Landau. Other places on the route are Edenkoben, Rhodt, Burrweiler and Siebeldingen. The road now runs past increasing numbers of castles, including the famous Hohenstaufen stronghold of Trifels – where the

Imperial regalia were kept and Richard Cœur de Lion was imprisoned – looming above the little town of Annweiler, a few kilometres off the road. Bergzabern is a well-known health resort (Kneipp cure). Schweigen, at the end of the Weinstrasse, lies close to the frontier with Alsace. Here there is an interesting "wine trail" demonstrating the different kinds of grapes grown in the Palatinate.

Dinkelsbühl

Land: Bavaria. – Vehicle registration: AN (DKB).
Altitude: 444 m. – Population: 11,000.
Post code: D-8804. – Dialling code: 0 98 51.

(i) Verkehrsamt, Marktplatz; tel. 30 13.

HOTELS. – Eisenkrug, Dr-Martin-Luther-Str. 1, 20 b.; Deutsches Haus, Weinmarkt 3, 23 b., old-style German restaurant; Goldene Rose, Marktplatz 4, 36 b.; Hecht, Schweinemarkt 1, 64 b. – YOUTH HOSTEL: Koppenstr. 10, 150 b. – CAMPING SITE: DCC-Campingpark Romantische Strasse, Durrwanger Str.

CAFÉS. – Bayer, Weinmarkt 10; Rohe, Segringer Str. 48. Lechler, Nördlinger Str. 17.

EVENTS. – Kinderzeche, a traditional festival with pageant play and parade (July) commemorating the occasion during the Thirty Years War when the children of the town saved it from being plundered by the Swedes.

Deutsches Haus, Dinkelsbühl

With its walls and towers of the 13th to 16th c., its moat and its gabled houses, this old Franconian Imperial city is a gem of medieval architecture. The Dinkelsbühl Boys' Choir, dressed in Rococo uniform, is widely famed. The "Romantic Road" links Dinkelsbühl with Rothenburg and Nördlingen.

HISTORY. – The origins of Dinkelsbühl reach back into the 7th c. It was defended by ramparts and a moat from an early period; the present walls, still completely intact, date from the 14th–15th c. The town's great period of prosperity began when it became directly subject to the Emperor towards the end of the 13th c. Since 1806 it has been in Bavaria.

SIGHTS. – In the MARKTPLATZ stands the late Gothic *St George's Church (1448–99: R.C.), one of the finest hall-churches in Germany, with a notable interior (Crucifixion, school of Hans Pleydenwurff, on high altar; tabernacle of 1480). – In the WEINMARKT, which adjoins the Marktplatz to the N, is the *Deutsches Haus, a beautiful half-timbered building of the 16th c. To the right is the Kornschranne, in which the pageant play "Die Kinderzeche" is performed every year. – SEGRINGER STRASSE, running W from the Marktplatz, is particularly charming, with its continuous range of old gabled houses. – S of the Marktplatz is the Deutschordenshaus (House of the Teutonic Order: 1761–64), with a fine chapel. – The town has four gates – the Rothenburg Gate in the N, the Nördlingen Gate in the S, the Segringen Gate in the W and the Wörnitz Gate in the E. There is a fascinating walk round the old town walls (1 hour).

SURROUNDINGS. – Feuchtwangen (12 km N), with a former collegiate church (12th–13th c.) and an interesting Heimatmuseum (including craftsmen's workshops). – Ellwangen (22 km SW), with a former collegiate church (13th c.), the palace of the Prince-Provosts (17th and 18th c.: museum) and the pilgrimage church of St Mary (17th c.) on the Schönenberg (522 m).

Donaueschingen

Land: Baden-Württemberg.
Vehicle registration: VS (DS).
Altitude: 675 m. – Population: 18,000.
Post code: D-7710. – Dialling code: 07 71.
ⓘ Städtisches Verkehrsamt, Karlstr. 41;
tel. 38 34.

HOTELS. – *Oschberghof, near golf-course, 90 b., SB, sauna, solarium, golf; Linde, Karlstr. 18, 35 b.; Zur Sonne, Karlstr. 38, 35 b.

RESTAURANTS. – Parkrestaurant, Parkanlage 8; Donau-Stuben (Donauhalle), Marktstr. 2; Fürstenberg-Bräustüble, Postplatz 1.

RECREATION. – Golf (18 holes); swimming pool in park.

EVENTS. – International Riding Championship (Sept.); International Donaueschingen music festival (Oct.).

The town of Donaueschingen lies on the eastern edge of the Black Forest on the River Brigach, which along with the "Source of the Danube" in the Schlosspark and the Breg which joins it below the town forms the Danube. From 1723 it was the seat of the Princes of Fürstenberg, whose territory passed to Baden and Württemberg in 1806.

SIGHTS. – On the E side of the town is the Schloss (rebuilt 1772 and 1893: open to visitors in summer). Facing it, to the W, is the Town Church (1724–47: R.C.). A short distance SE, in the park, is the so-called Source of the Danube ("To the sea, 2840 km").

To the N, above the Schloss, is the Karlsbau, with the Fürstenberg Collections (notable in particular for its fine *paintings of the Swabian and Franconian schools of the 15th and 16th c.).

In Haldenstrasse is the *Court Library, with many old German manuscripts, including Codex C of the "Nibelungenlied" (c. 1200: kept under lock and key).

SURROUNDINGS. – Entenburg (at Pfohren, 5 km SE). – *Wutach Gorge (15 km SW).

Dortmund

Land: North Rhineland-Westphalia.
Vehicle registration: DO.
Altitude: 86 m. – Population: 617,000.
Post code: D-4600. – Dialling code: 02 31.
ⓘ Verkehrspavillon,
Königswall 18;
tel. 14 03 41.

HOTELS. – *Römischer Kaiser, Olpe 2, 186 b.; *Drees, Hohe Str. 107, 150 b., SB, sauna, solarium; *Parkhotel Westfalenhalle, Strobelallee 41, 107 b., SB, sauna, solarium; Gildenhof, Hohe Str. 139, 80 b.; Drei Kronen, Münsterstr. 70, 76 b., sauna; Consul (no rest.), Hohe Str. 117, 60 b., SB, sauna, solarium; Stadthotel (no rest.), Reinoldistr. 14, 35 b.; Merkur (no rest.), Milchgasse 5, 30 b.; Atlanta (no rest.), Ostenhelweg 51, 27 b.; Union (no rest.), Arndtstr. 66, 40 b. – IN BRÜNNINGHAUSEN: Rombergpark, Am

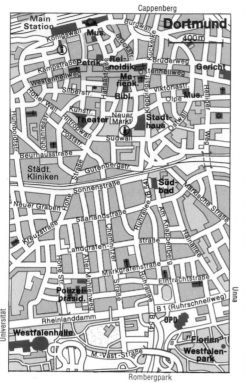

Rombergpark, 40 b. – IN KIRCHHÖRDE: *Haus Mentler*, Schneiderstr. 1 25 b. – IN SYBURG: *Landhaus Syburg*, Westhofener Str. 1, 37 b. – YOUTH HOSTEL: Richard-Schirrmann-Weg 1, Dortmund-Höchsten. – CAMPING SITE: Dortmund-Hohensyburg.

RESTAURANTS. – *Pfefferkorn*, Hoher Wall 38; *Krone*, Markt 10; *Mövenpick*, Kleppingstr. 9; *Kiepenkerl*, Markt 6; *Hövelpforte*, Hoher Wall 5; *Reinoldi*, Reinoldistr. 7; *Churrasco*, Westenhellweg 51 (Argentinian steak-house); *Turmrestaurant* (alt. 138 m), in Westfalenpark.

CAFÉS. – *Bristol*, Betenstr. 18; *Knüppel*, Ostenhellweg 62; *Orchidee*, in Rombergpark. – Bars and night-clubs.

EVENTS. – *Riding and Jumping Tournament*, in Westfalenhalle (March); *May Concerts*, in Alter Markt; *Amateur Theatre*, in Syburg open-air theatre (July–Aug.); *Six Day Race*, in Westfalenhalle (end Oct.); *Christmas Market*, in Alter Markt.

Dortmund, the largest city in Westphalia, lies on the eastern edge of the Ruhr, in the fertile Hellweg area traversed by the upper Emscher. The foundations of its economy are iron and steel working and engineering, but in addition it has huge breweries whose annual outputs puts even Munich in the shade. It is also a city of science and the arts, with its University, Max Planck Institute, Municipal Theatre and Museum, and a great sporting centre, with a total of almost 100 sports installations,

including the Westfalenhalle, Westfalenstadion and "Rote Erde" track. The pedestrian precinct in Westen- and Ostenhellweg is a popular shopping centre. In the N the city boundaries reach almost to the River Lippe; in the S, taking in an area which includes such attractive open spaces as the Westfalenpark and Rombergpark, they extend to the beautiful Hengsteysee at the foot of the Hohensyburg. Dortmund's harbour, one of the largest inland harbours in the Federal Republic, is linked with the Ems by the Dortmund-Ems Canal and with the Rhine by the Emscher and the Lippe Branch Canal.

HISTORY. – First recorded around 880 as *Throtmanni*, Dortmund grew out of a Carolingian royal fortress established to protect the Hellweg, an ancient trading route between the Rhine and the Weser. Between the 10th and 13th c. several Imperial diets and Church assemblies were held here. In 1220 it became a free Imperial city, and later a member of the Hanse. Around 1240 it was encircled by powerful fortifications, strong enough to withstand a 21-month siege by the Archbishop of Cologne in 1388–90. The town throve on its long-distance trade, but the prosperity of its citizens, then numbering some 8000, was destroyed by the Thirty Years War. When it passed to Prussia in 1815 the population was only 4000. From the middle of the 19th c. Dortmund developed into a city of heavy industry and mining and as a brewing centre. In the Second World War the old town was completely destroyed. Since then Dortmund has taken on a modern aspect, and as host to the Federal Garden Show in 1959 and 1969 has become known as a garden city; about half the area of the town consists of parks, woodland and gardens.

SIGHTS. – The OLD TOWN, now almost completely rebuilt, is enclosed within the circuit of the old town walls, now marked by a ring of "Wallstrassen". Its central feature is the ALTER MARKT, with the *Municipal and Provincial Library* (1957). – NE of the Markt is **St Reinhold's Church** (Evang.), one of the finest buildings in Westphalia (13th c.; late Gothic choir of the 15th c.); its 104 m high tower, with the heaviest peal of bells in Westphalia, is the emblem of the city. Opposite it is **St Mary's Church** (12th and 14th c.: Evang.), whose greatest treasure is an *Altar of the Virgin by the Dortmund master Konrad of Soest. – The WESTENHELLWEG and OSTENHELLWEG, which begin here, are the city's principal shopping streets (pedestrian precinct). – N of the Westenhellweg is **St Peter's Church** (14th–15th c.), with a beautiful carved *altar from Antwerp (*c.* 1521: 633 gilded figures). – S of the Westenhellweg is the *Propsteikirche* (14th c.; 15th c. high altar). Farther SW in the Hiltropwall, is the **Municipal Theatre** built 1958–66 (three main houses, with facilities for opera, operettas, drama and concerts). In the nearby Hansastrasse is the *Museum of the History of Art and Culture* (history of Dortmund). – In the Ostwall is the interesting **Museum am Ostwall** (20th c. art). In Münsterstrasse N of the city centre stands the *Museum of Natural Science*.

To the NW of the city are the harbour installations of the *Dortmund-Ems Canal* (272 km long). To the NE is the "Tropa Mare" all-weather recreation centre. – To the SW is a site with the Westfalenhalle (seating for 23,000, 5 satellite halls), a combined roller- and ice-skating stadium, the "Rote Erde" running-track and the *Westfalenstadion* (seating for 54,000). 3 km SW is the *University*, founded 1968. – In the S of the city is the WESTFALEN-PARK (70 hectares), where the Federal Garden Show was held in 1959 and 1969, with the 212 m high *Television Tower* known as "Florian" (revolving restaurant at 138 m) and the *German Rosarium*. Farther S is the ROMBERGPARK, with the *Botanic Garden* (tropical houses, arboretum) and the *Animal Park*.

SURROUNDINGS. – **Hohensyburg** (12 km S), above the 4 km long Hengsteysee (an artificial lake on the River Ruhr), with the Emperor William Memorial and the Vincke Tower (panoramic views). – **Cappenberg** (18 km NE), with a castle (occupied by the statesman Freiherr vom und zum Stein in his last years, and now the Freiherr vom Stein Archives) and a former collegiate church (12th and 14th c.; richly carved 16th c. choir-stalls; treasury, with a famous *reliquary in the form of a head of the Emperor Frederick Barbarossa, presented by the Emperor to his godfather Otto von Cappenberg c. 1165).

Duderstadt

Land: Lower Saxony.
Vehicle registration: GÖ (DUD).
Altitude: 175 m. – Population: 24,000.
Post code: D-3428. – Dialling code: 0 55 27.
ⓘ **Verkehrsbüro,** Rathaus;
tel. 8 15 10.

HOTELS: – *Zum Löwen,* Marktstr. 30, 60 b.; *Deutsches Haus,* Hinterstr. 29, 45 b.; *Kurmainzer Eck,* Am Sulberg 2, 24 b.

This medieval town of half-timbered houses in the Eichsfeld, SW of the

Harz, is huddled within a 3 km circuit of ramparts. Lying on the frontier with the German Democratic Republic, it is on two tourist routes – the Alps-Baltic Holiday Highway and the Harz-Heathland Highway.

HISTORY. – Duderstadt, lying at the meeting-place of important medieval traffic routes, is first recorded in 929. It became a town in the 13th c., and in 1334 was pledged by Duke Henry of Braunschweig-Grubenhagen to the Electorate of Mainz. Until 1802 it was a town within the principality of Eichsfeld, a territory belonging to Mainz. Thereafter it passed to Prussia, in 1816 to Hanover, in 1866 again to Prussia and in 1946 to Lower Saxony.

SIGHTS. – The central point of the town is the OBERMARKT, with the **Town Hall** (13th–16th c.: carillon), a handsome half-timbered building with three small towers and a two-tier sandstone arcade, and the Oberkirche or *Propsteikirche* of St Cyriacus (14th–16th c.: R.C.). Behind the Oberkirche stands *the Local Museum of the Eichsfeld.* In the Untermarkt is the Unterkirche or *parish church of St Servatius* (15th–16th c.: Evang.). In the MARKTSTRASSE are a number of notable *half-timbered houses* (in particular No. 20, of 1698, and No. 91, of 1752). – N of the Untermarkt is the *Westerturm,* the only surviving town gate; in front of it is a sandstone Madonna of 1752. A walk round the medieval ramparts is very much to be recommended (1 hour).

SURROUNDINGS. – Rhumesprung (15 km NE), the source of the River Rhume, is in a basin some 25 m across; NW lies the Seeburger See, a natural lake with an area of 1 sq. km.

Duisburg

Land: North Rhineland-Westphalia.
Vehicle registration: DU.
Altitude: 34 m. – Population: 570,000.
Post code: D-4100. – Dialling code: 02 03.
ⓘ **Stadtinformation,** Königstr. 53;
tel. 2 83 21 89.

HOTELS. – **Steigenberger Hotel Duisburger Hof,* Am König Heinrich Platz, 154 b.; *Plaza* (no rest.), Dellplatz 1, 95 b., SB, sauna; *Stadt Duisburg,* Düsseldorfer Str. 122, 60 b., sauna; *Haus Friedrichs,* Neudorfer Str. 35, 46 b.; *Haus Reinhard* (no rest.), Fuldastr. 31, 32 b., sauna; IN BUCHHOLZ: *Sittardsberg,* Sittardsberger Allee 10, 47 b. – IN HOMBERG: *Rheingarten,* Königstrasse 78, 52 b. – IN HUCKINGEN: *Haus Angerhof,* Düsseldorfer Landstr. 431, 16 b. – YOUTH HOSTELS: Kalkweg 148E, Duisburg-Wedau, 136 b.; Rheinanlagen 12, Duisburg-Homberg, 42 b.
RESTAURANTS. – *Mercatorhalle,* König-Heinrich-Platz; *La Provence,* Hohe Str. 29. – IN KAISERBERG:

Duisburg port from the air

Dante, Mülheimer Str. 213 (Italian); *Wilhelmshöhe*, at Botanic Garden; *Zoo-Terrassen*, Mülheimer Str. 277. – IN RAHM: *Hans Kornwebel*, Am Rahmer Bach 88. – IN RUMELN-KALDENHAUSEN: *Kuckeshof*, Düsseldorfer Str. 109.

CAFÉS. – *Dobbelstein*, Sonnenwall 8; *Heinemann*, Sonnenwall 5; *Kö-Café*, Königstr.

EVENTS. – *Carnival*, with Rose Monday parade; *Duisburger Akzente* (May); great firework display, "The Lower Rhine in Flames" (every four years in September); Film Weeks (November); rowing regattas in Duisburg-Wedau.

This industrial and commercial city on the western edge of the Ruhr, at the confluence of the River Ruhr with the Rhine, can claim two superlatives to its credit: it takes first place in Germany in the production of steel, and its harbour on the Ruhr is the largest island port in the world (area 918·6 hectares, 20 harbour basins, annual turnover 60 million tons). It was a university town in the Middle Ages, and it now has a Gesamthochschule (comprehensive higher educational establishment). The performances of the opera company it shares with Düsseldorf, the "Oper am Rhein", have an international reputation. The excellent regatta course in the Wedau sports park has made Duisburg a favoured choice for international rowing regattas. The famous cartographer Gerhard Mercator (1512–94) lived and taught in Duisburg.

HISTORY. – In Frankish times a trading and warehouse centre for the Rhine shipping trade grew up at the beginning of the Hellweg, the old traffic route between the Rhine and the Weser; and to protect it the Carolingian royal fortress of *Duisburch* was built in the 8th c. The settlement which grew up round the castle was enclosed within walls (on the line marked by the modern "Wallstrassen") around 1100. In the Staufen period Duisburg became an Imperial city and a member of the Hanse. An alteration in the course of the Rhine in the 13th c. put an end to a period of high prosperity. In 1290 the town was pledged to the Counts of Kleve, and in 1614 it passed to Brandenburg along with the county of Kleve. The

university founded by the Great Elector in 1655 was moved to Bonn in 1818. It was not until 1831 that Duisburg re-established a link with the Rhine through the construction of its outer harbour. In the latter part of the 19th c. mining and ironworking became established as major industries.

SIGHTS. – In the Burgplatz is the *Town Hall* (1897–1902: Mercator Room). In the *Salvatorkirche*, N of the Town Hall, can be seen Mercator's epitaph. – In KÖNIGSTRASSE (pedestrian precinct), the town's principal street, is König-Heinrich-Platz, with the *Municipal Theatre* and the **Mercatorhalle** (1962: an all-purpose hall for concerts, congresses, sporting events, performances of various kinds, exhibitions, etc.). – In Düsseldorfer Strasse, which runs S off Königstrasse, is the *Wilhelm Lehmbruck Museum (1964); 20th c. painting and sculpture (many works by the Duisburg-born sculptor Wilhelm Lehmbruck, 1881–1919). E of this, in Friedrich-Wilhelm-Strasse, is the *Lower Rhineland Museum* (history of the town, collection of maps). – On the Kaiserberg is the *Zoo, with spacious open enclosures, a large monkey-house, an *Aquarium* (the "House of a Thousand Fishes"), a *Dolphinarium* and a "Walarium" (with some European white whales; fresh-water dolphins).

The *Schwanentorbrücke* NW of the Town Hall, a bascule bridge, links the town centre with the northern district of RUHR-ORT, which has grown in size and importance through ironworking and the shipment of Ruhr coal. Its extensive *port installations* (918·6 hectares) include 20 harbour basins. At the "Harbour Mouth" the *Museum der Deutschen Binnenschiffahrt* (inland shipping) with the museum ship "Oscar Huber". The 1824 m long *Berliner Brücke* carries the North–South Highway over the River Ruhr and the Rhine-Herne Canal, linking the town centre with the district of MEIDERICH. – In the district of HAMBORN, farther N, are the large steelworks (Thyssen AG, etc.). From the Altmarkt, Alleestrasse runs SW to the former *abbey church* of a Premonstratensian abbey dissolved in 1805 but now again a convent of the order.

In the S of the city is the *Wedau Sports Park*, with a sports training school, a regatta course, a swimming stadium, an ice-rink and a football stadium. A popular recreation area is the *Sechs-Seen-Platte*, with facilities for sailing and swimming.

SURROUNDINGS. – **Moers** (12 km W), with a castle (15th–16th c.: Heimatmuseum).

Düsseldorf

Land: North Rhineland-Westphalia.
Vehicle registration: D.
Altitude: 38 m. – Population: 590,000.
Post code: D-4000. – Dialling code: 02 11
ⓘ **Verkehrsverein**, Konrad-Adenauer-Platz 12;
tel. 35 05 05.

HOTELS. – *Hilton*, Georg Glock Str. 20, 612 b., SB,
sauna, solarium; *Breidenbacher Hof*, Heinrich Heine
Allee 36, 220 b., *Nikko*, Immermannstr. 41, 600 b.,
SB, sauna, solarium; *Inter Continental*, Karl Arnold
Platz, 580 b., SP, sauna, solarium, golf; *Steigen-
berger Parkhotel*, Corneliusplatz 1, 230 b.; *Holiday
Inn*, Graf Adolf Platz 10, 204 b., SB, sauna; *Savoy*,
Oststr 128, 180 b.; Esplanade, Fürstenplatz 17, 110 b.,
SB, sauna, solarium; *Uebachs*, Leopoldstr. 3, 110 b.;
Excelsior (no rest.), Kapellstr. 1, 100 b.; *Börsenhotel*
(no rest.), Kreuzstr. 19a, 102 b.; *Graf Adolf* (no rest.),
Stresemannplatz 1, 130 b.
IN MÖRSENBROICH: *Ramada Renaissance*, Nördlicher
Zubringer 6, 389 b., SB, sauna, solarium. – IN BENRATH:
Rheinterrasse Benrath, Benrather Schlossufer 39, 24
b. – IN LOHAUSEN: *Fairport Hotel*, Niederrheinstr. 162,
70 b., SB, sauna, solarium. – IN OBERKASSEL: *Ramada*,
Am Seestern 16, 380 b., SB, sauna, solarium;
Rheinstern Penta Hotel, Emanuel Leutze Str. 17,
352 b., SB, sauna, solarium.

YOUTH HOSTEL: Düsseldorfer Str. 1, Düsseldorf
Oberkassel, 80 b. – CAMPING SITES: *Campingplatz
Lörick*, Düsseldorf Lörick; *Camp Unterbacher See*,
Düsseldorf Unterbach.

RESTAURANTS. – *"Top 180"*, in Rhine Tower;
Frickhöfer, Stromstr. 47; *KD* (Müllers and Fest).
Königsallee 12; *Naschkörbchen*, Wilhelm-Marx-
Haus, Heinrich-Heine-Allee; *Rheinterrasse*, Hofgar-
tenfer 7; *Schneider Wibbel Stuben*, Schneider Wibbel
Gasse 5–7; *Heinrich Heine Stuben*, Bolkerstr. 50 (1st
floor); *Benders Marie*, Andreasstr. 13. – IN GOLZHEIM:
Fischerstuben Mulfinger, Rotterdamer Str. 15. – IN
GRAFENBERG: *Zum Trotzkopf*, Rennbahnstr. 7a.
FOREIGN CUISINE: *Orangerie*, Bilker Str. 30, *Bateau
Ivre*, Kurze Str. 11, *La Vieille Auberge*, Grashofstr. 1
(all French); *Walliser Stuben*, Adersstr. 46 (Swiss);
Riccione, Pionierstr. 6 (Italian); *Daitokai*, Hunsrük-
kenstr. 2 (Japanese); *King Long*, Immermannstr. 19
(Chinese).

BEER-HOUSES (with "Obergäriges" – surface-
fermented beer). – *Zum Schiffchen*, Hafenstr. 5; *Zum
Schlüssel*, Bolkerstr. 45; *Zum Uerigen*, Berger Str. 1.;
Im Füchschen, Ratinger Str. 28.

CAFÉS. – *Rathaus Café*, Markt 6; *Hofkonditorei
Bierhoff*, Oststr. 128; *Nouvelle Stockheim*,
Kasernenstr. 1, *Funke Kaiser*, Marktplatz 6.

EVENTS. – *Carnival*, with Rose Monday parade. –
Shooting and local festival in Oberkassel (summer).

**Düsseldorf, capital of the Land of
North Rhineland-Westphalia, situated on the lower Rhine (here 310 m
wide), is the administrative centre
of North Rhineland-Westphalia's
heavy industry. It is a university city,
an art and fashion centre, a city of
congresses and trade fairs. This old
Electoral capital is a town of wide**
streets lined with many elegant
shops and crowded with traffic, of
spacious parks and gardens.

The old town with its friendly inns and
beer-houses has been called "the longest
bar-counter in Europe". The Opera House
and Theatre are among Germany's leading
houses. Other important features of the
city's life are the exhibitions of art, the
fashion shows, the brilliant literary and
political cabaret "Kom(m)ödchen", the
Carnival, the great shooting festival, and
the "Radschläger" (the small boys who
turn cartwheels for their own or for
visitors' pleasure – and have even had a
memorial dedicated to them). The 1987
Federal Horticultural Exhibition (Garten-
schau) will be held in Düsseldorf.

HISTORY. – Around the middle of the 12th c.
Düsseldorf was still a small fishing village. In 1288 it
was granted a charter by Count Adolf von Berg, and in
1386 Duke Wilhelm II selected the town as his capital.
After the Berg family died out (1609) their territory,
the Bergisches Land, passed to Palatinate-Neuburg,
and Düsseldorf became the capital of the splendour-
loving Elector Johann Wilhelm (known as Jan
Wellem, 1679–1716), who laid out the new town,
drew many artists to his court and founded the picture
gallery. His brother and successor Karl Philipp moved
his capital to Heidelberg in 1716 and Mannheim in
1720. The foundation of the Academy of Art in 1777
made Düsseldorf a centre of artistic life. In recent years
the city's economy has prospered, and a Japanese
Trade Centre has been established.

SIGHTS. – Düsseldorf's elegant shopping
street and promenade, the *KÖNIGSALLEE,
("Kö"), lined with elegant shops, galleries, restaurants and cafés, runs on both
sides of the old town moat from Graf-
Adolf-Platz northward to the Hofgarten. –
Parallel to the Königsallee on the W are the
BREITE STRASSE, with banks and the offices
of large industrial corporations, and the

Right bank of the Rhine, Düsseldorf

HEINRICH-HEINE-ALLEE, with the *Wilhelm-Marx-Haus*, the first German tower block, built by W. Kreis 1924–26. Farther N are the *Opera House* (on right) and the *Kunsthalle* (on left), with exhibitions. Beyond the Kunsthalle is the Baroque *St Andrew's Church*.

To the E of the Königsallee is the wide BERLINER ALLEE, with the Chamber of Industry and Commerce and the Rhineland-Westphalia Stock Exchange. In Jan-Wellem-Platz (overpass) is the **Thyssen Building**; nearby is the *Schauspielhaus* (1970).

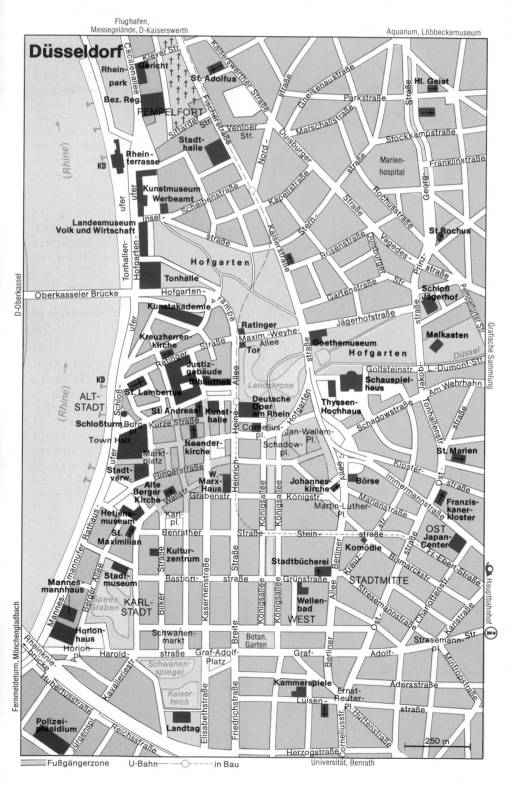

In the HOFGARTEN, laid out in 1767, is the former hunting lodge of **Jägerhof** (1752–63), with the *North Rhineland-Westphalia Art Collection* (Paul Klee collection, early Meissen porcelain). Nearby is the *Malkasten* ("Paint-Box"), headquarters of the Society of Artists. At Jägerhofstr. 1 is a *Goethe Museum* (Kippenberg Foundation). N of the Jägerhof is *St Roch's Church* with a high dome.

To the W, in the old town, is the MARKT, with the **Town Hall** (by H. Tussmann, 1567–73) and a handsome equestrian statue (cast by G. Grupello, 1711) of Elector *Johann Wilhelm II* ("Jan Wellem"). – In the Nesselrode Palace S of the Markt is the *Hetjens Museum* (ceramics of eight millennia), and beyond this, in the Spee Palace, is the *Municipal Museum*. To the E in Bilker Strasse is the *Cultural Centre* (including a puppet theatre). Still farther S of the Rhine rises the 24-storey *Mannesmann Building* and the *Rheinturm* (234 m, restaurants), a telecommunications tower. – N of the Markt is the *Alte Schlossturm* (since 1984 a shipping museum) and *St Lambert's Church* (13th–14th c. restored).

W of the old town the Schlossufer runs N to the Oberkasseler Brücke. On the S side of the Hofgartenrampe which leads up to the bridge is the *Academy of Art*. To the N is the **Ehrenhof**, with several buildings erected by W. Kreis in 1924–26: the *Tonhalle*, the *Landesmuseum Volk und Wirtschaft* ("People and Economy": a vivid presentation of the social and economical life of countries all over the world) and the *Museum of Art* (including in particular works by 19th and 20th c. Düsseldorf painters). – 2½ km NW are the TRADE FAIR GROUNDS, with the *Congress Centre* and the *Rheinstadion* (seating for 68,000). – In the Nordpark is a *Japanese Garden*.

SURROUNDINGS. – *Schloss Benrath (10 km SE in the district of Benrath), a Rococo palace built by N. de Pigage 1755–73, with a sumptuous interior and a beautiful park. – Kaiserswerth (10 km NW), with the ruins of a stronghold of the Emperor Frederick Barbarossa and the church of St Suitbertus (13th c.: reliquary of the saint). – Neandertal (10 km E), with a prehistoric museum and a game park. – Minidomm (16 km NE), at Breitscheid motorway junction with models of historic and modern German buildings.

East Frisian Islands

Land: Lower Saxony.

(i) **Fremdenverkehrsverband Nordsee-Niedersachsen-Bremen,** Gottorpstr. 18, D-2900 Oldenburg/Oldb.; tel. (04 41) 1 45 35.

The seven East Frisian islands form a protective screen off the coast of East Friesland between the Ems and Weser estuaries, washed on the N by the open sea and on the S by the Wattenmeer (which can be explored on conducted tours on any of the islands). Most of the islands are closed to motor vehicles: visitors can take their cars only to Borkum and Norderney.

The most westerly and the largest of the islands is **Borkum** (area 35 sq. km: 8 km long by 4 km across), lying in front of the Ems estuary, which can be reached by ferry from Emden in 2½ hours. A local railway runs from the landing-stage to the seaside resort of *Borkum*, with wide beaches to N and S and a covered swimming pool (sea-water, artificial waves).

E of Borkum is **Juist** (ferry from Norddeich), a long narrow island (17 km by only ½ km across) with a beautiful stone-free N beach fringed by a chain of dunes. On the S side is the resort of *Juist* (connected with the landing-stage by a railway 2·5 km long), with a covered swimming pool (sea-water, artificial waves). At the W end of the island is the *Bill* nature reserve, with the Hammersee and a birdwatchers' hide. Lying off Juist to the SW is the island of *Memmert* (bird reserve).

Norderney is the second largest of the islands (area 25 sq. km: 14 km long, up to 2 km across). At the W end is the resort of *Norderney* (car ferry from Norddeich), the oldest German North Sea resort (founded 1797) and the most fashionable. The covered swimming pool with sea-water and artificial waves, built in 1931, was the first of its kind in Germany. There is an interesting Heimatmuseum in a typical Norderney fisherman's house and a Museum of the Sea.

Baltrum, the "Sleeping Beauty of the North Sea", is the smallest of the islands

Wangerooge

(area 6·5 sq. km: 6 km long and up to 1·5 km across). Its beach of fine sand is popular with families. Here too there is a covered swimming pool with sea-water. The crossing from Norrdeich takes 1¾ hours, from Nessmersiel (in summer) only 20 minutes.

Langeoog, farther E, is 14 km long and 1–2½ km across. It is reached by ferry from Bensersiel in an hour. From the landing-stage a railway runs to the resort of *Langeoog* (covered swimming pool with sea-water and artificial waves), at the W end of the island. To the E of the *Melkörn dunes*, in the centre of the island, is the largest colony of seabirds on the North Sea, with thousands of herring gulls. A feature of Langeoog is its singing dunes.

Spiekeroog is reached by ferry from Neuharlingersiel (1 hour). The main feature of this island (over 8 km long by 2 km across: nature reserve) is an area of dunes, partly wooded, in its western half, with a stretch of grassland extending S towards the Wattenmeer. To the E extends a huge sandy beach, over 5 km long and 2 km wide, largely formed in the second half of the 19th c. It illustrates the slow but steady eastward movement of all the East Frisian islands. The island's church in *Spiekeroog*, built 1696, contains items salvaged from one of the ships of the Spanish Armada which ran aground here in 1588.

Wangerooge (boats from Harle), 9 km long and up to 1·5 km across, is the most easterly of the islands. In the middle of the island is the resort of *Wangerooge* (founded 1804: the place was destroyed by a high tide caused by a storm in 1854), the second oldest German North Sea resort (covered sea-water swimming bath). In the coastal dunes W of the resort is a heated open-air swimming pool (sea-

water: 25 °C). There are several bird reserves on the island. The Old Lighthouse (view; museum), the New Lighthouse, and the West Tower are all worth seeing.

Eichstätt

Land: Bavaria. – Vehicle registration: EIH.
Altitude: 388 m. – Population: 13,000.
Post code: D-8078. – Dialling code: 0 84 21.
ⓘ **Städtisches Verkehrsamt**, Domplatz 18; tel. 79 77.

HOTELS. – *Fuchs* (no rest.), Ostenstr. 8, 40 b.; *Adler*, Marktplatz 22, 35 b.; *Ochsbräu*, Westenstr. 17, 20 b. – YOUTH HOSTEL: Reichenaustr. 15.

RESTAURANT. – *Gasthof Krone*, Domplatz 3.

CAFÉ. – *Dom-Café*, Domplatz 1.

This picturesque old town in the Altmühl valley Nature Park at the foot of the Franconian Alb, with the massive Willibaldsburg looming over it, has the stamp of an ecclesiastical city; it is the see of a bishop and has a Roman Catholic Gesamthochschule (comprehensive higher educational establishment). It is a town of fine Baroque buildings, often with something of an Italian air. It is still surrounded by remains of its medieval walls.

HISTORY. – The bishopric of Eichstätt was established in 741 by St Boniface. During the Thirty Years War the whole town was destroyed, apart from the Cathedral and a few houses, and was later rebuilt in Baroque style.

SIGHTS. – In the DOMPLATZ stands the Romanesque and Gothic **Cathedral** (11th–14th c.), with a Baroque W front. In the W choir, on the rear side of the canopied altar, which contains the remains of St Willibald, first Bishop of Eichstätt (d. 787), is a seated figure of the saint, the finest work of the local sculptor Loy Hering (1514). In the N transept is the stone Pappenheim Altar by Veit Wirsberger (*c.* 1495), with numerous figures. On the SE side of the Cathedral is a two-storey *cloister* (1420–30), with the fine two-aisled hall of the *Mortuarium* (15th c.: "Beautiful Pillar" of 1489).

S of the Cathedral in the Baroque * RESIDENZPLATZ are the former *Residenz* of the Prince-Bishop (17th–18th c., by Angelini and Gabrieli), *Kavaliershöfe* and *Mariensäule* (1777: 19 m high) and the *Diocesan Museum*. – SE of the Cathedral, in LEONRODPLATZ, is the 17th c. **Schutzengelkirche** (Guardian Angel's Church), with a very beautiful Baroque interior. – From here Ostenstrasse leads to the *Summer Palace* of the Prince-Bishops (by Gabrieli, 1735), with the Hofgarten behind it. In the nearby *Capuchin Church* (17th c.) is a reproduction of the Holy Sepulchre (1189).

N of the Domplatz is the MARKTPLATZ, with the *Town Hall* (15th and 19th c.), the former *Provostry* (18th c.) and *St Willibald's Fountain* (1695). – NW of the Marktplatz by way of the Westenstrasse is the Baroque abbey church of *St Walburga* (17th c.), with the vault chapel of the saint (d. 779).

Above the town (¾ km drive) is the **Willibaldsburg**, built 1609–19 by the Augsburg municipal architect Elias Holl, which until 1725 was the residence of the Prince-Bishops, with a *Jurassic Museum* (fossils, skeleton of an archaeopteryx) and a museum of pre-history and early historical times. At the foot is *Rebdorf Monastery*.

Eifel

Land: Rhineland-Palatinate.
(i) **Fremdenverkehrsverband Rheinland-Pfalz**,
Löhrstr. 103, D-5400 Koblenz;
tel. (02 61) 3 10 79.

The Eifel, an upland region some 70 km long and 30 km wide between the Rhine, the Moselle and the Rur, is a residual range of hills averaging 600 m in height, with its highest point in the Hohe Acht (746 m), which was disrupted by more than 200 volcanoes. The lava flows of these extinct volcanoes are still visible today, particularly around the Laacher See and the Nürburgring

Also of volcanic origin are the romantically beautiful *Maare* found in the Eifel – volcanic craters, mostly now filled by small lakes. A particularly fine example of a *Maar* is the 52 m deep *Laacher See*, surrounded by over 40 lava vents. Equally beautiful are the *Maare* round Daun, particularly the *Gemündener Maar* and the melancholy *Totenmaar*.

In recent years several large dams have been built in the NW Eifel, producing attractive new landscape patterns, like the Urft Valley dam and the *Schwammenauel* artificial lake on the Rur. The rivers, *Maare* and lakes have great attractions for the angler and the water sports enthusiast, while the abundant snow of the Hocheifel and Schnee-Eifel attracts winter sports fans.

The austere beauty of these uplands, suitable only for forestry and stock-farming, is drawing increasing numbers of tourists to explore their winding valleys and wide forest-covered plateaux. Among places of artistic and historical interest is *Mayen*, with the Genovevaburg; and in many other places there are handsome castles and palaces, important churches and celebrated monastic houses (Maria Laach, Prüm).

Daun, in the heart of the volcanic Eifel, is a noted health resort (Kneipp cure, mineral springs). *Münstereifel*, still ringed by its 13th–14th c. walls, is another popular spa offering the Kneipp cure. The nearby Stockert and Effelsberg radio-telescopes are among the largest of the kind. At *Kommern* is the interesting Rhineland Open-Air Museum. *Monschau* in the Rur valley and *Adenau* are attractive little places with many half-timbered buildings.

The ***Nürburgring** (constructed 1925–27) S of Adenau is Germany's finest motor-racing circuit. It consists of the 20·8 km long northern loop and the new 4·5 km long Nürburgring. Until 1983 all races took place on the northern loop. From early 1984 there is a completely new circuit in use. It is 4·542 km in length and has 14 bends and 11 straights, with a maximum climb of 8·8% and a descent of 6·5% it surmounts a height of 56 m. The stands around the new track will accommodate 120,000 spectators. The northern loop which has been used until now remains fully operational and is to be connected to the new racing circuit. Members of the public can, on payment of a fee, drive on both circuits on certain days.

The Benedictine abbey of Maria Laach on the Laacher See

Emden

Land: Lower Saxony.
Vehicle registration: EMD.
Altitude: 4 m. – Population: 51,000.
Post code: D-2970. – Dialling code: 0 49 21.
ⓘ Amt für, Öffentlichkeitsarbeit,
Gräfin Anna Str. 2,
tel. 8 71.

HOTELS. – *Heerens Hotel*, Friedrich Ebert Str. 67, 40
b.; *Schmidt*, Friedrich Ebert Str. 79, 40 b.; *Deutsches
Haus*, Neuer Markt 7, 38 b.; *Goldener Adler*, Neutorstr.
5, 32 b.; *Faldernpoort*, Courbierestr. 6, 39 b. – YOUTH
HOSTEL: An der Kesselschleuse 5. – CAMPING SITE:
An der Knock, via Emden Wybelsum.

RESTAURANTS. – *Lindenhof*, Nordertorstr. 43;
Tschintau, Neutorstr. 50a (Chinese).

CAFÉ. – *Café am Stadtgarten*, Neutostr, 19.

This old Frisian town in the Dollart
inlet near the mouth of the Ems has
the most westerly German North
Sea harbour and the largest after
Hamburg and Bremen. Situated at
the end of the Dortmund-Ems Canal,
the port mainly serves the Ruhr
(coal, ore and grain; oil harbour).
The Ems-Jade Canal also provides a
connection with Wilhelmshaven.
Other important industries are shipbuilding, car manufacture and the
reception of North Sea gas. From the
outer harbour there is a ferry service
to the island of Borkum.

HISTORY. – Emden's first period of prosperity was in
the 16th c., when it had a merchant shipping fleet of
some 600 vessels. In 1683 the Great Elector made
Emden the main base of his fleet. During the
subsequent period of Prussian rule Frederick the Great
declared the town a free port (1751) and granted it
important trading privileges. The town's prosperity
was destroyed by Napoleon's continental blockade in
1806, and not until the construction of the port and
the Dortmund-Ems Canal did its fortunes take an
upward turn. After the destruction of the Second
World War Emden now has an entirely modern aspect.

SIGHTS. – On the *Ratsdelft* in the centre
of the town is the **Town Hall**, built
1959–62 on the foundations of the old
Renaissance town hall destroyed in 1944.
In addition to municipal offices it also
houses the *East Frisian Provincial
Museum* (unique municipal armoury,
with weapons of the 16th–19th c.). SW of
the Town Hall are the ruins of the *Great
Church* (late Gothic: tower restored
1965–66). – In the E part of the old town
is the rebuilt *New Church* (1643–48). –
Much to be recommended is a walk on the
Wall, a rampart (with windmills) which
runs in a semicircle round the town centre.

3 km W of the old town is the *port* (motor-
boat service from the Ratsdelft and trips
round the harbour), at the end of the
Dortmund-Ems and Ems-Jade Canals.

SURROUNDINGS. – **Wasserburg Hinte** (5 km N),
a 16th c. moated castle.

Essen

Land: North Rhineland-Westphalia.
Vehicle registration: E.
Altitude: 116 m. – Population: 649,000.
Post code: D-4300. – Dialling code: 02 01.
ⓘ Verkehrsverein,
Hauptbahnhof (S side); Freiheit 3;
tel. 2 04 21.

HOTELS. – *Sheraton*, Huyssenallee 55, 414 b., SB,
sauna; *Handelshof Mövenpick*, Am Hauptbahnhof 2,
260 b.; *Essener Hof*, Teichstr. 2, 160 b.; *Assindia*,
Viehofer Platz 5, 80 b.; *Manza* (no rest.), Gerlingstr.
45, 32 b.; *Europa* (no rest.), Hindenburgerstr. 35, 70
b.; *Luise* (no rest.), Dreilindenstr. 96, 40 b. – IN
BREDENEY: *Bredeney*, Theodor-Althoff-Str. 5, 550 b.;
Touring Hotel (no rest.), Frankenstr. 379, 64 b.;
Parkhaus Hügel, Freiherr-vom-Stein-Str. 209, 20 b.,
elegant restaurant. – IN KETTWIG: *Schloss Hugenpoet*,
August-Thyssen-Str. 51, 36 b.; *Rühl's Sengelmanns-
hof*, Sengelmannsweg 35, 43 b. – IN RÜTTENSCHEID:
Arosa, Rüttenscheider Str. 149, 85 b.; *Rütten-
scheider Hof*, Klarastr. 18, 36 b. – YOUTH HOSTEL:
Pastoratsberg 2, Essen-Werden, 152 b. – CAMPING
SITES: Haus Scheppen and Strandbad Scheppen, on
Baldeneysee; Am Bahnhof Werden and Deichklause,
Essen-Werden.

RESTAURANTS. – *Stadtgarten*, Huyssenallee 53;
Intercity Restaurant, at Main Station; *Rôtisserie Alter
Ritter*, Theatreplatz 3, (steaks a specialty); *Zum
Halben Hahn*, Kennedyplatz 5, *Kleiner Adler*, Akazien-
allee 12. – ON THE BALDENEYSEE: *Seeterrassen Schloss
Baldeney*, Freiherr von Stein Str. 386a; *Parkhaus
Hügel*, Freiherr von Stein Str. 9; *Schwarze Lene*,
Baldeney 38; *Heimliche Liebe*, Baldeney 31. – IN
KETTWIG: *Rôtisserie Ange d'or*, Ruhrtalstr. 326
(French). – IN RÜTTENSCHEID: *Silberkuhlshof*,
Lührmannstr 80.

CAFÉS. – *Overbeck*, Kettwiger Str. 15 (with terrace),
Limbecker Str. 45 and in Head Post Office at Main
Station.

EVENTS. – *Baldeney Festival*, with water sports,
parade of boats and fireworks (the climax of the
summer season); *Essener Lichtwochen* (beginning
Nov. to beginning Jan.); *Carnival*, with Rose Monday
parade.

**Essen, between the rivers Emscher
and Ruhr, is the largest city in the
Ruhr. It owes its importance as
metropolis of the Ruhr and the
headquarters of many large industrial corporations (including the
Ruhrkohle AG, the largest German
coal-mining undertaking and the
Rheinisch-Westfälische   Elek-
trizitäts AG) to its situation in the**

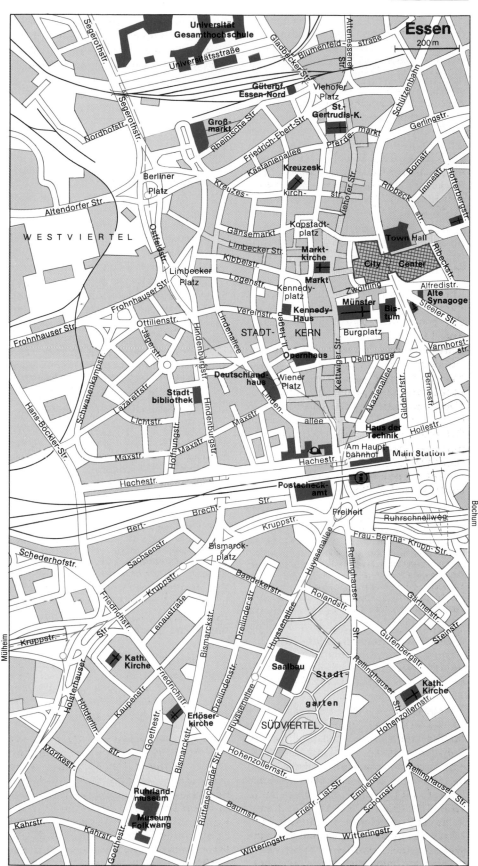

Essen

200 m

middle of the Rhineland-Westphalia industrial region. The town is the centre of important heavy industry (Krupp) and the headquarters of many other industries (electronics, chemical works, etc.). In addition Essen is the see of the Bishop of the Ruhr and the seat of a university and comprehensive higher educational establishment. The Ruhr State College of Music, Theatre and Dance and the Folkwang Academy of Music are institutions of recognised standing. The Grugapark was laid out for the great Ruhr Horticultural Show of 1929, and has since been enlarged. The transport facilities of the central area have been improved by the opening of an underground railway.

HISTORY. – On what is now the Burgplatz the Franks built a fortress in the middle of the 8th c. to provide protection against Saxon raids. Around 852 Bishop Altfried of Hildesheim built on his property of *Asnidhi* a religious house for the daughters of the Saxon nobility, which flourished under its abbesses of imperial blood (Mechthild and Theophanu, granddaughters of Otto I and II). The trading settlement which grew up round this house about the year 1000 was granted market rights in 1041, and in 1243–44, along with the convent, was enclosed by walls (on a line now marked by the "Alleestrassen"). Its patrons were the Counts of Berg and Altena in the 12th c., the Dukes of Jülich, Cleves and Berg from 1495 and the Electors of Brandenburg from 1609. In 1803 the convent, which had ruled the territory of Essen for nine centuries, was secularised and the territory was occupied by Prussia. From 1806 to 1813 Essen belonged to the Duchy of Berg, but in 1815 it became Prussian again and thereafter developed into one of Germany's principal industrial towns. Since the beginning of this century Essen's boundaries have been considerably extended by taking in land from neighbouring communes.

SIGHTS. – In the BURGPLATZ stands the *Minster (R.C.), one of the oldest churches in Germany (9th–14th c.). Among the most notable features of the interior are a seven-branched bronze candelabrum (*c.* 1000) and the "Golden Madonna" (before 1000). The rich Minster treasury is in the *Bishop's Palace* (1955–56). The principal shopping streets (pedestrian precinct) are the KETTWIGER STRASSE and the LIMBECKER STRASSE, which opens off the MARKTPLATZ. In this square is the little *Market Church* (probably 11th c., renovated 1952: Evang.). – E of here is the *City-Center* (shopping precinct) stands the new *Rathaus (106 m high) and the Alte Synagogue (memorial). – In the southern part of the city centre is the Opera

House and the *German Poster Museum* (Rathenaustr. 2).

To the W of the old town are the *Krupp Works*, once Europe's largest cast steelworks, founded by Friedrich Krupp in 1811 and developed by his son Alfred Krupp (1812–87), with exemplary welfare facilities.

S of the Main Station, Huyssenallee runs from the busy square FREIHEIT to the beautiful *Stadtgarten*, with the *Municipal Hall* (restaurant), built in 1949–54. – SW of this, in Bismarckstrasse, are the *Ruhr Museum* and the *Folkwang Museum (19th and 20th c. German and French works of all periods), since autumn 1983 both in one building. – Farther to the SW is the beautiful Grugapark (70 hectares), laid out for the Ruhr Horticultural Show in 1929 and enlarged in 1952 and 1965, with the *Grugahalle* (1958), an observation tower, exhibition halls, a botanic garden, animal enclosures, an aquarium, a recreation park, fountains and several restaurants. A light railway runs through the park for 3·5 km. – To the W, in Nachtigallental ("Nightingale Valley"), is the *Halbachhammer*, a 16th c. forge.

S of Essen are the *Stadtwald* (Town Forest), with a bird park (*c.* 1000 birds) and the *Heissiwald*, with a game park. – Above the northern shore of the 8 km long *Baldeneysee* (recreation area; boats) stands the *Villa Hügel, former home of the Krupp family (historical collection in the "Kleines Haus"; temporary exhibitions).

S of the Baldeneysee is *Werden Abbey Church*, which originally belonged to a Benedictine abbey founded by St Ludger in 796. It is one of the very finest late Romanesque churches in the Rhineland, with a late Baroque interior. The church treasury contains a bronze crucifix of 1060 and a chalice which belonged to St Ludger (*c.* 900).

Esslingen am Neckar

Land: Baden-Württemberg.
Vehicle registration: ES.
Altitude: 240 m. – Population: 90,000.
Post code: D-7300. – Dialling code: 07 11.
ⓘ Kultur- und Freizeitamt,
　Marktplatz 16;
　tel. 3 51 24 41.

HOTELS. – *Panorama-Hotel* (no rest.), Mühlberger Str. 66, 60 b. – IN OBERESSLINGEN: *Rosenau*, Plochinger Str. 65, 55 b, SB, sauna. – IN LIEBERSBRONN: *Traube*, Im Gehren 6, 66 b., SB, sauna.

Esslingen am Neckar: Fortress and Town Church

RESTAURANTS. – *Dicker Turm*, in the Burg; *Reichsstadt*, Rathausplatz 5; *Stadthalle*, Grabbrunnenstr. 21.

CAFÉS. – *Filderhof*, Pliensaustr. 46; *Theater-Café*, Strohstr. 6; *Fromm*, Beethovenstr. 5.

The industrial town of Esslingen lies in the middle Neckar valley with its extensive vineyards, a short distance upstream from Stuttgart. It preserves a number of important historic buildings dating from the time when it was a free Imperial city.

HISTORY. – The remains of Bronze Age settlements show that the Esslingen area was inhabited as early as 1000 B.C. In Roman times there was a villa at Oberesslingen. The place appears in the records for the first time in 777, when it featured as a settlement at the Neckar ford on the trading route between the Rhine and Italy. During the investiture dispute Esslingen was destroyed by the troops of the Emperor Henry IV. It received its municipal charter in 1219. The Swabian League was founded here in 1488. In 1531 the town council resolved that the Protestants should be free to preach the word of God in the town. The Thirty Years War and the incursions of French troops in the latter part of the 17th c. hit Esslingen hard. In 1803 it lost its status as a free Imperial city and became part of Württemberg. The Second World War left the town – which by this time had grown considerably as the result of industrial development and the incorporation of adjoining territory – relatively unscathed.

SIGHTS. – In the MARKTPLATZ is the twin-towered **Town Church** of St Dionys (Evang.), built on 8th c. foundations in the transitional style of the 13th–14th c., with a High Gothic choir. It has a fine interior, in which excavations in 1960–63 revealed remains of earlier churches, a crypt and a hut of the Urnfield culture (13th–11th c. B.C.; the remains can be seen by visitors). Opposite the choir is the *Speyerer Pfleghof*, a former hospice now occupied by a Sekt firm, Kessler – the oldest Sekt cellars in Germany (founded 1826). On the W side of the Marktplatz is the early Gothic *St Paul's Minster* (R.C.), one of the oldest surviving churches of a mendicant order in Germany (1233–68). N of St Paul's, beyond the ring of streets marking the line of the old fortifications (footbridge and underpass), is the High Gothic *Frauenkirche* (1321–1516), with a magnificent tower designed by Ulrich von Ensingen, architect of the Minster in Ulm. The nearby Stadttor (museum) leads out to the vineyards on the slopes of the Neckar valley.

In the RATHAUSPLATZ are the *New Town Hall* (formerly the Palmsches Palais, 1746) and the *Old Town Hall, a half-timbered building of 1430, rebuilt and provided with a Renaissance façade by H. Schickhardt in 1586–89 (clock with mechanical figures, carillon); it now houses the well-stocked Municipal Museum.

To the N the BURGBERG, planted with vines, rises above the old town, with a covered *flight of steps* and the Burgsteige leading up to the top. The **Burg** dates from the time of the Hohenstaufens; from the *Dicker Turm* ("Stout Tower") and the remains of the walls there are fine views; there is a restaurant in the Dicker Turm.

S of the Marktplatz and Rathaus is the OLD TOWN (mostly a pedestrian precinct). The *Innere Brücke* (with a small chapel) spans the two arms of the Neckar Canal, separated by the island known as the *Maille* (park).

SURROUNDINGS. – NE of Esslingen extends the **Schurwald**, a ridge of hills (highest point *Kernen*, 513 m) which is a popular recreation and excursion area.

(1757–62) and a famous figure of the Madonna by Pisano (14th c.) in the tabernacle of the high altar. In front of the church are the boarding school (until 1744 a Knights' Academy) and the grammar school.

SURROUNDINGS. – **Ettaler Mandl** (1634 m: 3 km N), 2½–3 hours' walk from Ettal or by the Laber cableway from Oberammergau. – **Oberammergau** (4 km NW), with the famous Passion Play theatre and a Heimatmuseum (Nativity figurines). – *****Schloss Linderhof** (11 km W), built by G. Dollmann for King Ludwig II of Bavaria in an extravagant Rococo style (1874–78); beautiful gardens with fountains.

Ettal

Land: Bavaria. – Vehicle registration: GAP.
Altitude: 878 m. – Population: 1000.
Post code: D-8101. – Dialling code: 0 88 22.
ⓘ **Gemeindeverwaltung**
  tel. 5 34.

HOTELS. – *Ludwig der Bayer*, Kaiser Ludwig Platz 10, 120 b. (with annex in monastery); *Benediktenhof*, 1 km on Oberammergau road, 36 b.

This health and winter sports resort in a high valley of the Ammergebirge at the foot of the Ettaler Mandl (1634 m) attracts many visitors to its Benedictine abbey with its famous church. The monks produce a fragrant herb liqueur, made according to an ancient recipe.

SIGHTS. – The *Benedictine abbey* was founded in 1330 by Emperor Ludwig the Bavarian. The *****abbey church**, originally a Gothic structure on a centralised plan, was converted into a Baroque domed church by Enrico Zuccali in 1710–26 and restored after a fire by Josef Schmuzer in 1744–52. In the sumptuous interior are a splendid dome painting (1752) by J. J. Zeiller of Reutte (his finest work), six beautiful side altars by J. B. Straub

Ettal Abbey, with the Krottenkopf group

Fichtelgebirge

Land: Bavaria.
ⓘ **Tourismusinformation Fichtelgebirge**,
  Schillerstr 1; 37, D-8672 Selb;
  tel. (0 92 87) 27 59.

This range of hills, largely covered with fir forests, lies in the NE corner of Bavaria, forming a link between the Erzgebirge and the Bohemian Forest (Franconian Forest and Upper Palatinate Forest). Weathering of the granitic rock has produced strikingly shaped mazes of crags and tumbles of rock which give the scenery a particular fascination.

This upland region of granites and slates contains the sources of the *Main*, the *Saale*, the *Eger* and the *Naab*, whose courses take them to all the points of the compass. It consists of three ranges of hills surrounding the Wunsiedel basin in horsehoe formation: the *Waldsteingebirge* (878 m) in the NW, the highest peaks (*Ochsenkopf*, 1024 m; *Schneeberg*, 1053 m) in the SW and the ridge formed by *Kösseine* (940 m) and the *Steinwald* (966 m) in the SE.

The charm of the Fichtelgebirge, which is traversed by the magnificent *Fichtelgebirgsstrasse* (B 303) and the 13 km long *Panorama-Strasse* (W and S round the Ochsenkopf), lies in the beautiful expanses of forest and the extraordinary mazes and scatters of rock produced by weathering, the most striking of which is the *Luisenburg*. Then there are the deeply cut valleys, particularly those of the *Weisser Main*, the *Ölschnitz*, the *Steinach* and the *Eger*. – *Selb*, in the E of the Fichtelgebirge, is the largest centre of the porcelain industry in the Federal Republic.

Holiday and health resorts include *Bischofsgrün, Fichtelberg, Warmensteinach* and *Wirsberg*. Warmensteinach is the most important winter sports resort in North Bavaria. S of Wunsiedel, the chief place in the Fichtelgebirge and the birthplace of the poet Jean-Paul, lies the pretty little *Bad Alexandersbad* (near the rock maze of Luisenburg, named in 1805 after Queen Louise of Prussia); NW of Wunsiedel, at the foot of the Waldstein, is the little town of *Weissenstadt*.

Flensburg

Land: Schleswig-Holstein.
Vehicle registration: FL.
Altitude: 20 m. – Population: 88,000.
Post code: D-2390. – Dialling code: 04 61.
ⓘ Verkehrsverein,
  Norderstr. 6;
  tel. 2 30 90.

HOTELS. – *Flensburger Hof*, Süderhofenden 38, 50 b.; *Europa*, Rathausstr. 1, 120 b.; *Am Rathaus* (no rest.), Rote Str. 32, 65 b.; *Am Wasserturm*, Blasberg 13, 35 b.; *Am Stadtpark*, Nordergraben 70, 30 b.; *Zoega*, Norderstr. 33, 30 b.; *Flensborghus*, Norderstr. 26, 25 b. – IN KRUSAU KUPFERMÜHLE: *Hotel an der Grenze*, 240 b. – YOUTH HOSTEL: Fichtestr. 16, Flensburg-Mürwick. – CAMPING SITES: *Jarplund*, on B 76 (south of the town); *Sankelmark*, in Bilschau; *Schwennau*, in Glücksburg; *Grenzblick*, in Drei (on the Holnis peninsula); *Fordefrieden*, in Bockholmwik; etc.

RESTAURANTS. – *Stadtrestaurant*, in the Deutschen Haus, Bahnhofstr. 15; *Fährkrog*, Schiffbrücke 37; *Alt Flensburger Haus*, Norderstr. 8; *Restaurant Harmonie*, Wilhelmstr. (fish).

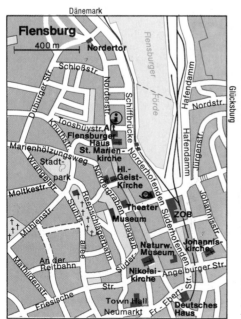
Dänemark
Flensburg
400 m
Husum   Hauptbahnhof

CAFÉS. – *Preusser*, Grosse Strasse 18; *Maass*, Angelburger Str. 4; *Charlott am Nordermarkt*, Grosse Str. 81. – Several discotheques.

Flensburg, Germany's most northerly port and the most important town in Schleswig, is attractively situated between wooded ranges of hills at the innermost tip of the fjord-like Flensburger Förde, which cuts inland between forest-fringed shores, the northern shore belonging to Denmark. It has a teachers' training college, a technical college and a Naval College at Mürwick for training officers for the Federal Navy. Its principal industries are shipbuilding and engineering. Local specialties are Flensburg rum and smoked eels.

HISTORY. – Flensburg received its municipal charter in 1284, and in the second half of the 16th c. enjoyed a first period of prosperity as a rising commercial town, In the 17th and 18th c. its trade prospered still further, with a large fleet of ships trading in the Baltic.

SIGHTS. – The principal shopping street of the OLD TOWN runs from S to N in three sections – Holm, Grosse Strasse and Norderstrasse. At the S end is the beautiful SÜDERMARKT, surrounded by gabled houses, with the large Town Church of **St Nicholas** (14th and 16th c.: Rococo high altar, Renaissance organ). To the E, in Süderhofenden, is the *Natural History Museum*. Near Angelburger Strasse stands St John's, the oldest church in the town (12th c.: wall-paintings, etc.).
In the NORDERMARKT, the old market-place of the town, are the *Neptune Fountain* (1758) and the *Schrangen* (1595), in which the bakers and butchers once sold their wares. To the SW are the little Gothic *Heiliggeistkirche* (Church of the Holy Ghost, 1386), a Danish church since 1588, and the *Municipal Museum (Lutherplatz 1), (culture, art and folk traditions of Schleswig.)
N of the Nordermarkt is the little brick-built hall-church of St Mary (13th and 15th c.: Renaissance altar). E of this, on the harbour, is the *Kompagnietor* (1583). At Norderstrasse 8 is the *Alt-Flensburger-Haus* (1780), parental home of the airship captain Hugo Eckener, who worked with Count Zeppelin. The massive *Nordertor* (1595) – the emblems of Flensburg – marks the northern end of the old town.

SURROUNDINGS. – *Schloss Glücksburg (9 km NE), built 1582–87; museum with a picture gallery and a collection of leather wall-hangings and Gobelin tapestries.

Frankfurt am Main

Land: Hesse. – Vehicle registration: F.
Altitude: 100 m. – Population:
Post code: D-6000. – Dialling code: 06 11.
(from August 1984 new local dialling code 0 69)

ⓘ **Verkehrsamt Frankfurt am Main,**
tel. 23 10 55.
Information Centre in the Hauptwache Passage;
tel. 28 74 86 and 29 10 18.

HOTELS. – *Steigenberger-Hotel Frankfurter Hof,*
Kaiserplatz 17, 600 b., ''Frankfurter Stubb'' restaurant;
Inter Continental, Wilhelm Leuschnerstr. 43, 1500 b.,
SB, sauna, solarium; *Canadian Pacific Frankfurt
Plaza Hotel,* Hamburger Allee 2, at Trade Fair Grounds
(Messegelände), 1182 b.; *Parkhotel,* Frankfurt,
Wiesenhüttenplatz 28–38, 420 b., sauna, solarium;
Hessischer Hof, Friedrich Ebert Anlage 40, 200 b.;
Savoy, Weisenhüttenstr. 42, 200 b., SB, sauna,
solarium; *Savigny,* Savignystr. 14, 160 b.; *National,*
Baseler Str. 50, 130 b.; *Turm Hotel* (no rest.),
Eschersheimer Landstr. 20, 130 b.; *Henninger Hof,*
Hanauer Landstr. 127, 100 b.; *Palmenhof* (no rest.),

Fernmeldeturm, Deutsche Bundesbank

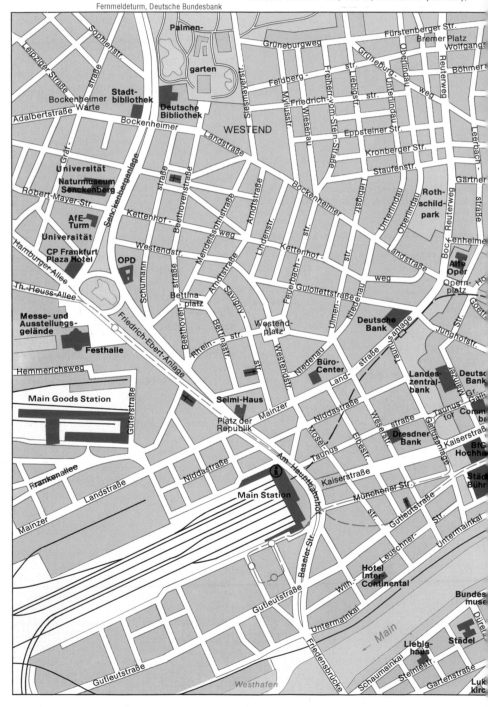

U-Bahn ———— ——O— — — —— under construction

Bockenheimer Landstr. 91, 80 b.; *Westfälischer Hof*, Düsseldorfer Str. 10, 80 b. – IN SACHSENHAUSEN: *Holiday Inn City Tower*, Mailänder Str. 1, 328 b.

AT THE RHEIN-MAIN AIRPORT: *Sheraton*, Am Flughafen, Terminal Mitte, 1110 b., SB, sauna, solarium; *Steigenberger Airport Hotel*, Flughafenstr. 300, 500 b., SB, sauna, solarium. – IN THE MAIN-TAUNUS SHOPPING CENTRE: *Holiday Inn*, 6231 Sulzbach, 580 b., SB, sauna, solarium; *Novotel*, 6236 Eschborn, 560 b. – IN NIEDERRAD: *Arabella Hotel*, Lyoner Str. 44, 600 b., SB, sauna, solarium; *Crest Hotel*, Isenburger Schneise 40, 413 b. – YOUTH HOSTEL: *Haus der Jugend*,

Deutschherrenufer 12, 550 b. – CAMPING SITES: *Hedderheim*, on the River Nidda; *Niederrad*, on the Schleuseninsel on the left bank of the Main; *Offenbach-Bürgel*, on the left bank of the Main.

RESTAURANTS. – *Weinhaus Brückenkeller*, Schützenstr. 6; *Skyline*, revolving restaurant (218 m) in the Telecommunications Tower; *Mövenpick*, Opernplatz 2; *Henninger Turm Panoramic Revolving Restaurant*, Hainer Weg 60, Sachsenhausen; *Börsenkeller*, Schillerstr. 11; *Hauptwache 68*, under the Hauptwache; *Dippegucker*, Eschenheimer Anlage 40.

FOREIGN CUISINE: *Churrasco*, Am Domplatz 6 (Argen-

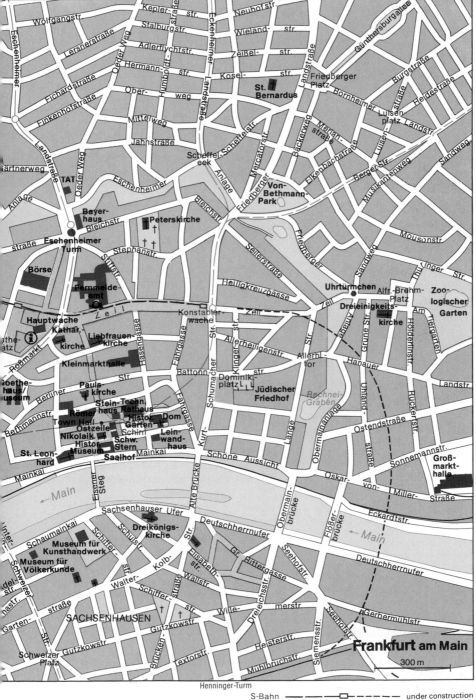

Tower blocks in Frankfurt am Main

tinian steakhouse); *Da Bruno*, Elbestr. 15 (Italian); *Peking*, Kaiserstr. 15 (Chinese).
IN SURROUNDINGS: *Flughafen-Rôtisserie 5 Continents*, at airport, above Departure Gate B; *Gutsschänke Neuhof*, Dreieich-Götzenhain (11 km S).

WINE BARS. – *Heylands Weinstuben*, Kaiserhofstr. 7; *Hahnhof, Pfälzer Weinstuben*, Scheffelstr. 1 and Berliner Str. 64; *Rheinpfalz-Weinstuben*, Gutleutstr. 1. – CIDER BARS: *Grauer Bock*, Grosse Ritterstr. 30; *Zum Gemalten Haus*, Schweizer Str. 67, Frankfurt-Sachsenhausen.

CAFÉS. – *Hauptwache*, in the old Hauptwache (garden terrace); *Bonaparte*, Römerberg; *Café am Opernplatz* (tables in square); *Odeon*, Seilerstr. 34 (in gardens on the line of the old walls); *Schwille*, Grosse Bockenheimer Str. 50; *Foerst*, Schillerstr. 12. – Night spots in Kaiserstrasse area.

EVENTS. – International **Frankfurt Fair** (Feb./March and Aug.); *Dippemess*, traditional fair, with stalls in the Ostpark (March–April and Sept.); *Cycle race* round the Henninger Turm (1 May); *Roses and Lights Festival* in Palmengarten (June); *Main Festival* on the Römer and the Main, with wine fountain, ox-roasting, boat tournament and illuminations on the river (July–Aug.); *International Motor Show* (every two years in autumn); *Sachsenhausen Fountain Festival* in Alt-Sachsenhausen, with selection of the Cider Queen (Aug.); **International Frankfurt Book Fair** (Oct.); *Christkindchesmarkt* on Römerberg (Dec.).

This old Imperial city on the Main, by virtue of its central situation an intermediary between North and South Germany, is one of the most important commercial and economic centres in the Federal Re- public. **The headquarters of the Bundesbank, the leading German stock exchange and numerous major banks are to be found in Frankfurt, and international trade fairs succeed one another here throughout the year. Frankfurt is also an international junction for rail, road and air traffic. Its University, theatres and museums foster an active cultural life. Most of the German Emperors were crowned in Frankfurt, Goethe was born in the town and the first German National Assembly met here. No other German town has had such a rapid and troubled development since the last war, both in the economic and in the intellectual and ideological fields.**

HISTORY. – Frankfurt first appears in the records in 794 as a royal stronghold, and in 876 it is described as capital of the East Frankish kingdom. From the Hohenstaufen period onwards the German kings were elected here, and from 1562 the Emperors were crowned in Frankfurt. Its thriving trade fairs made the town one of the principal markets of Central Europe. From 1815 to 1866 it was the seat of the Federal Diet, and in 1848–49 the first German National Assembly met in the Paulskirche here. The Second World War caused severe destruction in Frankfurt, particularly in the crowded old town. The city is now studded with modern tower blocks.

SIGHTS. – The central feature of the town is the square AN DER HAUPTWACHE (large shopping area in underpass; S- and U-

Bahn station), from which the main business and shopping streets take off, the ZEIL (pedestrian precinct), running E, and the KAISERSTRASSE, which runs SW by way of the Rossmarkt and Kaiserplatz to the **Hauptbahnhof** (built 1883–88 and recently modernised), one of the largest stations in Europe. – SW of Kaiserplatz, in Theaterplatz, is the *Municipal Theatre and Opera House*. Facing it, to the N, is the **BfG Building**, a tower block 156 m high.

N of the Rossmarkt is the *Stock Exchange* (Chamber of Commerce), built 1879, rebuilt 1957. S of the Rossmarkt, at Grosser Hirschgraben 23, is the **Goethe House*, completely rebuilt in 1946–51 on the basis of old plans, in which the great German writer was born on 28 August 1749 and lived until 1765. The rooms have been restored to their original state (museum). Adjoining the Goethe House is the *House of the German Book Trade* (built 1953), headquarters of the Federal book trade organisations.

S of the Hauptwache in Paulsplatz is the **Paulskirche** (St Paul's Church: built 1790–1833, restored 1948), a plain neo-classical building on a centralised plan in which the first German National Assembly met in 1848–49. The presentation of the Frankfurt Goethe Prize and the annual Peace Prize of the German Book Trade takes place here.

SE of St Paul's Church extends the **Römerberg*, with the fountain of justice as its central feature. On its western flank stands the **Römer*, the ancient City Hall; the *Kaisersaal* (Imperial Hall) was once the scene of brilliant coronation banquets. The Römer is a complex of eight originally separate 15th–18th c. houses; adjoining it is the *Neue Rathaus* (1900–08). To the S, on the Main, is the Gothic *St Leonard's Church* (14th c.: R.C.), with Romanesque doorways. – On the S side of the Römerberg is the Gothic *St Nicholas's Church* (carillon). Immediately S of this, extending to the Mainkai, is the *Historical Museum*, with material on the history of Frankfurt; it incorporates the *Rententurm* (1455) and the so-called *Saalhof*.

Well worth seeing is the **Ostzeile* on the east side of the Römerberg, with six buildings erected in the 1980s according to historic patterns; they are bordered on the south by the *Schwarzen Stern* (*Black Star*; partly rebuilt) and on the north by the

Steinernes Haus (*Stone House*), the headquarters of the Kunstverein (Art Union), which was restored between 1957 and 1960. From there the Alter Markt with the *Technical City Hall*, the modern district of "Freizeit und Kultur-schirn" together with the *Garden of History* lead to the Cathedral. The Gothic **Cathedral* (R.C.: badly damaged in 1944, but since restored), in red sand-stone, was built between the 13th and 15th c. Its tower, 95 m high, is one of the city's landmarks. From 1562 the Emperor was crowned under the crossing (Election Chapel on S side of choir). Among features in the interior are a **Crucifixion*

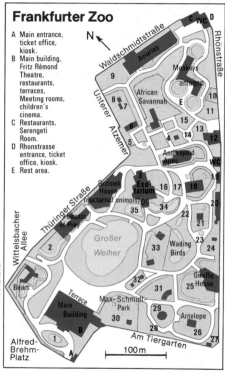

Frankfurter Zoo

A Main entrance, ticket office, kiosk.
B Main building, Fritz Rémond Theatre, restaurants, terraces, Meeting rooms, children's cinema.
C Restaurants, Serengeti Room.
D Rhonstrasse entrance, ticket office, kiosk.
E Rest area.

1 Flamingoes
2 Lions
3 Penguins, fish, reptiles, amphibians, insects
4 Children's zoo, donkeys, ponies, dwarf goats, pot-bellied pigs, lynx
5 Breeding aviaries
6 Hatcheries
7 Cheetahs
8 Wild dogs
9 Pheasantry
10 Gnomes
11 Prairie dogs
12 Animal nursery
13 Guineapig paddock
14 Racoons
15 Maze
16 Wild sheep and goats
17 Leopards
18 Elephants (performances), hippopotamuses, rhinoceroses
19 Owls, crows, etc.

20 Falcons
21 Emus, cassowaries cranes
22 Flamingo paddock
23 Coypus
24 Wolves
25 Giraffes, okapis, gazelles
26 Bongos, kudus
27 Porcupines
28 Dwarf civet cat
29 Rotunda: kangaroos, horned hogs, ant-bears, ducker, klipspringer (antelope)
30 Vicunas, nandus, water-hogs, Jabiru storks, griffon vultures, kangaroos
31 Zebras
32 Cavies (pampas hares)
33 Yaks, zebus, camels, dromedaries
34 Seals, sea-elephants, penguins
35 Pelican pond

by H. Backoffen (1509) under the tower; the Maria-Schlaf Altar (1434) in the Lady Chapel; the tombstone of the German king Günther von Schwarzburg (d. 1349 in Frankfurt) in the choir; the great organ (72 stops) in the S transept; and a number of carved wooden altars (15th–16th c.). The inner town is surrounded by a ring of gardens on the line of the fortifications, the finest relic of which is the *Eschenheim Gate* (1400–28). SE of the former Friedberg Gate is the *Zoo (c. 6000 animals), with an "exotarium" and a Nocturnal Animals House. – At the former Bockenheim Gate (Opernplatz) is the *Old Opera House* (reconstructed as a congress and concert hall). The Bockenheimer Landstrasse runs NW 1½ km to the beautiful **Palmengarten** (native, tropical and subtropical flora; Lilliputian railway), with a good restaurant. At the SW corner of the gardens is the *German Library* (1957–59). Opposite it, on the far side of the Bockenheimer Landstrasse, is the *Municipal and University Library* (1965). – E of the Palmengarten are the former offices of the IG-Farbenindustrie corporation, built 1928–30 by H. Poelzig, now occupied by the United States authorities. – NE of the Palmengarten is the *Grüneburg Park* (29 hectares), with the *Botanic Garden*. 1 km N of the Palmengarten is the new *Telecommunications Tower** (Fernmeldeturm, 1977), with a viewing platform, a restaurant and a café. – S of the Palmengarten, at Schubertstr. 20, is the *Heinrich Hoffmann Museum*, dedicated to the author of "Struwwelpeter" (material on the history of medicine). – ½ km W are the extensive buildings of the **Johann Wolfgang Goethe University** (opened 1914) and the *Senckenberg Nature Museum** (natural history, etc.). – ½ km S is the **Messegelände** (Trade Fair Grounds). Just N of the Messegelände is the *Canadian Pacific Frankfurt Plaza Hotel* (169 m high). To the SE, in the PLATZ DER REPUBLIK, is the *Selmi-Haus* (143 m high).

In the district of SACHSENHAUSEN on the left bank of the Main, on the SCHAUMAINKAI, a riverside promenade with a fine view of the old town, are the *Städel Art Institute and City Gallery** (No. 63: European painting from , the 14th c. to the present day, including Rembrandt's "Blinding of Samson"; engravings; modern graphic art), the **Liebieghaus Municipal Sculpture Collection** (No. 71), the **Federal**

Postal Museum (No. 53), the *Museum of Ethnography* (No. 29) and the *Museum of Handicrafts* (No. 51) and the German Architectural Museum. On the Sachsenhäuser Ufer is Germany's largest *flea-market*. In Grosse and Kleine Rittergasse, Rauschergasse, Textorgasse and Klappergasse are to be found Sachsenhausen's popular *cider bars*. Favourite dishes to accompany the "Ebbelwei" – hard cider – are *Rippchen mit Kraut* (pickled ribs of pork in sauerkraut) and *Handkäs mit Musik* (curd cheese with onions and vinaigrette dressing). – 1 km SE is the 120 m high **Henninger Turm** (revolving restaurant; *view). – 10 km SW is the *Rhein-Main Airport.

SURROUNDINGS. – **Königstein** (20 km NW), with a ruined castle. – **Grosser Feldberg**, the highest hill in the Taunus (880 m).

Freiburg im Breisgau

Land: Baden-Württemberg.
Vehicle registration: FR.
Altitude: 278 m. – Population: 175,000.
Post code: D-7800. – Dialling code: 07 61.
ⓘ **der Stadt Freiburg**,
　Rotteckring 14;
　tel. 2 16 32 89.

HOTELS: – *Colombi Hotel*, Rotteckring 16, 175 b.; *Panoramahotel am Jägerhäusle*, Wintererstr. 89, 140 b., SB, sauna, solarium; *Novotel*, Am Karlsplatz, 224 b.; *Victoria*, Eisenbahnstr. 54, 90 b.; *Central Hotel* (no rest.), Weberstr. 5, 84 b.; *Park Hotel Post* (no rest.), Eisenbahnstr. 35, 75 b.; *Zum Roten Bären*, Oberlinden 12, 60 b. (an historic inn, recorded in 1387); *City Hotel* (no rest.), Wasserstr. 2, 100 b.; *Atlanta* (no rest.), Rheinstr. 29, 72 b., SP; *Am Rathaus*, Rathausgasse 4–8, 38 b.; *Rappen*, Münsterplatz 13, 36 b.; *Markgräfler Hof*, Gerberau 22, 29 b. – YOUTH HOSTEL: Kartäuserstr. 151, 375 b. – CAMPING SITES: *Hirzberg*, Kartäuserstr. 99; *Kurbad Camping Mösle Park*, on the edge of the forest; *Breisgau Camping*, in Freiburg Hochdorf; *Tunisee*, in Freiburg Hochdorf Benzhausen.

RESTAURANTS. – *Zur Traube*, Schusterstr. 17 (old style Baden winebar); *Ratskeller*, Münsterplatz 11; *Wappen von Freiburg*, Münsterplatz 1; *Zum Roten Eber*, Münsterplatz 18; *Oberkirchs Weinstuben*, Münsterplatz 22; *Zum Storchen*, Schwabentorplatz 7; *Zähringer Burg*, Reutebachgasse 19; *Zum Kleinen Meyerhof*, Rathausgasse 27; *Taverne*, An der Mehlwaage 8; *Hongkong*, Auf den Zinnen 10 (Chinese). – ON THE SCHLOSSBERG: *Greifenegg-Schlössle* and *Schlossberg-Restaurant Dattler*.

CAFÉS. – *Münster-Café*, Münsterplatz 15; *Steinmetz*, Kaiser-Joseph-Str. 193.

EVENTS. – *Shrovetide Parade* on Rose Monday (last Monday before Lent); *Corpus Christi processions*;

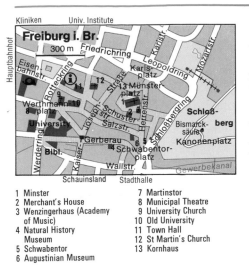

Kliniken   Univ. Institute

Hauptbahnhof

Freiburg i. Br.

300 m   Friedrichring

Eisenbahnstr.   Karlsplatz

Rottecking   St. Münsterplatz   Mozartstr.

Werthmann   Schusterstr.   Schloß-

8-platz   Salzstr.   Bismarck- **berg**
säule

University   Herrenstr.   Kanonenplatz

Gerberau   Schwabentorplatz
Bibl.
Wallstr.
Gewerbekanal

Schauinsland   Stadthalle

1 Minster
2 Merchant's House
3 Wenzingerhaus (Academy of Music)
4 Natural History Museum
5 Schwabentor
6 Augustinian Museum

7 Martinstor
8 Municipal Theatre
9 University Church
10 Old University
11 Town Hall
12 St Martin's Church
13 Kornhaus

Schauinsland Race for sports and racing cars (June); *Freiburg Wine Festival* (end June); *open-air performances* in Town Hall courtyard (end June and beginning July); *Theatrical Festival* (June/July); *Autumn Fair* in Messplatz (Oct.); *Christmas Market* in Rathausplatz; *Provincial Horticultural Exhibition* (1986).

Freiburg, a commercial and administrative centre as well as an episcopal and university city, situated between the Kaiserstuhl and the Black Forest at the point where the River Dreisam enters the Upper Rhine plain, is the gateway to the southern Black Forest. The 1284 m high Schauinsland, Freiburg's own domestic mountain, lies within the city boundaries, and only a short distance from its gates is the wild and romantic Höllental. Freiburg claims to be a "city of forests, of Gothic architecture and of wine". The Gothic Minster soars above the gables and roofs of the old town. The Colombi Park is surrounded by vineyards, and there are vines even on the Schlossberg in front of the Schwabentor. Freiburg is also a cultural centre, with a University, a State Academy of Music, a teachers' training college, a State training school for sculptors and stonemasons, museums, and a full programme of theatrical performances and concerts. It is also a conference centre and a sporting town. In the street called Oberlinden is what is believed to be Germany's oldest inn, the "Red Bear" (the names of its landlords being known as far back as 1311), and the streets of the Old Town still run side by side with the charming little streams called

"Bächle", as they did in the Middle Ages.

HISTORY. – At the end of the 11th c. the Dukes of Zähringen founded under their castle on the Schlossberg a trading and market settlement on the old Black Forest trade route between Swabia and Alsace. In 1120 Duke Berthold III and his brother Konrad gave it a municipal charter. The town's favourable situation, its market privileges and the rich deposits of silver in the Black Forest soon gave it a dominant position in the Breisgau. The Zähringen family died out in 1218 with Duke Berthold V and were succeeded by the Counts of Urach, who called themselves Counts of Freiburg. In 1368 the town bought its freedom from the Counts and submitted itself to the authority of the House of Habsburg. In 1457 Archduke Albrecht founded the University. Later Freiburg acquired some importance as a fortress. In 1805, at Napoleon's behest, Freiburg and the Breisgau were ceded by Austria to the newly created Grand Duchy of Baden. In 1827 the town became the see of an Archbishop. Between 1947 and 1952 it was the seat of the provincial government of Southern Baden, but in the latter year was incorporated in the newly established *Land* of Baden-Württemberg.

SIGHTS. – The main axis of the town (which suffered heavy damage during the Second World War but has been rebuilt) is the KAISER-JOSEPH-STRASSE, which divides the OLD TOWN (much of it now a pedestrian precinct) into an eastern half, with the Minster, and a western half, with the Town Hall and the University. Near the S end of the street is the old *Martinstor* (13th c.).

The **Minster* (13th–16th c.) is one of Germany's greatest masterpieces of Gothic architecture. The beautiful interior contains many works of art: 14th c. stained glass in the aisles; in the choir a

Freiburg Minster from the Schlossberg

painting on the high altar (1512–16) by Hans Baldung Grien (his finest work); in the University Chapel an altar painting (*c.* 1521) by Hans Holbein the Younger. From the platform of the delicately articulated **tower* (116 m high; completed 1320–30) there is a magnificent view. – In the MÜNSTERPLATZ a number of fine old buildings have survived: on the S side (No. 10) the red **Merchant House** (Kaufhaus), completed in 1532, with an arcade and crow-stepped gables, flanked by oriel windows with pointed roofs, and (No. 30) the *Wenzingerhaus* of 1761. On the N side the 15th c. *Kornhaus* (rebuilt 1969–71).

In SALZSTRASSE, occupying an old friary of the Augustinians, is the *Augustinian Museum*, with the artistic and historical collections of the city and the Upper Rhine region (including Matthias Grünewald's "Miracle of the Snow", stained glass and stone sculpture from the Minster, pictures by Baden painters). At the end of Salzstrasse is the 13th c. *Schwabentor* with wall paintings. – To the W, in the former *Adelshauser Kloster*, is the *Museum of Natural History and Ethnography*.

In the W part of the old town is the RATHAUSPLATZ, with a statue of the Franciscan *Berthold Schwarz*, who is believed to have invented gunpowder in 1359. On the W side of the square is the **Town Hall** (carillon daily at midday), the northern part of which dates from the 16th c. On its NE side is the Gothic *St Martin's Church*, with a beautifully restored interior and cloister wing. – In the neighbouring Franziskanerstrasse is the *Haus zum Walfisch*, a late Gothic burgher's house with a beautiful oriel window, built, it is believed, in 1516 as a residence for Emperor Maximilian in his old age.

In BERTHOLDSTRASSE are the *Old University* and the *University Church* (17th c., restored). Further W on the Ring are the *Municipal Theatre* (1910; exterior rebuilt 1963), the new *University Library* and the **University**, with three ranges of buildings laid out round a courtyard. Opposite the University, to the S, is the *Mensa* (students' refectory: 1963). N of the theatre stands the *Colombi Schlosschen* of 1859 with the Museum of prehistory and early history.

On the *Schlossberg* (460 m: cableway and lift), once occupied by the stronghold

of the Zähringen family, are the scanty remains of three castles and a column commemorating Bismarck. From the Kanonenplatz (formerly a bastion) there is a fine view of the town and the Minster.

SURROUNDINGS. – **Schauinsland** (1284 m: 21 km S), Freiburg's own mountain, reached either by road (many bends) or by cableway from Horben. – **Höllental** (20–25 km SE), with the *Stag's Leap Crag* and *Ravenna Gorge*. – **Titisee** (31 km SE), an attractively situated lake, 2 km long by ½ km wide, at the foot of the Feldberg. – **Feldberg** (by the Schauinsland road 39 km, via the Höllental and the Feldberg road 51 km), the highest point (1493 m) in the Black Forest (double chairlift to the Seebuck, 1148 m; television tower with viewing platform), excellent for winter sports.

Freudenstadt

Land: Baden-Württemberg.
Vehicle registration: FDS.
Altitude: 740 m. – Population: 20,000.
Post code: D-7290. – Dialling code: 0 74 41.
ⓘ **Städtische Kurverwaltung,**
Lauterbadstr. 5;
tel. 60 74.

HOTELS. – *Steigenberger Parkhostellerie*, Karl von Hahn Str. 129, 238 b., SB, sauna, solarium; *RWP Hotel Eden*, Im Nickentale 5, 125 b., SB, sauna, solarium; *Golfhotel Wandlust*, Lauterbadstr. 92, 146 b.; *Luz Posthotel*, Stuttgarter Str. 5, 76 b.; *Kurhotel Schwarzwaldhof*, Hohenrieder 74, 70 b.; *Kurhotel Sonne am Kurpark*, Turnhallestr. 63, 65 b., SB, sauna, solarium; *Hohenried*, Zeppelinstr. 5, 42 b., SB, solarium; *Württemberger Hof*, Lauterbadstr. 10, 35 b.; *Kurhotel Lauterbad*, 25 b.

RESTAURANTS. – *Ratskeller*, Markplatz 8; *Bärenschlössle*, Christophstr. 29; *Weinstube Bären*, Lange Str. 33. – *Café Bacher zum Falken*, Lossburgerstr. 5.

RECREATION. – Golf-course; tennis-courts; panorama swimming bath.

This health resort in the northern Black Forest is one of the most frequented holiday places in the region, and is also a popular winter sports resort.

HISTORY. – Freudenstadt was founded in 1599. Duke Frederick I of Württemberg settled in the town which was laid out on a grid plan and which was occupied mainly by miners from Christophstal and Protestant refugees from Salzburg. It received its present name when the foundation stone of the church was laid. In 1632 much of the town was destroyed by fire. In the 18th and 19th c. there was quite considerable glassmaking. In 1944–45 the centre of the town was completely destroyed, but the post-war rebuilding (1949–54) has produced a handsome and attractive replacement.

SIGHTS. – In the centre of the town is the spacious MARKTPLATZ (4½ hectares), surrounded by arcaded houses. In the middle of the square are the *Town House* (local museum) and *Post Office*. At the S corner is the *Town Church* (1601–08, restored 1951), with two naves at right angles to one another, one for men and the other for women (lectern, borne by the four evangelists, of 1140, 11th–12th c. font). The most southerly part of the town, which merges into the park-like natural firs forest (the "Palm Forest"), contains the SPA INSTALLATIONS – the *Kurhaus*, the *Kurgarten* and the *Kurmittelhaus* at the foot of the Kienberg.

SURROUNDINGS. – The *Schwarzwald-Hochstrasse* (Black Forest Ridgeway) runs from Freudenstadt via the Kniebis and Ruhestein areas and past the Mummelsee to Baden-Baden, giving access to the hills of the northern Black Forest and opening up extensive views. The SCHWARZWALD-TÄLERSTRASSE (Black Forest Valley Highway), running N to Karlsruhe and S to Wolfach, also passes through magnificent scenery.

In the Zeppelin Museum, Friedrichshafen

Friedrichshafen

Land: Baden-Württemberg.
Vehicle registration: FN.
Altitude: 402 m. – Population: 53,000.
Post code: D-7990. – Dialling code: 0 75 41.
ⓘ **Tourist Information,**
  Friedrichstr. 18;
  tel. 2 17 29 and 2 03 91.

HOTELS. – *Buchhorner Hof*, Friedrichstr. 33, 123 b.; *Krone* (no rest.), Schanzstr. 7, 120 b., SB; *Goldenes Rad*, Karlstr. 48, 120 b.; *Föhr*, Albrechtstr. 73, 28 b.; *Zeppelin* (no rest.), Eugenstr. 41, 20 b.

RESTAURANTS. – *Altstadt-Stuben Rommelspacher*, Seestr. 20; *Fischer*, Ailinger Str. 12.

EVENTS. – *Racing, motor sport and flying exhibition* (RMF; March); *International Lake Constance Fair* (IBO; May); *International Amateur Radio Exhibition* (ham-radio; June); *Seehasenfest* (July); *Interboot* boat show (Sept.).

Friedrichshafen, lying half-way along the northern shore of Lake Constance, is an important industrial town and tourist resort with excellent facilities (Lake Constance steamers) and connections to Switzerland.

HISTORY. – The town came into being in 1811 when King Frederick I of Württemberg promoted the amalgamation of the two villages of Buchhorn and Hofen, which were linked by the building of the "Neustadt" (New Town). In 1824 the maiden voyage of the steamer "Wilhelm" from Friedrichshafen marked the opening of shipping traffic on Lake Constance, and the town soon became the leading port on the lake. The first Zeppelin took to the air here in 1900. In 1944 most of Friedrichshafen was destroyed by bombing, but an energetic programme of rebuilding was carried through in the post-war years.

SIGHTS. – In the busy harbour is the modern *Harbour Station*, with a popular restaurant (terrace with view). The Uferstrasse which runs from here past the *Stadtgarten* affords magnificent views of the lake and the Alps. Near the yacht harbour is the conference and cultural centre "Graf Zeppelin House". In the town centre is the *Town Hall* (1956), with the *Lake Constance Museum* (art collection) and the Zeppelin Museum. At the W end of the town is the *Schloss* (former residence of Duke Carl of Württemberg), converted in 1824–30 from an old monastic house, with a prominent *church* (1695–1700).

SURROUNDINGS. – 12 km SE, on the shores of the lake, is *Langenargen*, with Schloss Montfort. 10 km farther on is the health resort of **Wasserburg**, on a peninsula, with a handsome church, castle and museum of fishing.

Fulda

Land: Hesse. – Vehicle registration: FD.
Altitude: 280 m. – Population: 60,000.
Post code: D-6400. – Dialling code: 06 61.
ⓘ **Städtisches Verkehrsbüro,**
  Schloss Str. 1, Stadtschloss;
  tel. 10 23 45 and 10 23 46.

HOTELS. – *Zum Kurfürst*, Schloss Str. 2, 94 b.; *Goldener Karpfen*, Simpliziusplatz 1, 43 b.; *Lenz*, Leipziger Str. 122, 87 b., sauna; *Peterchens Mondfahrt* (no rest.), Rhabanus Maurus Str. 7, 35 b.; *Kolpinghaus*, Goethestr, 13, 90 b. – IN NEUENBERG: *Europa*, Haimberger Str. 65, 120 b. – YOUTH HOSTEL: Neuenberger Str. 107, 150 b.

RESTAURANTS. – *Dianakeller*, in the Orangery; *Hauptwache*, Bonifatiusplatz 2.

CAFÉS. – *Thiele*, Mittelstr. 2; *Prüfer*, Bahnhofstr. 16.

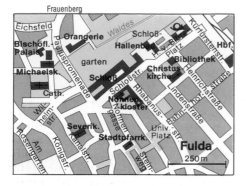

This old episcopal city is beautifully situated in the valley of the River Fulda among the foothills, crowned by churches, of the Rhön and Vogelsberg. The Prince-Bishops of the 18th c. endowed it with its Baroque architecture. The town is now a considerable industrial centre, with a ring of tower blocks on its outskirts. It has a Roman Catholic College of Theology and Philosophy, and is the meeting-place of an annual Bishops' conference.

HISTORY. – In 744 Sturmius, a disciple of St Boniface, founded a Benedictine abbey, which continued in existence until 1803. The Abbot of Fulda was from 969 Primate of all the Benedictines in Germany and France, and from 1220 a Prince-Abbot. Fulda was granted the right to hold markets and coin money in 1011, and received its municipal charter around 1114. Until the 14th c. it was the meeting-place of many court and princely diets. 1734 saw the foundation of its university (now a College of Theology and Philosophy). In 1752 the Abbots of Fulda became Prince-Bishops (until 1803). Fulda became the chief town of a Kreis (district) in 1866.

SIGHTS. – The **Stadtschloss** in Schloss Strasse, former residence of the imperial and Prince-Abbots was completed in 1730 and is today the administrative headquarters of the town. The historic rooms (including Princes' Hall and Hall of Mirrors) can be visited. On the N side of the Schlossgarten is the Baroque *Orangerie*, laid out according to the plans of Master Builder Maximilian von Welsch and now a conference and congress centre; in front of it stands the *Floravase*, a sculpture of 1728.

The Cathedral, in the DOMPLATZ, was built in 1704–12 by Johann Dietzenhofer and is the last resting place of St Boniface. In the *Cathedral Museum* can be seen a valuable reliquary, etc. N of the Cathedral stands *St Michael's Church*, one of the oldest churches in Germany (rotunda and crypt of 822) and the Bishop's Palace.

In the museum building in Universitätsstrasse is the *Vonderau Museum* (prehistory, ethnology, applied science). The *German Fire-service Museum* in St Laurentius Strasse in the SW of the town exhibits full-scale fire-engines from 1808 to 1937; the second part of the museum (documents about firefighting) can be found in the museum building in Universitätsstrasse.

In the *Provincial Library*, between the Schloss and the station, are valuable codices and Gospel books from the old Fulda Abbey school. – From *Frauenberg Friary* (founded *c.* 800, present building erected 1780; Baroque church), 10 minutes N of the Schlossgarte, there is a fine view of the town and the Rhön hills. – On the far side of the River Fulda, in the suburb of NEUENBERG, is *St Andrew's Church*, originally belonging to the Benedictine house of Andreasberg, with fine 11th c. paintings in the crypt.

SURROUNDINGS. – **Schloss Fasanerie** (*Adolphseck*: 6 km S), a Baroque castle of 1730–56, was once the summer residence of the imperial and Prince-Abbots of Fulda. Today it houses an interesting museum, with pictures, tapestries, porcelain, glass and a collection of antique sculpture. In the crypt of the Propsteikirche of **St Lioba** on the Petersberg (5 km NE; view) can be seen the oldest wall paintings in Germany (836–847).

Füssen

Land: Bavaria. – Vehicle registration: OAL.
Altitude: 800 m. – Population: 15,000.
Post code: D-8958. – Dialling code: 0 83 62.
ⓘ **Kurverwaltung,**
   Augsburger-Tor-Platz 1;
   tel. 70 77.

HOTELS. – *Sailer's Kurhotel*, Bildhauer Sturm Str. 14, 36 b., SB, sauna; *Hirsch*, Augsburger Tor Platz 2, 90 b.; *Sonne* (no rest.), Reichenstr. 37, 64 b.; *Kurhotel Filser*, Saulingstr. 3, 50 b. – IN BAD FAULENBACH: *Kurhotel Berger*, Alatseestr. 26, 50 b., SB, sauna; *Kurhotel Wiedemann*, Am Anger 3, 47 b. – YOUTH HOSTEL: Mariahilfer Str. 5, 150 b. – CAMPING SITE: *Hopfensee*, Füssen Hopfen a.S.

This old town on the Lech between the Ammergau and Allgäu Alps, framed by mountains, is a popular health and winter sports resort. Its suburb of Bad Faulenbach also makes it a spa town, with a sulphurous spring, the Kneipp water cure and mud baths. It lies at the end of the Romantische Strasse and is the starting point for visits to the famous royal castles of *Neuschwanstein and Hohenschwangau.

HISTORY. – The area round Füssen has been settled since very early times; there is evidence of temporary occupation in the Palaeolithic period. The Celts who lived here in historical times were followed in 15 B.C. by Roman colonists; the area then became part of the province of Raetia, and a military road, the Via Claudia, was built. On what is now the Schlossberg there was a fortress designed to provide protection against the Alemanni, who nevertheless later occupied the area. The present town goes back to a monastery founded by St Magnus (popularly called St Mang). The town received a municipal charter towards the end of the 12th c. From 1313 it was subject to the Bishop of Augsburg, and in 1802 passed to Bavaria. In 1921 the neighbouring Faulenbach was incorporated in the town.

SIGHTS. – Above the town is the *Hohes Schloss* (13th and 16th c.), formerly the summer residence of the Prince-Bishops of Augsburg, now the seat of the district court (Knights' Hall, chapel, collection of pictures). Below it is the former Benedictine abbey of *St Mang*, founded *c.* 728, now occupied by the Town Hall and Heimatmuseum (Princes' Hall, Papal apartments), with the Baroque *Town Church* (1701–17; tower and crypt of the 10th and 11th c.), the first work of the local architect Johann Jakob Herkomer. – A short distance W (reached by way of the 310 towards Kempten) is the district of BAD FAULENBACH, with a sulphurous spring, Kneipp cure, mud and natural baths. – 1 km N of Füssen is the 11½ km long **Forggensee**, an artificial lake created by a dam on the Lech (15·75 sq. km).

SURROUNDINGS. – *Schloss Neuschwanstein* (965 m, 5 km E: see photograph on cover), the towered and battlemented "fairy castle" built for King Ludwig II of Bavaria in 1869–86 by E. Riedel to the design of the scene-painter C. Jank (fine throne-room and minstrels' hall; beautiful views). – *Schloss Hohenschwangau* (865 m, 4 km E), in neo-Gothic style, built for King Maximilian II in 1832–36 to the design of the scene-painter D. Quaglio (frescoes by Moritz von Schwind).

Bad Gandersheim

Land: Lower Saxony.
Vehicle registration: NOM.
Altitude: 113 m. – Population: 12,500.
Post code: D-3353. – Dialling code: 0 53 82.
ⓘ **Kurverwaltung,**
Stiftsfreiheit 12;
tel. 7 34 40/1.

HOTELS. – *Kurpark Hotel Bartels*, Dr. Heinrich Jasper Str. 2, 165 b.; *Weisses Ross*, Markt 1, 60 b.; *Am Kantorberg*, Schanzensteig 2, 34 b. – YOUTH HOSTEL: Am Kantorberg 17. – CAMPING SITE: *Kur-Campingpark Bad Gandersheim*.

RESTAURANTS. – *Ratskeller*, Am Markt 10; *Kurhaus*, Hildesheimer Str. 6.

EVENTS. – *Domfestspiele* (in summer).

Bad Gandersheim is a well-known spa (recommended for rheumatism, gynaecological complaints, children's illnesses and catarrh of the respiratory organs) in the Leinebergland between the Harz and the Solling hills. It is famous as the home of Roswitha of Gandersheim, the first German poetess. The annual Domfestspiele, performed against the imposing backdrop of the Cathedral, provide a memorable experience.

HISTORY. – Gandersheim Abbey was taken under royal patronage by King Ludwig II in 877. In the 10th c. the nun Roswitha of Gandersheim wrote her Latin plays and poems in the nunnery here. The first miraculous cures by the medicinal springs took place at the beginning of the 13th c., but it was not until 1878 that Gandersheim began to be developed as a spa.

SIGHTS. – The town's principal landmark is the 11th c. Romanesque *Stiftskirche (Cathedral;* rich interior), to the E of which is the former *Abbey (c.* 1600), with a beautiful Renaissance gable (Imperial Hall of 1735). – In the nearby MARKT, ringed by handsome half-timbered houses, is the *Town Hall*, a charming Renaissance building which incorporates the old St Moritz's Church. – *St George's Church* (1550), on the W side of the town, has a Romanesque tower and a flat carved timber roof. – 1 km N of the town centre is the modern *spa establishment*.

Garmisch-Partenkirchen

Land: Bavaria. – Vehicle registration: GAP.
Altitude: 720 m. – Population: 27,500.
Post code: D-8100. – Dialing code: 0 88 21.
ⓘ **Verkehrsamt,** at Station;
tel. 25 70.
Kurverwaltung,
Schnitzschulstr. 19;
tel. 5 30 93.

HOTELS. – IN GARMISCH: *Alpina*, Alpspitzstr. 12, 70 b., SB, SP, sauna; *Obermühle*, Mühlstr. 22, 66 b., SB, sauna; *Königshof*, St. Martin Str. 4, 180 b., SB, sauna; *Clausing's Posthotel*, Marienplatz 12, 75 b.; *Zugspitz* (no rest.), Klammstr. 19, 72 b., SB, sauna; *Garmischer Hof* (no rest.), Bahnhofstr. 51, 59 b.; *Aschenbrenner* (no rest.), Loisachstr. 46, 43 b. – IN PARTENKIRCHEN: *Holiday Inn*, Mittenwalder Str. 2, 215 b., SB, sauna; *Reindl's Partenkirchner Hof*, Bahnhofstr. 15, 108 b. ("Reindl Grill"), SB, sauna; *Posthotel Partenkirchen*,

Ludwigstr. 49, 90 b.; *Leiner*, Wildenauer Str. 20, 73 b., SB, sauna. – IN THE SURROUNDINGS: *Forsthaus Graseck*, 74 b., SB, sauna; *Schneefernerhaus*, on Zugspitzplatt (2650 m), 23 b., sunbathing terrace. – YOUTH HOSTEL: Jochstr. 10, 290 b. – CAMPING SITE: *Zugspitze*, in the Schmölz.

RESTAURANTS. – *Reindle's Drei Mohren*, Ludwigstr. 65; *Stahls Badstuben*, in the Alpspitz Baths, Klammstr. 47; *Alpspitze*, Sonnenstr. 6; *Heuriger zum Melber*, Ludwigstr. 37.

CAFÉS. – *Krönner*, Achenfeldstr. 1; *Kneitinger*, Bahnhofstr. 7; *Riessersee*, on the Riessersee.

International Casino (roulette, baccarat), Marienplatz.

Garmisch-Partenkirchen in winter

Garmisch-Partenkirchen is one of the busiest tourist and holiday places in the Bavarian Alps, a well-known health resort and the leading German winter sports resort. The Winter Olympics of 1936 took place here, and in 1978 the alpine skiing world championships. The broad valley of the Loisach is enclosed within mighty mountain massifs – to the N Kramer and Wank, to the S the towering rock wall of the Wetterstein, with Kreuzeck, the jagged Alpspitze and Dreitorspitze and, rearing up behind the Grosser Waxenstein, Germany's highest mountain, the Zugspitze (2963 m). Garmisch-Partenkirchen is on the German Alpine Highway and the "Olympic Highway" (Olympiastrasse). It is the chief town of the Werdenfels district.

HISTORY. – The old settlement of Partenkirchen, the Roman *Parthanum*, was granted the right to hold a market in 1361. It was an important staging post on the trade route from Augsburg into Italy by way of Mittenwald, and enjoyed a period of great prosperity in the Middle Ages thanks to the thriving trade between Germany and Italy. Garmisch shared in this prosperity. Both places belonged to the Imperial county of Werdenfels, established by the Bishop of Freising at the end of the 13th c., which passed to Bavaria in 1803. After a period of economic decline in the 17th c. the town took on a new lease of life as a holiday centre around the middle of the 19th c. and at the beginning of the 20th c. the twin towns became a focus of the tourist trade.

SIGHTS. – GARMISCH, with its picturesque old peasants' houses (particularly in Frühlingstrasse), lies on the River Loisach W of the railway. In Richard-Strauss-Platz is the *Congress Building* and nearby the *Kurpark*. The *New Parish Church* of St Martin (by Joseph Schmuzer, 1730–33) has a rich Baroque interior, the *Old Parish Church* (15th and 16th c.) important remains of Gothic wall paintings. At the Zugspitze Station is the *Olympic Ice Stadium* and the Alpspitz Swimming Bath (with artificial waves).

Beyond the Loisach, at Zöppritzstrasse 42, is the *Richard Strauss Villa*, home of the composer, who died in Garmisch in 1949.

In PARTENKIRCHEN, between the River Partnach and the Wank, are a handsome *Town Hall* (1935) and the *Werdenfels Heimatmuseum* (in the "Wackerle-Haus" in Ludwigstrasse). From Florianplatz there is a magnificent *view of the Zugspitze*. Higher up (15 min.) are the *St. Anton Gardens* (fine view), with the *pilgrimage church of St Antony* (1704: beautiful interior). – S of Partenkirchen on the Gudiberg is the *Olympic Ski Stadium*, with two jumping platforms.

SURROUNDINGS. – *Wank* (1780 m, 3 km NE; circular cableway; mountain inn), with beautiful views of the valley and surrounding mountains. – *Kreuzeck* (1652 m, 4 km S; Zöppritz-Haus; cableway; mountain inn). – *Eckbauer* (1239 m, 4 km SE; mountain inn; cableway). – Osterfelderkopf (2050 m, 5 km SW; cableway; restaurant). Cableway to the *Hochalm* (1705 m). – *Partnachklamm* (3 km SE), a wild and romantic mountain gorge on the River Partnach, with tunnels and galleries. – *Höllentalklamm* (6 km SW). From the Höllentalklamm hut (1045 m) there is a road 1 km long, with numerous tunnels, galleries and bridges, to the end of the gorge (1161 m). – Riessersee (2 km S), a small mountain lake with views of the Kleiner and Grosser Waxenstein. – *Eibsee (7 km SW), a beautiful little mountain lake with views of the Waxenstein and the Riffelwand of the Zugspitze. Cableway (4·5 km) to the top of the Zugspitze. – **Zugspitze** (2963 m, 10 km SW), the highest mountain in Germany. There is an 18·7 km long rack railway from the *Zugspitzbahnhof* by way of *Riessersee*, *Grainau-Badersee*, *Eibsee* and *Riffelriss* to the *Hotel Schneefenerhaus* (2650 m), and from there a cableway to the peak (2950 m: viewpoint terrace). There is also a 4·5 km long cableway from *Eibsee* to the summit (see above). Magnificent views in all directions: to the S the Central Alps from the Hohe Tauern to Silvretta, with Ortler and Bernina; to the W the Lechtal and Allgäu Alps, with Tödi and Säntis beyond; to the N the Bavarian high plateau; to the E the Karwendel and the Tegernsee and Kitzbühel Alps. On the nearby *W summit* (2963 m) is a Bundespost radio station (1974–75: previously the Münchner Haus) and a chapel. On the *E summit* (2962 m: only for those with a good head for heights) is a cross. – The *Zugspitzplatt* (7·2 sq. km) is Germany's highest skiing area, with the best snow.

Giessen

Land: Hesse. – Vehicle registration: GI.
Altitude: 157 m. – Population: 76,000.
Post code: D-6300. – Dialling code: 06 41.
ⓘ Verkehrsamt,
   Berliner Platz 3;
   tel. 3 06 21 88.

HOTELS. – *Steinsgarten, Hein Heckroth Str. 20, 140 b., SB; Kübel, Bahnhofstr. 47, 79 b., SB; Am Ludwigsplatz 8, 74 b.; Liebig (no rest.), Liebigstr. 21, 55 b.; Köhler, Westanlage 35, 50 b., sauna; Parkhotel Friedrichstrasse, Friedrichstr. 1, 58 b.; Parkhotel Wolfstrasse, Wolfstr. 26, 30 b.; Motel an der Lahn (no rest.), Lahnstr. 21, 24 b. – YOUTH HOSTEL: Richard Schirrmann Weg 53 (on the Hardt). – CAMPING SITES: Am Schwimmbad, in Giessen Klein Linden; Campingplatz am Dutenhofener See, 6 km W from Giessen.

RESTAURANTS. – Kongresshalle-Ratsstuben, Berliner Platz 2; Martinshof, Liebigstr. 20.

CAFÉ. – Dach-Café, Ludwigsplatz 11.

This old university town on the Lahn, in the wide Giessen basin, is the largest town in central Hesse, with a number of large industrial undertakings. The great chemist Justus von Liebig, the originator of modern nitrogenous fertilisers and inventor of meat extract, lived and taught here from 1834 to 1852. In the Second World War the town suffered great destruction; a few old buildings were restored.

HISTORY. – The existence of a castle belonging to the Counts of Gleiberg is recorded in 1197, and by 1248 Giessen possessed a municipal charter. In 1265 it passed by purchase to the Landgraves of Hesse, who made it a powerful stronghold. In 1605 a "paedagogium" (residential school) was established in the town, and in 1607 this was raised to the status of a university. Two-thirds of the town was destroyed in 1944. The amalgamation of Giessen and Wetzlar with a further 14 other places to form the town of Lahn, was strongly resisted by the inhabitants, so that the new town of Lahn was broken up in 1979 and Giessen once more became independent.

SIGHTS. – In the Brandplatz stands the Altes Schloss (14th c.; destroyed in 1944 and rebuilt in 1980) with the Upper Hesse Museum (sculpture, paintings, furniture, etc.); other sections of this museum are in the nearby Burgmannenhaus (Georg Schlosser Strasse 2; civic history and ethnology) and in Haus Asterweg 9 (prehistory and early history, ethnology). A little way NE, in Landgraf-Philipp-Platz, are the Neues Schloss (16th c.), a half-timbered building. On the E edge of the old town is the Botanic Garden, the oldest in Germany (1609). In the S of the town is the Justus Liebig

University (founded 1607, present buildings 1880), at which the great chemist taught. The Liebig Museum at Liebigstr. 12 contains his laboratory, excellently preserved. In Bismarckstrasse is the University Library.

Goslar

Land: Lower Saxony.
Vehicle registration: GS.
Altitude: 265–320 m. – Population: 54,000.
Post code: D-3380. – Dialling code: 0 53 21.
ⓘ Tourist-Information,
   Markt 7;
   tel. 70 42 15/16.

HOTELS. – *Der Achtermann, Rosentorstr. 20, 184 b., old-style German Bierstube; Kaiserworth, Markt 3, 80 b. (a historic house dating from 1494, with "Dukatenkeller"); Das Brusttuch, Hoher Weg 1, 25 b. (a patrician mansion of 1526), SB; Harzhotel Bären, Krugwiese 11a, 340 b., SB, sauna; Niedersächsischer Hof, Klubgartenstr. 1, 120 b.; Schwarzer Adler, Rosentorstr. 25, 60 b.; Zur Tanne (no rest.), Bäringerstr. 10, 33 b. – IN GRAUHOF: Grauhof, at the Grauhof Fountain, 60 b., SB, sauna. – IN HAHNENKLEE: *Der Harz Stern, Triftstr. 25, 270 b., SB, sauna; *Dorint Harzhotel Kreuzeck, Kreuzeck 1, 180 b., SB, sauna; *Hahnenkleer Hof, Parkstr. 24a, 52 b., SB, sauna; Vier Jahreszeiten, Parkstr. 14, 250 b., SB, sauna; Diana, Parkstr. 4, 49 b., SB, sauna; Der Waldgarten, Lautenthaler Str. 36, 60 b., SB. – YOUTH HOSTEL: Rammelsberger Str. 25, 210 b. – CAMPING SITES: Sennhütte, on road to Clausthal-Zellerfeld; Am Kreuzeck, on road to Hahnenklee.

RESTAURANTS. – Ratskeller, Markt 1; Bistro, Bäkkerstr. 18, Lindenhof, Schützenallee 1. – IN HAHNENKLEE: Bergkanne, Am Kreuzeck; Eden am See, Grabenweg 10.

CAFÉ. – Anders, Hoher Weg.

This thousand-year-old Imperial city on the northern fringe of the Harz has its great Kaiserpfalz (Imperial palace) and its medieval churches and fortifications to bear witness to a great past. The old town has picturesque old-world streets of half-timbered houses. Goslar also takes in the well-known climatic and winter sports resort of Hahnenklee-Bockswiese at the foot of the 726 m high Bocksberg.

HISTORY. – The origin of Goslar was a trading settlement which as early as the 10th c. had achieved considerable economic importance by working the rich deposits of silver in the nearby Rammelsberg. At the beginning of the 11th c., therefore, Emperor Henry II moved his seat from Werla, above the Oker valley, to Goslar. The Kaiserpfalz at Goslar (rebuilt in the reign of Henry III) became the favourite residence of the Salian Emperors. A notable event in its history was Pope Victor II's visit to Henry III in 1056. The town was the meeting-place of many Imperial diets. In the 13th c. it became a member of the Hanse and in 1340 a

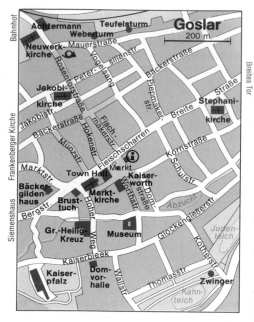

free Imperial city. After a period of great prosperity the town declined, following the loss of its mineral-working rights in the Rammelsberg and its involvement in the wars of the period. Only in recent times has it enjoyed an economic revival thanks to the development of industry and tourism.

SIGHTS. – In the old-world MARKTPLATZ, with its 13th c., *Market Fountain* decorated with the Imperial eagle, stands the *Town Hall (main building 15th c.). On the upper floor is the splendid Hall of Homage, with late Gothic wall and ceiling paintings and 16th c. carved woodwork (valuable Gospel book of 1230, silver can of 1477). On the S side of the square is the *Kaiserworth* (1494), the former guild house of the cloth-workers, now a hotel, with eight 17th c. figures of Emperors; to the left, at the corner, is the "Dukaten-männchen" ("Ducat Man"). From here Worthstrasse leads to the *Goslar Museum* which has collections on the history and culture of Goslar as well as on the geology and fauna of the Harz.

Well worth seeing are objets d'art from the former cathedral (including the altar) and the geological department which specialises in the Goslar "geological square mile".

Just W of the Town Hall is the late Romanesque **Market Church**, and facing its W front is the *Brusttuch*, a burgher's house (1526) with rich carved decoration. Nearby is the *Bakers' Guild House* (1501–57), now occupied by the Chamber of Industry and Commerce. Farther W is the *Siemenshaus* (1693), ancestral home of the Siemens family.

In the southern part of the old town, in the large square of Kaiserbleek, stands the *Kaiserpfalz (Imperial Palace), the largest surviving Romanesque palace in Germany, built in the reign of Emperor Henry III (1039–56) and rebuilt or altered several times. In the 47 m long Imperial Hall are mural paintings by Hermann Wislicenus (1879–97). In *St Ulrich's Chapel* is the tomb of Henry III, with his heart in a casket in the base. – E of the Kaiserpfalz is the *Cathedral Chapel*, the porch of the Cathedral (demolished 1820–22), in which is the Imperial throne with its stone rails (11th c.). A little way N, in the Hoher Weg, is the *Grosses Heiliges Kreuz* (formerly St John's Hospital, founded 1254), now an old people's home.

N of the Markt is the 11th–16th c. *St James's Church* (Jakobikirche: R.C.), with a fine Pietà of about 1525. A short distance W are the *Monks' House*, a half-timbered building of 1528, with the *Museum of Modern Art*, and the *Neuwerkkirche*, a monastic church founded c. 1186, with beautiful wall paintings in the choir. Opposite the church is the *Achtermannsturm* (1508: now a hotel), all that remains of one of the town gates, the Rosentor.

Other remains of the past on the line of the old fortifications are the *Breites Tor* (Broad Gate: 1505) to the E of the old town, the *Zwinger*, a round tower to the SE (1517: restaurant; medieval armoury and torture chamber) and the Romanesque *Frankenberg Church* (12th c.; wall paintings) to the W.

In the outlying district of HAHNENKLEE, 13 km SW, are a Scandinavian-style *stave church* (1908) and the grave of the composer, Paul Linke.

SURROUNDINGS. – The Augustinian **Riechenberg Monastery** (3 km NW), with the ruined church of St Mary (12th c.: crypt with richly ornamented pillars and capitals). – **Grauhof Stiftskirche** (4 km N), an 18th c. Baroque church with a rich interior. – *Oker valley (6 km SE), a wild and romantic river valley with magnificent rocky scenery and the *Romkerhalle Falls*.

Kaiserpfalz, Goslar

Göttingen

Land: Lower Saxony.
Vehicle registration: GÖ.
Altitude: 150 m. – Population: 130,000.
Post code: D-3400. – Dialling code: 05 51.
ⓘ **Fremdenverkehr verein Göttingen e.V.,**
Altes Rathaus, Markt 9;
tel. 5 40 00.
Tourist Office, at Main Station;
tel. 5 60 00.

HOTELS. – *Gebhards Hotel,* Goetheallee 22, 82 b.,
SB; *Eden* (no rest.), Reinhäuser Landstr. 22a, 59 b.,
SB, sauna; *Zur Sonne* (no rest.), Paulinerstr. 10,
120 b.; *Central* (no rest.), Jüdenstr. 12, 75 b.; *Stadt
Hannover* (no rest.), Goetheallee 21, 50 b. – IN GRONE:
*Parkhotel Ropeter, Kasseler Landstr. 45, 143 b., SB,
sauna; *Rennschuh,* Kesseler Landstr. 93, 90 b., SB,
sauna; *Groner Hof,* Kasseler Landstr. 64, 60 b. –
Autobahn-Rasthaus Göttingen-West, Rosdorf-
Mengershausen, 70 b. – YOUTH HOSTEL: Habichts-
weg 2, 150 b.

RESTAURANTS. – *Junkernschänke,* Barfüsserstr.
(half-timbered house of 1547); *Schwarzer Bär,* Kurz
Str. 12 (traditional student haunt); *Rathskeller,* Altes
Rathaus; *La Sicilia,* Wendenstr. 8a; *Peking* (Chinese),
Weender Landstr. 3.

CAFÉ. – *Cron und Lanz,* Weender Str. 25.

EVENTS. – *Film Festival* (April); *Art Market* (June);
Handel Festival (June); *University Week* (Oct.): *Jazz
Festival* (Nov.).

**Göttingen, in the Leine valley at the
foot of the Hainberg, is one of the
German university towns with the
richest heritage of tradition. Many
Nobel Prize winners have studied or
taught here, and the headquarters of
the Max Planck Society came here in
1945. Göttingen is also noted as a
city of congresses and of the
theatre. The old town, with many
half-timbered buildings, is still enclosed within the line of its walls. In
the outer districts of the town there
has been considerable industrial
development (precision engineering, optical equipment, metal-
working).**

HISTORY. – First recorded in 953, Göttingen received
its municipal charter in 1210. From 1351 to 1572 it
was a member of the Hanse. In 1734 elector George
II of Hanover founded the University, named the
Georgia Augusta University in his honour, which
became a fashionable university for young men of
good family and rapidly acquired a great reputation. In
our own day the University and its numerous institutes
(particularly in the faculties of science and medicine)
still play a major role in the town's life.

SIGHTS. – In the centre of the OLD
TOWN, in the MARKT, are the *Gänseliesel*
("Goose Lizzie") *Fountain* and the **Old
Town Hall** (1396–1443), with a fine
interior. Behind it is **St John's Church**

Town Hall and Markt, Göttingen

(14th c.), the oldest in the town. Its twin
towers have different tops; from the
gallery of the N tower there is a fine
panoramic view. To the NW is the
University Library (over 2 million volumes), to the SW the 14th c. *St Mary's
Church* (formerly belonging to the Teutonic Order).

In WEENDER STRASSE, Göttingen's principal
shopping street (pedestrian precinct), is
the Gothic **St James's Church**, with a
74 m high W tower (1426), a noted city
landmark, and a beautiful carved altar of
1402.

NE of the Markt in BARFÜSSERSTRASSE are
the old *Ratsapotheke* (Council Pharmacy), a fine half-timbered building
of 1553 (corner of Markt), the richly
decorated *Junkernschänke* of 1547–49
(No. 5: hotel) and the *Bornemann House*
of 1536 (No. 12). In Wilhelmsplatz is the
neo-classical **Great Hall** of the University (1837; sculpture by Ernst von
Bandel on the pediment). A short distance
E are *St Alban's Church* (15th c.; altar
with side-wings of 1499) and the *Stadthalle* (1964).

To the N, on the line of the old fortifications, is the THEATERPLATZ, with the
German Theatre, the **Museum of Ethnography** (interesting collection of material
from the South Seas) and the *University
Art Collection* (Italian, Dutch and German
painting, sculpture and graphic art from
the 14th to the 20th c.). Farther N is the
Botanic Garden. – In the Hardenberger

Hof (1592) on the Ritterplan is the *Municipal Museum* (prehistoric material, history of the town and university, religious art).

On the S side of the line of ramparts are the *Bismarckhäuschen*, an old bastion in which Otto von Bismarck lived as a student in 1832–33, and the *Wöhler and Gauss-Weber Memorial.* – Friedrich Wöhler, who discovered aluminium (1827), and Gauss and Weber, inventors of the electro-magnetic telegraph (1833), all taught at Göttingen University.

SURROUNDINGS. – In *Friedland Mollenfelde* (16 km S) is the European Bread Museum with exhibits illustrating the history of making bread from the time of the Pharaohs until the present day (bus connection).

Hagen

Land: North Rhineland-Westphalia.
Vehicle registration: HA.
Altitude: 86–438 m. – Population: 217,000.
Post code: D-5800. – Dialling code: 0 23 31.
(i) **Büro Hagen Information,**
Pavilion Mittelstr.;
tel. 1 35 73.

HOTELS. – *Crest Hotel,* Wasserloses Tal 4, 203 b., SB, sauna; *Lex,* Elberfelder Str. 71, 71 b.; *Deutsches Haus,* Bahnhofstr. 35, 55 b.; *Central* (no rest.), Dahlenkampstr. 2, 31 b. – IN DAHL: *Dahler Schweiz,* Hemker Weg 12, 25 b. – IN HOHENLIMBURG: *Bentheimer Hof,* Stennertstr. 20, 30 b. – IN RUMMENOHL: *Dresel,* Rummenohler Str. 31, 20 b., sauna. – IN SELBECKE: *Schmidt,* Selbecker Str. 220, 36 b. – YOUTH HOSTEL: Eppenhauser Str. 65a, 130 b.

RESTAURANTS. – *Ratskeller,* Friedrich-Ebert-Platz; *China Restaurant,* Altenhagener Str. 2; *Schlossrestaurant,* Alter Schlossweg 30, Hagen-Hohenlimburg.

Hagen, situated on the northern fringes of the Sauerland, extends its tentacles into the valleys, surrounded by wooded hills, of the rivers Ruhr, Ennepe, Lenne and Volme. The industries of this city at the junction of important traffic routes include ironworking and iron products, the manufacture of accumulators and the production of foodstuffs, textiles and paper. Since 1975 Hagen has been the seat of the Open University and here too is situated the German Institute for public educational work.

HISTORY. – The original nucleus of Hagen was an early medieval court under the jurisdiction of the Archbishop of Cologne on the trading route from Cologne to North Germany by way of Dortmund. St John's Church, round which the settlement grew up, was in existence around the year 1000. In 1392 Hagen

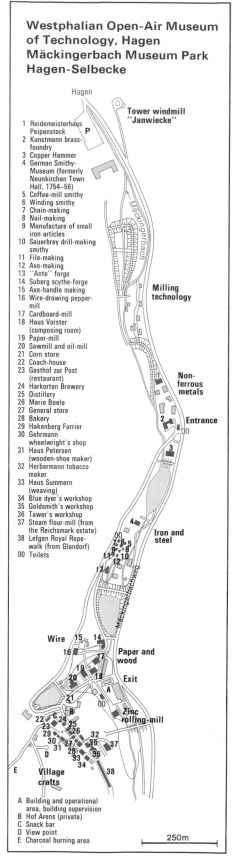

Westphalian Open-Air Museum of Technology, Hagen Mäckingerbach Museum Park Hagen-Selbecke

Hagen

1 Reidemeisterhaus Peipenstock
2 Kunstmann brass-foundry
3 Copper Hammer
4 German Smithy-Museum (formerly Neunkirchen Town Hall, 1754–56)
5 Coffee-mill smithy
6 Winding smithy
7 Chain-making
8 Nail-making
9 Manufacture of small iron articles
10 Sauerbrey drill-making smithy
11 File-making
12 Axe-making
13 "Ante" forge
14 Suberg scythe-forge
15 Axe-handle making
16 Wire-drawing pepper-mill
17 Cardboard-mill
18 Haus Vorster (composing room)
19 Paper-mill
20 Sawmill and oil-mill
21 Corn store
22 Coach-house
23 Gasthof zur Post (restaurant)
24 Harkorten Brewery
25 Distillery
26 Marie Boele
27 General store
28 Bakery
29 Hakenberg Farrier
30 Gehrmann wheelwright's shop
31 Haus Petersen (wooden-shoe maker)
32 Herbermann tobacco maker
33 Haus Summern (weaving)
34 Blue dyer's workshop
35 Goldsmith's workshop
36 Tawer's workshop
37 Steam flour-mill (from the Reichsmark estate)
38 Lefgen Royal Rope-walk (from Glandorf)
00 Toilets

Tower windmill "Janwiecke"

Milling technology

Non-ferrous metals

Entrance

Iron and steel

Wire

Paper and wood

Exit

Zinc rolling-mill

E Village crafts

A Building and operational area, building supervision
B Hof Arens (private)
C Snack bar
D View point
E Charcoal burning area

250m

passed from the Electorate of Cologne to the county of Mark, and in 1614, as part of that county, it fell to Brandenburg. Its industrial development began when the Great Elector settled swordsmiths from Solingen here in 1661. Soon afterwards paper-mills and cloth factories were established. In 1746 Hagen received its municipal charter from Frederick the Great. From 1876 the town grew rapidly in size by taking in land from neighbouring communes.

SIGHTS. – In Friedrich-Ebert-Platz in the centre of the town is the *Town Hall*. On its tower is a gilded sphere of special steel representing the sun, set up here in 1965. It has a diameter of 1·39 m, one thousand millionth of the sun's diameter, and the whole of the solar system is distributed about the town on the same scale, with bronze plates on the pavements marking the orbits of the planets. – To the W, in Elberfelder Strausse, is the *Municipal Theatre*. S of the Town Hall, at Hochstrasse 73, is the **Karl Ernst Osthaus Museum** (20th c. art), one of Henry van de Velde's huge Art-Nouveau buildings; (there are Art-Nouveau buildings throughout the town).

In the southern district of SELBECKE is the interesting **Westphalian Open-Air Museum of Technology**, covering an area of 34 hectares in the Mäckingerbach valley, with numerous industrial installations (including mills and smithics) brought together from various parts of Westphalia.

In the SW district of HASPE is *Haus Harkorten*, a slate-roofed house of 1756 in which the industrialist Friedrich Harkort, one of the pioneers of railway development, was born in 1793. – The villa development of *Hogenhagen* in the district of EPPENHAUSEN reflects the town-planning ideas of the Werkbund (founded in 1907 to promote good industrial design); its central feature is the house, *Hohenhof*, built by van de Velde 1906–08. – In the SE district of HOHEN-LIMBURG is **Schloss Hohenlimburg** (13th–14th c., with later rebuilding), with a Heimatmuseum. – In the courtyard in summer theatrical performances, ballet and concerts take place.

SURROUNDINGS. – **Hengsteysee** (10 km N), with the Emperor William Memorial on the Hohensyburg. – **Dechenhöhle** (15 km E), a limestone cavern 300 m deep, with beautiful stalactitic formations, discovered 1868 (conducted tours). – **Altena** (25 km SE), with the ancestral castle of the Counts of the March (Mark), beautifully situated above the Lenne valley (originally 13th c.: the oldest German youth hostel, opened 1912). In the castle are the interesting German Smithy-Museum and the German Wire Museum.

Hamburg

The Free Hanseatic City of Hamburg, a *Land* in its own right.
Vehicle registration: HH.
Altitude: 10 m. – Population: 1·6 million.
Post code: D-2000. – Dialling code: 0 40.

ⓘ **Fremdenverkehrszentrale**
(*Tourist Information Hamburg*),
Bieberhaus, at Main Station;
tel. 24 87 00.

HOTELS. – IN TOWN CENTRE: *Atlantic Hotel Kempinski*, An der Alster 72, 420 b. ("Atlantic Grill"), SB, sauna; *Vier Jahreszeiten*, Neuer Jungfernsteig 9, 263 b. ("Haerlin" restaurant); *Canadian Pacific Hamburg Plaza*, at Congress Centre, Marseiller Str. 2, 785 b. ("English Grill"), SB, sauna; *Inter-Continental*, Fontenay 10, 503 b. (roof-garden restaurant "Fontenay Grill", "Hulk Brasserie"), SB, sauna; *Ramada Renaissance*, Grosse Bleichen, 297 b., SB, sauna; *Europäischer Hof*, Kirchenallee 45, 620b.; *Reichshof*, Kirchenallee 34, 500 b.; *Ambassador*, Heidenkampsweg 34, 200 b., SB, sauna; *Oper*, Drebahn 15, 220 b.; *Alster Hof* (no rest.), Esplanade 12, 210 b.; *Baseler Hospiz*, Esplanade 11, 202 b.; *St. Raphael*, Adenauerallee 41, 160 b.; *Alte Wache* (no rest.), Adenauerallee 25, 106 b.; *Berlin*, Borgfelder Str. 1, 93 b.; *Prem*, an der Alster 9, 75 b. (garden terrace); *Fürst Bismarck*, Kirchenallee 49, 91 b.; *Graf Moltke* (no rest.), Steindamm 1, 200 b.; *Royal* (no rest.), Holzdamm 51, 44 b.; *Wedina* (no rest.), Gurlittstr. 23, 28 b., SB, sauna.
IN ALTONA: *Stadt Altona*, Louise-Schröder-Str. 29, 200 b. – IN BLANKENESE: *Standhotel*, Standstr. 13, 20 b. – IN EIMSBÜTTEL: *Norge*, Schäferkampsallee, 170 b., "Kon-Tiki Grill". – IN CITY NORD: *Crest Hotel Hamburg*, Mexikoring 1, 270 b. – IN HAMM: *Hamburg International*, Hammer Landstr. 200, 205 b. – IN HARVESTEHUDE: *Smolka*, Isestr. 98, 65 b. – IN STELLINGEN: *Falck*, Kieler Str. 333, 150 b. – YOUTH HOSTELS: *Auf dem Stintfang*, Alfred-Wegener-Weg 5, 350 b.; *Horner Rennbahn*, Rennbahnstr. 100, 326 b. – CAMPING SITES: *Camping Anders* and *Ramcke*, both in Eidelstedt; *Camping Brüning* and *Buchholz*, both in Stellingen.

RESTAURANTS. – *Schümanns Austernkeller*, Jungfernsteig 34 (turn of the century decor); *Cöllns Austernstuben*, Brodschrangen 1; *Ratsweinkeller*, Grosse Johannisstrasse 2; *Peter Lembke*, Holzdamm 49; *Michelsen*, Grosse Bleichen 10–14; *Globetrotter*, Jungfernsteig 36; *Überseebrücke*, Vorsetzen; *Fernsehturm*, Rentzelstr. (revolving restaurant at 132 m, with view over city); *Bavaria-Blick*, Bernhard-Nocht-Str. 99 (roof restaurant with view of harbour); *Alt Hamburger Aalspeicher*, Deichstr. 43 (fresh eels daily); *Finnlandhaus*, Esplanade 41 (view of Binnen- and Aussenalster); *Le Canard*, Martinstr. 11, Eppendorf; *Mühlenkamper Fährhaus*, Hans-Henry-Jahnn-Weg 1; *Fischereihafen-Restaurant*, Grosse Elbstr. 143; *Landhaus Scherrer*, Elbchaussee 130; *Landhaus Dill*, Elbchaussee 404; *Strandhof*, Strandweg 27, in Blankenese.
FOREIGN CUISINE: *L'Auberge Française*, Rutschbahn 34 (French); *Danmark*, Kieler Str. 333 (Danish); *Viking*, in Chilehaus, Depenau 3 (Scandinavian); *Tre Fontane*, Mundsburger Damm 45 (Italian); *Shalimar*, Dillstr./corner Rappstr. (Indian); *Pak Sun-Lam*, Ferdinardstr. 55; *Nanking*, Ness 1 (both Chinese); *Japan Grill Fuji*, Richardstr. 18 (Japanese).

CAFÉS. – *Alsterpavillon*, Jungfernsteig 54; *Mövenpick im Cafe Vernimb*, Spitalerstr. 9.

EVENTS. – *Hummelfest* (July–Aug.); **Hamburger Dom** (Nov.–Dec., on Heiligengeistfeld); *Interboot* international boat show (winter). – Numerous industrial, trade and craft fairs and congresses.

Hamburg Casino (roulette, baccarat, black jack, daily 3 p.m.–3 a.m.), Fontenay 10.

The Free Hanseatic City of Hamburg, Germany's largest city after Berlin, is one of the *Länder* of the Federal Republic. Its favourable situation at the head of the long funnel-shaped mouth of the Elbe has made it one of the leading centres of

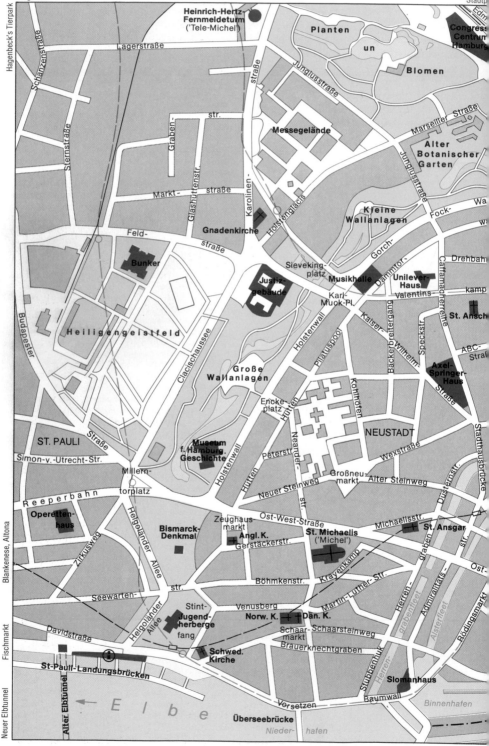

S-Bahn

European trade and a link between the sea and the network of inland waterways.

Hamburg has had a university since 1919, and it has also the Academy of Music, the College of Art and the World Economic Archives. The North German Broadcasting Corporation (Norddeutscher Rundfunk, NDR) has its headquarters and studios here. The State Opera House, the Deutsches Schauspielhaus and the Musikhalle make Hamburg the cultural centre of North Germany. It is also an important

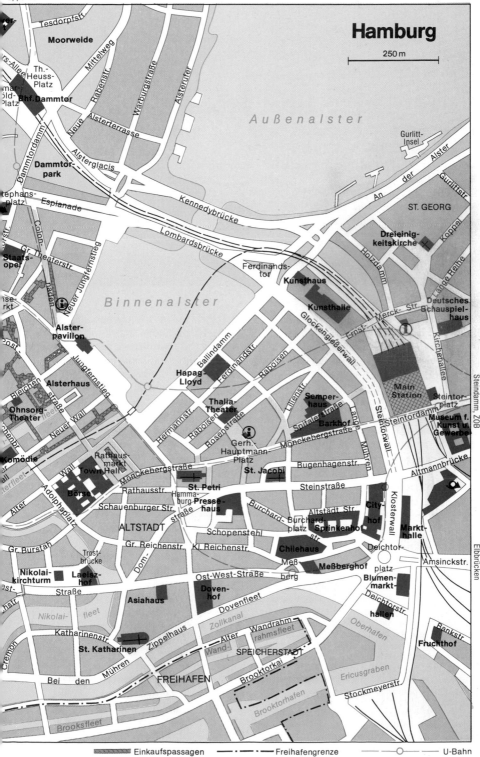

Hamburg: the Jungfernstieg on the Binnenalster

publishing and conference city. In the field of sport it has the German Derby, the German Jumping, Dressage and Driving Derby, the German International Tennis Championship and the Federal League football matches of the Hamburg Sports Club; while St. Pauli and the Reeperbahn cater for the needs of those seeking entertainment. Finally Hamburg is one of the Federal Republic's leading industrial centres (shipbuilding, oil, metal-working, engineering, car manufacture, electrical equipment, precision engineering, rubber, cosmetics, chemicals, foodstuffs, brewing, cigarette manufacture). – Hamburg is also a noted centre of light music.

HISTORY. – The settlement of *Hammaburg* on the Alster, founded in the 9th c., developed during the Middle Ages into an important ecclesiastical and commercial town, and in the 18th c. it became the intellectual centre of Germany, with Klopstock, Lessing and Matthias Claudius. In 1842 the town was devastated by a great fire. With the coming of steam the town and port entered a period of rapid development, and in 1937 Hamburg took in the neighbouring towns of Altona, Wandsbek and Harburg. The bombing of 1943–45 caused heavy destruction. During the post-war reconstruction the city's historic buildings were restored and modern business and residential districts were built. In February 1962 storm tides caused havoc in the city.

SIGHTS. – The townscape of Hamburg draws its particular charm from the large basin of the *Binnenalster (Inner Alster) in the centre of the city, round which run the elegant JUNGFERNSTIEG (with the well-known Alsterpavillon café and the landing-stage of the Alster boats) and the BALLINDAMM (with the offices of the Hapag-Lloyd shipping line, founded in 1847 as HAPAG). W of the Neuer Jungfernstieg, in Dammtorstrasse, is the **State Opera House** (1955).

The line of the old fortifications, with the Lombardsbrücke and Kennedy-Brücke, separates the Binnenalster from the *Aussenalster (Outer Alster) to the N, a sheet of water popular with sailing enthusiasts, with beautiful gardens along the W side. It can be reached by boat from the Jungfernstieg. Immediately W of the gardens is the district of PÖSELDORF, which has recently taken on a fresh lease of life (galleries, boutiques, cafés; painted house-fronts).

To the S the Binnenalster is linked with the Elbe by two canals (with locks), the Fleete, which divide the inner city into two parts, the Old Town and the New Town (Altstadt and Neustadt).

E of the Ballindamm, on the Glocken-giesserwall, is the *Kunsthalle (art gallery) (late works by Meister Bertram of Minden and Meister Francke, works by Philipp Otto Runge and Caspar David Friedrich and minor Dutch masters; important special exhibitions). In the grounds of the Kunsthalle at the Ferdinandstor are the Kunsthaus and Kunstverein.

The central feature of the OLD TOWN, reached from the Binnenalster by way of the Alsterarkaden, is the RATHAUSMARKT, with the sumptuous Renaissance-style Town Hall (1886–97). Behind the Town Hall is the Stock Exchange.

From the Rathausmarkt the wide MONCKE-BERGSTRASSE, Hamburg's principal shopping and business street, lined by imposing offices and business houses, runs past St Peter's Church (133 m high tower) to the Hauptbahnhof. E of the station are the Schauspielhaus and the **Museum of Arts and Crafts (Museum für Kunst und Gewerbe), which ranks with the Bavarian National Museum as the most comprehensive display of German, European and Asian applied art in Germany (in particular china, furniture and silver from Lower Germany and the Netherlands and Japanese art).

S of Mönckebergstrasse, in Steinstrasse, is St James's Church (St. Jakobi: originally 14th c., restored 1959 after severe war damage; medieval altars, organ by Arp-Schnitger). Farther S in Burchardplatz are the boldly conceived *Chilehaus (by Fritz Höger, 1920–23) and the massive Sprinkenhof (by Höger and Gerson, 1927–30), the handsomest of the large office buildings in Hamburg. To the E is the Cityhof (1956), four 42 m high office blocks.

On the busy Messberg stands the Messberghof, a brick building (1923–25) by H. and O. Gerson. From here the wide OST-WEST-STRASSE runs W past St Catherine's Church and the 147 m high tower of St Nicholas's Church, crossing the Nikolai-, Alster- and Herrengrabenfleet to enter the NEW TOWN. In this area is Hamburg's traditional emblem and landmark, the Baroque *St Michael's Church (by E. G. Sonnin, 1750–62), from the tower of which, known as "Michel" (lift), there are fine views. In a courtyard to the E are the Krameramts-

wohnungen (museum: streets of old houses).

The **PORT extends between the N and S Elbe from the Elbe bridges to the former fishing island of Finkenwerder, over about 100 sq. km. It is a tidal harbour, accessible at all states of the tide. The Free Port permits transhipment and warehousing of imports without payment of customs duty. Much to be recommended is a *trip round the harbour; the boats leave from the St. Pauli landing-stages, used by all shipping within the port and on the Unterelbe. Nearby is a domed structure which marks the entrance to the Old Elbe Tunnel (448·5 m long) to the island of Steinwerder, lined with quays.

At the St. Pauli landing-stages begin the Wallanlagen, the gardens laid out on the line of the former fortifications, with the Bismarck Memorial (on the model of the traditional figures of Roland, erected 1906), the *Museum on the History of Hamburg and the Old Botanic Garden. Adjoining the Botanic Garden to the NW is the popular park known as *Planten un Blomen (illuminated fountains after dark), with the *Congress Centre (1973) and the 32-storey Canadian Pacific Hamburg Plaza Hotel (118 m high). Opposite the Rentzelstrasse entrance to Planten un Blomen is the *Heinrich Hertz Tele-

Hamburg: Krameramtswohnungen and "Michel"

communications Tower (Fernmeldeturm), familiarly known as "Tele-Michel", completed in 1968 (271·5 m high: revolving restaurant at 132 m). N of the park, in Rothenbaumchaussee, is the *Museum of Ethnography and Prehistory* (Maori house, masks from the South Seas and Oceanian outrigger canoes). Immediately S of the park are the *Trade Fair and Exhibition Grounds* (Ernst-Merck-Halle). In FLOTTBEK, in the W of the town, lies the new *Botanical Garden*.

On the far side of the Grosse Wallanlagen and the Glacisschaussee is the large *Heiligengeistfeld*, scene of the Domfest in Nov.–Dec., and to the S of this is the harbour district of ST. PAULI, through which runs the **Reeperbahn**, famed for its bars and places of entertainment of all kinds. In the Grosse Freiheit, flanked by establishments of this kind, stands the Baroque *St Joseph's Church* (R.C.).

To the W, on the high right bank of the Elbe, is the district of ALTONA, with the once celebrated neo-classical street known as the *Palmaille* (houses protected as historical monuments) and the **Altona Museum** (geological history, landscape, settlement and economy of Schleswig-Holstein and the Lower Elbe). Fine *view of the port from the *Altonaer Balkon*. On the banks of the Elbe is the *fishing harbour*. In OTTENSEN is the Fabrik, a communications and pop music centre. To the N is the *Volkspark* with the Volkspark Stadium. – Farther N in the suburb of STELLINGEN lies *Hargenbeck's Zoo** with its open paddocks, which were the model for modern zoo layout, and its large stock of animals arranged accordingly to the different parts of the world from which they come; ("Troparium" and Dolphinarium). E of Stellingen in WINTERHUDE is the *Planatarium* (former water tower).

S of Altona the modern high-level *Köhlbrand Bridge** (3·9 km long and up to 54 m high) spans the Süderelbe. W of Altona the motorway (A7, E3) passes under the river in the **New Elbe Tunnel** (3·3 km long, up to 27 m under the surface; three lanes in each direction).

SURROUNDINGS. – An attractive drive on the *ELBCHAUSSEE to **Blankenese** (14 km W), an old fishing village with a ring of handsome villas on the *Süllberg* (85 m). 6 km farther downstream is the *Willkommhöft "ship-greeting point"*, at the

Schulau ferry house. – **Kiekeberg Open-Air Museum** at Ehestorf (14 km S). – *Schloss Ahrensburg (23 km NE), with a museum illustrating the aristocratic culture of Holstein. – **Curslack Open-Air Museum**, in the Vierlande district (27 km SE). –

Hamelin (Hameln)

Land: Lower Saxony.
Vehicle registration: HM.
Altitude: 68 m. – Population: 60,000.
Post code: D-3250. – Dialling code: 0 51 51.

(i) **Verkehrsbüro**,
Deisterallee;
tel. 20 25 17/18.

HOTELS. – *Dorint-Hotel Weserbergland*, Von-Dingelstedt-Str. 3, 165 b., SB, sauna; *Zur Krone*, Osterstr. 30, 80 b.; *Zur Börse*, Osterstr. 41, 48 b.; *Sintermann*, Bahnhofsplatz 2, 50 b.; *Hirschmann*, Deisterallee 16, 32 b.; *Bellevue am Roseplatz*, Klütstr. 34, 36 b. – YOUTH HOSTEL: Fischbekker Str. 33, 106 b. – CAMPING SITE: *Zum Fährhaus*, on left bank of Weser; *Camping am Waldbad* in Hamelin-Halvestorf.

RESTAURANTS. – *Weinstuben am Kamin*, Pyrmonter Str. 12 (open from 7 p.m.); *Klütturm*, on Klüt.

CAFÉS. – *Museums Café* (street café), Osterstr. 8; *Harms*, Osterstr. 34; *Kropp*, Münsterkirchhof 8.

EVENTS. – "**Pied Piper**" play (Rattenfängerspiele: mid May–mid Sept., every Sunday 12–12.30, at Hochzeitshaus).

Hamelin (Browning's "Hamelin Town in Brunswick"), delightfully situated in the broad Weser valley between the Schweineberg and Klüt, is famous as the city of the Pied Piper. The old town has many half-timbered houses and buildings in Weser Renaissance style. The principal industries are milling and carpet-manufacture.

HISTORY. – In the 9th c. monks from Fulda founded near the ancient village of *Hamala*, close to the Weser, a house which later became the monastery of St Boniface. Soon a market settlement was also established. About 1200 the three amalgamated to become a town. During the Middle Ages Hamelin prospered as a trading town, became a member of the Hanse and surrounded itself with strong walls and towers. Its cultural and economic heyday was in the 16th and early 17th c., but the Thirty Years War and Seven Years War were disastrous for the town. In 1757 the battle of Hastenbeck was fought just outside Hamelin. At the beginning of the 19th c. Napoleon ordered the demolition of its defences, which had been developed and improved during the 17th c. The line of the old walls is now marked by a ring of wide avenues.

SIGHTS. – In the MARKT stands the *Market Church* of St Nicholas, formerly the boatmen's and fishermen's church, as the golden ship on the spire indicates. Opposite it is the *Demptersches Haus* of 1607, with a fine oriel window.

E from the Markt runs OSTERSTRASSE (pedestrian precinct). At No. 2 is the magnificent **Hochzeitshaus** ("Marriage House": once used by the citizens for ceremonial occasions, now the Town Hall and Library), in Weser Renaissance style (1610–17), with a carillon and "Pied Piper" clock with mechanical figures (daily at 1.05, 3.35 and 5.35 p.m.). At No. 8 is the *Canons' House* of 1558, with fine carving. At No. 9 is the *Leisthaus* of 1589, now a museum (history of the town, local crafts and traditions, the Pied Piper legend). At No. 25 are the former *Garrison church* and the *Holy Ghost Foundation* of 1713 (now the Municipal Savings Bank). At No. 28 is the *Pied Piper's House (Rattenfängerhaus: restaurant) of 1603, a magnificent example of the Weser Renaissance style (inscription referring to the Pied Piper legend on the side wall in Bungelosenstrasse).

S of the Markt is BÄCKERSTRASSE (pedestrian precinct). At No. 16 is the *Rattenkrug* of 1568, in Weser Renaissance style (restaurant), at No. 12 the *Löwenapotheke* ("Lion Pharmacy"), with a Gothic gable of 1300. – Near the bridge over the Weser is the massive **Minster** of St Boniface (11th–14th c.: Romanesque crossing tower with Baroque crown). Features of the interior are a fine crypt under the choir, a 13th c. tabernacle and the 14th c. "Founders' Stone" (figures of the founders with a model of the church) on a pillar at the crossing.

The line of the old fortifications is marked by a ring of "Wallstrassen". In the Rathausplatz to the E stands the *Weserbergland-Festhalle*. To the S is the beautifully laid out *Bürgergarten*.

SURROUNDINGS. – **Klüt** (258 m, 2 km SW), with a restaurant and observation tower. – **Ohrbergpark** (4 km S), with rare trees and shrubs; particularly beautiful when the azaleas and rhododendrons are in flower. – *Fischbeck Collegiate Church (7 km NW), with a triumphal cross of 1250, a wooden statue of the foundress, Helmburg (c. 1300), silk embroidery and a 14th c. eagle lectern. A fine 16th c. tapestry relates the legend of the foundation. – **Schloss Hämelschenburg** (11 km S), a magnificent building with three wings, begun in 1588, which is one of the great masterpieces of the Weser Renaissance style. The Bridge Gate, with a figure of St George, dates from 1608. Some of the rooms are open to visitors (entrance from the park side).

Hanover (Hannover)

Land: Lower Saxony.
Vehicle registration: H.
Altitude: 58 m. – Population: 542,000.
Post code: D-3000.-Dialling code: 05 11.
ⓘ **Verkehrsbüro**, Ernst-August-Platz 8; tel. 32 10 33 and 1 68 23 19.

HOTELS. – *Inter-Continental*, Friedrichswall 11, 500 b., Prinz-Taverne; *Kastens Hotel*, Luisenstr. 1–3, 300 b.; *Am Stadtpark*, Clausewitzstr. 6, 420 b., SB, sauna; *Grand Hotel Mussmann* (no rest.), Ernst-August-Platz 7, 160 b.; *Am Leineschloss* (no rest.), Am Markt 12, 81 b.; *Körner*, Körnerstr. 24, 112 b., SB, garden terrace; *Loccumer Hospiz*, Kurt-Schumacher-Str. 16, 100 b.; *Thüringer Hof*, Osterstr. 37, 80 b.; *Bundesbahn Hotel*, Ernst August Platz 1, 75 b. – AT LANGENHAGEN AIRPORT: *Holiday Inn*, 300 b., SB. – IN ISERNHAGEN: *Parkhotel Welfenhof*, Prüssentrift 86, 44 b. – IN KIRCHRODE: *Crest Hotel*, Tiergartenstr. 117, 200 b. – AT LAATZEN: *Parkhotel Kronsberg*, opposite the exhibition grounds, 164 b. – YOUTH HOSTEL: Ferdinand-Wilhelm-Fricke-Weg 1, 181 b. – CAMPING SITES: *Blauer See*, Hannover-Garbsen; *Parksee Lohne*, Hannover Isernhagen.

RESTAURANTS. – *Georgenhof*, Herrenhäuser Kirchweg 20; *Mövenpick*, Georgstr. 35; *Altes Rathaus*, Köbelingerstr. 60; *Leineschloss*, Hinrich-Wilhelm-Kopf-Platz 1; *Parkrestaurant Stadthalle*, Theodor-Heuss-Platz 1; *Bakkarat Spielbank Restaurant*, Arthur Menge Ufer 3 (in casino on Maschsee). – IN THE EILENRIEDE: *Steuerndieb*, Steuerndieb 1. – IN DÖHREN: *Wichmann*, Hildesheimer Str. 230. – IN KLEEFELD: *Alte Mühle*, Hermann-Löns-Park 3.

BEER-HOUSES. – *Brauerei Gaststätten Herrenhausen*, Herrenhäuser Str. 99; *Wülfeler Brauerei Gaststätten*, Hildesheimer Str. 380.

WINE BARS. – *Wein-Wolf*, Rathenaustr. 2; *Fey's Weinstube*, Sophienstr. 6.

CAFÉS. – *Kröpcke*, Georgstr. 35; *Kreipe*, Bahnhofstr. 12.

Hannover Casino (roulette, baccarat, blackjack; daily from 3 p.m.). On N bank of Maschsees.

EVENTS. – *Hannover Trade Fair*, an international industrial show (end April); *Music and Theatre in Herrenhause*, with concerts, opera, drama and ballet (June–Aug.)

Hanover (in German usage Hannover), situated on the higher right bank of the Leine, is capital of the *Land* of Lower Saxony and an important industrial and commercial city, with a technological university, a medical school, a veterinary college and academies of music and drama. In recent decades its trade fairs have become of international importance. With the Mittelland Canal and its motorway and rail connections it is a major centre of communications. With its extensive parks like the Eilenriede, the

Maschpark and the gardens of Herrenhausen it can claim to be a "city in the country". It suffered heavy destruction during the war but has been rebuilt in exemplary modern fashion.

HISTORY. – The origin of Hanover was an old market settlement, first recorded in 1150 as *vicus Honovere*. It received its municipal charter from Henry the Lion. The division of the Guelf possessions in 1495 brought the town under the rule of the Calenberg family, and in

1636 Duke Georg von Calenberg moved his residence to Hanover. Under Elector Ernst August (1679–98) and his wife Sophie the town enjoyed a great flowering of culture, and the philosopher Gottfried Wilhelm Leibniz became court librarian and historian of the House of Guelf. This period too saw the creation of the Herrenhausen gardens, one of the great achievements of Baroque gardening art. In 1714 Elector George Ludwig of Hanover succeeded to the British throne as George I, and the Electorate (from 1815 Kingdom) of Hanover was joined with Britain in a personal union which lasted until 1837. Under King Ernst August (1837–51) Hanover had a period of economic prosperity, and the municipal architect

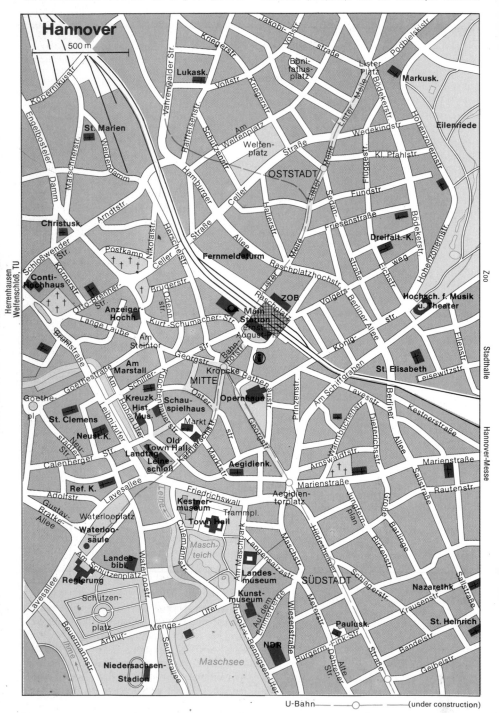

Georg Ludwig Friedrich Laves left his mark on the town's architecture. It suffered great destruction in the Second World War, but the post-war reconstruction directed by Professor Hillebrecht gave it a handsome modern face.

SIGHTS. – The hub of the modern city's life is the square called KRÖPCKE, which is approached from the station by Bahnhofstrasse, with the sunken shopping street *Passerelle* (750 m long and up to 20 m wide). Adjoining the **Kröpcke-Center**, a glass and concrete store almost 60 m high, are the new premises of Hanover's long-famous *Café Kröpcke*. To the SE, in the dignified GEORGSTRASSE, is the neo-classical **Opera House** (G. L. F. Laves, 1845–52). Georgstrasse begins at the square Am Steintor – to the N in Goseriede the **Anzeiger tower block** (by Fritz Höger, 1928) – and ends in the busy Aegidientorplatz. To the W of this square is the 14th c. *Aegidienkirche* (St Giles: ruins and memorial to the dead of both world wars; tower rebuilt, with carillon).

Hanover: Town Hall and Maschteich

SW of the Kröpcke is the MARKTPLATZ, in the centre of the OLD TOWN, with the late Gothic **Old Town Hall** (15th c.), in front of which is the graceful neo-Gothic *Market Fountain* (1881). To the W is the **Market Church** (14th c.: 15th c. bronze font and carved altar, 97 m high tower. NW stands the Leibnizhaus (originally 1652; re-opened in 1983. KRAMER-STRASSE, which opens off the Marktplatz, still preserves something of the atmosphere of old Hanover with its handsome old half-timbered buildings. Between Knochenhauerstrasse and Burgstrasse is the *Ballhof* (built 1649–65 for the then popular game of battledore and shuttlecock and for concerts: now a theatre), Hanover's finest half-timbered house. Beyond this, on the HOHES UFER, are the 14th c. *Beginenturm* and the **Historical Museum** (1966: history of the town and *Land*, folk traditions). On the southern edge of the old town, on the banks of the Leine, is the **Leineschloss**, built in the 17th c. for Duke Georg von Calenberg, altered in neo-classical style by Laves in 1817–42 and rebuilt in 1958–62 to house the Landtag of Lower Saxony. – NW of the palace is the *Neustädter Kirche* (17th c.), with the tomb of the philosopher Gottfried Wilhelm Leibniz (1646–1716).

On the FRIEDRICHSWALL is the *Wangenheim-Palais*, built by Laves in 1832 (restored: once the residence of King George V of Hanover, then used as

Town Hall, now occupied by a ministry). Adjoining it is the *Laveshaus* (1822), built by the architect for his own occupation (memorial room). Opposite the Inter-Continental Hotel is the modern *Kest-ner Museum (antiquities, including a fine Egyptian collection; applied art). In Trammplatz is the **Town Hall** (1901–13), in the style of the Wilhelmine period, with a domed tower almost 100 m high which dominates the town (lift: wide views). In the hall are models of the town; Hodler Room, with a huge picture by the noted Swiss artist, "The Oath of Loyalty". – S of the Town Hall is the *Maschpark*. At No. 5 in the street Am Maschpark is the *Provincial Museum of Lower Saxony*, with prehistoric, natural history and ethnographic collections and the Provincial Art Gallery (European art from the Romanesque period to the present day).

The **Maschsee**, a lake 2·4 km long and between 180 and 530 m across, was created in 1934–36. It is Hanover's largest sports and recreation area (bathing lido, sailing school, motor-boat services, beautiful walks). On the NW side are the *Lower Saxony Stadium* (seating for 60,000) and the *Stadium Baths*, on the NE side the *Funkhaus* (Broadcasting House) and the *Museum of Art* containing the *Sprengel Collection* (including 20th c. painting); to the N the newly built casino.

From Königsworther Platz (on right the modern *Continental Building*) the Nienburger Strasse runs parallel to the HERRENHAUSER ALLEE (laid out in 1726), past the *Technical University* (in the former Welfenschloss, built 1857–66), to the magnificent *Herrenhausen Gardens,*

2 km NW. To the left, in the *Georgengarten*, a beautiful English-style park, is the *Walloden-Palais*, with the *Wilhelm Busch Museum* (some 1200 drawings and paintings, together with letters and manuscripts of the 19th c. painter and poet Wilhelm Busch; also Heinrich Zille collection). – To the right is the *Berggarten*, a botanic garden with modern orchid and cactus houses. In the northern part of the gardens is the *Mausoleum* (1842–46) built by Laves for King Ernst August (d. 1851) and Queen Friederike (d. 1841), with marble figures by Rauch. The Mausoleum now also contains the sarcophagi of other members of the Guelf House, including George I of Britain.

The palace of Herrenhausen at the end of the Herrenhäuser Allee was destroyed during the war. The only surviving part of the palace is the *Gallery Wing* (1698), with a large series of Italian frescoes. In the middle section is the Baroque Hall, once the scene of court festivities, now a concert hall used for the summer festival, "Music and Theatre in Herrenhausen". – To the W of the Gallery Wing, in the *Fürstenhaus*, is the *Herrenhausen Museum*, with furniture and furnishings from the destroyed palace. – To the S is the geometrically designed *Great Garden* (1666–1714), the best preserved example of an early Baroque garden, with fountains, an orangery and a garden theatre (May–Sept.).

On the E side of the city is the beautiful municipal forest of **Eilenriede** (639 hectares: several restaurants), another large recreation area, with footpaths and bridle paths, playing areas and open spaces for relaxation and sunbathing. On its western edge are the **Zoo**, the *Stadt-*

On the Steinhuder Meer

halle congress centre, the *Niedersachsenhalle*, the *Glashalle* and the *Eilenriede Stadium*, adjoining which is the *Municipal Park*.

To the SE of the city is the **Messegelände** (Trade Fair Grounds: 970,000 sq. m), where every year at the end of April is held the Hanover Fair, one of the world's most important industrial shows, with the 83 m high *Hermesturm* or Hermes Tower (café; view). – The highest structure in the city is the 144 m high *Telecommunications Tower* (Fernmeldeturm), just off Raschplatz behind the Station.

SURROUNDINGS. – **Schloss Marienburg** (26 km S at Nordstemmen), Gothic-style, built 1860–68; former residence of Duchess Viktoria Luise. Museum, with picture gallery. – *Steinhuder Meer** (30 km NW), the largest inland lake in NW Germany (sailing regattas). On an artificial island is *Festung Wilhelmstein*, a fort built by Count Wilhelm von Schaumburg-Lippe in 1761–65. In Steinhude, on the SE shore of the lake, are eel-smoking establishments

The Harz

Land: Lower Saxony.

ⓘ **Harzer Verkehrsverband**,
Marktstr. 45,
D-3380 Goslar 1;
tel. (0 53 21) 2 00 31.

The *Harz, extending like a bastion into the North German plain, is an upland region of slates and greywackes, with numerous intrusions of granites and porphyries, covering an area some 95 km long by 30 km across and rising to a height of over 1000 m.

It is made up of two differing landscape patterns – the *Oberharz* (Upper Harz) in the W, an area of coniferous forest much broken up by valleys, and the *Unterharz* (Lower Harz) in the E, a rolling plateau on which beech-forests and arable land predominate. On the boundary between the two, within the German Democratic Republic, is the legendary *Brocken* (1142 m), the highest peak in North Germany. The economy of the Oberharz is based on forestry, mining and stock-rearing, that of the Unterharz on agriculture. Narrow rocky valleys, like the *Oker* valley and the *Bode* valley (in the GDR), cut deep into the hills, particularly on the N side. The Harz has numbers of charming old towns to attract the tourist, and its convenient situation in relation to many large towns in North Germany makes it a popular holiday and winter sports area.

The eastern part of the Harz, with the Brocken and places like Wernigerode, Elbingerode, Rübeland, Blankenburg and Thale, can be visited only by tourists with an entry permit for the German Democratic Republic. In the western Harz, however, there are the old Imperial city of **Goslar**, the well-known spa and health resort of **Bad Harzburg**, the health and winter sports resort of *Braunlage*, the ancient little mining towns of *St. Andreasberg*, *Altenau*, and **Clausthal-Zellerfeld** and smaller spa resorts such as *Wildemann*, *Bad Grund*, *Bad Lauterberg* and *Bad Sachsa*.

Heidelberg Castle

The highest peak within the Federal Republic is the 971 m high *Wurmberg* near Braunlage (cableway; ski-jump, toboggan run). Many of the rivers have been dammed, providing not only water supplies and hydroelectric power but also attractive recreation areas. The best known of the artificial lakes thus created are those on the rivers *Oker*, *Oder*, *Söse* and *Innerste*.

The HARZ-HOCHSTRASSE (Harz Ridgeway: B 242) gives access to the western Harz between Braunlage and Bad Grund. The HARZ-HEIDE-STRASSE (Harz-Heathland Highway) from Braunlage by way of Bad Harzburg, Brunswick, Gifhorn and Uelzen to Lüneburg links the Harz with Lüneburg Heath.

Heidelberg

Land: Baden-Württemberg.
Vehicle registration: HD.
Altitude: 110 m. – Population: 134,000.
Post code: D-6900. – Dialling code: 0 62 21.
ⓘ **Tourist-Information**, at Main Station; tel. 2 13 41.

HOTELS. – *Der Europäische Hof* (Hotel Europa), Friedrich Ebert Anlage 1a, 200 b. ("Kurfürstenstube" restaurant); *Atlas Hotel*, Bergheimer Str. 63, 225 b.; *Alt Heidelberg* (no rest), Rohrbacher Str. 29, 107 b.; Hirschgasse 3, 80 b.; *Holländer Hof*, An der Alten Brucke, 72 b.; *Zum Ritter*, Hauptstr. 178, 58 b. (a Renaissance building of 1592); *Parkhotel Atlantic* (no rest.), Schloss Wolfsbrunnenweg 23, 50 b.; *Kurfürst* (no rest.), Poststr. 46, 101 b.; *Diana* (no rest.), Rohrbacher Str. 152, 100 b.; *Schwarzes Schiff*, Neuenheimer Landstr. 5, 80 b. – IN KIRCHHEIM: *Crest Hotel*, Pleikartsförster Str. 101, 170 b. – YOUTH HOSTEL: Tiergartenstr. 5, 422 b. – CAMPING SITES: *Neckartal*, in Schlierbach on left bank of the Neckar; *Haide*, between Ziegelhausen and Neckargemünd on right bank on the Neckar.

RESTAURANTS. – *Kurpfälzisches Museum*, Hauptstr. 97; *Merien Stuben*, Neckarstaden 24; *Schinder-*

hannes, Theaterstr. 2 (grill); *Zum Roten Ochsen*, Hauptstr. 217 (a historic old student haunt of 1703). – IN THE HILLS: *Schloss Weinstuben*, in Schlosshof (with terrace); *Molkenkur* (301 m: above the Schloss); *Königstuhl*, on the Königstuhl (568 m).

CAFÉS. – *Schafheutle*, Hauptstr. 94; *Scheu*, Hauptstr. 137; *Gundel*, Hauptstr. 212.

EVENTS. – *"Heidelberger Frühling"* (traditional spring festival in the Karlsplatz); *Floodlighting of the castle* with fireworks (1st Saturday in June, July and Sept.); *Heidelberg Schloss-spiele* (July/Aug.); *Heidelberger Weindorf* (wine festival) on the Karlsplatz in Aug.; *Heidelberger Herbst* with festival in the castle and Old Town (last weekend in Sept.).

***Heidelberg, the old capital of the Palatinate and an ancient university town celebrated in song and poetry, lies at the point where the Neckar emerges from the hills of the Odenwald into the Rhine plain. Over the old town, caught between the river and the hills, looms its famous ruined castle. The best general view of the town in its beautiful setting is from the Theodor Heuss Bridge or the Philosophenweg.**

In Heidelberg are the Max Planck Institutes of Nuclear Physics, Medical Research, Astronomy and Foreign Public Law as well as the European Laboratory of Molecular Biology (EMBL). Its industry produces printing-presses, agricultural machinery, adhesives and sealing materials, and chemical and physical apparatus. Several publishing houses are based in the town.

HISTORY. – The place is first recorded in 1196. The Counts Palatine made it their residence, and in 1386 Count Ruprecht I founded the University. The first castle was also built in his time. In 1689 and 1693,

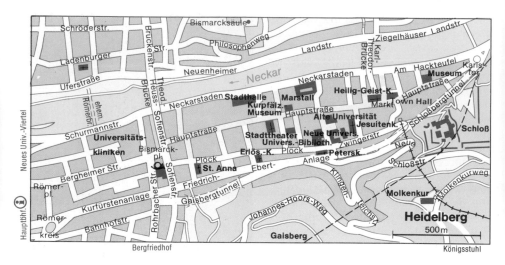

during the war over the Palatinate succession, the castle and the town were destroyed, and in 1720 Elector Karl Philipp moved his capital to Mannheim. In 1802 the territory of the Palatinate on the right bank of the Rhine passed to the Margraviate (later Grand Duchy) of Baden. In the Second World War Heidelberg remained untouched by bombing.

SIGHTS. – From BISMARCKPLATZ, S of the *Theodor Heuss Bridge* (viewpoint), the HAUPTSTRASSE (pedestrian zone) runs E for more than 2 km to the *Karlstor* (1775). In this street is the **Palatinate Museum** (Kurpfälzisches Museum), in the Baroque Palais Morass, with art and historical collections (*Windsheim Apostles' Altar by Tilman Riemenschneider; cast of the lower jaw of *Homo heidelbergensis*, some 500,000 years old). Farther E are the **Church of the Holy Ghost** (Heilig-geistkirche) of 1400–41, formerly the burial place of the Electors Palatine; the *Town Hall* (1701–03, view of the Castle from nearby Kornmarkt); the *Haus zum Ritter*, a splendid Renaissance building of 1592 (hotel); and the *Museum of Ethnography*, in the Palais Weimar (No. 235).

S of the Hauptstrasse is UNIVER-SITÄTSPLATZ, with the **Old University** of 1711. (In the beadle's house on its E side in Augustinergasse is the Karzer or student lock-up, used from 1778 to 1914.) Adjoining this is the *New University*, built 1928–31 with American help, and beyond it is the *Hexenturm* (Witches' Tower), part of the old fortifications. Opposite, in Grabenstrasse, are the richly stocked *University Library* (*''Manessische Handschrift'' of medieval songs, 14th c.) and the controversial *Triplex-Projekt* (a redevelopment project which houses the faculty of economic and social sciences). The little 15th c. *St*

Peter's Church is now mainly used as the University church. – Farther E, in KARLS-PLATZ, is the Academy of Science, in the Baroque *Grand-Ducal Palace*. In the nearby Pfaffengasse is the birthplace of the first President of Germany, *Friedrich Ebert* (1871–1925).

Between the Hauptstrasse and the Neckar are the narrow little lanes of the old town. On the NECKARSTADEN which runs along the left bank of the river are the old *Court Stables* (Marstall, 16th c.; now housing the student refectory, etc.) and *Hay-Barn* (Heuscheuer; now lecture theatres). Downstream is the former *Stadthalle* (1903, congress centre since 1980), (1786–88) or ''Old Bridge'', from which there are fine views.

From the KORNMARKT a rack railway (to the Castle, Molkenkur and Königstuhl), the Burgweg (15 minutes on foot) and the curving NEUE SCHLOSS-STRASSE lead up to the ****Castle**, one of the noblest examples of German Renaissance architecture, built of red Neckar sandstone on the terraced hillside (195 m). This once splendid Electoral residence was built principally in the reigns of Otto Heinrich (1556–59), Friedrich IV (1583–1610) and Friedrich V (1610–20). Since its destruction by the French, who devastated the Palatinate in 1689 and 1693, it has remained a ruin – in situation, size and picturesque beauty the most magnificent ruin in Germany. On the E side of the picturesque *courtyard (performances in summer) is the * *Ottheinrichsbau* (Otto Heinrich Building), the finest achievement of the early Renaissance in Germany (1557–66), on the lower floor of which is the *German Pharmacy Museum*. On the N side of the courtyard are the *Gläserner Saalbau* (Glass Hall) of 1544–49 and the *Friedrichsbau*, one of the outstanding monuments of the mature Renaissance style in Germany (by Johannes Schoch, 1601–07), with statues of rulers of the Palatinate (originals in the interior). On the W side are the *Frauenzimmerbau* (Women's Building, *c.* 1540), with the Königssaal (concerts), farther back the *Library* (*c.* 1520) and the Gothic *Ruprechtsbau* (*c.* 1400). A passage runs under the Friedrichsbau on to the *terrace*, with magnificent views. To the left of the Friedrichsbau, lower down, is the Cellar, with the famous *Great Tun* of 1751 (2200 hectolitres); opposite it is a wooden figure of the court fool *Perkeo* (*c.* 1728). – From the *Great Terrace* there is a magnificent view.

From the Theodor Heuss Bridge the **Philosophenweg** runs E along the slopes of the Heiligenberg, with a famous *view of the town and the castle. Also on the N side of the Neckar are the *Zoo* (Tiergartenstrasse) and *Botanic Garden* (Hofmeisterweg).

SURROUNDINGS. – **Heiligenberg** (443 m, 5½ km N), with ruins of St Michael's Basilica (11th c.). – *Königstuhl** (568 m, 7 km E; rack railway), with an 82 m high television tower (extensive views of Rhine plain, Neckar valley and Odenwald) and observatory. – SE near *Mauer*, where homo heidelbergensis was found, a museum of prehistory. **Schloss Schwetzingen** (12 km W), summer residence of the Electors of the Palatinate in the 18th c., with famous *gardens and a Rococo *theatre (by Pigage, 1746–52: festival performances). – **Weinheim** (17 km N), with Schlosspark, forest of exotic trees, ruins of Burg Windeck and Wachenburg.

Heilbronn

Land: Baden-Württemberg.
Vehicle registration: HN.
Altitude: 159 m. – Population: 113,000.
Post code: D-7100. – Dialling code: 0 71 31.
ⓘ **Verkehrsamt**, in Town Hall;
tel. 56 22 67.

HOTELS. – *Insel Hotel*, Friedrich Ebert Brucke, 180 b. (garden and roof terrace); *Götz*, Moltkestr 52, 153 b.; *Burkhardt*, Lohtorstr. 7, 67 b.; *Kronprinz*, Bahnhofstr. 29, 48 b.; *City Hotel* (no rest.), Allee 40, 40 b.; *Gästehaus Becker* (no rest.), Moltkestr. 24, 51 b.; *Beck*, Bahnhofstr. 31, 44 b.; *Gästehaus Allee Post* (no rest.), Titostr. 12, 24 b. – YOUTH HOSTEL: Schirrmannstr. 9 (at Trappensee), 145 b. – CAMPING SITE: Unterheinriet.

RESTAURANTS. – *Ratskeller*, Marktplatz 7; *Harmonie*, Allee 28 (garden terrace); *Heilbronner Winzerstüble*, Ludwig-Pfau-Str. 14. – IN THE JÄGERHAUSWALD: *Waldgaststätte Jägerhaus.* – ON THE WARTBERG: *Höhengaststätte Wartberg.*

St Kilian's Church, Heilbronn

CAFÉ. – *Noller*, Kirchbrunnenstr. 32.

EVENTS. – *Unterländer Volksfest* (July/Aug.); *Heilbronner Herbst* (wine festival).

The former free Imperial city of Heilbronn, the largest and most important industrial and commercial town of Lower Swabia, lies on both sides of the Neckar (here canalised), with a considerable harbour. The old town on the right bank of the river was almost completely destroyed in the last war, and only a few of its historic buildings survived. Heilbronn is the centre of an important wine-producing region. The town has a literary memorial in Heinrich von Kleist's play "Käthchen von Heilbronn".

HISTORY. – Heilbronn – the name comes from a sacred spring – developed as a trading town at the intersection of important traffic routes. The charming old town was destroyed by an air raid in 1944.

SIGHTS. – In the MARKTPLATZ in the reconstructed old town is the Renaissance **Town Hall** (restored), with an *astronomical clock* of 1580. The tall house at the SW corner of the square is known as *"Käthchen's House"*, although Kleist's play has no historical basis. The nearby **St Kilian's Church** dates from the 13th and 15th c.; its tower (62 m) was erected 1513–29. *High altar* by Hans Seyfer (1498). – S of the Marktplatz are the *Historical Museum*, the rebuilt *Church*

of SS. Peter and Paul (13th and 18th c.:
R.C.) and the *Deutschhof* (now the
Municipal Library; a museum is planned).
To the SW, on the Neckar, is the *Götzen-
turm* (1392), in which Goethe sets the
death of Götz von Berlichingen in his play
of that name (contrary to the facts of
history: Götz died in Burg Hornberg, on
the Neckar, in 1562). – E of the Marktplatz, in the ALLEE, is the festival hall
Harmonie (1958). Nearby in Moltke-
strasse is the *Robert Mayer Monument*,
commemorating the discoverer of the law
of the conservation of energy, born in
Heilbronn in 1814. In Berliner Platz,
corner of Allee and Weinsberger Strasse
stands the *theatre* (1982).

SURROUNDINGS. – **Neckarsulm** (6 km N), with
the German Two-Wheels Museum in the former castle
of the Teutonic Order. – **Bad Wimpfen** (15 km N),
with the *Knights' Church of St Peter* and the remains
of a Hohenstaufen stronghold (13th c.: very fine
*dwarf arcades).

Heligoland

Land: Schleswig-Holstein.
(i) **Kurverwaltung**, Südstrand;
tel. (0 47 25) 7 01.

**The red sandstone cliffs of the island
of** *Heligoland (in German Helgo-
land) tower up like a huge natural
fortress out of the wide expanse of
Heligoland Bay. The island (area
0·9 sq. km), lying 70 km off the
mouth of the Elbe, has belonged to
Germany only since 1890, when it
was exchanged by Britain for the
protectorate of Zanzibar. It was
developed as a naval base, and
served a strategic function during
the Second World War. On 18 April
1945 it was severely damaged by air
attack. After the end of the war
the remaining inhabitants were
evacuated, and in April 1947 the
fortifications were blown up, leading to the collapse of huge masses of
rock. Thereafter it was used as a
bombing target by the RAF. After its
restoration to Germany in March
1952 reconstruction began.**

Heligoland is now again a popular holiday
resort, not least because it is a duty-free
area. With its mild climate, its pure sea air
and its excellent facilities for "taking the
cure", it is also a much favoured health
resort. The only lobster-fishing grounds in
Germany, off Heligoland, are the preserve
of the local fishermen who also enjoy the

long-established privilege of bringing
visitors ashore, and incoming boats therefore discharge their passengers into small
boats in the anchorage. There are daily
boat services from Cuxhaven, and during
the season also from Hamburg, Wilhelmshaven, Bremerhaven and numerous
coastal resorts. The crossing from Bremerhaven takes a good 3 hours. A day trip
allows some $4\frac{1}{2}$ hours on the island.

Heligoland consists of three parts –
Unterland, Mittelland and Oberland – and
the little separate island of Düne. –
Unterland, on the SE side of the main
island, has been completely redeveloped
since 1952, with a *Kurhaus*, a *Town Hall*
(1961) and numerous hotels and pensions. To the N are the *Biological Research Establishment*, with a *sea-water
aquarium*, and the *Kur* installations, with a
heated open-air swimming pool (sea-
water; temperature *c.* 23 °C). – SW of
Unterland is the rather higher MITTELLAND,
formed when the fortifications were
blown up in 1947. S of Mittelland is the
artificially constructed *harbour* (trips
round the island from the landing-
stage).

Oberland, linked with Unterland by a lift
and a flight of 181 steps, is a triangle of
rock some 1500 m long and up to 500 m
across, largely flat and grass-covered,
rising to a height of 59 m above the sea.
On the E side is the village (rebuilt), with
St Nicholas's Church (1959; 33 m tower)
and the recently built *bird observatory*.
The former anti-aircraft tower to the W of
the village is now a *lighthouse*. At the
northern tip are an isolated crag known as
the *Hengst* (Stallion) or "Lange Anna"
and the *Lummenfelsen* (Guillemots'
Rock), the highest point on the island.
There is a very attractive walk round the
whole island on the *CLIFF-TOP PATH.

For bathers there are the N and S beaches on the little island of **Düne** (camping site), some 1·5 km E of Unterland and separated from it by an arm of the sea 10 m deep (ferry).

Herford

Land: North Rhineland-Westphalia.
Vehicle registration: HF.
Altitude: 68 m. – Population: 64,000.
Post code: D-4900. – Dialling code: 0 52 21.
ⓘ **Städtisches Verkehrsamt,**
Fürstenaustr. 7;
tel. 5 14 15.

HOTELS. – *Stadt Berlin*, Bahnhofsplatz 6, 61 b.; *Winkelmann*, Mindener Str. 1, 44 b.; *Hansa* (no rest.), Brüderstr. 40, 30 b.; *Motel Brandt*, Ahmser Str. 132, 14 b.; *Stadt Köln*, Bügelstr. 6, 12 b. – IN SCHWARZENMOOR: *Waldesrand*, Zum Forst 4, 25 b.; – IN ELVERDISSEN: *Ehaler*, Elverdisser Str. 337, 30 b. – CAMPING SITES: *Herforder Kanu-Klub*, on the Werre; *Elisabethsee*, in Herford-Eickum.

RESTAURANT. – *Ratskeller*, Rathausplatz 1.

CAFÉ. – *Café Wien*, Radewiger Str. 28.

Herford lies in the fertile hilly region between the Wiehengebirge , and the Teutoburg Forest, at the point where the Aa flows into the Werre. It has a variety of industry, in particular furniture manufacture and textiles. The Baroque architect Matthäus Daniel Pöppelmann was born in Herford in 1662.

HISTORY. – The nucleus of the town was a convent founded by a Saxon nobleman in 789 for the daughters of the Saxon nobility. Emperor Ludwig the Pious gave it the status of an Imperial foundation. The town received its charter about 1170. The new town (Neustadt) was founded about 1220. During the Middle Ages Herford became a member of the Hanse (1342) and a free Imperial city. In 1816 it became the chief town of a Kreis (district).

SIGHTS. – The OLD TOWN lies round the **Minster** of the former convent (13th c.; late Gothic font of 16th c.), the oldest of the large hall-churches of Westphalia. – NE, in the Neuer Markt, is the mid 14th c, *St John's Church*, with fine 14th and 15th c. stained glass. To the N is the 16th c. *Frühherrenhaus*, birthplace of Otto Weddigen, a well-known submarine commander of the First World War – W of the Minster is *St James's Church* (14th c.).

In HÖCKERSTRASSE (pedestrian precinct) is the former *Burgomaster's House* of 1538, with a fine late Gothic stepped gable, birthplace of Matthäus Daniel Pöp-

pelmann, architect of the famous Zwinger in Dresden. Another architectural gem is the *Remensnider-Haus* in the nearby Brüderstrasse, a half-timbered building with rich figural decoration. The *Linnenbauer* monument commemorates Herford's old linen trade. – On the Deichtorwall is the *Municipal Museum* (history, culture and art of the town and the former abbey). – The **Stiftsberg Church** (St Mary's) on the Lutterberg (high altar with late Gothic tabernacle) is one of the finest Gothic hall-churches in Westphalia.

SURROUNDINGS. – **Bad Salzuflen** (6 km SE), a brine spa with old burghers' houses, "graduation works" (for the evaporation of the saline water) and a beautiful Kurpark. – **Enger** (9 km NW). In the former collegiate church of St Dionysius (12th c.) is the sarcophagus of the Saxon Duke Wittekind, with a magnificent carved slab (*c.* 1100). – At **Bünde** (13 km NW), centre of the Westphalian tobacco industry, is the German Tobacco and Cigar Museum (with, among other things, the longest cigar in the world).

Bad Hersfeld

Land: Hesse. ↴ Vehicle registration: HEF.
Altitude: 242 m. – Population: 28,000.
Post code: D-6430. – Dialling code: 0 66 21.
ⓘ **Städtisches Verkehrsbüro**, Town Hall;
tel. 80 77.

HOTELS. – *Parkhotel Rose*, Am Kurpark 9, 40 b.; *Romantik Hotel Zum Stern*, Lingplatz 11, 58 b.; *Wenzel*, Nachtigallenstr. 3, 50 b.; *Sander*, at the Station, 90 b.; *Wilde Wässerchen*, Meisebacher Str. 31, 45 b. – YOUTH HOSTEL: Wehneberg 29. – CAMPING SITE: Geistal, on B 324.

RESTAURANTS. – *Ratskeller*, in Town Hall, Weinstr. 16; *Kurparkstuben*, in Stadthalle; *Stiftsschänke*, Linggplatz 17.

EVENTS. – *Hersfeld Festival*, in the ruins of the Stiftskirche (July/Aug.); *Lullusfest* (in the week of October 16).

Bad Hersfeld, a spa and festival city, lies amid wooded hills in a wide basin in the lower Fulda valley between the Rhön and Knüll ranges, at the point where the Hauna flows into the Fulda. Its mineral waters (containing sulphates of sodium and magnesium) are recommended in the treatment of liver, gall bladder, intestinal and stomach conditions and metabolic disturbances. The old town, still partly encircled by its walls, contains handsome old burghers' houses. The town's traditional industry is cloth-making.

Konrad Duden (1829–1911), compiler of an authoritative orthographical dictionary of German, lived in Bad Hersfeld.

HISTORY. – The town grew up round a Benedictine abbey founded in 769 by Archbishop Lullus of Mainz. In 1648 it passed to Hesse-Kassel as a secular principality. In 1806 Hesse became part of Napoleon's empire. The Lullus Spring was drilled in 1904, the Lingg Spring in 1928 and the Vitalis Spring in 1947. The Hersfeld Festival has been held in the ruins of the Stiftskirche since 1951.

SIGHTS. – The large MARKPLATZ is surrounded by handsome old burghers' houses. To the E is the 14th c. *Town Church*, with a massive tower and a late Gothic interior. Opposite it, to the S, is the *Town Hall*, a handsome Renaissance building (*c.* 1600). – To the W of the town are the imposing ruins of the *Stiftskirche, destroyed by the French in 1761 (11th and 12th c.: total length over 100 m), with a separate belfry. In the buildings adjoining it on the S is the *Municipal Museum.* – In the SW of the town is the *spa establishment* (Kurhaus; three mineral springs).

Nave of St Michael's Church, Hildesheim

Hildesheim

Land: Lower Saxony.
Vehicle registration: HI.
Altitude: 70 m. – Popularion: 105,000.
Post code: D-3200. – Dialling code: 0 51 21.
ⓘ **Verkehrsverein,**
   Markt 5;
   tel. 19 95.

HOTELS. – *Gollart's Hotel Deutsches Haus,* Carl Peters Str. 5, 80 b., HB, sauna; *Rose am Markt,* Markt 7, 68 b. ("Knockenhauer" restaurant); *Bürgermeisterkappele,* Osterstr. 60, 65 b.; *Dittmann's Hotel zum Hagentor,* Kardinal Bertram Str. 35, 36 b.; *Gästehaus Klocke,* Humboldtstr. 11, 20 b.; *Berghölzchen,* at Berghölzchen, 16 b.; *Dittmann* (no rest.), Almsstr. 15, 38 b. – IN EINUM: *Hansa-Hotel,* Hirschberger Str. 7, 20 b. – YOUTH HOSTEL: Schirrmannweg, 81 b.

RESTAURANTS. – *Ratskeller,* Markt 1; *Zur Roten Nase,* Bruhl 27; *China-Restaurant,* Kaiserstr. 17. – IN OCHTERSUM: *Kupferschmiede,* Steinberg 6.

WINE-BARS. – *Schlegel,* Am Steine 4; *Insel Café,* Bischofsmühle, Dammstr. 30.

This old episcopal city lies in the north-western foreland of the Harz, in the fertile valley of the Innerste. The church-building of Bishop Bernward (993–1022) and his successors made Hildesheim a treasurehouse of early Romanesque architecture, and the numerous half-timbered buildings contributed to producing an effect that was almost unique. Then on the night of 22 March 1945 all this splendour was destroyed by fire. Accordingly the town now has a predominantly modern aspect, with a fine pedestrian precinct and well-designed shops and offices, and only a few islands of tradition here and there in the form of rebuilt and restored historic buildings.

The town's principal industries are the manufacture of hardware and electronics. Its port is linked with the Mittelland Canal by a branch canal 13 km long. S of the town is the attractive Hohnsensee recreation centre.

HISTORY. – Hildesheim grew out of an 8th c. trading settlement, in which Emperor Ludwig the Pious built a cathedral around 815. In the 11th c. the town was granted the right to hold a market and enjoyed a great cultural flowering under Bishops Bernward, Godehard and Hezilo. The "new town" (Neustadt) was founded about 1220. After a first union in 1583 the new town and the old town were finally united in 1803. With the secularisation of the ecclesiastical states in that year the principality of Hildesheim, which had previously been directly subject to the Emperor, passed to Prussia. After a period when it belonged to Hanover it returned to Prussia in 1866.

SIGHTS. – In the centre of the old town, which is still enclosed within its moats, is the ALTSTÄDTER MARKT, with the *Fountain* of 1540. On the E side of the square is the late Gothic **Town Hall** (restored). Facing it, to the S, is the *Tempelhaus* (14th and 15th c.; Renaissance oriel window of 1592), with the new building of the *Municipal Savings Bank* adjoining it. – In Andreasplatz, to the SW beyond the HOHER WEG (pedestrian precinct), the lively main shopping and business street of Hildesheim, is **St Andrew's Church** (Evang.), with a Gothic choir of 1389 (rebuilt).

In the W of the old town is the 13th c. *Magdalene Church* (R.C.), which preserves in its treasury the so-called St Bernward's Cross (11th c.). – A little way N, on a commanding eminence, is ***St Michael's Church** (Evang.), one of Germany's finest basilican churches (begun by Bishop Bernward in the 11th c., altered in the 12th.; restored). The most notable features of the interior are the *painted timber roof of the nave (genealogy of Christ, 12th c.) and the Angel Choir. In the crypt is the stone sarcophagus of St Bernward.

In the SW of the Old Town rises the Romanesque **Cathedral** (1054–79, built on the remains of a 9th c. basilica and reconsecrated in 1960 after considerable war damage had been made good. The church contains notable *works of art (St Bernwards Doors 1015; column with carved scenes from the life of Christ, etc.). On the outer wall of the E door is the "thousand-year-old rose-bush"; in the cloister garden is *St Anne's Chapel* (1322). The *Cathedral Treasury can be seen in the adjoining *diocesan museum*. W of the Cathedral, in the square Am Steine, is the ***Roemer-Pelizaeus Museum**, which has the finest collection of Egyptian antiquities in Germany after the Egyptian section of the State Museums in Berlin, in addition to outstanding collections of natural history and ethnography. – On a terrace E of the Cathedral is the *Church of the Holy Cross* (R.C.), rebuilt in Baroque style in the 18th c.

On the southern edge of the old town is **St Godehard's Church** (1133–72: R.C.), one of the best preserved Romanesque churches in Germany, with a beautiful interior; the church treasury contains a very fine 13th c. Romanesque chalice. On the *Lappenberg*, is the *Kehrwiederturm* ("Come back again") of 1465, the only

surviving tower from the town's fortifications, and in the street called the *Brühl* near St Godehard's Church there are still some handsome old half-timbered houses. – In MORITZBERG the Mauritiuskirche (11th c.) with a well-preserved cloister and the tomb of Bishop Hezilo (1054–79).

Hof

Land: Bavaria.
Vehicle registration: HO.
Altitude: 495 m. – Population 53,000.
Post code: D-8670. – Dialling code: 0 92 81.
ⓘ **Amt für Öffentlichkeitsarbeit**, Rathaus; tel: 81 52 33.

HOTELS. – *Kongress Hotel*, Kulmbacher Str. 100 b. (autumn 1984); *Strauss*, Bismarckstr. 31, 95 b.; *Am Kuhbogen*, Marienstr. 88, 55 b. – YOUTH HOSTEL: Beethovenstr. 44, 125 b.

Hof, on the upper Saale, between the Fichtelgebirge and the Franconian Forest, is the most important industrial town of northern Bavaria (textiles, metal working and finishing).

HISTORY. First mentioned in 1214, Hof was from 1373 the property of the Burgraves of Nuremberg. In 1792 it passed to Prussia and in 1810 to the Kingdom of Bavaria.

SIGHTS. – On the Klosterstrasse, W of the Saale, stands the **Town Hall**; opposite, on the E, the Parish *Church of St Michael* (1380–86; severely damaged by fire in the 19th c.). The street known as "Altstadt" and Lorenzstrasse lead to the *Church of St Laurence* (1292; altered on several occasions) with a late Gothic winged altar (Hertnid Altar; 1480). N of the Rathaus at the Lower Gate is the *Hospital Church*, a Gothic building with a Baroque coffered roof (1688–89) and a carved altar of 1511.

In the NE of the town lies the Stadtpark Theresienstein (70 hectares) with the Botanical Garden, a miniature zoo and a viewing tower (on the Labarinth-Berg). In the W of Hof in Kulmbacher Strasse stands the *Freiheitshalle*. Some 3 km S on the Rosenbuhl (579 m) is the *Bismarck Tower*.

Holsteinische Schweiz ("The Switzerland of Holstein")

Land: Schleswig-Holstein.

(i) **Fremdenverkehrsgemeinschaft Holsteinische Schweiz,**
D-2320 Plön;
tel. (0 45 22) 27 17.

The "Switzerland of Holstein" is a region of hills and lakes – the remains of an Ice Age ground and terminal moraine – on the Wagrien peninsula in East Holstein, between Kiel Bay and Lübeck Bay. With its beautiful beech forests and its shimmering sheets of water it is one of the most attractive stretches of country in Germany. The name dates from the 19th c. when holidaying in Switzerland was extremely fashionable.

The centre of the Holsteinische Schweiz is the friendly little climatic and health resort (Kneipp water cure) of *Malente-Gremsmühlen*, delightfully situated between the Dieksee and the Kellersee, the starting-point of the popular "Five Lakes" trip. The nearby town of **Eutin** was once a favourite resort of writers and painters, and its summer festival, with opera performances in the Schlosspark, is widely famed. **Plön** has a castle in the style of the late Renaissance and is a water-sports centre. The old 12th c. church of undressed stone at *Bosau* recalls the missionary work of Bishop Vicelin, the "apostle of the Slavs". The **Grosser Plöner See** is the largest (30 sq. km) and most impressive of the lakes. At the other extreme is the idyllic little *Ukleisee*, quiet and secluded in its forest setting, although it lies within the boundaries of Eutin.

The north-westerly outpost of the Holsteinische Schweiz is the old shoemakers' town of *Preetz* with its brick-built Gothic church. Its north-eastern bastion is the *Bungsberg* near Schönwalde, the highest point in Schleswig-Holstein (164 m); from the television tower on top of the hill there are magnificent views. There is skiing in winter here.

Those who want a holiday region with abundant facilities for recreation and relaxation and with an abundance of light, air and sun, and not a trace of industrial smoke or pollution, will find what they are looking for in the "Switzerland of Holstein".

Bad Homburg vor der Höhe

Land: Hesse. – Vehicle registration: HG.
Altitude: 200 m. – Population: 53,000.
Post code: D-6380. – Dialling code: 0 61 72.

(i) **Kurverwaltung,**
in Kaiser Wilhelm Bad (in the Kurpark);
tel. 2 20 87.

HOTELS. – *Maritim Kurhaus Hotel,* Ludwigsstr. 3, 230 b.; *Geheimrat Trapp,* Kaiser Friedrich Promenade 55, 80 b.; *Hardtwald,* at the end of Philosophenweg, 80 b.; *Haus Daheim* (no rest.), Elisabethenstr. 42, 32 b.; *Villa Kissleff* (no rest.), Kissleffstr. 19, 18 b.; *Darmstadter Hof* (no rest.), Louisenstr. 7, 34 b. – IN DORNHOLZ-HAUSEN: *Haus von Noorden,* Kälberstückweg 41, 18 b., garden terrace, tennis. – YOUTH HOSTEL: Meiereiberg 1, 96 b.

RESTAURANTS. – *Ratsstuben,* in Stadthaus; *Landgrafen,* in Schloss; *Table,* Kaiser Friedrich Promenade 85; *Schildkröte,* Mussbacherstr. 19. – IN DORNHOLZ-HAUSEN: *Hirschgarten.* – AT THE SAALBURG: *Saalburg.*

CAFÉS. – *Peter Kofler,* Louisenstr. 42; *Schleiermacher,* Louisenstr. 28; *Eiding,* Schuttberg 13.

Casino (roulette, baccarat) in Kurpark.

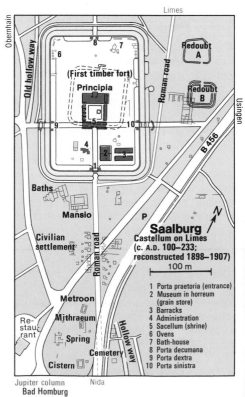

Saalburg
Castellum on Limes
(c. A.D. 100–233;
reconstructed 1898–1907)
|—— 100 m ——|

1 Porta praetoria (entrance)
2 Museum in horreum (grain store)
3 Barracks
4 Administration
5 Sacellum (shrine)
6 Ovens
7 Bath-house
8 Porta decumana
9 Porta dextra
10 Porta sinistra

Jupiter column   Nida
Bad Homburg

Bad Homburg vor der Höhe, at the foot of the Taunus, is one of the most famous of German spas. Its hot saline springs (chalybeate) are set in a splendid Kurpark.

HISTORY. – The town grew up round a castle, first recorded about 1180, which was replaced by the present Schloss in 1680–85. From 1622 to 1866 Homburg was the residence of the Landgraves of Hesse-Homburg. It began to be developed as a spa in 1834, and the Casino was established in 1841. As the Emperor William II's favourite spa it became the resort of the German aristocracy, and it was frequently visited by King Edward VII as Prince of Wales.

SIGHTS. – The town's principal street is LOUISENSTRASSE, in which is the **Kurhaus** (Festival Room, Hotel). N of the Kaiser-Friedrich-Promenade, which runs parallel to Louisenstrasse, is the *Kurpark (44 hectares), laid out in the English style by P. J. Linné in 1854, with the *Kaiser-Wilhelm-Bad* (1890), the *Casino*, an indoor promenade, several carbonic mineral springs, a Siamese Temple, and beautiful gardens and clumps of trees. On the W side of the town, dominated by the *White Tower* (13th c.), is the **Schloss** (17th–19th c.: banqueting hall, Pompeian Room, Hall of Mirrors).

SURROUNDINGS. – *Saalburg (7 km NW): a unique reconstruction of a Roman fort on the Limes (see p. 172), built 1898–1907 on the foundations of the fort which stood on this site. The fort measures 221 by 147 m. Remains of other buildings surround it. Museum, with material recovered by excavation.

*Grosser Feldberg (24 km NW), the highest hill in the Taunus (880 m), with a 70 m high telecommunications tower erected by the Federal Post Office; from the *Kleiner Feldbergturm* (40 m) there are wide views, extending as far as the Spessart and the Odenwald.

Höxter

Land: North Rhineland-Westphalia.
Vehicle registration: HX.
Altitude: 90 m. – Population: 35,500.
Post code: D-3470. – Dialling code: 0 52 71.
ⓘ **Verkehrsamt,**
　Am Rathaus 7;
　tel. 6 32 44.

HOTELS. – *Niedersachsen,* Möllinger Str. 4, 90 b.; *Weserberghof,* Godelheimer Str. 16, 64 b.; *Corveyer Hof,* Westerbachstr. 29, 22 b.; *Braunschweiger Hof,* Corbiestr. 3, 10 b. – YOUTH HOSTEL: Am Ziegenberg, 176 b. – CAMPING SITE: *Städtischer Campingplatz,* at sports ground.

RESTAURANTS. – *Ratskeller,* Weserstr. 11; *Schloss-Restaurant,* at Schloss Corvey, 2 km E.

EVENTS. – *Corvey Music Weeks* (March/June).

Corvey Abbey, near Höxter

Höxter lies on the left bank of the Weser in an attractive setting of wooded hills, those on the right bank belonging to the Solling range. It has preserved numerous 16th c. half-timbered buildings, and in the nearby Corvey Abbey possesses one of the great centres of Western culture.

HISTORY. – Höxter, situated at the intersection of old traffic routes, goes back to the *Villa Huxori* which Emperor Ludwig the Pious presented to Corvey Abbey in 823. In the 13th c. it received its municipal charter and the right to build walls, and it is referred to as a Hanseatic town in 1295. Until 1792 Höxter was capital of the ecclesiastical territory held by Corvey Abbey directly from the Emperor, from 1792 to 1802 of the Prince-Bishopric of Corvey, and from 1803 to 1806 of the Orange-Nassau principality of Corvey.

SIGHTS. – In the OLD TOWN are numerous Renaissance half-timbered houses dating from the 16th c. Among the finest are the twin-gabled **Dechanei** (Deanery) of 1561, once the town house of the noble Amelunxen family (oriel window, beautiful rosette-patterned timber-work) in MARKTSTRASSE; *Haus Hütte* (1565) at NIKOLAISTRASSE 10; in WESTERBACHSTRASSE, a relatively wide street by which the old trading route the Hellweg entered the town, the *Tillyhaus* of 1598 (No. 33), where the Imperial general Count Tilly is said to have stayed several times during the Thirty Years War, *Haus Hottensen* (1537) at No. 34 and a charming group of houses (restored) at Nos. 2–10; opposite the W front of St Kilian's Church is the *Küsterhaus* (Verger's House), now occupied by the municipal tourist office, a fine half-timbered building of 1595.

The **Town Hall**, with a richly carved oriel window and an octagonal staircase tower, dates from 1610 to 1613. In the entrance hall is a late Romanesque stone carving (*c.* 1260) showing the municipal weighhouse-master; in the tower a carillon with 35 bronze bells. – NE of the Town

Hall is the Romanesque **St Kilian's Church** (12th–13th c.: Evang.), with two prominent W towers of unequal height. In the interior are a Crucifixion of 1520 (on high altar), a pulpit of 1597 and a font of 1631. – To the N is the early Gothic *St Mary's Church* (13th c.), originally belonging to a Minorite friary.

SURROUNDINGS. – *Corvey Abbey (2 km NE), the most distinguished Benedictine abbey in North Germany, founded by Ludwig the Pious in 822 and secularised in 1803 (now owned by the Duke of Ratibor). Of the old *abbey church* there survives the projecting**west front, the oldest building of the early medieval period in Westphalia (in the interior the two-storey Imperial Chapel, with remains of 9th c. wall paintings). The present abbey church has a magnificent Baroque interior; on the S side is the tomb of *A. H. Hoffmann von Fallersleben*, author of the German national anthem, "Deutschland über alles", who was librarian of Schloss Corvey. Of the Baroque period, too, are the plain undecorated buildings of the former abbey, now the *Schloss* (the Abbot's Gallery, the Imperial Hall and the Library being particularly notable). – **Neuhaus im Solling** (16 km E), a health and winter sports resort in the heart of the Solling hills, with a former hunting lodge (1768–91) of the Kings of Hanover. – *Köterberg (17 km NW), a 497 m high hill with a television tower and the Köterberghaus restaurant: beautiful panoramic views of the Solling, Vogler, Lippisches Bergland and Eggegebirge hills.

Husum

Land: Schleswig-Holstein.
Vehicle registration: NF.
Altitude: 5 m. – Population: 25,000.
Post code: D-2250. – Dialling code: 0 48 41.
ⓘ **Tourist Information**, Town Hall, Grosse Str. 25;
tel. 66 61 33.

HOTELS. – *Thomas*, Zingel 9, 70 b.; *Carstens am Wasserturm* (no rest.), Hinter der Neustadt 28, 50 b.; *Obsens Hotel*, Hafenstr. 2, 31 b.; *Osterkrug*, Osterende 56, 50 b.; *Zur Grauen Stadt am Meer*, Schiffsbrücke 9, 40 b.

RESTAURANTS. – *Ratskeller*, Grosse Str. 27; *Storm-Café*, Markt 11.

Husum, situated on the W coast of Schleswig-Holstein, in the Husumer Au, which serves as a natural harbour, is the cultural centre of northern Friesland. As the birthplace of the poet and novelist Theodor Storm (1817–88) this "grey city by the sea" features in many of his stories.

SIGHTS. – In the MARKTPLATZ is the *Town Hall*, rebuilt many times on the model of the original Renaissance building of 1601. On the E side of the square is

the neo-classical **St Mary's Church**: (1829–33: bronze font of 1643). At No. 9 is the *birthplace of Theodor Storm*; at No. 31 Wasserreihe the *Theodor Storm Haus Husum* (museum).

The former **Schloss** (1577–82) now contains local government offices. Beyond the cemetery is the **Ostenfelder Bauernhaus** (16th–17th c.), a farmhouse re-erected here as an open-air museum in 1899.

SE of the Marktplatz is the brick-built **Nissenhaus** (1937–39), with the *Museum of North Friesland* (natural history, local history and traditions, pictures).

The *harbour*, to the W of the town, is the starting point for trips to the Halligen islands and the North Frisian Islands.

SURROUNDINGS. – 10 km SW of Husum, near Simonsberg, is the **Roter Hauberg**, a handsome old farmhouse, now a hotel (no rest.).

Idar-Oberstein

Land: Rhineland-Palatinate.
Vehicle registration: BIR.
Altitude: 260 m. – Population: 35,000.
Post code: D-6580. – Dialling code: 0 67 81.
ⓘ **Städtisches Fremdenverkehrsamt**, Pavillon at Main Station;
tel. 2 70 25.

HOTELS. – *Merian-Hotel*, Mainzer Str. 34, 212 b.; *Park-Hotel*, Hauptstr. 185, 65 b.; *Schützenhof*, Hauptstr. 141, 42 b.; *Zum Schwan*, Hauptstr. 25, 37 b. – IN TIEFENSTEIN: *Handelshof*, Tiefensteiner Str. 235, 28 b. – YOUTH HOSTEL: Alte Treibe, 23, 160 b. – CAMPING SITES: *Im Staden*, on outskirts of town on Trier road; *Fischbachtal*, Niederwörresbach; *Oberes Idartal*, Sensweiler-Katzenloch; *Campingpark Waldwiesen*, Birkenfeld.

CAFÉS. – *Benner*, Kobachstr. 3.

Attractively situated at the outflow of the Idar into the Nahe, with crags of melaphyre (basaltic rock) towering above it to a height of 125 m, Idar-Oberstein is one of Germany's leading centres of the trade in precious stones and the jewellery industry, with well-known establishments for grinding and polishing precious stones and agates.

HISTORY. – The town's fame was based on the rich reserves of agates which it once possessed. Its supplies originally came from the agate blocks washed out of the local melaphyre, but since the mid 19th c., when supplies from overseas became increasingly available, only imported stones have been processed.

SIGHTS. – Above the district of **Oberstein** (*Idar-Oberstein Museum*) is a *rock church* in a cave (1482). Higher up still, on the sheer crags, are two ruined castles (11th and 12th c.). – The district of **Idar** extends up the Idar valley, with the 22-storey *Diamond and Precious Stone Exchange*; on the first floor is the interesting* *German Museum of Precious Stones*. In Tiefensteiner Strasse is the *Weiherschleife*, an old grinding and polishing establishment. In ALGENROTH the agate mines in the *Steinkaulenberg* can be visited.

Ingolstadt

Land: Bavaria. – Vehicle registration: IN.
Altitude: 365 m. – Population: 90,000.
Post code: D-8070. – Dialling code: 08 41.
ⓘ **Städtisches Fremdenverkehrsamt,**
Hallstr. 5;
tel. 30 54 17.

HOTELS. –*Holiday Inn,* Goethestr. 153, 200 b.; SB, sauna; *Rappensberger,* Harderstr. 3, 169 b.; *Donau Hotel,* Münchener Str. 10, 89 b.; *Bavaria,* Feldkirchener Str. 67, 74 b., SB, sauna; *Scholze* (no rest.), Ziegeleistr. 64, 36 b.; *Adler* (no rest.), Theresienstr. 22, 80 b. – IN GAIMERSHEIM-FRIEDRICHSHOFEN: *Heidehof,* Ingolstädter Str. 121, 30 b., SB, sauna. – YOUTH HOSTEL: Oberer Graben 4, 100 b. – CAMPING SITE: *Auwaldsee,* on the Auwaldsee.

RESTAURANTS. – *Bastei,* Schlosslände 1; *Chaton,* Beckerstr. 19 (grill).

CAFÉ. – *Westermeier,* Harderstr. 7.

This former stronghold and residence of the Dukes of Bavaria lies on the southern fringe of the Franconian Alb in a wide plain in the Danube valley. The old town (pedestrian precinct) with its numerous historic buildings is still surrounded by considerable remains of its medieval fortifications. It is now an important industrial town, with large oil refineries (pipeline from the Adriatic) and car assembly plants.

HISTORY. – Ingolstadt first appears in the records in 806. Around 1260 Duke Ludwig the Severe built a castle here, and in 1472 Duke Ludwig the Rich founded a university, which Johann Eck, Luther's opponent, built up into a stronghold of the Counter-Reformation. The university continued to exist until 1800.

SIGHTS, – In the centre of the OLD TOWN is the RATHAUSPLATZ (recently reconstructed), with the *Old Town Hall* (1882), the *New Town Hall* (1959) and the *Spitalkirche* (15th c.). – The LUDWIG-STRASSE runs E to the massive old

Kreuztor, Ingolstadt

Herzogsschloss (Ducal Castle: 15th c.), with some of the finest secular Gothic apartments in Germany (Bavarian Army Museum, opened 1972). Farther S, between the New Town Hall and the Schloss, is the *Herzogkasten,* now the municipal library.

From the Rathausplatz THERESIENSTRASSE runs W to the massive late Gothic **Minster** (Liebfrauenmünster: 15th–16th c.), with two towers placed diagonally to one another and a fine interior (tombstone of Luther's opponent Johann Eck). To the N is the * **Church of Maria de Victoria**, built 1732–36 by the Asam brothers, with an interior which is a masterpiece of Bavarian Rococo. W of this church is an old gateway with seven towers and turrets, the * **Kreuztor** (1385). In the *Old Anatomy Building* in the nearby Anatomiestrasse is the *German Museum of the History of Medicine.* In the restored "Cavalier Hepp" is the Town Museum. – On the S bank of the Danube are neo-classical fortifications by Leo van Klenze.

Kaiserslautern

Land: Rhineland-Palatinate.
Vehicle registration: KL.
Altitude: 236 m. – Population: 100,000.
Post code: D-6750. – Dialling code: 06 31.
ⓘ **Verkehrsamt,** in Town Hall;
tel. 85 23 16.

Town Hall, Kaiserslautern

kirche (13th–14th c.: Evang.) with its three towers; in the porch is a memorial, with figures of Luther and Calvin, commemorating the union of the two Protestant denominations (1818). A little way NE is *St Martin's Church* (14th c.: R.C.), and to the W of this is the *Fruchthalle* (1843–46), where fruit and vegetables were once sold, with a large banqueting hall. Farther W is the RATHAUSPLATZ, with the modern **Town Hall** (1968), a tower block 84 m high (the tallest town hall in Europe). Of the old "Barbarossa castle" (originally built by Charlemagne, enlarged by the Emperor Frederick Barbarossa 1153–58) which stood nearby only fragments remain. – In MUSEUMSPLATZ, in the N of the town, is the Palatinate Craft Institute, with the *Palatinate gallery* (19th and 20th c. art).

SURROUNDINGS. –.**Grosser Humberg** (430 m, 4 km S), with wide views. – **Hohenecken** (7 km SW): ruined castle. – **Otterberg church** (8 km N).

HOTELS. – *Dorint*, St Quentin Ring 1, 225 b., SB, SP, sauna; *City* (no rest.), Rosenstr. 28, 35 b., SB, sauna; *Zepp* (no rest.), Pariser Str. 4, 82 b.; *Bonk* (no rest.), Riesenstr. 13, 39 b.; *Pfälzer Hof*, Fruckthallstr. 15, 35 b.; *Reitz*, G. M. Pfaff Platz 1, 18 b. – ON THE GELTERSWOOG: *Seehotel Gelterswoog*, Gelterswoog, 88 b., SB, SP, sauna. – CAMPING SITE: Gelterswoog, Kaiserslautern-Hohenecken.

RESTAURANTS. – *Rathaus Restaurant*, on 21st floor of Town Hall; *Zur Burg*, Steinstr. 18; *Bella Casa*, Pirmasenser Str. 59; *Bremer Hof*, 2·5 km SW on the Bremer Strasse.

WINE-BARS. – *Kelterstubchen*, Alleestr. 11; *Spinnradl*, Schillerstr. 1 (half-timbered house of 1509); *Hahnhof*, Eisenbahnstr. 27.

CAFÉ. – *Fegert*, Mühlstr. 11.

The old "Barbarossa town" of Kaiserslautern, situated at the intersection of important traffic routes, is the cultural and economic centre of the Palatinate Forest, with Kaiserslautern University and the Palatinate Theatre as well as a variety of industry (car components, assembly of sewing machines, engineering and iron-working).

SIGHTS. – In the STIFTSPLATZ in the centre of the town is the early Gothic **Stifts-**

Karlsruhe

Land: Baden-Württemberg.
Vehicle registration: KA
Altitude: 116 m. – Population: 272,000.
Post code: D-7500. – Dialling code: 07 21.
ⓘ **Verkehrsverein**, Bahnhofplatz 6;
tel. 38 70 85.

HOTELS. –* *Hilton International*, Mendelssohnplatz, 432 b. ("La Cave" wine cellar);* *Parkhotel*, Ettlinger Str. 23, 240 b. (Bavarian wine room);* *Schlosshotel*, Bahnhofplatz 2, 130 b.; *Kübler* (no rest.), Bismarckstr. 39, 122 b.; *Hansa Hotel*, Bahnhofplatz 16, 113 b.; *Eden*, Bahnhofstr. 17, 101 b.; *Erbprinzenhof* (no rest.), Erbprinzenstr. 26, 83 b.; *Berliner Hof* (no rest.), Douglasstr. 7, 80 b. – IN DURLACH: *Maison Suisse*, Hildebrandstr. 24, 23 b. – YOUTH HOSTEL: Moltkestr. 2b (in Engländerplatz). – CAMPING SITE: *Turmbergblick*, Tiengener Str. 40, in Durlach.

RESTAURANTS. – *O'Henry's Spezialitätenrestaurant*, Breite Str. 24; *Balkan Grill*, Herrenstr. 36; *Unter den Linden*, Kaiserallee 71; *Santa Lucian*, Badenwerkstr. 1 (Italian); *Brauhaus Moniger*, Kaiserstr. 142; *Burghof*, Haid und Neu Str. 18; *Zum Hasen*, Gerwigstr. 47. – IN DAXLANDEN:* *Zur Krone*, Pfarrstr. 18 (frequented by artists). – IN MAXAU: *Hofgut Maxau*.

WINE-BARS. – *Oberländer Weinstube*, Akademiestr. 7 (with garden); *Badische Weinstuben*, in Botanic Garden; *Badische Weinstube*, Ritterstr. 10.

CAFÉS. – *Schlossmuseum* (with terrace); *Barany*, in Festplatz; *Nancy*, at Nancyhalle in Stadtgarten; *Tiergarten-Café*, Bahnhofplatz 4 (with terrace); *Feller*, Am Marktplatz.

This former Grand-Ducal capital lies close to the Rhine in the north-western foothills of the Black Forest, laid out in a fan-shaped pattern centred on the palace. It is the seat of the Federal High Court and Federal Constitutional Court and has a University (College of Technology), Academy of Art and Academy of Music. The German Nuclear Research Centre is based here. The port on the Rhine, 7 km away, has promoted the establishment of a varied range of industries, including large refineries linked with the Marseilles–Karlsruhe–Ingolstadt pipeline.

Karlsruhe was the birthplace in 1785 of Karl von Drais, inventor of a foot-propelled bicycle, and in 1844 of Carl Benz, originator of the petrol-engine. He constructed his first petrol-driven vehicle in 1885.

HISTORY. – Karlsruhe owes its origin to Margrave Karl Wilhelm of Baden-Durlach, who established his new capital here in 1715. It was given its neo-classical stamp by the restrained and elegant buildings, both public and private, erected in the early 19th c. by the architect Friedrich Weinbrenner, who had been trained in Rome. Repeated air raids during the Second World War caused heavy destruction in the town, but the damage was made good by an impressively conceived post-war reconstruction programme.

SIGHTS. – The town's focal point is the SCHLOSSPLATZ, with the **Palace**, built by Friedrich von Kesslau in 1752–85, partly on the basis of plans by Balthasar Neumann (rebuilt after war damage). It now contains the rich *Baden Provincial Museum* (prehistoric material, antiquities, applied art, folk traditions). Behind the palace are the extensive *gardens* (Schlossgarten). – On the SW side of the Schlossplatz, at Hans-Thoma-Str. 2, is the *State Art Gallery* (Staatliche Kunsthalle), with an important collection of pictures (early German masters like Cranach, Grünewald, Holbein and Striegel; Dutch and French painting of the 17th and 18th c.; major works of the modern Baden school); built on to it is the *Hans Thoma Museum*, with works by the landscape painter Hans Thoma (1839–1924); in the Orangery is a permanent display of German painting from 1890 to the present day. N of the Kunsthalle is the *Federal Constitutional Court* (Bundesverfassungsgericht: 1968). 1 km NE of the Palace is the *Wildpark Stadium*.

S of the Schlossplatz is the MARKTPLATZ, with the 6·5 m high red sandstone **Pyramid** which has become the emblem of the town. It contains the burial vault of Karlsruhe's founder. On either side of the square, which divides the long Kaiser-strasse into two parts, are the **Town Church** (Evang.) and the **Town Hall** (both by Weinbrenner; restored). KAISER-STRASSE runs W past the handsome Post Office to the Mühlberger Tor, to the W of which, at Röntgenstr. 6, is the *Museum of Upper Rhineland Writers* (manuscripts, first editions, letters, etc.). In the eastern half of the street, which leads to the Durlacher Tor, is the *Technical University* (founded 1825), which extends NW to the Schlossplatz. Here Heinrich Hertz discovered electro-magnetic waves in 1885–89.

SW of the Marktplatz, in FRIEDRICHSPLATZ, is **St Stephen's Church** (R.C.), built by

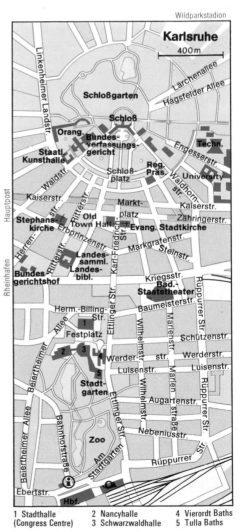

| 1 Stadthalle | 2 Nancyhalle | 4 Vierordt Baths |
| (Congress Centre) | 3 Schwarzwaldhalle | 5 Tulla Baths |

Weinbrenner in 1814 (restored). On the S side of the square is the *Natural History Museum* (vivarium); behind it, in the Nymphengarten, is the *Baden Provincial Library* (1964). A little to the SW is the former Erbgrossherzogliches Palais (1893–97), occupied since 1950 by the **Federal High Court** (Bundesgerichtshof).

From the Marktplatz Karl-Friedrich-Strasse runs S by way of the RONDELL-PLATZ, with the *Constitution Column* and the *Margrave's Palace*, one of Weinbrenner's finest buildings (rebuilt 1963 and now occupied by a bank), to the recently reconstructed street intersection at the *Ettlinger Tor*. To the SE is the new **Baden State Theatre** (opera and drama), built 1970–75.

From here Ettlinger Strasse continues S to the FESTPLATZ (on right), with the **Stadthalle** (1915: at present being converted into a modern congress centre – opening 1985), the **Schwarzwaldhalle**, with a bodly contoured roof (1953–54: sporting events, etc.), and the *Nancyhalle* (1966). – The beautiful *Stadtgarten* extends S from here to the railway station, with a restaurant, the Vierordt Baths, the Tulla Baths and the *Zoo*. E of the Vierordt Baths, at Werderstr. 63, is a small *Transport Museum*. W of the station stands the *Europahalle*, a huge sports hall.

SURROUNDINGS. – **Turmberg** (225 m: 7½ km E), with the Durlacher Warte (fine views of Karlsruhe and the Upper Rhine plain). – **Bruchsal** (21 km NE) with an 18th c. castle (staircase by B. Neumann). **Rastatt** (22 km SW) also has a castle, a Military Museum, a Local Museum and a Baroque "Favorite".

Kassel

Land: Hesse. – Vehicle registration: KS.
Altitude: 132 m. – Population: 203,000.
Post code: D-3500. – Dialling code: 05 61.
ⓘ **Stadtinformation**, Main Station; tel. 7 87 80 06.
Informationsstelle, am Friedrichsplatz; tel. 7 87 80 22.

HOTELS. – *Dorint Hotel Reiss*, Werner Hilpert Str. 24, 150 b.; *Parkhotel Hessenland*, Obere Königsstr. 2, 203 b.; *Domus*, Erzbergerstr. 1, 75 b.; *Hospiz Treppenstrasse* (no rest.), Treppenstr. 9, 60 b.; *Seidel* (no rest.), Holländische Str. 27, 50 b. – IN BETTENHAUSEN: *Holiday Inn*, Heiligenröder Str. 61, 268 b., SB, sauna. – IN NIEDERZWEHREN: *Gude*, Frankfurter Str. 299, 110 b., SB, sauna. – IN WILHELMSHÖHE: *Schlosshotel Wilhelmshöhe*, Schlosspark 2, 185 b., SB, sauna; *Schweizer Hof*, Wilhelmshöhe Allee 288, 93 b. – AT KASSEL MITTE ENTRANCE TO MOTORWAY: *Autobahn*

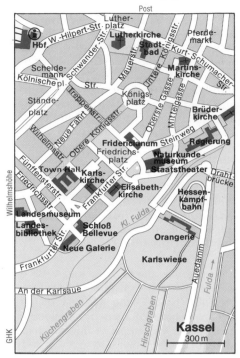

Post

Kassel
300 m

Rasthaus Kassel, Lohfelden, 140 b. – YOUTH HOSTEL: Schenkendorfstr. 18, 220 b. – CAMPING SITES: Giesenallee and Fulda Freizeitzentrum, both on the Fulda.

RESTAURANTS. – *Henkel im Hauptbahnhof*, in Station; *Ratskeller*, in Town Hall, Obere Königsstr. 8; *Stadthallen-Restaurant*, Friedrich-Ebert-Str. 152; *Schloss Schönfeld*, at Botanic Gardens.

WINE-BARS. – *Weinstuben Boos*, Wilhelmshöher Allee 97; *Weinkruger*, Oberste Gasse 6.

CAFÉS. – *Paulus*, Friedrichsplatz and Treppenstr. 13; *Lange*, Friedrich-Ebert-Str.72.

EVENTS. – *Löwenburg Serenades* (Sat. evenings in summer); *documenta*, an exhibition of modern art (July–Sept.). *Festival of Light* in Wilhelmshöhe Park (Sept.).

Kassel, the cultural, economic and administrative centre of northern Hesse, is delightfully situated at the foot of the Habichtswald in a basin in the Fulda valley. Numerous cultural establishments (including a Gesamthochschule or comprehensive higher educational establishment) and official agencies (Federal Labour Court, Federal Social Court) are based here. In the artistic field Kassel is noted for the avant-garde "documenta" exhibitions. Wilhelmshöhe, within the city limits, is a popular health resort (Kneipp cure). Kassel has many different industries; engineering, the

manufacture of locomotives and public transport vehicles, as well as electro-technical and chemical plants. In addition its position on the N–S motorway makes Kassel an important traffic junction.

The town centre has an attractive modern aspect, with fine traffic arteries, spacious squares and pedestrians-only shopping streets.

HISTORY. – The first nucleus of Kassel was a Frankish royal stronghold at the crossing of the Fulda. By the 12th c. it had acquired a municipal charter and the right to build walls. In 1277 Landgrave Heinrich I made Kassel his residence. the town's great periods of economic and cultural flowering were in the 15th and particularly the 18th c. Landgrave Karl laid out the Karlsaue, Wilhelm VIII founded the famous picture gallery and Wilhelm IX built Schloss Wilhelmshöhe. The reverse of the medal was that Friedrich II enlisted soldiers from all over his territories to fight for Britain in North America (1775). – In October 1943 most of the old town was destroyed; it was later rebuilt in modern style.

SIGHTS. – The main business and shopping street in the town centre is the OBERE KÖNIGSSTRASSE (pedestrian precinct), which runs from Königsplatz by way of Friedrichsplatz (on right the 300 m long "Treppenstrasse" – with steps, as its name implies) and Opernplatz to Brüder-Grimm-Platz. – On the NE side of Friedrichsplatz is the former **Museum Fridericianum**, a neo-classical building (by Simon du Ry, 1769–79) which after an interval of several years has been used since 1955 for the "documenta" temporary exhibitions of modern art. On the S side of the square is the **State Theatre**, rebuilt 1958–59, with two houses (Grosses Haus and Kleines Haus). N of the theatre, in the **Ottoneum** (16th c.), Germany's earliest permanent theatre, is the *Natural History Museum* (Steinweg 2). S of the theatre, along the banks of the Fulda, is the *****Karlsaue**, a beautiful natural forest park (160 hectares), with the *Orangery* (1701–11: destroyed), the *Marble Baths*, a magnificent structure built in 1720 to the design of the sculptor Pierre Etienne Monnot, and the flower-covered island of *Siebenbergen*. – In Opernplatz is a sculpture by V. Sidur, "Man in Chains" (1974). Farther SW in Obere Königsstrasse is the imposing **Town Hall** (with Ratskeller) built 1905–09.

In BRÜDER-GRIMM-PLATZ are the *Wachthaus*, in which the brothers Jakob and Wilhelm Grimm (famous for their collection of fairy tales and their German dictionary) lived from 1814 to 1822, and the **Hessian Provincial Museum** (medieval tapestries, applied art, astronomy and physics, folk traditions, and the unique *German Wallpaper Museum*). Behind the Museum, to the SE, is the *Murhard and Hessian Provincial Library* *manuscript of the famous "Hildebrandlied" written in Fulda Abbey *c.* 800; *"documenta" archives*). A short distance E, at Schöne Aussicht 2, is the little *Schloss Bellevue*, with the *Grimm Brothers Museum* (manuscripts of their tales, scientific works, letters, pictures, translations of the tales from all over the world). Opposite it, to the SW, is the *Neue Galerie* (pictures and sculpture of the 19th and 20th c.). – NW of Obere Königsstrasse is the long STÄNDEPLATZ, with the *Town Museum* and imposing modern tower blocks.

From Brüder-Grimm-Platz the 5 km long Wilhelmshöher Allee runs in a dead straight line to WILHELMSHÖHE, a health resort (Kur Hesse Baths) within the city boundaries, passing close to the **Stadthalle**, the *Federal Labour Court* and the *Federal Social Court*. The neo-classical **Schloss Wilhelmshöhe** (287 m long) was built by Simon Louis du Ry and Heinrich Christoph Jussow in 1786–1801 for Landgrave Wilhelm IX (later Elector Wilhelm I). From 1807 to 1813 it was the residence of Napoleon's brother Jérôme, King of Westphalia, in 1871 Napoleon III of France was lodged here after his capture at the battle of Sedan, and it later became a summer residence of Emperor William II. In the magnificent interior are the *Schlossmuseum* and the *****Gallery of Old Masters*, a collection begun by Landgrave Wilhelm VIII which now contains more than 600 pictures. It is rich in works by Dutch painters (including 17 Rembrandts and 11 Van Dycks) and Italian and Spanish masters (Titian, Tintoretto, Murillo); there are also collections of *engravings, antiquities* and *prehistoric material*.

On the eastern slopes of the Habichtswald is the *****Bergpark Wilhelmshöhe** (250 hectares), described by the art scholar Dehio as "perhaps the most grandiose achievement of the Baroque style in the combination of architecture and landscape", with the *Löwenburg* (a castle ruin, built 1793–97), the *Great Fountain* (53 m) and artificial *waterfalls* and *cascades*, all crowned by the *Octagon* (525 m), which has a pointed column 32 m high bearing an 8 m high copper figure of Hercules, in whose club there is room to accommodate eight people. It is a fascinating sight when the fountain, the cascades and the figure of Hercules are floodlit in the evening.

SURROUNDINGS. – *Schloss Wilhelmsthal (11 km NW). The Elector's summer palace, built by François de Cuvilliés 1753–67, is one of the most charming Rococo palaces in Germany (sumptuous interior; Gallery of Beauty, with paintings by Johann Heinrich Tischbein). – Oberkaufungen (11 km E), with a church which originally belonged to a Benedictine nunnery founded in 1017 by Empress Kunigunde, Henry II's wife.

Hofgarten, Kempten im Allgäu

Kempten im Allgäu

Land: Bavaria. – Vehicle registration: KE.
Altitude: 695 M. – Population: 57,000.
Post code: D-8960. – Dialling code: 08 31.
ⓘ Verkehrsamt, Rathausplatz 14;
tel. 2 52 52 37.

HOTELS. – Fürstenhof, Rathausplatz 8, 144 b.; Peterhof, Salzstr. 1, 98 b.; Bahnhof Hotel, Mozartstr. 2, 70 b.; Bayerischer Hof, Füssener Str. 96, 65 b.; Haslacher Hof, Immenstädter Str. 74, 50 b.

RESTAURANTS. – Kreuz-Stuben, Rathausplatz 23; Haubenschloss, Haubenschloss-str. 37; Weinhaus zum Strittigen Winkel, Fischerstr (external staircase); Hummel, Immenstädter Str. 2 (garden inn).

The chief town of the Allgäu in Upper Swabia is attractively situated on the banks of the Iller, on a site once occupied by a Celtic settlement. Since 1982 the remains of "Cambodunum", founded by the Romans in the 1st c. A.D. have been excavated. In its present form the town arose from a princely foundation in the 17th and 18th c. and is the centre of the Allgäu diarying industry.

SIGHTS. – In the RESIDENZPLATZ is the extensive Baroque Palace of the Prince-Abbots, built 1651–74, now occupied by government offices. Adjoining the W wing is the domed Baroque abbey church of St Lawrence (1652–66). In the nearby Kornhaus (18th c.) is the Allgäu Heimatmuseum; in the Zumsteinhaus Roman material and a geological collection (Alpine relief).

The Town Hall, originally built in 1474, was reconstructed in Renaissance style in the 16th c. S of the Town Hall is the late Gothic church of St. Mang (St Magnus,

patron saint of the Allgäu), with a Baroque interior. – From the Burghalde (open-air theatre) above the bridge over the Iller there are beautiful views of the mountains.

SURROUNDINGS. – Up the Iller valley to the S is the old town of Immenstadt (Hirsch, 50 b.; Lamm, 47 b.; Goldener Adler, 50 b.; Alpengasthof Buhlerhöh, 40 b; in Buhl), with a Schloss of 1620 and the Upper Allgäu Heimatmuseum (in September the "Immenstädter Viehscheid"); to the W are the Grosser and Kleiner Alpsee, popular with water sports enthusiasts (excellent recreational facilities).

Kiel

Land: Schleswig-Holstein.
Vehicle registration: KI.
Altitude: 5 m. – Population: 257,000.
Post code: D-2300. – Dialling code: 04 31.
ⓘ Verkehrsverein,
Auguste-Viktoria-Str. 16;
tel. 6 22 30 and 6 36 60.

HOTELS. – *Maritime Bellevue, Bismarckalle 2, 200 b., SB, sauna; *Conti-Hansa, Am Schlossgarten 7, 167 b., SB, sauna (closed until June 1984); *Kieler Kaufmann, Niemannsweg 102, 72 b., SB, sauna; *Keiler Yacht Club, Hindenburgufer 70, 100 b.; *Astor, Holstenplatz 1, 72 b.; Berliner Hof, Ringstr. 6, 100 b.; Muhl's Hotel, Lange Reihe 5, 67 b.; Wiking, Schützenwall 1, 61 b.; Erkenhof (no rest.), Dänische Str. 12, 50 b.; Zum Fritz Reuter (no rest.), Langer Segen 5a, 70 b. – IN HOLTENAU (5 km N): Waffenschmiede, Friedrich-Voss-Ufer 4, 21 b. – IN SCHILKSEE (15 km N): Olympia (no rest.), Drachenbahn 20, 200 b. – YOUTH HOSTEL: Johannisberg 1, Gaarden, 467 b. – CAMPING SITES: Falckenstein, on W shore of Firth of Kiel (2 km N of Friedrichsort); Möltenort, in Heikendorf; Fördeblick, Stein bei Laboe.

RESTAURANTS. – *Restaurant im Schloss*, Wall 76 (view of harbour); *Friesenhof*, in Town Hall; *Rauchfang*, Brunswiker Str. 26; *Jever Böön*, Dänische Str. 22; *La bonne Auberge*, Holtenauer Str. 53; *Schiffer Ausschank*, Walkerdamm 11; *Tai Ping*, Wilhelminenstr. 21 (Chinese). – IN SCHILKSEE: *Am Olympiahafen*, Fliegender Holländer 45.

CAFÉS. – *Fiedler*, Holstenstr. 92; *Heningsen*, Kehdenstr. 1; *Arkaden Cafe*, on the Reventloubrücke; *Das Kaffeehaus*, Waisenhofstr. 7.

EVENTS. – *Kieler Umschlag* (a traditional popular festival, Feb.); *Kieler Woche* (Kiel Week: sailing regattas and programme of cultural events, June).

Kiel, capital of the *Land* of Schleswig-Holstein and a university town, is attractively situated at the S end of the Kieler Förde, an arm of the Baltic which extends some 17 km inland. It is an important port (ferry service to Scandinavia) with a considerable range of industries (engineering, manufacture of electrical precision instruments, fish-processing). It is also a naval base, with naval command posts and training establishments.

During the Second World War the town's importance as a naval base brought it heavy air attacks, and the post-war reconstruction has produced a fine modern town. Kiel's business and shopping district with its pedestrian precinct, set a standard for the creation of modern town centres.

HISTORY. – Kiel was founded by Count Adolf IV von Schauenburg in the 13th c., and under his son Count Johann I it received a municipal charter on the model of Lübeck (1242). In 1283 the town became a member of the Hanse. The University was founded by Duke Christian Albrecht of Holstein-Gottorf in 1665. In 1848 the provisional government of Schleswig-Holstein met in Kiel in order to maintain the province's rights against Denmark. When the base of the Prussian fleet was moved to Kiel in 1865 (with the status of an Imperial naval base following in 1871) the town entered on a period of rapid growth. In 1882 the first sailing regatta was held in the Firth of Kiel. The Kiel Canal (originally called the Kaiser-Wilhelm-Kanal, now the Nord-Ostsee-Kanal) was opened in 1895. The sailing events of the Summer Olympics were held in the Firth of Kiel in 1936 and 1972.

SIGHTS. – In the MARKT in the centre of the OLD TOWN stands **St Nicholas's Church** (late Gothic, altered in the 19th c., restored after war damage), with a beautiful altar, font and pulpit. In front of the church is a sculpture by Ernst Barlach, "The Spiritual Fighter" (1928). – From here Kiel's main shopping street, HOLSTEN-STRASSE (pedestrian precinct) runs SW to Holstenplatz.

W of the Markt is the *Kleiner Kiel*, a relic of an arm of the firth which once encircled the old town. To the SW are the *Opera House* (1952–53, extension 1973) and the **New Town Hall** (1907–11), with a tower 106 m high (view of town and firth; lift). A short distance away, on higher ground, is the *Ostseehalle* (1951).

N of the Markt is the former *refectory* (rebuilt in 1950 as a student residence) of the Franciscan friary, founded 1241,

Sailing boats in the Firth of Kiel

which was the original site of the University. E of the Markt, on the shores of the firth, is the town's CULTURAL CENTRE (built on the foundations of the Schloss, destroyed during the war), with the *Provincial Library*, the *Provincial Historical Hall* (material on the history of Schleswig-Holstein), a *Concert Hall* and other amenities; adjoining it is the beautiful *Schlossgarten*. In front of it is the **Oslo-Kai**, used by the shipping services to Scandinavia (cars carried). Farther N are the *University Library*, the *Museum of Ethnography*, the **Kunsthalle** (mainly works by Schleswig-Holstein artists), the *Zoological Museum*, the *Institute of Oceanography* (with an *aquarium*). To the S of Oslo-Kai is the Kiel Shipping Museum (Wall 65) and the Schweden-Kai.

A very beautiful part of the town is the district of DÜSTERNBROOK, set in wooded hills. On the shores of the firth are the **Landeshaus** (seat of the parliament and government of the *Land*) and the *World Economic Institute* (Institut für Weltwirtschaft). On the beautiful Hindenburgufer is the *Düsternbrook boating harbour.* – In the W of the town is the *Christian Albrecht University.*

In the INNENFÖRDE (trips round the firth from the Bahnhofskai) in the district of HOLTENAU, is the end of the 99 km long *Kiel Canal* (Nord-Ostsee-Kanal, opened in 1895 as the Kaiser-Wilhelm-Kanal), the busiest canal for seagoing vessels in the world. – On the AUSSENFÖRDE, in the district of SCHILKSEE, is the **Olympic Centre**, with the *Olympic Harbour*, where the sailing events of the 1972 Olympics were contested.

In the southern district of RAMMSEE is the ***Schleswig-Holstein Open-Air Museum**, with peasant houses and

craftsmen's workshops from all over the *Land.*

SURROUNDINGS. –***Laboe Naval Memorial** (20 km N), a 72 m high monument in the form of a ship's stem commemorating the naval dead of both world wars, erected 1927–36 (viewing platform; lift). In front of it is *U 995* (Submarine Museum).

Bad Kissingen

Land: Bavaria. – Vehicle registration: KG.
Altitude: 201 m. – Population: 24,000.
Post code: D-8730. – Dialling code: 09 71.
 Staatliche Kurverwaltung,
Am Kurgarten 1;
tel. 30 43.

HOTELS. – **Steigenberger Kurhaus Hotel*, Am Kurgarten 3, 140 b., SB, sauna, solarium (with "Kurhaus" restaurant); * *Kur Center*, Frühlingstr. 9, 332 b., SB, sauna, solarium; * *Kurotel 2002*, Von der Tann Str. 18, 278 b., SB, SP, sauna, solarium; *Dorint Hotel*, Frühlingstr. 1, 200 b.; sauna, solarium; *Kissinger Hof*, Bismarckstr. 14, 140 b.; *Bristol*, Bismarckstr. 8, 101 b., SB, sauna, solarium; *Kurhotel "Das Ballinghaus"*, Martin Luther Str. 3, 100 b., SB, sauna, solarium; *Vier Jahreszeiten*, Bismarckstr. 23, 95 b.; *Kurhaus Tanneck*, Altenbergweg 6, 37 b., SB, sauna, solarium. – IN REITERSWIESEN: * *Sonnenhügel*, Burgstr. 15, 340 b., bath with artificial waves, sauna, solarium. – YOUTH HOSTEL: Karl-Straub-Weg 34, Bad Kissengen-Garitz, 50 b. – CAMPING SITE: *Tabbert-Campingplatz*, on the Saale.

RESTAURANTS. – *Casino Restaurant "Le Jeton"*, in Luitpold Park 1; *Ratskeller*, Rathausplatz 1; *Bratwurstglöckle*, Grabenstr. 6.

WINE-BARS. – *Weinstuben Schubert*, Kirchgasse 2; *Stadtschänke-Weinstuben*, Marktplatz 7.

CAFÉS. – *Kurgarten-Café*, in Kurgarten; *Café Jagdhaus Messerschmidt*, on Staffelberg.

Casino (roulette, blackjack: daily from 3 p.m.) in Luitpold Park.

EVENTS. – *Rakoczy Festival*, with parade, ball and firework display (end July).

Bad Kissingen, lying in the beautiful valley of the Franconian Saale, surrounded by wooded hills, is one of the most frequented spas in Bavaria. Its hot brine springs, containing carbonic acid and usually iron, are used in both drinking and bathing cures for affections of the digestive organs, metabolism and cardio-vascular system and gynaecological conditions.

HISTORY. – Salt was worked here as early as the 9th c. The Rakoczy Spring was discovered by B. Neumann in 1737 during work on the diversion of the river, and the recognition of its therapeutic virtues soon led to the development of the spa. Tolstoy and Bismarck were among those who came to take the cure here.

SIGHTS. – The activity of the spa centres on the *Kurgastzentrum* (resort and spa administration, travel bureau, swimming bath, etc.). On the W side of the KURGARTEN is the **Regentenbau** (1911–13), with a great hall and lounges, on the S side the large **Wandelhalle** or indoor promenade (1910–11) and in Prinzregentenstrasse the **Kurhausbad** (1927), all designed by Max Littmann. In the cross wing of the Wandelhalle are two main springs, the *Rakoczy* (11·1 °C) and the *Pandur*. On the N side of the Kurgarten is the *Maxbrunnen* (10·4 °C). – Opposite the Wandelhalle on the right bank of the Saale is the LUITPOLD PARK, with the **Luitpold Baths** and the Luitpold Casino. – $2\frac{1}{2}$ km N of the Kurgarten, on the left bank of the Saale (15 minutes by motor-boat), are the *Gradierhaus* ("graduation house" for the evaporation of brine) and the Liver Clinic, with a 94 m deep artesian brine well (19·1 °C, 2% salt content) which alternately rises and falls, with a variation in height of up to 3 m. – At the Ballingham is a fine *terrace swimming pool.*

SURROUNDINGS. – There are Bundespost coaches to **Bad Bocklet** (10 km N), in the romantic Saale valley, and to *Schloss Aschach* (rebuilt 1571: art collection, conducted tours). In Münnerstadt (12 km NE) the *Henneberg Museum* (castle of the Teutonic Order: Folk art). **Bad Brückenau** (29 km NW), another spa resort situated in the forest-fringed Wiese valley on the southern edge of the Rhön hills, with a state hydropathic establishment founded in 1747 and a municipal establishment on the E side of the Kurpark. The *Staatsbad* (298 m; Dorint Kurhotel, 200 b.; SB; Regina-Kursanatorium, 174 b., SB), with three medicinal springs, is recommended for affections of the kidneys and bladder, anaemia and gynaecological conditions. Its main features are the Kurhäuser, largely dating from the spa's period of development in the time of King Ludwig I of Bavaria, the Kurmittelhaus, the pumproom and a number of country houses. – The *Städtisches Heilbad* (312 m; Deutsches Haus, 25 b., sauna; Central, 35 b.) dates back to the end of the 19th c. Recommended for metabolic disturbances of the stomach and intestinal tract and anaemia. Outdoor swimming pool, indoor swimming bath; Heimatmuseum. – *View from the *Dreistelzberg* (660 m: 6 km SW).

Koblenz

Land: Rhineland-Palatinate.
Vehicle registration: KO.
Altitude: 60 m. – Population: 115,000.
Post code: D-5400. – Dialling code: 02 61.
ⓘ **Fremdenverkehrsamt,**
Pavilion opposite Main Station;
tel. 3 13 04.

HOTELS. – *City Hotel Metropol*, Münzplatz 54, 90 b., SB, sauna, solarium; *Brenner* (no rest.), Rizzastr. 20,

48 b.; *Trierer Hof*, Deinhardplatz 1, 57 b.; *Kleiner Riesen* (no rest.), Rheinanlagen 18, 55 b.; *Continental Pfälzer Hof*, Bahnhofsplatz 1, 50 b.; *Hamm* (no rest.), St Josefstr. 32, 50 b.; *Höhmann* (no rest.), Bahnhofsplatz 5, 49 b.; *Im Stüffje*, Hohenzollernstr. 5, 31 b. – IN EHRENBREITSTEIN: *Diehls Hotel*, on Rhine, 120 b., SB, solarium. – IN METTERNICH: *Fährhaus am Stausee*, An der Fähre 3, 50 b., terrace overlooking Mosel. – YOUTH HOSTEL: in Ehrenbreitstein fortress (lower E front), 207 b. – CAMPING SITE: *Rhein-Mosel*, in Koblenz-Neuendorf (at mouth of Mosel, opposite Deutsches Eck).

RESTAURANTS. – *Rhein-Mosel-Halle*, Julius-Wegeler-Str. (at Pfaffendorf Bridge); *Rheinanlagen*, in Rheinanlagen (concerts on Sat. and Sun. in summer); *China-Restaurant Asia*, Münzplatz 14; *Weindorf*, Julius-Wegeler-Str. (with garden on banks of Rhine; dancing daily in summer). – IN MOSELWEISS: *Zur alten Post*, Koblenzer Str. 68. – IN PFAFFENDORF: *Le Bastion*, on Rheinhöhe (with terrace).

WINE-BARS. – *Alt Koblenz*, Am Plan 13 (music from 8 p.m. onwards); *Weinhaus Hubertus*, Florinsmarkt 6; *Weihwasserkessel*, An der Liebfrauenkirche (music from 8 p.m. onwards); *Zum Schwarzen Bären*, Koblenzer Str. 35.

CAFÉS. – *Besselink*, Emil-Schüller-Str. 45, opposite Main Station (specialty Koblenzer Herrentorte); *Café im Allianz-Haus*, Friedrich-Ebert-Ring 32–34. – Several dancing places and night-clubs.

EVENTS. – *Carnival*, with Rose Monday parade (Feb.); music and dancing in the "Wine Village" (April–Oct.); *Flower Festival* in Güls (early May); concerts in Music Pavilion in Rheinanlagen (May to mid Sept.); *Serenades* in Blumenhof (July); "The Rhine Aflame" (illuminations and fireworks, Aug.); *Wine and Harvest Festival* in the district of Lay (Sept.).

This former residence of the Electors of Trier, beautifully situated at the junction of the Moselle with the Rhine, is an important traffic junction, the seat of numerous government offices, one of the leading centres of the wine trade on the Rhine and the largest garrison town in the Federal Republic, with the Federal Agency of Defence Technology and Procurement. The town is dominated by the fortress of Ehrenbreitstein on the right bank of the Rhine.

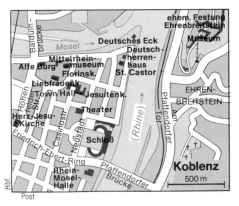

Deutsches Eck, Koblenz

HISTORY. – In 9 B.C. the Roman fort *Castrum ad Confluentes* was established to protect the Moselle crossing. In 1018 Koblenz fell into the hands of the Archbishops (later Electors) of Trier, who frequently resided here from the 13th to the beginning of the 19th c. The town then became the capital and stronghold of the Prussian province of Rhineland. In 1937 the town extended on to the right bank of the Rhine with the incorporation of Ehrenbreitstein. During the Second World War Koblenz suffered severe destruction, and after the war, though the old town centre was largely rebuilt in traditional style, the rest of the city took on a modern aspect. – From 1827 to 1872 the publishing house of *Karl Baedeker* (1801–59) was based in Koblenz.

SIGHTS. – Below the Pfaffendorf Bridge, close to the banks of the Rhine, stands the neo-classical **Schloss**, built 1777–86 by the last Elector of Trier, Clemens Wenzeslaus (now occupied by government offices: art exhibitions). – Downstream is *St Castor's Church, founded in 836 on a site which was then outside the town; the present building mostly dates from the 12th c. – Beyond this is the **Deutsches Eck** ("German Corner"), the tongue of land between the Rhine and the Moselle, named after the former House of the Teutonic Order (Deutschherrenhaus: evening "Serenades" in the Blumenhof in summer) which stands here. On the point is the *Monument to German Unity* (fine *view, particularly downstream).

On the highest point in the OLD TOWN stands the **Liebfrauenkirche** (12th–15th c.: R.C.). To the E is the *Town Hall* (1695–1700). A short distance N is the FLORINSMARKT, with the 12th–14th c. *St Florinus's Church* (Evang.) and the *Middle Rhineland Museum* (in the Altes Kaufhaus). – On the banks of the Moselle is the *Alte Burg* (1276–80), a stronghold of the Electors of Trier (Municipal Archive and Library). Close by is the *Balduinbrücke* (1343–1420), which crosses the Moselle to the suburb of Lützel. Upstream is the *New Moselle Bridge* (1954), and from there to the Langemarck Barracks, with a technical military collection.

The beautiful Rheinanlagen (Rhine Gardens) extend for some 4 km upstream from the Schloss to the island of *Oberwerth* (bathing lido, stadium). Just above the Pfaffendorf Bridge is the **Weindorf** ("Wine Village"), built 1925, rebuilt 1951; nearby is the Rhein-Moselle-Halle.

The *Pfaffendorf Bridge* (rebuilt 1952) leads to *EHRENBREITSTEIN, on the right bank of the Rhine, dominated by the **Fortress of Ehrenbreitstein** (118 m: access by chair-lift or by a road branching off B 42), built 1816–32 on the site of an earlier fortress of the Electors of Trier. The

State Collection on the Prehistory and Early History of the Middle Rhine, the Rhine Museum and a youth hostel. From the terraces there are views Koblenz, the Rhine, the mouth of the Mosel and the Vordereifel.

SURROUNDINGS. – **Rittersturz** (166 m: 4½ km S), viewpoint on an outlier of the Hunsrück which rises sheer from the Rhine. – **Schloss Stolzenfels** (154 m, 6 km S: 15 min. walk – no cars), neo-Gothic, built by Schinkel 1836–42. – **Burg Lahneck** (164 m, 8 km SE: café). From the castle, 19th c., above the town of Lahnstein, there are beautiful views of the mouth of the Lahn, the Rhine and Schloss Stolzenfels.

Konstanz

Land: Baden-Württemberg.
Vehicle registration: KN.
Altitude: 407 m. – Population: 70,000.
Post code: D-7750. – Dialling code: 0 75 31.
ⓘ **Tourist-Information**, Bahnhofsplatz 13;
tel. 28 43 76.

HOTELS. – *Steigenberger Insel-Hotel*, Auf der Insel 1, 180 b. (in a former Dominican monastery), lakeside terrace, bathing lido; *Seeblick* (no rest.), Neuhauser Str. 14, 120 b., SP; *Mago Hotel* (no rest.), Bahnhofplatz 4, 48 b.; *Buchner Hof* (no rest.), Buchner Str. 6, 19 b.; *Deutsches Haus*, Marktstätte 15, 55 b.; *Eden* (no rest.), Bahnhofstr. 4, 32 b. – IN ALLMANNSDORF: *Mainauer Hof* (no rest.), Mainaustr. 172a, 50 b. – IN STAAD: *Schiff*, William-Graf-Platz 2, 50 b. – YOUTH HOSTEL: *Otto-Moericke-Turm*, Zur Allmannshöhe 18, 207 b. – CAMPING SITES: *Klausenhorn* and *Am Fliesshorn*, in Dingelsdorf; site in Konstanz-Mainau-Litzelstetten.

RESTAURANTS. – *St. Stefanskeller*, Am Stefansplatz 41; *Casino-Restaurant*, Seestr. 21; *Konzil-Gaststätte*, Hafenstr. 2; *Capri-Fischerstube*, Neugasse 10; *Schwedenschenke*, on the island of Mainau.

CAFÉS. – *Mahler*, Münzgasse 1; *Dischinger*, Untere Laube 49.

International Casino (roulette, blackjack: daily from 2 p.m.), Seestr. 21.

Konstanz, beautifully situated close to the Swiss frontier on the stretch of the Rhine between the Obersee and the Untersee, is the largest town on Lake Constance, an important cultural centre with a University and a College of Engineering and an active theatrical and musical life. It is also a favourite congress and conference centre, and has two limnological institutes and a meteorological observatory. The main elements in its economy, apart from tourism, commerce and wine-growing, are electrical and metal-processing industries, pharmaceuticals and textiles.

The picturesque old town with its medieval buildings extends between the Rhine and the Swiss frontier. The spaciously laid out new town clings to the gentle slopes of the Bodanrück. The town also includes the flower island of *Mainau, much frequented by visitors.

HISTORY. – Konstanz (Constance) developed out of a Roman camp of the 1st c. A.D. The bishopric, then the largest in German territory, was founded in 590. Situated as it was at the intersection of important trading routes to Italy and France, the town prospered in the Middle Ages, was granted the right to hold a market around 900 and from 1192 to 1548 was a free Imperial city. At the important Council of Constance of 1414–18 Martin V was elected Pope and the Bohemian reformer Jan Hus was condemned to be burned at the stake. During the Second World War the town escaped any air raids. The University was founded in 1966.

SIGHTS. – On the **harbour** (the base of the Federal Railways' ships on Lake Constance) is the picturesque **Council Building** (Konzilsgebäude), built in 1388 as a warehouse for the linen trade with Italy and since 1970 a concert and congress hall. The conclave of cardinals which in 1417 elected the Italian Cardinal Oddone Colonna Pope as Martin V – the only Papal election to be held on German soil – met in the upper room of this building. – N of the Stadtgarten, on an island in the lake, is a former *Dominican monastery*, dissolved in 1785 and now a hotel (beautiful cloisters). Count Zeppelin, inventor of the steerable rigid airship, was born here in 1838. From 1966 to 1969 it was occupied by **Konstanz University**, now permanently housed in avant-garde *terraced buildings on the Giessberg (440 m: views) N of the town.

In the OLD TOWN, in the MÜNSTERPLATZ with its handsome old canons' houses, is the **Minster** (11th, 15th and 17th c.: R.C.), with a beautiful main doorway (carved decoration of 1470) and a fine interior (choir-stalls of 1460). In the Mauritiusrotunde is a 13th c. *Holy Sepulchre; from the tower (1850–57) there are fine views. A short distance W, in KATZGASSE, are the *Lake Constance Nature Museum* and the *Wessenberg Picture Gallery*. – To the S, in the OBERMARKT, is the *Hohenzollernhaus zum Hohen Hafen*, in which Burgrave Friedrich of Nuremberg was invested with the fief of Mark Brandenburg on 18 April 1417. Close by is the *Town Hall* (1593). In ROSGARTEN-STRASSE are the **Rosgarten Museum**, with a collection of local and regional material, and the *Trinity Church* (Driefaltigkeitskirche: fine frescoes of 1407). – Of the town's medieval fortifications there remain three towers, the *Rheintorturm*, the *Pulverturm* (Powder Tower) and the *Schnetztor*.

SURROUNDINGS. – **Mainau (7 km N). This island (45 hectares) near the S shore of the Überlinger See attracts many visitors with its beautiful*parks and gardens, planted with subtropical and even tropical vegetation. It is now owned by a foundation of which the Swedish Count Lennart Bernadotte is director. *Schloss* (1739–46) which belonged to the Grand Duke of Baden.

*Reichenau (6 km W: access by causeway), in the Untersee; the largest island in Lake Constance (428 hectares); cultivation of fine vegetables (18 hectares under glass). The churches belonging to the once world-famed Reichenau Monastery founded by Charles Martel, Charlemagne's grandfather, in 724 are among the finest examples of early Romanesque art in Germany, both for their architecture and their magnificent frescoes. They are *St George's Church in *Oberzell*, the *Minster of St Mary and St Mark in *Mittelzell* and SS. Peter and Paul in *Niederzell.*

Lahn Valley

Land: Hesse.
ⓘ **Hessischer Fremdenverkehrsverband,**
   Abraham-Lincoln-Str. 38–42,
   D-6200 Wiesbaden;
   tel. (0 61 21) 7 37 25.
   Fremdenverkehrsverband Rheinland Pfalz,
   Lohrstrasse 103/105,
   D-5400 Koblenz;
   tel. (02 61) 3 10 79.

The Lahn rises at an altitude of 600 m in the southern Rothaargebirge and enters the Rhine at Lahnstein.

From its source the river flows E by way of the holiday resorts of *Laasphe* and *Biedenkopf*, turns S past the university town of **Marburg** and **Giessen**, and then bears W through **Wetzlar** and *Weilburg*. The hills are now crowned with castles – *Burg Runkel, Schloss Diez*, the ruins of *Burg Balduinstein, Schloss Schaumburg*, the ruined *Laurenburg, Burg Nassau* and *Burg Stein, Burg Lahneck*. At Obernhof *Arnstein Abbey* rears above the valley. The Lahn then breaks through the Rhenish Uplands in innumerable meanders and flows past picturesque old towns like the cathedral city of **Limburg,** *Nassau* (birthplace of Freiherr vom Stein) and **Bad Ems**, a town rich in tradition. After a course of 218 km the Lahn flows into the Rhine at *Lahnstein*. As the crow flies it is only 80 km from its source to the junction with the Rhine.

The LAHN HOLIDAY ROUTE along the river is waymarked

Between Wetzlar and Lahnstein the charming LAHN-NÖHENWEG (Lahn Ridgeway) runs along the left bank of the river. For those who prefer to travel by water there are canoe trips from Marburg and excursions by motor-boat from Bad Ems. In the scenically attractive lower course of the Lahn the road and railway run close to the river.

Landshut

Land: Bavaria. – Vehicle registration: LA.
Altitude: 393 m. – Population: 58,000.
Post code: D-8300. – Dialling code: 08 71.
ⓘ **Verkehrsverein**, Altstadt 315;
   tel. 2 30 31.

HOTELS. – *Kaiserhof*, Papiererstr. 2, 280 b.; *Fürstenhof*, Stethaimer Str. 3, 42 b., sauna; *Goldene Sonne*, Neustadt 520, 70 b.; *Luitpold*, Luitpoldstr. 43, 30 b. – In Schönbrunn: *Obermeier*, 50 b. – YOUTH HOSTEL: *Jugendhaus Ottonianum*, Richard-Schirmann-Weg 6, 64 b. – CAMPING SITE: *Städtischer Campingplatz*, on the Isar.

RESTAURANTS. – *Herzog Georg im Vitztumb*, Obere Land 51; *Weinstube Isarklause*, Land 124; *Klausenberg*, Klausenberg 17.

CAFÉ. – *Belstner*, Altstadt 295; *Wildegger*, Altstadt 254.

EVENTS. – Historical *pageant play, "**Die Landschuter Hochzeit**" ("The Landshut Wedding"), with wedding procession, dances and tournaments (every four years: the next May 1985).

The old Ducal town of Landshut is picturesquely situated on the Isar. The attractive pattern of the town centre is set by two wide streets, Altstadt and Neustadt, with 15th and 16th c. gabled houses. The town with its numerous towers is dominated by Burg Trausnitz to the S. Most of the town's industry

Landshut

has developed to the N (electrical and mechanical engineering, car manufacture, textiles, dyestuffs, building).

HISTORY. – Landshut first appears in the records around 1150. It grew out of a settlement at the bridge over the Isar, beside which Duke Ludwig I founded the town, at the foot of the Burgberg. In 1255 Landshut became capital of the Duchy of Lower Bavaria. Its heyday was in the 15th c., and during this period, in 1475, it was the scene of one of the most splendid court festivities of the Middle Ages, the marriage of the last Landshut Duke, Georg, with Hedwig, daughter of the King of Poland. From 1800 to 1826 the Bavarian Provincial University was in Landshut. The town suffered little damage in the last war.

SIGHTS. – In the town's main street, ALTSTADT, lined with handsome late Gothic gabled houses, is the *Town Hall* (14th–15th c.). Opposite it is the old Ducal *Stadtresidenz*, a splendid Renaissance palace (16th and 18th c.), with the *Residenzmuseum* (magnificent residential apartments), a rich *picture gallery* and the *Town and District Museum*. To the S is the late Gothic *St Martin's Church* (14th–15th c.), the finest achievement of Hans Stethaimer, with a strikingly slender tower (132 m high). In the church is a notable carved figure of the Virgin by Hans Leinberger (c. 1520). At the N end of the Altstadt is the *Church of the Holy Ghost* (1407–61), also in part by Hans Stethaimer.

Above the town, on a steep hill (by road 2 km; on foot from Dreifaltigkeitsplatz 15 min.), is *Burg Trausnitz (464 m), founded by Duke Ludwig I along with the town about 1204. Until 1503 it was the seat of the Wittelsbach Dukes of Lower Bavaria. Between 1568 and 1578, under Hereditary Prince Wilhelm, it was rebuilt as an imposing palace in the Italian style (Fürstenbau, with state apartments and the "Narrentreppe" or "Fools' Staircase";

late Romanesque chapel belonging to the original castle; conducted tours). On the eastern slopes of the Burgberg is the *Hofgarten* (fine viewpoints).

Lauenburg Lakes

Land: Schleswig-Holstein.
(i) Fremdenverkehrsverband Schleswig-Holstein, Niemannsweg 31, D-2300 Kiel; tel. (04 31) 56 30 27.

Between the Elbe-Lübeck Canal in the W and the frontier with the German Democratic Republic in the E, Gross-Grönau in the N and Büchen in the S extends the *Lauenburg Lakes Nature Park, a region of forests and lakes covering some 400 sq. km.

With more than 40 lakes, the area is a paradise for water sports enthusiasts, offering endless scope for bathing, sailing and rowing. From Lübeck it is possible to take a motor-boat up the River Wakenitz to reach the elongated **Ratzeburger See**. The delightfully situated cathedral city of **Ratzeburg**, on an island connected with the mainland by causeways, separates the Ratzeburger See to the N from the Küchensee to the S. An "Academy of rowing" was established here by Karl Adam. On the *Küchensee*, famous in Germany as the practice and regatta course of the national eight, important rowing competitions are held.

Round **Mölln**, the town of Till Eulenspiegel (tombstone, Eulenspiegel Monument and Museum, commemorating the legendary jester who is supposed to have died here in 1350) are a number of smaller lakes – the *Möllner See, Lankauer See, Schmalsee, Lütauer See, Drüsensee* and *Krebssee*. To the S are the *Sarnekower See, Gudower See* and

Rowing on the Ratzeburger See

Segrahner See – all formed during the Ice Age. The largest of the Lauenburg lakes is the *Schaalsee* (23 sq. km, with numerous bays and inlets), the eastern part of which is in the Democratic Republic.

The Lauenburg Lakes Nature Park also offers excellent walking. It contains some 80 sq. km of forest, and there are numerous footpaths leading through beautiful beech-woods and along the shores of the lakes. Altogether there are more than 800 km of marked footpaths.

Access to the Nature Park is provided by major tourist routes like the OLD SALT ROAD and the ALPS-BALTIC HOLIDAY HIGHWAY, and there are very beautiful roads through the park itself.

Leer in East Friesland

Land: Lower Saxony.
Vehicle registration: LER.
Altitude: 6 m. – Population: 31,000.
Post code: D-2950. – Dialling code: 04 91.
(i) **Reise-und Verkehrsbüro,**
Am Denkmal;
tel. 31 03.

HOTELS. – *Central Hotel*, Pferdemarktstr. 47, 60 b.; *Oberledinger Hof*, Bremer Str. 33, 65 b.; *Voigt*, Wörde 10, 34 b. – IN NETTELBURG: *Lange*, Zum Schöpfwerk 1, 60 b.

RESTAURANT. – *Zur Waage*, Neue Str. 1.

EVENTS. – *Gallimarkt* (Oct.); *East Friesian Show* (alternate years; 1984, etc.).

This old town on the Leda, near its junction with the Ems, calls itself the "gateway to East Friesland". Its red brick buildings show the influence of the early Baroque style of the Netherlands. Leer's economy is based on its harbour, its large cattle-market and its active industries (including the Libby milk canning factory).

HISTORY. – Leer, situated at the intersection of important trade routes, was the starting point of the missionary travels of the 8th c. "apostle of the Frisians", Liudger. Later it became the seat of a provostry. In 1508 it obtained the right to hold a market. In the 16th c. weavers and merchants who had fled from the Netherlands for religious reasons made the town a centre of the linen-weaving industry. Leer's development as a port began in the 18th c. The Dortmund-Ems Canal came into service in 1899. The barrage on the River Leda was completed in 1954.

SIGHTS. – By the harbour are the **Town Hall** (1892) and the *Old Weigh-House* (1714: good restaurant). Close by are *Haus Samson* (1643), occupied by Wolff's wine business (with old-style East Frisian interior), and the *Heimatmuseum* (prehistoric material, history of the town,

natural history). – Also of interest are the *Hanenburg* (17th c.: now an old people's home), the castle of a Frisian notable, the Evenburg (*c.* 1650) and the *Harder-wykenburg* (in private ownership). In the old Protestant cemetery is a 12th c. *crypt*, one of the oldest buildings in East Friesland (now a war memorial). W of the town is the *Plytenberg*, a hill which features in local legend and is thought to have served some pagan cult. The *Leda barrage* is a modern installation providing protection against high tides. – In the district of LOGABIRUM are the interesting **East Friesland Zoo** and the leisure centre *Waldzoo-Park*.

Town Hall and Old Weigh-House, Leer

Leinebergland

Land: Lower Saxony.
(i) **Verkehrsverein Leinebergland,**
Ständehausstr. 1, D-3220 Alfeld (Leine);
tel. (0 51 81) 2 31 22.

The Leinebergland is a hilly region of varied scenery between the Weserbergland and the Harz through which the River Leine flows. The river (281 km long, navigable for 112 km) rises in the Eichsfeld in Thuringia (GDR) and flows into the Aller at Schwarmstedt.

W of the Leine are a series of hills – *Külf* (260 m), *Thüsterberg* (433 m), *Duinger Berg* (330 m), *Duinger Wald* (221 m) and *Selter* (396 m). To the rear are the long ridge of *Ith* (439 m), with its picturesque limestone crags, and the ear-shaped *Hils* (477 m: sandstone), which already show a transition towards the Weserbergland. – E of the river are *Heber* (305 m), *Sackwald* (330 m) and the limestone uplands of the **Sieben Berge** (398 m), where the tale of Snow-White and the seven dwarfs has become firmly established. Beyond this is the *Hildesheim Forest* (281 m).

Town Hall, Einbeck

At Nordstemmen *Schloss Marienburg*, a neo-Gothic castle built in 1860–68 by George V, the last King of Hanover, rears up over the Leine. – At Benstorf in the Saale valley is the *Rastiland* leisure centre old-time railway, etc.). – *Salzhemmendorf*, on Ith, is a friendly little health resort with fine half-timbered buildings. – The *Duing Lakes* are a paradise for water sports enthusiasts, with camping sites and good walking. – **Alfeld** is an attractive old town of historic buildings. – The *Lippoldshöhle* ("Lippold's Cave") recalls the story of Lippold, the robber who is said to have held the Burgomaster of Alfeld's daughter captive here. – **Bad Gandersheim** is famous for its Domfestspiele. – The medieval little town of **Einbeck** is the home of bock beer. – In the NE of the area is the *Eulenspiegel Park*.

Lemgo

Land: North Rhineland-Westphalia.
Vehicle registration: DT (LE).
Altitude: 101 m. – Population: 40,000.
Post code: D-4920. – Dialling code: 0 52 61.
ⓘ **Städtisches Verkehrsbüro,** Am Markt; tel. 21 33 47.

HOTELS. – *Stadtpalais,* Papenstr. 24, 41 b. (in a nobleman's mansion of the 16th c.); *Lemgoer Hof,* Detmolder Weg 14, 30 b.; *Gästehaus Lindau* (no rest.), Franz-Liszt-Str. 52, 11 b.; *Hansa,* Breite Str. 14, 40 b.; *Stadtwappen,* Mittelstr. 54, 11 b. – CAMPING SITE: At the open-air swimming pool, near Regenstorplatz.

RESTAURANTS. – *Ratskeller,* Am Markt 1, *Zur Krone,* Leopoldstr. 26.

CAFÉS. – *Stadtcafé,* Papenstr. 12; *Schmidt,* Mittelstr. 122; *Kracht,* Breite Str. 66.

EVENT. – International *Organ Festival*.

Lemgo lies in the valley of the Bega amid the forest-covered Lippe uplands. The oldest town in the territory of Lippe, it preserves a charming *medieval aspect.

HISTORY. – The town was founded by Bernhard II of Lippe in 1190 and developed into a prosperous trading community, becoming a member of the Hanse in the 13th c. Its cultural and economic heyday was in the 15th and 16th c., which saw the building of the magnificent Town Hall and many burghers' houses bearing witness to the prosperity of their owners. In the 17th c., however, the town went through an unhappy period of "witch fever" under its "Hexenbürgermeister" ("witch burgomaster") Hermann Cothmann (1667–83).

SIGHTS. – In the MARKT, lined with handsome gabled houses, stands the **Town Hall,** with a Gothic stepped gable, an arcade and a splendid oriel window (Renaissance). Behind it is **St Nicholas's Church** (13th c., later enlarged in Gothic style), with an early Baroque high altar and a fine railed-in font (1597). – MITTELSTRASSE, a pedestrian shopping street, is lined with old stone and half-timbered houses – at No. 17 the *Gasthof Alt-Lemgo* (1587), at No. 24 *Haus Sonnenuhr* (1546), at No. 27 *Haus Sauerländer* (1569), at No. 36 the *Planetenhaus* (1612). To the W and E of the street are two old towers belonging to the old fortifications, the *Johannisturm* and the *Pulverturm* (Powder Tower).

In BREITE STRASSE, which runs S from the Markt, is the *****Hexenbürgermeisterhaus,** a fine patrician house (1571) in Weser Renaissance style (Heimatmuseum; Engelbert Kämpfer Room, with mementoes of the 17th c. traveller to Japan, born in Lemgo in 1651). Close by, in Stiftstrasse, is **St Mary's Church,** a

Hexenbürgermeisterhaus (witch-burgomaster's house), Lemgo

Gothic hall-church of 1320 (organ of 1600), scene of the annual Lemgo Organ Festival. – S of the town is **Schloss Brake**, a 13th c. moated castle with a 16th c. N wing and tower in Weser Renaissance style (now offices).

SURROUNDINGS. – **Burg Sternberg** (13 km NE). This 13th c. castle, once the seat of the Counts of Sternberg, was taken over by the musical instrument maker Peter Harlan. Interesting collection of old instruments; concerts with historic instruments in the Knights' Hall.

Limburg an der Lahn

Land: Hesse. – Vehicle registration: LM.
Altitude: 108 m. – Population: 29,000.
Post code: D-6250. – Dialling code: 0 64 31.
ⓘ **Städtisches Fremdenverkehrsamt**,
   Hospitalstr. 2;
   tel. 20 32 22 and 61 66.

HOTELS: – *Dom Hotel*, Grabenstr. 57, 102 b.; *Huss Bahnhofsplatz* 3, 85 b.; *Zimmermann*, Blumenöder Str. 1, 45 b.

RESTAURANTS. – *Georgs-Stuben*, in the Stadthalle, Hospitalstr. 4; *Goldener Löwe*, Kornmarkt 7.

Limburg an der Lahn lies in the fertile Limburg Basin between the hills of the Taunus and the Westerwald. It is a town of picturesque half-timbered houses dominated by the Cathedral. Since 1972 the medieval layout of the town has been thoroughly restored. It has a variety of industries (hardware, textiles, plastics).

HISTORY. – Limburg grew up round its church and its castle, and is first recorded as a town in 1277. In 1344 the Counts of Lahn pledged half their territory to the Elector of Trier, and from 1420 to 1803 the whole of the territory belonged to Trier. It then passed to Nassau, and in 1866 to Prussia. From 1336 to 1398 the town clerk, Tileman Elhen von Wolfhagen, wrote the famous "Limburg Chronicle", which throws interesting light on the life of the period.

SIGHTS. – Above the *OLD TOWN with its beautiful half-timbered houses, on a steep crag high above the Lahn, stands the ***Cathedral** (R.C.) with its seven towers, one of the finest creations of late Romanesque (13th c.). Inside are 13th–16th c. wall paintings, recently uncovered. Behind the Cathedral is the old **Schloss** of the Counts of Lahn (partly 13th c.). – At the foot of the Schloss is the 15th c. *Town Church*, and adjoining it is the Bishop's residence, which contains the valuable Cathedral treasury (reliquary with cross of 959). From the *Old Lahn Bridge* (1315) and the large motorway bridge there are fine views of the Cathedral.

SURROUNDINGS. – **Burg Runkel** (7 km E), the ancestral castle of the Princes of Wied (12th c., with some 17th and 18th c. work: open to visitors).

Limes

The Limes was a Roman frontier fortification of the 1st–3rd c. A.D. which ran for 548 km from the Rhine to the Danube. Remains of this defensive line, mainly in the form of earthworks, can still be identified on the ground.

The northern part, 382 km long, is known as the **Upper German Limes**. It started from the Rhine, below Rheinbrohl (between Koblenz and Bonn) and ran through the Westerwald and Taunus and along the Wetterau to reach the Main at Hanau, and then continued S through the Odenwald and the Neckar region to Lorch. This part of the Limes consisted of a palisade, an earth rampart and a ditch, and was defended with the help of watch-towers and forts a few kilometres behind the Limes. The fort at **Saalburg** (see p. 154), re-erected on the old foundations in 1897–1907, gives an excellent impression of a permanent Roman camp on the Limes.

The defensive line was continued S by the **Raetian Limes**, 166 km long, which ran through the Franconian Alb and crossed the Altmühl valley at Weissenburg to

Limburg Cathedral and the Lahn

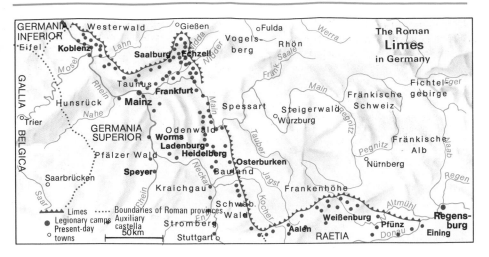

The Roman **Limes** in Germany

Limes ····· Boundaries of Roman provinces
● Legionary camps   Auxiliary
○ Present-day   castella
  towns |——50km——|

reach the Danube, coming to an end at Eining (W of Kelheim). This section was strengthened at the beginning of the 3rd c., the palisade being replaced by a stone wall some 1 m thick and 3 m high. *Limes Museum* at Aalen; *Welzheim Ostkastell* in Welzheim.

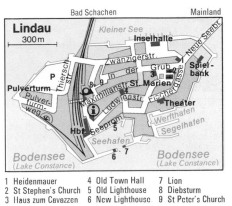

Lindau 300 m

1 Heidenmauer   4 Old Town Hall   7 Lion
2 St Stephen's Church 5 Old Lighthouse   8 Diebsturm
3 Haus zum Cavazzen   6 New Lighthouse   9 St Peter's Church

Lindau in Lake Constance

Land: Bavaria. – Vehicle registration: LI.
Altitude: 400 m. – Population: 25,000.
Post code: D-8990. – Dialling code: 0 83 82.
ⓘ **Städtisches Verkehrsamt**
  (*Verkehrsverein*),
  Bahnhofplatz (on the island);
  tel. 50 22.

HOTELS. – ON ISLAND, ROUND HARBOUR: *Bayerischer Hof*, 172 b., terrace, heated SP; *Reutemann*, 68 b., terrace, heated SP; *Helvetia*, 80 b., terrace; *Seegarten*, 51 b., garden heated SP; *Lindauer Hof*, 45 b., SB, sauna (all on Seepromenade or Hafenplatz). – ON ISLAND IN TOWN CENTRE: *Insel Hotel* (no rest.), Maximilianstr. 42, 44 b.; *Goldenes Lamm*, Schafgasse 3, 72 b.; *Zum Stift*, Stiftsplatz 1, 50 b. – ON MAINLAND IN AESCHACH: *Am Holdereggenpark*, Giebelbachstr. 1, 58 b.; *Toscana* (no rest.), Am Aeschacher Ufer 12, 28 b. – IN REUTIN: *Köchlin*, Kemptener Str. 41, 35 b. – IN BAD SCHACHEN: *Bad Schachen*, 215 b., terrace, park, SB, heated SP; *Strandhotel Tannhof*, Oeschländer Weg 24, 54 b., terrace; *Parkhotel Eden* (no rest.), Schachener Str. 143, 43 b.; *Schachen-Schlössle* (no rest.; with block of flats), Enzisweiler Str. 3, 80 b., SB, sauna. – YOUTH HOSTEL: Herbergsweg 11a, Reutin. – CAMPING SITES: *Lindau-Zech*, on the lake; *Hammergut*, Hammerweg 34.

RESTAURANTS. – *Spielbank-Restaurant*, Oskar-Groll-Anlage 2 (terrace); *Zum lieben Augustin*, Ludwigstr. 29; *Walliser Stuben*, Ludwigstr. 7; *Zum Sünfzen*, Maximilianstr. 1; *Samos*, In der Grub 32; *China Restaurant*, In der Grub 11.

WINE-BARS. – *Frey*, Hauptstr. 15; *Müller*, In der Grub 30.

CAFÉS. – *Lindauer Hof*, Schreier, *Reutemann*, all on Seepromenade (Hafenplatz); *Café Restaurant am See* (in the Inselhalle), Am Kleinen See; *Café Vis à Vis*,

Bahnhofplatz 4. – Several discotheques and night spots.

International Casino (roulette, baccarat, blackjack: daily from 3 p.m.), Oskar-Groll-Anlage 2.

EVENTS. – *Sailing Regatta* (May–June); Meeting of Nobel Prizewinners (June–July); *Children's Festival* (July).

Lindau, the largest town on the Bavarian shores of Lake Constance, consists of the picturesque *old town on an island in the lake (area recently increased to 68·6 hectares by land reclamation to provide car parking in the NW), with the harbour used by ships of the Lake Constance "White Fleet", and the garden city of Lindau (housing, recreation, industry), spaciously laid out amid orchards on the morainic slopes of the mainland. The two parts of the town are linked by the Seebrücke ("Lake Bridge") and a causeway carrying the railway. In summer Lindau is a popular tourist resort, but it is also developing into an important conference venue; the Inselhalle seats 1100.

Lindau Harbour

HISTORY. – Lindau was originally a fishing village, taking its name (first recorded in 882) from a convent dedicated to Our Lady under the Lime Trees (Unter den Linden) founded in the early 9th c., which from the 16th c. held its territory directly from the Emperor. Lindau soon obtained the right to hold markets, became a free Imperial city in 1220 and rose to prosperity through its trade and its shipping, becoming known as the "Swabian Venice". At the Imperial Diet held at Lindau in 1496–97 the Estates refused Emperor Maximilian I their support against France and Russia. The townspeople became early converts to the Zwinglian Reformation (adopting the "Confessio Tetrapolitana" in 1530 along with Memmingen, Konstanz and Strasbourg), but in 1548 were compelled by Charles V to accept the Augsburg Interim. In 1647 the town was bombarded by the Swedes. After centuries of conflict between the town and the convent, both of them passed to Austria in 1804 and in the following year were ceded to Bavaria under the Peace of Pressburg. After the Second World War the town and district were occupied by the French – the only part of Bavaria within the French occupation zone – and until 1956 enjoyed a special status. Since 1972 the town has been part of the rural district (Landkreis) of Lindau.

SIGHTS. – On the S side of the island is the *Harbour, with the *Old Lighthouse* or *Mangturm* (13th c.), between the Hafenplatz and the Seepromenade. At the ends of the outer breakwaters are Lindau's best-known landmarks, the 6 m high Bavarian *Lion* of Kelheim marble and the 33 m high *New Lighthouse* (*views of the town and the Alps).

The OLD TOWN (much of it now pedestrians-only) has preserved beautiful old *streets of Gothic, Renaissance and Baroque buildings, in particular the MAXIMILIANSTRASSE with its trim patrician houses, arcades, fountains and street cafés. To the S, in Reichsplatz, is the **Old Town Hall** (built 1422–36, rebuilt in Renaissance style 1578), in which are the *Municipal Archives* and the old *Municipal Library* of the free Imperial city. To the NW, in Schrannenplatz, is the former *St Peter's Church* (founded *c.* 1000, converted into a war memorial in 1928), with the only surviving *frescoes by Hans Holbein the Elder (*c.* 1480). Close by is the *Diebsturm* (Thief's Tower) of 1420 (view).

In the E part of the old town is the MARKTPLATZ, with the *Neptune Fountain* (1841) and the **Haus zum Cavazzen** (1729), which contains the *Heimatmuseum* (domestic life, weapons) and the *Municipal Art collections*. On the E side of the square are **St Stephen's Church,** the Evang. parish church (built 1180, reconstructed in Baroque style 1782) and **St Mary's Church,** the R.C. parish church (Rococo interior). St Mary's, originally belonging to the convent (dissolved 1802), was built in 1748–52 on the site of a Romanesque Minster destroyed in a great fire in 1729–30. A short distance to the NE is the so-called *Heidenmauer* ("Pagan Wall"), a medieval watch-tower. In the N of the island is the Inselhalle, in the NE the Casino. – There is a pleasant walk round the island on the *Uferweg.

On the mainland NW of the island is the district of BAD SCHACHEN, with a bathing lido and a beautiful *park; in the Villa Lindenhof a *"Museum of Peace".

Lübeck

Land: Schleswig-Holstein.
Vehicle registration: HL.
Altitude: 11 m. – Population: 220,000.
Post code: D-2400. – Dialling code: 0451.
ⓘ **Lübecker Verkehrsverein e.V.,**
Beckergrube 95;
tel. 7 23 00.
Kurverwaltung Travemünde,
Strandpromenade 1b;
tel. 8 43 63.

HOTELS: *Lysia Mövenpick, Biem Holstentor, 230 b.; Kaiserhof (no rest.), Kronsforder Allee 13, 110 b., sauna; Hotel am ZOB (no rest.), Hansestr. 3, 108 b.; Jensen am Holstentor, Obertrave 4, 102 b.; Autel-Auto-Hotel (no rest.), Bel der Lohmühle 19, 69 b.; Schweizerhaus, Travemünder Allee 51, 38 b., SP; Wakenitzblick, Augustenstr. 30, 27 b.; Lindenhof (no rest.), Lindenstr. 1a, 90 b.; Berlin, Moislinger Allee 18, 75 b.; Stadtpark (no rest.), Roeckstr. 9, 35 b. – IN TRAVEMÜNDE: *Maritime Strandhotel (roof restaurant "Uber den Wolken"), Trelleborgallee 2, 480 b., sea water SB and SP, sauna, solarium; Kurhaus Hotel, Aussenallee 10, 130 b., SB, sauna, solarium; Deutscher Kaiser, Vorderreihe 52, 80 b., SP, Strandhaus Becker (no rest.), Strandpromenade 7, 50 b.; Sonnenklause (no rest.), Kaiserallee 21, 37 b.; Villa Charlott (no rest.), Kaiserallee 5, 32 b. – YOUTH HOSTELS: Folke-Bernadotte-Haus, Am Gertrudenkirchhof 4, 180 b.; Jugendfreizeitstätte Priwall, Mecklenburger Landstr. 69, 108 b. – CAMPING SITES: Auto-Camping Lübeck, at motorway exit; Grüner Jäger, Lübeck-Ivendorf; Strandcamping, Travemünde-Priwall; Auto-Camping, Travemünde-Priwall.

RESTAURANTS. – *Schabbelhaus, Mengstr. 48 (in an old merchant's house); Ratskeller, in Town Hall,

Markt 13; Haus der Schiffergesellschaft, Breite Str. 2 (historic house of 1535; ship models); Die Gemeinnützige, Königstr. 5 (with Picture Room) Stadtrestaurant Lübeck, Am Bahnhof 2; Rathaushof, at Town Hall; Lübecker Hanse, Kolk 5; Grillrestaurant Jagdzimmer, Obertrave 4.
IN TRAVEMÜNDE: *Casino-Restaurant, Kaiserallee 2 (terrace; light music); Hermannshöhe, Brodtener Steilufer (view); Skandinavia, Skandinavienkai.

WINE-BARS. – Weinstuben unter dem Heiliggeistspital, Koberg 5.

CAFÉS. – *Niederegger, Breite Str. 89 (noted for its marzipan); Junge, Breite Str. 1; Maret, Markt 17 (Marktplatz).

Casino (roulette, baccarat, punto banco and blackjack), Kaiserallee 2, Travemünde.

EVENTS. – Evening recitals of church music (June–Sept.); Travemünde Week (July–Aug.); Baltic Rally (beginning of Sept.).

The former free Imperial and Hanseatic city of Lübeck is now a busy port and industrial town. The oval *old town, ringed by water, presents a striking image of a medieval German Hanseatic city. The Trave, which flows into the Baltic 20 km N of the town, enables seagoing vessels of up to 6 m draught to reach the town's harbour, while the Elbe-Lübeck Canal, opened in 1900, gives river shipping access to the Baltic. The 12 docks in the harbour handle timber, coal, machinery, meat, salt and other products. The town has important industries, including the manufacture of machinery, electrical and oxygen equipment, structural ironwork and ceramic tiles, fish canning and shipbuilding. Lübeck has long been noted for its red wine trade and its marzipan. The town's economic development is hampered by the nearness of the East German frontier.

Lübeck has a School of Seamanship, several vocational colleges, a medical school, an Academy of Music and the North German Organ School. It also has a theatre.
The fashionable Baltic resort of **Travemünde** falls within the town's boundaries.

HISTORY. – Lübeck was founded by Count Adolf II of Holstein in 1143, and became a free Imperial city in 1226. Conveniently situated for the purposes of trade, it soon developed into an important staple port and achieved a dominant position in the Hanse, an association formed by the North German towns to protect their trade. In the 16th c., with the slow decline

Holstentor, Lübeck

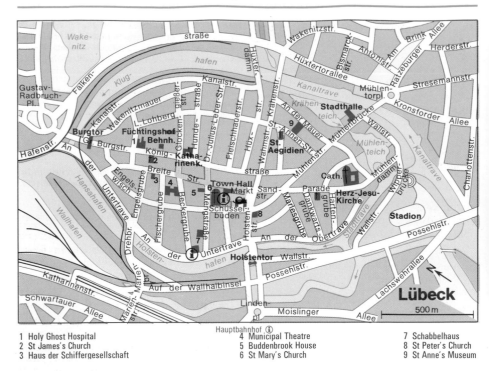

1 Holy Ghost Hospital
2 St James's Church
3 Haus der Schiffergesellschaft

4 Municipal Theatre
5 Buddenbrook House
6 St Mary's Church

7 Schabbelhaus
8 St Peter's Church
9 St Anne's Museum

of the Hanse, Lübeck's predominance began to fade. The last meeting of the Hanse took place in 1630, attended only by Lübeck, Hamburg and Bremen. In the early 19th c. Lübeck suffered severely under French rule. After the fall of the Napoleonic empire Hamburg, Bremen and Lübeck joined in a league of free Hanseatic towns. In 1900 the Elbe-Lübeck Canal was opened, and this was followed in the 20th c. by the development of industry. In 1937 the town lost its independent status and was incorporated in Schleswig-Holstein. During the Second World War much of the old town was destroyed in an air raid (1942). Since the division of Germany Lübeck has been a frontier town.

Lübeck was the birthplace in 1875 of *Thomas Mann*, whose novel "Buddenbrooks" (1901) depicts the decline of a Lübeck patrician family.

SIGHTS. – At the W entrance to the OLD TOWN stands the emblem of Lübeck, the massive twin-towered ****Holstentor** (1477), with a *museum on the history of the town* (large model of Lübeck around 1650). Near the Holsten Bridge is the *Museum Ship "Mississippi"*. – In the MARKT stands the **Town Hall*, one of the most splendid in Germany, partly faced with glazed tiles (13th–15th c., with a front building in Renaissance style added in 1570). N of the Markt is **St Mary's Church* (13th–14th c., restored), the prototype of many brick-built churches in the Baltic area. Fine interior, with a Gothic tabernacle (1476–79); in the S tower is a memorial chapel with the bell which crashed to the ground during the fire caused by bombing in 1942.

N of St Mary's, at MENGSTRASSE 4, is the *Buddenbrook House* (originally 1758, rebuilt; belonged to the novelist's family 1841–91). At Nos. 48–50 is the *Schabbelhaus* (rebuilt after war damage; restaurant). – In BREIT STRASSE (partly pedestrians-only), at No. 2, is the *Haus der Schiffergesellschaft* (Shipping Company's House) of 1535, now a restaurant, which with its old furniture and furnishings give a vivid impression of one of the old business houses of Lübeck. Opposite it is **St James's Church** (14th c.), with the 16th c. Brömbse Altar and a late Gothic organ. – In Königstrasse, which runs parallel to Breite Strasse, are the former *St Catherine's Church*, a noble example of High Gothic (14th c.; in the niches in the façade nine figures by Ernst Barlach and Gerhard Marcks), the neo-classical *Behnhaus* of 1783 (collection of 19th and 20th c. art; works of the Romantic school, including in particular pictures by Friedrich Overbeck); adjoining is the *Drägerhaus Museum* (19th and 20th c. art and culture) and the ***Holy Ghost Hospital** (13th c.: now an old people's home), the best preserved medieval hospice in Germany (entrance hall with late Gothic wall paintings; early 14th c.). At the end of Grosse Burgstrasse, the continuation of Königstrasse to the N, is the *Burgtor* (1444), with remains of an old circuit of walls. In Glockengiesserstrasse, which branches off Königstrasse to the E, is the snug and attractive *Füchtingshof*, built in 1639 as a residence for the widows of merchants and ship-captains.

SW of the Markt is *St Peter's Church* (13th–14th c., restored), with a tower from which there are wide *views. – On the southern edge of the old town is the **Cathedral** (Evang.) with its two towers, founded by Henry the Lion in 1173 and enlarged in Gothic style in the 13th and 14th c. (restored after severe war damage). In the nave are a font of 1455 and a *Triumphal Cross group by the Lübeck master Bernt Notke (1477). In an adjoining building is the *Natural History Museum* and the Hansa archives of Lübeck. – NE of the Cathedral is *St Anne's Museum (in a former convent dedicated to St Anne), which presents an excellent survey of Lübeck art from the early Middle Ages to the 19th c. Of particular interest are works by the town's leading sculptors and painters, together with numerous works of art salvaged from Lübeck churches in 1942.

Travemünde is the most fashionable and liveliest German resort on the Baltic, with its *Kurhaus, Kursaal, Casino*, indoor *swimming bath* (sea-water, with artificial waves), *Kurpark* and wide *Strandpromenade*, all dominated by the 158 m high *Hotel Maritim* (viewing platform). The OLD TOWN huddles round the 16th c. parish church of *St Lawrence*. In the Passat Harbour on the Priwall peninsula is moored the four-masted barque *Passat*, which once sailed the world's seas and is now used by the German-French Youth Welfare Organisation (Jugendwerk) during the summer months as a hostel and training school (open to visitors during the season).

SURROUNDINGS. – *Brodtener Steilufer (1½ km N), a steeply scarped coastal strip 18 m high which extends for some 4 km round the curve of land between Travemünde and Niendorf; golf-course, Hermannshöhe restaurant. – *Hansaland Recreation Park*, Sierksdorf (19 km NW).

Ludwigsburg

Land: Baden-Württemberg.
Vehicle registration: LB.
Altitude: 295 m. – Population: 80,000.
Post code: D-7140. – Dialling code: 0 71 41.
ⓘ **Fremdenverkehrsamt**, Wilhelmstr. 24; tel. 1 82 52.

HOTELS. – *Schiller Hospiz*, Gartenstr. 17, 68 b.; *Heim* (no rest.), Schillerstr. 19, 55 b.; *Alte Sonne*, Bei der

Kath. Kirche 3, 20 b. – IN HOHENECK: *Hoheneck*, Uferstr., 20 b. – AT SCHLOSS MONREPOS: *Schlosshotel Monrepos*, 123 b., SB, sauna. – IN OSSWEIL: *Kamin*, Neckarweihinger Str. 52, 21 b. – YOUTH HOSTEL: Gemsenbergstr. 21, 130.

RESTAURANTS. – *Ratskeller*, Wilhelmstr. 13; *Hongkong*, Untere Marktstr. 5; *Post-Cantz*, Eberhardstr. 6. – AT SCHLOSS MONREPOS: *La Perle* (many specialties); *Gutsschenke* (Swabian dishes).

CAFÉ. – *Kunzi*, Myliusstr. 15.

EVENTS. – *"Blühendes Barock"* ("Flowering Baroque") horticultural show and Castle Festival in summer.

With its palaces and parks Ludwigsburg, situated on a plateau above the Neckar a few kilometres from Stuttgart, preserves unchanged the aspect and atmosphere of a princely capital of the Baroque period. There are several establishments of higher education and institutes in the town.

HISTORY. – Ludwigsburg owes its name to Duke Eberhard Ludwig of Wurttemberg, who built a palace here from 1709 onwards. The town grew up round the palace, receiving its charter in 1709. In 1717 it became the Ducal capital. In 1758 Duke Karl Eugen founded the porcelain manufactory.

SIGHTS: – The **Residenzschloss**, built by various architects between 1704 and 1733, the largest of the palaces built in Germany on the model of Versailles, is a magnificent Baroque building with a sumptuous interior in Baroque, Rococo and Empire style (452 rooms: conducted tours, festival in summer) and a beautiful SCHLOSSPARK ("Blühendes Barock" horticultural show in summer). In the New Wing is a section of the Württemberg Provincial Museum devoted to Baroque court art. N of the palace is the *Favoritepark* (nature reserve and game park), with the little Baroque palace of *Favorite* (1718–23). Farther NW is *Schloss Monrepos* (1760–64), Duke Karl Eugen's "lake palace".

SW of the Schloss, in the MARKTPLATZ (fountain with a figure of Duke Eberhard Ludwig, founder of the town), are the twin-towered Baroque *Town Church* (1718–26: Evang.), the plain *Trinity Church* (1721–27: R.C.) and the birthplace of the poet *Justinus Kerner* (1786–1862: No. 8). Nearby is the 16-storey *Marstall-Center* (1974). In Schillerplatz is a *statue of Schiller*, who lived in Ludwigsburg in 1768–73 and 1793–94. Near here too are the birthplaces of the poet *Eduard Mörike* (1804–75: Kirchstr.

2), the writer on aesthetics *Friedrich Theodor Fischer* (1807–87: Stadtkirchenplatz 1) and the theologian *David Friedrich Strauss* (1808–74: Marstallstr. 1).

SURROUNDINGS. – **Hohenasperg Fortress** (356 m: 5 km W). In this old fortress (now a penal establishment), set high on a conical hill, the writer Christian Schubart was confined in 1777–87 and the economist Friedrich List in 1824–25. Wide views; restaurant. – **Marbach** (8 km NE), with *Schiller's birthplace and the *Schiller National Museum (rich collections, with works of Swabian authors).

Lüneburg

Land: Lower Saxony.
Vehicle registration: LG.
Altitude: 17 m. – Population: 63,000.
Post code: D-2120. – Dialling code: 0 41 31.
ⓘ **Verkehrsverein**, Town Hall, Market Place; tel. 3 22 00.

HOTELS. – *Seminaris Luneburg*, Soltauer Str. 3, 200 b., SB, sauna, solarium; *Residenz am Kurpark*, Munstermannskamp 10, 60 b.; *Wellenkamp's Hotel*, Am Sande 9, 73 b.; *Am Kurpark*, Uelzener Str. 41, 67 b.; *Kurpension Erika*, Uelzener Str. 73b, 30 b.; *Parkhotel*, Uelzener Str. 27, 24 b.; *Bremer Hof*, Luner Str. 13, 76 b.; *Heiderose*, Uelzener Str. 29, 33 b.; *Zum Heidekrug*, Am Berge 5, 14 b. (half-timbered building of 1455). – ON THE B 4: *Motel Landwehr*, Hamburger Str. 15, 70 b. – YOUTH HOSTEL: Soltauer Str. 133, 112 b. – CAMPING SITES: *Rote Schleuse*, off the B 4; *Radenbeck*, in E Lüneburg Heath: *Bockelmann*, on the Neetze in Neu-Rullstorf.

RESTAURANTS. – *Ratskeller*, in Town Hall; *Zur Krone*, Heiligengeiststr. 41.

This old salt-working and Hanseatic town lies on the navigable River Ilmenau, on the edge of the Elbe lowlands and in the NE of Lüneburg Heath. It is one of the principal centres of North German brick-built architecture, with numerous public buildings and burghers' houses in late Gothic and Renaissance style. It is the chief town of an administrative region (*Bezirk*), with a university college, a specialist college and the East German Academy. It is also visited as a health resort (saline baths, mud baths, Kneipp cure). It has a variety of industries (chemicals, woodworking, wallpaper manufacture, paper-making, metal-working), mostly situated to the N of the town. Lüneburg is the terminal point of the Harz Heathland Highway and the starting point of the Old Salt Road to Lübeck. – A new inland harbour on the Elbe Branch Canal is now in operation.

HISTORY. – Lüneburg rose to importance at an early stage thanks to the castle built by Duke Hermann Billung of Saxony on the Kalkberg in 951 as a fortress and administrative centre, the important Ilmenau bridge, which also had legal status and the abundant brine springs. But it was not until after the destruction of the powerful neighbouring town of Bardowick by Henry the Lion in 1189, the confirmation of Lüneburg's municipal charter in 1247 and its admission to the Hanse that the town achieved the almost complete independence of a free Imperial city. After the destruction of the castle on the Kalkberg during the war over the Lüneburg succession (1371), the citizens of Lüneburg shook off the rule of the Dukes of Brunswick-Lüneburg, whose residence the town had hitherto been. In the 16th c. Lüneburg was one of the wealthiest towns in North Germany, but thereafter its prosperity declined, until the development of the spa and the coming of industry gave it a new lease of life.

SIGHTS. – The central feature of the town is the charming square *AM SANDE, surrounded by old brick-built houses with magnificent stepped gables. At its W end is the *Schwarzes Haus* ("Black House": built in 1548 as a brewhouse, now occupied by the Chamber of Industry and Commerce). At the E end, dominating the square, is *St John's Church (14th c.: 49 m long, 43 m wide), with a tower 180 m high; fine high altar (1485), beautiful choir stalls (1589), numerous monuments. A short distance SE is the richly stocked *Museum of the Principality of Lüneburg*.

From Am Sande KLEINE and GROSSE BÄCKERSTRASSE (pedestrian precinct) run N to the MARKT, with the *Diana Fountain* or "Luna Fountain" (1530). On the W side of the square is the *Town Hall, a group of buildings of the 13th to 18th c. with a Baroque façade of 1720 richly decorated with figures. Of the many well-preserved rooms in the interior the arcaded *Court Room (*c.* 1330), the Cloth

Old Crane, Lüneburg

Hall (c. 1450, containing the famous Lüneburg silver plate), the Old Chancery (1433), the Large Council Chamber (1466–84: fine carving) and the Princes' Hall (15th c.) are particularly notable. – NE of the Markt is St Nicholas's Church (consecrated 1409). To the E of the church, on the Ilmenau, is the Kaufhaus (1745), with a Baroque façade; in front of it is the *Old Crane, which is mentioned in the records as early as 1336. – On the outskirts of the town to the NE is the former nunnery of Lüne (14th and 15th c.: now occupied by a women's religious house),

house), with a rich *collection of old tapestries (on show only for one week in August).

On the western edge of the old town is St Michael's Church (14th–15th c.), at the foot of the Kalkberg (57 m: fine view). A little way SE of the church is the East Prussian Hunting Museum (Salzstr. 26). – Farther S are the former salt springs and the KURPARK (laid out in 1907), with the Kurhaus, baths and brine bath with artificial waves.

SURROUNDINGS. – Bardowick Cathedral (SS. Peter and Paul: 6 km N), with a late Romanesque W front and a Gothic triple-aisled nave; carved altar with two wings (1425), magnificent late Gothic choir stalls. – Scharnebeck ship-lift (10 km NE: lifts a max. of 1350 tons 38 m in 3 min.) for the Elbe Branch Canal.

Lüneburg Heath

Land: Lower Saxony.

ⓘ Fremdenverkehrsverband
Lüneburger Heide,
Am Sande 5, D-2120 Lüneburg;
tel. (0 41 31) 420 06/7.

The *Lüneburg Heath is the largest expanse of heathland in Germany. It lies between the River Aller and the

Sheep and shepherd, Lüneburg Heath

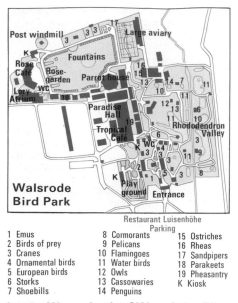

Walsrode Bird Park

1 Emus	8 Cormorants	15 Ostriches
2 Birds of prey	9 Pelicans	16 Rheas
3 Cranes	10 Flamingoes	17 Sandpipers
4 Ornamental birds	11 Water birds	18 Parakeets
5 European birds	12 Owls	19 Pheasantry
6 Storks	13 Cassowaries	K Kiosk
7 Shoebills	14 Penguins	

lower Weser in the SW and the Elbe in the NE, and reaches its highest point in the Wilseder Berg (169 m).

The dry and infertile stretches of higher ground, between which lie tracts of bog, are covered for much of their extent with heather, which during the flowering season in August and September brings a touch of life and colour to the rather melancholy landscape. Variety is given by the curiously misshapen juniper bushes, the tracks caught between clumps of birches and the red-brick heath farm-houses nestling amid groups of oak-trees. Numerous "Hünengräber" (megalithic tombs) are a reminder that men lived here in prehistoric times. The main occupation of the heath people are sheep-rearing, forestry and farming, but industry (gravel-working, oil drilling) is now also develop-ing. The traditional bee-keeping has declined.

The finest heath scenery is to be found in the central part of the Heath. Here in 1921 an area of 200 sq. km round the heath village of **Wilsede** (Heath Museum) was designed as the *LÜNEBURG HEATH NATURE RESERVE (the first nature park in Ger-many). Popular features in the park are the *Totengrund* and the *Steingrund.* The SÜDHEIDE NATURE PARK (500 sq. km) between Uelzen, Soltau and Celle is also very attractive, particularly round *Un-terlüss, Müden* and *Hermannsburg.*

The *grave of Herman Löns,* amid beautiful juniper plantations near Fallingbostel, draws thousands of this local writer's admirers every year. More difficult of access are the *"Seven Stone Houses"* (megalithic tomb chambers with huge capstones); they lie in the middle of a military training area, and access to them is usually permitted only on the first and third Sunday in the month.

W of Fallingbostel is the *Walsrode Bird Park (10 hectares), with 4000 birds, which attracts crowds of visitors. Its *Paradise Hall is one of the largest aviaries for tropical birds in Germany.

400 animals live in the **Wildpark Lüneburger Heide** (open all year; restaurant). The majority of the larger European species are represented in this park near the Hamburg–Hanover motorway – elks, bison, bears, lynx, wolves, ibex, red-azis- and roe deer.

The Lüneburg Heath is the favourite recreation area of the people of Hamburg, and is now increasingly popular with holidaymakers from other parts of the Federal Republic, who come here to find rest and relaxation in unspoiled natural surroundings. Many places in the Heath are now favourite holiday resorts, the best-known being *Amelinghausen, Bispingen, Dorfmark, Fallingbostel, Her-mannsburg, Müden, Schneverdingen, Unterlüss, Walsrode* and *Wilsede. –* Coach-trips through the wide expanses of the Heath are popular with visitors. In autumn there are Heather Festivals in many places (crowning of the "Queen of the Heath", etc.).

Main Valley

Länder: Bavaria and Hesse.
ⓘ **Fremenverkehrsverband Franken,** Am Plärrer 14, D-8500 Nuremberg 81; tel. (09 11) 26 42 02/04.
Hessischer Fremdenverkehrsverband, Abraham-Lincoln-Str. 38–42, D-6200 Wiesbaden; tel. (0 61 21) 7 37 25.

The River Main, with a total length of 524 km, is formed by the junction of the Weisser Main or White Main, which rises on the Ochsenkopf in the Fichtelgebirge, and the Roter Main or Red Main coming from the Fran-conian Jura, which meet below Kulmbach.

The river follows a tortuous course with many windings, some large and some small: if it flowed in a straight line it would be only half as long. It breaks through the *Franconian Jura* at Lichtenfels, cuts through the Keuper hills between the *Hasseberge* and the *Steigerwald* in its westward course between Bamberg and Hassfurt, describes a wide bend at Kitzingen through the wine-growing Muschelkalk region known as the *Franconian Plateau*, flows round the Bunter sandstone plateau of the *Spessart* in a great rectangle from Gemünden to Aschaffenburg – with the red cliffs of the Spessart in the N and the Odenwald to the S coming right up to the river at certain points – and reaches the *Middle Rhine plain* just before Aschaffenburg. It then flows through the Rhine-Main industrial region and into the Rhine opposite Mainz.

The river gives its name to the smiling region of *Mainfranken. Here are grown a whole range of delectable wines – Würzburger Stein, Escherndorfer Lump, Randersackerer Pfülben and many more – which come to the table in their characteristic rounded bottles, the "Bocksbeutel". (Hence the name of the tourist route, the Bocksbeutelstrasse, which runs along the river.) Here too the visitor will find a series of picturesque little medieval wine towns like *Ochsenfurt* and *Marktbreit*, as well as strongly defended medieval towns like **Miltenberg** and **Wertheim**.

The splendours of Baroque and Rococo are also to be found in the Main valley. The pilgrimage church of *Vierzehnheiligen*, the palaces at *Banz* and *Veit schöchheim*, the old princely residence and festival town of **Bayreuth**, the episcopal cites of **Bamberg** and **Würzburg** may be taken as tokens of the abundance that awaits the visitor. Among the architects the great names are Balthasar Neumann and Johann Dientzenhofer. But Gothic art too is represented by the magnificent works of Tilman Riemenschneider. *Schloss Johannisburg* in **Aschaffenburg** is a great Renaissance creation. Tradition and progress are both to be found in Goethe's town of **Frankfurt**, once the place of coronation of German Emperors, now an important industrial centre in the Rhine-Main region.

Mainz

Land: Rhineland-Palatinate.
Vehicle registration: MZ.
Altitude: 82 m. – Population: 185,000.
Post code: D-6500. – Dialling code: 0 61 31.
ⓘ**Verkehrsverein**, Bahnhofplatz 2;
tel. 23 37 41.

HOTELS. – ON THE RHINE: *Hilton International*, Rheinstr. 68, 840 b. (Rhine Grill, Römische Weinstube, Rhine Terrace); *Mainzer Hof*, Kaiserstr. 98, 114 b. (panoramic restaurant). – NEAR THE MAIN STATION: *PLM Europahotel*, Kaiserstr. 7, 160 b. (grill restaurant "La Poularde"); *Central Hotel Eden*, Bahnhofsplatz 8, 91 b.; *Grünewald* (no rest.), Frauenlobstr. 14, 90 b. – IN THE "GREEN BELT": *Am Römerwall* (no rest.), Römerwall 53, 62 b.; *Stiftswingert* (no rest.), Am Stiftswingert 4, 42 b. – IN FINTHEN (7 km SW): *Kurmainz* (no rest.), Flugplatzstr. 44, 80 b., SB, sauna, solarium. – IN BRETZENHEIM: *Novotel*, Essenheimer Str. 200, 242 b., SP. – IN WEISENAU: *Bristol*, Friedrich Ebert Str. 20, 157 b. – YOUTH HOSTEL: At Forst Wiesenau, 150 b. – CAMPING SITE: *Maarau*, on the island of Maaraue.

RESTAURANTS. – *Rats- und Zunftstuben "Heilig Geist"*, Rentengasse 2 (in the restored 13th c. Heiliggeistspital; original vaulting); *Stadtpark-restaurant an der Favorite*, Karl-Weiser-Str. 1 (terrace with beautiful view of the Rhine, the mouth of the Main and the Taunus); *Drei Lilien*, Ballplatz 2; *Bauernschänke*, Haugasse 6/Corner Rheinstr.; *Rhein-goldterrace*, Auf dem Rathausplatz 1 (view of the Rhine); *Walderdorff*, Karmeliterplatz 4 (French); *Bei Mama Gina*, Holzstr. 34 (Italian); *China Restaurant Man Wah*, Am Brand 42. – IN GONSENHEIM: *Zum Löwen*, Mainzer Str. 2.

WINE-BARS. – *Haus des Deutschen Weines*, Gutenbergplatz 3–5 (with wines from all the German wine-growing regions); *Gutsschänke "Zum Schildkneckt"*, Leichhofstr. 5; *Zur Reblaus*, Schottstr. 5; *Weinhaus Quintin*, Kleine Quintinstr. 2; *Gebert's Weinstuben*, Frauenlobstr. 94.

CAFÉS. – *Dom-Café*, Markt 12–16; *Janson*, Schillerstr. 40; *Dinges*, Mailandsgasse 2–6.

EVENTS. – **Mainzer Fastnacht** (Shrovetide), with *Rose Monday procession; Open Ohr Festival* (Whitsun); *Mainzer Johannisnacht* (mid June), summer programme, "Mainz lives in its squares"; *Wine Market* (Aug.–Sept.); *Mainzer Tage der Fernsehkritik* (end Oct.); Christmas Market.

Mainz, capital of the *Land* of Rhineland-Palatinate and a university city, a former Electoral and archiepiscopal capital with a his-

Market Fountain outside Mainz Cathedral

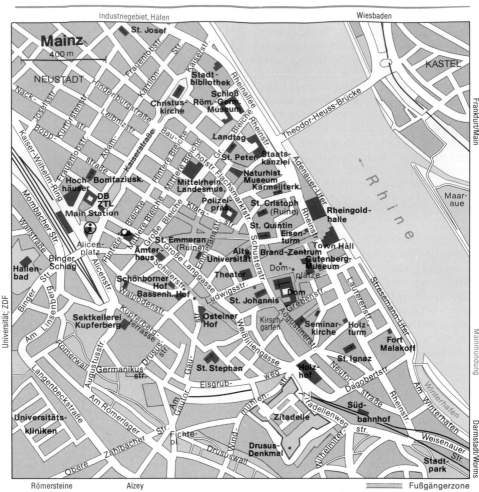

Römersteine   Alzey   ▬▬ Fußgängerzone

toric past, is situated on the left bank of the Rhine opposite the mouth of the Main. It lies in the fertile Mainz Basin, the most northerly part of the Upper Rhine plain, and is the focal point of the western end of the Rhine-Main economic region, encircled by a ring of motorways. It is the city of Gutenberg, but it is also the centre of the Rhine wine trade (with Sekt cellars), an important traffic junction and commercial and industrial centre, with the headquarters of radio and television corporations (ZDF, SWF) and publishing houses; and it is one of the great centres of the Carnival.

HISTORY. – In 38 B.C. the Romans established a camp, *Moguntiacum*, close to a Celtic settlement, and from about A.D. 10 this was the chief stronghold and headquarters of the commander of Upper Germany (Germania Superior). In 742 St Boniface founded the archbishopric, and Mainz became the metropolis of Christianity in Germany. The building of the Cathedral was begun in 975 under Archbishop Willigis. In 1184 the Emperor Frederick Barbarossa held a splendid Imperial festival on the Maaraue. The town – "golden Mainz", Aurea Moguntia – reached its peak of

prosperity in the 13th c. as chief town of the Rhenish League of Towns, established in 1254. Around 1450 Johannes Gutenberg, the inventor of printing with movable type, set up his press in Mainz. The town lost all its privileges in 1462 as a result of a dispute with the ecclesiastical authorities. The University was founded by Archbishop Diether von Isenburg in 1476–77. During the Thirty Years War Mainz was taken by the Swedes. The heyday of the Electorate of Mainz was in the 17th and 18th c., when the town took on a Baroque stamp. In 1792 Mainz was declared a republic, and Goethe gives an eye-witness account of the devastating bombardment of the town in that year. In 1801 it became chief town of the French *département* of Donnersberg, in 1816 capital of the province of Rhine-Hesse. During the Second World War four-fifths of the old town was destroyed. The city became capital of the *Land* of Rhineland-Palatinate in 1950.

SIGHTS. – In the centre of the city stands the six-towered *Cathedral of SS. Martin and Stephen (begun 975; mostly 11th–13th c.), which ranks with the cathedrals of Speyer and Worms as one of the supreme achievements of Romanesque religious architecture on the Upper Rhine; fine *bishops' tombs in the interior. (Photograph, p. 45.) In the cloister is the *Cathedral and Diocesan Museum*. On the

N side of the Cathedral are the **Dom-plätze** (Cathedral Squares), newly laid out in 1975, with a *Market Fountain of 1526. At the NE corner is the *Guten-berg Museum, a museum of world printing (42-line **Gutenberg Bible of 1452–55; reproduction of *Gutenberg's printing-house). Behind it is the *"Am Brand" shopping centre* (1974), and beyond this, on the RHEINUFER, the *Town Hall (1970–73) and the *Rheingoldhalle* (1968), together with two relics of the medieval fortifications, the *Eisenturm* (Iron Tower, *c.* 1240) and the *Holzturm* (Wooden Tower, 14th c.).

In the old town with its narrow streets and half-timbered houses, to the S of the Cathedral, are two fine Baroque churches, the *Seminary Church* and *St Ignatius's.* – In GUTENBERGPLATZ (lat. 50° N marked on the roadway), opposite the **Theatre**, is a *statue of Johannes Gutenberg* (1398–1467), born in Mainz, who invented printing about 1440. To the W, in SCHILLERPLATZ, are the handsome *Adels-palais* and the *Shrovetide Fountain* (1966). – To the S, higher up, is the Gothic **St Stephen's Church** (14th c.; *Chagall window).

Just below the bridge over the Rhine is the **Electoral Palace** (17th and 18th c.), with fine state apartments and the *Roman-Germanic Central Museum. Opposite it, to the SE, are the **Landtag** (parliament of the *Land*: formerly House of the Teutonic Order) and the *Staats-kanzlei* (*Land* government offices). To the N of the Palace is the *Municipal Library*, to the NW the large *Christuskirche* (1903: Evang.). In GROSSE BLEICHE is the twin-towered *St Peter's Church* (originally 1752–56). In the former Court Stables (Nos. 49–51: 1765–71) is the **Middle Rhineland Provincial Museum** (antiquities, pictures). A little way E is the *Natural History Museum* (Reich-Klara-Str. 1).

The *Theodor Heuss Bridge* (1950) leads over the Rhine to KASTEL, a former suburb of Mainz now incorporated in Wiesbaden, the Roman bridgehead post of Castellum Mattiacorum. – On the plateau W of the city is the campus of the **Johannes Gutenberg University**, to the SE of which are the *Römersteine* (remains of a Roman aqueduct, 1st c. A.D.) – Between the western suburbs of Mombach and Gonsenheim is the *Main-

zer Sand* nature reserve (interesting steppe flora).

On the *Lerchenberg* (205 m), 7 km SW of the town centre, is the **ZDF Radio and Television Centre**, with an office block 70 m high; modern sculpture in forecourt.

The "Six Little Men of Mainz" devised by the cartoon film artist Wolf Gerlach have been a great draw on the ZDF television service.

SURROUNDINGS. – **Ingelheim** (16 km W), with 14th–15th c. church and remains of a Carolingian royal stronghold. – **Oppenheim** (20 km S), with *St Catherine's Church (13th–15th c.), one of the finest Gothic churches on the Rhine, and German Museum of Viticulture.

Mannheim

Land: Baden-Württemberg.
Vehicle registration: MA.
Altitude: 97 m. – Population: 307,000.
Post code: D-6800. – Dialling code: 06 21.
ⓘ **Verkehrsverein**, Bahnhofplatz 1;
tel. 10 10 11.

HOTELS. – *Steigenberger Hotel*, Mannheimer Hof, Augusta-Anlage 4, 280 b. ("Holzkistl" basement restaurant); *Novotel*, Auf dem Friedensplatz 6, 360 b., SB; *Warburg* F4, 4–11, 272 b.; *Augusta*, Augusta-Anlage 43, 140 b.; *Basler Hof*, Tattersallstr. 27, 96 b.; *Wegener* (no rest.), Tattersallstr. 16, 70 b.; *Holländer Hof* (no rest.), U1, 11–12, 64 b.; *Intercity Hotel*, Bahnhofplatz 15, 63 b.; *Seitz* (no rest.), Sekkenheimer Str. 132, 47 b. – YOUTH HOSTEL: Rheinpromenade 21, in Lindenhof, 134 b. – CAMPING SITES: *Strandbad Nord*, on the Rhine in Neckerau; *Am Neckar*, in Neuostheim.

RESTAURANTS. – *L'Epi d'Or*, H 7/3 (French); *Kopenhagen*, Friedrichsring 2a (Danish); *Savarin*, in Rosengarten Congress Centre, Friedrichsplatz; *Zeppelin*, revolving restaurant in Television Tower (125 m) in Luisenpark; *Bit am Theatre*, Goethestr. 16 (Yugoslav); *Garda*, P 6/12 (Italian).

BEER-HOUSES. – *Habereckl-Bräustübl*, Q 4/13; *Eichbaum-Stammhaus*, P 5/9.

WINE-BARS. – *Henningers Gutsschänke*, at National Theatre; *Mannemer Stub*, Augusta-Anlage 43; *Goldene Gans*, Tattersallstr. 19 (Palatinate wines).

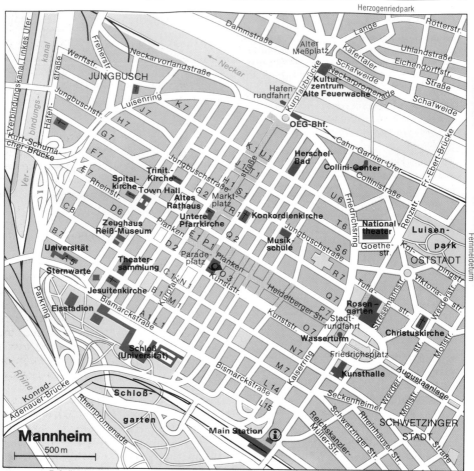

Fußgängerzone

CAFÉS. – *Kiemle*, Plankenhof Passage; *Gmeiner*, Friedrichsplatz 12; *Herrdegen*, E2, 8; Kettemann, L15, 10.

EVENTS. – **May Market** (end April/beginning May with exhibition and riding tournament); *Upper Rhine Rowing Regatta* (mid May); *Midsummernight's Festival* in Luisenpark (end June); *Autumn Amusement Fair* on Messplatz in Herzogenried Park (Sept./Oct.).

Thanks to its favourable situation on the right bank of the Rhine at the outflow of the canalised Neckar this former capital of the Electors of the Palatinate has become an important commercial and industrial centre. Here Drais demonstrated his first foot-propelled bicycle in 1817, Benz his first motor vehicle in 1885.

Mannheim has one of the largest inland harbours in Europe (conducted tours: at Bonadies Dock is the world's largest oil-mill.

A notable feature of the town is its regular grid pattern, in which each block is designated by a letter and a number.

Mannheim has numerous educational and cultural institutions, including its University, the Academy of Music and Drama, and specialist colleges of fashion, technology, etc. It earned a place in theatrical history in 1782 with the first performance of Schiller's drama "Die Räuber" in the National Theatre.

Opposite Mannheim on the left bank of the Rhine is the industrial city of **Ludwigshafen**, known throughout the world as the headquarters of BASF (Badische Anilin- und Sodafabrik): BASF tower block, oil harbours). Modern Town Hall.

HISTORY. – The town grew out of the boatmen's and fishermen's village of *Mannenheim* ("Manno's home"), on the site of the present Palace on the high bank of the Rhine, which appears in the records as early as 766. In 1606 Elector Friedrich IV built a Dutch-style fortress on the site of the village and established a trading settlement which obtained its municipal charter in 1607. During the war over the Palatinate succession the French General Mélac devastated the Palatinate and destroyed Mannheim.

Thereafter Elector Johann Wilhelm had the town rebuilt in 136 rectangular blocks. The town and fortress were now brought together and enclosed within a common circuit of fortifications. In 1720 Elector Karl Philipp moved his principal residence from Heidelberg to Mannheim, and the present Palace was built on the site of the old citadel. Karl Philipp and his successor Karl Theodor attracted leading French and Italian architects to their court, as well as sculptors, painters and workers in porcelain. A Palatine Academy of Science was founded in 1763. This splendid cultural flowering came to an end when Karl Theodor (who had become Elector of Bavaria in 1778) moved his capital to Munich. Under the treaty of Lunéville (1801) the Palatinate territory on the right bank of the Rhine passed to Baden, that on the left bank to France, and Mannheim became a frontier town. At the Congress of Vienna in 1815, however, Bavaria recovered the left-bank territory, and King Ludwig I founded Ludwigshafen in that territory in 1843. The opening up of the Rhine to shipping made Mannheim the terminal point of traffic on the Upper Rhine and set it on the way to further economic

Telecommunications Tower, Luisenpark, Mannheim

development. The port was constructed between 1834 and 1876. During the Second World War 51% of the town and 95% of the port was destroyed; post-war rebuilding has given both of them a very modern aspect.

SIGHTS. – The principal streets (pedestrian zone) of the chequerboard-patterned inner city are the **Planken** and the *Kurpfalzstrasse* (Breite Strasse) which intersect at the *Paradeplatz*. By the MARKET PLACE stand the *Old Town Hall* (rebuilt) and the *Lower Parish Church* (R.C.), a double structure built 1701–23. – In the spacious FRIEDRICHSPLATZ (fountains), reached by way of Planken and Heidelberger Strasse, are the **Water Tower** (1888), Mannheim's emblem and landmark, and the great congress and

meeting centre known as the *Rosengarten*. S of the Water Tower is the *Kunsthalle*, extended in 1983, with an excellent collection of paintings and sculpture of the 19th and 20th c. At the near end of the Augusta-Anlage is a *monument to Carl Benz* (1844–1929).

N of Friedrichsplatz, on the FRIEDRICHSRING, is the **National Theatre** (two houses, Grosses and Kleines Haus), built here in 1955–57. The original theatre, built 1779, famous as the scene of the first performances of Schiller's plays "Die Räuber", "Fiesco" and "Kabale und Liebe" in 1782 and 1784, stood N of the Palace; it was destroyed during the war.

To the E of the theatre is the LUISENPARK, with a lake-stage, horticultural exhibition buildings, gondoletta, animal enclosures and the 205 m high **Telecommunications Tower** (1975: revolving restaurant at about 125 m). – On the far side of the Neckar is the HERZOGENRIED PARK, with a modern multi-purpose hall, an open-air swimming pool and a cycle racing-track.

Near the bank of the Rhine is the Baroque **Electoral Palace** (1720–60), one of the largest in Germany (rebuilt: now occupied by the University and the District Court; conducted tours of historic rooms), with the *palace church* (rebuilt 1952–56). NW of the Palace is the *Jesuit Church*, a fine Baroque building of 1733–60 (restored). To the N of the church are the *Theatre Museum* and the *Arsenal* (Zeughaus: 1777–78), which houses the *Reiss Museum*, named after Carl and Anna Reiss, honorary citizens of Mannheim, with the municipal collections (archaeology, ethnography, history of the town).

The **Port of Mannheim** consists of the *Commercial Harbour* (on the 3 km long tongue of land between the Rhine and the Neckar), the *Industrial Harbour* (on the N side of the Neckar), *Rheinau Harbour* (11 km upstream in Rheinau), the *Old Rhine Harbour* and the *Oil Harbour* (on the Friesenheimer Insel) – a total of 3 river harbours and 17 harbour basins. There are trips round the port from the Kurpfalzbrücke (left bank of Neckar).

SURROUNDINGS. – **Ludwigshafen** (1 km W), with the pilgrimage church of the Assumption, Municipal Museum, Schiller House and the beautiful Ebert Park. – **Schloss Schwetzingen** (15 km SE), summer residence of the Electors of the Palatinate in the 18th c., with celebrated *gardens and *Rococo theatre (built by Pigage 1746–52: festival performances).

Marburg an der Lahn

Land: Hesse. – Vehicle registration: MR.
Altitude: 176–387 m. – Population: 74,000.
Post code: D-3550. – Dialling code: 0 64 21.
ⓘ **Verkehrsamt**, Neue Kasseler Str. 1
(at Station);
tel. 20 12 49.

HOTELS. – *Europäischer Hof* (no rest.), Elisabethstr.
12, 180 b.; *Waldecker Hof*, Bahnhofstr. 23, 60 b.;
Bahnhofshotel Rump (no rest.), Bahnhofstr. 29, 34 b.;
Hamburger Hof, Gutenbergstr, 25, 18 b.; *Zur Sonne*,
Markstr. 14, 18 b.; *Haus Müller* (no rest.),
Deutschhausstr. 29, 17 b. – IN GISSELBERG: *Fasanerie*,
46 b. – IN MARBACH: *Berggarten*, Emil-von-Behring-
Str. 26, 49 b., Kneipp treatment, sauna. – IN WEHRS-
HAUSEN: *Dammühle*, 18 b., garden terrace. – YOUTH
HOSTEL: Jahnstr. 1, 200 b. – CAMPING SITES:
Lahnaue, at the Sommerbad; *Kernbach*, Kernbach;
Dammhammer, Brungershausen. *Niederasphe*, on the
Aspha.

RESTAURANTS. – *Zur Krone*, Markt 11; *Santa Lucia*,
Deutschhausstr. 35 (Italian); *Stadthallen-Restaurant*,
Biegenstr. 15; *Zur Stiftsschänke*, Ockershauser Str.
71.

**This Hessian university town is at-
tractively situated on the Lahn. The
picturesque old town with its narrow winding streets and stepped
lanes extends in a semicircle up the
steep slopes of the Schlossberg.
A modern note is added by the
various institutes and clinics of
the University; and Marburg also
has considerable pharmaceutical
and optical industries.**

HISTORY. – Marburg grew up under the protection of
a castle belonging to the Gisonen, which later passed
to the Landgraves of Thuringia. It first appears in the
records as a town in 1228. In the 13th c. the castle was
the residence of St Elizabeth, wife of Landgrave
Ludwig IV of Thuringia, who moved from the
Wartburg to Marburg after her husband's death and
devoted herself to the care of the sick and the poor. In
1527 Landgrave Philipp the Magnanimous founded
the university which still bears his name – the first
Protestant university in Germany. In 1529 the castle
was the scene of the famous Colloquy of Marburg
between Luther and Zwingli. In 1604 Marburg passed
to Hesse-Kassel; from 1806 to 1813 it belonged to the
kingdom of Westphalia; and in 1866 it became
Prussian.

SIGHTS. – Marburg's finest building is
the famous *St Elizabeth's Church*,
along with the Liebfrauenkirche in Trier
the earliest church in Germany in purely
Gothic style (1235–83; towers *c.* 1340).
The original furnishings have been almost
completely preserved, including the
golden *shrine of St Elizabeth (*c.* 1249) in
the sacristy, a carved wooden *figure of St
Elizabeth (15th c.) and 13th and 14th c.
*stained glass in the choir, and the tombs

Marburg an der Lahn

of Hessian rulers (13th–16th c.) in the S
transept. In the chapel under the N tower
is the tomb of President Paul von Hindenburg (1847–1934). – To the S, attractively situated above the Lahn at the foot
of the Schlossberg, is the *Philipp University* (founded 1527; present building
1874–91), with the 14th c. *University
Church*. A little higher up is the MARKT,
with the *Town Hall* (1525). N of the Town
Hall, half way up the Schlossberg, is the
Lutheran Church (1297); fine view of the
old town from the churchyard.

High above the old town rears the
Castle (287 m), in the 15th and 16th c.
seat of the Landgraves of Hesse and in
1529 scene of the Colloquy of Marburg
between Luther and Zwingli. It contains
the valuable religious collection of the
University. Magnificent Knights' Hall (*c.*
1300); chapel (13th c.). Behind it, to the
W, is the *Schlosspark* (with an open-air
theatre). – In the Ernst-von-Hülsen-Haus
in Biegenstrasse is the richly stocked
University Museum (history and culture
of northern Hesse; painting and graphic
art of the 19th and 20th c.).

Meersburg

Land: Baden-Württemberg.
Vehicle registration: FN.
Altitude: 410 m. – Population: 5000.
Post code: D-7758. – Dialling code: 0 75 32.
ⓘ **Kur- und Verkehrsamt**,
Schlossplatz 4;
tel. 8 23 83.

HOTELS. – *Strandhotel Wilder Mann*, Bismarktplatz 2,
60 b., SP (garden terrace); *Terrassen Hotel Weisshaar*,
Stefan Lochner Str. 24, 50 b.; *Rothmund am See* (no
rest.), Uferpromenade 11, 35 b., SP; *Bad Hotel*

Meersburg (no rest.), von Lassberg Str. 23, 24 b., SB, sauna; *Villa Bellevue* (no rest.), Am Rosenhag 5, 20 b.; *Seehotel Zur Münz*, Seepromenade 7, 32 b. (roof sunbathing terrace); *Bären*, Marktplatz 11, 28 b. (inn since 1605); *Seegarten*, Uferpromenade 47, 22 b.

RESTAURANTS. – *Weinstube zum Becher*, Höllgasse 4 (at Neues Schloss; oldest wine-house on Lake Constance; Baden wines); *Ratskeller*, in Town Hall.

CAFÉS. – *Droste*, Seepromenade 9; *Dagobertsklause*, Steigstr. 31; *Gross*, Unterstadtstrasse.

EVENTS. – *Wine tasting for visitors* (Tue. and Fri.); *Serenades in the Neues Schloss* (Mon., May–Oct.); *Open-air concerts* (Thur., June–Sept.); *International concerts in the Castle* (Sat., June–Sept.)

The little town of *Meersburg on Lake Constance, noted for its wine, is picturesquely situated on the steeply sloping shores of the lake at the point where the Überlinger See merges into the Obersee. The pattern of the town was set mainly during the period when it was the residence of the Bishops of Konstanz (1526–1803). There is a ferry service between Meersburg and Konstanz, on the other side of the lake (20 min.).

SIGHTS. – In the UPPER TOWN is the **Altes Schloss**, the "Meersburg", which has a history going back to the 7th c.; its four round towers date from 1508. From 1526 to 1803 it was the residence of the Bishops of Konstanz. It became the property of Freiherr Joseph von Lassberg in 1838, and the poetess Annette von Droste-Hülshoff, his sister-in-law, stayed here for much of the time between 1841 and her death; the room in which she worked and died is shown to visitors. – To the E, in SCHLOSSPLATZ, is the **Neues**

Schloss, built 1741–50 by Balthasar Neumann as a new residence for the Bishops of Konstanz; in it are the *Dornier Museum* and the *Heimatmuseum*. To the N of this palace, in Vorburggasse, is the *Wine-growing Museum* ("Türkenfass", a huge tun with a capacity of over 50,000 litres), occupying a house in which Franz Anton Mesmer, inventor of mesmerism, died in 1815. – The MARKTPLATZ is exceedingly picturesque, with its half-timbered houses and old town gate, the *Obertor*. A short distance E of the Obertor, among the vineyards, is the *Fürstenhäusle*, built in 1640 as a wine-grower's house, now a *Droste Museum*, with mementoes of the poetess.

SURROUNDINGS. – *Pile-dwellings of Unteruhldingen* (6 km NW). The *Open-Air Museum of German Prehistory*, founded by the archaeologist Hans Reinerth in 1922, contains two reconstructed settlements of pile-dwellings and a museum containing material recovered by excavation. The five houses of the Bronze Age village in the lake are being rebuilt after their destruction by arson in 1976.

Bad Mergentheim

Land: Baden-Württemberg.
Vehicle registration: TBB (MGH).
Altitude: 210 m. – Population: 20,000.
Post code: D-6990. – Dialling code: 0 79 31.
ⓘ **Städtisches Kultur- und Verkehrsamt**,
Marktplatz 3;
tel. 5 72 32.

HOTELS. – *Parkhotel*, Lothar Daiker Str. 6, 180 b., SB, sauna; *Kurhotel Victoria*, Poststr. 2, 140 b.; *Deutschmeister*, Ochsengasse 7, 100 b.; *Kurhotel Haus Bundschu*, Cronbergstr. 15, 80 b.; *Garni am Markt*, H. H. Ehrler Platz, 40, 52 b.; *Garni in den Herrenwiesen*, Herrenwiesenstr. 30, 40 b.; *Kurhotel Steinmeyer*, Wolfgangstr. 2, 25 b. – CAMPING SITE: Willinger Tal.

RESTAURANTS. – *Kettlers Weinstube Zum Rebstöckchen*, Krummer Gasse 12, *Solymar*, Erlenbachweg (near Kurpark).

Bad Mergentheim lies in the valley of the Tauber, ringed by hills covered with forests and vineyards. It has three mineral springs containing carbonic acid and a high proportion of salt (the Karls-, Wilhelms- and Albertquelle) and one brine spring (the Paulsquelle), which are used in both drinking and bathing cures for affections of the gall bladder, liver, stomach and intestines. The historic old town forms an attractive counterpart to the modern spa installations.

The Meersburg

Castle of Teutonic Order, Bad Mergentheim

HOTELS. – *Riesen*, Hauptstr. 97, 24 b. (one of the oldest inns in Germany: 1590); *Brauerei Keller*, Hauptstr. 66, 34 b.; *Schönenbrunnen*, Mainstr. 75, 32 b., terrace overlooking Main; *Deutscher Hof*, Mainstr. 33, 27 b.

RESTAURANTS. – *Fränkische Weinstube*, Hauptstr. 111; *Hopfengarten*, Ankergasse 16; *Anker*, Hauptstr. 31.

This picturesque little Lower Franconian town with its beautiful half-timbered houses and narrow lanes, still enclosed within its walls and gate towers, is attractively situated between the Odenwald and the Spessart on the narrow left bank of the Main, under a steep wooded hill crowned by the Mildenburg. Along with Wertheim, Miltenberg is the most visited tourist resort between Aschaffenburg and Würzburg.

HISTORY. – First recorded in 1058, Mergentheim became a base of the Teutonic Order in 1229, and from 1525 to 1809 it was the residence of the High Master of the Order. In 1828 a shepherd discovered its medicinal springs, and a hundred years later, in 1929, the bathing establishment and pump room were built and the town developed as a spa.

SIGHTS. – In the pretty Marktplatz stands the *Town Hall* (1564), with the late Gothic *Town Parish Church* (13th c.: R.C.) just N of it. S of the square is *St Mary's Church* (14th c.: R.C.). – On the edge of the old town is the 16th c. **Deutschordensschloss**, formerly the residence of the High Master of the Teutonic Order (now the Museum of the Teutonic Order, etc.), with the *Schlosskirche* (Evang.), built 1730–35 to the design of Balthasar Neumann and François Cuvilliés. – From here the *Schlosspark* leads to the spa establishment on the right bank of the Tauber, with the **Kursaal**, *pump room* and *indoor promenade, visitors' centre and bathing facilities* and the *Kurpark*.

SURROUNDINGS. – **Stuppach Church** (6 km S), with a famous *Madonna by Grünewald. – *Schloss **Weikersheim** (11 km E), with a magnificent Knights' Hall.

Miltenberg

Land: Bavaria. – Vehicle registration: MIL.
Altitude: 128 m. – Population: 9800.
Post code: D-8760. – Dialling code: 0 93 71.
ⓘ **Städtisches Verkehrsbüro**, Town Hall;
tel. 6 72 72.

Schnatterloch, Miltenberg

HISTORY. – The old settlement here was incorporated by the Romans in the Limes, which reached the Main at this point. Miltenberg obtained its municipal charter about 1237. It went through many vicissitudes in the course of its history, belonging successively to Mainz, Leiningen, Baden and Hesse before becoming Bavarian in 1816.

SIGHTS. – The charming old-world *MARKTPLATZ is lined with half-timbered buildings; *Market Fountain* of 1583. On the N side of the square is *St James's* parish church (14th c.: R.C.), with towers of 1829. Other features of interest are the 15th c. *house at No. 185*; the former *Amtskellerei* (municipal cellars: 16th c.), with the *Heimatmuseum*; a former inn, *Zur güldenen Cron*; and the *Schnatterloch*, a gate-tower which gives access to the **Mildenburg** (13th–16th c.: civic property), in the forest above the town. – In the HAUPTSTRASSE, a little way E of the Marktplatz, is the *Hotel Zum Riesen*, a half-timbered building of 1590 patronised by King Gustavus Adolphus of Sweden, Wallenstein and Prince Eugene of Savoy. (Photograph, p. 261.) In Engelplatz is the Baroque *Franciscan Church* (1667–87). At the E end of the Hauptstrasse is the *Würzburg Gate* (1379). – At the *Spitzer Turm* (Pointed Tower) or Mainz Gate, on the W side of the town, is *St Lawrence's Chapel* (15th–16th c.).

SURROUNDINGS. – Amorbach Abbey Church (8 km S), with a sumptuous Rococo· interior and a famous Baroque *organ.

Minden

Land: North Rhineland-Westphalia.
Vehicle registration: MI.
Altitude: 46 m. – Population: 78,000.
Post code: D-4950. – Dialling code: 05 71.
ⓘ **Verkehrs- und Werbeamt,**
Ritterstr. 31,
tel. 8 93 85.

HOTELS. – *Exquisit*, in den Barenkampen 2a, 78 b., SB, sauna; *Bad Minden*, Portastr. 36, 66 b.; *Kruses Parkhotel*, Marienstr. 108, 40 b.; *Silke* (no rest.), *Fischerglacis* 21, 34 b., SB; *Victoria* (no rest.), Markt 11, 68 b., sauna; *Marienhöhe* (no rest.), Marienglacis 45, 40 b. – *Naturfreundehaus Häverstädt*, in Minden Häverstädt, Am Hang 5, 35 b.

RESTAURANTS. – *Ratskeller*, Markt 1 (with "Die Tonne" beer-cellar); *Laterne*, Hahler Str. 38; *Domschänke*, Kleiner Domhof 14; *Akropolis*, Brüderstr. 2 (Greek). – IN HADDENHAUSEN: *Landgasthaus Niemeier*, Bergkirchener Str. 244.

EVENTS. – *Harbour concerts* (May–Sept., Sat. 10.30 a.m.), at Schachtschleuse; organ recitals.

The cathedral city of Minden, comprised of an upper and a lower town, lies in the Weser lowlands N of the Porta Westfalica. It is the chief town of a Kreis (district) and an important railway junction, as well as the point of intersection between two major waterways, the Weser and the Mittelland Canal. Although it is not usually thought of as a spa, it possesses a brine bathing establishment.

HISTORY. – The town grew out of a fishing settlement at the ford on the Weser. In 798 Charlemagne founded the bishopric of Minden, and

this led to the emergence of a second nucleus of settlement round the bishop's fortified residence and cathedral. In the 10th c. a trading settlement came into being round the market square. In the 15th c. the town became a member of the Hanse. After the Thirty Years War Minden fell to Brandenburg, and the Great Elector developed it into a fortress and garrison town. One of the battles of the Seven Years War was fought at Minden (1759). In 1873 the old fortifications were pulled down and gave place to streets and gardens. In our own day this former town of officials and soldiers has developed into a flourishing commercial and industrial city.

SIGHTS. – In the DOMHOF in the LOWER TOWN stands the ***Cathedral** (11th–13th c., restored after war damage: R.C.), the most important early Gothic hall-church in Westphalia, with an early Romanesque W end and a late Romanesque choir and transept. The *Treasury contains valuable works of religious art, including the Minden Cross of 1070. In the nearby MARKTPLATZ is the **Town Hall**, with a vaulted arcade of the 13th c. (restored). In the adjoining SCHARN, Minden's principal business and shopping street, is the *Hagemeyer House*, a handsome Weser Renaissance mansion of 1592.

To the NW, on the highest point of the UPPER TOWN, is **St Mary's Church** (11th c., rebuilt in 14th c.: Evang.), with a tower 57 m high. S of this church is *St Martin's Church*, a Gothic rebuilding of an earlier Romanesque basilica (late Gothic choir-stalls, Renaissance font, Baroque organ); behind it is the *Windloch*, a picturesque narrow half-timbered house – the smallest in the town. From here RITTERSTRASSE runs S past the *Museum of History, Local History and Ethnology* to the late Gothic *St Simeon's Church* and the immediately adjoining *St Maurice's Church* (15th c.). – To the N of the town is the **waterway crossing**, where a 375 m long aqueduct carries the Mittelland Canal over the Weser at a height of 13 m. A link between the two waterways is provided by a lock, the *Schachtschleuse*.

SURROUNDINGS. – ***Porta Westfalica** (6 km S), where the Weser breaks through the Wesergebirge and Wiehengebirge in a breach 800 m wide. To the W, on the Wittekindsberg, is the *Emperor William Monument*, inaugurated 1896 (magnificent view of Weser valley); to the E, on the steep Jakobsberg (236 m), is a *telecommunications tower*. – **Potts Park**, in Dützen (5 km W), a paradise for children, with a model railway layout, an aerodrome, a veteran steam locomotive, an aeroplane, a submarine, a children's railway and a variety of other attractions. **Mühlenstrasse** in the district of Minden-Lübbecke (within the town boundaries; 34 mills).

Mittenwald

Land: Bavaria. – Vehicle registration: GAP.
Altitude: 920 m. – Population: 8600.
Post code: D-8102. – Dialling code: 0 88 23.
ⓘ **Kurverwaltung/Verkehrsamt,**
Dammkarstr. 3;
tel. 10 51.

HOTELS. – *Post,* Obermarkt 7, 165 b., terrace, SB, sauna, solarium; *Rieger,* Dekan Karl Platz 28, 80 b., SB, sauna, solarium; *Jägerhof,* Partenkirchner Str. 35, 120 b.; *Wetterstein,* Dekan Karl Platz 1, 60 b., SB, sauna, solarium; *Gästehaus Sonnenbichl* (no rest.), Klausnerweg 32, 47 b., sauna, solarium; *Gästehaus Franziska* (no rest.), Innsbrucker Str. 24, 35 b., sauna, solarium; *Wipfelder* (no rest.), Riedkopfstr. 2, 30 b., sunbathing terrace. – *Berghotel Café Latscheneck,* Kaffeefeld 1 (1100 m), 35 b., SB, sauna; *Lautersee,* on the Lautersee, 10 b.

RESTAURANTS. – *Arnspitze,* Innsbruker Str. 68; *Bozner Weinstuben,* Obermarkt 54 (with café).

The health and winter sports resort of Mittenwald, a town of violin-makers and of beautiful old houses decorated with frescoes, is magnificently situated in the green valley of the Isar immediately under the towering Karwendel chain, framed in the S and W by wooded hills above which the Wetterstein rears its handsome peak.

HISTORY. – In the Middle Ages Mittenwald was an important trading station on the road from Augsburg into Italy and on the River Isar, from this point navigable by rafts. In the 17th c. Matthias Klotz, who had served his apprenticeship with Amati in Cremona, introduced the craft of violin-making.

SIGHTS. – The best places to see the houses with frescoed fronts, set in staggered formation along the street, are the UNTERMARKT and OBERMARKT. In front of the beautiful Baroque **Parish Church** (by Josef Schmuzer, 1738–45), with a

Pünderich, on the Moselle

tower painted by Matthäus Günther, stands a *monument to Matthias Klotz* (1653–1743), founder of the Mittenwald violin-making industry. In the nearby Ballenhausgasse is the *Violin-Making and Heimatmuseum.*

SURROUNDINGS. – *Western Karwendel peak (2385 m: to E); cableway to *Hohe Karwendelgrube* (2244 m: restaurant). – **Hoher Kranzberg** (1391 m: to W); chair-lift to *St. Anton,* cableway from there. – **Lautersee** (1010 m: 3 km W), with hotel, swimming pool and hire of rowing-boats.

Moselle Valley

Land: Rhineland-Palatinate.
ⓘ **Fremdenverkehrsverband Rheinland-Pfalz,**
Löhnstr. 103–105, D-5400 Koblenz;
tel. (02 61) 3 10 79.

The beautiful River *Moselle (German: Mosel) is one of the longest of the Rhine's tributaries, with a total course of 514 km, of which 242 km are in Germany. It rises at the Col de Bussang in the French Vosges. It owes its name to the Romans (Mosella, the "little Meuse").

After entering German territory the river passes through the wide Trier basin and then makes its way in countless meanders through the Rhenish Uplands between the Hunsrück and the Eifel to flow into the Rhine at Koblenz. From Perl to Trier is the UPPER MOSELLE, from Trier to Bullay the MIDDLE MOSELLE, from Bullay to Koblenz the LOWER MOSELLE. Since 1964 the Moselle has been canalised, with a series of ten dams (at Trier, Detzem, Wintrich, Zeltingen, Enkirch, St. Aldegund, Fankel, Müden, Lehmen and Koblenz) to regulate its flow.

The Moselle flows through a landscape of steep slaty slopes planted with vines, upland forests and hills crowned with castles. The Romans brought the vine to the Moselle valley, and the "Neumagen wine-ship" in Trier Museum bears early artistic witness to the practice of wine-growing. From the 12th c. onwards the princes of the Church promoted the production of wine with the help of the monasteries and other religious houses. Among the best-known wine towns are *Bernkastel-Kues, Zell, Traben-Trarbach, Wehlen* and *Cröv;* Bernkasteler Doktor and Wehlener Sonnenuhr rank among the finest Moselle wines.

The ancient traffic route which runs through the Moselle valley is now followed by a host of tourists. The principal tourist centres are the old episcopal city of **Trier** with its Cathedral and ****Porta Nigra**, **Bernkastel-Kues** with its delightful nooks and corners of half-timbered houses and **Cochem**, over which looms the frowning Reichsburg, rebuilt between 1869 and 1877. Above a lateral valley on the lower Moselle rears ***Burg Eltz** with its high gables, towers and oriel windows, one of Germany's finest castles.

A BOAT TRIP on the Moselle offers many attractions. The MOSELLE WINE HIGHWAY also follows the river's numerous windings. The railway, on the other hand, takes a short cut, making its way across the great loop at Cochem in a tunnel 4·2 km long. Regrettably, the once famous "drinkers' railway" between Bullay and Trier no longer runs.

Münden

(Hannoversch Münden)

Land: Lower Saxony.
Vehicle registration: GÖ.
Altitude: 120–320 m. – Population: 28,000.
Post code: D-3510. – Dialling code: 0 55 41.
(i) **Städtisches Verkehrsbüro**, Town Hall; tel. 7 53 13.

HOTELS. – *Schmucker Jäger*, Wilhelmshäuser Str. 45, 64 b.; *Berghotel Eberburg*, Tillyschanzenweg 14, 51 b.; *Jagdhaus Heede*, Hermannshäger Str. 81, 34 b; *Schloss-schänke*, Vor der Burg 7, 24 b. – IN WERRA VALLEY: *Gästehaus Weitemeyer* (no rest.), 22 b. – YOUTH HOSTEL: Prof.-Oelkers-Weg 10, 180 b. – CAMPING SITES: *Oberer Tanzwerder*, on an island in the Fulda; *Zella im Werratal*, near Laubach; *Camping Hemeln*, on right bank of Weser.

RESTAURANT. – *Brauereischänke*, Tanzwerderstr. 9.

CAFÉ. – *Café Beer*, Lange Str. 61.

EVENTS. – *"The Play of Dr Eisenbart"* (from Whit Sunday – on Sundays in summer at 11.15 a.m. in front of the Rathaus).

This old-world little town is attractively situated on a tongue of land between the rivers Werra and Fulda (which join here to form the Weser) in a basin surrounded by the hills of the Reinhardswald, Bramwald and Kanfunger Wald. Alexander von Humboldt held that it was one of the world's seven most beautifully situated towns. It is a town of 16th and 17th c. half-timbered houses, still preserving some of its old defensive towers. It is also celebrated as the home of the notorious quack, Dr Johann Andreas Eisenbart, who died here in 1727.

HISTORY. – Excavations in St Blaise's Church have revealed that there was a substantial settlement here in the time of Charlemagne. The town is said to have been founded by Henry the Lion about 1170. By 1247 it had obtained the right of staple, which promoted its rise to prosperity, since it meant that all ships arriving in the town must discharge their goods and offer them for sale for three days at preferential prices, after which the goods must be conveyed on their way by Münden shippers or carriers. – In the 16th c. Duke Erich I of Brunswick-Lüneburg made Münden .his capital. In 1626, during the Thirty Years War, the town was captured, after a stout defence, by the Imperial general Tilly. The abolition of the right of staple in 1823 led to the town's economic decline, but it was given a fresh lease of life by the establishment of a Hanoverian garrison here in 1850, the foundation of the Prussian School of Forestry (until the mid 20th c. the faculty of forestry of Göttingen University) in 1868 and the development of industry and commerce. In 1973 the town's area was considerably increased by the incorporation of adjoining communes.

SIGHTS. – In the MARKTPLATZ, lined with half-timbered buildings, stands the **Town Hall**, a Gothic building to which Georg Crossmann added an imposing Weser Renaissance façade in 1603–13. Opposite it, to the S, is **St Blaise's Church** (13th–16th c.), with a bronze font of 1392, a sandstone pulpit of 1493 and the tombstone of Duke Erich I (a fine piece of carving by Loy Hering). – On the S side of the old town, adjoining the gardens which mark the site of the old fortifications, is the 17th c. *St Giles' Church*, with the *tombstone* of the famous *Dr Eisenbart* (1663–1727) on the N outside wall. – To the NE of the old town, close to the Werra, is the **Schloss** (16th and 18th c.), with an excellent *Heimatmuseum* (china, models of half-timbering, history and crafts of the town; "White Horse Room" and "Roman Room", with 16th c. frescoes). A little way W are the Kunsthandwerkerhof "Ochsenkopf" (skilled artisan's court, called "Ox-head") and a stone *bridge* over the Werra (1397–1402). On the island of Unterer Tanzwerder between the Fulda and the Werra is the **Weserstein**, near which is the landing-stage used by the Upper Weser steamers.

SURROUNDINGS. – **Ziegenhagen Fairytale Zoo**, (about 10 km SE, with a car, motorcycle and iron-founding museum). – ***Bursfelde Abbey Church** (17 km N). The oldest part is the Romanesque W church (1104), to which the E church was added in 1130–40; both churches have rich fresco decoration. – ***Sababurg** (25 km NW), a former hunting lodge of the Landgraves of Hesse, still impressive as a ruin, on a basaltic hill in the Reinhardswald. The old chancery building is now a *hotel*. *Game park*, with fallow deer, wild boars, moufflons, wild horses, aurochs and bison.

Munich (München)

Land: Bavaria. – Vehicle registration: M.
Altitude: 520 m. – Population: 1,300,000.
Post code: D-8000. – Dialling code: 0 89.
ⓘ **Verkehrsamt,** Am Bahnhof (Bayerstr. exit);
tel. 23 91 256/259.
Information Bureau in Stachus-Passage.

HOTELS. – **Vier Jahreszeiten,* Maximilianstr. 17, 591
b. (*"Walterspiel"* restaurant), SB, sauna, solarium;
*Hilton International, Am Tucherpark 7, 982 b., SB,
sauna, solarium; **Bayerischer Hof und Palais Mont-
gelas,* Promenadenplatz 2, 663 b., SB, sauna,
solarium; **Grand Hotel Continental,* Max Joseph Str.
5, 222 b. ("Conti-Grill"); **Der Königshof,* Karlsplatz
25, 200 b.; *Eden Hotel Wolff,* Arnulfstr. 4, 319 b.;
Bundesbahnhotel, at Main Station, Bahnhofplatz 2,
300 b.; *Deutscher Kaiser,* Arnulfstr. 2, 300 b.;
Excelsior, Schützenstr. 11, 200 b.; *Drei Löwen,*
Schillerstr. 8, 190 b.; *Ambassador,* Mozartstr. 4, 100
b.; *Reinbold* (no rest.), Adolf Kolping Str. 11, 100 b.;
Torbräu, Tal 37, 160 b.; *Haberstock* (no rest.),
Schillerstr. 4, 116 b.; *Ariston* (no rest.), Unsöldstr. 10,
112 b.; *Schlicker* (no rest.), Tal 74, 109 b.; *Concorde*
(no rest.), Herrnstr. 38, 97 b.

IN BOGENHAUSEN: **Sheraton,* Arabellastr. 6, 1300 b.,
SB, sauna, solarium; **Arabella,* Arabellastr. 5, 431 b.,
SB, solarium; **Crest Hotel,* Effnerstr. 99, 303 b. – IN
HAIDHAUSEN: *Penta Hotel,* Hochstr. 3, 1176 b., SB,
sauna, solarium. – IN OBERWIESENFELD: **Olympiapark
Hotel,* Helene Mayer Ring 12, 105 b., sauna, solarium.
– IN SCHWABING: **Holiday Inn,* Leopoldstr. 194, 720 b.
("Yellow Submarine" night-spot), SB, sauna, sola-
rium; **Residence,* Artur Kutscher Platz 4, 300 b., SB;
Motel Vitalis, Kathi Kobus Str. 24, 250 b., SP.

YOUTH HOSTELS. – Wendl-Dietrich-Str. 20, 585 b.;
Jugendgästehaus, Miesingstr. 4, 344 b. – CAMPING
SITES. *Campingplatz Thalkirchen,* Thalkirchen;
Waldcamping, Obermenzing; *Nordwest,* Ludwigs-
feld; *Langwieder See,* 50 m from lake.

RESTAURANTS. – **Boettner,* Theatinerstr. 8; **Kafer-
schänke,* Schumannstr. 1; *Maximilianstuben,*
Maximilianstr. 27; **Aubergine,* Maximiliansplatz 5;
Mövenpick, in Künstlerhaus, Lenbachplatz 8; *Im
Olymp,* Spiridon-Louis-Ring 7 (revolving restaurant
at 182 m); *Dallmayr,* Dienerstr. 14; *Ratskeller,*
Marienplatz 8; *Haxnbauer,* Münzstr. 5; *Donisl,*
Weinstr. 1.
FOREIGN CUISINE: **Tantris,* Johann-Fichte-Str. 7; **Le
Gourmet,* Ligsalzstr. 46 (French); **Piroschka,* Prinz-
regentenstr. 1 (Hungarian); **El Toula,* Sparkassenstr.
5 (Italian); *Chesa Rüegg,* Wurzerstr. 18 (Swiss).

WINE-RESTAURANTS. – **Weinhaus Schwarzwäl-
der,* Hartmannstr. 8; *Weinkruger,* Maximilianstr. 21;
Torggelstubend, Am Platzl 6; *Pfälzer Weinprobier-
stube,* Residenzstr. 1.

BEER-HOUSES. – **Hofbräuhaus,* Platzl 9 (a famous
old establishment; brass music daily); *Augustiner-
Keller,* Arnulfstr. 52; *Franziskaner-Fuchsenstuben,*
Perusastr. 5; *Mathäser Bierstadt,* Bayerstr. 5; *Salvator-
Keller,* Hochstr. 77; *Pschorr-Bierhallen,* Neuhauser
Str. 11; *Spatenhof,* Neuhauser Str. 26.

CAFÉS. – *Café am Dom,* Marienplatz 2; *Feldherrnhalle,* Theatinerstr. 38; *Glockenspiel,* Marienplatz 28;
Hag, Residenzstr. 26; *Kreutzkamm,* Maffeistr. 4;

Luitpold, Brienner Str. 11; *Zur Schönen Münchnerin,*
Karl-Scharnagl-Ring 60.

EVENTS. – **Fasching** (Shrovetide carnival, with
Fasching ball); *Maidult* (May Fair); **Oktoberfest*
(beer festival) on the Theresienwiese, with ceremonial
entry of innkeepers and parade in traditional costume;
Christkindlmarkt (Christmas Market) in Marienplatz.

BAVARIAN FILM TOUR. – From 1 Apr. to 31 Oct. the
Bavarian film town Geiselgasteig can be visited (one
and a half hours, daily 9 a.m. to 4 p.m.; prior notice
necessary for parties of 20 and over).

The capital of the *Land* of Bavaria
and Germany's third largest city lies
on the Isar some 40–60 km from the
Alps. It is famed as a centre of art and
learning, thanks to its higher educational establishments (University,
Technical University, Academies of
Television, the Cinema and Music),
scientific institutes, museums and
theatre. It is an attractive city, with
fine examples of Gothic, Renaissance, Baroque and neo-classical
architecture. Munich likes to call
itself a "world city with a heart", a
city which has preserved its charm in
spite of its irresistible growth, a city
of elegance and fashion and at the
same time a city of popular beer-
gardens.

Munich is the see of both a Roman
Catholic archbishop and an Evangelical
bishop, the headquarters of radio and
television corporations, a tourist centre,
an important road and rail junction, an
international airport, a great sporting city
(host to the Summer Olympics of 1972)
and a noted Carnival city.
The city's principal industries are precision engineering, the manufacture of
optical and electrical apparatus, the
construction of machinery and motor
vehicles, printing and publishing, clothing manufacture, brewing and the
marketing of fruit and vegetables.

HISTORY. – Munich owes its origin to Duke Henry
the Lion, who diverted the old salt road from
Reichenhall to Augsburg to cross the Isar here on a
new bridge near a monastic establishment: hence the
name Munich and the little monk (the "Münchner
Kindl") who figures in the city's coat of arms. In 1180
the town passed to Count Palatine Otto von
Wittelsbach, and became under Ludwig the Severe
(1253–94) the permanent residence of the Wit-
telsbachs, in 1506 capital of the united Duchy of
Bavaria and in 1806 capital of the Kingdom of Bavaria.
The real creator of modern Munich was King Ludwig I
(1825–48; d. 1868), who made it an art city of
European standing and a centre of German intellectual life. During the Second World War the city
suffered severe destruction by bombing.

Munich, with the Frauenkirche

SIGHTS. – The central point of old Munich is the busy MARIENPLATZ (flower-market), with the *Mariensäule* (1638) and the neo-Gothic **New Town Hall** (1867–1908). On the tower is a clock with mechanical figures (11 a.m. daily, and at 5 and 9 p.m. in summer); from the gallery there are magnificent views of the city and surrounding area, with the Alps to the S. On its E side is the *Old Town Hall* (15th c.), with the original Council Chamber above the arched carriage entrance. To the S is **St Peter's Church**, probably founded about 1050 as the town's first parish church, with a tower familiarly known as "Alter Peter" (famous *view). SE of the church is Munich's well-known **Food Market** (Viktualienmarkt: fruit and vegetables, meat and cheese). SW of the church, in St.-Jakobs-Platz, are the **Municipal Museum** (history and culture of the town; museum of photography and film; collections of puppets and musical instruments; brewing museum) and the Baroque *Ignaz Günther Houses*. – W of St.-Jakobs-Platz, in SENDLINGER STRASSE (at the far end of which is the 14th c. *Sendlinger Tor*), is the *Asamkirche (St John of Nepomuk), one of the most fanciful creations of South German Rococo, built by the Asam brothers in 1733–46 close to their own house.

E of Marienplatz is the street called the TAL ("Valley"), leading to the 14th c. *Isartor* (restored 1972: unusual Karl Valentin Museum). At the near end of this street, on right, is the Gothic *Church of the Holy Ghost* (13th–14th c.). A short distance N is the *Alter Hof*, the first residence of the Dukes of Bavaria (1252). In the nearby Platzl is the popular *Hofbräuhaus*.

W of Marienplatz are KAUFINGER STRASSE and NEUHAUSER STRASSE (pedestrian precinct). Off Kaufinger Strasse to the N is the *Frauenkirche, Munich's Cathedral, an imposing late Gothic brick-built church (by Jörg Ganghofer, 1468–88), whose twin domed towers are a characteristic Munich landmark. The interior (restored) has fine 15th and 16th c. *stained glass. Under the S tower is the *tomb (1622) of Emperor Ludwig the Bavarian (1282–1347). In the lower church (restored 1950) is the episcopal and ducal burial vault. – Farther W along

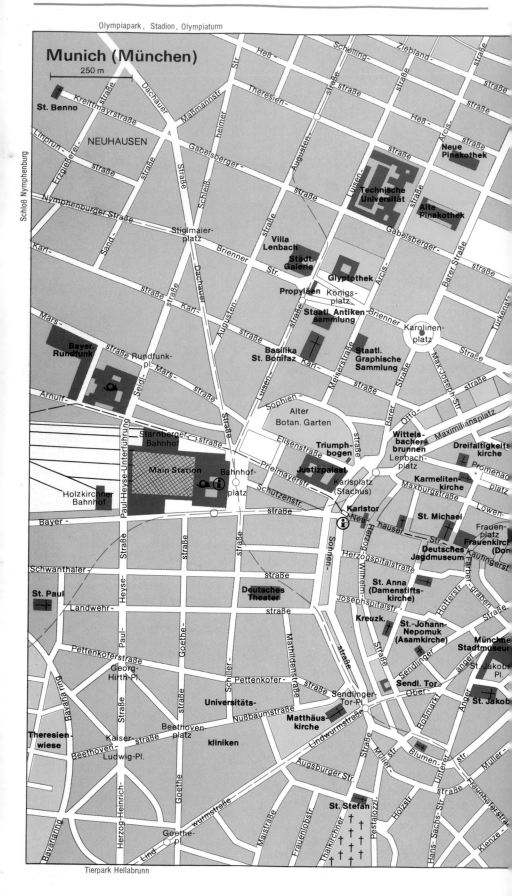

Olympiapark, Stadion, Olympiaturm

Munich (München)

250 m

Schloß Nymphenburg

St. Benno

NEUHAUSEN

Neue Pinakothek

Technische Universität

Alte Pinakothek

Stiglmaier-platz

Villa Lenbach

Städt. Galerie

Glyptothek

Propyläen Königs-platz

Staatl. Antiken-sammlung

Bayer. Rundfunk

Rundfunk-pl.

Basilika St. Bonifaz

Staatl. Graphische Sammlung

Karolinen-platz

Alter Botan. Garten

Starnberger Bahnhof

Triumph-bogen

Wittels-bacher-brunnen

Dreifaltigkeits-kirche

Lenbach-platz

Promenade

Main Station

Bahnhof-platz

Justizpalast

Karmeliten-kirche

Maxburgstraße

platz

Holzkirchner Bahnhof

Schützenstr.

Karlsplatz (Stachus)

Karlstor

St. Michael

Löwen-

Frauen-platz

Frauenkirch (Dom)

Deutsches Jagdmuseum

Herzogspitalstraße

St. Anna (Damenstifts-kirche)

Schwanthaler-

St. Paul

Landwehr-

Deutsches Theater

Josephspitalstr.

Kreuzk.

St.-Johann-Nepomuk (Asamkirche)

Münchne Stadtmuseu

Pettenkoferstraße

Georg-Hirth-Pl.

Pettenkofer-

Sendlinger-Tor-Pl.

Sendl. Tor

St. Jakobs-Pl.

St. Jakob

Universitäts-

Matthäus-kirche

Theresien-wiese

Beethoven-platz

kliniken

Ludwig-Pl.

Augsburger Str.

Goethe-pl.

St. Stefan

Tierpark Hellabrunn

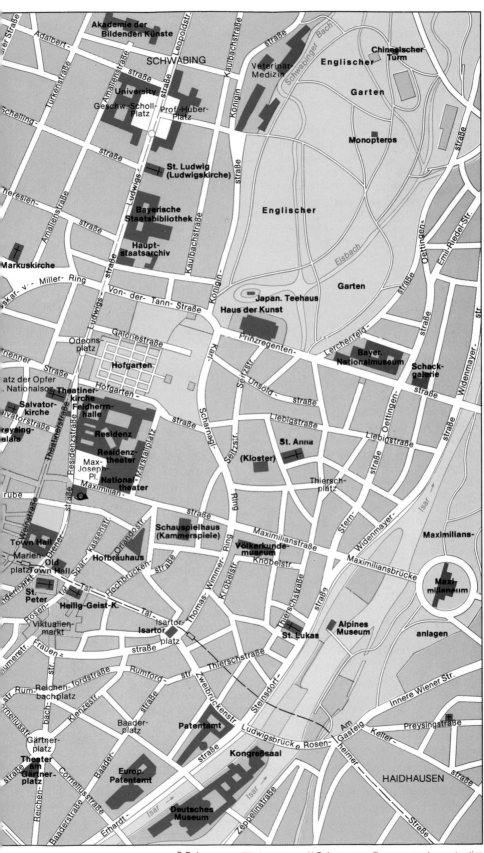

Neuhauser Strasse are the *German Hunting and Fishing Museum* (in the former
Augustinian church) and *St Michael's
Church* (Jesuit Church; formerly the
court church), a Renaissance building (by
F. Sustris, 1583–97) with an interior of
impressive spatial effect which marked an
epoch in the church architecture of
Catholic southern Germany. The burial
vault contains the remains of more than
30 members of the Wittelsbach family,
including King Ludwig II. – At the end of
the street is the 14th c. *Karlstor*, which
leads into the busy KARLSPLATZ, usually
known as **Stachus** (after an old · inn
which stood here), with a large underground shopping centre. On the W
side of the square are the *Law Courts*
(Justizpalast).

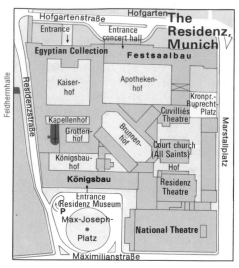

N of Karlsplatz is the *KÖNIGSPLATZ, a
masterly neo-classical composition by
Leo von Klenze (1816–48), the character
of which was altered by stone paving and
new building on the E side in 1935–37.
On the N side is the **Glyptothek** (by
Klenze, 1816–30; rebuilt), with an important collection of Greek and Roman
sculpture, including the famous *figures
from the Aegina temple. Opposite the
Glyptothek is the imposing neo-classical
building (1838–48; restoration completed 1967) which contains the *State
Collection of Antiquities** (gold and
silver articles, pottery, small sculpture,
glass, etc.). On the W side of the square
are the *Propylaea*, a triumphal gateway
(by Klenze, 1846–62) modelled on the
prototype on the Acropolis in Athens. – N
of the Königsplatz are the **Lenbach
House** (residence and studio of the
famous   painter   Franz   Lenbach,
1836–1904), now housing the *Lenbach
Gallery* and the *Municipal Gallery*, the
Technical University and the **Alte
Pinakothek** (by Klenze, 1826–36) as
well as the *New Pinakothek** (opened
1981), both important picture galleries.

From Königsplatz the elegant BRIENNER
STRASSE runs by way of KAROLINENPLATZ
(*obelisk* commemorating the 30,000
Bavarians who died in Russia in 1812) to
the ODEONSPLATZ, one of Munich's finest
squares, from which the imposing LUDWIG-
STRASSE (the grandest of Ludwig I's
monumental creations, 1 km long), runs N
past the *State Library*, *Ludwigskirche* and
University towards SCHWABING (an
artists', students' and entertainment
quarter). To the SW of the Odeonsplatz is

the *Theatinerkirche (17th–18th c.), in
Roman Baroque style, with a massive
dome 71 m high; the interior has rich
stucco decoration. SW at Prannerstrasse
10 we come to the *Siemens Museum*; E of
the church is the **Feldherrnhalle** (by
Friedrich Gärtner, 1840–44), modelled on
the Loggia dei Lanzi in Florence (statues
of the 17th c. general Tilly and Prince
Wrede, by Schwanthaler). – Farther E is
the **Residenz**, a complex of buildings
of the 16th–19th c., badly damaged
during the last war and since restored. In
Residenzstrasse is the Old Residenz
(1611–19), with the State Coin Collection; in Max-Joseph-Platz is the Königsbau, with the *Residenz Museum* (rooms
in period style, porcelain, silver, etc.) and
the *Treasury* (in E wing); on the Hofgarten
side are the Festsaalbau (like the Königsbau, built by Klenze 1826–42) and the
State Collection of Egyptian Art. In
the   Apotheken-Pavillon   ("Pharmacy
Pavilion") is the rebuilt *Old Residenz
Theatre* or Cuvilliés Theatre (fine Rococo
interior), formerly on the site now occupied by the New Residenz Theatre.

The **Hofgarten** (laid out 1613–15) on
the N side of the Residenz is enclosed on
its W and N sides by arcades; in the N
wing is the *German Theatre Museum*,
with portraits of artists, sketches of
scenery, manuscripts, etc. From the NE
corner of the Hofgarten PRINZREGENTEN-
STRASSE runs along the S side of *English
Garden**, a park of 350 hectares laid out
1789–1832, with clumps of trees and
areas of grass, a *monopteral temple*, a
Chinese tower and the *Kleinhesseloher
See*. At the near end of this street,

on the right, is the **Prinz-Carl-Palais** (1803–11), now housing the Academy of Fine Arts. Farther along, on the left, are the **Haus der Kunst** (**Bavarian State Picture Collections*; periodic special exhibitions and the *State Gallery of Modern Art*), the *****Bavarian National Museum**, one of the leading collections of German art and applied art (early German sculpture, tapestries, collection of Nativity groups) and the **Schack Gallery* (19th c. German painting). In Lerchenfeldstrasse, which goes off on the left, is the *State Prehistoric Collection*.

MAX-JOSEPH-PLATZ, S of the Residenz, is surrounded by monumental buildings. On the E side of the square is the *National Theatre* (Opera House, built 1811–18, restored 1959–63). Adjoining it is the *New Residenz Theatre*, a State theatre built in 1948–51 on the site of the Old Residenz Theatre, burned down in 1944. On the N side of the square is the Königsbau of the Residenz, on the S side the former Head Post Office (now Post Office No. 1).

From Max-Joseph-Platz MAXIMILIANSTRASSE, laid out 1852–59 under King Maximilian II in uniform architectural style, runs E to the Isar. At the near end, on right, is the *Mint*, with a beautiful inner courtyard (1565: entrance in Hofgraben); on left, where the street opens out into a little square, the *Regierungsgebäude* (Government Buildings, 1856–64); then, on right, the *State Museum of Ethnography*. At the end of the street, on the high right bank of the Isar, is the **Maximilianeum** (1857–74), now the seat of the Bavarian parliament, the Landtag.

Farther upstream the Ludwigsbrücke spans the Isar, crossing the MUSEUMSINSEL which here divides the river into two channels. On the left bank of the Isar is the *German and European Patent Office*. On the island is the *****German Museum** (Deutsches Museum), the largest museum of technology in the world, founded by Oskar von Miller, an engineer, in 1903. Here scientific discoveries and technological inventions are shown not only in splendidly conceived displays but in working models.

S of the city, at Thalkirchen, is ****Hellabrunn Animal Park**, a nature park in which the animals live in large open enclosures arranged according to the part of the world from which they come.

In the SW of Munich ($1\frac{1}{2}$ km from Karlsplatz) is the **Theresienwiese**, where the Oktoberfest is held. On the W side of the park is a figure of "Bavaria" (by Schwanthaler, cast 1850), 30 m high including the base (views). Behind it is the *Ruhmeshalle* (Hall of Fame; by Klenze, 1843–53), and adjoining this is the *Exhibition Park* (halls used for trade fairs, etc.). – In UNTERSENDLING lies the Westpark, the site of the IGA 83 (4th International Horticultural Exhibition in Germany).

To the NW of the city is ****Schloss Nymphenburg** (1664–1728), a group of buildings laid out round a large roundel and surrounded by a beautiful park with fountains. The main building contains sumptuously decorated apartments; particularly notable is King Ludwig I's "gallery

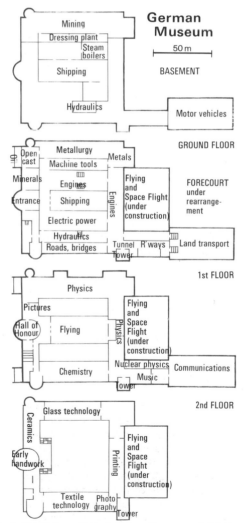

German Museum

50 m

BASEMENT

GROUND FLOOR

FORECOURT
under
rearrangement

1st FLOOR

2nd FLOOR

3rd FLOOR: Space Flight, Agriculture, Measures and Weight, Measurement of Time, Observatory.
5th FLOOR: Astronomy. 6th FLOOR: Planetarium.

In the Olympic Park, Munich

of Beauty'', with 24 portraits of women by the court painter Josef Stieler; in the S wing is the *Marstallmuseum* (Court Stables Museum). Among the buildings in the park the *Amalienburg*, a little hunting lodge built by François de Cuvilliés in 1734–38, is particularly fine. (Photograph, p. 49.) In the NE part of the main roundel is the *Nymphenburg State Porcelain Manufactory*, founded 1741. – N of the park is the beautiful *Botanical Garden* (café).

In the *Olympic Park (formerly called the Oberwiesenfeld), some 5 km NW of the city centre, are the 290 m high Olympic Tower (1965–68: revolving restaurant), the Olympic Stadium (80,000 spectators), the *Swimming Hall* (9000 spectators) and the *Sports Hall* (11,000 spectators), all covered by a *tent roof with a total area of 76,000 sq. m. To the W is the *Cycling Stadium*, to the N the *Olympic Village*. – To the E are the *BMW tower block* and the *BMW Automobile Museum*.

SURROUNDINGS. – "Concentration Camp" Memorial at **Dachau** (17 km N.). – **Schloss Oberschleissheim** (13 km N), with *Baroque gallery*. – **Schäftlarn Monastery church** (20 km S), with stucco work and frescoes by Johann Baptist Zimmermann. – **Starnberger See** (20 km SW to Starnberg). – **Ammersee** (30 km SW to Herrsching).

Münster

Land: North Rhineland-Westphalia.
Vehicle registration: MS.
Altitude: 62 m. – Population: 275,000.
Post code: D-4400. – Dialling code: 02 51.
ⓘ **Verkehrsverein**, Berliner Platz 22;
   tel. 4 04 95.

HOTELS. – *Mövenpick*, Kardinal von Galen Ring 65, on the Aasee, 220 b., sauna; *Kaiserhof* (no rest.), Bahnhofstr. 14, 150 b.; *Conti* (no rest.), Berliner Platz 2a, 84 b.; *Coerdehof*, Raesfeldstr. 2, 82 b.; *Martinihof*, Hörsterstr. 25, 50 b.; *Feldmann*, Klemenstr. 24, 48 b.; *Windsor* (no rest.), Warendorfer Str. 177, 42 b.; *Steinburg*, Mecklenbecker Str. 80, 23 b.; *Schloss Wilkinghege* (3 km N), Steinfurter Str. 374, 66 b. (golf); *Parkhotel Schloss Hohenfeld* (6 km W), 78 b.

– ON HILTRUPER SEE: *Waldhotel Krautkrämer*, 110 b., terrace overlooking lake, SB. – IN HANDORF: *Hof zur Linde*, 54 b.; *Deutscher Vater*, 36 b. – IN WOLBECK: *Thier-Hülsmann*, 31 b. – YOUTH HOSTEL: *Bernhard-Salzmann-Jugendherberge*, Bismarckallee 31 (by the Aasee), 148 b. – CAMPING SITE: *Wersewinkel*, Handorf.

RESTAURANTS. – *Pinkus Müller*, Kreuzstr. 4–10 (Münsterland specialities, Altbierbowle); *Altes Gasthaus Leve*, Alter Steinweg 37; *Stuhlmacher*, Prinzipalmarkt 6; *Wielers*, Spiekerhof 47; *Ratskeller*, Prinzipalmarkt 8.

WINE-BAR. – *Westfälischer Friede 1648* (17th c. setting; Baden wines, French cuisine).

CAFÉS. – *Schucan*, Prinzipalmarkt 24; *Grotemeyer*, Salzstr. 24.

EVENTS. – *Carnival*, with Rose Monday procession; *Send* (a fair held every year in March, June and Oct.); Christmas Market.

Münster, capital of Westphalia, situated on the River Aa and on the Dortmund-Ems Canal, is the geographical and economic centre of the Münsterland, the see of a Roman Catholic bishop and a university town. After heavy destruction during the last war it has been rebuilt in its old familiar style. Münster is a city of churches, of aristocratic mansions and handsome old burghers' houses. The *old town is now surrounded by a ring of gardens on the line of the old fortifications.

HISTORY. – The bishopric of Münster was founded by Charlemagne in 805, the first bishop being Liudger, the "apostle of the Frisians". In the 12th c. the town

Town Hall, Münster

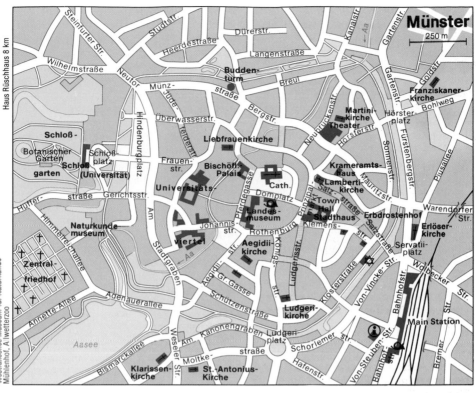

obtained its municipal charter and a circuit of walls, and in the 13th c. it became a member of the Hanse. In 1534–35 it was the scene of fearful atrocities by the Anabaptists, who sought to establish a "new Zion" in Münster. In 1648 the Peace of Westphalia, which ended the Thirty Years War, was signed at Münster and Osnabrück. Until 1803 Münster was the residence of a Prince-Bishop, and in 1816 it became capital of the Prussian province of Westphalia. After the Second World War it became part of the *Land* of North Rhineland-Westphalia.

SIGHTS. – In the PRINZIPALMARKT, surrounded by arcades and gabled houses, stands the Gothic **Town Hall** (14th c.; rebuilt), with the fine *Peace Chamber, in which the peace treaty between Spain and the Netherlands was signed in 1648. Next to it is the *Municipal Wine House*, a gabled building of the late Renaissance period. – At the N end of the Prinzipalmarkt is the magnificent *St Lambert's Church** (14th–15th c.); on the W tower are the three iron cages in which the bodies of the Anabaptists Johann von Leyden, Knipperdollinck and Krechting were displayed. A little way N is the *Krameramtshaus* of 1588 (now the Municipal Library). In SALZSTRASSE (No. 38) is the **Erbdrostenhof**, an aristocratic mansion built by the great Westphalian Baroque architect Johann Conrad Schlaun in 1754 (faithfully restored 1953–70). Behind it is the Baroque *St*

Clement's Church, another building by Schlaun which has been excellently restored.

W of the Prinzipalmarkt, in the spacious DOMPLATZ, stands the *Cathedral (1225–65: transitional style), the largest church in Westphalia (restored). On the S side, in the porch ("Paradise") of the western transept, are 13th c. figures of apostles and saints. Notable features of the interior, which is of impressive spatial effect, are the numerous tombs of bishops and canons (including Cardinal von Galen, d. 1946) and an astronomical clock of 1542 on the wall of the choir. The chapterhouse has fine panelling.

On the S side of Domplatz is the *Westphalian Provincial Museum of Art and Cultural History*, reopened in 1974, with sculpture, pictures, folk art and a remarkable collection of stained glass; S, on the Rothenburg, the *Westphalian Provincial Museum of Archaeology*. On the W side of the square is the *Bishop's Palace*. – A short distance NW of Domplatz is the Gothic *Liebfrauenkirche* or *Überwasserkirche* (1340–46), with a richly articulated tower.

On the W side of the Old Town is the former **Prince-Bishop's Palace** (by Johann Conrad Schlaun, 1767–73), which now houses the *Wilhelm University of Westphalia*. Behind it is the magnificent SCHLOSSGARTEN (restaurant), with a *Botanic Garden*.

Still farther S is the **Aasee** (40 hectares) Münster's paradise for water sports enthusiasts (sailing school, hire of sailing boats and canoes). – SW of the lake on the Sentruper Höhe are the *Mühlenhof Open-Air Museum* and the *All-Weather Zoo, opened 1974 (2000 animals of 470 species); display by dolphins; nearby stands the new *Westphalian Provincial Museum of Natural History* (Planetarium).

A notable example of modern design is the *Central Clinic* in Roxeler Strasse.

SURROUNDINGS. – **Rüschhaus** (7 km NW): a Baroque house built by J. C. Schlaun in 1745–49 as a summer residence, later occupied by the Westphalian poetess Annette von Droste-Hülshoff (Droste Museum). – **Haus Hülshoff** (10 km W): a charming moated castle (16th c.) in which Annette von Droste-Hülshoff was born in 1797 (Droste Museum). – **Baumberge** (20 km W): a ridge of hills over 180 m high (Longinus Tower) in the middle of the wide park-like landscape of the Münsterland; a favourite outing of the citizens of Münster. – **Burg Vischering**, Lüdinghausen (28 km SW): once a castle belonging to the Bishops of Münster, now housing an interesting *Münsterland Museum*. The **Heimathaus Munsterland** in Telgte (12 km E) is a centre of Westphalian ethnology.

Münsterland

Land: North Rhineland-Westphalia.
ⓘ **Landesverkehrsverband Westfalen,**
Balkenstr. 40, D-4600 Dortmund 1;
tel. (02 31) 57 17 15 or 54 22 21 75.

Between the Teutoburg Forest and the River Lippe lies the Münsterland, a region which is sometimes flat and sometimes rolling or hilly (Baumberge, Beckumer Berge), with much fertile soil but also with large areas of sand and heathland and extensive stretches of moorland.

It is a land of hedged fields, of beechwoods, of substantial farmhouses; of moated castles and country houses, of cathedrals and village churches, of roadside crosses; of lonely "Pättkes" and of busy and friendly inns in which the local people still speak the homely Low German dialect of the Münsterland as they eat their ham and drink their *Korn*.
The centre of the region is the cathedral city of **Münster**. *Telgte*, a short distance

away, is a popular place of pilgrimage. *Warendorf* is noted as the Westphalian horse-breeding centre and the headquarters of the German Olympic Riding Committee. *Rheda-Wiedenbrück*, with its fine old half-timbered houses, was once the residence of a count, as was *Burgsteinfurt. Ahaus* was the summer residence of the Prince-Bishops of Münster. *Rheine, Gronau* and *Bocholt* are thriving textile towns. *Beckum* is noted for its cement works, whose presence can be detected from afar by their plumes of white smoke.

The *Borkenberge* near Haltern are a favourite gliding area; the *Halterner Stausee* (reservoir) caters for water sports enthusiasts, and canoeists can practise their sport on the rivers *Ems* and *Lippe, Werse* and *Vechte*.

Among the numerous MOATED CASTLES **Schloss Nordkirchen**, the "Westphalian Versailles", takes a leading place. **Burg Hülshoff**, near Münster, was the birthplace in 1797 of Annette von Droste-Hülshoff, Germany's finest woman poet. **Burg Vischering**, at Lüdinghausen, houses the interesting Münsterland Museum. **Burg Gemen**, near Borken, is now a Roman Catholic youth centre. – Westphalia's leading architect, who built palaces and country houses, churches and monasteries, fortifications and factories, was *Johann Conrad Schlaun* (1695–1773).

Nahe Valley

Land: Rhineland-Palatinate.
ⓘ **Fremdenverkehrsverband Rheinland-Pfalz,**
Löhrstr. 103–105, D-5400 Koblenz;
tel. (02 61) 3 10 79.

The Nahe, the little sister of the Moselle, rises in the Hunsrück and follows a winding course past forests and pastureland, sunny vine-clad slopes and sometimes sheer rock faces.

Along its banks are a series of picturesque little towns: **Idar-Oberstein**, the town of jewellery and precious stones, with its rock church; *Kirn*, over which looms the ruined Kyrburg; the health resort of *Sobernheim*, specialising in the Felke cure; **Bad Münster** *am Stein-Ebernburg*, at the foot of the porphyry wall of the *Rheingrafenstein*, which is exceeded in steepness only by the *Rotenfels*. Opposite Bad Münster is the *Ebernburg*, birthplace of the celebrated knight Franz von Sickingen (1481–1523) and refuge of the

Houses on the bridge, Bad Kreuznach

humanist Ulrich von Hutten. Bad Münster am Stein-Ebernburg and **Bad Kreuznach** have radioactive brine springs. A charming feature of Bad Kreuznach is its houses built on a bridge over the river. After a course of 116 km the Nahe flows into the Rhine at *Bingen*.

The vine was originally brought to the Nahe valley by Roman legionaries. The quartzites and slates, the Bunter sandstone, the clay and loess which make up its soil produce a **wine** whose special characteristic is its richness of colour. The Nahe wine-growing region thus offers the wine-lover ample opportunity of enlarging his experience.

Bad Nauheim

Land: Hesse. – Vehicle registration: FB.
Altitude: 144 m. – Population: 25,000.
Post code: D-6350. – Dialling code: 0 60 32.
(i) **Verkehrsamt der Kurverwaltung,**
    Ludwigstr. 20;
    tel. 34 41.
    Verkehrsverein, pavilion in Parkstr.;
    tel. 21 20.

HOTELS. – *Am Hockwald*, Carl Oelemann Weg 9, 210 b., SB, sauna; *Parkhotel am Kurhaus*, Nördlicher Park 16, 168 b., SB, sauna; *Grand Hotel Accadia*, Lindenstr. 15, 72 b. (Kosher food); *Blumes Hotel am Kurhaus*, Auguste Viktoria Str. 3, 28 b.; *Spöttel*, Luisenstr. 5, 50 b.

RESTAURANTS. – *Gaudesberger*, Hauptstr. 6; *Kurhaus-Restaurant*, Im nördlichen Park 12.

This spa resort in the Wetterau, situated on the eastern slopes of the Taunus with the River Usa flowing through it, is a town of regular streets and beautiful parks and gardens. Its hot brine springs, rich in carbonic acid, are used particularly

in the treatment of cardio-vascular disease, rheumatism and nervous complaints; it also provides courses of treatment for those who want to give up smoking.

SIGHTS. – In the **Sprudelhof** (Fountain Court), surrounded by Art-Nouveau bath-houses, are the *Friedrich-Wilhelm-Sprudel* (34 °C), the *Grosser Sprudel* (30°) and the *Ernst-Ludwig-Sprudel* (32°), with a total flow of 2½ million litres of brine a day. To the W, merging into the Taunus Forest, is the **Kurpark** (800 hectares), with the *Kurhaus* (large terrace) and the *hot brine bath*. To the NE is the *Grosser Teich* (rowing). – Along the S edge of the Kurpark runs PARKSTRASSE, the town's principal business and shopping street. – Farther S is the **Pump Room** (Trinkkuranlage), with numerous drinking fountains. On the SE of the town are extensive *"graduation works"* for the evaporation of brine. – To the W is the *Johannisberg* (269 m: observatory), from the top of which there is a view of the Steinfurt rose-growing region.

SURROUNDINGS. – A few kilometres S is the former free Imperial city of **Friedberg**, with a 14th–15th c. castle, a Baroque country house surrounded by a beautiful garden, and the Wetterau Museum.

Neckar Valley

Land: Baden-Württemberg.
(i) **Fremdenverkehrsverband   Neckarland-Schwaben,**
    Wollhaustr. 14, D-7100 Heilbronn;
    tel. (0 71 31) 6 90 61.

The Neckar, with a total length of 371 km, rises at Villingen-Schwenningen, on the eastern fringe of the Black Forest and enters the Rhine at Mannheim.

The first place of any size on its course is **Rottweil**, noted for its traditional Shrovetide "Fool's Leap". The picturesque little town of *Horb* still retains some of its walls and towers. *Rottenburg*, with its churches, is the see of a Roman Catholic bishop (jointly with Stuttgart). **Tübingen**, dominated by its castle, is an old and famous university town. **Esslingen**, has its fine Gothic Frauenkirche and Old Town Hall. Then come **Stuttgart**, capital of the *Land*, the old Baroque residence town of **Ludwigsburg** and Schiller's

Marbach. One of the most charming little towns in Germany is *Besigheim*, where the Neckar flows through a narrow passage in the limestone hills. It then passes the former free Imperial city of **Heilbronn**, known to tourists as the town of Käthchen, heroine of Kleist's play "Käthchen von Heilbronn". Between Heilbronn and Bad Wimpfen the valley becomes wider to accommodate not only the industrial area of *Neckarsulm* but also vineyards, orchards and fields of vegetables. *Bad Wimpfen* has the remains of an Imperial castle of the Staufen dynasty. Here the *Kocher* and the *Jagst* flow into the Neckar, as if to give it strength for its winding passage of 50 km through the Odenwald hills. The lower Neckar valley

Burg Hornberg on the Neckar

with its many castles offers some of the most beautiful river scenery in southern Germany. Particular highlights are *Schloss Guttenberg* (with the "Library of Wood"), *Burg Hornberg* (once the home of the famous knight Götz von Berlichingen, who died here in 1562), the picturesque *Zwingenberg, Hirschhorn* and the little town of *Neckarsteinach* with its four castles. At the famous and romantic old university town of **Heidelberg** the Neckar enters the Rhine plain, and at **Mannheim** it flows into the Rhine.

Between 1921 and 1968 the Neckar was canalised on the 200 km stretch from Plochingen to Mannheim (the *Neckar Canal*, with 30 regulatory dams). – PASSENGER SHIPS ply between Stuttgart and Besigheim, Heilbronn and Neckarzimmern, Heidelberg and Hirschhorn.

Nördlingen

Land: Bavaria. – Vehicle registration: DON (NÖ).
Altitude: 430 m. – Population: 18,500.
Post code: D-8860. – Dialling code: 0 90 81.
ⓘ **Verkehrsamt,** Marktplatz 15;
tel. 43 80.

HOTELS. – *Sonne,* Marktplatz 3, 54 b.; *Am Ring,* Bürgermeister-Reiger-Str. 14, 48 b.; *Altreuter* (no rest.), Marktplatz 11, 25 b.; *Schützenhof,* Kaiserwiese 2, 22 b.; *Mondschein,* Bauhofgasse 4, 18 b.; *Goldenes Lamm,* Schäfflesmarkt 3, 17 b. – YOUTH HOSTEL: Kaiserwiese 1, 80 b.

RESTAURANTS. – *Klösterle,* Beim Klösterle; *Goldenes Rad,* Löpsinger Str. 8.

CAFE. – *Eickmann,* Marktplatz 7.

EVENT. – *Open-air performances* in the Alte Bastei (summer).

Nördlingen, lying between the Swabian and the Franconion Alb, is the chief town of the fertile Ries depression (a crater 20–25 km across caused by the fall of a meteorite). It is one of the three charming old free Imperial cities (the others being Rothenburg and Dinkelsbühl) on the "Romantic Highway". In the *town centre stands St George's Church, surrounded by a circular core of old houses, two outer rings of 16th and 17th c. houses and a completely preserved circuit of medieval town walls.

HISTORY. – Nördlingen first appears in the records in 898 as a royal estate. From 1215 to 1803 it was a free Imperial city. In a battle fought here during the Thirty Years War (1634) an Imperial army defeated the Swedes.

SIGHTS. – In the MARKT, in the centre of the town, stands the late Gothic **St George's Church** (originally 1427–1505: Evang.). It has a Baroque high altar with late Gothic carved figures. From the 90 m high tower ("Daniel") there are splendid wide-ranging views. – N of the church is the late Gothic **Town Hall** (restored 1934), with a beautiful

Nördlingen from the air

Renaissance flight of steps (1618). Farther N, in the Hospital of the Holy Ghost, is the *Municipal Museum* (department of geology, prehistory and early history, history of art and history of the town). To the E, by the Eger are old tanners' houses. – There is a very attractive walk (¾ hour) on the wall-walk of the *town walls, with their gateways and towers (14th–16th c.).

North Frisian Islands

Land: Schleswig-Holstein.

ⓘ Fremdenverkehrsverband Schleswig-Holstein,
Niemannsweg 31, D-2300 Kiel;
tel. (04 31) 56 30 27.

The North Frisian Islands lie off the N part of the W coast of Schleswig-Holstein. Numerous prehistoric burial places bear witness to early human settlement in this area. The freedom-loving inhabitants of the islands asserted their independence against the kings of Denmark. Then in the 19th c. bathing resorts began to develop on the islands, with their health-giving oceanic climate and their unrestricted sunshine.

The most northerly and the largest of the islands is *Sylt (see p. 240), which can be reached either by rail over the 11 km long *Hindenburg Causeway* (cars loaded at Niebüll) or by air from Hamburg. This "pearl of the North Sea" attracts visitors with its mighty dunes, its spacious beaches and its wide range of recreational facilities. Its chief town is the fashionable North Sea health resort of *Westerland*, with its treatment establishment, indoor sea-water swimming pool (artificial waves), Casino and deep-sea aquarium. *Kampen*, on the Rotes Kliff, is a favourite resort of the "jet set", with old thatched Frisian houses. *List* is the most northerly German seaside resort, with the last moving dunes in Germany. The Lister Ellenbogen ("List Elbow") is a nature reserve, the home of many seabirds.

Föhr, the second largest of the islands (82 sq. km), lies in a sheltered position between Amrum and the coast. There is a ferry service from Dagebüll to its chief place, *Wyk*. The island offers excellent bathing and pleasant walks along the shoreline.

Amrum (area 20 sq. km: 10 km long, 3 km across) is an ideal place for family holidays. Its main bathing beach is *Kniepsand*, on the W side, with a beach 1 km in width and a great sweep of surf. From the resort of *Wittdün* at the NE tip of the island there are boat services to Wyk (on Föhr) and from there to the mainland.

Nordstrand (45 sq. km), off Husum, is connected with the mainland by a road causeway. A 24 km long dike surrounds the fenland area which until a devastating storm tide in 1634 was part of the mainland. In spite of its name ("North Strand") the island has no bathing beach. Trips to the seal banks are possible. – The island of **Pellworm** (38 sq. km), to the W, has a number of bathing places; boat service from Husum.

The neighbouring **Halligen** are ten fenland islands torn off the mainland in the 1634 storm tide, some of them inhabited. Their farmhouses are built on artificial mounds 4–6 m high. The largest of the Halligen are the two islands, protected by dikes, of *Langeness* (9·6 sq. km: linked with the mainland by a causeway, via the island of Oland) and *Hooge* (5·7 sq. km: boat connection with Pellworm).

One of the Halligen in a storm

North Sea Coast

Länder: Schleswig-Holstein, Lower Saxony and Bremen.

ⓘ Fremdenverkehrsverband Schleswig-Holstein,
Niemannsweg 31, D-2300 Kiel;
tel. (04 31) 56 30 27.
Fremdenverkehrsverband
Nordsee-Niedersachsen-Bremen,
Gottorpstr. 18, D-2900 Oldenburg/Oldb.;
tel. (04 41) 1 45 35.

The German North Sea coast, some 300 km long as the crow flies, is divided into two parts, the East

Frisian and the North Frisian areas, by the Elbe estuary. Off both stretches of coast lie a chain of islands, which have developed into popular holiday resorts (see East Frisian Islands, p. 113, and North Frisian Islands, p. 203). The coastal territory is flat fenland protected by dikes, outside which extends the Watt, formerly part of the mainland, now dry only at low tide. This is one of the largest bird reserves in Europe. – The mouths of the East Frisian rivers are protected from the inflow of sea-water by the "Siele", gate-like sluices which close automatically at high tide. – Off the North Frisian coast lie the Halligen, fenland islands, usually not protected by dikes, some of which are connected with the mainland by causeways.

A road runs along the coastal dikes of East Friesland to the departure points of the island boat services, where visitors can leave their cars in large parking garages. There are ferry services from *Norddeich* (for Juist, Norderney and Baltrum), *Nessmersiel* (for Baltrum), *Bensersiel* (for Langeoog), *Neuharlingersiel* (for Spiekeroog) and *Harle* (for Wangerooge).

The only bathing resorts of any size off the East Frisian coast are the islands of

Lighthouse on Amrum

Borkum (boats from Emden), *Juist, Norderney, Baltrum, Langeoog, Spiekeroog* and *Wangerooge*. There are also a number of smaller coastal resorts which offer bathing at high tide and walks on the Watt at low tide. **Cuxhaven** at the mouth of the Elbe, with its modern spa establishment is very popular; the small resorts of *Duhnen* and *Döse* and the nearby *Sahlenburg* have good beaches usable at any stage of the tide.

On the North Frisian coast is the attractive resort of *St. Peter-Ording*, with a beautiful sandbank which can be reached at low tide by car (sand yachting). The old crab-fishing port of *Büsum* is now also a seaside resort. A modern tourist attraction is walks on the Watt accompanied by music. Apart from these places the best known resorts are on the islands of **Sylt, Föhr* and *Amrum*. In summer there are boat services from *Dagebüll* to the Halligen and the North Frisian islands. – The island of *Heligoland* (see p. 150) is also a popular bathing resort.

Nuremberg (Nürnberg)

Land: Bavaria. – Vehicle registration: N.
Altitude: 330 m. – Population: 483,000.
Post code: D-8500. – Dialling code: 09 11.
ⓘ **Verkehrsverein**, Eilgutstr. 5.
　　Tourist Information, in Town Hall, Hauptmarkt, and Station (Mittelhalle); and Craft Centre (Information kiosk);
　　tel. 2 33 60.

HOTELS. – **Atrium Hotel*, Münchener Str. 25, 300 b., SB, sauna; **Grand Hotel*, Bahnhofstr. 1, 273 b., sauna; **Carlton*, Eilgutstr. 13, 175 b.; *Merkur*, Pillenreuther Str. 1, 240 b.; *Novotel*, Münchener Str. 340, 234 b., SB, sauna; *Crest Hotel*, Münchener Str. 283, 211 b.; *Am Sterntor*, Tafelhofstr. 8, 170 b.; *Deutscher Hof*, Frauentorgraben 29, 70 b. ("Holzkistl" restaurant). – YOUTH HOSTELS: Auf der Kaiserburg, 340 b.; *Jugend Hotel Nürnberg*, Rathsbergstr. 180 b. – CAMPING SITE.

RESTAURANTS. – *Zum Waffenschmied*, Obere Schmiedgasse 22; *Almosenmühle*, Mühlegasse 3 (Swiss); *Essigbrätlein*, Am Weinmarkt 3; *Pfeffermühle am Sterntor*, Vordere Sterngasse 30; *Ratsstuben*, Rathausplatz 2; *Till Eulenspiegel*, Am Weinmarkt 12.

"SAUSAGE PARLOURS". – *Bratwurst-Häusle*, Rathausplatz 1; *Bratwurst-Röslein*, Obstmarkt 1; *Bratwurst-Herzle*, Brunnengasse 11.

BEER-HOUSES. – *Bauhofstübla*, Johannesgasse 59; *Pilsstubhbe, Schnorrwastl*, Grasergasse 9; *Anno Domini 1438*, Augustinerstr. 7.

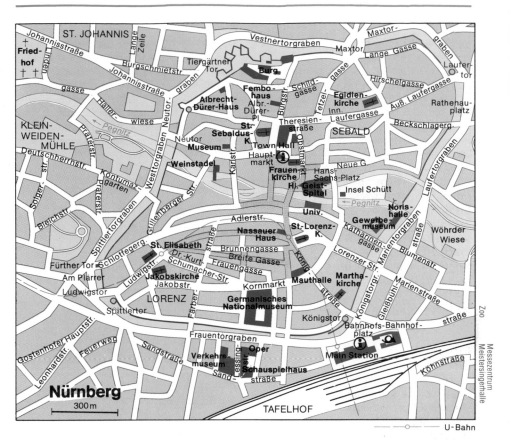

Nürnberg

300 m

TAFELHOF

——○—— U-Bahn

WINE RESTAURANTS. – *Böhms Herrenkeller*, Theatergasse 19; *Goldenes Posthorn*, Glöckleinsgasse 4; *Heiliggeistspital*, Spitalgasse 12; *Nassauer Keller*, Karolinenstr. 2 (historic old wine-house; music in the evening).

CAFÉS. – *Kröll*, Hauptmarkt 6; *Neef*, Winklerstr. 29; *Café "W"*, Johannesgasse 51.

EVENTS. – *Kaïserburg Concerts* (May–Aug.); *International Organ Week* (July); *Hans Sachs Plays* (July–Aug.); *Nuremberg Bardic Meeting* (early Aug.); *Autumn Fair* (end Aug.–mid Sept.); *Old Town Festival* (Sept.); **Christkindlmarkt* (end Nov.–24 Dec.).

The ancient and famous town of Nuremberg (German: Nürnberg), situated in the well-wooded plain of the Middle Franconian basin, on the River Pegnitz and the Rhine-Main-Danube Canal (the "Europa-Kanal"), is the second largest city in Bavaria, the capital of Franconia and one of the leading industrial and commercial towns of South Germany (manufacture of electrical equipment, cars, office machinery, toys, meat products and bakery and brewing). Nuremberg gingerbread (Lebkuchen) and sausages (Rostbratwürste) are famous. An International Toy Fair is held here every year. The faculties of economic and social sciences and of educational theory of the Friedrich Alexander University of Erlangen-Nuremberg are based in Nuremberg.

In the rebuilding of Nuremberg after severe destruction during the war the layout of the historic old town was preserved; and present-day Nuremberg, with its walls and towers, its castle and the restored parish churches of St Lawrence and St Sebaldus, presents a striking image of the old city.

HISTORY. – Nuremberg first appears in the records in 1050. Previously Emperor Conrad II had established a royal stronghold on the left bank of the Pegnitz and Henry III had set up a castle on the Nürnberg, a projecting crag on the right bank. At first the two settlements developed separately round their parish churches of St Lawrence and St Sebaldus, amalgamating to form a single community only at the beginning of the 14th c. The town received its charter from King Frederick II in 1219, and soon developed into the greatest trading town in Franconia (sharing with Augsburg the right of staple on the trade route from the East to northern Europe via Venice), to reach its greatest economic and cultural flowering at the beginning of the 16th c. In Nuremberg lived the humanist Willibald Pirkheimer (1470–1530), the cosmographer Martin Behaim (1459–1506), maker of the first globe, the poet Hans Sachs (1494–1576), Peter Henlein, who produced the first pocket watch, the "Nuremberg egg", in 1500, the sculptors Adam Kraft (1450–1509) and Veit Stoss (1445–1533), and the brassfounder Peter Vischer the Elder

The "Beautiful Fountain", Nuremberg

* tabernacle by Adam Kraft (1493–96), the crucifix by Veit Stoss on the high altar, the Krell Altar at the E end of the church (with the oldest surviving representation of the town, *c.* 1480) and the splendid stained glass in the choir (1477–93). – Outside the church, to the NW, is the *Fountain of Virtue* (1589), and opposite this is the tower-like *Nassauer Haus* (13th–15th c.: restaurant).

The Museum Bridge leads over the Pegnitz to the **Hauptmarkt** on St Sebaldus's Side, with the 14th c. *"Beautiful Fountain"*, decorated with numerous figures. On the E side of the square is the Gothic *Frauenkirche (R.C.: rebuilt). Above the fine porch is the "Männleinlaufen", an old clock with mechanical figures (the seven Electors pacing round Charles IV, in commemoration of the Golden Bull of 1356: noon daily). In the interior are the very fine *Tucher Altar (*c.* 1440) and two beautiful tombstones by Adam Kraft. – On the N side of the Hauptmarkt is the new **Town Hall** (1954), with the old building behind it (by Jakob Wolff, 1616–22, rebuilt: magnificent doorways on W side; dungeons). Between the two buildings is the famous *Gänsemännchen*, a fountain (*c.* 1555) in the form of a Franconian peasant carrying two geese from whose beaks water flows.

(1460–1529) and his sons. The Nuremberg school of painters of the 15th and 16th c. produced Michael Wolgemut (1434–1519) and his greatest pupil Albrecht Dürer (1471–1528), one of the great commanding figures in the history of German art. A major event in technological history was the opening of Germany's first railway line between Nuremberg and Fürth in 1835; and the continuing improvement in means of transport gave a fresh lease of life to the old trading routes and brought a new period of prosperity to Nuremberg.

SIGHTS. – The OLD TOWN is divided by the Pegnitz into two parts, named St Lawrence's Side and St Sebaldus's Side after their principal churches. The hub of the city's traffic is the Bahnhofplatz, in which are the Main **Railway Station**, The *Head Post Office*, the Frauentorturm and *Handwerkerhof Nürnberg* (old craftsman's house). From here the busy KÖNIG-STRASSE runs NW through St Lawrence's Side. At the near end of the street, on right, is *St Martha's Church* (14th c.), in which the mastersingers held their singing schools from 1578 to 1620. Farther along, on the left, is the old *Mauthalle* (1489–1502), originally built as a granary, later a custom house; "Mautkeller" restaurant.

In Lorenzer Platz is the Gothic *St **Lawrence's Church** (Evang.), Nuremberg's largest church (13th–15th c., restored). Outstanding among the many works of art it contains are the *"Annunciation" hanging in the choir (by Veit Stoss, 1517–18; restored 1971), the

W of the Town Hall is *St Sebaldus's **Church** (1225–73: R.C.), with a magnificent Gothic choir of 1379 (restored). On the outside of the choir is the Schreyer-Landauer tomb, a masterpiece by Adam Kraft (1492). Inside the church, on a pillar in the N aisle, is a "Madonna in an Aureole" (1420–25); in the choir is the **Tomb of St Sebaldus (1508–19), an outstanding example of the brass founder's art by Peter Vischer and his sons (silver sarcophagus of 1397 containing the saint's relics; on the E side Peter Vischer with his leather apron and chisel); behind the tomb is a striking *"Crucifixion" by Veit Stoss (1507 and 1520); new organ with 6000 pipes. – To the W, at Karlstr. 13, is the *Toy Museum*.

At the N end of Albrecht-Dürer-Strasse, under the Burgberg, is the **Albrecht Dürer House** (15th c., restored), in which Dürer lived from 1509 until his death in 1528; it contains copies of his works. At the nearby *Tiergärtner Tor* a complete little medieval square has been preserved. – In Burgstrasse, which runs from the Town Hall to the Burg (No. 15, on left), is the **Fembo House** (1591–c. 1600), the best preserved example of an old Nuremberg patrician house; it contains an *Old Town Museum*.

To the N of the old town is the * **Burg** (351 m), in which all legitimate German kings and emperors from 1050 to 1571 resided and many Imperial diets and courts were held. It covers a total area of 220 m by 50 m. Below is the so-called *Kaiserstallung* or Imperial Stables (built in 1495 as a granary, now a youth hostel; Noricama exhibition), and immediately W of this is the "Five-Cornered Tower", the oldest structure in the town (*c.* 1040), originally part of a Hohenzollern castle which stood here. Farther up is the *Kaiserburg* (Imperial castle), built in the 12th c. and several times altered, with the Sinnwell Tower (wide views) and the "Deep Well"; the interior (conducted tours) contains a number of fine rooms, including the 12th c. * Imperial chapel, and works of art. – In the NW suburb of St. Johannis is **St John's Cemetery**, with the graves of many famous citizens of Nuremberg, including Dürer, Veit Stoss, Willibald Pirkheimer and Hans Sachs (see plan).

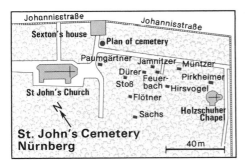

St. John's Cemetery
Nürnberg
40 m

In EGIDIENPLATZ, in the eastern part of St Sebaldus's Side, is **St Giles's Church** (Egidienkirche: 1711–18, restored), Nuremberg's only Baroque church (Tetzel Chapel, Gothic, with the Landauer tomb by Adam Kraft). NW of the church is the handsome new **Municipal Library**, with the arcades of the Peller House (1605), destroyed during the war. – A little way S, in Hans-Sachs-Platz, is a monument to the poet and mastersinger *Hans Sachs* (1494–1576), whose cobbler's workshop was somewhere near here. On the S side of the square is the *Hospital of the Holy Ghost* (founded 1331, now restored and used as an old people's home: winebar); in the courtyard is a "Crucifixion" by Adam Kraft. From here the Spitalbrücke leads on to *Insel Schütt*, between two

arms of the Pegnitz, with the 14th c. *Männerschuldturm* ("Men's Fault Tower"). To the SE are the *Katharinenbau* (serenades), the *Museum of Applied Art* and the National History Museum.

In JAKOBSPLATZ, in the SW part of St Lawrence's Side, is *St James's Church* (14th c., restored: Evang.). On the N side of the square is *St Elizabeth's Church* (18th–19th c., restored: R.C.). – A short distance SW is the *Spittlertor*, and outside the town walls is the PLÄRRER, Nuremberg's most heavily trafficked square. – Between the Spittlertor and the former Maxtor are the finest sections of the 5 km long circuit of * **town walls** (14th–17th c.; some parts occupied by houses; 46 towers). The best view of the walls is to be had from the *Fürther Tor*. – There are fine views of the town from the bridges over the Pegnitz, particularly the MAXBRÜCKE, the area near the *Weinstadel* (15th c.).

On the S side of the old town is the ** **National Germanic Museum**, partly housed in a former monastery (main entrance in Kornmarkt), with a unique and extraordinarily rich collection covering many aspects of German art and culture (pictures, sculpture, engravings, arts and crafts, collection on the history of music). – Nearby, at Lessingstr. 6, is the interesting * **Transport Museum** (railway and postal systems; *first German railway). To the W the *Nicolaus Copernicus Planetarium* (41 Am Plärrer).

In the *Luitpoldhain*, to the SE of the town, is the **Meistersingerhalle** (1963). ½ km N is the 17-storey tower block occupied by the *Federal Labour Institute* (1973: 78 m high). S of the Luitpoldhain is *Dutzendteich Park*. Still farther S, in the district of LANGWASSER, is the **Trade Fair Centre** (Messezentrum). 5 km SW is the **Harbour** (sightseeing trips), at the temporary terminal point of the Rhine-Main-Danube Canal or Europa-Kanal (passenger as well as cargo ships). 5 km NW of the harbour rises a *television tower* in the district of SCHWEINAU. – To the E of the town, on the Schmausenbuck, is the popular **Zoo** (with dolphinarium; restaurant).

SURROUNDINGS. – **Schloss Neunhof** (9 km N): the best preserved example of the country houses (at one time 50–60) belonging to Nuremberg patrician families in the surrounding countryside. – **Erlangen** (19 km N), with Schloss (now the University) and Margravial theatre.

Oberammergau

Land: Bavaria. – Vehicle registration: GAP.
Altitude: 840 m. – Population: 4800.
Post code: D-8103. – Dialling code: 0 88 22.
ⓘ **Verkehrsbüro**, Schnitzergasse 6–8;
tel. 49 21.

HOTELS. –*Alois Lang*, St. Lukas Str. 15, 80 b.
(garden terrace); *Parkhotel Sonnenhof*, König Ludwig Str. 12, 170 b., SB; *Böld*, König Ludwig Str. 10,
110 b.; *Wittelsbach*, Dorfstr. 21, 90 b.; *Wolf*, Dorfstr. 1,
76 b., SP; *Alte Post*, Dorfstr. 19, 58 b. – Conference
Centre *Ammergauer Haus* (opening 1984).

**Oberammergau, situated in a wide
basin in the Ammer valley, surrounded by the foothills of the
Ammergau Alps, is a popular health
and winter sports resort. There is a
State School of Woodcarving in the
town, and many of its inhabitants
are woodcarvers. The* Passion Play
(every ten years: 1984 (special) and
next in May 1990) has made the little
town world-famous.**

HISTORY. – There was a settlement here in Roman
times. The town prospered in the Middle Ages as a
result of its situation on the trade route between
Augsburg and Italy. Woodcarving has been practised
here since the 17th c., and the Passion Play dates from
the same period: it was first performed in 1634,
following a vow taken by the people of Oberammergau during an outbreak of plague in the previous
year.

SIGHTS. – Numerous houses have frescoes on their external walls by the
Ammergau painter Franz Zwink
(1748–92), a practitioner of this
"Lüftlmalerei" – e.g. the *Pilatushaus*
(1784) and the *Geroldhaus* (1778). The
magnificent Rococo **parish church**
(1736–42) is one of Josef Schmuzer's
finest creations; the very fine ceiling
paintings in the interior are by Matthäus
Günther. At Dorfstrasse 8 is the *Heimatmuseum*, with old Oberammergau wood-

Parish church, Oberammergau

carving and a collection of Nativity
groups. At the N end of the village is the
Passion Play Theatre (1930), with an
open stage which incorporates the natural
setting into the backdrop and seating for
4800 spectators (open to visitors).

SURROUNDINGS. – **Laber** (1684 m: to SE),
cableway from St. Gregor. –* **Schloss Linderhof**
(11 km SW): see p. 120.

Oberstdorf

Land: Bavaria. – Vehicle registration: SF.
Altitude: 843 m. – Population: 12,000.
Post code: D-8980. – Dialling code: 0 83 22.
ⓘ **Kurverwaltung und Verkehrsamt**,
Marktplatz 7;
tel. 19 0.

HOTELS. –*Parkhotel Frank*, Sachsenweg 11, 120 b.,
SB;* *Wittlsbacher Hof*, Prinzenstr. 24, 140 b., SB, SP;
Kur und Ferienhotel Filser, Freibergstr. 15, 113 b.,
SB; *Kurhotel Exquisit*, Prinzenstr. 17, 80 b., SB;
Kappeler Haus (no rest.), Am Seeler 2, 90 b., SP;
Alpenhof, Zweistapfenweg 6, 45 b., SB, SP; *Gäste-
haus Weller* (no rest.), Fellhornstr. 22, 30 b. – IN
JAUCHEN:* *Kurhotel Adula*, in der Leite 6, 130 b., SB.

RESTAURANTS. – *Sieben Schwaben*, Pfarrstr. 9;
Sonnenkeller, Weststr. 5; *Kurhaus Restaurant*,
Prinzenstr.; *La Provence*, Kirchstr. 3.

RECREATION. – Golf-course (9 holes); tennis; open-
air and indoor swimming pools; ice-rink; ski-jumps.

**The substantial market town of
Oberstdorf lies at the end of the Iller
valley, which cuts deep into the
Allgäu Alps. The three streams
which combine to form the Iller – the
Trettach, the Stillach and the Breitach – flow together below the
town. Its excellent climate and very
beautiful *situation within a ring of
towering mountains have made
Oberstdorf the most popular health
resort, walking and climbing centre
and winter sports town in the
Allgäu. Most of the town centre was
rebuilt after a great fire in 1865.**

SIGHTS. – Behind the neo-Gothic *parish
church* is the old churchyard, with a war
memorial chapel. A short distance S is the
Kurplatz, with an indoor promenade; from
here there is a splendid *view of the
mountains. SW of the church is the **Cure
and Congress Centre**, completed 1973,
with the *Kurhaus* and the *Kurmittelhaus* (Treatment Building); close by is the
wave bath. To the E of the church are the
Heimatmuseum, the lower station of the
cableway up the Nebelhorn and, beyond

Oberstdorf (Allgäu)

the Trettach, the *Ice Stadium* (artificial ice: Bundesleistungszentrum für Eiskunftlauf =federal training centre) and the Schattenberg ski-jump.

SURROUNDINGS. – Some 2·5 km N of Oberstdorf the road to the *Breitach Gorge branches W off B 19. From the large parking place at the end of the gorge continue on foot up the footpath through the gorge to the Gasthaus Walser Schanz (1 hour). – 5 km up the Stillach valley, then off the road on the right to the *Heini Klopfer Ski-jump (max. jump 170 m); lift to start (fine view of Freibergsee). The road ends at the lower station of the large-cabin cableway up *Fellhorn (2037 m: magnificent views), with a great expanse of walking and skiing country (beautiful Alpine flora; numerous ski-lifts). – *Nebelhorn (2224 m). Large-cabin cableway from SE side of Oberstdorf to the upper station at 1932 m (ski-lifts); from there a chair-lift to the summit. 4 km SW, on the B19, is the Söllereck railway.

Odenwald

Länder: Baden-Württemberg and Hesse.
ⓘ **Fremdenverkehrsamt Odenwald**,
Landratsamt, D-6120 Erbach/Odenwald;
tel. (0 60 62) 7 02 17.

The *Odenwald is one of the most attractive of Germany's upland regions. In the W it rises steeply from the Upper Rhine rift valley, in the NE it is bounded by the Main and in the S by the Neckar. Roughly along the line from Heidelberg to Aschaffenburg runs a 150 m high terrace which separates the Vorderer Odenwald from the Hinterer Odenwald.

The VORDERER ODENWALD is a region of rounded hills built up of crystalline rock,

covered by deciduous forest and much pitted by valleys. Its highest point is *Melibokus* (517 m), E of Zwingenberg on the Bergstrasse. In this part of the Odenwald there are numerous quarries, mainly of granite and porphyry. A geological curiosity is the *Felsenmeer*, a "sea" of huge granite blocks S of the *Felsberg* (515 m) near Lautertal-Reichenbach.

In the HINTERER ODENWALD beds of New Red sandstone and Bunter sandstone overlie the crystalline basement rock. The landscape pattern is characterised by long broad ridges of hills, mainly covered with coniferous forest. The highest point is the *Katzenbuckel* (626 m), near Eberbach, in the NE of the range. The Roman Empire's frontier with Germany, the *Limes* (see p. 172), ran through the eastern Odenwald. – The *Bergstrasse-Odenwald Nature Park*, opened in 1960, has an area of 2320 sq. km and an extensive network of footpaths.

Town Hall, Michelstadt

Two major tourist routes, the **Nibelung Highway** (Worms–Bensheim–Lindenfels–Erbach–Amorbach–Miltenberg–Wertheim) and the **Siegfried Highway** (Worms–Lorsch–Heppenheim–Fürth–Hetzbach–Amorbach), run through the hills from W to E. In addition there is the "Odenwald Farmhouse Museum Highway". BUNDESSTRASSE 45 (Hanau–Dieburg–Höchst–Michelstadt–Hetzbach–Beerfelden –Eberbach), following the Mümling valley for much of the way, provides a N–S connection between the Main and the Neckar.

The Odenwald has a whole series of climatic and health resorts to attract the visitor. Among the best known are *Amorbach* (with a famous *Benedictine abbey church, *Baroque organ and neo-classical library), *Bad König, Beerfelden*,

Erbach (an ivory-carving centre, with a castle), *Fürth, Grasellenbach* (near which is the well where Hagen is supposed to have killed Siegfried), *Höchst, Lindenfels* (a health resort in the shadow of a ruined castle), *Michelstadt* (with a half-timbered *Town Hall of 1484 and a Carolingian *basilica erected by Einhard), *Schönau, Waldbrunn* and *Wald-Michelbach.*

Offenbach

Land: Hesse. – Vehicle registration: OF.
Altitude: 103 m. – Population: 112,000.
Post code: D-6050. – Dialling code: 06 11.
ⓘ **Verkehrsbüro,** Frankfurter Str. 35;
tel. 80 65 29 46.

HOTELS. – *Tourhotel Frankfurt/Offenbach,* Kaiserleistr. 54, 480 b., SB; *Novotel,* Strahlenberger Str. 12, 260 b., SP; *Offenbacher Hof,* Ludwigstr. 37, 75 b.; *Kaiserhof,* Kaiserstr. 8a, 60 b.; *Graf,* Ziegelstr. 2, 40 b.; *Hansa,* Bernradstr. 101, 36 b. – YOUTH HOSTEL: *Jugendgästehaus,* at the Waldschwimmbad 30, 60 b. – CAMPING SITE: *Offenbach-Bürgel,* by the Main.

RESTAURANTS. – *Alt Offenbach,* Domstr. 39; *Lucullus,* Bieberer Str. 61; *Kupferpfanne,* Karlstr. 32. – IN BÜRGEL: *Zur Post,* Offenbacher Str. 33.

This busy industrial town on the left bank of the Main above Frankfurt is noted as the centre of the German leather industry and the headquarters of the central office of the German Meteorological Service. The International Leather Goods Fair is held here every year. The Kaiser-Friedrich-Quelle, drilled in 1885, is a soda water spring with the highest alkaline content in Germany (table water).

HISTORY. – Although Offenbach appears in the records as early as 977, it did not obtain its municipal charter until 1800. From 1486 to 1815 it was held by the Counts of Isenburg; in 1816 it passed to Hesse-Darmstadt.

SIGHTS. – On the banks of the Main stands the early Renaissance **Isenburg Castle** (1564–78), formerly residence of the Counts of Isenburg. – At Frankfurter Str. 86 is the unique *German Leather Museum/German Shoe Museum (collection of objects made of leather and cultural history of the shoe). At Herrnstr. 80 is the *Klingspor Museum* (Institute of 20th c. literary art).

SURROUNDINGS. – **Heusenstamm** (4½ km SW), with Schloss Schönborn and the parish church of SS. Cecilia and Barbara (by Balthasar Neumann).

Offenburg

Land: Baden-Württemberg.
Vehicle registration: OG.
Altitude: 161 m. – Population: 51,000.
Post code: D-7600. – Dialling code: 07 81.
ⓘ **Städtisches Verkehrsamt,** Steinstr. 2;
tel. 8 22 48.

HOTELS. – *Am Messeplatz,* Schutterwälder Str., 179 b.; *Palmengarten,* Okenstr. 17, 120 b.; *Union* (no rest.), Hauptstr. 19, 65 b.; *Sonne,* Hauptstr. 94, 59 b.; *Haus Hubertus,* Kolpingstr. 4, 40 b.; *Centralhotel* (no rest.), Poststr. 5, 35 b. – IN ZELL-WEIERBACH: *Rebenhof,* Talweg 48/32a, 56 b., SB.

RESTAURANT. – *Traube,* Fessenbacher Str. 115, Offenburg-Fessenbach (Baden and Alsatian specialities).

EVENTS. – *Wine Market* in the Oberrheinhallen (mid May); *Ortenau Wine Festival* (last weekend in Sept.); *Baden Quality Brand Wine Market* (first Sat. in Nov.).

Situated at the point where the River Kinzig emerges from the vine-clad foothills of the Black Forest into the fertile Upper Rhine plain, Offenburg is the chief town of the Ortenau district, the "golden land" of wine and fruit. It also has a large publishing house, printing, electronic, chemical and engineering works, as well as several breweries.

HISTORY. – First recorded in 1101, Offenburg obtained its municipal charter in 1223 and from 1289 to 1803 was a free Imperial city. From 1551 to 1701 and from 1771 to 1803 it belonged to Austria; thereafter it passed to Baden.

SIGHTS. – In the MARKT are the **Town Hall** (1741) and the **Landratsamt** (district government offices, originally headquarters of the Imperial governor: 1714–17). In the nearby Ritterstrasse is the *Ritterhausmuseum* (history of the town and region, colonial history).

W of the Hauptstrasse is the **Town Church of the Holy Cross** (rebuilt in the early 18th c.: R.C.). In front of the church is a sculpture representing *Christ on the Mount of Olives* (1524). – There are some remains of the old *town walls.* – W of the Kinzig are the *Oberrheinhallen* and the Messeplatz.

SURROUNDINGS. – **Kinzig valley** (to SE), with Gengenbach (11 km), Haslach (28 km; costume museum) and Hausach (35 km); near Hausach in Gutach is the *Vogtsbauernhof Open-Air Museum.

Oldenburg

in Oldenburg

Land: Lower Saxony. – Vehicle registration: OL.
Altitude: 7 m. – Population: 135,000.
Post code: D-2900. – Dialling code: 04 41.
ⓘ **Verkehrsverein**, Lange Str. 3;
tel. 2 50 96.

HOTELS. – *Wieting*, Damm 29, 100 b.; *Parkhotel*,
Cloppenburger Str. 418, 57 b.; *Beyer*, Alexanderstr.
105, 55 b.; *Schützenhof*, Hauptstr. 36, 55 b.; *Sprenz*
(no rest.), Heilingengeiststr. 15, 53 b.; *Posthalter*,
Mottenstr. 13, 50 b., SB, sauna; *Harmonie*,
Dragonerstr. 59, 14 b. – YOUTH HOSTEL: Huntestr. 6,
70 b. – CAMPING SITE: *Flötenteich* (grass area within
town boundary).

RESTAURANTS. – *La Cuisine*, Wallstr. 13; *Patent-
krug*, Wilhelmshavener Heerstr. 359; *Ratskeller*, Markt
1; *Sartorius-Stuben*, Herbertgang 6; *Shangri-La*,
Ammerländer Heerstr. 61.

CAFÉ. – *Klinge*, Theaterwall 47.

**This former Grand-Ducal residence,
now the chief town of the Bezirk
(region) of Oldenburg, lies on the
River Hunte. It is a university town
and the seat of a Higher Administrative Court, the marketing centre
of a rich agricultural area and a town
of varied industries, which has
developed considerably since the
improvement of the Küstenkanal
(Coastal Canal) to the Ems.**

HISTORY. – First recorded in 1108 as *Aldenburg*, in
1150 it became the residence of the Counts of
Ammerland, the last and greatest of whom, Count
Anton Günther, died in 1667, whereupon the town
passed to Denmark. From 1773 to 1918 Oldenburg
was the residence of the Dukes (later Grand Dukes) of
Holstein-Gottorf and enjoyed a further period of high
prosperity. From 1918 to 1933 it was the capital of the
Free State of Oldenburg. The University was founded
in 1970.

SIGHTS. – In the centre of the OLD
TOWN, surrounded by the line of its
ramparts and by water-courses, is the
MARKT, with the *Town Hall* (1887) and **St
Lambert's Church** (13th, 18th and 19th
c.). W of the Markt is the *Haus Degode*, a
fine half-timbered house of 1617.

A short distance SE of the square is the
Grand-Ducal Palace (17th and 18th
c.), with the interesting *Provincial Museum of Art and Cultural History*; behind it
is the attractive *Schlossgarten*. In the
former *Augusteum* is a picture gallery. In
the Damm, which runs SE from the
Schlossplatz, is the *State Museum of
Natural History and Prehistory*. – On the

northern edge of the old town is the
Lappan (tower of the Chapel of the Holy
Ghost, 1468), the oldest building in the
town and a noted landmark.

Farther N, at Raiffeisenstr. 32–33, is the
Municipal Museum. – N of the station is
the *Weser-Ems-Halle* (1954). – In the
NW of the town is the *Botanic Garden*.

SURROUNDINGS. – **Zwischenahner Meer** (17
km NW), a lake over 3 km long and up to 2½ km across
in the S of the Ammerland region round Oldenburg.
On its S side is the resort of *Bad Zwischenahn* (mud-
baths, Kneipp cure).

*Cloppenburg **Museum Village** (42 km SW), in
the Münsterland region of Oldenburg: the largest
open-air museum in Germany, with peasants' houses,
windmills and workshops. Its prize exhibit is the
farmstead of Wehlburg (1750) from the Artland area.

Osnabrück

Land: Lower Saxony.
Vehicle registration: OS.
Altitude: 64 m. – Population: 155,000.
Post code: D-4500. – Dialling code: 05 41.
ⓘ **Städtisches Verkehrsamt**, Markt 22;
tel. 3 23 22 02.

HOTELS. – *Hohenzollern, Heinrich-Heine-Str. 17,
136 b., SB, sauna, solarium; *Parkhotel*, Am Heger
Holz, 150 b., SB, sauna; *Kulmbacher Hof*, Schlosswall
67, 75 b.; *Residenz*, Johannisstr. 138, 41 b.; *Intour-
hotel* (no rest.), Maschstr. 20, 45 b.; *Gretescher Hof*,
Sandforter Str. 1, 44 b.; *Westerkamp*, Bremer Str. 120,
42 b.; *Welp*, Natruper Str. 227, 25 b.; *Neustadt* (no
rest.), Miquelstr. 34, 42 b.; *Klute*, Lotterstr. 30, 24 b. –
IN NAHNE: *Himmelreich* (no rest.), Zum Himmelreich
11, 54 b., SB. – YOUTH HOSTEL: Am Tannenhof 6,
120 b. – CAMPING SITES: *Niedersachsenhof*,
Nordstr. 109; *Attersee*, on Attersee.

RESTAURANTS. – *Vitischanze*, Vitihof 15a; *Rats-
keller*, Markt 30; *Der Landgraf*, Domhof 9; *Ellerbrake*,
Neuer Graben 7; *Aldermann*, Johannisstr. 92;
Steckenpferd, Stadhalle, Schlosswall 1.

WINE-BARS. – *Weinkrüger*, Marienstr. *Joducus*,
Kommenderiestr. 116.

CAFÉS. – *Leysieffer*, Krahnstr. 61; *Brüggemann*,
Bierstr. 13; *Terfort*, Am Markt 26–27.

EVENTS. – *Street Carnival* (Feb., Sat. before Rose
Monday); *May week*, inner-city festival (2nd week in
May); *Folk Festival* (weekend before Easter and last
weekend in Oct.); *Osnabrück Music Festival* (annually in summer); *"In Praise of Peace"*, with riding of
hobby-horses by school-children (25 Oct.).

**The old episcopal city and new
university town of Osnabrück lies in
the Hase valley, attractively framed
by the hills of the Wiehengebirge
and Teutoburg Forest. It is a busy
commercial and industrial city (car**

manufacture, metal-working, textiles, paper-making) linked by a branch canal with the Mitelland Canal.

HISTORY. – The town, made an episcopal see by Charlemagne in 785, grew up round its Cathedral. In 889 King Arnulf of Carinthia granted it the right to hold a market, levy tolls and coin money. It first appears in the records as a town in 1147, and in 1157 the Emperor Frederick Barbarossa granted it the right to build fortifications. The "new town" which grew up round St John's Church was also surrounded by walls. By the 13th c. Osnabrück was a member of the Hanse and the Westphalian League of Towns. In 1306 the old and new towns were united, and in subsequent centuries their defences were strengthened. In 1643–48 the negotiations between the Protestant powers, the Swedes and the Emperor which led to the Peace of Westphalia took place in Osnabrück. In 1876–77 the old fortifications, with the exception of the Herrenteichswall, were pulled down, and the town began to expand outside its old boundaries. The University was founded in 1970. – Osnabrück was the birthplace of Erich Maria Remarque (1898–1970), who achieved world fame with his novel "All Quiet on the Western Front".

SIGHTS. – The historic centre of the city, in the heart of the OLD TOWN, is the **Cathedral** of St Peter (R.C.), founded by Charlemagne at the end of the 8th c. and dating in its present form, with its massive SW tower and the slenderer NW tower, from the 13th c. Notable features of the interior are the fine bronze font of 1225, the triumphal cross of 1250 and the 16th c. statues of Apostles on the pillars of the nave. The adjoining **Diocesan Museum** (entrance in Kleine Domsfreiheit) contains among much else the valuable *Cathedral Treasury. In the Domhof is the *Löwenpudel*; in the Grosse Domsfreiheit are the *Episcopal Chancery*, the *Bishop's Palace* and the *Möser Monument* (by Drake), commemorating the statesman and writer Justus Möser (1720–94), whose "Patriotic Fancies" impressed Goethe.

A short distance W of the Cathedral is the MARKT, surrounded by gabled houses (rebuilt in the original style), with the **Town Hall** (1487–1512: interesting treasury), containing the *Peace Chamber in which the treaty between the Emperor, the Protestant Estates and the Swedes was signed in 1648. Also in the square are the Gothic **St Mary's Church** (13th–15th c.: Evang.), with a beautiful 16th c. altar with side-panels from Antwerp, a 14th c. triumphal cross and the tomb of Justus Möser; the *Municipal Weigh-House* (16th c.), now the registry office; and the *Möserhaus* (rebuilt) in which Möser was born.

In KRAHNSTRASSE and BIERSTRASSE are a number of old half-timbered houses, like *Haus Willmann* at Krahnstr. 7 (1586, restored 1891) and the *Gasthof Walhalla* at Bierstr. 24 (1690). HEGER STRASSE, with its old inns and antique shops, leads to the **Heger Tor** or Waterloo Gate, part of the old fortifications. Other remains of the fortifications to be seen in the "Wallstrassen" which now mark their line are the *Bocksturm* (medieval instruments of torture and weapons: conducted tours), the *Bürgergehorsam*, the *Vitischanze* and the *Pernickelturm*. In HEGER-TOR-WALL are the **Museum of Cultural History** (local traditions, history, art) and the *Natural History Museum*. In the NEUER GRABEN, which marks the boundary between the old town and the new town, are the modern *Stadthalle*, the **Prince-Bishop's Palace** (1668–90), now occupied by the University, and the *Ledenhof*, a stone-built medieval building with a handsome Renaissance bell-gable; and behind this *St Catherine's Church* (14th c.: Evang.), with a tower 103 m high.

The hub of the modern city's life, always busy with traffic, is the NEUMARKT, off which open (to N) the GROSSE STRASSE (pedestrian precinct), the main business and shopping street, and (to S) JOHANNISSTRASSE. **St John's Church** (13th c.: R.C.) is the parish church of the NEW TOWN, which grew up around it; it has a high altar (1525) of the school of the "Master of Osnabrück". – Farther S is the **Waldzoo** (Forest Zoo) on the Schölerberg (open enclosures, Seal Pool, South American House).

SURROUNDINGS. – **Bad Iburg** (16 km S), a health resort (Kneipp cure) in the TEUTOBURG FOREST (Dörenberg, 331 m: observation tower), with a castle. – **Tecklenburg** (22 km SW), a little hill town in the Teutoburg Forest with a ruined castle (open-air theatre). – **Bad Essen** (24 km NE), a brine spa in the WIEHENGEBIRGE.

Osnabrück

Paderborn

Land: North Rhineland-Westphalia.
Vehicle registration: PB.
Altitude: 119 m. – Population: 110,000.
Post code: D-4790. – Dialling code: 0 52 51.
ⓘ **Verkehrsverein**, Marienplatz 2a;
tel. 2 95 95.

HOTELS. – *Hotel Ibis*, Am Paderwall 1–5, 180 b.;
Arosa, Westernmauer 38, 155 b., SB, sauna; *Zur
Mühle*, Mühlenstrasse (Paderaue), 44 b. ("Au Cygne
Noir" restaurant); *Krawinkel*, Karlsplatz 33, 41 b.;
Südhotel, Borchener Str. 23, 37 b. – IN ELSEN:
Kaiserpfalz, von-Ketteler-Str. 20, 38 b. – YOUTH
HOSTEL: Meinwerkstr. 16, 129 b. – CAMPING SITE:
Am Waldsee, Husarenstr. 130; *Stauterrassen*, Auf der
Thune 14.

RESTAURANTS. – *Schweizer Haus*, Warburger Str.
99 (Swiss); *Ratskeller*, Rathausplatz; *Domhof*, Markt
9.

EVENTS. – *Feast of St Liborius* (end July), with a
nine-day fair.

**This old Westphalian Imperial, epis-
copal and Hanseatic city lies at the
source of the Pader in the eastern
part of the Münster basin, to the W
of the Eggegebirge. Rebuilt after
severe destruction during the last
war, it is now a busy commercial and
industrial centre and a university
town (with a Gesamthochschule or
comprehensive higher educational
establishment).**

HISTORY. – A settlement grew up here at an early
stage, at the intersection of important trade routes. In
777 Charlemagne held his first Imperial Diet in the
newly conquered Saxon territory in Paderborn, and he
had his important meeting with Pope Leo III here in
799. The year 806 saw the foundation of the
bishopric, which enjoyed a great flowering of art in the
11th c. under Bishop Meinwerk. In 1180 the town
was surrounded by a powerful circuit of walls. By
1294 it was a member of the Hanse, and in 1497 it
became one of the Hanse's principal towns. The
University was founded in 1614, the first in Westphalia (until 1844: re-founded as a College of
Catholic Theology).

SIGHTS: – In the DOMPLATZ, in the centre
of the town, is the *Cathedral
(11th–13th c.: R.C.), with a tower 94 m
high which forms a distinctive landmark.
The S main doorway (the Paradise
Doorway) has fine Romanesque sculpture (*c.* 1250–60); the interior has notable
monuments and a rich treasury; in the
crypt (12th c.) is an ebony reliquary with
the remains of St Liborius. On the N side
of the Cathedral is *St Bartholomew's
Chapel* (1017), Germany's oldest hall-
church. From 1945 excavation, also on
the N side, uncovered a Carolingian and
an Ottonian-Salisian *imperial palace*. The
latter was rebuilt and now houses a

museum. The **Diocesan Museum**, W of
the Cathedral, has as its greatest treasures
the Shrine of St Liborius (1627) and the
*Imad Madonna (*c.* 1050). Opposite is
St Ulrich's Church* (12th c.: R.C.), the
town's oldest parish church, with an
octagonal tower.

From the Domplatz the busy shopping
street SCHILDERN (pedestrian precinct)
runs SW to the RATHAUSPLATZ, which is
dominated by the **Town Hall**, a magnificent three-gabled building of the late
Renaissance (1613–15; rebuilt). – NW of
the Domplatz is the Romanesque **Ab-
dinghof Church** (11th c.: Evang.), and
below this, in beautiful gardens, is the
source of the Pader. In the N of the old
town, which is surrounded by a ring of
streets on the line of the old walls, is the
Adam and Eve House (Museum of Civic
History), and in the E the *Busdorf Church*
(11th c.; R.C.); to the S are the Baroque
Franciscan Church (1691) and the *Jesuit
Church* (1682–84), formerly the University church. – **Schloss Neuhaus**
(13th–16th c.), a four-winged building
with massive corner towers, was once the
residence of the Prince-Bishops of Paderborn.

SURROUNDINGS. – **Wewelsburg** (17 km SW), a
mighty fortified castle of the 17th c. – **Büren** (28 km
SW), with a Baroque Jesuit church.

Passau

Land: Bavaria. – Vehicle registration: PA.
Altitude: 290 m. – Population: 51,000.
Post code: D-8390. – Dialling code: 08 51.
ⓘ **Fremdenverkehrsverein**,
Nibelungenhalle;
tel. 5 14 08/88.

HOTELS. – *Weisser Hase*, Ludwigstr. 23, 240 b.;
Passauer Wolf, Rindermarkt 6, 60 b.; *Schwarzer
Ochse*, Ludwigstr. 22, 127 b.; *Dreiflüsse Hof*, Dan-
ziger Str. 42, 125 b.; *Schloss Ort*, am Dreiflusseck, 58
b.; *Abrahamhof*, Abraham 1, 50 b.; *Zum König*,
Rindermarkt 2, 31 b. – YOUTH HOSTEL: in Veste
Oberhaus, 125 b. – CAMPING SITES: in the courtyard
of Veste Oberhaus; *Dreiflüsse Camping Irring*, on left
bank of the Danube (8 km W); *Ferienzentrum
Bayerwald*, near Gottsdorf (28 km SE).

RESTAURANTS.   – *Heilig-Geist-Stiftsschänke*,
Heiliggeistgasse 4 (with medieval cellar and garden);
Ratskeller, Rathausplatz; *Nibelungen* Restaurant,
Neuburger Str. 7.

BEER-HOUSES.   –   *Hacklberger   Bräustüberl*,
Bräuhausplatz 7; *Innstadtbräustüberl*, Schmiedgasse
23; *Schlossbräukeller*, Schrottgasse; *Löwenbräu-
stüberl*, Kleiner Exerzierplatz 16.

CAFÉS. – *Greindl*, in Rosstränkenhof (garden café);
Wittgasse 8; *Hoft*, Ludwigstr. 17; *Theresiencafé*,
Theresienstr. 14; *Torten König*, Grabengasse 25;
Oberhaus, Oberhaus 1.

EVENTS. – *Spring Trade Fair* in Nibelungenhalle; *Maidult* (May Fair), with a parade of local costumes and marksmen; *European Weeks*, with concerts and dramatic performances (June–July); costume festivals; *Herbstdult* (Autumn Fair: first week Sept.); *Christkindlmarkt* in Nibelungenhalle (Dec.).

The old episcopal city of Passau is magnificently situated at the junction of the Danube (here only 240 m wide) with the Inn (290 m wide) and the little River Ilz. With its houses in the Italian style typical of the towns on the Inn and the Salzach, dominated by the Oberhaus fortress and the Mariahilf church, it presents a *townscape of arresting beauty. Alexander von Humboldt counted this "city of the three rivers" among the seven most beautifully situated towns in the world. The University was founded in 1978. Passau lies on the frontier with Austria, and is the terminus of the passenger boat services on the Danube. The Passau Spring Trade Fair is held every year in the Nibelungenhalle.

HISTORY. – Passau, in early times a fortified settlement (*Bojodurum*) of a Celtic tribe, the Boii, takes its name from the Roman camp of Castra Batava (occupied by a cohort of Batavian troops) which was established around A.D. 200 on the S bank of the Inn. In the 7th c. a Bavarian ducal castle was built on the ruins of the Roman fort. The bishopric was founded about 735, and later extended its bounds to the frontier with Hungary. The energetic Bishop Piligrim (971–91) is praised in the "Nibelungenlied", and in 1217 Bishop Ulrich II was raised to the dignity of Prince of the Empire (Reichsfürst). In the Middle Ages Passau's excellent situation made it an important trading town. Its most brilliant days came in the 16th c., when the Treaty of Passau (1552) between the Emperor Charles V and Elector Maurice of Saxony paved the way for the Augsburg religious settlement. In 1662 and 1680 the town was ravaged by two devastating fires; and the rebuilding was carried out by Italian architects summoned to Passau by the Prince-Bishops, who endowed the town with its splendid Baroque architecture. In 1784 the bishopric lost its territory in Austria, and in 1803 it was secularised and incorporated in Bavaria. The bishopric was re-established in 1821.

SIGHTS. – In the OLD TOWN, crowded between the Danube and the Inn, the busiest traffic intersection is the LUDWIGSPLATZ, the starting point of LUDWIGSTRASSE, which with its continuation the Rindermarkt is Passau's main business and shopping street. In the Rindermarkt is the Baroque *St Paul's Church* (1678).

In the DOMPLATZ, with its old canons' houses, is the *Cathedral of St Stephen (15th–17th c.), which has Italian-style stucco decoration by G. B. Carlone (1680–86). The *organ is the largest church organ in the world, with more than 17,300 pipes and 231 stops (daily recitals May–Sept.). – The appealing little RESIDENZPLATZ, with the *New Bishop's Palace* (1712–72) lies to the E of the Choir of the Cathedral.

On the right bank of the Danube is the RATHAUSPLATZ, with the **Town Hall**, a complex of buildings (including a Ratskeller) dating from 1298 onwards (tower, 68 m high, built 1893). – On the left bank of the Inn is the former *Jesuit church of St Michael* (Studienkirche: 17th c.), with a magnificent interior. Beyond this is the former Benedictine nunnery, founded in the 8th c., of **Niedernburg** (now occupied by the order known as the English Ladies), with the former *St Mary's Church* (11th–17th c.). In the Maria Parz Chapel is the imposing tomb of Abbess Gisela (d. *c.* 1060), sister of the Emperor

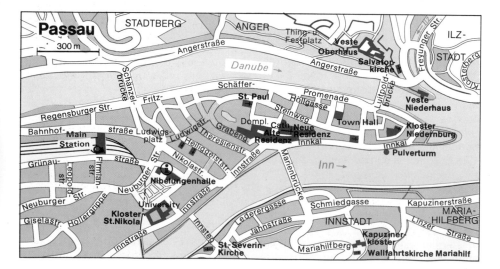

The old town of Passau, between the Danube (left) and the Inn (right)

Henry II and widow of St Stephen, King of Hungary. – From the *Dreiflusseck* (landing-stage used by the Danube passenger ships to Linz, Vienna and the Black Sea) there is an interesting view of the confluence of the yellow-green Danube, the grey Inn and the peat-brown Ilz.

On the right bank of the Inn, occupying the site of the Celtic settlement of Bojodurum, is the INNSTADT district, at the W end of which stands *St Severinus's Church* (originally 8th c.). Here in 1974 were discovered the foundations of the late Roman fort of *Boiotro*; museum in the so-called "Gruberhaus". On the hill above the Innstadt (358 m: view) is the pilgrimage church of **Mariahilf** (1627).

Above the left bank of the Danube stands the former episcopal stronghold of *Veste Oberhaus** (408 m: on foot 15 min., by road 1 km), dating from the 13th–16th c., with the *Municipal Museum, Picture Gallery, Bohemian Forest Museum* and *Fire Brigade Museum*. From the restaurant and the observation tower there are magnificent views. – A wall-walk links the Oberhaus with the former fortress of *Niederhaus* (now private property), on the tongue of land between the Ilz and the Danube. A little to the N, beyond a gateway in the rock, is the unusual *St Salvator's Church* (15th c.), now a concert hall.

SURROUNDINGS. – **Schloss Neuburg** (11 km S), on the high bank above the Inn (European Academy of the Gustav Stresemann Institute). In **Schloss Obernzell** (14 km E) there is a *Pottery Museum* (branch of the Bavarian National Museum). – *Jochenstein** Hydroelectric Station (21 km E), on the Danube, one of the largest hydroelectric installations in Western Europe.

Pforzheim

Land: Baden-Württemberg.
Vehicle registration: PF.
Altitude: 274 m. – Population: 106,000.
Post code: D-7530. – Dialling code: 0 72 31.
ⓘ **Stadtinformation**, Marktplatz 1; tel. 39 21 90.

HOTELS. – *Eden Hotel Ruf*, Bahnhofsplatz 5, 98 b. ("Schüttelfass" restaurant), sauna; *Schlosshotel*, Lindenstr. 2, 48 b.; *Gute Hoffnung*, Dillsteiner Str. 9, 50 b. ("Rôtisserie Le Canard"); *Schwarzwaldhotel* (no rest.), Am Schlossgattor 7, 50 b.; *Europa* (no rest.), Kronprinzenstr. 1, 34 b; *City* (no rest.), Bahnhofstr. 8, 27 b. – YOUTH HOSTEL: Kräheneckstr. 4, 90 b. – CAMPING SITE: Pforzheim-Schellbronn.

RESTAURANTS. – *Ratskeller*, Marktplatz 1; *Goldener Adler*, Leopoldplatz; *Ketterers Bräustüble*, Jahnstr. 10; *Martinsbau*, Dillsteiner Str. 3a.

Pforzheim, situated on the northern fringe of the Black Forest in a basin at the confluence of the rivers Enz, Nagold and Würm, is the gateway to the northern Black Forest, an excellent base from which to explore the beautiful valleys of these rivers and the three ridgeway footpaths of the Black Forest. It is widely famed as a centre of the goldsmithing and jewellery industry.

HISTORY. – Pforzheim grew up at the foot of the Schlossberg in the 13th c., and until 1565 was the residence of the Margraves of Baden-Durlach. The goldsmithing and jewellery industry was established here in 1767 by Margrave Karl Friedrich of Baden. In February 1945 the town was almost completely destroyed in an air raid, and the post-war rebuilding has produced a handsome modern town.

SIGHTS. – Of the old residence of the Margraves of Baden-Durlach there remain only the *Archives Tower* and the

In the Jewellery Museum, Pforzheim

Schlosskirche (11th c., rebuilt; tomb monuments of the Margraves in the choir) on the Schlossberg. To the S. in the MARKTPLATZ (pedestrian zone), is the *Town Hall* (carillon). Farther S, in the triangle formed by the Enz and the Nagold, is the *Town Church*; from the detached tower (76 m high: lift) there are extensive views. To the SW, on the N side of the STADTGARTEN, is the **Reuchlinhaus**, in which is the *Jewellery Museum*. The *Heimatmuseum* (In der Westliche 243) has among its exhibits the original Oechsle Scales.

In the E of the town is the Romanesque **St Martin's Church** (12th c.), with late Gothic wall paintings in the choir. – In the western district of ARLINGER is the modern tent-shaped *St Matthew's Church* (by Egon Eiermann, 1953). – In the *Wildpark* in Tiefenbronner Strasse are indigenous and foreign animals as well as threatened species; in the district of WÜRM is an *Alpine Garden*.

SURROUNDINGS. – **Maulbronn** (18 km NE), with a *Cistercian abbey*, the best preserved medieval religious house in Germany (founded 1146), now occupied by an Evangelical Theological Seminary. – **Bad Liebenzell** (24 km S), in the Nagold valley, in the shadow of an old castle (447 m: international Youth Forum).

Recklinghausen

Land: North Rhineland-Westphalia.
Vehicle registration: RE.
Altitude: 76 m. – Population: 120,000.
Post code: D-4350. – Dialling code: 0 23 61.
ⓘ **Verkehrsamt**, Town Hall;
   tel. 58 71.

HOTELS. – *Barbarossa-Hotel*, Löhrhof 8, 90 b., SB; *Landhaus Quellber*, Holunderweg 9, 63 b., SP, sauna; *Die Engelsburg*, Augustinessenstr. 10, 40 b.; *Wüller*, Hammer Str. 1, 100 b.; *Bahnhofshotel*, Kunibertistr. 40, 42 b.; *Bergedick*, Hochlarmarkstr. 66, 22 b.

RESTAURANTS. – *Ratskeller*, in Town Hall; *Zum Drübbelken*, Münsterstr. 5.

EVENTS. – *Ruhr Festival* (May–July).

The busy industrial town of Recklinghausen lies in the area known as the Neues Revier between the rivers Emscher and Lippe. Its economy revolves mainly round coal-mining, but it has also made a name for itself in the cultural field with its annual Ruhr Festival.

HISTORY. – Recklinghausen is one of the oldest towns in the Neues Revier, having grown up round a Carolingian royal stronghold. From about 1150 it belonged to the Archbishopric of Cologne, being then the seat of a district court. In 1236 it was granted extended municipal privileges, and in 1316 became a member of the Hanse. During the 14th and 15th c. it prospered. In the 16th and 17th c. it was ravaged by several large fires. In 1802 it became the administrative headquarters of the Duke of Arenberg; then in 1815, along with the surrounding district, it passed to Prussia. From the middle of the 19th c. the development of coal-mining brought it a further period of prosperity. In 1926 the town extended its area by taking in land from neighbouring communes.

SIGHTS. – In the middle of the OLD TOWN with its narrow lanes is **St Peter's** Church (13th c., with later extensions: R.C.). Opposite it, to the W, is the *Icon Museum*, with a collection of icons (some 600, dating from the 15th–19th c.) which is unique in Western Europe. – Farther W is the *Engelsburg* (1701), now a hotel. – To the N of the old town, in Wickingplatz, is the *Kunsthalle* (modern art; special exhibitions during the Ruhr Festival). – In the Stadtgarten, to the NW of the town, are the modern **Festival Hall** (opened 1965), the *Zoo* and the *Observatory* (with a Planetarium).

Regensburg

Land: Bavaria. – Vehicle registration: R.
Altitude: 333 m. – Population: 131,000.
Post code: D-8400. – Dialling code: 09 41.
ⓘ **Verkehrsamt**, Altes Rathaus;
   tel. 5 07 21 41.

HOTELS. – *Parkhotel Maximilian*, Maximilian Str. 28, 103 b.; *Avia Hotel*, Frankenstr. 1, 120 b.; *Karmeliten*, Dachauplatz 1, 120 b.; *Bischofshof*, Krauterermarkt 3, 106 b.; *St. Georg*, Stielerstr. 8, 104 b.; *Kaiserhof am Dom*, Kramgasse 10, 56 b.; *Casino Hotel*, Puricellistr. 32, 104 b.; *Straubinger Hof*, Adolf Schmetzer Str. 33, 100 b.; *Apollo 11*, Neuprüll 17, 80 b., SB, sauna; *Weidenhof* (no rest.), Maximilianstr. 23, 65 b. – YOUTH HOSTEL: Wöhrdstr. 60, 250 b. – CAMPING SITE: *Dunnerkeil*, am Weinweg 40 (on bend of Danube).

RESTAURANTS. – *Ratskeller*, Rathausplatz 1 (specialty wels, a Danube fish); *Historisches Eck Zur Stritzelbäckerin*, Watmarkt 6; *Leerer Beutel*, Bertoldstr. 9; *Historische Wurstküche*, Weisse-Lamm-Gasse 3 (specialty Schweinswürstl).

BEER-HOUSES. – *Brandl-Bräu*, Ostengasse (with garden); *Kneitinger-Brauerei*, Arnulfplatz 3; *Hofbraühaus*, Rathausplatz; *Zum Weissbierbrauer*, Schwanenplatz.

CAFÉ. – *Deutzer*, Kohlenmarkt 6, Pfauengasse 8.

The old Imperial city of Regensburg (Ratisbon), chief town of the Bezirk (region) of Upper Palatinate and the see of a bishop, lies at the most northerly point in the course of the Danube, which is here joined by the Regen and is navigable below the town (river harbour, with passenger services to Walhalla, Kelheim/ Weltenburg and Passau). Regensburg has the same significance for the art and culture of the early and high Middle Ages as have Nuremberg and Augsburg for later centuries. The *medieval townscape is made up of numerous churches, towers belonging to the great noble families and patrician houses of the 13th and 14th c., such as are found nowhere else N of the Alps. – Regensburg has the fourth Bavarian university, a School of Church Music and other training colleges.

The town's industries include electrical engineering, chemical plants, clothing factories, sugar-refining, carpet-making and brewing.

HISTORY. – The site of Regensburg was once occupied by the Celtic settlement of *Radasbona*. This was followed in A.D. 77 by a Roman camp accommodating a cohort, and in 179 by the large legionary camp of *Castra Regina* established by Marcus Aurelius. At the beginning of the 6th c. Regensburg became the residence of the Dukes of Bavaria of the Agilolfing line. The bishopric was founded by St Boniface in 739. In 788 Charlemagne put an end to the rule of the Agilolfings, and the town became a residence of the Carolingian rulers. In the 12th and 13th c. Regensburg, which became a free Imperial city in 1245, developed into the most populous and wealthiest city in southern Germany, carrying on a thriving trade with Venice over the Brenner. In the 14th c., however, a slow decline began, caused by the rise of Augsburg and Nuremberg. The Reformation came to Regensburg in 1542. From 1663 to 1806 the "Permanent Imperial Diet", the first German parliament, sat in Regensburg. In 1748 the Princes of Thurn and Taxis – who had been responsible for running the German postal service since 1595, a service which continued to operate in the smaller states of central Germany until 1866 – took up their residence in Regensburg as principal commissioners of the Diet. In 1803 Regensburg, now a secular principality, passed to the former Elector of Mainz, Karl von Dalberg (d. 1817). In 1809 the town was captured by the French, and in 1810 it was united with Bavaria. During the Second World War the older quarters of Regensburg escaped unscathed, apart from the destruction of the Obermünster church.

The best *view of Regensburg is from the 310 m long **Stone Bridge** over the Danube (12th c.), a masterpiece of medieval engineering. Downstream by the Werftstrasse lies the Museum Ship "Ruthof"; then comes the *Nibelungen Bridge*. – A short distance from the Stone Bridge is the hub of the city's life, the DOMPLATZ, in which is the *Cathedral (13th–16th c.: R.C.), the finest Gothic building in Bavaria, with two spires 105 m high on its magnificent W front. Its greatest treasures are inside: splendid stained glass, mostly of the 14th c.; a late Gothic stone pulpit (1482); a fine Annunciation (*c.* 1280), with the "Angel of Regensburg", on the two W pillars of the crossing; the beautiful cloisters (in their present form mostly 14th–16th c.), with the Romanesque *All Saints' Chapel* (wall paintings). The rich *Cathedral Treasury contains fine reliquaries, processional and reliquary crosses, chalices, vestments, etc. – The Cathedral has a famous boys' choir, the "Domspatzen" ("Cathedral sparrows").

Close by, to the N, are *St John's Church* (14th c.) and the former *Bischofshof*, now a hotel, which was the bishop's residence from the early 11th c. onwards and frequently provided lodging for the Emperor. On the N side of the Bischofshof are the arches and E tower of the **Porta Praetoria**, the N gate of the Roman legionary fort of *Castra Regina* (2nd c. A.D.). – On the S side of the Domgarten is the early Gothic *St Ulrich's Church* (*c.* 1250). Nearby, adjoining the Bishop's

Regensburg Cathedral

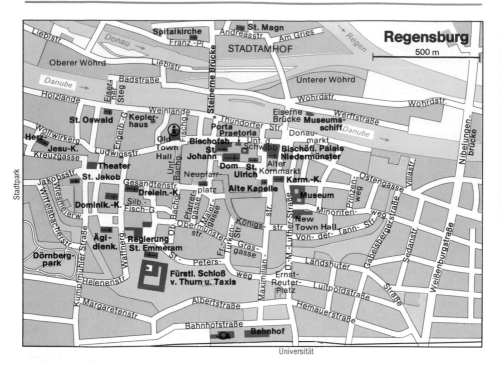

Palace, is the *Niedermünster church*, where extensive excavations have been carried out.

In the ALTER KORNMARKT are the so-called *Roman Tower* and the Herzogshof, a residence of the Dukes of Bavaria which appears in the records as early as 988 (Ducal Hall). On the S side of the square is the **Old Chapel** (built 1002; choir 1441–52), with a sumptuous Rococo interior, and on the E side is the Baroque *Carmelite Church* (after 1660). Beyond this church, in Dachauplatz (56 m stretch of *Roman walls*), is the *Municipal Museum*, housed in a former Minorite friary, with exhibits covering 2000 years of art and culture. To the S is the *New Town Hall* (1936–38).

In the old merchants' quarter round the Old Town Hall are several fortified houses belonging to noble families with tall towers after the Italian model. – In Haidplatz is the "Neue Waage", formerly a tavern, the scene of a famous disputation between Melanchthon and Johann Eck in 1541. – The picturesque *Old Town Hall* dates from the 14th–18th c. In the large Imperial Hall the "Permanent Imperial Diet" held its sessions (museum). On the ground floor is a medieval court-room. The Baroque eastern part of the building, connected with the older part by the tower, dates from 1661. – A short distance NW of the Old Town Hall, at Keplerstr. 5,

is the house in which the astronomer Johannes Kepler died in 1630 (mementoes). The Ducal Palace (Prebrunntor 4) houses the *East Bavarian Museum of Natural Science*. S in the Stadtpark is the *East German Gallery*.

At the W end of the old town is the 12th c. **St James's Church**, originally belonging to a house of Irish-Scottish Benedictines. The *N doorway has enigmatic sculpture showing Northern influence. – To the SE is the 13th c. *Dominican Church*, notable for its spaciousness.

On the S side of the old town is EMMERAMSPLATZ, with the *Regierungsgebäude* (government buildings) and the former *Benedictine monastery of St Emmeram*, one of the oldest in Germany, founded in the 7th c. on the site of a late Roman building. It has a Romanesque porch (c. 1170), on the left of which is the entrance to *St Rupert's Church* (rebuilt in Baroque style); straight ahead is the doorway of *St Emmeram's Church*, with three very early limestone figures (Christ and SS. Emmeram and Dionysius: c. 1050). St Emmeram's (8th–12th c.) has a magnificent Baroque interior by the Asam brothers (1731) and contains very fine *tombs of the 12th–15th c. (Hemma, wife of King Ludwig the German, etc.). Under the church are three crypts (St Emmeram's,

8th–9th c.; St Ramwold's, end of 10th c.; St Wolfgang's, 1052). – The former monastic buildings were from 1812 the *residence of the Princes of Thurn and Taxis*, German postmasters-general until 1866 (valuable art treasures in S wing; beautiful Gothic cloisters; *Stables Museum*, library).

SURROUNDINGS. – *Walhalla, Donaustauf (11 km E), a marble imitation of the Acropolis (by Leo von Klenze, 1830–42), designed as a German Temple of Fame. (Photograph, p. 103.) – *Hall of Liberation, Kelheim (26 km SW), a 59 m high rotunda on the Michelsberg above the Danube, erected 1842–63 to commemorate the Wars of Liberation (1813–15); designed by Friedrich Gärtner and Leo von Klenze; in the interior 34 goddesses of victory by Ludwig von Schwanthaler.

Bad Reichenhall

Land: Bavaria. – Vehicle registration: REI.
Altitude: 470 m. – Population: 18,000.
Post code: D-8230. – Dialling code: 0 86 51.
ⓘ **Kur- und Verkehrsverein**, at station; tel. 14 67.

HOTELS. – *Steigenberger-Hotel Axelmannstein*, Salzburger Str. 4, 218 b., SP, SB, sauna; *Kurhotel Luisenbad*, Ludwigstr. 33, 118 b., SB, sauna; *Residenz Bavaria*, Am Münster, 400 b.; *Panorama*, Baderstr. 6, 126 b., SB; *Bayerischer Hof*, Bahnhofsplatz 14, 93 b.; *Kurhotel Alpina*, Adolf-Schmid-Str. 5, 51 b.; *Deutsches Haus*, Poststr. 32, 55 b.; *Tiroler Hof*, Tiroler Str. 12, 52 b., SB. – IN NONN: *Alpenhotel Fuchs*, 58 b. – ON THUMSEE: *Haus Seeblick*, 94 b., SB. – CAMPING SITE: *Staufeneck*, Piding near Bad Reichenhall.

RESTAURANT. – *Schweizer Stuben*, Nonner Str. 8; *Die Holzstub'n*, Ludwigstr. 33.

CAFÉS. – *Reber*, Ludwigstr. 10; *Dreher*, at Kurpark.

Casino (roulette, baccarat) in Kurhaus.

Bad Reichenhall has a sheltered situation in a wide basin in the Saalach valley framed by hills. It

Cableway up Predigtstuhl, Bad Reichenhall

lies at the entrance to the Berchtesgadener Land near the Austrian frontier. The nearest peaks are the Predigtstuhl (1613 m) and the Hochstaufen (1771 m). The spa has strong brine springs which are used in the treatment of asthma, bronchitis, affections of the upper respiratory passages and rheumatism.

HISTORY. – The bishopric of Salzburg acquired land in Reichenhall about 700, but the place does not appear in the records as a town until 1159. In 1507 numerous springs were tapped; at first the brine was used only for the production of salt, but from the early 18th c. it began to be used for therapeutic purposes. The treatment facilities were brought into use in 1846, and Reichenhall was officially recognised as a spa in 1890.

SIGHTS. – The activity of the resort centres on the **Kurgarten**, with the Kurhaus, Gradierhaus (for the evaporation of brine), pump-room and treatment building. – In the southern part of the town are the *Town Hall*, the Salt-Works (conducted tours of the underground structures containing the springs) and the *parish church* (founded 1181; frescoes by Moritz von Schwind). To the E, higher up, is *Schloss Gruttenstein* (13th–17th c.: flats). – At the NE corner of the town is the former Augustinian house of *St Zeno* (now occupied by the order of English Ladies), with a notable Romanesque *church (12th and 16th c.).

SURROUNDINGS. – Cableway up the *Predigtstuhl (1613 m: extensive views; chair-lift to the Spechtenalm (100 m)).

Rendsburg

Land: Schleswig-Holstein. – Vehicle registration: RD.
Altitude: 7 m. – Population: 32,000.
Post code: D-2370. – Dialling code: 0 43 31.
ⓘ **Amt für öffentliche Einrichtungen und Fremdenverkehr**, Rathaus; tel. 20 62 22.

HOTELS. – *Conventgarten*, Hindenburgstr. 38, 96 b.; *Töpferhaus*, 10 km N on Bistensee, 30 b.; *Hansen*, Bismarkstr. 29, 28 b.; *Schützenheim*, Itzehoer Chaussee 2, 14 b.

RESTAURANTS. – *Zum Landsknecht*, Schleifmühlenstr. 2 (a house dating from 1541); *Alt Nürnberg*, Pastor-Schröder-Str. 16.

RECREATION. – Golf-course (9 holes), open-air and indoor swimming pools.

The old town of Rendsburg, a considerable industrial centre in Schleswig-Holstein, between the two parts of which it forms a link, is

attractively situated between the River Eider, which here opens out in to the semblance of a lake, and the Kiel Canal. It is the most important inland port on the canal.

SIGHTS. – The OLD TOWN is on an island in the Eider. In the Markt is the **Town Hall**, a half-timbered building of 1566, with the *Municipal* and *Heimatmuseum*. The nearby *St Mary's Church* (13th c.) has a fine Baroque altar of 1649. – In the S part of the old town is the NEUWERK district, built 1690–95, with the large Paradeplatz, in which is the interesting *Christkirche* (1695–1700), with the "royal throne". – Also of interest are the *Elektro Museum* (Kieler Strasse 19) and the *Eisenkunstguss Museum* (ironcasting) in BÜDELSDORF.

SE of the town is the **Rendsburg High-Level Bridge* (with a transporter bridge underneath it), on which the railway crosses the Kiel Canal in an elliptical loop. W of the town is a **road tunnel*.

SURROUNDINGS. – Eckernförde (26 km NE), between Eckernförde Bay and the Windebyer Noor, a coastal lagoon. The Gothic St Nicholas's Church has a fine Baroque carved altar and a carved pulpit of 1605; wall paintings (1578) in the choir. In the district of Borby is a Romanesque church of undressed stone.

Reutlingen

Land: Baden-Württemberg.
Vehicle registration: RT.
Altitude: 375 m. – Population: 96,000.
Post code: D-7410. – Dialling code: 0 71 21.
ⓘ **Verkehrsbüro**, Listplatz 1;
tel. 30 35 26/27.

HOTELS. – *Ernst*, Leonhardsplatz, 120 b., SB; *Fürstenhof*, Kaiserpassage 90 b.; *Württemberger Hof*, Kaiserstr. 3, 72 b.; *Reutlinger Hof* (no rest.), Kaiserstr. 33, 55 b., SB.

RESTAURANTS. – *Stadt Reutlingen*, Karlstr. 55; *Ratskeller*, Marktplatz 22.

RECREATION. – Tennis; indoor and open-air swimming pools; ice-rink.

This former free Imperial city lies on the NW slopes of the Swabian Alb. It is now an important centre of the textile, engineering and leatherworking industries, with the West German School of Tanning.

SIGHTS. – **St Mary's Church* (13th–14th c.: Evang.) is one of the finest creations of the High Gothic period in Swabia, with a tower (73 m) of 1343. The nearby "Spendhaus", originally a municipal warehouse, now houses the *Municipal Library*, a natural history museum and temporary art exhibitions. Not far away, in a 15th c. half-timbered building, is the *Heimatmuseum*, with a room devoted to the economist *Friedrich List* (1789–1846), son of a Reutlingen tanner. A little way W is the *Town Hall* (1963–65), with the *List Archives*.

In the W part of the town is the former workers' housing area of *Gmindersdorf* (1903). – To the E of the town is the isolated hill of *Achalm* (707 m; remains of a castle, observation tower: 1 hour on foot).

SURROUNDINGS. – 20 km E, charmingly situated in the Erms valley, is the little town of **Bad Urach**, with half-timbered houses (15th and 16th c.: photograph p. 240), a late Gothic church and a 15th c. castle (rich collections) which was the birthplace of Count Eberhard im Bart, founder of Tübingen University. To the W is the new spa establishment, with thermal baths and "Aquadrome" wave-bath. Above the town are the ruins of Hohenurach Castle; nearby are the Urach Falls (26 m high).

Rhine Valley

The **Rhine (Celtic *Renos*, Latin *Rhenus*; "Vater Rhein", "Father Rhine") is Europe's most important waterway and scenically its most beautiful. With a total length of 1320 km, it rises in the Swiss canton of Grisons, where the Vorderrhein and Hinterrhein unite to form the Alpenrhein or Alpine Rhine. It then flows through Lake Constance, forms the Rhine Falls at Schaffhausen and continues on its way to Basle as the Hochrhein (Higher Rhine). From Basle it turns N and flows through the Upper Rhine plain. Between Mainz and Bingen it follows a westerly course and then bears NW through the Rhenish Uplands as the Middle Rhine. Below Bonn it is known as the Lower Rhine. Within the Netherlands it divides into a number of arms which flow separately into the North Sea.

The UPPER RHINE PLAIN, a rift valley some 30–40 km wide, is bounded on the E by the Black Forest, the Kraichgau and the Odenwald, on the W by the Vosges, the Haardt and the uplands of the northern Palatinate. Its deposits of loess form a

fertile fruit- and wine-growing region
(the Markgräflerland, Ortenau, Deutsche
Weinstrasse and Bergstrasse areas). The
old stronghold of Breisach rears above the
river on its steep crag, and beyond this are
Karlsruhe, with its palace, Mannheim with
its regular grid of streets, and the cathedral
cities of Speyer, Worms and Mainz.

In its middle course the Rhine flows
between the RHEINGAU (on right) and
RHEINHESSEN (on left) for some 100
km. Both of these areas lie within the
MAINZ BASIN, which forms the northern
termination of the trough-like depression
of the Upper Rhine plain and, like it, was
the result of a rift in Tertiary times. – The
Rheingau and the Rheinhessen uplands
were at one stage submerged by water
and were separated from one another only
in geologically recent times. How far the
water extended at one time is shown by
the interesting fossil-rich deposits which
can be seen in sand and marl pits at Gau-
Algesheim, Sprendlingen and Weinheim.
At Bingen the river, which at Mainz had
come up against the wall of the Taunus
and made a sharp turn westward, changes
its course again and flows through the
Rhenish Uplands against the grain of the
rock, cutting across the hard quartzites of
the Hunsrück and Taunus. In this resistant
rock it is confined to a narrow gorge-like
valley. The hills rose slowly from the
middle Tertiary onwards, while the Rhine
cut its way in stages into a pre-existing
trough, creating a terraced landscape
pattern; and accordingly boulder clay
deposited by the Rhine is found at varying
altitudes.

The PASSAGE THROUGH THE RHINE SLATES,
with its changes of gradient, creates
difficulties of navigation – at the Binger
Loch ("Bingen Hole"), the legendary
Loreley Rock and St. Goar. In the more
open loess basins between these places
there is space for prosperous living, for the
growing of vines and fruit. These variations, together with the castles crowning
the steep **hills** on either side and the
islands in the river, produce an ever-
changing pattern of scenery. Oestrich,
Rüdesheim and Assmannshausen are
well known for their wines. Bacharach
and Oberwesel are fascinating little medieval towns. At St. Goarshausen are the
two castles known as the "Cat" and the
"Mouse", at Kamp-Bornhofen two others
called the "Enemy Brothers". Burg Lahneck watches over the entrance to the

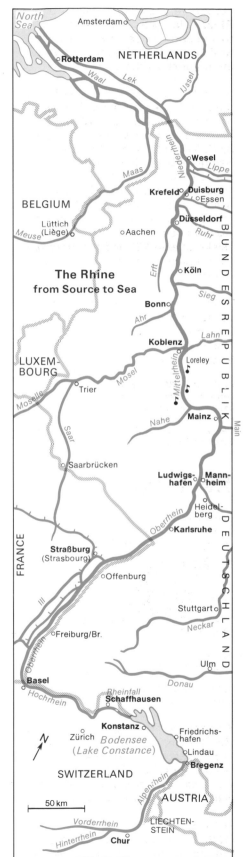

The Rhine
from Source to Sea

Burg Stahleck and Bacharach, on the Rhine

Lahn valley. Below Koblenz, where the Moselle flows into the Rhine at Deutsches Eck, the valley opens out into the little *Neuwied basin*, in which active industry has developed. Shortly before the river enters the Lower Rhine plain it passes on the right an outlier of the Westerwald, the distinctively shaped Siebengebirge (460 m), which takes its name from the seven hills of which it is composed and forms a striking landmark at the lower end of the Middle Rhine.

The river then enters the COLOGNE or LOWER RHINE PLAIN, a gently undulating region with a number of major towns like the Federal capital of Bonn, the cathedral city of Cologne, the art city of Düsseldorf and the port town of Duisburg. The Lower Rhine really begins at Duisburg. The towns here are smaller but show evidence of a long history. Wesel was an important fortress town, Xanten a Roman station, Kalkar was famed for its school of woodcarving, Kleve (Cleves) was once a Ducal capital. Then after passing Elten, under a hill crowned by a monastery, the Rhine crosses the frontier into the Netherlands.

The **water-level** of the Rhine is the most regular of any German river. It is only rarely (in September or October) that there is insufficient water for navigation. The numerous tributaries have an equalising effect. The largest of these is the *Main*, which joins the Rhine at Mainz (canalised: work in progress on development of Rhine-Main-Danube waterway for large vessels); others are the *Nahe* (which comes in from the S at Bingen), the *Lahn* (from the E at Lahnstein) and the *Moselle* (from the SW at Koblenz).

With its mild climate, the Rhine seldom freezes over, though there may sometimes be drift-ice. – The Rhine has a relatively steep **gradient**, falling from 250 m above sea level at Basle to 80 m at Mainz, 60 m at Koblenz and only 10 m at Emmerich.

The Rhine's greatest **width**, between Mainz and Bingen, is from 400 to 800 m. In its passage through the Rhenish Uplands it narrows to 250 m at the Binger Loch and 90–150 m at the Loreley Rock, but at Cologne it widens again to 350 m. – The river tends to wander a little and form **islands**, known as "Aue" above Bingen and "Werthe" below, which add variety to the scenery.

Navigation presents the greatest difficulty between Bingen and St. Goar on account of the steep gradient and the narrowness of the channel. The river authorities devote considerable effort to maintaining the navigability of the river by dredging and the blasting away of dangerous rock faces. The artificially created shipping channel is marked by buoys, beacons and floating booms, and at points where visibility is restricted the traffic upstream and downstream is regulated by warning signs (lamps, flags, balls, revolving signs). Navigation on the Rhine, which within German territory is subject to the authority of the Federal Ministry of Transport, was internationalised in 1831. – On both banks of the Middle Rhine run *railway lines* and *roads* (on the left bank B 9, the "Rheingoldstrasse", on the right bank B 42, the "Loreley-Burgenstrasse"), which carry heavy traffic.

The **Köln-Düsseldorfer Deutsche Rheinschiffahrt** company (*KD*: head office at Frankenwerft 15, 5000 Köln 1, tel. 02 21-2 08 80, telex 08-88 27 23) runs regular PASSENGER SERVICES on the Rhine with a fleet of comfortable and well-equipped motor-ships and steamers (at times the paddle-boat "Goethe" and the hydrofoil "Rheinpfeil"; restaurants on board). The services begin at Easter and end in mid October (main season July and Aug.). – A joint service is provided by KD and the Federal Railways, under which (at KD offices only) a rail ticket can be exchanged for a boat ticket, or vice versa. – KD also offers *organised trips* on the Rhine (Switzerland-France-Germany-Netherlands), in well-equipped vessels with cabin accommodation.

The beautiful riverside scenery and the excellent state of the river-bed offer the prospect of trips by MOTOR-BOAT or CANOE. The German Canoe Club (*Deutscher Kanu-Verband*) has many boat-houses, hostels, camping sites and canoe stations on the Rhine, listed in the "Deutsches Fluss- und Zeltwanderbuch". Information and advice can also be obtained from ADAC, the German Automobile Club (pleasure boating information section). Numerous boating maps of the river can be obtained in bookshops.

In consequence of the heavy pollution of the water – though considerable efforts are now being made to combat this – the FISH STOCKS of the Rhine have been decimated and the catch of fish (in the past chiefly salmon) has fallen practically to zero. Bathing in the Rhine should be avoided at all costs.

Rhön

Länder: Bavaria and Hesse.

ⓘ Fremdenverkehrsverband Rhön,
Wörthstrasse 15,
D-6400 Fulda;
tel. (06 61) 10 63 05.

The Rhön is an upland region between Fulda and Bad Kissingen, with hills rising to 950 m. The southern and eastern parts, with Bruckenau and Bischofsheim on the Kreuzberg, belong to Bavaria, the NW, with Gersfeld and the Wasserkuppe, to Hesse and the northeastern tip to Thuringia (GDR). Tertiary volcanic flows have overlaid a basement of Bunter sandstone and Muschelkalk limestone with a massive layer of basalts and phonolites, in which the later carving-out of valleys between 200 and 400 m deep has created the present curiously formed hills, often with rounded tops.

The HOHE RHÖN is a plateau region at 700–900 m, covered with grass and high moorland. To the W is the VORDERRHÖN, with isolated hills, either conical in form (like the Wachtküppel, a basaltic cone 706 m high) or hog-backed (Milseburg, 835 m, a rugged crag of phonolite), and to the S the highest hill in the Rhön, the *Wasserkuppe* (950 m), a favourite resort of gliding and hang-gliding enthusiasts. To the S of Bischofsheim and Gersfeld extends the FORESTED RHÖN, with long ridges covered with mixed forest, reaching its highest point in the *Kreuzberg* (932 m, with wide views; Franciscan friary, Crucifixion group).

The most beautiful part of the Rhön is the area round Gersfeld, with roads up to the Wasserkuppe and the Wachtküppel. – Much of the range is now a nature park. Following the "Hochrhönring" (silver thistle emblem) one gets to know the north of the nature park (Guckaisee Leisure Park near Poppenhausen).

The main health and holiday resorts are *Gersfeld* and *Bischofsheim,* where there are also facilities for winter sports. Popular health resorts are *Bad Brückenau* in the Sinn valley and *Bad Neustadt an der Saale.* The leading spa in the Rhön area, and indeed in the whole of Bavaria, is *Bad Kissingen* in the beautiful valley of the Franconian Saale.

Rothenburg
ob der Tauber

Land: Bavaria. – Vehicle registration: AN (ROT). Altitude: 425 m. – Population: 13,000. Post code. D-8803. = Dialling code. 0 90 01.

ⓘ Kultur- und Fremdenverkehrsamt,
Rathaus, Marktplatz;
tel. 20 38.

HOTELS. – *Eisenhut,* Herrngasse 3, 145 b.; *Goldener Hirsch,* Untere Schmiedgasse 16, 145 b.; *Markusturm,* Rödergasse 1, 55 b., sauna; *Burg Hotel* (no rest.), Klostergasse 1, 40 b.; *Mittermeier,* Vorm Würzburger Tor 9, 25 b., SB, sauna; *Stadt Rothenburg,* An der Hofstatt 3, 65 b.; *Reichs Küchenmeister,* Kirchplatz 8, 64 b.; *Adam,* Burggasse 29, 20 b.; *Roter Hahn,* Obere Schmiedgasse 21, 70 b. – YOUTH HOSTEL: *Rossmühle,* 141 b.; Spitalhof, 90 b. – CAMPING SITE: *Tauber-Idyll,* on N side of Detwang.

RESTAURANTS. – *Baumeisterhaus,* Obere Schmiedgasse 3; *Ratsstube,* Marktplatz 6.

CAFÉ. – *Prezel,* Marktplatz 5.

EVENTS. – Pageant play, "**The Master Draught**", Shepherds' Dance (at Whitsun and several times during the summer); *Reichsstadt Festival* (Sept.).

This old Franconian Imperial city is picturesquely situated on the steep bank of the Tauber. With its surrounding walls and towers, almost untouched since the Thirty Years War, it is of unique charm and interest as a completely preserved little ** medieval town.

HISTORY. – Rothenburg grew up under the protection of a Hohenstaufen castle in the 12th c. It became a free Imperial city about 1274, and under its energetic burgomaster Heinrich Toppler rose to prosperity at the end of the 14th c. During the Thirty Years War the town, which supported Gustavus Adolphus, was taken by storm by Imperial troops under Tilly.

SIGHTS. – In the MARKTPLATZ stands the *Town Hall, one of the finest in southern Germany. The side which faces on to Herrngasse is Gothic (13th c.), with a 16th c. tower (50 m: view); the main front on the Marktplatz is Renaissance (1572–78); fine Imperial Hall (drama, concerts). On the N side of the square is the former *Ratstrinkstube* (1466): clock with mechanical figures representing the "master draught" with which Burgomaster Nusch saved the town from plundering by Imperial forces in 1631 (daily 11 a.m., noon, 1, 2, 3 p.m. and 9, 10 p.m.). Here the pageant play commemorating the occasion is performed at Whitsun and on certain Sundays during the summer. – At the entrance to HERRNGASSE (Gothic and Renaissance patrician houses), on left, is the town's most beautiful fountain, the *Herterich* or *St George's Fountain* (1608). Farther along the street is the early Gothic *Franciscan Church* (Evang.),

The Plönlein, Rothenburg ob der Tauber

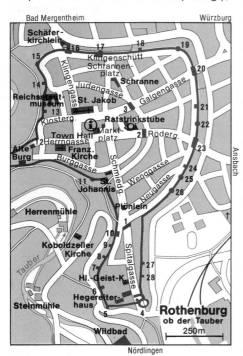

THE FORTIFICATIONS

1 Siebersturm
2 Markusturm with Röderbogen (arch)
3 Weisser Turm (White Tower)
4 Spitalbastei (Hospital Bastion)
5 Sauturm (Sow's Tower)
6 Stöberleinsturm
7 Kalturm (Limestone Tower)
8 Fischturm (Fish Tower)
9 Kohlturm
10 Koboldzeller Bastei
11 Johanniterturm
12 Burgturm (Castle tower with bastion)

13 Bettelvogtsturm
14 Klosterturm (Monastery Tower: passage for pedestrians)
15 Strafturm (Punishment Tower)
16 Klingentor (Sword Gate)
17 Pulverturm (Powder Tower)
18 Henkersturm (Hangman's Tower)
19 Kummerecksturm/Ganserturm
20 Galgentor (Gallows gate)
21 Thomasturm
22 Weiberturm (Women's Tower)
23 Rödertor
24 Hohennersturm
25 Schwefelturm (Sulphur Tower)
26 Faulturm
27 Grosser Stern (Great Star)
28 Kleiner Stern (Little Star)

with fine tombstones. Herrngasse ends at the *Burgtor* (close by, the *Puppet Theatre*), which leads into the **Burggarten**, on the site of the Hohenstaufen castle destroyed in an earthquake in 1356 (magnificent *view).

Just N of the Town Hall is *St James's Church* (1373–1436: Evang.), with a high altar which in composition and total effect is one of the finest in Germany. In the W choir is the *Altar of the Holy Blood by Tilman Riemenschneider (1501–04). – To the NW of the church is the *Imperial City Museum*, in a former Dominican nunnery.

From the Marktplatz OBERE SCHMIEDGASSE runs S. On the left (No. 3) is the *Baumeisterhaus* (1596: restaurant), and adjoining it (No. 5) is the *Gasthaus zum Greifen*, once the residence of Burgomaster Heinrich Toppler (d. 1408). Farther along, on the right, is *St John's Church* (1393–1403). Nearby at Burggasse 3 is the interesting *Kriminalmuseum*. At the end of UNTERE SCHMIEDGASSE, at a street intersection, is the *Plönlein, one of the most picturesque corners of the town. – From here under the *Siebersturm* into SPITALGASSE, passing the early Gothic *Spitalkirche* (on right) and the *Spital* (1574–78; in the picturesque courtyard the "Hegereiterhäuschen" of 1591), to the massive 16th c. **Spitaltor**.

There is an interesting and attractive walk (25 min.) round the *town walls on the wall-walk, from the Spitaltor by way of the *Rödertor* (view) to the *Klingentor* and *St Wolfgang's Church* (1473–92). – Outside the town in the Tauber valley is the **Topplerschlösschen**, a tower-like house built by Burgomaster Toppler in 1388.

SURROUNDINGS. – **Detwang** (3 km NW), in the Tauber valley, with a *Crucifixion by Tilman Riemenschneider (*c*. 1512–13) in the central shrine of the high altar in the little Romanesque-Gothic church. – **Creglingen** (17 km NW), also in the Tauber valley, with an arresting carved altar by Tilman Riemenschneider, the **Marienaltar (*c*. 1505–10), in the Herrgottskirche (1386–96).

Rottweil

Land: Baden-Württemberg.
Vehicle registration: RW.
Altitude: 600 m. – Population: 24,000.
Post code: D-7210. – Dialling code: 07 41.
(i) **Städtisches Verkehrsbüro**, Town Hall; tel. 9 42 80/81.

HOTELS. – *Bären*, Hochmaurenstr. 1, 59 b.; *Johanniterbad*, Johannsergasse 12, 42 b.; *Lamm*, Hauptstr. 45, 35 b.

RECREATION. – Tennis, riding, swimming, skiing.

EVENTS. – **Rottweiler Narrensprung** ("Fools' Dance": Rose Monday and Shrove Tuesday).

This former free Imperial city is picturesquely situated above the steep bank of the upper Neckar and has many interesting old buildings. It is celebrated for its Carnival ("Fasnet"), with *masks.

SIGHTS. – In the HAUPTSTRASSE is the late Gothic **Town Hall** (1521), opposite which is the *Municipal Museum* (collection of Carnival masks). A little way N is the Gothic *Minster* of the Holy Cross (13th–15th c.: R.C.), with numerous carved altars; above the high altar is a crucifix, perhaps by Veit Stoss. – In Friedrichsplatz is the *Evangelical Parish Church*, formerly a Dominican church, with ceiling paintings (1755). Nearby is *St Lawrence's Chapel* (16th c.), with a collection of medieval sculpture in stone and wood. *Market Fountain* of 1540 (partly reproduction). In Hochbrücktorstrasse is the Baroque *Kapellenkirche* (R.C.), with a Gothic tower. In the Unteres Bohrhaus is the *Salt Museum*. To the SE are *Roman baths*.

Ruhr

Land: North Rhineland-Westphalia.
(i) **Landesverkehrsverband Westfalen e. V.**, Balkenstr. 40, D-4600 Dortmund 1; tel. (02 31) 57 17 15.

The Ruhr, between the rivers Ruhr and Lippe, is one of the largest industrial regions in Europe and a major element in the economy of Federal Germany. Founded on coal-mining, it has developed into a huge industrial complex centred particularly on iron and steel, chemicals, engineering and textiles. A dense network of roads, railways and waterways covers this heavily populated region in which housing areas and industrial installations often merge imperceptibly into one another. The amalgamation of rural communes and towns in 1929 produced a number of agglomerations of considerable size.

The largest city in the Ruhr is **Essen** (pop. 645,000), a coal-mining centre with much heavy industry which in 1812 had no more than 3500 inhabitants. The former Hanseatic town of **Dortmund** owes its prosperity to coal, iron and beer. **Duisburg** has Europe's largest inland port. **Bochum** has the Ruhr University and the Institute of Space Research. **Recklinghausen** has made its cultural mark with its Ruhr Festival.

In spite of the predominance of industry the Ruhr also has excellent facilities for recreation, like the forests between the Emscher and the Lippe or the Ruhr valley, with scope for water sports on the *Baldeneysee*, *Harkortsee* and *Hengsteysee*. The cities too have provided themselves with lungs like the *Grugapark* in Essen and the *Westfalenpark* in Dortmund.

The Ruhr also has such historic buildings as the *Minster* in Essen, *Werden Abbey Church* and *St Reinold's Church* in Dortmund, as well as more modern technological achievements like the *Television Tower* in Dortmund's Westfalenpark, the *Planetarium* in Bochum and the *Henrichenburg Ship-Lift* near Datteln.

Saarbrücken

Land: Saar. – Vehicle registration: SB.
Altitude: 182 m. – Population: 199,000.
Post code: D-6600. – Dialling code: 06 81.
(i) **Amt fur Öffentlichkeitsarbeit,
Kongresswesen und Fremdenverkehr,**
Rathaus,
tel. 300 13 04/05;
Städtischer Informationspavillon,
Trierer Str. 2,
tel. 3 65 15.

Ludwigskirche, Saarbrücken

HOTELS. – *Etap Kongress Hotel,* Hafenstr. 8, 300 b.,
SB, sauna; *Novotel,* Zinzingerstr. 9, 198 b., SB; *Etap
Hotel Haus Berlin,* Faktoreistr. 2, 120 b.; *Am Triller,*
Trillerweg 57, 240 b., SB, sauna ("Chez Marianne"
rôtisserie); *Christine,* Gersweiler Str. 39, 100 b., SB,
sauna; *Windsor,* Hohenzollernstr. 41, 71 b., sauna;
Park Hotel, Am Deutsch Französischen Garten, 66 b.
– YOUTH HOSTEL: Meerwiesertalweg 31, 170 b. –
CAMPING SITES: *Saarbrücken,* on Spicherer Berg;
Burbach, Mettlacher Str.

RESTAURANTS. – *Welsch,* Breite Str. 12; *Ratskeller,*
in Rathaus, Rathausplatz; *Handleshof,* Wilhelm Heinrich Str. 17; *La Tourain,* in the Kongrasshalle, Hafenstr.
2; *Schloss Halaberg,* right of Mainzer Str.

WINE-BARS. – *Winzerstube d'Alsace,* Deutschherrenstr. 3; *Weinstube Hauck,* St. Johanner Markt 7.

CAFÉS. – *Menn,* Victoriastr. 32; *Fretter,* corner of
Hohenzollernstr. and Eisenbahnstr.

**Saarbrücken, situated in the forest-
fringed valley of the Saar, in the
middle of the Saar coalfield, is the**
capital and the economic and cultural centre of the *Land,* with a
University, a Teachers' Training College and an Academy of Music as
well as the headquarters of the Saar
radio and television comporation.
Situated in the frontier area between Germany and France, it is also
notable for its trade fairs.

HISTORY. – There was originally a Celtic settlement
on the site; and later the Romans built a stone bridge
over the Saar and a fortress to protect it. Later still
there was a Frankish royal stronghold here, *Villa
Sarabrucca.* In more modern times Saarbrücken was
the residence of the Counts (later Princes) of Nassau-
Saarbrücken, and in the 18th c. had a period of
brilliance under Prince Heinrich (1741–68), whose
court architect Friedrich Joachim Stengel embellished the town with a number of imposing Baroque
buildings. In the 19th and 20th c., thanks to its large
reserves of iron ore and coal, the town developed into
an important industrial centre.

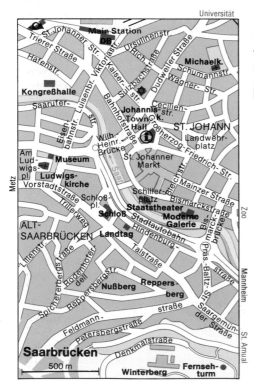

Saarbrücken

500 m

SIGHTS. – On the right bank of the Saar is
the lively district of ST. JOHANN, with
the principal business and shopping
streets, the *station* and the *Town Hall*
(1897–1900). S of the station, on the
banks of the Saar, is the *Congress Hall*
(restaurant). S of the Baroque ST. JOHAN-
NER MARKT are the *Municipal Theatre* and
the *Modern Gallery* with the richly stocked *Saarland Museum* (Rococo and
Biedermeier art, modern art), near which
is *St John's Church* (1758: R.C.).

In the SCHLOSSPLATZ, in the district of
ALT-SAARBRÜCKEN on the left bank of
the Saar, are the *Old Town Hall* and
Hereditary Prince's Palace (both 18th c.)
and the **Castle** (19th c.: now government
offices). From the castle grounds there is a
fine view of the town. A little lower down
is the late Gothic *Schlosskirche* (modern
*stained glass by G. Meistermann, tombs
of Princes). NW of the Schlossplatz, in
the middle of LUDWIGSPLATZ with its
fine Baroque houses, is the **Ludwigskirche** (1762–65, by F. J. Stengel,

restored, with modern interior: Evang.). At Ludwigsplatz 15 is the *Museum of Prehistory and Early History.*

In the district of ST. ARNUAL, 3 km SE, is the former * **Collegiate Church of St. Arnual** (13th–14th c.: Evang.), with numerous tombs of members of the House of Nassau-Saarbrücken. In the SW of the town is the *German-French Garden* (amusement park with a water-organ and *"Gulliver's Mini-World"*).

5 km NE of the town centre, in wooded country at the foot of the Schwarzenberg, are the modern buildings of the **Saarland University.** – On the outskirts of the town, on the road to St. Ingbert (B 40), are (on right) the *Halberg* (castle; Saarland Radio) and (on left) the entrance to the *Zoo* (more than 600 animals).

Saar Valley

Länder: Saar and Rhineland-Palatinate.
ⓘ **Fremdenverkehrsverband Saarland e. V.**,
Am Stiefel 2, D-6600 Saarbrücken;
tel. (06 81) 3 53 76.

The River Saar, known to the Romans as the Saravus, rises in the Vosges, flows into the Moselle and has a total length of 246 km. Between Saargemünd (Sarreguemines) and Saarbrücken it forms the frontier between Germany (the Saarland) and France (Lorraine).

In the wide Saar valley are industrial towns like **Saarbrücken** (see above), *Völklingen, Saarlouis* and *Dillingen.* At *Merzig,* where the river is bordered by rich orchards, the valley becomes narrower. Near *Mettlach* (manufacture of ceramics; former Benedictine abbey) is the long forest-fringed *Saar bend, one of the great beauty spots of the Saar valley. The best view is to be had from the viewpoint at *Cloef* or the ruined *Montclair Castle.* The river then pursues a winding course through the hills. *Saarburg,* dominated by its castle, is the centre of the Saar wine trade. In the centre of the little town is a 20 m high waterfall on the Leukbach. The river then continues past a series of idyllic wine villages – *Ockfen, Schoden, Wiltingen, Kanzem, Filzen, Könen* – and flows into the Moselle at *Konz.*

Sauerland

Land: North Rhineland-Westphalia.
ⓘ **Landesverkehrsverband Westfalen e. V.**,
Balkenstr. 4, D-4600 Dortmund 1;
tel. (02 31) 57 17, 15.
Kreisverkehrsverband Südsauerland e. V.,
Seminarstr. 22, D-5960 Olpe/Biggesee;
tel. (0 27 61) 68 22.

The attractive Sauerland ("south land") area is a beautifully wooded upland region to the S of the industrial belt of the Rhineland and Westphalia, slashed by numerous winding river valleys and rising to a height of 843 m in the Hegekopf and Langenberg near Willingen and 841 m in the Kahler Asten (Rothaargebirge) near Winterberg. The largest river in the Sauerland, which is bounded on the S by the Sieg, is the Ruhr, reinforced by the Möhne at Neheim-Hüsten and the Lenne at Hohensyburg. The hills are largely slate, with intrusions of eruptive rock and limestones. The area is fairly densely populated; its main industry is the manufacture of hardware.

In the valley bottoms and on the hillsides are picturesque old towns like *Altena, Arnsberg, Attendorn, Brilon, Hohenlimburg, Iserlohn* and *Marsberg,* and there are many health and holiday resorts. *Willingen* and **Winterberg** are popular winter sports resorts. Many of the rivers have been dammed to provide water supplies and electric power (*Bigge, Diemel, Ennepe, Henne, Lister, Möhne, Sorpe* and *Verse* dams). Among the features which make up the particular scenic charm of the Sauerland are the deeply hewn valleys of the *Hönne, Lenne, Möhne, Ruhr, Sorpe* and *Volme,* hills like the *Kahler Asten* (841 m) near Winterberg

The Biggesee in the southern Sauerland

and the *Hohe Bracht* (584 m) near Bilstein with their wide-ranging views, the impressive porphyry crags of the *Bruchhauser Steine*, the extensive *Felsenmeer* (Sea of Rocks) at Hemer and bizarre stalactitic caves like the *Attahöhle* (Attendorn), *Dechenhöhle* (Iserlohn) and *Bilsteinhöhle* (Warstein). A tourist attraction of a different kind is *Fort Fun*, near Olsberg, with a Wild West town, a holiday village and castle hotel, a double chair-lift (to the 732 m high Stüppel), chutes, facilities for riding and tilt-cart rides.

Schleswig

Land: Schleswig-Holstein.
Vehicle registration: SL.
Altitude: 14 m. – Population: 30,000
Post code: D-2380. – Dialling code: 0 46 21.
(i) **Städtisches Touristburo**,
     Plessenstr. 7;
     tel. 8 14 – 2 26.

HOTELS. – *Strandhalle*, Strandweg 2, 45 b., SB, SP, sauna, garden terrace; *Skandia*, Lollfuss 89, 50 b.; *Waldhotel am Schloss Gottorf*, An der Stampfmühle 1, 20 b.; *Zum Weissen Schwan*, Gottorsstr. 1, 26 b. – IN PULVERHOLZ: *Waldschlösschen*, Kolonenweg 152, 75 b. – IN HADDEBY (2·5 km SE): *Historisches Gasthaus Haddeby*, 30 b. – YOUTH HOSTEL: *Nordmark-Jugendherberge*, Spielkoppel 1, 129 b.

RESTAURANTS. – *Schlosskeller*, in Schloss Gottorf; *Schleimöve*, Süderholm 8 (specially gulls' eggs, May–June fish dishes).

CAFÉ. – *Wikingturm*, in Wikingturm.

EVENTS. – *Spring Market* (end Apr.–beginning May); *Shooting Festival* (in summer); *Peermarkt* (end Aug.–beginning Sept.); **Schlei Week** with sailing regatta (July).

Schleswig, the old residence town of the Dukes of Gottorf, is attractively situated at the head of the Schlei, a fjord-like arm of the sea. The harbour is only used for sporting and leisure purposes. It is the seat of the Supreme Court and Administrative Court of the *Land* and other government agencies and the see of an Evangelical bishop. Its position and historic importance have made the town of interest to visitors.

HISTORY. – The forerunner of the town was the old trading settlement of Haithabu. Schleswig itself first appears in the records in 808 as *Sliesthorp* and *Slieswic*. In 947 it became the see of a bishop, and about 1200 it obtained its municipal charter. From 1544 to 1713 Schloss Gottorf was the seat of the Dukes of Schleswig-Holstein-Gottorf, a collateral line of the Danish royal house. From 1867 Schleswig was capital of the newly established province of Schleswig-Holstein. After the Second World War the government of the *Land* was transferred to Kiel.

SIGHTS. – In the heart of the OLD TOWN is the Romanesque-Gothic **Cathedral** (12th–15th c.), with a tower (110·5 m) of 1894. It contains the famous ****Bordesholm Altar** by Hans Brüggemann, a masterpiece of late Gothic carving with 392 figures crowned by the Virgin, and the magnificent free-standing marble tomb of King Frederick I of Denmark, who had previously been Duke of Schleswig and died in the town in 1533; fine cloisters with 14th c. wall paintings. – To the E of the old town is the old fishermen's quarter of HOLM, with *St John's Convent* (fine 13th c. stalls in chapterhouse). In the Schlei is the *Möweninsel* (Gull Island: 1000 gulls' eggs a day in spring).

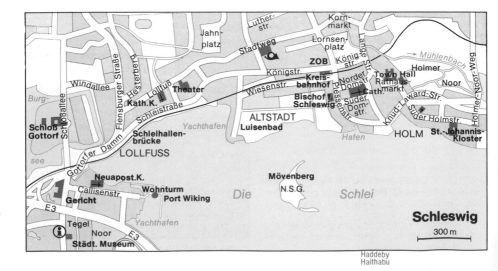

In the FRIEDRICHSBERG district at the W end of the Schlei is **Schloss Gottorf**, a large palace of the 16th–18th c. (particularly fine are the sumptuous chapel, the Royal Hall and the Stags' Hall), once a fortress and Ducal residence, now housing the two most important museums in Schleswig-Holstein, the *Provincial Museum of the History of Art and Culture, with art treasure from all over the *Land* from the Middle Ages to the 20th c., and the *Provincial Museum of Prehistory and Early History. The Museum of Prehistory is the largest of its kind in Germany, since Schleswig-Holstein has yielded the richest harvest of finds. Items of outstanding interest are the 23 m long **Nydam Boat (*c.* A.D. 400), a skull, found in a bog, corpses found in bogs and runic stones from Haithabu. – A short distance S of Schloss Gottorf, in a house at Friedrichstr. 9 built for a Persian embassy in 1834–36, is the *Municipal Museum.* – At the Port Wiking yachting harbour is the *Wikingturm*, a tower block of flats 85 m high.

SURROUNDINGS. – **Haithabu** (2 km S), a Viking harbour and trading settlement on the Haddebyer Noor with a semicircular rampart, destroyed in the 11th c. Finds from archaeological excavations will be on show from 1985 in a *Haithabu Museum*, specially built for the purpose. – **Danewerk** (to SW), an earthwork 15 km long, first built in the 9th c. and maintained and strengthened until the 13th, designed to defend the southern frontier of Danish territory. In the 12th c. the central section was reinforced by the Waldemarsmauer, a brick wall 3·5 km long, 7 m high and 2 m thick (still readily identifiable at Klein-Dannewerk, 4½ km SW of Schleswig). – **Tolk Fairytale Park** (9 km NE).

Schwäbisch Gmünd

Land: Baden-Württemberg.
Vehicle registration: AA (GD).
Altitude: 321 m. – Population: 56,000.
Post code: D-70 70. – Dialling code: 0 71 71.
ⓘ **Städtisches Verkehrsamt,**
Kulturzentrum Prediger,
Johannisplatz 3;
tel. 6 03 – 41 50.

HOTELS. – *Pelikan*, Freudental 26, 51 b.; *Bahnhofhotel Arche*, Bahnhofstr. 12, 32 b.; *Patrizier*, Kornhausstr. 25, 30 b.; *Goldene Krone* (no rest.), Marktplatz 18, 27 b.; *Weber* (no rest.), Ledergasse 14, 25 b. – YOUTH HOSTEL: Taubentalstr. 46/I, 70 b. CAMPING SITE: *Schurrenhof*, near Schwäbisch Gmünd, Rechberg.

RESTAURANTS. – *Postillion*, Königsturmstr. 3 (Swabian and international dishes); *s'Zapfle*, Ledergasse 1.

CAFÉ. – *Zieher*, Marktgässle.

This former free Imperial city lies in the valley of the Rems, on the northern edge of the Swabian Alb. It is noted for its goldsmith's and silversmith's work (vocational training school) and for its glassworks, maintaining Bohemian traditions. It was the birthplace of the 14th c. master-builder Peter Parler and of the painters Hans Baldung, known as Grien, and Jörg Ratgeb.

HISTORY. – Schwäbisch Gmünd was founded during the reign of the first Staufen King, Konrad III (1138–52) as the first Staufen town. After the end of Staufen rule it became a free Imperial city (until 1803), known mainly for its goldsmith's work. During the Second World War the town remained largely unscathed. After 1945 the Gablonz glass and jewellery industry, transferred here from Czechoslovakia, made a major contribution to the town's economy. Today, however, the principal factor in the economy is the metal industry.

SIGHTS. – In the charming elongated MARKET PLACE are the *Town Hall* (1783–85) and the important late Romanesque **St John's Church** (*c.* 1210–30: R.C.), with rich sculptured ornament. A short distance away to the SW is the Gothic *Minster of the Holy Cross (R.C.), basically designed at the beginning of the 14th c. by the Gmünd master-builder Heinrich Parler (father of Peter Parler, who built Prague (Cathedral), one of the earliest large hall-churches in southern Germany. – A few towers belonging to the 15th c. *fortifications* have survived.

The former Dominican monastery, now the "Prediger" cultural centre, houses the *Civic Museum* (history of the countryside and culture). – Beyond the station is the pilgrimage chapel of *St Salvator* hewn out of the rock (1617–20: fine view). – In the western part of the town are remains of the Roman fort of *Schirenhof*.

SURROUNDINGS. – **Hohenrechberg** (707 m: 9 km S), with a ruined castle and a pilgrimage chapel; wide-ranging views. – **Hohenstaufen** (684 m: 15 km SW), site of the ancestral castle of the Staufen family, destroyed in the peasant war of 1525 and later razed to the ground; magnificent *view.

Schwäbisch Hall

Land: Baden-Württemberg.
Vehicle registration: SHA.
Altitude: 270 m. – Population: 32,500.
Post code: D-7170. – Dialling code: 07 91.
(i) **Informations- und Kulturamt,**
Am Markt 9;
tel. 75 13 21.

HOTELS. – *Hohenlohe*, Weillertor 14, 150 b., brine bath, sauna; *Ratskeller*, Am Markt 12, 100 b., SB, sauna; *Scholl* (no rest.), Klosterstr. 3, 31 b.; *Goldener Adler*, Am Markt 11, 30 b.; *Simon* (no rest.), Schweikkerweg 25, 24 b.

RESTAURANT. – *Schuhbäck*, Untere Herrengasse 1 (grill-room).

EVENTS. – Historical *cakes and springwater festival of the Salt-Boilers* (Whitsun); **Open-air performances** on steps of St Michael's (June–Aug.); *Summernight's festival* (Aug.); *Street plays* (Sept.); *Muzzle-loader shooting* (Sept.).

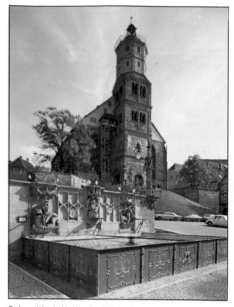

Schwabisch Hall – St. Michael

The former free Imperial city of Hall lies in the deeply indented valley of the Kocher on the north-eastern fringe of the Swabian Forest. Within the town, on the right bank of the river, is the brine spring which was once used to produce salt but now serves therapeutic purposes. It is a charming little town, with the church of St Michael (patron saint of the town) and its great flights of steps, the covered wooden footbridges over the Kocher, the half-timbered houses rising in tiers up the slope, the old defensive towers and the many picturesque nooks and crannies about the town.

HISTORY. Schwäbisch Hall owes its prosperity to salt which was worked here as early as Celtic times. About 1180 the Haller Pfennige (coins known as "Heller") were struck; about 1280 Schwäbisch Hall became an imperial city. After internal constitutional struggles in the 15th and 16th c. the town gained a civil administration. In 1802/03 Hall and its territory passed to Württemburg which propriated the brine springs in return for the payment of a perpetual sum. The spring is now used as a brine-bath.

SIGHTS. – In the *MARKTPLATZ, one of the most impressive market squares in Germany in its compact and consistent architectural setting, is the Baroque *Town Hall* (1728–35). A flight of steps (on which the festival performances are given in summer) leads up to **St Michael's Church** (15th c.: Evang.), with a notable interior (high altar of 1470). Above the church are the *Crailsheim Gate* (1515) and the handsome *Neubau* ("New Build-

ing": erected 1527 as an arsenal; Great Hall). In the nearby Untere Herrengasse is the *Keckenburg Museum* (history of the town). Attractive old footbridges span the Kocher and the island of Unterwöhrd. On the left bank of the Kocher, in the district of ST. KATHARINA, are *St Catherine's Church* (choir of 1343 with valuable stained glass) and the *Powder Tower* (1490). – In the suburb of UNTERLIMPURG, S of the Marktplatz, is *St Urban's Church* (13th c.). From here there is a footpath to the scanty remains of the *Limpurg*, a 13th c. castle which was later enlarged.

SURROUNDINGS. – **Comburg** (Gross-Comburg, 3 km SE). This former Benedictine abbey (1079, now a teachers' training college) on a 340 m high conical hill above the right bank of the Kocher is a magnificent example of a fortified Benedictine house dating from the heyday of the order. 6 km W of Schwäbisch Hall the *Hohenlohe Open-air Museum Wackershofen* is in course of development.

Schweinfurt

Land: Bavaria. – Vehicle registration: SW.
Altitude: 218 m. – Population: 53,000.
Post code: D-8720. – Dialling code: 0 97 21.
(i) **Städtisches Verkehrsamt**
und Verkehrsverein,
Rathaus, Metzgergasse;
tel. 5 14 97/8.

HOTELS. – *Dorint Panorama Hotel* (no rest.), Am Oberen Marienbach 1, 154 b.; *Ross*, Postplatz 9, 120

b., SB, sauna; *Central* (no rest.), Zehntstr. 20, 74 b.;
Parkhotel, Hirtengasse 6a, 55 b. – YOUTH HOSTEL:
Niederwerrner Str. 17½, 125 b.

RESTAURANTS. – *Weinrestaurant Gösswein*, Fis-
cherrain 67; *Ratskeller*, Markt 1.

RECREATION. – Open-air and indoor swimming
pools; riding; ice-rink.

**This former free Imperial city on the
Main has important factories producing ball bearings, small motors
and specialised machinery as well as
dyeworks.**

SIGHTS. – In the MARKT is the **Town Hall**
(1570–72), a masterpiece of German
Renaissance architecture by the Saxon
architect Nikolaus Hofmann. At the corner of Rückertstrasse is the birthplace of
the poet *Friedrich Rückert* (1788–1866);
there is a monument to him in the Markt.
St John's Church (originally late Romanesque), N of the Markt, has a beautiful
Bride's Door. Opposite the church, to the
N, is the *Municipal Museum*, with a
collection of birds. In the NW of the town
is *St Kilian's Church* (1953: R.C.), with
a beautiful stained glass window (250
sq. m) in the choir.

Half-timbered houses in Freudenberg

district) in the Federal Republic. The chief
town of the Kreis, **Siegen**, once the seat
of the Princes of Nassau-Orange and
birthplace of Rubens, is the cultural and
economic centre of the region (steel and
iron-working). Tourism has an important
place in the economy; the motorways
(A45 "Sauerlandlinie" and A4
Cologne–Olpe) provides good connections to the towns of the Rhine, Main and
Ruhr. Waymarked footpaths (over 1000
km) open up the forest. In the villages
many country customs have survived.

Among the most popular HEALTH AND
HOLIDAY RESORTS are **Freudenberg* with
its many half-timbered houses, *Hilchen-
bach, Netphen, Erndtebrück*, etc. *Bad
Berleburg* and *Laasphe* are much frequented health resorts (Kneipp cure).

Siegerland/
Wittgenstein

Land: North Rhineland-Westphalia.
ⓘ **Landesverkehrsverband Westfalen**,
Balkenstr. 40, D-4600 Dortmund 1;
tel. (02 31) 57 17 15.
**Kreisverkehrsverband
Siegerland/Wittgenstein e. V.**,
Koblenzer Str. 73, D-5900 Siegen 1;
tel. (02 71) 3 37 74 78.

**The Siegerland, a region with sub-
stantial industry traversed by the
beautiful valley of the Sieg, is bounded on the N by the Sauerland, on
the W by the Bergisches Land, on the
S by the Westerwald and on the E by
the Wittgensteiner Land round the
old residence town of Berleburg,
with which it has much in common
in terms of both landscape and
economy.**

This upland region of rounded hills
up to 800 m in height is extensively
covered with forest: it is indeed the most
densely forested Kreis (administrative

Soest

Land: North Rhineland-Westphalia.
Vehicle registration: SO.
Altitude: 98 m. – Population: 43,000.
Post code: D-4770. – Dialling code: 0 29 21.
ⓘ **Verkehrsamt**, Am Seel 5;
tel. 10 33 23.

HOTELS. – *Garni Soest*, Siegmund Schultze Weg 100,
50 b.; *Andernach zur Börse*, Thomästr. 31, 36 b.; *Stadt-
Soest* (no rest.), Brüderstr. 50, 33 b.; *Im Wilden Mann*,
Markt 11, 23 b.; *Pilgrim Haus Anno 1304*, Jakobistr.
75, 18 b. – YOUTH HOSTEL: Jahnstadion, Arnsberger
Str., 80 b.

RESTAURANTS. – *Brauerei Christ*, Walburger Str. 36;
Zum Eselstall, Leckgadum 37; *Rocholls Schlemmer-
grill*, Rathausstr. 4; *Hopfenstube*, Brüderstr. 50; *Im
Osterkamp*, Walburger Str. 10.

**This old Westphalian town lies in the
fertile Soester Börde on the northern edge of the Sauerland. It has a**

number of fine churches, charming old half-timbered houses and well-preserved town walls.

HISTORY. – The "Soester Schrae" (c. 1120) is the oldest charter of municipal rights in Germany, providing a model which was followed as far afield as the Baltic region. Soest was an important Hanseatic town, and at the height of its economic power was able to throw off the authority of the Archbishopric of Cologne (in the famous "Soester Fehde", 1444–49). Later the town passed to Brandenburg.

SIGHTS. – In the centre of the town stands the massive *Cathedral of St Patroclus (12th c., restored), one of the most important early Romanesque churches in Westphalia; the choir has 12th C. wall paintings and 13th c. stained glass. To the W is the Romanesque *St Peter's Church* (c. 1150: Evang.), to the E *St Nicholas's Chapel* (R.C.), with wall paintings in mature Romanesque style (mid 13th c.) and an altar-piece by Konrad of Soest (15th c.). To the S, in Thomasstrasse, is the *Wilhelm Mogner House*, with the *Municipal Art Collection*. N of the Cathedral is the *Town Hall* (1713), with the *Municipal Archives* ("Soester Schrae"; two copies of the "Sachsenspiegel", the oldest and most important law-book of the medieval period in Germany).

In the N of the town is the church of **St. Maria zur Höhe** or *Hohnekirche* (completed c. 1225: Evang.), with *wall paintings which are among the finest 13th c. work known. Nearby is the church of *St. Maria zur Wiese or *Wiesenkirche* (14th–15th c.: Evang.), the finest Gothic building in Soest; in the north aisle is the "Westphalian Last Supper" (stained glass of c. 1500). – The most notable feature of the old town walls is the *Osthofentor*, which contains a collection of historic weapons.

SURROUNDINGS. – **Bad Sassendorf** (5 km NE), a small spa (brine and mud-baths), with a Kurpark. – *Möhne Dam (10 km S). The dam (bombed during the last war) is 650 m long and 40 m high; the reservoir is 10 km long and 3½ km wide.

Spessart

Länder: Hesse and Bavaria.
ⓘ **Fremdenverkehrsverband Hessen,**
Abraham-Lincoln-Str. 38–42,
D-6200 Wiesbaden;
tel. (0 61 21) 7 37 25.
Fremdenverkehrsverband Franken,
Am Plärrer 14, D-8500 Nürnberg 81;

The Spessart ("Spechteshart" or "Woodpecker Forest") is a small upland region of deciduous forest at an altitude of some 500 m, bounded on the W, S and E by the rectangular course of the Main (Hanau-Miltenberg-Wertheim-Gemünden) and extending in the N to the area of Schlüchtern in Hesse. The undulating plateau, with no individual peaks of dominating height, is broken up into a series of broad ridges by winding valleys between 150 and 200 m deep with narrow strips of meadowland along the bottom.

To the S is the HOCHSPESSART, covered with a magnificent natural forest of oak and beech, reaching its highest point in the *Geiersberg* (585 m). N of a line from Aschaffenburg to Lohr is the HINTERSPESSART, in which afforestation since the late 18th c. has produced a predominance of fir-trees. The VORSPESSART, N of Aschaffenburg, is a fertile region of Bunter sandstone, gneiss and micaceous schist, reaching a height of 437 m in the *Hahnenkamm*.

Human settlement in this area was long discouraged by the princes of the Church, concerned to preserve their hunting grounds, and a movement of population into the valleys did not get under way until the 13th and 14th c.

The most attractive spots in the Spessart are the picturesque moated castle of *Mespelbrunn* and the areas round *Rohrbrunn* and the old monastic house of *Lichtenau*, with the finest stands of 400-

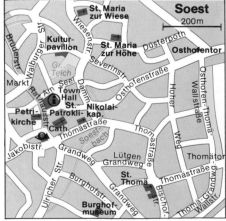

and 500-year-old oaks in Germany ("Metzgergraben"). – The **Main valley** enclosing the Spessart offers the tourist its old-world little towns, *Miltenberg* and *Wertheim* being among the most charming. In the north-western foothills of the Spessart lies the popular resort of *Bad Orb*.

Speyer

Land: Rhineland-Palatinate.
Vehicle registration: SP.
Altitude: 104 m. – Population: 44,000.
Post code: D-6720. – Dialling code: 0 62 32.
ⓘ **Verkehrsamt,**
    Maximilianstr. 11;
    tel. 1 43 92.

HOTELS. – *Goldener Engel,* Mühlturmstr. 27, 66 b.; *Kurpfalz* (no rest.), Mühlturmstr. 5, 25 b.; *Schlosser* (no rest.), Maximilianstr. 10, 23 b., café – ON E BANK OF RHINE: *Rheinhotel Luxhof,* at bridge, 104 b. – YOUTH HOSTEL: Am Leinpfad 4 (at municipal open-air swimming pool), 150 b.

RESTAURANTS. – *Zum Domnapf,* Domplatz; *Weisses Ross,* Johannesstr. 2; *Stadthalle,* Obere Langgasse 11.

CAFÉ. – *Hindenburg,* Maximilianstr. 91.

This old Imperial city, the see of a bishop from the 7th c. and the meeting-place of many Imperial diets, lies on the left bank of the Rhine, dominated by its Romanesque Cathedral.

HISTORY. – The origin of the town was the Roman *Civitas Nemetum.* The name *Spira* first occurs in the 7th c., when Speyer became the see of a bishop. From 1294 to 1797 it was a free Imperial city, in which numerous Imperial diets were held (including the Diet of 1529 at which the Protestant princes and estates made their "Protest" against the anti-Reformation resolutions of the majority). In the 16th and 17th c. it was the seat of the Reichskammergericht (Imperial High Court). In 1689, during the war over the Palatinate succession, the town suffered severe destruction.

SIGHTS. – The six-towered ***Cathedral** (R.C.), the largest and most imposing cathedral of the High Romanesque period in Germany, was begun about 1030 by the Salian Emperor Conrad II and consecrated in 1061. Between 1082 and 1125, in the reigns of Henry IV and V, a major rebuilding took place. In the W porch are statues of the eight Emperors buried in the Cathedral. Raised choir (the "Royal Choir"); *crypt (consecrated 1039) and *Imperial burial vault, with the remains of the Imperial tombs, some of which were plundered by the French in 1689 (including the tombs of Conrad II, d. 1039; Henry III, d. 1056; Henry IV, d. 1106; Henry V, d. 1125; and Rudolf of Habsburg, d. 1291). In front of the Cathedral is the *Domnapf* (1490), a stone basin which was filled with wine at the induction of a new bishop. – A short distance S of the Cathedral are the **Palatinate Historical Museum,** with an outstanding collection of material from ancient, medieval and modern times, the *Diocesan Museum* and an interesting *Wine Museum.* At the end of the nearby Judenbadgasse, lying almost 10 m under ground level in a little garden, is the *Jews' Bath,* belonging to a synagogue which once stood here.

From the Cathedral the wide MAXIMILIANSTRASSE, Speyer's principal street, runs W to the *Altpörtel,* a handsome gate-tower of the 13th and 16th c. – In the SW of the town is the *Gedachtniskirche* (1893–1904), erected to commemorate the Protest of 1529. To the E, at Allerheiligenstr. 4, is the *Feuerbach Museum.* – E of the station is *St Bernard's Church of Peace* (1953–54), built jointly by French and Germans.

SURROUNDINGS. – ***Hassloch Holiday Park** (14 km NW), a large recreation park (350,000 sq. m), with a Fairytale Park, "Lilliput", a dolphinarium, a circus, a 180° cinema and other attractions. – **Schloss Schwetzingen** (17 km NE): see p. 185.

Speyer Cathedral

30 m

1 Main doorway	7 Speyer Madonna	14 Steps down to
2 Side doorways	8 Ambo	crypt, antecrypt
3 Entrance to	9 High altar	and Imperial vault
St Afra's Chapel	10 Baptismal chapel	(4 emperors,
4 Organ	11 Sacristy	4 kings, 1 princess,
5 Pfarraltar	12 Bishop's throne	3 empresses,
6 Royal Choir	13 St Afra's Chapel	5 bishops)

Staffelstein

Land: Bavaria. – Vehicle registration: LIF.
Altitude: 264 m. – Population: 9900.
Post code: D-8623. – Dialling code: 0 95 73.
ⓘ **Verkehrsamt,**
    "Alte Darre", at the Stadtturm;
    tel. 2 00.

HOTELS. – *Rödiger,* Zur Herrgottsmühle 2, 37 b. – IN VIERZEHNHEILIGEN: *Haus Frankenthal,* 69 b. – IN BANZ CASTLE: *Schlossgasthof,* 40 b.

The ancient little town of Staffel-stein, birthplace of the 16th c. arithmetician Adam Riese, lies in the Main valley on the fringes of the Franconian Alb. Above it rises the Staffelberg (539 m), from the top of which there are wide-ranging views.

SIGHTS. – The beautiful **Town Hall**, a half-timbered building of 1687, contains the *Heimatmuseum*. – There is a thermal brine-bath (over 50 °C).

To the NE, half way to Lichtenfels, is Grundfeld-Vierzehnheiligen, dominated by the much visited pilgrimage church of ** **Vierzehnheiligen**, the finest achievement of Franconian Baroque architecture, standing high above the left bank of the Main (387 m). It was built between 1743 and 1772 by Balthasar Neumann. The name reflects its dedication to the Fourteen Auxiliary Saints (Nothelfer).

The plan of the church is unique, with its interplay of ovals and circles, and the spatial concept of the interior (decorated by Johann Michael Feuchtmayr and Johann Georg Übelherr) is bold and imaginative. The beautiful ceiling paintings are by Giuseppe Appiani. Above the spot where the Fourteen Auxiliaries are said to have appeared to a shepherd in 1445 stands the sumptuous Shrine of the Fourteen (Gnadenaltar) by Johann Michael Küchel.

SURROUNDINGS. – Opposite Staffelstein, standing high above the right bank of the Main, is the former **Benedictine monastery of Banz**. It was begun in 1695 by Johann Leonhard Dientzenhofer, and the massive rectangular complex of buildings was completed by the addition of a gatehouse wing by

Balthasar Neumann. The magnificent twin-towered *church* was built by Johann Dientzenhofer 1710–19; the interior is sumptuously decorated with stuccowork and ceiling paintings, with a high altar by Balthasar Esterbauer (1714). Notable features of the monastic buildings are the Abbot's Chapel and the Imperial Hall. There are also a small Egyptian collection and a collection of local Jurassic fossils.

Starnberger See

Land: Bavaria.

 **Fremdenverkehrsverband München-Oberbayern e. V.,** Sonnenstr. 10, D-8000 München 2; tel. (0 89) 59 73 47.

The *Starnberger See or Würmsee, with the River Würm flowing out of its northern end, is a lake in the Alpine Foreland 25 km SW of Munich. It occupies a basin 20 km long and 2–5 km wide gouged out by a glacier and is surrounded by forest-covered morainic hills. Its total area is 57·2 sq. km, its greatest depth 123 m.

The lake, which on a fine summer day is dotted with countless sailing boats and excursion vessels, offers a varied pattern of great scenic beauty, with its wooded hills, the popular holiday and weekend resorts round its shores, its groups of villas and its beautiful parks and gardens, all set against the backdrop of the distant Alpine chain. To the S. there is good bathing at the various places round the lake. The fish most commonly caught in the lake are whitefish.

Starnberg, at the N end of the lake, is a favourite residence of prominent people. A popular weekend resort is *Schloss Berg*, a beach hotel on the E side of the lake. In front of the nearby *Votivkirche* a cross in the lake marks the spot where King Ludwig II of Bavaria was drowned on Whit Sunday in 1886. *Feldafing*, on the W side of the lake, has a well-known golf-course. In the nearby *Schloss Possenhofen* the Empress Elizabeth of Austria, wife of the Emperor Francis Joseph, spent her early years. The health resort of *Tutzing* is noted for its Evangelical Academy and its musical festival. From the 728 m high *Ilkahöhe* there is a magnificent *view of the lake, with the resort of *Seeshaupt* at its S end and beyond this the peaks of the Alps.

Pilgrimage Church of
Vierzehnheiligen

ALTARS
1 Shrine of the Fourteen
2 High altar
3 St Francis
4 St Antony
5 St Blaise
6 St George

CEILING PAINTINGS
a Adoration of the Kings
b Abraham's Sacrifice
c Jacob's Ladder
d Emperor Henry II and Empress Kunigunde
e The Fourteen with the Trinity
f Annunciation
g Joseph's Dream
h Adoration of the Shepherds
P Pulpit O Organ

Straubing

Land: Bavaria. – Vehicle registration: SR.
Altitude: 332 m. – Population: 43,000.
Post code: D-8440. – Dialling code: 0 94 21.
ⓘ **Städtisches Verkehrsamt,**
Town Hall, Theresienplatz;
tel. 1 63 07

HOTELS. – *Heimer,* Schlesische Str. 131, 65 b., sauna;
Seethaler, Theresienplatz 25, 50 b.; *Schedlbauer,*
Landshuter Str. 78, 35 b.; *Motel Lermer* (no rest.),
Landshuter Str. 55, 33 b.; *Regensburger Hof,* Regens-
burger Str. 46, 24 b.; *Gäubodenhof,* Theresienplatz 8a,
16 b. – YOUTH HOSTEL: Friedhofstr. 12, 66 b. –
CAMPING SITE: *Campingplatz Stadt Straubing,* on
left bank of Danube.

RESTAURANT. – *Taxis-Stuben,* Mühlsteingasse 12

CAFÉS. – *Krönner,* Theresienplatz 22; *Isabell,* Stett-
haimerplatz.

EVENTS. – *Agnes Bernauer Festival* in the Schlosshof
(July in even-numbered years); *Gäuboden Fair*
(August).

Theresienplatz, Straubing

**Straubing lies on the right bank
of the Danube at the foot of the
Bavarian Forest, in the fertile
Gäuboden plain, the granary of
Bavaria. Known for its association
with the tragic story of Agnes
Bernauer, it is also an important
agricultural centre and has a number
of breweries.**

HISTORY. – The old town grew up round St Peter's
Church, on the site of the Roman settlement of
Sorviodurum. The fortified "new town" founded in
1218 was from 1353 to 1425 capital of an independent Duchy, which then passed to Duke Ernst of
Bavaria. In 1432 Duke Ernst's son Albrecht III married
the beautiful Agnes Bernauer, daughter of an
Augsburg barber: whereupon his father had her
accused of witchcraft and drowned in the Danube
(1435). She has her literary memorial in Hebbel's
tragedy "Agnes Bernauer".

SIGHTS. – In the middle of the NEW
TOWN, between THERESIENPLATZ in the W
and LUDWIGSPLATZ in the E, stands the
14th c. *Stadtturm* (68 m high: view).
Opposite it, to the N, is the Gothic *Town
Hall* (1382); to the W are the *Tiburtius
Fountain* (1685) and the *Trinity Column*
erected in 1709 after a siege of the town.
To the N of Theresienplatz is **St James's
Church** (15th–16th c., designed by Hans
Stethaimer), with an 86 m high tower and
a fine interior. – In Ludwigsplatz is *St
James's Fountain* (1644). In the Löwen-
apotheke (No. 11) the painter *Karl
Spitzweg* worked as an apprentice phar-
macist 1828–30. In Fraunhofergasse,
which runs N from the middle of the
square, are (No. 1) the birthplace

of the physicist *Joseph Fraunhofer*
(1787–1826) and (No. 9) the *Gäuboden
Museum* (history of the town, local
traditions, prehistoric material; the Roman
*Straubing Treasure, discovered 1950). A
short distance E are the *Carmelite Church,*
also by Hans Stethaimer, altered in
Baroque style in the 18th c., with the tomb
of Duke Albrecht II (d. 1397) behind the
high altar, and the sumptuous *Ursuline
Church* (1738) by the Asam brothers. To
the N, on the Danube, is the old Ducal
palace (15th c.). – To the W of the new
town is the *Stadtpark,* laid out in 1905,
with the *Zoo.*

E of the new town, in the countrified OLD
TOWN, is **St Peter's Church** (1180),
a Romanesque pillared basilica, with
towers of 1886; above the high altar is a
fine crucifix (*c.* 1200). In the churchyard
is the *Agnes Bernauer Chapel,* with the
tomb of the Augsburg barber's daughter
who married Duke Albrecht III. Nearby is
the *Totentanzkapelle* (1486: burial vault),
with frescoes of the Dance of Death
(1763).

SURROUNDINGS. – **Oberalteich** (10 km NE):
monastery church (completed 1630), with a
sumptuous Rococo interior.

Stuttgart

Land: Baden-Württemberg.
Vehicle registration: S.
Altitude: *c.* 245 m. – Population: 580,000.
Post code: D-7000. – Dialling code: 07 11.
ⓘ **Touristik-Zentrum i-Punkt,**
Klett-Passage, Main Station (until 10 p.m.);
tel. 2 22 80.

HOTELS. – *Steigenberger Hotel Graf Zeppelin*, Arnulf Klett Platz 7, 400 b., SB, sauna (Grill Restaurant, Zeppelin Stüble and Weinstube); *Am Schlossgarten*, Schillerstr. 23, 175 b.; *Parkhotel*, Villastr. 21, 100 b. (Weinstube); *Intercity Hotel*, Arnulf-Klett-Platz 2, 136 b.; *Royal*, Sophienstr. 35, 130 b.; *Ruff*, Friedhofstr. 21, 116 b., SB, sauna; *Wartburg Hospiz*, Lange Str. 49, 96 b.; *Rieker* (no rest.) Friedrichstr. 3, 80 b.; *Ketterer*, Marienstr. 3, 100 b.; *Unger* (no rest.), Kronestr. 17, 94 b.; *Azenberg* (no rest.), Seestr. 114–116, 80 b.; *Mack*, Krieger Str. 7, 71 b.; *Haus von Lippe* (no rest.), Rotenwaldstr. 68, 49 b.; *Höhenhotel Wielandshöhe* (no rest.), Alte Weinsteige 71, 36 b.; *Bäckerschmide*, Schurwaldstr. 44, 17 b. – IN BOTNANG: *Hirsch*, Eltinger Str. 2, 60 b. – IN FEUERBACH: *Europe*, Siemensstr. 26, 300 b. – IN MÖHRINGEN: *Stuttgart International*, Plieninger Str. 100, 282 b. SB. – IN PLIENINGEN: *Traube*, Brabandtgasse 2, 28 b. – IN VAIHINGEN-BÜSNAU: *Waldhotel Schatten*, Gewand Schatten 2, 66 b. – AT THE AIRPORT: *ASH Flughafen-hotel*, Randstr., 160 b. – YOUTH HOSTEL: Haussmannstr. 27, 300 b. – CAMPING SITE: *Cann-statter Wasen*, between Bad Cannstatt and the Neckar.

RESTAURANTS. – *Alte Post*, Friedrichstr. 43; *Alter Simpl*, Hohenheimer Str. 64; *Scheffelstuben*, Haussmannstr. 5; *Alte Kanzlei*, Schillerplatz 5a; *Mövenpick*, Kleiner Schlossplatz 11; *Ratskeller*, Marktplatz 1; *Eulenspiegel*, Bärenstr. 3; *Greiner Stuben*, Hindenburg building, Arnulf Klett Platz 1; *Bopserwirt*, Neue Weinsteige 8.

FOREIGN CUISINE: *Schwyzer Eck*, Nekkarstr. 246 (Swiss); *China Garden*, Königstr. 17 (Chinese); *Mira*, Calwer Str. 46 (Yugoslavian); *Come Prima*, Steinstr. 3 (Italian).

ON THE HILLS: *Fernsehturm Restaurant*, Jahnstr. 20; *Killesbergstube*, Stresemannstr. 1.

WINE-BARS. – *Bäcka-Metzger*, Aachener Str. 20, Bad Cannstatt; *Hirsch-Weinstuben*, Maierstr. 3, Möhringen; *Paule*, Augsburger Str. 643, Obertürk-heim.

CAFÉS. – *Königsbau*, Königstr. 28; *Schlossgarten*, in Schlossgarten Hotel (terrace); *Schapmann*, Königstr. 35; *Sommer*, Charlottenplatz 17.

EVENTS. – *Spring Festival* on Cannstatter Wasen (April); *Cannstatt Brezel Festival* (June); Lichterfest on the Killesberg, with fireworks (July); *Stuttgart Weindorf* (end Aug.–beginning Sept.); **Cannstatt Folk Festival** (Sept./Oct.); *Christmas Market* (Dec.).

Stuttgart, capital of the *Land* of Baden-Württemberg, is beautifully situated in a basin enclosed by forest-covered hills, orchards and vineyards, open only on the E to-wards the Neckar. From the valley bottom, where the older part of the town and the historic buildings are to be found, the houses climb up the surrounding slopes; when these are too steep for streets access is by flights of steps and stepped lanes.

Stuttgart has two Universities (Stuttgart and Hohenheim), an Academy of Fine Art,

an Academy of Music and Dramatic Art and numerous specialised higher educa-tional establishments. It has an active theatrical and musical life, the Stuttgart Ballet and Stuttgart Chamber Orchestra have an international reputation, and the popular Fishermen's Choirs are also based in the city. Stuttgart's industries include car manufacture (Daimler-Benz, Porsche), electrical equipment, engineer-ing, precision mechanical and optical equipment, textiles, paper-making and publishing.
Stuttgart is also one of Germany's largest fruit-growing and wine-producing centres, and in Berg and Bad Cannstatt, both within the city boundaries, there are the most productive mineral springs in Europe after those of Budapest.

HISTORY. – The name Stuttgart comes from a stud farm ("Stutkarten") established here by the Aleman-nic Duke Liutolf about 950: hence the black horse which features in the city's coat of arms. Under the protection of a moated castle built by Ulrich I (1241–65), its founder, the town soon developed into an important fortified market for the fertile Filder plain to the S. In 1321, after the destruction of his ancestral castle of Wirtemberg on the Rotenberg, Count Eberhard I moved his seat to Stuttgart, and as residence of the Counts of Württemberg the town quickly grew out beyond its old circuit of walls. In 1495 the Emperor Maximilian raised Count Eberhard im Bart to the dignity of Duke, and Stuttgart became the capital of a Duchy. Thereafter the extended area of the town was enclosed within a new ring of walls which took in the upper and lower suburbs as well. In 1717 Duke Eberhard Ludwig, who maintained an extravagant court on the French model, moved his seat to his new palace at Ludwigsburg; but Duke Karl Eugen (1737–93) later returned to Stuttgart. In 1770 he founded the famous Karlsschule (first at Schloss Solitude, from 1775 in Stuttgart), whose most celebrated pupil was Friedrich Schiller. In 1803, under the Reichsdeputationshauptschluss, Duke Friedrich II became an Elector, and in 1805 Napoleon made him King under the style of Friedrich I. Stuttgart thus became capital of the kingdom of Württemberg. In 1813 Friedrich broke with Napoleon, and in 1815 entered the German Confederation. Under King Wilhelm I (1816–64) a constitution was introduced (1819), and a period of great building activity began. The town grew in size, and most of its old walls were pulled down. In 1845 the first railway in Württemberg began to operate, and in 1868 the first horse-drawn tram (Stuttgart to Cannstatt). In 1918 King Wilhelm II abdicated and the Free State of Württemberg came into being, with Stuttgart as its capital. The Second World War caused great destruction in the city, particularly in the old town. In 1945 Stuttgart became the seat of the provincial government of Württemberg-Baden, and in 1952 capital of the *Land* of Baden-Württemberg.

SIGHTS. – In ARNULF-KLETT-PLATZ (underground shopping gallery) is the massive *Hauptbahnhof* with its 58 m high tower (1914–27, by P. Bonatz and F. E. Scholer). Opposite the station is

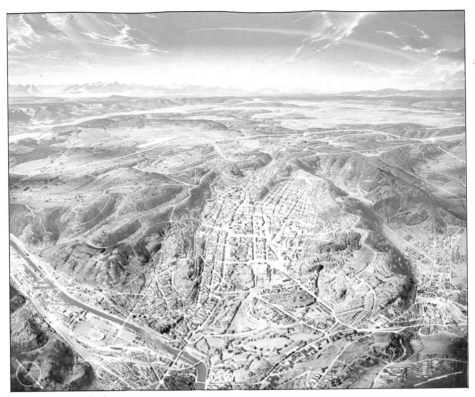

Stuttgart: panoramic view

the *Hindenburgbau* (1927–28; extension 1951), and beyond this, in Lautenschlagerstrasse, are the *Zeppelinbau* (hotel) and the *Post Office Headquarters* (1926–27). Farther left (looking from the station) is the *Schlossgartenbau* (1960–61: hotel). – The city's main business and shopping street, KÖNIGSTRASSE (pedestrian precinct), runs SW from the station past *St Eberhard's Church* (rebuilt 1955), the Roman Catholic cathedral, to the Schlossplatz and beyond this the Wilhelmsbau.

The *Schlossplatz** is surrounded by buildings dating from the time when Stuttgart was a Ducal capital. In the middle of the gardens is the *Jubilee Column*, erected in 1841 to commemorate King Wilhelm I's 25th year of rule. On the NW side of the square is the *Königsbau* (1856–60, restored 1957–59), with a pillared hall. To the SW, on a higher level, is the KLEINER SCHLOSSPLATZ (1968), with shops, offices and restaurants (and sometimes fleamarkets). At the NE corner of the square is the *Kunstgebäude* (1912–13, rebuilt 1956–61), with the Municipal Gallery (and temporary exhibitions). Along the SE side, dominating the square, is the **Neues Schloss** (1746–1807, rebuilt

1959–62: state apartments), which houses the Ministries of Culture and Finance.

To the SW, on the PLANIE, is the **Altes Schloss** (built 1553–78 by A. Tretsch, restored 1948–69), with a picturesque courtyard. It contains the richly stocked and excellently arranged *Württemberg Provincial Museum* (medieval collection, religious and secular applied art, the Württemberg crown jewels, watches and clocks, astronomical and musical instruments, costumes of various periods, archaeological finds, etc.). In the S wing is the *Schlosskapelle* (1560–62).

Behind the Altes Schloss is the *SCHILLERPLATZ (underground car park), with a *monument to Schiller* by Thorwaldsen. On the NE side of the square is the *Old Chancery* (c. 1500). On the NW side is the *Prinzenbau* (begun in 1605 by Schickhardt, finished a hundred years later by Matthias Weiss), which during the reign of Duke Eberhard Ludwig (1677–1733) was the residence of his heir, Prince Friedrich Ludwig; it is now occupied by the Ministry of Justice. On the SW side of the square is the *Fruchtkasten* (1390), now containing a lapidarium of Roman material. Adjoining it is the choir of the Stiftskirche.

The *Stiftskirche (Evang.), with its two towers, was founded in the 12th c. and rebuilt in late Gothic style in the 15th c. by Aberlin Jörg and others; restored in 1958 after heavy war damage. In the choir is a magnificent series of 11 fine Renaissance statues of Counts of Württemberg by Simon Schlör (1576–1608). – A short distance away to the SE is the MARKT-PLATZ, with the **Town Hall** (1956: carillon; Ratskeller). – On the southern edge of the Old Town are the 61 m high *Tagblatt Tower* (built 1927/28) with the culture centre "Kultur unterm Turm") and *St Leonard's Church* (15th c.).

In CHARLOTTENPLATZ, with its constant flow of traffic (underpass, on several levels, for road traffic, trams and pedestrians), is the *Wilhelmspalais* (built by Salucci in 1840, burned down 1944, rebuilt 1964–65), formerly the residence of the last king of Württemberg, Wilhelm II, now housing a collection of material on the history of Stuttgart and the Municipal Library. From here KONRAD-ADENAUER-STRASSE runs NE. On the right-hand side of this street is the **Provincial Library** (1970: exhibitions). Beyond this, on the left, are the **Landtag** (parliament: 1960–61) of Baden-Württemberg and the **State Theatre**, an effective group consisting of two buildings originally built by Max Littmann in 1907–12. The *Grosses Haus* (opera) is still Littmann's building; the *Kleines Haus* (theatre) is a new building erected in 1960–62 to replace the original building destroyed during the war. Then comes (on right) the excellent *State Gallery** (works by Dutch masters, including a Rembrandt self-portrait; numerous Swabian artists of the 15th c.; 19th and 20th c. Swabian painting; a large range of modern works and a collection of graphic art). Beyond the gallery, on the right, is the entrance to the *Wagenburg Tunnel* (824 m long: min. speed 30 km p.h.), which carries traffic to the eastern districts of the town; straight ahead is NECKARSTRASSE, which runs 3 km NE to the Berg district.

Along the W side of Konrad-Adenauer-Strasse and Neckarstrasse lies the **Schlossgarten**, which extends from the

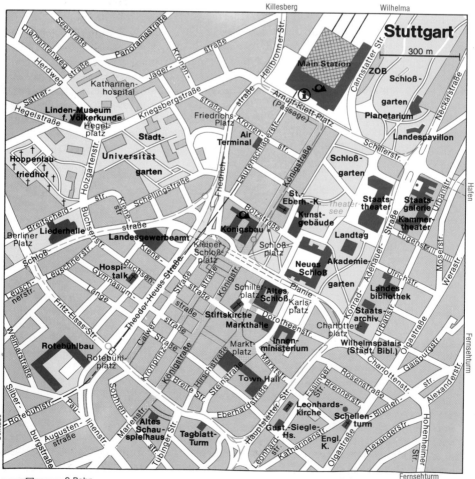

Stiftskirche, Stuttgart

Neues Schloss to Berg and Bad Cannstatt on the Neckar (mineral springs; spa treatment, open-air swimming baths). In the gardens are a *Planetarium (near the intersection of Schillerstrasse and Neckarstrasse), pretty ponds and unusual fountains.

On a low hill in the district of BERG, on the left bank of the Neckar, is Schloss Rosenstein (1824–29), housing the Natural History Museum until the completion of a new building. Below it extends the *Wilhelma Zoological Botanic Garden (named after a little Moorish-style palace built in 1842–53 and rebuilt in 1962), beautifully laid out, with hothouses, animal houses (especially apes and pachyderms), open enclosures and an *aquarium (1967).

On the right bank of the Neckar is the old district of BAD CANNSTATT (220 m), with the Kursaal (two mineral springs, restaurant) and Kurpark. In Taubenheimstrasse, which begins here, Gottlieb Daimler had his workshop (No. 13, with memorial museum; monument in the garden, in which Daimler drove his first car in 1885). Just off the Cannstatter Wasen (Canstatt Meadows) are the large Neckar Stadium and the Hanns Martin Schleyer Halle.

In the NW part of the city, near the Ministry of the Economy, is the massive structure of the Provincial Industrial Museum (Design Center, extensive collections, temporary exhibitions). In the

Stadtgarten, is the University of Technology, with a number of new buildings occupied by various institutes. In Berliner Platz, a short distance SW, is Stuttgart's concert hall (with restaurant), the Liederhalle (rebuilt 1955–56). In the nearby Hegelplatz is the richly stocked *Linden Museum (geography and ethnography: at present closed).

Above the city to the N, near the Academy of Fine Art, are the Weissenhof (1927), a pioneering and influential housing development, and the beautiful Killesberg Park (383 m, restaurant), with exhibition halls, a chair-lift, a swimming pool and a restaurant. – In the northern industrial district of ZUFFENHAUSEN is the Porsche Works Museum.

In the SW of the city is the Birkenkopf (511 m: *view), a hill built up of rubble from demolished buildings. – On the Hoher Bopser (481 m), a wooded hill in the S of the city, is the *Television Tower of the South German Broadcasting Corporation, a slender concrete pillar 217 m high (including aerial) with a restaurant at 150 m and above it a viewing platform (access by lift only).

E of the city, in the outlying district of UNTERTÜRKHEIM, is the *Daimler-Benz Museum, illustrating in the most comprehensive way the development of car and car engine manufacture (at present closed). Between Untertürkheim and Obertürkheim is the Neckar Harbour, opened in 1958.

In UHLBACH is the Stuttgart Museum of Viticulture.

SURROUNDINGS. – *Schloss Solitude (10 km W), a Rococo palace built by Louis Philippe de la Guêpière for Duke Karl Eugen in 1763–67 (restaurant in annexe).

Swabian Alb (Schwäbische Alb)

Land: Baden-Württemberg.

ⓘ Fremdenverkehrsverband Neckarland-Schwaben, Wollhausstr. 14, D-7100 Heilbronn; tel. (0 71 31) 6 90 61.

The Swabian Alb ("mountain pasture"), an upland region of Jurassic limestone of around 700 m in height,

Half-timbered houses in Urach

extends for 210 km, varying in width between 15 and 40 km, from the SE edge of the Black Forest to the Ries round Nördlingen, reaching its greatest height in the Lemberg (1015 m), E of Rottweil. In the NW the hills drop down to the valleys of the Neckar, the Fils and the Rems in a steep scarp some 400 m high, which is broken up by valleys reaching deeply into the hills and has a series of celebrated castle ruins on outlying crags. To the SE the Alb slopes gently down to the Danube, forming a slightly undulating plateau of permeable limestone through which most surface water seeps away, forming caves, swallow-holes and dry valleys.

The great attraction of the Alb is the variety of its scenery – fertile fruit-growing valleys with trim villages and little towns containing treasures of art and architecture; steep-ended valleys with abundant springs (the best known being the Blautopf at Blaubeuren) and huge caves, like the Nebelhöhle, the Bären-höhle and the Falkenstein cave, not yet properly explored; rocky hillsides with splendid beech forests and numbers of ruined castles (Hohenneuffen, Teck, etc.); and the austere beauty of the plateaux with their mountain pastures and lonely expanses of heath.

Among the areas most popular with visitors are the HONAU VALLEY, with the *Wilhelm Hauff Museum* in Lichtenstein-Honau, *Schloss Lichtenstein* and the nearby *Nebelhöhle* and *Bärenhöhle*; the ERMS VALLEY, with the charming little town of *Bad Urach*; the LENNINGEN VALLEY, from which *Teck* and *Hohenneuffen* can be visited; the area

between Göppingen and Schwäbisch Gmünd, with the *Hohenstaufen* and *Hohenrechberg*; and, in the SW, the Zollarnalb, with the *Hohenzollern*, and the *Heuberg*, with the highest hills.

There are many popular HEALTH and HOLIDAY RESORTS in the Swabian Alb, and in the volcanic region around Kirchheim and Bad Urach there are aspiring spas of *Beuren, Boll, Ditzenbach, Überkingen* and *Bad Urach*.

The **Swabian Alb Highway** (signposted by a silver thistle on a green ground) runs from *Nördlingen* via *Heidenheim* and *Geislingen* to *Bad Urach* and then continues via *Ebingen* to *Tuttlingen* or *Trossingen*, offering a very attractive trip along the whole length of the Alb.

Sylt

Land: Schleswig-Holstein.
Vehicle registration: NF.
Altitude: 0–50 m. – Area: 102 sq. km.
(i) **Fremdenverkehrszentrale,**
Bundesbahnhof, D-2280 Westerland;
tel. (0 46 51) 2 40 01.

HOTELS. – IN WESTERLAND: *Stadt Hamburg*, Strandstr. 2, 125 b.; *Wulff* (no rest.), Margaretenstr. 9, 80 b., SB; *Roth*, Strandstr. 31, 80 b.; *Dünenburg*, Elisabethstr. 9, 65 b.; *Wünschmann* (no rest.), Andreas-Dirks-Str. 4, 54 b. IN WENNINGSTEDT: *Wüstefeld*, 54 b.; *Strandhörn*, 25 b.; *Seehotel Heidehof* (no rest.), 65 b. – IN KAMPEN: *Rungholt*, 100 b; *Walter's Hof*, 70 b., SB; *Cliff's Herberge* (no rest.), 28 b.; *Kamphörn* (no rest.), 21 b. – IN LIST: *Silbermöve*, 28 b. – IN KEITUM: *Benen-Diken-Hof*, 35 b., SB; *Wolfshof* (no rest.), 24 b., SB. – IN HÖRNUM: *Appartement Hotel Helene*, 75 b., SB; *Seepferdchen*, 25 b.

RESTAURANTS. – IN WESTERLAND: *Käpt'n Hahn*, Trift 10; *Kleines Restaurant*, Strandstr. 8. – IN WENNINGSTEDT: *La Bonne Auberge*. – IN KAMPEN: *Kupferkanne*. – IN KEITUM: *Fisch-Fiete*. – IN TINNUM: *Landhaus Stricker*.

RECREATION. – Beaches; indoor sea-water baths with artificial waves (Westerland, Keitum); tennis; riding; numerous naturist bathing beaches on the W coast.

ACCESS. – The land route to Sylt is by rail over the 11* km long **Hindenburg Causeway** (Hindenburg-damm), built 1923–27 (cars carried: *c.* 1 hour), which cuts across the Wattenmeer (nature reserve). – Airstrip at Westerland.

The island of *Sylt, a popular summer resort, is the most northerly German island and the largest of the North Frisian Islands (37 km long). It is shaped rather like a large pickaxe; its central portion is a sandy ridge mostly covered with heath. Its particular attractions are the dunes and the 40 km of wave-swept *beach.

Half way along the W coast, on the open sea, is the fashionable bathing resort of **Westerland**, founded 1857 (pop. 10,000, post code D-2280, dialling code 0 46 51; air-strip), the chief town of the island, with a long beach of fine sand, extensive treatment facilities, an indoor sea-water bath with artificial waves, a North Sea Aquarium, a Casino and an old village church of the 17th–19th c. (sun-dial of 1789).

A road 35 km long (bus services) runs N from Westerland via the seaside resorts of **Wenningstedt** (4 km: pop. 2200, post code D-2283, dialling code 0 46 51; Kurverwaltung (administrative office), tel. 4 10 81), with a long beach, treatment facilities and the Denghoog "Hun's grave", and **Kampen** (6 km: pop. 1100, post code D-2285, dialling code 0 46 51; Kurverwaltung, tel. 4 10 91), with reed-thatched houses and the 4 km long *Rotes Kliff*, falling sheer to the sea for anything up to 27 m, and then through the LISTLAND nature reserve (large dunes; bird-watchers' hide) to the seaside resort of **List** (16 km: pop. 3200, post code D-2282, dialling code 0 46 52; Kurverwaltung, tel. 2 15, on the S side of the large Royal Harbour, now silted up, which is enclosed on the N by the 4 km long arc of land known as the "Ellenbogen" ("Elbow": two lighthouses). From here there is a car ferry to the Danish island of Rømø.

Promenade, Westerland (Sylt)

The road S from Westerland runs through the beautiful *dunes of the narrow HÖR-NUM PENINSULA by way of the village of *Rantum* (7 km: pop. 600, post code D-2280, dialling code 0 46 51; Kurverwal-tung, tel. 60 76), to the NW of which a large bird reserve, and a cluster of houses

at *Puan Klent* (13 km) to **Hörnum** (18 km: pop. 1400, post code D-2284, dialling code 0 46 53; Kurverwaltung, tel. 10 65), a seaside resort near the southern tip of Sylt (powerful beacon) with a small harbour (boats to Heligoland).

E of Westerland extends the peninsula of SYLT-OST, mostly fenland. There is a good road via *Tinnum* (2 km: pop. 1800, post code D-2280), with the ring fort of Tinnumburg, to **Keitum** (5 km: pop. 1800, post code D-2286, dialling code 0 46 51; Kurverwaltung, tel. 3 10 50), formerly chief town of the island, with typical Frisian houses (including the "Altfriesisches Haus" of 1739), the Sylt Heimatmuseum and the late Romanesque church of St Severinus, standing on higher ground to the N. – From Keitum it is another 7 km SE to *Morsum* (12th c. church), near the eastern tip of Sylt where the Hindenburg Causeway begins.

Taunus

Land: Hesse

ⓘ **Fremdenverkehrsverband Hessen,** Abraham-Lincoln-Str. 38–42, D-6200 Wiesbaden; tel. (0 61 21) 7 37 25.

The Taunus is a ridge of hills some 70 km long between the rivers Rhine, Main and Lahn and the Wetterau. It reaches its highest point in the Grosser Feldberg (881 m), the high-est peak in the Rhenish Uplands. It is made up of slates, with beds of quartzite and some rounded basaltic summits of volcanic origin. The higher levels are covered by fine beech and oak forests, with some conifers. On the side nearest Frank-furt the Taunus presents its steep southern slopes which, sheltered from the harsh north winds, have one of the mildest climates in Ger-many, producing excellent fruit, almonds and – at Kronberg – sweet chestnuts. The Taunus is also the region in Germany which is richest in mineral springs. The most impor-tant springs, along the southern fringe of the hills, have led to the establishment of famous spas.

One of the most scenically attractive spots in the Taunus is the little town of

Königstein, from which a good road runs up the *Grosser Feldberg* (881 m: telecommunications tower), with magnificent wide-ranging views. There is also a road from *Oberursel*. – From *Bad Homburg* with its beautiful Kurpark B 456 runs N to the **Saalburg*, with the only reconstructed Roman fort on the Limes (see p. 172). From here an Educational Walk leads to the Hessenpark Open-Air Museum. – In the north-western Taunus, not far from Wiesbaden, are the attractive little resorts of *Bad Schwalbach* and *Schlangenbad*, from which the "Spa Highway" (B 260) runs through the north-western outliers of the range to Bad Ems in the Lahn valley.

Numerous places in the Taunus are popular HEALTH and HOLIDAY RESORTS, including in particular, in addition to those already mentioned, *Königstein, Kronberg, Falkenstein, Eppstein, Oberreifenberg* and *Schmitten*.

Teutoburg Forest

Länder: North Rhineland-Westphalia and Lower Saxony.
ⓘ **Landesverkehrsverband Westfalen,**
Balkenstr. 4, D-4600 Dortmund;
tel. (02 31) 57 17 15.

The Teutoburg Forest (Tentoburger Wald) runs along the N side of the park-like landscape of the Münster lowlands for some 100 km, beginning at the point where the Mittelland Canal joins the Dortmund–Ems Canal and rising from NW to SE to end in its highest peak, the Preussische Velmerstot (468 m). The hills consist of Upper Cretacous limestones and sandstones, the difference between the two being reflected in the vegetation (beech forests on the limestone, spruces on the sandstone).

The principal beauty spots are the *Dörenther Klippen* at Brochterbeck, the *Dörenberg* (331 m) at Bad Iburg, the *Ravensburg* at Borgholzhausen, the **Hermannsdenkmal* near Detmold and the **Externsteine* not far from Horn–Bad Meinberg. Other tourist attractions are "*Big Game Safari Land*" (lions, tigers, elephants, rhinoceroses, antelopes, zebras, ostriches, monkeys, etc.) at *Stukenbrock*, S of the Dörenschlucht, the *Eagle Observatory* at

Hermannsdenkmal, Teutoburg Forest

Berlebeck and the *Bird and Flower Park* at Heiligenkirchen.

There are numerous HEALTH and HOLIDAY RESORTS in these beautiful wooded hills – the picturesque little hill town of *Tecklenburg*, the resort of *Bad Iburg* (Kneipp cure), the brine spas of *Bad Laer* and *Bad Rothenfelde*, the gingerbread town of *Borgholzhausen*, the hill town of *Oerlinghausen*, the old Lippe residence town of Detmold, the health resorts of *Hiddessen* and *Berlebeck*, as well as *Horn-Bad Meinberg* and many more.

Immediately S of the Teutoburg Forest is the **Eggegebirge**, a 35 km long range of hills bounded on the S by the Diemel valley. In the Senne, an extensive area of heath and sand to the W, is *Bad Lippspringe*, while to the E of the hills are *Bad Driburg* and the charming health resort of *Willebadessen*.

In this region two nature parks have been established, the *Northern Teutoburg Forest – Wiehengebirge Park* and the *Southern Teutoburg Forest – Eggegebirge Park*.

Trier

Land: Rhineland-Palatinate.
Vehicle registration: TR.
Altitude: 124 m. – Population: 101,000.
Post code: D-5500. – Dialling code: 06 51.
ⓘ **Tourist-Information,**
at the Porta Nigra;
tel. 71 82 80 68.

HOTELS. – *Dorint Hotel Porta Nigra*, Porta Nigra Platz 1, 176, sauna; *Holiday Inn*, Zurmaiener Str. 164, 335 b., SB, sauna ("La Brochette" restaurant); *Europa Parkhotel*, Kaiserstr. 29, 170 b.; *Deutscher Hof*, Südallee 25, 172 b.; *Fassbenders Central Hotel*, Sichelstr. 32, 60 b.; *Petrisberg* (no rest.), Sickingerstr. 11, 60 b.; *Am Hügel* (no rest.), Bernhardstr. 14, 32 b.; *Deutschherrenhof* (no rest.), Deutschherrenstr. 32, 24 b. – IN EUREN: *Eurener Hof*, Eurener Str. 171, 130 b., SB, sauna. – IN PFALZEL: *Klosterschenke*, Klosterstr. 10, 16 b. – IN OLEWIG: *Blesius Garten*, Olewiger Str. 135, 115 b. – YOUTH HOSTEL: Maarstr. 156, 312 b. – CAMPING SITES: *Trier City*, on the Moselle; *Horsch Camping*, Konz-Könen.

RESTAURANTS. – *Pfeffermühle*, Herzogenbuscher Str. 1; *Brasserie*, Fleischstr. 12; *Ratskeller Zur Steipe*, Hauptmarkt 14; *Brunnenhof*, in Simeonstift; *Zum Krokodil*, Böhmerstr. 10.

WINE-BARS. – *Kurtrierische Weinstube Zum Domstein*, Hauptmarkt 5 (with "Roman Wine-Cellar" and dishes prepared from old Roman recipes); *Römischer Weinkeller Küferstube*, Domfreihof 9.

Trier, the busy capital of an administrative region (Bezirk), lies in a basin in the valley of the Moselle, here navigable (port installations). It ranks as Germany's oldest town, its importance in ancient times being attested by impressive Roman remains such as are found nowhere else north of the Alps. Numerous churches reflect its long-established status as the see of a bishop (since the 4th c.). It is a university town; it has a College of Philosophy and Theology as well as a technical college and is a considerable centre of the wine trade.

HISTORY. – The Roman town of *Augusta Treverorum* was founded by Augustus in 16 B.C. on the site of a settlement of the Celtic Treveri, who had been subjugated by Caesar. In A.D. 117 it became capital of the province of Belgica and later an Imperial capital, the residence of several Roman Emperors, including Constantine the Great (306–312). As one of the major cities of the Empire it had a great cultural flowering. In the 4th c. it became the see of a bishop, the first bishopric N of the Alps, and in the 9th c. Charlemagne made it an archbishopric. From the 12th to the 18th c. it was the capital of an Electorate, the Archbishop of Trier being until 1794 one of the three ecclesiastical Electors of the Holy Roman Empire.

SIGHTS. – At the N entrance to the OLD TOWN stands the imposing ****Porta Nigra**, one of the fortified gates in the late 2nd c. Roman walls, converted into a church *c.* 1040 and restored to its original state in 1804–17 (interior open to visitors). In the adjoining *Simeonstift* (11th c.) is the *Municipal Museum* and nearby the *Trier Academy of Craftsmen*.

From here Simeonstrasse (*Dreikönigenhaus, c.* 1230) runs SW to the *HAUPT-*MARKT* (pedestrian precinct), with the late Gothic *St Gangolf's Church*. A little way W, in Dietrichstrasse, is the *Frankenturm*, one of the earliest surviving tower-dwellings in Germany (11th c.).

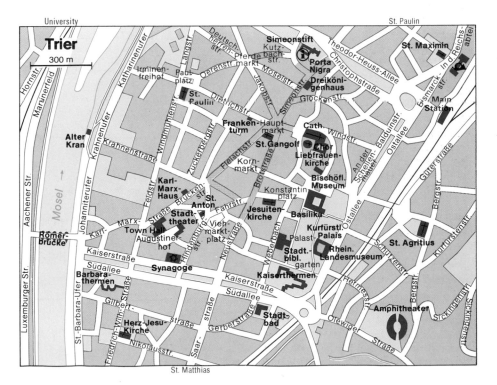

Porta Nigra, Trier

E of the Hauptmarkt is the *Cathedral, one of the oldest churches in Germany (4th, 11th and 12th c.; restored 1964–74). It contains a number of very fine monuments of the 16th–18th c. and a rich *treasury (including the 10th c. portable altar of St Andrew, one of the great masterpieces of Ottonian art; the Cathedral's most precious relic, the Holy Coat, is kept in the cathedral sacristy). Adjoining the Cathedral is the *Liebfrauenkirche, one of the earliest Gothic churches in Germany (completed c. 1270). – ½ km SW of the Hauptmarkt, at Brückenstr. 10, is the birthplace of Karl Marx (museum).

SE of the Hauptmarkt, in KONSTANTIN-PLATZ, are the Episcopal Museum and the Roman *Aula Palatina (Basilica), now restored and used as a church (Evang.), built in the time of Constantine the Great, who resided in Trier from 306 to 312. Adjoining it is the former Electoral Palace (17th and 18th c.), now the regional government offices. To the S of the palace, beyond a stretch of the medieval town walls which bound the palace gardens (Baroque sculpture), is the Rhenish Provincial Museum, with finds and objects d'art of prehistoric, Roman, Early Christian and Franconian times.

Farther S are the ruins of the Roman Imperial Baths (4th c. A.D.; in medieval times a castle; with a labyrinth of subterranean rooms). From here the Südallee runs W to the remains of other baths, the Barbarathermen (2nd c. A.D.). The nearby Roman Bridge over the Moselle still rests on Roman foundations. – To the E of the

Imperial Baths, reached by way of Olewiger Strasse, is the interesting Roman Amphitheatre, built about A.D. 100, which had seating for some 25,000 spectators.

NE of the Porta Nigra, near the road along the Moselle valley (Paulinstrasse), is the church of *St Paulinus, one of the finest Baroque buildings in the Rhineland (by Balthasar Neumann, 1732–54). – On the southern outskirts of the town is the pilgrimage church of St Matthias (12th c., restored), with the remains of the disciple Matthias, which belonged to a Benedictine house (re-founded 1097) on the site of an early Christian building.

SURROUNDINGS. – 8 km SW, where the Saar joins the Moselle, lies the wine town of **Konz** (educational vineyard path; wine tasting), with the open-air *Roscheiderhof Museum.* Following the left bank of the Moselle one reaches (9 km SW of Trier) the village of Igel. Here stands the *Igeler Saule, a 22 m high funeral monument (pillar with rich relief decoration) of a Gallo-Roman family of the 3rd c. A.D.

Tübingen

Land: Baden-Württemberg.
Vehicle registration: TÜ.
Altitude: 332 m. – Population: 72,000.
Post code: D-7400. – Dialling code: 0 70 71.
ⓘ **Verkehrsverein**, at Eberhardsbrücke;
tel. 3 50 11.

HOTELS. – *Krone,* Uhlandstr. 1, 85 b.; *Hospiz,* Nekkarhalde 2, 80 b.; *Stadt Tübingen,* Stuttgarter Str. 97, 72 b.; *Barbarina,* Wilhemstr. 94, 36 b.; *Haus Katharine* (no rest.), Lessingweg 2, 14 b. – YOUTH HOSTEL: Gartenstr. 22, 200 b. – CAMPING SITE: on left bank of Neckar, on western outskirts of town.

RESTAURANTS. – *Museumsgaststätte,* Wilhelmstr. 3; *Rosenau,* at New Botanic Garden. – IN BEBENHAUSEN: *Waldhorn,* Hauptstr. 31.

WINE-BAR. – *Forelle,* Kronenstr. 8.

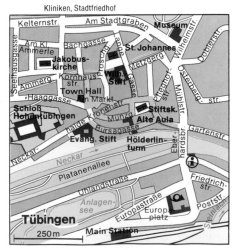

This ancient and famous Swabian university town is attractively situated in the middle Neckar valley near the point where it is joined by the Ammer, NW of the Swabian Alb. Between the Schlossberg and the Österberg (438 m) with its tower the picturesque *old town climbs up the steep slopes on the left bank of the Neckar. The best view of the river frontage of the old town is from the Platanenallee on the right bank.

HISTORY. – Tübingen, which first appears in the records in 1078, grew out of two settlements on the Neckar and the Ammer. For a time it was the seat of the Dukes of Württemberg, and Count Eberhard im Bart founded the University in 1477. Another important centre of intellectual life in Württemberg was the Evangelical theological seminary founded in 1536. The famous Cotta-Verlag, established here in 1659, published the works of the leading German writers.

SIGHTS. – In the HOLZMARKT stands the late Gothic **Stiftskirche** (15th c.: Evang.), with handsome monuments commemorating members of the princely House of Württemberg (including Count Eberhart im Bart and Duke Ludwig) and 15th c. stained glass in the choir. Behind it are the oldest parts of the **University** – the *Alte Aula* (Old Assembly Hall), the *Alter Karzer* (lock-up) and the fine *Bursa*, in which the reformer Philip Melanchthon lectured in 1514–18. Below, on the Neckar, is the *Hölderlin Tower*, in which the poet Friedrich Hölderlin lived from 1807 until his death, insane, in 1843. At the end of Bursagasse is the *Stift*, an Evangelical theological seminary founded in 1536 whose pupils included Kepler, Schelling, Hegel, Hölderlin, Mörike and Wilhelm Hauff. Higher up are the birthplace of the poet *Ludwig Uhland* (1787–1862), at Neckarhalde 24, and the *Muncipal Musem* (No. 31).

In the nearby MARKET SQUARE is the picturesque **Town Hall**, a half-timbered building of 1435, with the *Market Fountain* (1617) in front of it. Above the square the Burgsteige runs steeply up, affording wide views, to the 16th c. **Schloss Hohentübingen** (372 m), built on the remains of an earlier castle of the Counts Palatine.

In the busy WILHELMSTRASSE is the *Neue Aula* (New Assembly Hall) of the University (extended 1930–31). Beyond this, on the right, is the *University Library*. To the N, on the slopes of the Schnarrenberg, are the *University clinics*, and above them,

on the Morgenstelle, are the new buildings of the Faculty of Science.

SURROUNDINGS. – *Bebenhausen Abbey (5 km N), a Cistercian house founded about 1185, which ranks with Maulbronn Abbey as one of the finest and best preserved monastic houses in Germany (now occupied by government offices). – **Wurmlingen Chapel** (475 m: 9 km SW), celebrated in a well-known poem of Uhland's. – **Rottenburg** (12 km SW), see of a Roman Catholic bishop (jointly with Stuttgart), with St Martin's Cathedral and the Stiftskirche of St Maurice.

Ulm
an der Donau

Land: Baden-Württemberg.
Vehicle registration: UL.
Altitude: 478 m. – Population: 100,000.
Post code: D-7900. – Dialling code: 07 31.

ⓘ **Verkehrsbüro**, Münsterplatz 51;
tel. 6 41 61.

HOTELS. *Intercity Hotel*, Bahnhofplatz 1, 165 b.; *Neutor Hospiz*, Neuer Graben 23, 130 b.; *Stern*, Sterngasse 17, 85 b.; *Am Rathaus*, Kronengasse 8, 65 b.; *Ulmer Spatz*, Münsterplatz, 52 b.; *Goldenes Rad* (no rest.), Neue Str. 65, 34 b. – AT ULM-OST MOTORWAY EXIT: *Rasthaus Seligweiler*, 211 b., SB. – IN NEU-ULM: *Mövenpick Hotel*, Silcherstr. 40, 189 b., SB; *Donau Hotel*, Augsburger Str. 34, 110 b. – YOUTH HOSTEL: Grimmelfinger Weg 45, 179 b.

RESTAURANTS. – *Zum Pflugmerzler*, Pfluggasse 6 (wine-bar); *Ratskeller*, in Town Hall; *Kornhauskeller*, Hafengasse 19; *Zur Forelle*, Fischergasse 25.

CAFÉ. – *Tröglen*, Münsterplatz 5.

EVENTS. – City-Fest in Münsterplatz (June); Schwörmontag, with the "Nabada", a parade of boats on the Danube (July); Fischerstechen (Fishermen's Tournament) on the Danube, with dancing (July event four years: next in May 1985).

This old Imperial city on the Danube, at the inflow of its left-bank tributary the Blau, still retains many

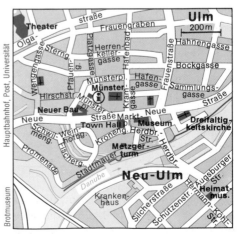

Ulm Minster from the Danube

features from its past – the Minster with its soaring spire, the richly ornamented Town Hall, the picturesque fountains, idyllic lanes and quaint old corners in the old town and Blau quarter, the beautiful silhouette of the town seen from the Danube. In its modern aspect it is the economic and cultural centre of upper Württemberg, the seat of a university and an engineering college, and a busy commercial and industrial town (car manufacture, electrical engineering, textiles, leather goods). It is the starting-point of the "Upper Swabian Baroque Highway". – On the right bank of the Danube is the Bavarian town of Neu-Ulm.

HISTORY. – Thanks to its situation on the Danube and at the intersection of major traffic routes Ulm developed during the Middle Ages into a commercial centre. It obtained its municipal charter in 1164 and became a free Imperial city in 1274. During the Second World War it suffered severe destruction. – Ulm was the birthplace of Albert Einstein (1879–1955).

SIGHTS. – In the middle of the town stands the **Minster (Evang.), Germany's largest Gothic church after Cologne Cathedral (1377–1529, further work 1844–90). The soaring *spire crowning the tower (climb to top recommended: in clear weather view of Alps), begun by Ulrich von Ensingen in 1392 and completed 1880–90 on the basis of drawings left by Matthäus Böblinger, is the highest church tower in the world (161 m: Cologne Cathedral 157 m). In the interior are notable *choir-stalls by J. Syrlin the Elder (1469–74) which are among the finest in Germany. – NE of the

Minster is the *Kornhaus* (1591, restored: now a concert hall). In the Friedrichsau is an *Aquarium* with a tropical house.

S of the Minster, in the MARKET SQUARE, is the handsome Gothic **Town Hall** (destroyed by fire in 1944 but since restored), with frescoes of 1540. In front of it is a beautiful fountain known as the *Fischkasten*, by J. Syrlin the Elder (1482). – The *Municipal Museum (Neue Str. 92) has an interesting collection of material on art and municipal history. – Along the Danube a stretch of the 15th c. town walls has been preserved, with the *Metzgerturm*, a leaning tower 2·05 m off the vertical. – In the SW of the town (Fürstenecker Str. 17) is the *German Bread Museum* (history of bread and baking). – In the southern district of WIBLINGEN is the late Baroque *St Martin's Church* (18th c.: frescoes by J. Zick), built as a monastic church. In the N wing of the monastery buildings (1714–60) is a beautiful Rococo *Library*.

SURROUNDINGS. – 20 km W, at Blaubeuren, is the * **Blautopf**, a small lake 20 m deep which is the source of the River Blau (2000 litres per sec.). High Altar (*c.* 1493) in the monastery church at **Blaubeuren**.

Upper Swabia (Oberschwaben)

Länder: Baden-Württemberg and Bavaria.
ⓘ **Fremdenverkehrsverband Bodensee-Oberschwaben**,
Schützenstr. 8, D-7750 Konstanz;
tel. (0 75 31) 2 22 32.
Landesfremdenverkehrsverband Baden-Württemberg,
Bussenstr. 23, D-7000 Stuttgart 1;
tel. (07 11) 48 10 45.

Upper Swabia is bounded in the N by the Danube, in the W by the foothills of the Black Forest and in the S by Lake Constance, while in the E it merges gradually into the Allgäu. The landscape pattern was set by deposits laid down during the Ice Age. Out of the gently undulating and rolling country individual hills rise to above 750 m; the highest and most prominent of these is Bussen (757 m), near the Danube. Scattered over the whole area are numbers of small lakes, some of them reduced to bogs.

Upper Swabia is rich in religious houses and Baroque churches. **Ulm**, with its

Obertor, Ravensburg

**Minster, is the starting point of the "Upper Swabian Baroque Highway", which runs close to some of the greatest achievements of South German Baroque – the finest perhaps *Obermarchtal* (monastery church by Michael Thumb), *Zwiefalten* (*Minster by Johann Michael Fischer), *Bad Schussenried* (Library by Dominikus Zimmermann) and *Weingarten* (*monastery church by Michael Thumb, Franz Beer, G. D. Frisoni and others).

The former free Imperial cities of *Biberach* and **Ravensburg** have well-preserved medieval fortifications. *Bad Waldsee, Bad Buchau* and *Bad Wurzach* are well-known spas (mud-baths). At *Tettnang* asparagus and hops are grown; those who would like to sample first-class asparagus dishes should try the Hotel Rad.

Wangen im Allgäu

Land: Baden-Württemberg.
Vehicle registration: RV (WG).
Altitude: 556 m. – Population: 24,000.
Post code: D-7988. – Dialling code: 0 75 22.
ⓘ Städtisches Gästeamt, Town Hall; tel. 40 81/2.

HOTELS. – *Romantik-Hotel Alte Post, Postplatz 2, with *Hotel-Villa Alte Post*, Leutkircher Str. 20, together 50 b.; *Waltersbühl*, Max-Fischer-Str. 4, 96 b., SB, SP; *Alpina* (no rest.), Am Waltersbühl 6, 50 b., SB.

RESTAURANTS. – *Fidelisbäck*, Paradiesstr. 3; *Fuggerstuben*, Saumarkt 1.

RECREATION. – Heated open-air swimming pool and lake bathing lido; tennis; riding.

EVENT. – *"Fasnet"* (Shrovetide carnival); *Cycle Union tour* of the "Upper Swabian Baroque Road" (Sept.); *Wangen Heimattage* (every two years).

The former free Imperial city of Wangen, chief town of the Württemberg Allgäu, lies above the River Argen. It is a much frequented health resort and a centre of the dairying and cheese-making industry (with a teaching and research institute). By virtue of its almost perfectly preserved medieval streets and buildings the whole of the *old town (8 hectares) was designated in 1976 as a protected national monument.

HISTORY. – The town was already in existence in the early medieval period, and obtained its municipal charter in 1217. It became a free Imperial city in 1281, and from the 13th to the 15th c. was a flourishing centre of the linen trade (particularly with Italy). In 1539 and again in 1793 the town was ravaged by devastating fires. The Thirty Years War reduced it to poverty. In 1802 it passed to Bavaria, in 1810 to Württemberg.

SIGHTS. – In the *MARKET SQUARE stands the **Town Hall**, originally built in the 13th c.; part of the building dates from the 15th c., but it was largely rebuilt in Baroque style in 1719–21. To the left is a gate tower known as the *Ratloch*. To the right is the late Gothic parish church of **St Martin** (13th c.; interior re-done in Baroque style in 1684), with 19th c. altar and ceiling paintings.

From the Marktplatz Herrenstrasse runs N to the **Ravensburg Gate** or *Liebfrauentor* of 1608 (originally 13th c.), with a clock and sundial.

The charming Paradiesstrasse runs W from the SW corner of the Marktplatz to the painted **Martinstor** or *Lindau Gate* (1608: originally 14th c.). Beyond the gate, to the right, is the Italian-style **Old Cemetery** (now a municipal park), with *St Roch's Chapel* (1593: painted wooden roof).

Through the Ratloch a street runs E to the picturesque POSTPLATZ (Kornhausplatz, Kornmarkt), the main square of lower town, with *Kornhaus* (1595). From here Spitalstrasse runs NE to the *Old Hospital*, with the Rococo **Hospital Church** (1719–32), and the *Eselmühle* (Heimatmuseum). Here, round the NE and E sides of the old town above the River Argen, there is a stretch of the old *town walls*, with the 15th c. *Powder Tower*.

About 1 km SE of the old town, on the *Atzenberg* (584 m), is the **Eichendorff Museum** (with archives), devoted to the Silesian writer Joseph von Eichendorff (1788–1857). Here too are the archives of the later Silesian author *Hermann Stehr* (1864–1940) and the **Gustav Freytag Museum**, with archives and mementoes of the Silesian novelist and historian of culture (1816–95).

1 km SW, on the *Gehrenberg* (582 m), is the large **St Wolfgang's Cemetery** or New Cemetery, with *St Wolfgang's Chapel* (choir 15th c., nave 17th c.: beautiful *views). The cemetery lies on the attractive FOOTPATH, offering wide-ranging views, which makes a 16 km circuit round Wangen.

SURROUNDINGS. – 20 km E is the old-world little town of **Isny**, with a 17th c. Town Hall, the Romanesque St Nicholas's Church, St George's Church (1635–71: Rococo interior) and a former Benedictine monastery (17th c.). S of Isny in Wengen can be found the **Miniland** layout, with a model railway in a naturalistic landscape (from the sea to the Alps).

Weserbergland

Länder: Hesse, North Rhineland-Westphalia and Lower Saxony.

(i) **Fremdenverkehrsverband Weserbergland-Mittelweser,**
Falkenstr. 2, D-3250 Hameln 1;
tel. (0 51 51) 2 45 66.

The **Weserbergland (Weser hill country) is made up of several ranges of hills on both sides of the Weser between Münden and Minden. To the N it is bordered by the North German plain, while on the W it merges into the Lippe hills, on the E into the Leinebergland and on the S into the hills of Hesse.**

EAST OF THE WESER, below Münden, is the **Bramwald**, reaching a height of 400 m in the basalt cone of the *Bramburg* and 408 m in the *Totenberg*. Next come the **Solling** hills, a plateau of Bunter sandstone 500 sq. km in extent with beautiful deciduous and coniferous forests, rising to 528 m in the *Grosse Blösse*, the highest hill in the Weser region. Between Stadtoldendorf and Bodenwerder is the **Vogler**, a smaller massif of Bunter sandstone with flat-bottomed depression and deeply indented valleys between the hills, its highest point being *Ebersnacken* (460 m: views).

Beyond this are two beautifully wooded ridges of Jurassic limestone – the **Hils**, with the *Blosse Zelle* (477 m) and the *Grosser Sohl* (472 m: view), and the long and often precipitous **Ith** ridge, with the *Knüllbrink* (439 m.: view). – N of the B 1 (Hamelin–Elze) are the *Osterwald* (419 m) and the *Saupark* chain of hills (Bison Park). NW of B 217 (Hamelin–Springe–Hanover) are the **Deister** range, with the *Annaturm* (405 m) and *Normannsturm* (379 m), and the **Süntel**, with the *Hohe Egge* (437 m: view) and the magnificent limestone cliffs of the *Hohenstein*. – To the W is the **Wesergebirge**, reaching a height of 320 m in the *Amelungsberg*, with the **Bückeberge** (367 m: large sandstone quarries) lying to the N.

WEST OF THE WESER, below Münden, is the **Reinhardswald**, the largest single area of forest in Lower Hesse (210 sq. km, with a 70 hectare nature reserve round the *Sababurg*), reaching its highest point in the *Staufenberg*, a rounded basalt hill 472 m high. – Between Höxter and Vlotho extends the **Lippisches Bergland** (Lippe hills), with the 497 m high *Köterberg* (wide views; television tower, Köterberghaus). Finally the northern limit of the Weserbergland is reached in the long-drawn-out **Wiehengebirge** (*Heidbrink* and *Wurzelbrink*, 320 m), the continuation of the Wesergebirge W of the Porta Westfalica.

The most attractive part of the Weserbergland is seen on the WESER VALLEY HIGHWAY between Münden and Minden, with its ever-changing scenery and numerous pretty villages and towns. Among these are "Hannoversch" **Münden**, beautifully situated at the point where the Fulda and the Werra join to form the Weser, with many half-timbered houses; *Bad Karlshafen*; **Höxter**, with *Corvey Abbey*;

Porta Westfalica in the Weserbergland

Wetzlar: old bridge over the Lahn and Cathedral

Bodenwerder, the town of Baron Münchhausen; the Pied Piper's town of **Hamelin** with its beautiful buildings in Weser Renaissance style; the former university town and fortress of *Rinteln*; and the cathedral city of **Minden**, with the crossing of the Weser and the Mittelland Canal. – There are, too. a whole range of rewarding excursions t. be made: between Münden and afen into the Reinhardswald, with the *Sababurg*; from Höxter to the *Köterberg* with its wide-ranging views and to the health resort of *Neuhaus im Solling*; from Emmern to the imposing *Schloss Hämelschenburg* and *Bad Pyrmont* with its beautiful Kurpark. The climax of a trip down the Weser valley, however, is the *Porta Westfalica* or Westphalian Gates where the Weser breaks through the hills just above Minden; from here an excursion can be made to the interesting old residence town of Bückeburg.

The best known of the numerous HEALTH and HOLIDAY RESORTS in the Weserbergland are **Porta Westfalica**, *Bodenwerder*, *Polle* and *Neuhaus im Solling*; of the HEALTH RESORTS *Bad Karlshafen*, **Bad Pyrmont**, *Bad Eilsen*, *Bad Münder am Deister*, *Bad Nenndorf*, *Bad Oeynhausen* and *Bad Essen*.

Wetzlar

Land: Hesse. – Vehicle registration: WZ (L).
Altitude: 145 m. – Population: 52,000.
Post code: D-6330. – Dialling code: 0 64 41.
ⓘ **Städtisches Verkehrsamt Wetzlar,**
Domplatz 8;
tel. 40 53 38/48.

HOTELS. – *Team Hotel and Kongresszentrum Wetzlar,* Friedenstr. 20, 250 b. (opening 1984); *Bürgerhof,* Konrad Adenauer Promenade 20, 50 b.; *Wetzlarer Hof,*

Obertorstr. 3, 48 b.; Euler Haus (no rest.), Buderusplatz 1, 40 b. – YOUTH HOSTEL: Brühlsbachstr. 49, 170 b. (completion 1984). – CAMPING SITES: *Fischerhütte*, on banks of Lahn; *Iserbachtal*, Braunfels near Wetzlar; *Campingplatz am Duterhofener See,* near Wetzlar (6 km E).

RESTAURANTS. – *Zehntscheune*, Ludwig Erkplatz 1; *Zum Goldenen Ross*, Langgasse 11; *Wöllbacher Tor,* Goethestr. 14.

This old free Imperial city is picturesquely situated on the Lahn above the inflow of the Dill, below the ruined 13th c. castle of Kalsmunt. It has important industrial plants (including Leitz, Hensoldt, Philips and Buderus).

HISTORY. – Wetzlar grew up around a collegiate foundation. It first appears in the records in 1142 as *Witflaria*. It became a free Imperial city at an early stage (1180) and prospered greatly through its working and trade in iron. It was ringed with walls in the 13th–14th c. From 1693 to 1806 it was the seat of the Reichskammergericht, the highest court of the Holy Roman Empire. With the opening up of the iron-mining areas on the Lahn and the Dill by the railway Wetzlar developed in the second half of the 19th c. into a centre of the iron and optical-mechanical industries.
A recent plan to unite Wetzlar and Giessen into the new town of Lahn had to be abandoned because of strong local resistance.

SIGHTS. – The OLD TOWN on the slopes above the left bank of the Lahn, with its narrow lanes and many handsome old burghers' houses, is dominated by the tall bulk of the **Cathedral** of St Mary (Evang.-R.C.), a richly articulated building of the 12th–16th c. In the Fischmarkt, SW of the cathedral square, a double eagle marks the building once occupied by the **Reichskammergericht** (German Supreme Court), where Goethe worked as a young lawyer in 1772. E of the cathedral square, at Lottestr. 8, is *Lotte's House* (in the former buildings of the Teutonic Order), home of Charlotte Buff, who won Goethe's heart during his stay in Wetzlar and became the heroine of his "Werther" (museum). – The former tithe barn houses the *Wetzlar Industrial Museum*.

Wiesbaden

Land: Hesse. – Vehicle registration: WI.
Altitude: 117 m. – Population: 273,000.
Post code: D-6200. – Dialling code: 0 61 21.
ⓘ **Verkehrsbüro,** Rheinstr. 15;
tel. 31 28 47 and 37 43 53.
In Main Station; tel. 31 28 48.

HOTELS. – **Aukamm Hotel*, Aukamm Allee 31, 300 b.; **Naussauer Hof*, Kaiser Friedrich Platz 3, 270 b.;

Schwarzer Bock, Kranplatz 12, 220 b., thermal SB, sauna, roof restaurant; *Penta Hotel*, Auguste Viktoria Str. 15, 340 b., sauna; *Forum Hotel*, Abraham Lincoln Str. 17, 310 b., SB, sauna; *Fürstenhof-Esplanade*, Sonnenberger Str. 32, 120 b.; *Klee am Kurpark*, Parkstr. 4, 75 b.; *Hansa Hotel*, Bahnhofstr. 23, 130 b.; *Oranien*, Platter Str. 2, 110 b.; *Hôtel de France*, Taunusstr.49, 66 b. – YOUTH HOSTEL: Blücherstr. 66, 257 b. – CAMPING SITES: *Rheininsel Maaraue*, in Mainz Kostheim: *Rheinwiesen Biebrich*, near N approach to Schierstein bridge; *Rheininsel Rettbergsaue*, at Biebrich.

RESTAURANTS. – *Alte Münze*, Kranzplatz 5; *Le Gourmet*, Kleine Frankfurter Str.; *Alte Krone*, Sonnenberger Str. 82; *Mövenpick*, Sonnenberger Str. 2; *Kurhaus-Restaurant*, Kurhausplatz; *Alt-Prag*, Taunusstr. 41 (Bohemian specialities); *Steakhouse Cattle Baron*, Büdingenstr. 4; *Ratskeller*, Schlossplatz 6; *Bobbeschänkelsche*, Röderstr. 39; *China Restaurant "Asia"*, Friedrichstr. 43. – IN BIEBRICH *Weihenstephan*, Armenruhstr. 6.

CAFÉS. – *Mocca Stube*, Webergasse 8; *Rathaus-Café*, Rathauspassage; *Maldaner*, Marktstr. 34.

Wiesbaden Casino, in Kurhaus (roulette, blackjack).

EVENTS. – Carnival ceremonies, balls and Shrovetide-Sunday procession; *Riding tournament* in the Schlosspark in Biebrich (May); *International May Festival*; Summer Festival with fireworks and dancing in the Kurpark (Aug.); *Rheingau Wine Week* in the pedestrian precinct (Aug.); *Rheingau Wine Festival* in the Kurhaus (Sept.); *St Andrew's Market* on the Elsasser Platz (Dec.).

The capital of the *Land* of Hesse lies at the foot of the wooded Taunus hills, extending with its suburbs to the Rhine. The 27 thermal springs, the mild climate and the beautiful surroundings make it a much frequented health resort. Wiesbaden is also noted for its theatre and its modern shopping facilities, and it is the seat of the Federal Criminal Department, the Federal Statistical Office, the Federation of the German Film Industry and well-known publishing houses. Most of the large German Sekt (sparkling wine) cellars are in the Wiesbaden area.

HISTORY. – Wiesbaden's healing springs were known to the Romans, who called the place *Aquae Mattiacorum* (after the local tribe, the Mattiaci, who were a branch of the Chatti). There was a Roman fort here, probably established in the time of Claudius (A.D. 41–50); the Roman baths were near the present hot spring. In 406 the Romans finally abandoned the Rhine frontier, and thereafter the Franks made it a local capital, erecting a fortified tower in the area where the Schloss now stands. The name *Wisibada* ("bath in the meadows") is first recorded by Einhard, Charlemagne's biographer, in 829. At the beginning of the 13th c. the town's development into a free Imperial city began. In 1236 Frederick II celebrated Whitsun in Wiesbaden, but six years later the town was conquered and destroyed by the Archbishop of Mainz. About 1270 it passed to the Counts of Nassau, who made it a subsidiary residence town. In 1744 Prince Karl of Nassau-Usingen moved his seat to his

newly built palace in Biebrich. In 1816 Wiesbaden became capital of the new Duchy of Nassau and enjoyed its first period of prosperity as a modest Biedermeier-style residence town and spa to which the great ones of Europe (among them Goethe, 1814–15) came to take the cure. Dukes Friedrich August (1803–16) and Wilhelm (1816–39) laid out wide and handsome streets and erected imposing public buildings. In 1868 the Duchy of Nassau was incorporated in Prussia, and Wiesbaden became the chief town of an administrative region (Bezirk). Until the First World War the spa had a further period of splendour as the summer resort of the Emperor and the court. In 1926–28 the town increased considerably in size by taking in land from neighbouring communes. After the last war it became capital of the *Land* of Hesse.

SIGHTS. – The town's main traffic artery is the wide WILHELMSTRASSE, at the N end of which, on right, is the *spa district (Kurbezirk), bounded on the S by the *Theatre Colonnade* and the *State Theatre* (1892–94) and on the N by the *Fountain Colonnade*. To the E is the **Kurhaus** (by Friedrich von Thiersch, 1905–09), an imposing building with a massive Ionic pillared porch; in the left wing is the *Casino*. Behind the Kurhaus extends the well-groomed *Kurpark*. – To the E, in Aukamm-Allee, is the *Indoor thermal Bath*. – To the NW is the *Hot Spring* (closed), with the *Kaiser Friedrich Baths* (1910–13) and Rheumatism Clinic a little way away to the SE.

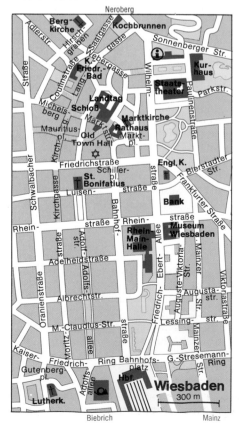

Wiesbaden

300 m

Biebrich   Mainz

In the SCHLOSSPLATZ in the town centre (W of Wilhelmstrasse) is the **Castle** (1837–41), which now houses the Landtag and government offices. Between the Schlossplatz and the MARKET SQUARE are the *Town Hall* (1884–88; restored 1951) and the *Market Church* (1855–62: Evang.). – At the S end of Wilhelmstrasse is the *Municipal Museum* (Friedrich-Ebert-Allee 2), with collections of antiquities and natural history and a picture gallery. Opposite is the **Rhein-Main-Halle,** a congress and exhibition centre.

N of the town is the wooded *****Neroberg** (245 m: rack railway), with the conspicuous *Greek Chapel* (185 m: Orthodox), the beautifully situated *Opel-Bad* (open-air swimming pool) and a café-restaurant. – In the NW of the town (Schützenhausweg) is the **Fasanerie Animal and Plant Park** (red deer, moufflons, bison, wild pigs, raccoons, wolves, etc.). – 5 km S of the town centre, in the district of BIEBRICH, is **Schloss Biebrich,** a Baroque palace built (1698–1744) as the seat of the Dukes of Nassau (rebuilt: now occupied by the Federation of the German Film Industry).

SURROUNDINGS. – *Eberbach Monastery (17 km W), with a church of 1186 and well-preserved monastic buildings of the 12th–14th c. (German Wine Academy; concerts in summer).

Wieskirche

Land: Bavaria. – Altitude: 870 m.
Post code: D-8924 Steingaden/Oberbayern.
Dialling code: 0 88 62.
ⓘ **Verkehrsamt Steingaden,**
Krankenhausstr. 1;
tel. 2 00 and 2 83.

ACCOMMODATION. – AT THE WIESKIRCHE: *Moser,* 30 b. – IN STEINGADEN: *Graf,* 40 b.; *Post,* 35 b.

The widely famed *****Wieskirche or Kirche in der Wies ("church in the meadow") is situated in a forest meadow near Steingaden in the Bavarian Oberland, some 45 km NW of Garmisch-Partenkirchen. This pilgrimage church, built 1746–54, is the finest achievement of the great architect Dominikus Zimmermann (1685–1766) and one of the maturest creations of German Rococo. The exterior is beautifully adapted to the mountain setting. The church, with windows arranged in groups, is

linked by a cupola-topped tower with two residential buildings.

The INTERIOR, with its consummate assimilation to one another of architecture and decoration, creates a magnificent effect of light and space. A porch leads into the oval nave with its shallow-vaulted roof, in which eight columns form a kind of ambulatory. The choir, with a painting of the Incarnation on the altar, is narrow and elongated, and is also surrounded by an ambulatory. The choir and the pulpit are supreme examples of what has been called the "fairy-tale architecture" of Baroque. The stucco work and ceiling paintings are by Johann Baptist Zimmermann, the architect's brother. Dominikus Zimmermann himself spent the last years of his life in the nearby inn run by his son.

SURROUNDINGS. – 5 km NW is **Steingaden** (763 m: pop. 2500), with many old houses. The Premonstratensian house founded here in 1147 was dissolved in 1802. The twin-towered *church has preserved its Romanesque exterior; the choir was redone in Baroque style in 1740–45 and decorated with stucco work of the Wessobrunn school; the Renaissance stalls date from 1534. One wing of the beautiful late Romanesque cloisters (early 13th c.; vaulting late Gothic) has been preserved. In the churchyard is the small Romanesque St John's Chapel.

Wildbad
im Schwarzwald

Land: Baden-Württemberg.
Vehicle registration: CW.
Altitude: 426 m. – Population: 11,000.
Post code: D-7547. – Dialling code: 0 70 81.
ⓘ **Verkehrsbüro,**
König-Karl-Str. 7;
tel. 1 02 80.

HOTELS. – *Sommerberg-Hotel,* on the Sommerberg, 140 b., SB; *Badhotel,* Kurplatz 5 (re-opening 1984); *Post,* Kurplatz 2, 100 b., SB; *Valsana,* Kernerstr. 182, 75 b.; *Bären,* Kurplatz 4, 60 b.; *Traube,* König Karl Str. 31, 55 b.; *Bergfrieden,* Bätznerstr. 78, 79 b.

RESTAURANTS. – *Kurpark-Restaurant,* in Kurpark; *Ratsstuben,* Uhlandplatz 5.

RECREATION. – Tennis; riding; water sports.

Wildbad, in the deeply indented Enz valley, is second only to Baden-Baden in popularity among the spas of the Northern Black Forest. Its thermal springs (35–41 °C) are effective particularly in the treatment of rheumatism, gout, sciatica and nervous complaints and in the follow-up treatment of paralysis and injuries.

SIGHTS. – In the KURPLATZ are the **Graf Eberhard Baths** (beautiful mosaic basin), now protected as a national monument, and, to the rear, the new *Treatment Centre* (1977), a terraced building close to the springs. In Olga-strasse are the *Swimming and Thermal Baths*, and farther upstream are the *Kurtheater* and the *Pump Room and Promenade*. On the left bank of the Enz are the Haus des Gastes *"König Karl Baths"*, and behind them, in Neuer Weg, the *Thermal Swimming Baths* (two indoor baths and one open-air pool); upstream is the *Kurhaus* (Kursaal). On both sides of the Enz are the beautiful KURANLAGEN (gardens).

To the W of the town is the wooded **Sommerberg** (733 m), which can be ascended either by an electric mountain railway (8 min.) or by a road which starts from above the railway station ($2\frac{3}{4}$ km; gradient of 16%). On the summit there are numerous footpaths (including one to the Wildsee-Hochmoor Nature Reserve).

SURROUNDINGS. – 14 km E, in the Nagold valley, is the well-known health resort of **Hirsau**, with the picturesque *ruins of a Benedictine monastery (founded 1059) and a hunting lodge (celebrated in one of Uhland's poems). – 3 km farther on is the town of **Calw**, with many half-timbered houses, birthplace of the writer Hermann Hesse (1877–1962). On the bridge over the Nagold is the tiny Gothic St Nicholas's Chapel.

Wolfenbüttel

Land: Lower Saxony.
Vehicle registration: WF.
Altitude: 75 m. – Population: 51,000.
Post code: D-3340. – Dialling code: 0 53 31.
ⓘ **Verkehrsverein**,
   Breite Herzogstr. 25;
   tel. 23 37.

HOTELS. – *Landhaus Dürkop*, Alter Weg 47, 25 b., sauna; *Waldhaus*, Adersheimer Str. 75, 45 b.; *Forst-haus*, Neuer Weg 5, 17 b.; *Antoinette*, Neuer Weg 91, 10 b. – YOUTH HOSTEL: *Städtisches Jugendheim*, Schlossplatz 13, 64 b. – CAMPING SITE: *Städtischer Campingplatz*, at Stadtbad (Municipal Swimming Pool).

RESTAURANT. – *Ratskeller*, Stadtmarkt 2.

This old Ducal town situated be-tween two arms of the River Oker and surrounded by attractive gardens on the line of the old fortifications,

Thermalbad, Wildbad

with many fine half-timbered build-ings, still preserves almost intact the aspect of a princely residence town. It has canning plants which handle the fruit and vegetables grown in the fertile surrounding area.

HISTORY. – The town grew up round a castle which was destroyed in 1255 and replaced by a moated castle erected by Duke Heinrich Mirabilis in 1283. From 1308 to 1753 Wolfenbüttel was the seat of the Dukes of Brunswick and a centre of culture and scholarship. Duke Heinrich Julius (1589–1613), who was himself the author of dramas in prose, summoned to his court a troupe of English players, the first professional actors in Germany. Duke August (1635–66) founded the famous library which bears his name, where Leibniz and Lessing were later to work.

SIGHTS. – In the SCHLOSSPLATZ stands the **Schloss**, dominated by the Hausmanns-turm. Built in the 16th c. and rebuilt in Baroque style at the beginning of the 18th c. (Baroque façade by Hermann Korb, 1716), it now houses the *Town and District Heimatmuseum*. On the N side of the square is the former *Arsenal* (Zeug-haus: 1613–18), a handsome Renais-sance building with a four-storey gable. To the W is the *Lessing House* (Lessing Museum), in which the great dramatist and critic lived from 1777 and in which he completed his play "Nathan der Weise" (1779). Behind it is the **Herzog August Library** (present building erec-ted 1882–87: the original building by Hermann Korb, 1705, in which Leibniz and Lessing worked, was pulled down in 1887), which contains 450,000 books, 4000 incunabula and 8000 manuscripts, including the 10th c. *Reichenau Gospel Book, the **Gospel Book of Henry the Lion (12th c.) and the 14th c. *'Sachsen-spiegel".

In the STADTMARKT, E of the Schloss, is the *Town Hall* (*c.* 1600), a beautiful half-timbered building with timber arcades. A short distance E is the Renaissance **Chancery** (Kanzlei), until 1753 seat of the provincial government, now housing the *Museum of Prehistory and Early History*. – To the S, in the centre of the town, is the **Hauptkirche** (*St Mary's Church*), built by Paul Francke in 1607–23, a curious blend of Gothic and Renaissance forms and one of the major examples of early Protestant church-building in Germany. It contains a Baroque high altar of 1618, a carved pulpit of 1623, choir-stalls of 1625, 16th c. tombstones and a Ducal burial vault.

Wolfsburg

Land: Lower Saxony.
Vehicle registration: WOB.
Altitude: 70 m. – Population: 131,000.
Post code: D-3180. – Dialling code: 0 53 61.
ⓘ **Informationspavillon,**
Porschestrasse, Rathausvorplatz;
tel. 1 43 33.

HOTELS. – *Holiday Inn*, Rathausstr. 1, 414 b., SB, sauna; *Primas*, Büssingstr. 18, 67 b.; *Parkhotel*, Unter den Eichen 55, 59 b.; *Simonshof*, Braunschweiger Str. 200, 50 b.; *Goya*, Poststr. 34, 32 b. – IN VORSFELDE: *Vorsfelder Hof*, Achtenbütteler Weg 2, 46 b. – CAMPING SITE: *Am Allersee*, at Allerwiesen Friends of Nature House.

RESTAURANTS. – *Stadtkeller*, Porchestr. 50; *Ratskeller*, in Town Hall (Dalmatiner Stuben); *König in der Porschestrasse*, Porschestr. 41d.

EVENTS. – *International Jazz and Folk Festival* (June); *Lichterfest in Schlosspark* (July); *City-Fest* (Sept.)

The town of Wolfsburg, established on the Mittelland Canal only in 1938, is the location of the Volkswagen car factory. The excellently landscaped town has a green city belt and a long waterfront on the Aller Lake. Half-timbered houses can still be seen in the Old Town.

HISTORY. – The castle of Wolfsburg on the Aller appears in the records as early as 1135. The Volkswagen works were established here in 1938, and this marked the beginning of a rapid development from a hamlet of 150 inhabitants to a considerable modern town.

SIGHTS. – E of the **Volkswagen works** (guided tours Mon.–Fri.), the largest car factory in Europe, rises the **Schloss Wolfsburg** (16/17th c.; municipal gallery, Heimatmuseum). To the S the *Badeland am Allersee*, with a wave-bath, massage parlours with water-jets, as well

as indoor and outdoor pools. Among modern buildings within the extensive boundaries of the town the following are of particular interest: the **Theatre** (by Hans Scharoun, opened 1973); the **Cultural Centre** by the famous Finnish architect Alvar Aalto, adjoining the *Town Hall* (1958) in PORSCHESTRASSE (the town's principal business and shopping street); Aalto's *Church of the Holy Ghost* (1962) on the Klieversberg and *St Stephen's Church* (1968) in the Detmeroder Markt. – To the E, near the **Stadthalle** is a *Space-flight Planetarium* (1983, projection equipment by Zeiss Jena).

SURROUNDINGS. – **Fallersleben** (6 km W), with the Hoffmann House, birthplace of August Heinrich Hoffman von Fallersleben (1798–1874), author of the German national anthem "Deutschland über alles"; Hoffmann Museum (Schlossplatz 12).

Worms

Land: Rhineland–Palatinate.
Vehicle registration: WO.
Altitude: 100 m. – Population: 74,000.
Post code: D-6520. – Dialling code: 0 62 41.
ⓘ **Verkehrsverein**, Neumarkt 14;
tel. 2 50 45.

HOTELS. – *Dom Hotel*, Obermarkt 10, 96 b.; *Nibelungen Hotel*, Martinsgasse 8, 94 b.; *Hüttl* (no rest.), Petersstr. 5, 40 b.; *Central Hotel* (no rest.), Kämmererstr. 5, 38 b.; *Kriemhilde*, Hofgasse 2, 32 b.; – IN PFEDDERSHEIM: *Pfeddersheimer Hof*, Zellertalstr. 35, 34 b. – YOUTH HOSTEL: Dechaneigasse 1, 139 b. – CAMPING SITE: at Nibelungenbrücke.

Worms Cathedral

RESTAURANTS. – *Domschänke*, Stephansgasse 16; *Neue Post*, Rheinstr. 2. – IN RHEINDÜRKHEIM: *Rôtisserie Dubs*, Kirchstr. 6.

CAFÉ. – *Schmerker*, Wilhelm-Leuschner-Str. 9.

EVENT. – *Backfischfest* (end Aug./beginning of Sept.).

The cathedral city of Worms, on the left bank of the Rhine, is one of the oldest towns in Germany. It is a noted centre of the wine trade and has considerable industry. The vineyards round the Liebfrauenkirche produce the famous Liebfraumilch.

HISTORY. – Worms goes back to an old Celtic settlement (*Borbetomagus*) and a later Roman fort (*Civitas Vangionum*). A bishopric was established here in the 4th c., and during the great migrations it became the capital of the Burgundian kingdom which was destroyed by the Huns in 437. The events of this period provided the basis for the story of the Nibelungs. During the medieval period more than 100 Imperial diets were held in Worms, the most celebrated being the Diet of 1521 at which Luther defended his doctrines.

SIGHTS. – In the centre of the OLD TOWN is the *Cathedral of SS. Peter and Paul (R.C.), a four-towered building with two domes, which ranks along with the larger cathedrals of Speyer and Mainz as one of the finest achievements of the High Romanesque style (11th and 12th c.). The interior is 110 m long and 27 m wide; the nave is 26 m high, the towers 40 m. In the N aisle are five fine late Gothic sandstone reliefs from the demolished Gothic cloisters; the choir has beautiful stalls and a high altar by Balthasar Neumann. To the E of the Cathedral in the MARKET SQUARE are *Trinity Church* (1709–25; rebuilt 1954–59 after major war damage), with a fine interior, and the *Town Hall* (1956–58). A little way NE is

the Romanesque *St Paul's Church*, with two round towers topped by cupolas.

SW of the Cathedral are the late Romanesque church of *St Magnus* (10th–14th c.: Evang.), with a spire, the town's first church, and the former *St Andrew's Church* (12th–13th c., restored 1927–29), which along with the adjoining monastic buildings now houses the *Municipal Museum* (excavation material, works of art and other remains of the past from the Worms area). A short distance NW of the two churches, in Andreasring, is the oldest and largest *Jewish cemetery* in Europe (tombstones of the 11th–12th c.). Since 1970 the former Jewish quarter has been redeveloped.

N of the Cathedral is the *Kunsthaus Heylshof*, a mansion erected in 1884 on the site of the former Bishop's Palace (painting of the 16th–19th c., sculpture, stained glass, porcelain, etc.). Still farther N, in Lutherplatz, is the **Luther Monument** (by Ernest Rietschel, 1868), commemorating Luther's appearance before the Diet of Worms in 1521. To the E of this, in the Judengasse (protected as a national monument), is the *Synagogue* (originally 12th–13th c.: ritual bath of 1186), rebuilt in 1961 after its destruction in 1938. – Just off the road (B 9) which runs N to Mainz is the *Liebfrauenkirche* or Church of Our Lady (13th–15th c.: R.C.), surrounded by vineyards; it contains a 15th c. Madonna and tabernacle.

Wuppertal

Land: North Rhineland-Westphalia.
Vehicle registration: W.
Altitude: 146 m. – Population: 400,000.
Post code: D-5600. – Dialling code: 0202.

(i) **Informationszentrum,**
Pavillon Döppersberg,
Wuppertal-Elberfeld;
tel. 5 63 22 70 and 5 63 21 80.

HOTELS. – IN BARMEN: *Haus Juliane*, Mollenkotten 195, 126 b., SB, SP, sauna; *City-Hotel* (no rest.). Fischertal 21, 33 b.; *Imperial* (no rest.), Heckinghauser Str. 10, 40 b.; *Waldhof Vesper* (no rest.), Mollenkotten 183a, 35 b.; *Lunkenheimers Parkhotel* (no rest.), Mollenkotten 245, 30 b.; *Villa Christina* (no rest.), Richard Strauss Allee 18, SB; *CVJM Gasteheim*, Bundeshöhe, 85 b. – IN CRONENBERG: *Zur Post* (no rest.), Hauptstr. 49, 25 b. – IN ELBERFELD: *Kaiserhof*, Döppersberg 50, 200 b., sauna; *Zur Post* (no rest.), Poststr. 4, 80 b.; *Haymann* (no rest.), Mäuerchen 4, 60 b.; *Rathaus Hotel* (no rest.), Wilhelmstr. 7, 44 b.; *Rubin* (no rest.), Paradestr. 59, 26 b. – YOUTH HOSTELS: Obere Lichtenplatzer Str. 70, Barmen, 141 b.; In der Gelpe 79, Cronenberg, 40 b.

RESTAURANTS. – IN BARMEN: *Palette-Röderhaus*, Sedanstr. 68; *Taverne Aramis*, Alter Markt 5; *Jagdhaus Mollenkotten*, Mollenkotten 144; *China-Restaurant Wah-Nam*, Fischertal 21; *Rôtisserie Wicküler an der Oper*, Friedrich-Engels-Allee 378. – IN ELBERFELD: *Ratskeller*, Neumarkt 10; *Orangerie*, Döppersberg 50; *Pilken*, Fouriersgasse. – IN VOHWINKEL: *Scarpati*, Scheffelstr. 41 (Italian).

This university and industrial city, attractively situated in the Bergisches Land, consists principally of the districts of Barmen, Elberfeld and Vohwinkel (formerly separate towns), strung out along the narrow valley of the Wupper for a distance of 19 km and linked by the unique *overhead railway constructed in 1898–1901 (13·3 km long: now with modern articulated trains).

HISTORY. – Elberfeld grew up in the 10th c. round a moated castle belonging to the lords of Elverfelde and obtained its municipal charter in 1610. Barmen, recorded in 1070 as belonging to the monastery of Werden, was until the end of the 17th c. no more than a cluster of peasants' houses; it obtained its charter as a town only in 1808. The textile industry of the two towns was given a powerful boost by Napoleon's continental blockade (1806), which cut out English competition. In 1929 the towns of Elberfeld, Barmen, Vohwinkel, Cronenberg and Ronsdorf, together with

parts of neighbouring communes, were amalgamated to form a new city, which in 1929 took the name of Wuppertal.

SIGHTS: – In BARMEN are the *Town Hall* (1913–22) and, to the SE, the *Haus der Jugend* (House of Youth), with the Municipal Library (temporary exhibitions). In FRIEDRICH-ENGELS-ALLEE are the *Opera House* (1956) and the *Engelshaus*, with records of Friedrich Engels, the co-founder of scientific socialism. To the W, on the Hardt, is the *Missionshaus* containing the Rhineland Missionary Society's ethnographical collection. – S of Barmen is the *Toelleturm* (access road), with beautiful views of the Wupper valley.

Mungsten Railway Bridge

ELBERFELD: In the Neumarkt is the former *Town Hall* (now offices). At Turmhof 8 is the **Von der Heydt Museum** (French Impressionists, 19th and 20th c. German painting). To the E, at Poststr. 11, is the *Wuppertal Clock Museum* (history of time-keeping). In BUNDESALLEE is the *Schauspielhaus* (1966). On the Johannisberg, near the *Stadthalle*, is the *Stadtbad* (1956), a municipal swimming pool of ultra-modern design. On the western outskirts of Elberfeld is the

300 m   ●——●——● Schwebebahn   ══════ Fußgängerzone

Zoo (3500 animals, open enclosures). To the SE is the two-level *Kiesberg Tunnel* (upper carriageway 854 m long, lower 1043 m).

SURROUNDINGS. – *Klütert Cave (9 km E), in the Ennepe valley, one of the largest natural caves in Germany (total length 5·2 km), which has been used since 1951 for the treatment of asthmatics. – *Müngsten Bridge (13 km S), Europe's highest railway bridge (107 m high, 500 m long).

Würzburg

Land: Bavaria. – Vehicle registration: WÜ.
Altitude: 182 m. – Population: 126,000.
Post code: D-8700. – Dialling code: 09 31.
ⓘ **Fremdenverkehrsamt,**
Haus zum Falken;
tel. 5 22 77.
Tourist-Information, pavilion outside Station.

HOTELS. – *Rebstock*, Neubaustr. 7, 112 b. (Franconian wine room); *Amberger* (no rest.), Ludwigstr. 17, 118 b.; *Walfisch*, Am Pleidenturm 5, 60 b.; *Wurzburger Hof* (no rest.), Barbarossaplatz 2, 80 b.; *Franziskaner*, Franziskanerplatz 2, 64 b.; *Bahnhofhotel Excelsior*, Haugerring 2, 58 b.; St. *Josef* (no rest.), Semmelstr. 28, 51 b.; *Grüner Baum* (no rest.), Zeller Str. 35, 48 b.; *Schönleber* (no rest.), Theaterstr. 5, 48 b.; *Central Hotel* (no rest.), Koellikerstr. 1, 32 b.; *Alter Kranen* (no rest.), Kärnergasse 11, 26 b. – ON THE STEINBERG: *Schloss Steinburg*, 75 b., garden terrace, SP. – YOUTH HOSTELS: Burkader Str. 44 (temporarily closed for conversion); Frau Holle Weg 27, Heidingsfeld, 65 b. – CAMPING SITES: *Kalte Quelle*, Heidingsfeld, Winterhäuser Str.; *Camping Estenfeld*, Estenfeld.

RESTAURANTS. – *Ratskeller*, in Town Hall, Langgasse 1; *Klosterschänke*, Franziskanerplatz 2; *Schiffbäuerin*, Katzengasse 7 (fish dishes); *Diocletian*, Domstr. 24 (Yugoslav specialties).

WINE-BARS. – *Hofkellerei*, Residenzplatz 1 (in Gesandtenbau of Residenz); *Bürgerspital*, Theaterstr. 19; *Juliusspital*, Juliuspromenade 19; *Zum Stachel*, Gressengasse 1 (Würzburg's oldest wine-house: 1413); *Maulaffenbäck*, Maulhardgasse 9.

CAFÉS. – *Ludwig*, Kaiserstr. 5; *Hofgartencafé*, Residenzplatz; *Am Dom*, Kürschnerhof 2.

EVENTS. – *Mozart Festival*, with concerts in the Imperial Hall of the Residenz and serenades in the Hofgarten (June); *Wine-growers' Festival* (end Sept.–beginning Oct.); *Würzburg Bach Festival* (end Nov. –beginning Dec.).

This old Franconian capital and episcopal city is beautifully situated in a vineyard-fringed basin in the Main valley. It has a University and an Academy of Music and is the principal centre of wine production and marketing in Franconia. The Bürgerspital, the Juliusspital and the Staatsweingut (State Wine Estate), with the Hofkeller (Court Cellars) are the largest vine growing estates in Germany, and an excellent wine is produced by the vineyards on the slopes of the Schlossberg and the Steinberg. The destruction of the last war has been made good, and the old town has recovered much of its original aspect, with its numerous churches and the magnificent buildings erected by the Prince-Bishops. High above the town rears the medieval fortress of Marienberg.

HISTORY. – The beginnings of the settlement at the ford on the Main, under the protection of the Würzberg – which first appears in the records, as *Castellum Virteburg*, in 704 – go back to the 7th c., when a Frankish ducal stronghold was established on the right bank of the river. The work of the Irish-Scottish monks led by the "Apostle of the Franks", St Kilian (murdered 689), made this the principal place in the territory of the Franks. In 706 Duke Hedan II built a chapel dedicated to the Virgin Mary on the Würzberg, which later became known as the Marienberg. The first bishop was St Burchard (d. 758), who was consecrated by St Boniface in 741. Under the Salian and Staufen emperors some 20 churches were built between 1000 and 1200. During the 12th c. the Emperor Frederick Barbarossa held five Imperial diets in Würzburg, and in 1156 his marriage with Beatrice of Burgundy was celebrated here. It was Frederick, too, who elevated the Bishops of Würzburg to the rank of Dukes of Franconia. His son Henry VI also held many Imperial diets and assemblies of dignitaries in Würzburg, and his Chancellor Konrad von Querfurt (from 1201 Bishop of Würzburg) built a massive keep, the beginning of the castle which was to serve as a place of refuge and a stronghold to curb the rising power of the burghers. In the 15th and 16th c. the great sculptor and woodcarver Tilman Riemenschneider worked in the town, and also became burgomaster. The 17th and 18th c. saw a period of furious building activity by the Prince-Bishops of the House of Schönborn, and Balthasar Neumann (1678–1753) created his greatest work in the Wurzburg Residenz. After being secularised in 1803 the Grand Duchy of Würzburg, under the Habsburg Grand Duke Ferdinand of Tuscany, became a member of the Confederation of the Rhine (1806–14). In 1815 it was incorporated in Bavaria.

SIGHTS. – In the spacious RESIDENZPLATZ is the most important secular building in the Baroque style in Germany, the *Residenz of the Prince-Bishops, built 1719–44, mainly under the direction of Balthasar Neumann. It was burned down in 1945 with the exception of the middle range of buildings and the church, but has for the most part been rebuilt; the furniture and furnishings were almost completely preserved. Among those parts which survived, apart from the *church*, are the monumental *staircase hall with a huge fresco by G. B. Tiepolo, the White Room with its beautiful rococo stucco work and the splendidly decorated Imperial Hall. In

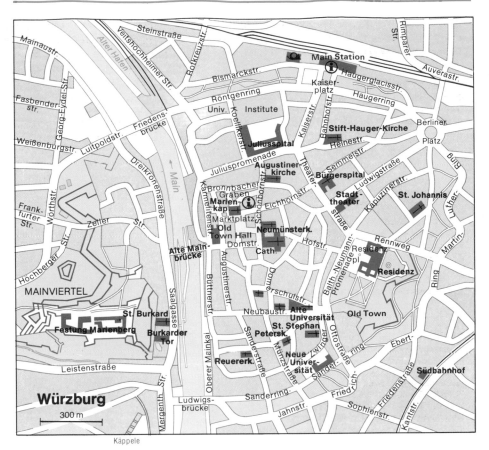

the S wing of the Residenz is the *Martin von Wagner Museum* belonging to the University (antiquities, pictures, graphics). – Behind the Residenz is the *Hofgarten* (18th c.), with magnificent wrought-iron gates.

W of the Residenz is the *Cathedral (11th–13th c.); the interior was destroyed by fire in 1945 but has been restored, partly in modern style. It contains some fine bishops' tombs, including the *tombs of Rudolf von Scherenberg and Lorenz von Bibra, by Tilman Riemenschneider. In the N transept is the *Schönborn chapel* (by Balthasar Neumann, 1721–36). – Immediately N of the Cathedral is the **Neumünsterkirche**, with a Romanesque E end (11th and 13th c.) and a Baroque W end (1711–19). Under the dome are a figure of the Virgin and a crucifix, both by Riemenschneider. In the W crypt is the stone sarcophagus of the Irish monk St Kilian, murdered here in 689. In the former cloisters (the "Lusamgärtlein") on the N side of the church is a memorial stone commemorating *Walther von der Vogelweide*, greatest of the German minnesingers, who died in Würzburg about 1230.

A short distance NW of the Neumünsterkirche is the MARKET SQUARE, with *St Mary's Chapel, the finest late Gothic building in Würzburg, built 1377–1479, destroyed by fire 1945, restored 1945–61 (fine doorways; tomb of Balthasar Neumann on third pillar in nave; monument of Konrad von Schaumberg, d. 1499, by Tilman Riemenschneider).

Just E of the chapel is the **Haus zum Falken**, with the finest Rococo façade in Würzburg (restored, and now occupied by the Tourist Office). – SW of the MARKET SQUARE, in Domstrasse, is the **Old Town Hall**, a group of buildings of varying date (13th–19th c.) – On the Kranenkai along the Main is the *Old Crane* of 1773. – In Juliuspromenade is the large *Juliusspital* (18th c., restored) and in Theaterstrasse the *Bürgerspital* (18th c.), both with famous old wine-bars.

In the southern part of the old town is the **Old University** (1582–92). In the E wing are sections of the *University Library*, in the S wing the *University Church* or *Neubaukirche*, one of the few important churches in German Renaissance style (adapted for use as concert hall, etc.). – Farther S, in Sanderring, is the **New University** (1892–96); most of the university buildings are now in the E of the town (Universität am Hubland).

The *Old Main Bridge (1473–1543), decorated with Baroque statues of saints, leads into the districts on the left bank of the Main, dominated by the old fortress of *Marienberg (266 m: access road), seat of the Prince-Bishops from the mid 13th c. until the construction of the Residenz. In the Arsenal (Zeughaus) is the *Franconian Museum, containing work by artists who were either born in Franconia or worked there (including an important collection of work by *Riemenschneider). Close to the keep (1201) is St Mary's Church, a Merovingian rotunda of 706. Magnificent views from the Fürstengarten. – Upstream from the Old Main Bridge is the parish church of St Burkard (St Burchard: 11th, 12th and 15th c.), and beyond it is the Burkarder Tor. Beyond this again is a stepped footpath with Stations of the Cross leading up to the *Käppele, a picturesque pilgrimage church by Balthasar Neumann (1747–50), with frescoes by Matthias Günther; beautiful view, particularly in the evening.

On the N edge of the town runs the Würzburg Steinweinpfad an educational path through the Würzburg Stein, one of the best-known German vineyard areas (information and pictorial illustration of different kinds of grape, etc.).

SURROUNDINGS. – **Schloss Veitshöchheim** (7 km NW: accessible also by boat), a country palace of the Prince-Bishops of Würzburg (1682). The *Hofgarten (1703–74), laid out according to French models is the best preserved rococo garden in Germany and is equipped with numerous garden sculptures. At the heart of the layout lies a large lake; on an island is the "Parnassus", a group of sculptures crowned by a Pegasus

Xanten

Land: North Rhineland-Westphalia.
Vehicle registration: WES.
Altitude: 24 m. – Population: 17,000.
Post code: D-4323. – Dialling code: 0 28 01.
ⓘ **Verkehrsamt**, Town Hall;
tel. 3 72 38 and 3 72 98.

HOTELS. – Hövelmann, Markt 31, 36 b.; Limes Hotel, Niederstr., 80 b.; Van Bebber, Klever Str. 14, 21 b. – IN MARIENBAUM: Deckers, Kalkarer Str. 71, 46 b. – IN WINNENTHAL: Burg Winnenthal, 60 b.

This old city is today a culture and leisure centre on the Lower Rhine. Siegfried, the hero of the Niebelungenlied is supposed to have been born in Xanten. The town has many relics of its Roman past.

HISTORY. – About 15 B.C. the Roman Castra Vetera was established on the Fürstenberg, S of Xanten, and it was from here that Varus and his legions set out on the campaign which ended in defeat in the Teutoburg Forest. In A.D. 100 Trajan founded, to the N, the civil town of Colonia Ulpia Traiana. Present-day Xanten developed further S over the grave of the martyr Victor and his companions. In the 8th c. there was already a religious foundation here which soon developed into a medieval trading settlement. Xanten received its charter in 1228 and in 1263 Archbishop Friedrich von Hochstaden laid the foundation stone of the Cathedral. In the 16th c. the Rhine shifted its course for 2 km and this caused a recession. In the Second World War the town and the Cathedral suffered damage. In 1975 (European year of protection of monuments) Xanten was chosen as a model town for its successful reconstruction of the town centre.

SIGHTS. – The *Cathedral of St Victor (originally a monastic church) in the market place is, after Cologne Cathedral, the most important Gothic church on the Lower Rhine (1190–1516; restored). The most notable feature of the interior is the large Altar of Our Lady by H. Douvermann (1525). – N of the Cathedral are the conventual buildings; in the chapterhouse is the interesting Cathedral Museum. To the S is the Regional Museum. In the Old Town are the Gothic House and other medieval buildings. In the NW of the town stands the Klever Gate (1393; Roman museum).

NE of the town on the far side of the B57 an *Archaeological Park is being laid out with reconstructions of Roman buildings (including an amphitheatre and a port temple). Gradually the entire site of Colonia Ulpia Traiana will be incorporated.

SURROUNDINGS. – Kalkar (15 km NW), with St Nicholas's Church (important examples of the work of the Kalkar school of woodcarvers). A fast-breeder atomic reactor is under construction nearby.

Practical Information

Hotel Riesen, Miltenberg

Safety on the Road. Some Reminders for the Holiday Traveller

Always wear your seat-belt, and make sure that your passengers wear theirs.
This is compulsory in the Federal Republic.
Note: Compensation for injury may be reduced by up to 50% if seat-belts are not worn.

Change the brake fluid in your car at least every two years.
This vitally important fluid tends to lose its effectiveness in the course of time as a result of condensation of water, dust and chemical decomposition.

Change your tires when the depth of tread is reduced to 2 mm ($\frac{3}{32}$ in.).
Tires must have enough depth of tread to get a good grip on the road and hold the car steady even on a wet surface. In the case of wide sports tires, with their long water channels, a 3-mm ($\frac{1}{8}$ in.) tread is advisable.

You will see better, and be more easily seen, if your car lights are functioning properly.
It is important, therefore, to check your sidelights and headlights regularly. This can be done even without getting out of the car. When you stop at traffic lights in front of a bus or truck you can see whether your rear lights and brake lights are working from the reflection on the front of the other vehicle, and you can check up on your headlights and front indicators in your own garage or in a shop window.

When driving at night on wet roads you should stop in a parking place every 50 or 100 km and clear your headlights and rear lights.
Even the thinnest coat of dirt on the glass reduces the strength of your headlights by half, and a heavy coating may reduce their output by as much as 90%.

The best place for fog lamps is on the front bumper.
This gives them the maximum range without dazzling oncoming traffic. If they are mounted below the bumper they will have a range of only 5 or 10 m. Fog lamps are most effective when used in conjunction with parking lights only: for safe driving, therefore, they must have an adequate range.

It is always advisable to carry a first-aid kit and drivers of vehicles registered in the Federal Republic are required to do so by law. It is compulsory for all drivers, including visitors, to carry a warning triangle and anyone driving a vehicle registered in the Federal Republic must carry a triangle which conforms to the national design. Remember, however, that if these items are kept on the rear shelf they can become dangerous projectiles in the event of an accident.

The first-aid kit should be kept inside the car, either secured in a holder or under a seat; the warning triangle should be kept ready to hand in the trunk. If there is no more room in the trunk any items of equipment or pieces of luggage inside the car should be stowed carefully and securely.

If there is so much luggage in the back of the car that the view through the rear window is obstructed it is a wise precaution, as well as a statutory requirement, to have an outside mirror on the passenger's side. This is useful in any event when driving in heavy traffic on multi-lane highways. It should be of convex type.

Drivers who keep their left foot on the clutch pedal after changing gear may be letting themselves in for a heavy repair bill.

This very rapidly wears down the clutch release bearing, giving rise to whining and grating noises.

As a lamp bulb grows older its efficiency falls off very markedly. A dark-coloured deposit inside a bulb – wolfram from the filament – is an indication of age.
All bulbs should therefore be checked at least once a year. It is advisable to change those which have darkened glass as well as those which are clearly defective.

You can save fuel when driving on motorways by keeping the accelerator pedal at least 2 cm (¾ in.) short of the "foot-down" position.
The nearer to its maximum speed a car is travelling the more steeply does fuel consumption increase. A slightly lighter touch on the accelerator will make little difference to your speed but quite a difference to the amount of fuel you use.

If you wear glasses you will increase the safety of night driving by getting special coated lenses; and all drivers should avoid wearing tinted glasses after dusk and at night.
All glass reflects part of the light passing through it, and even through a clear windscreen only about 90% of the light outside reaches the driver's eyes inside the car. If the driver is wearing glasses there is a further light loss of 10%. With a tinted windscreen and tinted glasses only about half the light outside reaches the driver's eyes, and in these conditions driving at night is not possible.

If you have an accident

However carefully you drive, you may nevertheless find yourself involved in an accident. If this does happen do not lose your temper, however great the provocation: remain polite, keep cool and take the following action:

1. Warn other road users: switch on your hazard warning lights and set out your warning triangle at a sufficient distance from the scene of the accident.

2. Attend to the injured. Expert assistance should be summoned immediately. Unless you have a knowledge of first aid you should be extremely cautious about attending anyone injured in an accident. Call an ambulance if required.

3. If anyone has been injured, if there has been major damage to the cars involved or if there is disagreement between you and the other party, inform the police.

4. Get the names and addresses of other parties involved; note the registration number and make of the other vehicles and the time and place of the accident. Ask the other parties for the name of their insurers and their insurance number.

5. Note down the names and addresses of witnesses; take photographs and/or make sketches of the scene of the accident.
After a minor accident the police are usually more concerned to get the road clear for traffic than to make a full record of the incident. What you should try to

record in your photographs is not the damage to the cars involved – that can be established later – but the general situation at the scene of the accident. It is particularly important to photograph each of the cars in the direction of travel from a sufficient distance.

6. If possible fill in the "European Accident Statement" (which you will have received along with your green card) and have it signed by the other party. Do not sign any admission of liability. If the other party asks you to sign an accident form not written in English and you are in doubt of its meaning, add the words "without prejudice to liability" above your signature.

7. Inform your own insurance company by letter, if possible, within 24 hours of the accident.

8. If the accident involves injury to persons (other than yourself and your passengers) or damage to property, inform the bureau named on the back page of your green card. In the Federal Republic the bureau is the HUK-Verband, Glockengiesserwall 1, D-2000 Hamburg 1, tel. (0 40) 32 10 71.

9. Follow the instructions of your insurance company – which you will normally have received along with your green card – concerning repair of damage to your car.

When to Go

The summer months are the best for the North Sea and Baltic coasts, the East Friesian Islands and for the mountainous regions in the Bavarian Alps. The central highland area is very attractive in spring, and autumn is a good time to visit the vine-growing regions of the Rhine, the Main and the Moselle. The best places for winter-sports are to be found in the Alps, the Bavarian Forest, the Black Forest, the Hochsauerland and in the Harz.

Climate

The climate of Germany is temperate, and fluctuations in temperature are comparatively slight. In winter the mountains are deeply covered with snow, and winter sports are possible at heights from 500 m upwards. The average temperature in January (the coldest month in the year) is around 0 °C; in the mountains it is about −10°. The winter lasts from December to March, in the Alps until May.

In April skiing is still possible in the Alps, while the fruit-trees are already in blossom on the Bergstrasse, in the Palatinate and in the areas of Black Forest and Lake Constance.

In summer the average temperature in the valleys and plains is around 20 °C. The best time for bathing is between June and August.

For a fuller account of the climate see p. 36.

Time

Germany is on Central European Time (Mitteleuropäische Zeit – MEZ). This is an hour ahead of Greenwich Mean Time and the same as British Summer Time. This is 6 hours ahead of New York time.

Summer Time in Germany (two hours ahead of Greenwich Mean Time/MEZ+1) is in force approximately during the same period as in the UK.

Passport and Customs Regulations

For entry into the Federal Republic a valid passport is normally all that is required. Visitors from the EEC countries and some other Western European countries require only an identity card (in the U.K. a Visitor's Passport). For nationals of most countries, including holders of U.K., Commonwealth and U.S. passports, no visa is required for a visit of up to 3 months. Visitors may not, however, take up employment or practise any profession on the basis of a visa-free entry.

Special regulations apply to **travel to West Berlin** through the territory of the German Democratic Republic:

For *travel by air* GDR transit visas are not required.

For *travel by rail* GDR transit visas are required, and are issued free of charge on the train. Full Passports are necessary, since Visitor's Passports, etc., are not recognised.

For *travel by scheduled coach services* (which run from many places in the Federal Republic) GDR transit visas are required, and are issued free of charge at frontier checkpoints. Passports are necessary.

For *travel by car* passports and GRD transit visas are required. Visas are issued at frontier checkpoints and cost DM 5 for the single journey and DM 10 return. Visitors are recommended to get their return visa at the point of entry: it is not necessary to return by the same route. For access routes, see below (p. 268).

Visitors to the Federal Republic can take in without formality all normal personal effects and equipment. In addition visitors may take in limited quantities of tobacco, alcohol, etc., free of duty. For EEC nationals the present limits are 300 cigarettes or 150 small cigars or 75 large cigars or 400 g of tobacco; $1\frac{1}{2}$ litres of spirits or 3 litres of liqueurs, aperitifs, sparkling wines or fortified wines; 3 litres of ordinary wine; 750 g of coffee (beans) or 300 g of instant coffee; 150 g of tea or 60 g of instant tea; 75 g of perfume; and $\frac{3}{8}$ litre of toilet water. These limits apply to goods bought in ordinary shops; there are lower limits for goods bought in duty-free shops. Slightly lower allowances apply to visitors from other European countries, slightly higher allowances to overseas visitors. Visitors are also allowed to bring in reasonable quantities of other food-stuffs for their own consumption.

There are no restrictions on the import or export of German or any other currency.

Currency

The unit of currency is the **Deutsche Mark** (*DM*), which is divided into 100 *pfennigs*.

There are banknotes for 5, 10, 20, 50, 100, 500 and 1000 marks and coins in denominations of 1, 5, 10 and 50 pfennigs and 1, 2 and 5 marks.

Exchange rates fluctuate. The rates at the beginning of 1984 were approx. as follows:

1 pound sterling = DM 4
DM 1 = 25 p
1 US dollar = DM 2.70
DM 1 = 37 cents
Canadian dollar = DM 2.00
DM 1 = 50 cents

Postal Rates

The inland postage rate for a letter (up to 20 g) is DM 0.80, for a postcard 0.60. These rates also apply to letters and postcards to Andorra, Belgium, France, Holland, Italy, Liechtenstein, Luxembourg, Monaco, San Marino, Switzerland and Vatican City. Letters to all other countries cost DM 0.90, postcards DM 0.60.

Airmail rates vary according to destination. There is no airmail surcharge for letters to European countries, which normally go by airmail.

Check-lists

Have you got everything ready for your journey? Is everything under control at home? These check-lists may help you to make sure that you haven't forgotten anything. (Not all of the items listed necessarily apply to a direct journey to the Federal Republic.)

Six weeks or so before the date of departure:
Passport still valid?
Visas, if required?
International driving permit, if required.
Registration document.
Fuel coupons, if available.
Green card (international insurance certificate).
Travel insurance.
Tickets (air, boat, train).
Visit doctor and dentist if required.
Vaccinations, etc.?
Check first-aid kit.
Confirm hotel, etc., reservations.
Check-up on car, caravan, etc.
List of service garages for car.
Maps.
Inform friends and neighbours.

Before a motoring holiday:
Look over car and caravan.
Wash car.
Fill up windscreen washer reservoir.
Check tire pressures.
Check first-aid kit.
Check adjustment of seat-belts and head-rests.
Check visibility.
International Distinguishing Sign.
Warning triangle.
Flashing lamp.
Pocket torch.
Fire extinguisher.
Wheel spanner.
Tow-rope.
Spare light bulbs and fuses.
Check tool-kit and jack.
Second outside mirror (if towing a caravan).

A week or so before leaving:
Arrange for payment of bills (telephone, electricity, gas, water, insurance premiums, television licence, rent, rates, shops, etc.).
Stop papers, milk, etc.
Make arrangements for dealing with mail.
Valuables into bank safe deposit.
Arrange for house plants and animals to be looked after.
Get foreign currency and/or travellers' cheques.
Leave details of holiday program and addresses and spare keys with friends or neighbours.
Make photocopies of important papers.
Begin packing.
Use up perishable foodstuffs.
Empty, de-frost and switch off refrigerator.

Immediately before departure:
Put on comfortable clothing.
Don't eat too heavy a meal.

Turn off water.
Turn off gas.
Pull out electric plugs (except deep-freeze).
Pull out radio and television aerial plug.
In summer switch off heating system; in winter turn it down (checking oil level where appropriate) and take precautions against freezing of heating and water system.
Take sun-glasses – children's toys – personal medicines.
Empty trash cans.
Check documents (papers, money, checks, tickets, etc.), make sure that you have everything necessary and distribute them among the members of the party.
Give second set of car keys to passenger.
Pack food – tissues – toilet paper – bag for rubbish.
Lock garage.
Children into back seat of car.
Check doors and windows.
Close curtains – blinds – shutters.
Switch on burglar alarm, if any.
Fill up with fuel and check oil.

Medical Treatment

Hospital, other medical and dental treatment is free in the Federal Republic. You may have to pay a small charge for prescribed medicine.

Travellers who are in the habit of taking certain medicines should make sure that they have a sufficient supply to last for their trip since they may be very difficult to get abroad.

Those who suffer from certain diseases (diabetes or coronary artery diseases, for example) should get a letter from their doctor giving treatment details. Some continental doctors will understand a letter written in English, but it is better to have it translated into the language of the country that it is intended to visit.

Travellers, who for legitimate health reasons carry drugs or appliances (hypodermic syringe, etc.) may have difficulty with Customs or other authorities. Others may have a diet problem which would be understood in hotels but for a language problem. The letter which such persons carry should, therefore, supply treatment details, a statement for Customs, and diet requirements.

It should be remembered that some medicines may affect your speed of reaction and thus your driving ability. Pay heed to any warnings on the packet.

Getting about in the Federal Republic

Motoring

Visitors may drive their car in the Federal Republic for up to one year if they have a national or international driving permit and car registration certificate. A national driving licence is valid in the case of nationals of EEC countries and of Austria, Finland, Greece, Hong Kong, New Zealand, Norway, Portugal, Senegal, Sweden, Switzerland and USA; nationals of other countries must have either a German translation of their national licence or an international driving permit. The car registration papers of EEC countries are accepted; visitors from other countries are advised to have an international certificate for motor vehicles. All foreign cars must display the appropriate international distinguishing sign.

Third party insurance is compulsory in the Federal Republic. Foreign visitors, other than nationals of the EEC countries, Austria, Czechoslovakia, Finland, Hungary, Norway, Sweden and Switzerland, must either have a green card (international insurance certificate) or take out third party insurance at the frontier. You should consult your insurers prior to any overseas visit to confirm your cover is adequate.

Traffic goes on the right, with overtaking on the left. Main road traffic has priority; at junctions of two main roads or two minor roads traffic from the right has priority, unless otherwise indicated; traffic on motorways has priority over traffic entering or leaving the motorway.

Drivers and front seat passengers must wear their safety belts. Children under 12 must not sit in the front.

Dipped headlights must be used after dark and when visibility is poor: driving on sidelights is not allowed.

Traffic signs are in accordance with international standards.

Speed limits for private cars and other vehicles under 2·8 tons in weight are 50 km per hour (31 mph) in built-up areas and 100 km per hour (62 mph) on the open road, except on motorways and dual highways (which have a "recommended" speed limit of 130 km per hour (81 mph)). Vehicles towing a caravan or trailer are limited to 80 km per hour (49 mph) on all roads outside built-up areas. Some roads may be subject to special limits, as indicated by traffic signs.

The Federal Republic has an extensive network of **motorways** (*Autobahnen*), identified by the letter A and a number. A 1 to A 9 are the main long-distance through routes, usually coinciding with European highways (lettered E); motorways with a two-digit number are important trunk routes and connecting routes; those with a three-digit number are mainly of regional importance. Motorways with even numbers mostly run from east to west, those with odd numbers from north to south.

The motorway network has been extensively developed in recent years, and normally enables traffic to keep moving over long distances at high speed. In the main holiday season, however, there may be occasional hold-ups. In particular there may be considerable delays at frontier crossings, and if you have to cross a frontier it may be well worth while leaving the motorway at some suitable point and making for a smaller frontier crossing.

The ordinary roads (*Bundesstrassen*, identified by the letter B and a number) are also excellent.

Radio traffic reports

Information about traffic conditions is broadcast by local radio stations (VHF). The timings of these broadcasts, the frequencies used and the areas covered are posted up on motorways and major trunk roads. The traffic areas are shown on the map on p. 269.

Where there are serious hold-ups on the motorways **diversions** may be indicated, signposted by blue signs with the letter U and a number.

In case of accident or emergency on the motorway help can be summoned by using the orange-coloured **emergency telephones** (illuminated at night) which are set at intervals of 2 km. This will bring breakdown assistance, a towing vehicle, the police, fire brigade or ambulance as required. Black triangles on the posts along the side of the motorway indicate the direction of the nearest telephone. In the event of an accident do not forget to put out your warning triangle. If there is a major traffic hold-up a lane must be left in the middle for emergency vehicles.

In reporting an accident you should give details of the place and nature of the accident and of any injury to persons.

Access Routes to West Berlin

There are four recognised routes from the Federal Republic to West Berlin through the territory of the German Democratic Republic:

1. *From Hamburg*
   Frontier crossing at Gudow/Zarrentin – motorway to Nauen exit – then trunk road No. 5 – checkpoint Staaken/Heerstrasse Berlin (West).

2. *From Hanover*
   Frontier crossing at Helmstedt/Marienborn – motorway – checkpoint Drewitz/Dreilinden Berlin (West).

3. *From Frankfurt am Main*
   Frontier crossing at Herleshausen/Wartha – motorway – checkpoint Drewitz/Dreilinden Berlin (West).

4. *From Munich*
   Frontier crossing at Rudolphstein/Hirschberg – motorway – checkpoint Drewitz/Dreilinden Berlin (West).

On passport and visa requirements, see p. 265.

Traffic regulations are in general similar to those of the Federal Republic. Speed limits are 50 km per hour in built-up areas, 90 km per hour on the open road, 100 km per hour on motorways. There is an absolute ban on driving after taking any alcohol.

It is forbidden to leave the direct route, to pick up hitch-hikers and to distribute or leave behind while travelling any newspapers, magazines or other printed matter.

Traffic offences attract substantial on-the-spot fines, payable in Federal German currency.

In the event of a breakdown help can be obtained by telephoning a central unit in each area. The telephone number can be obtained from petrol stations, motorway telephones, service areas and telephone directory enquiries.

Air Services

The principal cities in the Federal Republic are served by **Deutsche Lufthansa**, which provides domestic services to and from the following airports: Bremen, Düsseldorf-Lohausen, Frankfurt am Main (Rhein-Main Airport), Hamburg-Fuhlsbüttel, Hanover-Langenhagen, Cologne/Bonn, Munich-Riem, Nuremberg-Langwasser, Saarbrücken-Ensheim, Stuttgart-Echterdingen.

The *Deutsche Luftverkehrsgesellschaft (DLT)* provides connecting services, with smaller aircraft, to and from Bayreuth, Hof, Münster/Osnabrück and Paderborn/Lippstadt, linking these smaller airports with Bremen, Düsseldorf-Lohausen, Frankfurt am Main, Hanover-Langenhagen, Saarbrücken-Ensheim and Stuttgart-Echterdingen. This company's aircraft sometimes also fly short-distance services between the major airports.

The *Ostfriesische Flug-Dienst (OFD)* is mainly concerned with passenger traffic to the coastal resorts, with services to the airports of Borkum, Juist, Norderney, Baltrum, Langeoog, Wangerooge, Heligoland and Norddeich. It also serves Düsseldorf-Lohausen, Emden, Bremen and Bremerhaven (in summer also from Heligoland to East Friesian Islands).

BERLIN. – Services between the Federal Republic and West Berlin (Tegel Airport) are provided, in accordance with the city's four-power status, by Air France, British Airways and Pan American Airways. There are services to Berlin-Tegel from Bremen, Düsseldorf-Lohausen, Frankfurt am Main (Rhein-Main Airport), Hamburg-Fuhlsbüttel, Hanover-Langenhagen, Cologne/Bonn, Munich-Reim, Nuremberg-Langwasser, Saarbrücken-Ensheim and Stuttgart-Echterdingen.

Information: *Deutsche Lufthansa* (Head Office), Von-Gablenz-Str. 2–6, D-5000 Köln 21;
tel. (02 21) 82 61.
(Offices in all large towns.)

Deutsche Luftverkehrsgesellschaft (DLT),
Flughafen, D-6000 Frankfurt am Main 75;
tel. (06 11) 6 90 53 45.

Ostfriesischer Flug-Dienst (OFD),
Flugplatz, D-2970 Emden;
tel. (0 49 21) 4 20 57 and 4 16 29.

Motorways

Traffic Broadcast Areas

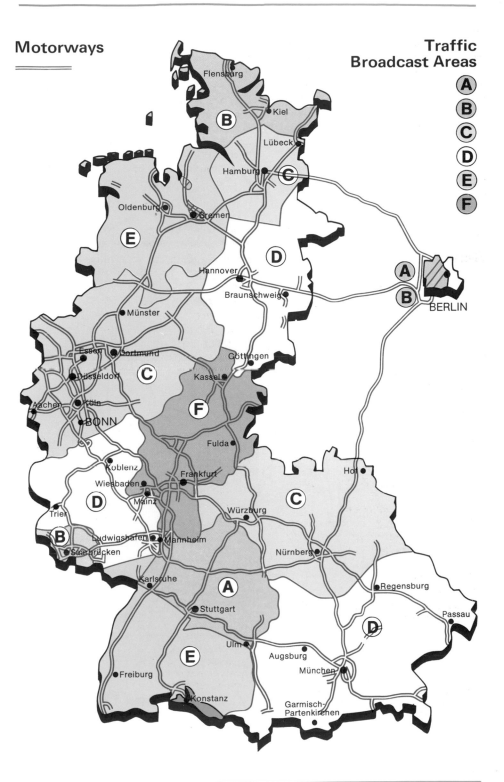

Motorway Traffic Broadcasts

The motorway network of the Federal Republic is one of the densest in the world, but the volume of traffic it carries may sometimes – particularly during the main holiday season – lead to delays. To enable motorists to take alternative routes and reduce pressure on the motorways, local radio stations broadcast regular reports on traffic conditions. For this purpose the territory of the Federal Republic is divided up into areas, as shown on this map.

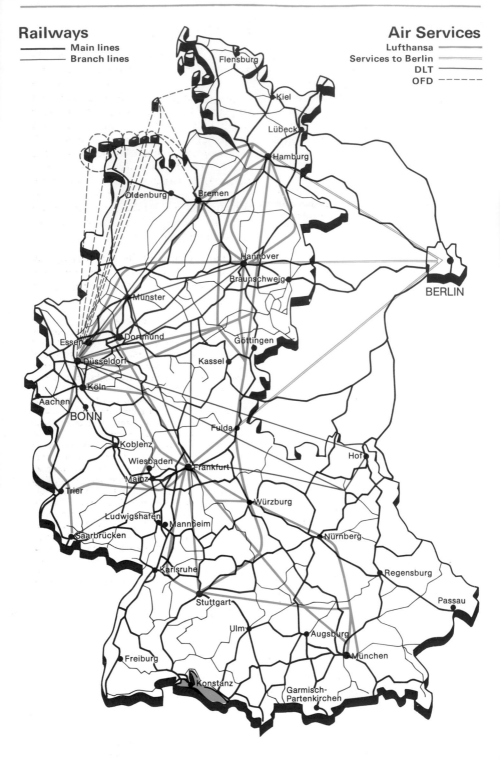

Railways

—— Main lines
—— Branch lines

Air Services

Lufthansa ——
Services to Berlin ══
DLT ——
OFD ------

Railways · Air Services

Before the advent of the motor car the most important means of transport were the railways, and in recent years they have been trying to draw back some of the traffic they have lost by developing the most modern types of train. Their great asset is their ability to provide rapid and comfortable services between the larger centres of population. – Domestic air services are provided by Lufthansa and two smaller companies, DLT and OFD, mainly providing local services.

Rail Services

Although the **Deutsche Bundesbahn** (German Federal Railways) system has been pruned in recent years on economic grounds, it still provides convenient access to the great majority of the places described in this Guide. Rail travel is made particularly attractive by a great variety of REDUCED FARES and special offers:

> Privilege, mini-group, junior, family, senior citizen and monthly "tramper" tickets; national and regional "rail rover" tickets, circular tour tickets; combined rail-boat tickets on the Rhine and Moselle; package tours, etc., etc.

There are **Motorail** services within the Federal Republic and to various stations in other countries.

At many stations the Federal Railways operate a **bicycle hire** service.

Information can be obtained from offices of the Federal Railways and the DER Travel Service. In the United Kingdom:

German Federal Railways,
Wellington Road,
Folkestone, Kent.

DER Travel Service, Ltd,
15 Orchard Street,
London W1;
tel. 01–486 4593.

Boat Services

In recent years there has been a considerable increase of interest in tourist travel by boat. On many inland waters there are motor-launch and motor-boat services opening up areas of beautiful lake and river scenery and offering a new experience to tourists accustomed to going everywhere in their own car. On the North Sea and Baltic coasts there are not only the excursion vessels but the passenger and car ferries which provide connections with the offshore islands.

There are passenger services on the following coastal and inland waters:
North Sea coast. – Baltic coast. – Schlei. – Plön lakes. – Ratzeburger See. – River Elbe. – River Aller. – Mittelland Canal. – River Weser. – River Hamme. – River Fulda. – Zwischenahner Meer. – Maschsee. – Steinhuder Meer. – Oker reservoir. – Möhne reservoir. – Sorpe reservoir. – Bigge reservoir. – Baldeneysee. – Schwammenauel reservoir on River Rur. – River Rhine. – River Moselle. – River Main. – River Neckar. – River Danube. – Starnberger See. – Ammersee. – Tegernsee. – Staffelsee. – Chiemsee. – Königssee. – Lake Constance. – West Berlin lakes.

Language

German, like English, is a Germanic language, and the pronunciation of German usually comes more easily to English-speakers than does a Romance language like French. Much of the basic vocabulary, too, will be familiar to those whose native language is English, though they may have more difficulty with more complex terms incorporating native Germanic roots rather than the Latin roots used in English. The grammar is not difficult, but has retained a much more elaborate system of conjugations and declensions than English.

Standard German (*Hochdeutsch*) is spoken throughout the country, although many people speak a strong local dialect as well.

Pronunciation. – The *consonants* are for the most part pronounced broadly as in English, but the following points should be noted: *b*, *d* and *g* at the end of a syllable are pronounced like *p*, *t* and *k*; *c* (rare) and *z* are pronounced *ts*; *j* is pronounced like consonantal *y*; *qu* is somewhere between the English *qu* and *kv*; *s* at the beginning of a syllable is pronounced *z*; *v* is pronounced *f*; and *w* is pronounced *v*. The double letter *ch* is pronounced like the Scottish *ch* in "loch" after *a*, *o* and *u*; after *ä*, *e*, *i* and *ü* it is pronounced somewhere between that sound and *sh*. *Sch* is pronounced *sh*, and *th* (rare) *t*. – The *vowels* are pronounced without the diphthongisation normal in standard English; before a single consonant they are normally long, before a double consonant short. Note the following: short *a* is like the flat *a* of northern English; *e* may be either closed (roughly as in "pay"), open (roughly as in "pen") or a short unaccented sound like the *e* in "begin" or in "father"; *ä* is like an open *e*; *u* is like *oo* in "good" (short) or "food" (long); *ö* is like the French *eu*, a little like the vowel in "fur"; *ü*, like the French *u*, can be approximated by pronouncing *ee* with rounded lips. Diphthongs: *ai* and *ei* similar to *i* in "high"; *au* as in "how"; *eu* and *äu* like *oy*; *ie* like *ee*.

Vocabulary

Good morning	Guten Morgen
Good day	Guten Tag
Good evening	Guten Abend
Good night	Gute Nacht
Goodbye	Auf Wiedersehen
Do you speak English?	Sprechen Sie Englisch?
I do not understand	Ich verstehe nicht
Yes	Ja
No	Nein
Please	Bitte
Thank you (very much)	Danke (sehr)
Yesterday	Gestern
Today	Heute
Tomorrow	Morgen
Help!	Hilfe!
Have you a single room?	Haben Sie ein Einzelzimmer?
Have you a double room?	Haben Sie ein Doppelzimmer?
Have you a room with private bath?	Haben Sie ein Zimmer mit Bad?

Numbers

0	Null	21	einundzwanzig	
1	eins	22	zweiundzwanzig	
2	zwei	30	dreissig	
3	drei	40	vierzig	
4	vier	50	fünfzig	
5	fünf	60	sechzig	
6	sechs	70	siebzig	
7	sieben	80	achtzig	
8	acht	90	neunzig	
9	neun	100	hundert	
10	zehn	101	hundert und eins	
11	elf	153	hundert dreiundfünf-	
12	zwölf		zig	
13	dreizehn	200	zweihundert	
14	vierzehn	300	dreihundert	
15	fünfzehn	1000	tausend	
16	sechzehn	1001	tausend und eins	
17	siebzehn	1021	tausend einundzwan-	
18	achtzehn		zig	
19	neunzehn	2000	zweitausend	
20	zwanzig	1,000,000	eine Million	

Ordinals

1st	erste	6th	sechste
2nd	zweite	7th	siebte
3rd	dritte	8th	achte
4th	vierte	9th	neunte
5th	fünfte	10th	zehnte
		11th	elfte
		20th	zwanzigste
		100th	hundertste

Fractions

$\frac{1}{2}$	Hälfte
$\frac{1}{3}$	Drittel
$\frac{1}{4}$	Viertel
$\frac{3}{4}$	drei Viertel

vocabulary *continued*

What does it cost?	Wieviel kostet das?
Please wake me at six	Wollen Sie mich bitte um sechs Uhr wecken?
Where is the lavatory?	Wo ist die Toilette?
Where is the bathroom?	Wo ist das Badezimmer?
Where is the chemist's?	Wo ist die Apotheke?
Where is the post office?	Wo ist das Postamt?
Where is there a doctor?	Wo gibt es einen Arzt?
Where is there a dentist?	Wo gibt es einen Zahnarzt?
Is this the way to the station?	Ist dies der Weg zum Bahnhof?

Days of the week

Sunday	Sonntag
Monday	Montag
Tuesday	Dienstag
Wednesday	Mittwoch
Thursday	Donnerstag
Friday	Freitag
Saturday	Samstag, Sonnabend
Day	Tag
Public holiday	Feiertag

Festivals

New Year	Neujahr
Easter	Ostern
Ascension	Christi Himmelfahrt
Whitsun	Pfingsten
Corpus Christi	Fronleichnam
Assumption	Mariä Himmelfahrt
All Saints	Allerheiligen
Christmas	Weihnachten
New Year's Eve	Silvester

Road and traffic signs

Abstand halten!	Keep your distance
Achtung!	Caution
Baustelle	Road works
Durchfahrt verboten	No thoroughfare
Einbahnstrasse	One-way street
Einordnen!	Get into line
Gefahr	Danger
Halt!	Halt
Kurve	Bend
Langsam	Slow
Rollsplit	Loose stones
Stadtmitte	Town centre
Stop	Stop
Strasse gesperrt	Road closed
Vorsicht!	Caution
Zoll	Customs

Rail and air travel

Airport	Flughafen
All aboard!	Einsteigen!
Arrival	Ankunft
Baggage	Gepäck
Baggage check	Gepäckschein
Bus station	Autobushof
Departure	Abfahrt, Abflug (aircraft)
Flight	Flug
Halt	Haltestelle
Information	Auskunft
Lavatory	Toilette(n)
Line	Gleis
Luggage	Gepäck
Non-smoking	Nichtraucher
Platform	Bahnsteig

Porter	Gepäckträger	Bauernhaus	farmhouse
Restaurant car	Speisewagen	Bauernhof	farm, farmstead
Sleeping car	Schlafwagen;	Becken	basin, pool
	Liegewagen	Berg	hill, mountain
	(couchettes)	Bergbahn	mountain railway
Smoking	Raucher	Bergbau	mining
Station	Bahnhof	Bezirk	region (an administrative
Stewardess	Stewardess		subdivision of a *Land*)
Stop	Aufenthalt	Bhf. = Bahnhof	railway station
Ticket	Fahrkarte	Bibliothek	library
Ticket collector	Schaffner	Börse	(stock) exchange
Ticket window	Schalter	Brücke	bridge
Timetable	Fahrplan, Flugplan (air)	Brunnen	fountain
Train	Zug	Bücherei	library
Waiting room	Wartesaal	Bucht	bay, bight
Window seat	Fensterplatz	Bund	federation, league

Bundes-   Federal
Burg   (fortified) castle

Months

Damm   causeway, breakwater, dike

January	Januar	DB =	(German Federal
February	Februar	Deutsche Bundesbahn	Railways)
March	März	Denkmal	monument, memorial
April	April	DER =	(German Travel Agency,
May	Mai	Deutsches Reisebüro	a subsidiary of the
June	Juni		Federal Railways)
July	Juli	Dom	cathedral
August	August	Dorf	village
September	September	Dreieck	triangle
October	Oktober	Einkaufzentrum	shopping centre
November	November	Eisenbahn	railway
December	Dezember	Fähre	ferry

Fels   rock, crag
Fernmeldeturm   telecommunications tower

At the post office

Fernsehturm   television tower
Feste   fortress, citadel
Festhalle   festival hall, banqueting-hall

Address	Adresse	Festung	fortress, citadel
Express	Eilboten	Flügel	wing
Letter	Brief	Flughafen	airport
Letter-box	Briefkasten	Fluss	river
Parcel	Paket	Förde	firth, fjord
Postcard	Postkarte	Forst	forest
Poste restante	Postlagernd	Freilichtmuseum	open-air museum
Postman	Briefträger	Fremdenverkehrsverein	tourist information office
Registered	Einschreiben	Friedhof	cemetery
Small packet	Päckchen	Furt	ford
Stamp	Briefmarke	Garten	garden
Telegram	Telegramm	Gasse	lane, street
Telephone	Telefon	Gau, Gäu	region; area of flat
Telex	Fernschreiben		country (Bavaria)

Gebäude   building
Gebirge   (range of) hills, mountains

Glossary

Gelände   tract of land, grounds
Gemeinde   commune (the smallest administrative unit)

(mainly of topographical terms)

Gericht   court (of law)

This glossary is intended as a guide to the meaning of terms which visitors will encounter frequently on maps, plans and signposts. They may occur independently, or sometimes as part of a compound word.

Gesamthochschule   comprehensive higher educational establishment (combining functions of university, technical colleges, teachers' training college, etc.)

Allee	avenue, walk		
Alt	old		
Amt	office	Gewerbe	trade, industry, craft
Anlage	gardens, park	Grab	tomb, grave
Anstalt	institution	Graben	ditch, moat
Auskunft	information	Gross	large, great
Ausstellung	exhibition	Gut	estate; country house,
Bach	brook, stream		farm
Bahn	railway; lane (in road)	Hafen	harbour, port
Bahnhof	railway station	Halbinsel	peninsula
Bau	building	Halde	hillside

Halle	hall
Hallenbad	indoor swimming bath
Hauptpost	head post office
Hauptstrasse	main street
Haus	house
Hbf=Hauptbahnhof	main railway station
Heide	heath
Heim	home
Heimatmuseum	local or regional museum (bygones, folk traditions)
Hochhaus	multi-storey building, tower block
Hochschule	higher educational establishment, university
Hof	courtyard; farm; (royal) court
Höhe	hill, eminence
Höhle	cave
Holz	wood
Hospital	hospital, hospice
Hügel	hill
Insel	island
Jagdschloss	hunting lodge
Jugendherberge	youth hostel
Kai	quay
Kaiser-	imperial
Kammer	chamber, room
Kapelle	chapel
Keller	cellar
Kirche	church
Klamm	gorge
Klein	small
Klippe	cliff
Kloster	monastery, convent, monastic house
Kran	crane
Krankenhaus	hospital
Kreis	district (an administrative subdivision of a Bezirk)
Krkhs.=Krankenhaus	hospital
Kunst	art
Kur	cure (at a spa or health resort)
Kurhaus	spa establishment
Kurort	spa, health resort
Kurverwaltung	management authorities of spa
Land	land; specifically, one of the Länder or provinces of the Federal Republic
Landes-	provincial; relating or belonging to a Land
Landkreis	rural distict
Laube	arcade, loggia
Maar	small volcanic lake (in Eifel)
Markt	market (square)
Marstall	court stables
Mauer	(masonry) wall
Meer	sea
Messe	trade fair
Moor	marsh (land)
Moos	moss, bog
Mühle	mill
Münster	minster, monastic church; cathedral (in S Germany)
Neu	new
Nieder-	lower
Noor	coastal inlet, lagoon (in N Germany)
Nord	north
Ober-	upper
OPD=Oberpostdirektion	GPO
Oper	opera (house)
Ost	east
Palais, Palast	palace
Pfad	path, trail
Pfalz	(royal) palace, stronghold
Pfarrkirche	parish church
Pforte	doorway
Platz	square
Post	post office
Propstei	provostry, reśidence or jurisdiction of a provost (eccl.)
Quelle	spring, source
Rasthaus, Raststätte	"rest-house" (in motorway service area)
Rathaus	town hall
Ratskeller	cellar (restaurant) of town hall
Reisebüro	travel agency
Rennbahn	race-track
Residenz	residence, seat of a ruling prince; princely capital
Ruine	ruin
Rundfunk	radio
S-Bahn-Stodtbahn	urban railway, tramway
Saal	hall, room
Säule	column
Schatzkammer	treasury
Schauspielhaus	theatre
Schiffshebewerk	ship-lift
Schlachthof	slaughterhouse
Schleuse	lock, sluice
Schloss	castle, palace, country house (usually designed for show rather than defence)
Schlucht	gorge
Schnellweg	fast motor road
Schule	school
Schwarz	black
See	lake; sea
Seilbahn	cableway (either aerial or on rails)
Sperre	dam, barrage
Spielbank	casino
Spital	hospital
Staats-, staatlich	state, national
Stadel	barn, shed, stall
Stadt	town, city
städtisch	municipal
Standseilbahn	mountain railway
Stätte	place, spot
Stausee	lake formed by dam, reservoir
Steig	path
Steige	staircase, steep ascent
Stein	stone
Sternwarte	observatory
Stiege	staircase
Stift	religious house; chapter, college; foundation
Strassenbahn	tramway
Stiftskirche	collegiate church; monastic church
Strand	beach
Strasse	street, road
Süd	south
Sund	sound, straits
Tal	valley
Teich	pond, small lake
Theater	theatre
Tiergarten, Tierpark	zoo, animal park
Tonhalle	concert-hall

Tor	gate(way)	Wallfahrtskirche	pilgrimage church
Turm	tower	Wand	wall
U-Bahn =		Wasser	water
Untergrundbahn	underground railway	Wasserburg, -schloss	moated castle
Ufer	shore, coast	Weg	way, road
Unter-	lower	Weiler	hamlet
Verkehr	traffic, transport	Weinstube	wine-bar, -house
Verkehsamt, -büro,		Weiss	white
-verein	tourist information office	Werder	small island in river
Veste	fortress, citadel	Werft	shipyard, wharf
Viertel	quarter, district	West	west
Vogelpark	bird park	Wildpark	game park, wildlife park
Vorstadt	suburb, outer district	Zeughaus	arsenal
Waage	weigh-house	Zitadelle	citadel
Wald	wood, forest	ZOB =	
Wall	rampart	Zentralomnibusbahnhof	central bus station

Water Sports

The provisions regulating water sports, particularly sailing and boating, vary from place to place, and it is therefore not possible to give detailed information here. Enquiry should be made locally about the regulations in force.

On many lakes there are restrictions on the size, draught and horsepower of sailing and motor boats. Frequently motor-propelled boats are banned altogether. British visitors taking a boat to the Federal Republic must hold a Helmsman's Certificate of Competence, obtainable from the Royal Yachting Association, Victoria Way, Woking, Surrey GU21 1EQ. – In shipping lanes and coastal waters the skippers of sailing-boats with auxiliary motors or motor-boats of over 3·68 kW (5 h.p.) must have an official licence (*Sportbootführerschein*). Special conditions apply on Lake Constance, where it is necessary to have a special licence (*Bodensee-Patent*) for sailing-boats with a sail area of over 12 sq. m and motor-boats of over 4·41 kW (6 h.p.). – There are also special regulations controlling water-skiing.

Information: *Deutscher Motoryacht Verband, Gründgensstr. 18, D-2000 Hamburg 60*

Deutscher Segler Verband, Gründgensstr. 18, D-2000 Hamburg 60.

Deutscher Wasserski Verband, Luxemburger Str. 91, D-5500 Trier.

Tourist Highways

The territory of the Federal Republic is covered by a network of named and specially signposted tourist highways which allow visitors to explore particular areas or pursue particular interests. They are listed below in alphabetical order.

Alte Salzstrasse (Old Salt Road)
Lübeck – Ratzeburg – Mölln – Schwarzenbek – Lauenburg – Lüneburg.
For centuries this was the route along which salt – "white gold" – was transported from the Lüneburg salt-workings to Lübeck.

Artlandroute (Artland Route)
Dinklage – Bersenbrück – Ankum – Berge – Börstel – Quackenbrück – Dinklage.
A circuit through the Artland (="arable land") district of Lower Saxony, a region of large fields, lonely farmhouses and huge areas of pastureland.

Badische Weinstrasse (Baden Wine Highway)
Baden-Baden – Kappelrodeck – Oberkirch – Offenburg – Ettenheim – Oberbergen – Ihringen – Freiburg – Lörrach – Basle.
On both sides of the road – in the Ortenau, on the Kaiserstuhl and in the Markgräfler Land – are a whole series of little wine towns and villages bearing names familiar to wine-lovers and connoisseurs.

Bäderstrasse (Spa Highway)
Niederlahnstein – Bad Ems – Nassau – Bad Schwalbach – Schlangenbad – Wiesbaden.
The healing powers of the mineral springs along this road have been known since Roman times.

Bayerische Ostmarkstrasse (Bavarian Eastern Marches Highway)
Marktredwitz – Weiden – Cham – Viechtach – Regen – Passau.
An excellent road which runs through Germany's greatest area of forest (Fichtelgebirge, Upper Palatinate Forest, Bavarian Forest), with many attractive holiday places, lakes for bathing and fishing, castles and palaces.

Bergstrasse (Hill Road)
Darmstadt – Bensheim – Weinheim – Heidelberg – Wiesloch – Bruchsal.
On this old Roman "via strata montana" spring comes early: the blossom is out when elsewhere cold east winds are still blowing.

Bier- und Burgenstrasse (Beer and Castles Highway)
Kulmbach – Weissenbrunn – Kronach – Mitwitz – Neundorf – Förtschendorf – Ludwigsstadt – Lauenstein.
Beer has been brewed in the Franconian Forest for some thousands of years, and has been subject to standards of purity since 1349. Proud castles and trim little towns bear witness to a historic past.

Bramgauroute (Bramgau Route)
Neuenkirchen – Engter – Hagenbeck – Dalum – Westerholte – Neuenkirchen.
A trip through the attractive upland country round Bersenbrück – fertile farm land, forests, ancient little towns where you will be served anchovies with your schnaps.

Burgenstrasse (Castle Highway)
Mannheim – Heidelberg – Mosbach – Bad Wimpfen – Heilbronn – Öhringen – Rothenburg o.d. T – Ansbach – Nuremberg.
Romantic medieval country – 28 castles, from the Age of Chivalry, quiet villages, little towns with old half-timbered houses.

Deutsche Alpenstrasse (German Alpine Highway)
Lindau – Sonthofen – Garmisch-Partenkirchen – Rottach-Egern – Reit im Winkl – Berchtesgaden.
A road running right through the Alps at a height of between 800 and 1000 m, on German territory all the way.

Deutsche Edelsteinstrasse (German Precious Stone Highway)
Idar-Oberstein – Kirschweiler – Allenbach – Herrstein – Fischbach or Herborn – Vollmersbach – Idar-Oberstein.
This route through the attractive hills and valleys of the Hunsrück takes in 17 places engaged in the precious-stone industry and 60 establishments in which the processes of cutting and polishing can be watched.

Deutsche Ferienstrasse Alpen-Ostsee (German Alps-Baltic Holiday Highway)
Puttgarden – Oldenburg in Holstein – Plön – Lübeck – Mölln – Lauenburg – Celle – Gifhorn – Helmstedt – Goslar – Braunlage – Göttingen – Eschwege – Büdingen – Gelnhausen – Michelstadt – Schwäbisch Hall – Ellwangen – Dinkelsbühl – Kelheim – Landshut – Wasserburg – Traunstein – Berchtesgaden.
More than 100 towns and rural districts combined to create this route, 1720 km long.

Deutsch-Französische Touristik-Route (Franco-German Tourist Route)
Schweigen – Siebeldingen – Neustadt an der Weinstrasse – Dahn – Fischbach – Bitche – Saverne – Obersteinbach – Schweigen.
A round trip through German and French wine villages and forests, holiday resorts and spas.

Deutsche Hopfenstrasse (German Hop Highway)
Zolling – Au – Abensberg.
B 301, through the hop-growing uplands of the Hallertau area. The main hop-growing centre is Au.

Deutsche Märchenstrasse (Germany Fairytale Highway)
Hanau – Steinau – Marburg – Kassel – Göttingen – Hamelin – Minden – Bremen.
Through towns and country districts noted for their legends and fairytales.

Deutsche Schuhstrasse (German Shoe Highway)
Waldfischbach – Burgalben – Leimen – Pirmasens – Lemberg – Bruchweiler – Dahn.
Passes 200 shoe factories. The centre of the industry is Pirmasens.

Deutsche Weinstrasse (German Wine Highway)
Schweigen – Bergzabern – Edenkoben – Neustadt – Deidesheim – Bad Dürkheim – Bockenheim.
In this sheltered and sunny strip of vineyards on the left bank of the Rhine there are 150 million vines covering an area of 20,000 hectares.

Deutsche Wildstrasse (German Game Highway)
Daun – Manderscheid – Bitburg – Prüm – Gerolstein – Daun.
An area of 120,400 hectares containing 24,000 head of small game, 8500 roedeer and 2900 red deer, wild pigs and moufflons.

Eichenlaubstrasse (Oakleaf Highway)
Oberlenken – Orscholz – Mettlach – Nonnweiler – Oberkirchen.
The River Saar is at its most beautiful in the great bend at Mettlach. The road continues through extensive deciduous and coniferous forests.

Elbufer-Strasse (Elbe Highway)
Schnackenburg – Gorleben – Hitzacker – Bleckede – Niedermarschacht.
Along the Elbe from the GDR frontier to the outskirts of Hamburg.

Elmhochstrasse (Elm Highway)
Helmstedt – Schöningen – Schöppenstedt – Wolfenbüttel.
The Elm is Germany's largest uninterrupted area of beech forest, with numerous footpaths and trails.

Feldbergstrasse (Feldberg Highway)
Freiburg – Kirchzarten – Titisee – Neustadt – Feldberg.
One of the most beautiful and most popular routes in the Black Forest, with magnificent views.

Ferienstrasse Südeifel (Southern Eifel Holiday Highway)
Baustert – Waxweiler – Schönecken – Nattenheim – Rittersdorf – Bettingen – Baustert.
Extensive forests, beautiful valleys, good footpaths and attractively situated holiday places.

Fichtelgebirgsstrasse (Fichtelgebirge Highway)
Bad Berneck – Bischofsgrün – Wunsiedel – Marktredwitz.
From the valley of the Franconian Saale through the foothills of the Hassberge.

Frankenwaldhochstrasse (Franconian Forest Ridgeway)
Steinwiesen – Nordhalben – Teuschnitz – Reichenbach – Rothenkirchen.
Runs at altitudes between 600 and 700 m, with views extending from the hills of the Franconian Forest to the Fichtelgebirge and the Thuringian Forest.

Frankenwaldstrasse (Franconian Forest Highway)
Mitwitz – Kronach – Zeyern – Wallenfels – Schwarzenbach – Naila – Hof.
The deeply indented valleys give the Franconian Forest its particular charm.

Freundschaftsstrasse (Friendship Highway, Route de l'Amitié)
Stuttgart – Freudenstadt – Kehl – Strasbourg – Obernai – Metz.
A Franco-German route running through the beauties of Lorraine with its lakes and hills, the Vosges with their great expanses of mixed forests, the Rhine plain, Strasbourg and the romantic Black Forest.

Glasstrasse (Glass Highway)
Fichtelberg – Fleckl – Warmensteinach – Weidenberg – Bayreuth.
This route through the Fichtelgebirge runs through glass-making towns. The chief centre of the industry is Weidenberg.

Grüne Küstenstrasse (Green Coastal Highway)
From Scandinavia via Niebüll – Heide – Itzehoe – Hamburg – Bremen – Oldenburg to Holland.
Along the North Sea coast through heathland, forests and beautiful countryside.

Grüne Strasse (Green Highway, Route Verte)
Domrémy – Epinal – Colmar – Freiburg – Donaueschingen; then either Stockach – Friedrichshafen – Lindau or Radolfzell – Konstanz.
From Lorraine through romantic Vosges valleys to the Upper Rhine, then through the Black Forest to the Baden-Swabian plateau and on to Lake Constance.

Grüne Strasse Eifel-Ardennen (Eifel-Ardennes Green Highway)
Bad Neuenahr – Kelberg – Daun – Manderscheid – Kyllburg – Bitburg – Roth – Dasburg – Clervaux (France) – Bouillon (Belgium) – Rethel (France).
One-third of the way along the road enters a region famed for its red wines, where the slates and volcanic rocks store up the sun's warmth for 500 hectares of vines.

Hamaland-Route (Hamaland Route)
Ahaus – Borken – Winterswijk (Holland) – Haaksbergen – Ahaus.
For a third of the way the road runs through the Achterhoek in Holland; the rest goes through the western Münsterland, known in the Middle Ages as Hamaland.

Harz-Heide-Strasse (Harz-Heathland Highway)
Lüneburg – Uelzen – Brunswick – Bad Harburg – Braunlage – Göttingen.
A fast route on B 4 from the romantic heathland to the forests and rivers of the Harz.

Harz-Hochstrasse (Harz Ridgeway)
Seesen – Clausthal-Zellerfeld – Braunlage.
Although the name Harz means wooded hills the route offers a variety of other scenery as well – the rolling plateau round Clausthal-Zellerfeld with its 70 little lakes, deeply indented valleys, high moorland and waterfalls.

Hochrhönring (High Rhön Circuit)
Kleinsassen – Dietges – Obernhausen – Gersfeld – Poppenhausen – Kleinsassen.
A circuit round the Wasserkuppe (950 m).

Hochrhönstrasse (High Rhön Highway)
Bischofsheim – Leubach – Fladungen.
Long ridges of hills, with few trees and great expanses of grass and high moorland, alternating with isolated hills, valleys covered with meadowland and forests.

Hochtaunusstrasse (High Taunus Highway)
Bad Homburg – Oberursel – Sandplacken – Schmitten – Weilnau – Camberg.
Extensive forests, quiet valleys, health resorts and idyllically situated villages.

Hunsrück-Höhenstrasse (Hunsrück Ridgeway)
Koblenz – Kastellaun – Kappel – Morbach – Hermeskeil – Kell – Zerf – Saarburg.
Wide plateaus, forest regions well stocked with game, snug villages.

Hünsrück-Schieferstrasse (Hunsrück Slate Highway)
Kirn – Bundenbach – Rhaunen – Simmern.
For fossil-hunters and amateur geologists, with good exposures of rock, mines and quarries.

Idyllische Strasse (Idyllic Highway)
Welzheim – Ebni – Muurhardt – Spiegelberg – Mainhardt – Gaildorf – Sulzbach – Eschach – Gschwend – Welzheim.
A circuit through the Swabian Forest.

Kannenbäckerstrasse (Kannenbäcker Highway)
Neuhäusel – Hillscheid – Höhr-Grenzhausen – Hilgert – Ransbach-Baumbach – Mogersdorf – Siershahn – Wirges – Moschheim – Boden.
In the south-western Westerwald, through the Kannenbäckerland which takes its name from the pottery trade which has long flourished here.

Kehlsteinstrasse (Kehlstein Highway)
Obersalzberg – Kehlstein.
The road starts at a height of 1000 m on the Obersalzberg, climbs another 700 m in hairpin bends and cuts across the NW side of the Kehlstein.

Kesselbergstrasse (Kesselberg Highway)
Kochel am See – Kesselberg – Urfeld/Walchensee.
A hill road from one lake to another, with 32 bends and an 858 m pass.

Liebfrauenstrasse (Our Lady's Highway)
Worms – Oppenheim – Nierstein – Mainz.
The celebrated Liebfraumilch wine (Our Lady's Milk) is produced in huge vineyards round the Gothic pilgrimage church of Our Lady (Liebfrauenkirche) near Worms.

Loreley-Burgenstrasse (Loreley and Castles Highway)
Kamp – Dahlheim – Weyer – Auel – St. Goarshausen – Weisel – Kaub.
A road on the right bank of the Rhine – opposite the Rheingoldstrasse – which pursues an uphill-downhill course past vineyards, through little medieval towns and under castles and ruins.

Moselweinstrasse (Moselle Wine Highway)
Perl – Konz – Trier – Schweich – Bernkastel – Zell – Karden, then along both banks of the Moselle to Koblenz.
On both banks of the Moselle are old wine towns and villages of beautiful half-timbered houses with grey-blue slate roofs, and behind them the steepest vineyards in the world.

Nahe-Weinstrasse (Nahe Wine Highway)
Bad Kreuznach – Sobernheim – Martinstein – Wallhausen – Guldental – Schweppenhausen – Langenlonsheim – Bad Kreuznach.
A circuit taking the tourist from wine villages to wine-producers' cellars, from vineyards to wine-testing rooms.

Nibelungenstrasse (Nibelung Highway)
Worms – Lorsch – Michelstadt – Amorbach.
The Odenwald, an inhospitable forest region in the time of the Nibelungs, is now attractive tourist country.

Nordstrasse (Northern Highway)
Flensburg – Langballig – Gelting – Gundelsby – Kappeln.
B 199, the quickest route between Flensburg and Kappeln.

Oberschwäbische Barockstrasse (Upper Swabian Baroque Highway)
Ulm – Ehingen – Zwiefalten – Bad Waldsee – Ravensburg – Friedrichshafen – Isny – Bad Wurzach – Ulm.
A circuit round the churches and monasteries of the great Baroque architects.

Obstmarschenweg (Fruit Fenlands Highway)
Itzwörden – Hörne – Frieburg/Elbe – Hamelwörden – Drochtersen – Stade – Grünendeich – Jork – Neuenfelde.
The road runs along the edge of the fenlands which extend N to the Elbe, through the Kehdingen district (Neuhaus – Stade) and the Altes Land (Stade – Hamburg-Harburg), in an area protected by dikes built by 12th c. Dutch settlers.

Ostsee-Bäderstrasse (Baltic Resorts Highway)
Travemünde – Timmendorfer Strand – Scharbeutz/ Haffkrug – Sierksdorf – Neustadt – Grömitz – Kellenhusen – Dahme – Grossenbrode – Burg auf Fehmarn – Weissenhäuser Strand – Schönwalde – Hohwacht – Schönberg – Laboe – Eckernförde – Glücksburg.
Along the 384 km long Baltic coast between Lübeck and Flensburg there are 17 leading health and bathing resorts.

Panoramastrasse (Panoramic Highway)
Bischofsgrün – Ochsenkopf – Fichtelberg.
A route through forested country, passing the Ochsenkopf (1024 m), the highest peak in the Fichtelgebirge.

Panoramastrasse (Panoramic Highway)
Heppenschwand – Attlisberg – Amrigschwand – Strittberg – Höchenschwand.
Over the plateau of the Southern Black Forest, with views of the Alps.

Panorama- und Saaletalstrasse (Panoramic and Saale Valley Highway)
Rudolphstein – Eisenbühl – Blankenberg – Lichtenberg.
The road runs along the Saale and the Selbitz through the wild and romantic Franconian Forest.

Porzellanstrasse (Porcelain Highway)
Selb – Marktredwitz.
Selb is the centre of the German porcelain industry. the stone markers along the edge of this road (B 15) are made from waste products of the industry.

Rheingauer Riesling-Route (Rheingau Riesling Route)
Lorch – Assmannshausen – Rüdesheim – Geisenheim – Eltville – Rauenthal – Schierstein – Wiesbaden – Hochheim – Wicker.
The road runs through the Rheingau vineyards, on south-facing slopes sheltered by the Taunus hills.

Rheingoldstrasse (Rheingold Highway)
Oberspay – Boppard – St. Goar – Perscheid – Bacharach – Niederheimbach.
Runs over the hills on the left bank of the Rhine, between the river and the A 61 motorway. From here,

according to the legend, the sinister Hagen sank the treasure of the Nibelungs, the Rheingold, in the Rhine.

Romantische Strasse (Romantic Highway)
Würzburg – Tauberbischofsheim – Rothenburg o.d. T. – Nördlingen – Augsburg – Landsberg – Füssen.
Through the romantic country between the Main and the Alps – old free Imperial cities ringed by walls and towers, pretty wine villages, Baroque *putti* figures in palace gardens, richly clad Madonnas in churches and convents.

Rossfeld-Ringstrasse (Rossfeld Circuit)
Berchtesgaden – Rossfeld – Berchtesgaden.
A mountain road up the Rossfeld (1600 m), with beautiful views of the Berchtesgaden hills.

Schauinslandstrasse (Viewpoint Highway)
Freiburg – Todtnau.
This 11 km stretch of road, on which car and motorcycle rallies are held, runs for most of its course through beautiful forest scenery, with 170 bends.

Schwäbische-Alb-Strasse (Swabian Alb Highway)
Nördlingen – Heidenheim – Geislingen – Urach – Burladingen – Tuttlingen – Trossingen.
A tour through Swabia which offers endless scope for recreation and relaxation – rock-climbing, stalactitic caves, ruined castles, great expanses of forest.

Schwäbische Bäderstrasse (Swabian Spa Highway)
Bad Buchau – Bad Schussenried – Aulendorf – Bad Waldsee – Bad Wurzach – Ottobeuren – Bad Wörishofen.
This road, running at some distance from the northern edge of the Alps, links up some of the many health resorts (peat-baths, Kneipp cures) in Upper Swabia and Bavarian Swabia.

Schwäbische Dichterstrasse (Swabian Poets' Highway)
Bad Mergentheim – Jagsthausen – Marbach – Ludwigsburg – Stuttgart – Esslingen – Tübingen – Biberach – Meersburg – Konstanz.
From Franconia to Lake Constance, passing through more than 30 places with houses and museums connected with famous poets and writers like Schiller, Mörike, Hauff, Schwab, Kerner and Hölderlin.

Schwäbische Weinstrasse (Swabian Wine Highway)
Gundelsheim – Bad Friedrichshall – Heilbronn – Besigheim – Waiblingen – Esslingen.
A route along the Neckar, past vine-clad slopes and wine-producers' cellars, castles and palaces, little medieval towns and romantic villages.

Schwarzwald-Bäderstrasse (Black Forest Spa Highway)
Pforzheim – Bad Liebenzell – Calw – Wildberg – Nagold – Freudenstadt – Enzklösterle – Wildbad – Bad Herrenalb – Pforzheim.
A circuit of the famous mineral and thermal resorts of the Northern Black Forest.

Schwarzwald-Hochstrasse (Black Forest Ridgeway)
Baden-Baden – Mummelsee – Ruhestein – Kniebis – Freudenstadt.
Reached in a series of sharp bends, the road runs over moorland and heath, past tumbles of rock and glaciated valleys, and always the great forests of firs.

Schwarzwald-Tälerstrasse (Black Forest Valley Highway)
Karlsruhe – Rastatt – Gaggenau – Gernsbach –

Forbach – Schwarzenberg – Freudenstadt – Alpirsbach – Schenkenzell.
Through the heart of the central Black Forest into the Kinzig, Schiltach and Gutach valleys.

Siegfriedstrasse (Siegfried Highway)
Worms – Lorsch – Fürth – Hüttenthal – Kailbach – Amorbach.
The hunting grounds of the heroes of the "Nibelungenlied" were in the Odenwald, now a favourite holiday region.

Spessart-Höhenstrasse (Spessart Ridgeway)
Steinau – Flörsbach – Wiesen – Hösbach.
The world of the Grimm brothers' fairytales, the hunting grounds of German Emperors, now a popular holiday region.

Spitzingstrasse (Spitzing Highway)
Schliersee – Spitzingsee.
Across the Aurach valley, then a gentle climb, through forest country to the Spitzing saddle (1128 m), then down to the lake (1083 m), with many bends.

Steigerwald-Hohenstrasse (Steigerwald Ridgeway)
Ebelsbach – Ebrach – Geiselwind – Schlüsselfeld – Neustadt/Aisch; then (northern alternative) Hassfurt – Unterschleibach or (southern alternative) Burghaslach – Scheinfeld – Uffenheim.
Through the upland scenery of Franconia.

Störtebeker-Strasse (Störtebeker Highway)
Leer – Emden – Norden – Bensersiel – Wilhelmshaven – Varel – Bremerhaven – Cuxhaven.
Along the North Sea coast, from which the 14th c. pirate Störtebeker set out on his raids.

Strasse der Staufer (Staufen Highway)
Göppingen – Bad Boll – Kloster Lorch – Schwäbisch Gmünd – Rechberg – Donzdorf – Salach – Hohenstaufen – Göppingen.
A circuit taking in almost all the places of importance closely connected with Staufen history and culture.

Totenkopfstrasse (Death's Head Highway)
Neustadt – Maikammer – St. Martin – Elmstein – Johanniskreuz.
The road runs through Maikammer, the second largest wine-growing commune in Germany, and then through the Palatinate Forest to the Johanniskreuz.

Wesertalstrasse (Weser Valley Highway)
Hannoversch Münden – Höxter – Holzminden – Bodenwerder – Hamelin – Minden.
This road down the Weser valley passes many spas and holiday villages, palaces, castles and pretty little towns of half-timbered houses.

Westfälische Mühlenstrasse (Westphalian Mill Road)
Minden – Schlüsselburg – Petershagen – Rahden – Preusisch Oldendorf – Lübbecke – Minden.
On the Weser and on both sides of the Mittelland Canal stand many wind and water mills, which can be visited on this tour. A few old bakehouses are again working.

Emergency Telephone Numbers

Police: dial **110**
Fire brigade: dial **112**
These numbers apply throughout almost the entire territory of the Federal Republic.

There are **emergency telephones**, from which help can be summoned in case of accident or breakdown, on all motorways and many main roads.

Emergency broadcasts. All German radio stations transmitting traffic news will also transmit emergency messages received from abroad through the proper channels. If you hear such a message concerning you, contact the Hessischer Rundfunk in Frankfurt, tel. (06 11) 15 51, for full details.

AA Continental Emergency Centre

G. A. Gregson and Sons,
Tour Damremont (18ème) Bd Chanzy,
F-62201 Boulogne-sur-Mer;
tel. (21) 30 22 22.
24-hour service daily, including Sundays, from 1 July to 30 September; 1 October to 30 June daily, including Sundays but excluding Christmas, 9 a.m. to 6 p.m. and for scheduled ferry sailings.

Breakdown services

The motoring clubs run 24-hour breakdown services in a number of large towns:

Club	Town	Tel.
ACE	Stuttgart	(07 11) 5 06 71
ADAC	Berlin	(0 30) 86 86 86
	Bremen	(04 21) 44 62 62
	Dortmund	(02 31) 17 19 81
	Düsseldorf	(02 11) 1 92 11
	Frankfurt/M	(06 11) 7 43 06
	Hamburg	(0 40) 2 39 99
	Hanover	(05 11) 8 50 02 22
	Munich	(0 89) 76 76 76
	Nuremberg	(09 11) 5 39 02 22
	Stuttgart	(07 11) 2 80 01 11
AvD	Frankfurt/M	(06 11) 6 66 16 66
	(central emergency no.)	
DTC	Munich	(0 89) 8 11 12 12
	(central emergency no.)	

FRANKFURT
New local dialling code
from August 1984:
069

Accommodation

Hotels and Inns

Limitations of space make it impossible to give more than a selection of hotels and other accommodation in this Guide; and the omission of a particular establishment does not of course imply any reflection on its standards. The information given is based on personal experience and enquiry and on various official lists. In the following paragraph some indications about the level of charges are given, but these should be taken only as guidelines, which may be overtaken by general rises in price. The figures given are for single rooms.

The leading hotels in cities and the major resorts are up to normal international standards, with charges per night ranging from perhaps 150 to 220 DM. In establishments offering high standards of comfort and amenity charges are likely to range between 80 and 140 DM all in; in those of the next category, with above-average standards, between 40 and 100 DM; and in those of good normal standard between 30 and 90 DM. In remote areas the charges may well be lower. Breakfast is usually included in the charge for accommodation. Reduced rates are often given for groups.

Useful Addresses

Room reservation service
Allgemeine Deutsche Zimmerreservierung (ADZ),
Beethovenstr. 69,
D-6000 Frankfurt am Main 1;
tel. (06 11) 7 57 21.

Hotels and inns catering for special diets
IKD Gesellschaft für medizinischen tourismus,
Westenrieder Str. 29,
D-8000 München 2;
tel. (0 89) 22 93 22.

Youth hostels
Deutsches Jugendherbergswerk,
Hauptverband für Jugendwandern und Jugendherbergen
Bülowstr. 26,
Postfach 220,
D-4930 Detmold;
tel. (0 52 31) 3 10 91.

Camping
Deutscher Camping-Club (DCC),
Mandlstr. 28,
D-8000 München 40;
tel. (0 89) 33 40 21.

Farmhouse and country holidays
Lists from
*Reisedienst der Deutschen
Landwirtschaftsgesellschaft (DLG) Agrartour GmbH,*
Rüsterstr. 13,
D-6000 Frankfurt am Main,
tel. (06 11) 72 28 76

Landschriften-Verlag,
Kurfürstenstr. 55,
D-5300 Bonn 1;
tel. (02 28) 21 75 90.

Riding holidays
Deutsche Reiterliche Vereinigung,
Freiherr-von-Langen-Str. 13,
D-4410 Warendorf 1;
tel. (0 25 81) 80 41.

Hobby holidays
Information about hobby holiday courses can be obtained from local and regional tourist offices.

Family holidays
Bundeszentrale für gesundheitliche Aufklärung,
Postfach 91 01 52,
D-5000 Köln 91;
tel. (02 21) 8 99 21.

Deutscher Familiendienst,
Rheinallee 33,
D-5300 bonn 2;
tel. (02 28) 36 10 01.

Holidays for the handicapped
Bundesarbeitsgemeinschaft "Hilfe für Behinderte",
Kirchfeldstr. 149,
D-4000 Düsseldorf;
tel. (02 11) 34 00 85.

Spas and Health Resorts

There are numerous spas and health resorts throughout the Federal Republic, catering for those who want to "take the cure" or enjoy a relaxing and health-giving holiday in the hills or by the sea.

Drosselgasse, Rüdesheim

Medicinal springs are mostly to be found along the fringes of the Alps and in upland regions, while the coasts of the North Sea and the Baltic have numbers of resorts offering the benefits of sea-water bathing and sea air.

Most of the spas and health resorts belong to the German Resort Association (Deutscher Bäderverband). A distinction is made between health resorts (with medicinal springs or mud-baths), seaside resorts and resorts offering the Kneipp water cure. Detailed information about health resorts is given in the "Deutscher Bäderkalender" of the German Resort Association (published by the Flöttmann-Verlag, Gütersloh).

Information: Deutscher Bäderverband e.V., Schumannstr. 111, D-5300 Bonn 1; tel. (02 28) 21 10 88/89.

Gastronomy

Restaurants

Lunch is usually served in restaurants between noon and 2 p.m., dinner from 7 p.m. – sometimes earlier in South Germany. The main meal is usually taken at midday; in international hotels and restaurants in the evening. A table d'hôte meal will cost between 30 and 80 DM in leading hotels and restaurants, between 25 and 40 DM in middle-range establishments, from 15 DM up in the general run of restaurants both in towns and in the country. There are frequently set menus at very reasonable prices and special rates for children and pensioners. Some restaurants cater for special diets.

Food and Drink

German cooking is nourishing and varied, with many local specialties, most easily found in the smaller restaurants. As a general rule more vegetables and potatoes are eaten in North Germany, while in the south there is a preference for soups and pasta dishes.

In NORTH GERMANY, with its proximity to the sea, there are – in addition to the excellent sausages – numerous fish dishes. Among them are the very filling *Hamburg eel soup*, *Heligoland lobsters*, *herring*, *smoked Kiel sprats*, *smoked eel* and the fresh-water fish of the Holstein lakes. – Meat dishes include *lobscouse* (sometimes made with fish), *pea-soup with pig's snout and trotters*, *stuffed rib of pork*, *Bokweeten Janhinnerk* (bacon pancake of buckwheat flour), *Kohl mit Pinkel* (cabbage with coarse sausage) and *Holsteiner Katenschinken* (ham). – A popular dessert is *Mehlpüt*, a kind of pudding with pears and butter

sauce. Another favourite sweet is *Lübeck marzipan*. – The principal drinks are *tea* (with sugar-candy and cream), *grog* (the traditional formula being "rum you must have, sugar you can, water you can do without") and *corn brandy*.

In LOWER SAXONY, lying farther inland, meat and sausages come to the fore. On Lüneburg Heath there is *Heidschnuckenbraten* (roast lamb), and another favourite dish is *Braunkohl mit Brägenwurst* (kale with brain sausage). The streams of the Harz yield *trout*, the Weser and its tributaries *eels*. – Brunswick is noted for its excellent *sausages* and its *honey-cake*. – *Braunschweiger Mumme* is a very strong dark beer with a malt content of over 50%, once an important element in the provisioning of sailing ships, now usually drunk mixed with ordinary beer. – A Hanover speciality is the "*lüttje Lage*", a glass of beer and a glass of schnaps drunk together. *Einbeck beer* is also famous. The heath regions produce *Haidmärker* (corn brandy, schnaps).

In WESTPHALIA too meat dishes predominate. Smoked meat products are popular, particularly *Westphalian ham*, accompanied by dark *pumpernickel* bread. Other substantial dishes are *Puffbohnen mit Speck* (broadbeans and bacon), *Pfefferpotthast* (highly spiced boiled beef), *Mettwurst mit Linsen* (pork and beef sausages with lentils) and *Westfälische Reibekuchen* (made of grated raw potatoes and buckwheat flour). Fresh-water fish add variety to the menu. – The popular drink is *beer*, mainly brewed in the Dortmund area. With sausage dishes *Steinhäger* (corn brandy) is drunk.

In HESSE there is a preference for substantial pork dishes. *Frankfurter* sausages have of course achieved international fame. Other specialties are *Speckkuchen* (bacon pie), *Kasseler Rippchen* (smoked pickled loin of pork: named after a Berlin butcher named Kassel), *Bauernfrühstück* ("peasant breakfast" – ham, potatoes and egg) and *Handkäse* (curd cheese). – *Bethmännchen* and *Frankfurter Brenten* are popular types of biscuit. – The favourite drink is *wine* or, particularly round Frankfurt, "*Äppelwoi*" (hard cider).

Popular dishes in the RHINELAND are *Sauerbraten* (braised pickled beef), "*Himmel und Erde*" ("heaven and earth" – a purée of apples and potatoes with blood sausage), *Hämmchen* (knuckle of pork), *Hunsrücker Festessen* (sauerkraut and pease pudding with potatoes, horse-radish and ham), *Schweinepfeffer* (jugged pork) and *fish* from the tributaries of the Rhine and the volcanic lakes in the Eifel. During the season many restaurants offer *mussel* dishes. – A *Halver Hahn* is a sandwich of rye bread and cheese, accompanied by beer. – There are a great variety of cakes and biscuits such as *Spekulatius*, *Muzenmandeln*, *Aachener Printen*, etc. – The most popular drink is *wine*, here of excellent quality (particularly Rhine, Moselle and Nahe wines). Beer is also drunk, in particular "*Kölsch*", a light-coloured surface-fermented beer, and "*Alt*", also surface-fermented, which is dark.

The people of SOUTH-WESTERN GERMANY like meat dishes and farinaceous food (dumplings, pasta). In Swabia there is a great range of soups, such as *Flädlesuppe* (with the addition of pancakes cut into strips) and *Gaisburger Marsch* (a thick soup of meat stock, potatoes, Spätzle and beef). *Spätzle* are a form of pasta made of flour, eggs and salt, grated and boiled. *Maultaschen* are also made of pasta, filled with minced meat, spinach, onions, etc. They are eaten either in soup or with onions browned in fat.

Sauerkraut is served with *Ripple* (pickled rib of pork), blood and liver sausage or pig's stomach. In the Black Forest there are *trout* and the well-known *Black Forest ham*. A favourite accompaniment of new wine is onion pasty. – In addition to *beer*, mostly brewed in Stuttgart and the Black Forest, the main drink is *wine*, produced in Württemberg and on the Bergstrasse in Baden. *Most* (fermented apple or pear juice), once the chief drink in country areas, is now rarely found. Excellent *fruit brandies* (Kirschwasser from cherries, Zwetschgenwasser from plums, Himbeergeist from raspberries) are distilled in the Black Forest.

BAVARIA has many local dishes, often with names in Bavarian dialect. A popular mid-morning snack or second breakfast is *Weisswürste* (spiced veal and pork sausages), which are skilfully extracted from their skins and eaten with sweet mustard. Another favourite snack is *Leberkäs*, a meat paste which is eaten either hot or cold. – Among main dishes there are *Ochsenbrust* (breast of beef), *Schweinebraten mit Semmelknödeln* (roast pork with bread dumplings) and *Züngerl* (pig's tongue) or *Wammerl* (pig's stomach) with cabbage. In the Main and Altmühl valleys there are fish dishes, Altmühl *carp* being famous for their high quality. In Lower Bavaria potato dumplings (*Klösse*) are often served in place of bread dumplings. The little *Nürnberger Bratwürste* are a well-known local speciality. – The national drink is *beer*, brewed not only in Munich but in many other towns. Everywhere the summer visitor will find shady beer-gardens in which to quench his thirst. The beer may be accompanied by a "*Radi*", a large white radish cut into thin spirals and salted. In Franconia the regular drink is white *wine*.

The cuisine of BERLIN offers a number of substantial dishes. Pork is in great demand, particularly the famous *Eisbein* (knuckle of pork), which is accompanied by sauerkraut and pease pudding. The *Berliner Schlachtplatte* consists of fresh blood and liver sausage, pig's kidney and fresh-boiled pork. Other favourite dishes are *chops* with mixed vegetables, *leg of pork* with red cabbage, *neck of pork* and *goose* cooked in various ways. Fish dishes include *Aal grün* (eel cooked in a rich sauce), *roast pike* with bacon salad, *carp* and *tench*. – Well-known kinds of cake and pastry are *Kranzkuchen, Baumkuchen, Windbeutel* and *Berliner Pfannkuchen* (Berlin pancakes). – The usual drink is beer, brewed by several large breweries. *Berliner Weisse mit Schuss* is a glass of wheaten beer with a shot of raspberry juice or woodruff extract.

Useful addresses

Diabetics
Diabetiker-Verband e.V.,
Hahnbrunnerstr, 46,
D-6750 Kaiserslautern;
tel. (06 31) 7 64 88.

Bund diabetischer Kinder und Jugendlicher e.V.,
Hahnbrunnerstr. 46,
D-6750 Kaiserslautern;
tel. (06 31) 7 64 88.

Diet Care
Gütegemeinschaft Diätverpflegung e.V.,
Moorenstr. 5,
D-4000 Düsseldorf 1;
tel. (02 11) 3 11 85 31.

Wine

Although wine-growing in Germany is confined to the southern part of the country the vineyards are among the most northerly in the world. As a result of this geographical situation the quality of the wine depends very largely – as it does not in the southern countries – on the weather in a particular year; though when conditions are favourable the wine achieves a balance and perfection which spreads its fame far beyond the bounds of Germany.

Most German wines are white: red wines account for only some 15% of total production and are little drunk outside the area where they are produced.

After the grapes are harvested (October) they are crushed between rollers and then pressed. The resulting must soon begins to ferment. When the yeast has settled and the wine clears (mid to end November) it is filtered out from the lees, a dose of sulphur is added, and the wine is put into fresh casks, which are filled up to the bung. In the following spring it is then fined and filtered, and during the summer or autumn it is bottled. In bad years grape-musts from the poorer plots of vineyards may be improved by the addition of sugar. Well-made wines keep for 10–20 years but acquire a taste which does not appeal to everyone. Rhine wines have brown bottles, Moselle and South German wines green ones.

Under a new wine law passed in 1971 German wines are no longer graded according to the vineyard of origin but solely according to their grape-sugar content. There are now three basic classes of wine – Tafelwein (table wine), Qualitätswein (quality wine) and Qualitätswein mit Prädikat (quality wine with some specific distinction). The five specific distinctions, in ascending order of quality, are Kabinett, Spätlese, Auslese, Beerenauslese and Trockenbeerenauslese: they are explained in the next section. There is also the classification Qualitätswein aus bestimmten Weinbaugebieten (quality wine from a particular wine town or village), which ranks somewhat below Qualitätswein mit Prädikat.

Understanding the Wine Label
(Source: Deutsche Wein-Information, Mainz)

The label on a bottle of German wine will show the region (and where appropriate the wine town or village) from which it comes, the year it was made, usually the grape from which it was made, and its classification. The following paragraphs explain the official classifications and describe the grapes used in making German wines.

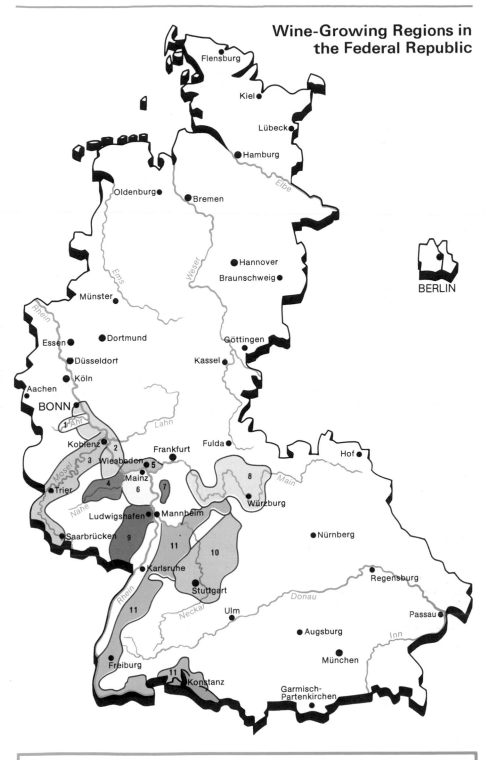

Wine-Growing Regions in
the Federal Republic

There are eleven regions:

1 Ahr
2 Middle Rhine (Mittelrhein)
3 Moselle-Saar-Ruwer
4 Nahe
5 Rheingau
6 Rhineland-Hesse (Rheinhessen)
7 Hessische Bergstrasse
8 Franconia (Franken)
9 Rhineland-Palatinate
  (Rheinpfalz)
10 Württemberg
11 Baden

Classifications of German Wine

Deutscher Tafelwein (German table wine)
These are light and wholesome wines for everyday drinking. They must come from one of the four large regions into which the German wine-growing areas have been divided for this purpose – the Rhine and Moselle, the Main, the Neckar and the Oberrhein regions. They can come only from approved vineyards and from approved kinds of grapes. They may have a more exact indication of origin (sub-region, area or commune) in addition to the regional designation.

Qualitätswein aus bestimmten Anbaugebieten (QbA) (Quality wine from particular areas)
These are good-quality wines with the characteristics of their area. They must have passed a test of quality and bear an official testing number on the label: this guarantees that they have been accepted as typical of their place of origin and of the kind of grape used and as free from any defect of colour, clarity, aroma or taste. They must come from one of the 11 regions shown on the map opposite.

Qualitätswein mit Prädikat (QmP) (Quality wine with some specific distinction)
These are the wines which have given Germany its international reputation for high-quality wine, with an elegance, a richness of bouquet and a fullness of taste which appeal to the discriminating wine-lover. Prädikat wines must come from one particular area within one of the 11 wine-growing regions. The grapes must be fully ripe, with a harmonious balance between sweetness and acidity; the addition of sugar is not permitted. All Prädikat wines must be typical of their area and of the type of grape, and are assigned their Prädikat after a stringent testing procedure. The qualities expected of each of the five categories are as follows:

Kabinett. – The grapes must be gathered when ripe in accordance with the provisions of the harvesting regulations. Kabinett wines are light and fresh, but they also have a characteristic distinction and elegance.

Spätlese. – The grapes are gathered when fully ripe, after completion of the normal harvest. The wines are rounded, elegant and full-flavoured.

Auslese. – The grapes are picked separately and pressed separately after all imperfect grapes have been discarded. The wines are prized for their maturity, fullness of bouquet and elegance of style.

Beerenauslese. – Over-ripe grapes and grapes with "noble rot" (which concentrates the sugar in the grapes) are individually selected to make this wine, a wonderfully mature, full-flavoured and full-bodied wine with a distinctive, almost honey-like, sweetness. It is amber-coloured, or may have a gold or coppery tone.

Trockenbeerenauslese. – This Prädikat is given only to wines of the very highest standard. They are made from grapes which have dried on the vine into a raisin-like state and have been attacked by noble rot. In appearance and taste they are similar to Beeren-auslese wines, only more so.

In addition there is **Eiswein**, which stands in a category of its own. It is made from grapes whose water content has been turned to ice by frosts of at least – 7 °C, and only the residual concentrate of grape juice, rich in sugar and in aroma, is pressed. The designation can be earned by a wine in any of the five classes.

Types of Grape

Müller-Thurgau. – Large heavy grapes, which prefer clay and loess soils; very early ripening. They produce full-flavoured and very palatable aromatic wines with a strong bouquet and a taste of muscatel. Grown mainly in Rheinhessen, Rheinpfalz, the Nahe, Baden and Franconia.

Riesling. – Small grapes which ripen late. They prefer slate soils, marls and areas of Tertiary and eruptive rocks. Riesling wines are notable for their extraordinary variety of flavour, ranging from fruity acidity to the most aristocratic elegance. The grapes are grown in all areas, particularly in Moselle-Saar-Ruwer, the Middle Rhine and the Rheingau.

Silvaner. – Medium-sized grapes. The wine is mild, harmonious, rounded and succulent, with slight acidity and a delicate bouquet. Grown mainly in Rheinhessen, Rheinpfalz and Franconia.

Ruländer. – Medium-sized golden-brown grapes, which need good soil and a warm climate; ripening medium early to late. The wines are amber-coloured, full and spicy. Grown particularly in Rheinpfalz and Baden.

Traminer. – Bright red grapes, late ripening. The wine is full and aromatic, with a rich bouquet and a perfume of roses. The Gewürztraminer belongs to the same family. The Traminers are ideal dessert wines. Grown mainly in Rheinpfalz, Baden and Rheinhessen.

Spätburgunder. – Small blue grapes which produce excellent red wines, full-flavoured, full-bodied, aromatic and when mature velvety smooth. Grown mainly in Baden and the Ahr valley.

Trollinger. – Large sweet grapes, bright red in colour; ripen very late. They prefer deep Muschelkalk and Keuper soils. The wine is pleasantly fresh and palatable. Grown almost exclusively in Württemburg.

Portugieser. – Deep blue grapes; early ripening; undemanding as to soil and situation. A pleasant tasty wine for everyday drinking. Grown mainly in Rheinpfalz and Rheinhessen.

Lemberger. – A large and productive vine with small bitter-sweet grapes, reddish blue to blackish blue in colour. Prefers deep soils. the wine, dark red in colour with a hint of purple, is full-flavoured, full-bodied, dry, ranging from fresh and robust to fiery and aromatic. Grown almost exclusively in Württemberg.

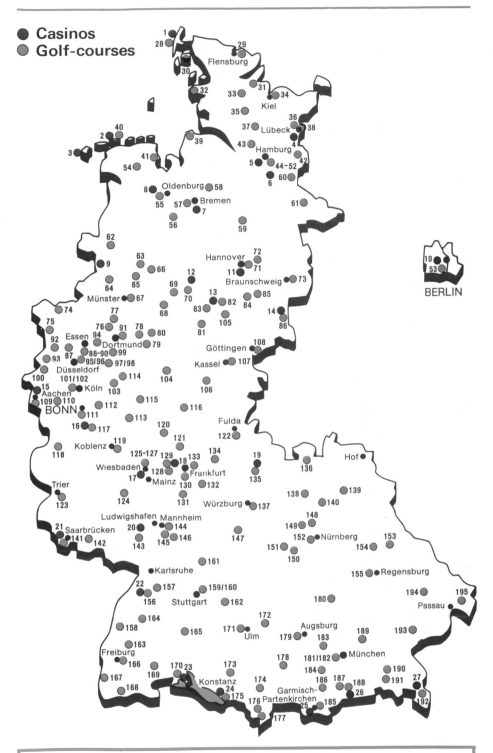

● Casinos
◐ Golf-courses

Casinos · Golf-courses

Golf is still an exclusive sport in Germany; but the map demonstrates strikingly the wide spread it has now achieved in the Federal Republic.

Gaming is apparently becoming increasingly popular in the Federal Republic. In recent years a number of new casinos have been established alongside the traditional establishments, and others are planned.

Information can be obtained from the German Golf Association – the *Deutscher Golf Verband*, Rheinblickstr. 24, D-6200 Wiesbaden; tel: (0 61 21) 8 80 91. The Association also publishes a yearbook, "Golf in Deutschland".

Casinos and Golf-Courses

● Casinos

1 Westerland/Sylt. – **2** Norderney. – **3** Borkum. – **4** Lübeck/Travelmünde. – **5** Hamburg. – **6** Seevetal. – **7** Bemen. – **8** Bad Zwischenahn. – **9** Bad Bentheim. – **10** Berlin. – **11** Hanover. – **12** Bad Oeynhausen. – **13** Bad Pyrmont. – **14** Bad Harzburg. – **15** Aachen. – **16** Bad Neuenahr. – **17** Wiesbaden. – **18** Bad Homburg. **19** Bad Kissingen. – **20** Bad Dürkheim. – **21** Saarbrücken. – **22** Baden-Baden. – **23** Konstanz. – **24** Lindau. – **25** Garmisch – Partenkirchen. – **26** Bad Wiessee. – **27** Bad Reichenhall.

● Golf-courses

28 Westerland/Sylt (6). – **29** Glücksburg (9). – **30** Nieblum auf Föhr (9). – **31** Eckernförde (9). – **32** St Peter-Ording (9). – **33** Rendsburg (9). – **34** Kiel/ Kitzeberg (9). – **35** Aukrug (9). – **36** Timmendorfer Strand (36). – **37** Bad Bramstedt (9). – **38** Lübeck/ Travemünde (9). – **39** Cuxhaven (18). – **40** Norderney (9). – **41** Wilhelmshaven (9). – **42** Grambeck/Molln (9). – **43** Quickborn/Renzel (6). – **44** Hamburg/ Ahrensburg (18). – **45** Hamburg/Falkenstein (18). – **46** Hamburg/Grossflottbek (6). – **47** Hamburg/ Kisdorf (18). – **48** Hamburg/Lüneburger Heide (18). – **49** Hamburg/Hoisdorf (18). – **50** Hamburg/Reinbek (9). – **51** Hamburg-Walddörfer (18). – **52** Hamburg/ Wendlohe (18). – **53** Berlin/Wannsee (9). – **54** Wiesmoor/Hinrichsfelden (18). – **55** Oldenburg/ Oldb. (9). – **56** Wildeshausen (9). – **57** Bremen/Vahr (27). – **58** Worpswede (9). – **59** Fallingbostel/ Tietlingen (9). – **60** St Dionys (18). – **61** Brassche (9). – **63** Lingen (9). – **63** Velpe (9). – **64** Burgsteinfurt (9). – **65** Tecklenburg (9). – **66** Osnabrück (9). – **67** Münster (9). – **68** Gütersloh (18). – **69** Bielefeld (9). – **70** Bad Salzuflen (9). – **71** Hanover (18). – **72** Burgdorf (18). – **73** Brunswick (9). – **74** Anholt (9). – **75** Issum (18). – **76** Recklinghausen (9). – **77** Nordkirchen (9). – **78** Werl (9). – **79** Neheim-Hüsten (9). – **80** Soest (9). – **81** Bad Driburg (9). – **82** Bad Pyrmont (9). – **83** Blomberg-Cappel (18). – **84** Rheden (9). – **85** Bad Salzdetfurth (9). – **86** Bad Harzburg (9). – **87** Duisburg (9). – **88** Essen (9). – **89** Essen/Heidhausen (9). – **90** Essen/Haus Oefte (9). – **91** Dortmund (18). – **92** Krefeld (18). – **93** Mönchengladbach (18). – **94** Bochum (9). – **95**

Düsseldorf (18). – **96** Düsseldorf/Hubbelraht (36). – **97** Wuppertal (18). – **98** Wuppertal/Barmen (18). – **99** Hagen (9). – **100** Wegberg (9). – **101** Cologne/ Marienburg (9). – **102** Cologne (18). – **103** Gummersbach/Georghausen (18). – **104** Winterberg (9). – **105** Polle/Holzminden (9). – **106** Bad Wildungen (9). – **107** Kassel (18). – **108** Göttingen (9). – **109** Aachen (9). – **110** Düren (9). – **111** Bonn-Bad Godesberg (18). – **112** Hennef/Sieg (9). – **113** Hachenburg (9). – **114** Kierspe/Varmert (9). – **115** Siegen/Olpe (9). – **116** Marburg (9). – **117** Bad Nauenahr (18). – **118** Hillesheim (9). – **119** Bad Ems (18). – **120** Braunfels (18). – **121** Bad Nauheim (9). – **122** Fulda (9). – **123** Trier/Ebsch-Birkenheck (9). – **124** Bad Kreuznach (14). – **125** Wiesbaden (9). – **126** Wiesbaden/Delkenheim (9). – **127** Wiesbaden/ Rheinblick (18). – **128** Kronberg/Taunus (18). – **129** Bad Homburg (15). – **130** Frankfurt/Main (18). – **131** Darmstadt (9). – **132** Aschaffenburg (9). – **133** Hanau (18). – **134** Bad Orb (10). – **135** Bad Kissingen (18). – **136** Coburg (9). – **137** Würzburg/Kitzingen (18). – **138** Bamberg (9). – **139** Bayreuth (9). – **140** Kanndorf (9). – **141** Saarbrücken (18). – **142** Blieskastel (9). – **143** Neustadt/Weinstrasse (18). – **144** Mannheim (9). – **145** Schwetzingen (18). – **146** Heidelberg (18). – **147** Bad Mergentheim (9). – **148** Erlangen (9). – **149** Herzogenaurach (9). – **150** Lichtenau/Weickershof (9). – **151** Ansbach (9). – **152** Nuremberg (9). – **153** Neunburg v.W. (9). – **154** Schmidmühlen (9). – **155** Regensburg (18). – **156** Baden-Baden (18). – **157** Bad Herrenalb (9). – **158** Lahr/Reichenbach (9). **159** Stuttgart/Kornwestheim (18). – **160** Stuttgart/ Mönsheim (9). – **161** Heilbronn (9). – **162** Göppingen (9). – **163** Gutach im Breisgau (9). – **164** Freudenstadt (9). – **165** Hechingen/Hohenzollern (9). – **166** Freiburg im Breisgau (9). – **167** Baden-weiler (9). – **168** Rickenbach (9). – **169** Donaue-schingen (9). – **170** Konstanz (9). – **171** Ulm (9). – **172** Günzburg (9). – **173** Bad Waldsee (18). – **174** Wiggensbach/Oberallgäu (9). – **175** Lindau/Bad Schachen (18). – **176** Ofterschwang (18). – **177** Oberstdorf (9). – **178** Bad Wörishofen (18). – **179** Augsburg (9). – **180** Ingolstagt (6). – **181** Munich (27). – **182** Munich/Dachau (9). – **183** Olching (18). – **184** Feldafing (18). – **185** Garmisch-Partenkirchen (two courses, each 9). – **186** St Eurach/Iffeldorf (18). – **187** Bad Tölz (9). – **188** Bad Wiessee (18). – **189** Erding/Grünbach (9). – **190** Höslwang (9). – **191** Prien (9). – **192** Berchtesgaden (9). – **193** Eggen-felden (9). – **194** Deggendorf (9). – **195** Waldkirchen/ Niederbayern (9).

●Castles, Palaces and Country Houses

(The terms used to differentiate the various types of castle are explained in the Glossary on p. 273. The post code is given in brackets after the name of the place.)

1 Glücksburg (D-2392)
Wasserschloss (16th c.)

2 Schleswig (D-2380)
Schloss Gottorf (13th, 16th–18th c.)

3 Emkendorf (D-2371)
Schloss (18th c.)

4 Schierensee (D-2301)
Herrenhaus (18th c.)

5 Kiel-Holtenau (D-2300)
Gut Knoop (18th c.)

6 Eutin (D-2420)
Schloss (17th–18th c.)

7 Altenkrempe (D-2430 Altenkrempe, Post Neustadt in Holstein)
Herrenhaus Hasselberg(18th c.)

8 Ahrensburg (D-2070)
Schloss (16th c.)

9 Winsen/Luhe (D-2090)
Schloss (12th–16th c.)

10 Dornum (D-2988 Dornum/Ostfriesland)
Wasserburg (17th c.)

11 Hinte (D-2971)
Wasserburg (16th c.)

12 Jever (D-2942)
Schloss (14th–18th c.)

13 Gödens (D-2945 Sande)
Wasserschloss (17th c.)

14 Oldenburg (D-2900)
Schloss (17th c.)

15 Sögel (D-4475)
Schloss Clemenswerth (18th c.)

16 Celle (D-3100)
Herzogsschloss (17th c.)

Schloss Bürresheim near Mayen, the Eifel

17 **Gifhorn** (D-3170)
Wasserschloss (16th–19th c.)
18 **Wolfsburg** (D-3180)
Schloss (17th c.)
19 **Berlin** (D-1000)
Jagdschloss Grunewald (17th c.)
20 **Berlin** (D-1000)
Schloss Charlottenburg (17th–18th c.)
21 **Berlin** (D-1000)
Schloss Bellevue (18th c.)
22 **Berlin** (D-1000)
Schloss Tegel (19th c.)
23 **Berlin** (D-1000)
Schloss Pfaueninsel (ruined: 18th c.)
24 **Berlin** (D-1000)
Schloss Kleinglienicke (19th c.)
25 **Bentheim** (D-4444)
Schloss (12th, 15th, 17th c.)
26 **Langenhorst** (D-4434 Ochtrup)
Wasserburg Welbergen (16th–18th c.)
27 **Ahaus** (D-4422)
Wasserschloss (17th c.)
28 **Burgsteinfurt** (D-4430)
Wasserschloss (12th c.)
29 **Darfeld** (D-4428 Rosendahl)
Wasserschloss (17th–19th c.)
30 **Havixbeck** (D-4401)
Wasserburg (16th–18th c.)
31 **Münster** (D-4400)
Wasserburg Haus Hülshoff (16th–18th c.)
32 **Münster** (D-4400)
Schloss Rüschhaus (18th c.)
33 **Bad Iburg** (D-4505)
Schloss (17th–18th c.)
34 **Schledehausen**
(D-4516 Bissendorf/Kreis Osnabrück)
Schloss Schelenburg (15th–16th c.)
35 **Gesmold** (D-4520 Meile)
Wasserburg (16th c.)
36 **Bückeburg** (D-3062)
Schloss (16th–19th c.)
37 **Steinhude** (D-3050)
Festung Wilhelmstein (18th c.)
38 **Stadthagen** (D-3060)
Schloss (16th c.)
39 **Rehren** (D-3262 Auetal 1)
Schloss Schaumburg (11th–15th c.)
40 **Hanover** (D-3000)
Schloss Herrenhausen
(partly destroyed: 17th–18th c.)

41 **Nordstemmen** (D-3204)
Schloss Marienburg (19th c.)
42 **Brunswick** (D-3300)
Schloss Richmond (18th c.)
43 **Wolfenbüttel** (D-3340)
Schloss (16th c.)
44 **Isselburg** (D-4294)
Wasserschloss (16th c.)
45 **Gemen** (D-4280)
Wasserschloss (15th–17th c.)
46 **Raesfeld** (D-4281)
Wasserschloss (17th c.)
47 **Lembeck** (D-4270 Dorsten 12)
Wasserburg (15th–17th c.)
48 **Dorsten** (D-4270)
Schloss Beck (18th c.)
49 **Lüdinghausen** (D-4710)
Wasserburg Vischering (16th c.)
50 **Nordkirchen** (D-4717)
Wasserschloss (18th c.)
51 **Herborn** (D-4715)
Schloss (13th–17th c.)
52 **Wolbeck** (D-4400 Münster)
Drostenhof (16th c.)
53 **Lippborg** (D-4775 Lippetal)
Wasserburg (17th c.)
54 **Rheda** (D-4840 Rheda-Wiedenbrück)
Schloss (13th–17th c.)
55 **Lippstadt** (D-4780)
Wasserschloss Schwarzengraben (18th c.)
56 **Neuhaus** (D-4790 Paderborn)
Schloss Wilhelmsburg (16th c.)
57 **Wewelsburg** (D-4793 Büren)
Burg (17th c.)
58 **Brenken** (D-4793 Büren)
Schloss Erpenburg
59 **Detmold** (D-4930)
Schloss (16th c.)
60 **Brake** (D-4920 Lemgo 1)
Wasserschloss (16th–17th c.)
61 **Emmern** (D-3254 Emmerthal)
Schloss Hämelschenburg (16th–17th c.)
62 **Hehlen** (D-3452)
Schloss (16th c.)
63 **Bevern** (D-3454 Bevern/Kreis Holzminden)
Schloss (17th c.)
64 **Fürstenberg** (D-3476 Fürstenberg/Weser)
Burg Fürstenberg (14th c.)
65 **Karlshafen** (D-3522)
Ruine Krukenburg

66 **Trendelburg** (D-3526)
Burg (15th c.)
67 **Daseburg** (D-3530 Warburg)
Ruine Desenberg
68 **Brüggen** (D-3211 Brüggen/Leine)
Schloss (16th–18th c.)
69 **Sillium** (D-3201 Holle bei Hildesheim)
Burg (partly destroyed: 13th c.)
70 **Adelebsen** (D-3404)
Burg (17th–18th c.)
71 **Hardegsen** (D-3414)
Schloss (14th c.)
72 **Nörten-Hardenberg** (D-3412)
Ruine Hardenberg (11th c.)
73 **Liebenburg** (D-3384)
Schloss (18th c.)
74 **Goslar** (D-3380)
Kaiserpfalz (11th, 17th–18th c.)
75 **Herzberg** (D-3420)
Schloss (16th c.)
76 **Scharzfeld** (D-3420 Herzberg)
Ruine Scharzfels (13th c.)
77 **Weeze** (D-4179)
Schloss Wissen (16th–18th c.)
78 **Geldern** (D-4170)
Wasserburg Haag (17th c.)
79 **Krefeld** (D-4150)
Wasserburg Linn (14th–18th c.)
80 **Mönchengladbach** (D-4050)
Wasserburg Myllendonck (14th–16th c.)
81 **Rheydt** (D-4050)
Schloss (16th c.)
82 **Linnich** (D-5172)
Wasserschloss Kellenberg (15th c.)
83 **Jülich** (D-5170)
Zitadelle (ruined: 16th c.)
84 **Bedburg** (D-5012 Bedburg/Erft)
Schloss (13th–16th c.)
85 **Kettwig** (D-4300 Essen 18)
Schloss Landsberg (13th c.)
86 **Düsseldorf** (D-4000)
Schloss Benrath (18th c.)
87 **Düsseldorf-Kaiserswerth** (D-4000)
Kaiserpfalz (ruined: 12th c.)
88 **Altena** (D-5990)
Burg (13th c.)
89 **Attendorn** (D-5952)
Burg Schellenberg (17th c.)
90 **Oberhundem** (D-5942 Kirchhundem)
Schloss Adolfsburg (17th c.)
91 **Arolsen** (D-3548)
Schloss (18th c.)
92 **Waldeck** (D-3544 Waldeck/Hessen)
Ruine Weidelsburg (13th–14th c.)
93 **Waldeck** (D-3544 Waldeck/Hessen)
Schloss (12th–16th c.)
94 **Bad Wildungen** (D-3590)
Schloss Friedrichstein (18th c.)
95 **Kassel** (D-3500)
Schloss Wilhelmshöhe (18th c.)
96 **Kassel** (D-3500)
Schloss Wilhelmsthal (18th c.)
97 **Felsberg** (D-3582 Felsberg/Hessen)
Burgruine (9th–11th c.)
98 **Mollenfelde** (D-3403 Friedland)
Schloss Berlepsch (14th, 16th, 19th c.)
99 **Wendershausen** (D-3430 Witzenhausen 8)
Burg Ludwigstein (15th c.)
100 **Spangenberg** (D-3509)
Schloss (13th c.)
101 **Rotenburg/Fulda** (D-6442)
Schloss (16th c.)
102 **Nentershausen** (D-6446)
Burg Tannenberg
(partly destroyed: 14th c.)
103 **Friedewald** (D-6431 Friedewald/Hessen)
Wasserschloss (ruined: 15th c.)
104 **Cologne-Frens** (D-5000)
Schloss (15th–16th, 19th c.)

105 **Bensberg** (D-5060 Bergisch Gladbach 1)
Neues Schloss (18th c.)
106 **Gymnich** (D-5042 Erftstadt)
Schloss (16th–18th c.)
107 **Lechenich** (D-5042 Erftstadt)
Burgruine (14th c.)
108 **Brühl** (D-5040)
Schloss Augustusburg (18th c.)
109 **Bonn** (D-5300)
Poppelsdorfer Schloss (18th c.)
110 **Gudenau** (D-5307 Wachtberg-Villip)
Wasserburg (16th–18th c.)
111 **Königswinter** (D-5330)
Ruine Drachenfels (12th c.)
112 **Nideggen** (D-5168)
Burgruine (12th–14th c.)
113 **Monschau** (D-5108)
Burgruine (12th–13th c.)
114 **Friesenhagen** (D-5221)
Wasserschloss Crottorf (16th–17th c.)
115 **Siegen** (D-5900)
Oberes Schloss (13th c.)
116 **Siegen** (D-5900)
Unteres Schloss (17th–18th c.)
117 **Greifenstein** (D-6331)
Burgruine (14th–17th c.)
118 **Giessen** (D-6300 Lahn 1)
Neues Schloss (16th c.)
119 **Krofdorf-Gleiberg** (D-6301 Wettenberg)
Burg Gleiberg (12th–14th c.)
120 **Marburg** (D-3550)
Schloss (15th–16th c.)
121 **Schweinsberg** (D-3570 Stadtallendorf)
Schloss (partly destroyed: 13th c.)
122 **Eisenbach** (D-6420 Lauterbach/Hessen)
Schloss (13th c.)
123 **Herzberg** (D-6320)
Burg (12th, 15th, 17th c.)
124 **Schlitz** (D-6407)
Burg (16th–17th c.)
125 **Fulda** (D-6400)
Schloss (14th, 17th–18th c.)
126 **Altenahr** (D-5481)
Burg Are (ruined: 12th, 14th–15th c.)
127 **Dernau** (D-5481)
Ruine Saffenburg (11th–12th c.)
128 **Bad Hönningen** (D-5462)
Schloss Arenfels (13th c.)
129 **Dierdorf** (D-5419)
Schloss (17th c.)
130 **Bad Breisig** (D-5484)
Burg Rheineck (19th c.)
131 **Rheinbrohl** (D-5456)
Ruine Hammerstein (12th c.)
132 **Neuwied** (D-5450)
Schloss (18th c.)
133 **Bendorf** (D-5413 Bendorf/Rhein)
Burgruine (13th c.)
134 **Koblenz** (D-5400)
Kurfürstl Burg (13th–16th c.)
135 **Koblenz** (D-5400)
Feste Ehrenbreitstein (19th c.)
136 **Nürburg** (D-5489)
Ruine Nürburg (12th c.)
137 **Monreal** (D-5441)
Burgruine (13th c.)
138 **Mayen** (D-5440)
Genovevaburg (13th–18th c.)
Schloss Bürresheim (13th–16th c.)
139 **Koblenz-Stolzenfels** (D-5400)
Schloss Stolzenfels (19th c.)
140 **Lahnstein** (D-5420)
Burg Lahneck (13th–19th c.)
141 **Moselkern** (D-5401)
Burg Eltz (13th–16th c.)
142 **Moselkern** (D-5401)
Burg Thurant (18th c.)
143 **Brodenbach** (D-5401)
Ruine Ehrenburg (13th c.)

144 **Braubach** (D-5423)
Marksburg (13th c.)
145 **Kamp-Bornhofen** (D-5424)
Burg Liebenstein (ruined: 13th c.)
146 **Kamp-Bornhofen** (D-5424)
Burg Sterrenberg (ruined: 13th c.)
147 **Klotten** (D-5592)
Ruine Coraidelstein
148 **Cochem** (D-5590)
Burg (19th c.)
149 **Beilstein** (D-5591)
Reichsfeste Beilstein
(ruined: 13th c.)
150 **Alf** (D-5584)
Burg Arras (10th c.)
151 **Zell** (D-5583)
Schloss (16th c.)
152 **Bernkastel-Kues** (D-5550)
Burg Landshut (ruined: 13th c.)
153 **Kastellaun** (D-5448)
Burgruine (destroyed 1689)
154 **Wellmich** (D-5422 St. Goarshausen)
Burg Thunberg
(known as the "Maus": 14th c.)
155 **St. Goar** (D-5401)
Burg Rheinfels (ruined: 13th c.)
156 **St. Goarshausen** (D-5422)
Burg Katz (14th–19th c.)
157 **Oberwesel** (D-6532)
Ruine Schönburg (10th c.)
158 **Kaub** (D-5425)
Burg Gutenfels (13th c.)
159 **Kaub** (D-5425)
Burg Pfalzgrafenstein (14th c.)
160 **Bacharach** (D-6533)
Burg Stahleck (ruined: 12th c.)
161 **Lorch** (D-6223)
Burg Nolling (ruined: 12th c.)
162 **Niederheimbach** (D-6531)
Burg Hoheneck (13th–19th c.)
163 **Trechtingshausen** (D-6531)
Burg Sooneck (13th–19th c.)
164 **Trechtingshausen** (D-6531)
Burg Reichenstein 12th c.)
165 **Geroldstein** (D-6209 Heidenrod 7)
Burgruine
166 **Stromberg** (D-6534)
Ruine Stromburg
(11th c., destroyed 1689)
167 **Stromberg** (D-6534)
Schloss Gollenfels
(11th–12th c., destroyed 1614)
168 **Simmern** (D-6540)
Schloss (15th c.)
169 **Rüdesheim** (D-6220)
Burg Ehrenfels (ruined)
170 **Bingen** (D-6530)
Burg Klopp (13th–19th c.)
171 **Oestrich** (D-6227 Oestrich-Winkel)
Schloss Reichartshausen
172 **Ingelheim** (D-6507)
Kaiserpfalz (ruined: 9th c.)
173 **Blankenheim** (D-5378 Blankenheim/Ahr)
Burg (12th c.)
174 **Pelm** (D-5531)
Ruine Kasselburg (13th–14th c.)
175 **Lissingen** (D-5530 Gerolstein)
Burg (12th, 15th–18th c.)
176 **Mürlenbach** (D-5531)
Ruine Bertradaburg (14th c.)
177 **Manderscheid** (D-5562)
Ruine Oberburg (10th c.)
178 **Manderscheid** (D-5562)
Ruine Niederburg (12th c.)
179 **Balduinstein** (D-6251)
Schloss Schaumburg (19th c.)
180 **Burgschwalbach** (D-6251)
Burgruine (14th c.)

181 **Runkel** (D-6251)
Burg (12th, 17th–18th c.)
182 **Weilburg** (D-6290)
Schloss (16th–18th c.)
183 **Braunfels** (D-6333)
Schloss (13th, 17th, 19th c.)
184 **Wiesbaden-Biebrich** (D-6200)
Schloss (18th c.)
185 **Idstein** (D-6270)
Schloss (17th c.)
186 **Münzenberg** (D-6309)
Burgruine (12th c.)
187 **Friedberg** (D-6360 Friedberg/Hessen)
Burg (14th–15th c.)
188 **Hanau** (D-6450)
Schloss Philippsruhe (18th c.)
189 **Büdingen** (D-6470)
Schloss (15th–17th c.)
190 **Geinhausen** (D-6460)
Kaiserpfalz (ruined: 12th c.)
191 **Aschaffenburg** (D-8750)
Schloss Johannisburg (17th c.)
192 **Aschaffenburg** (D-8750)
Schloss Schönbusch (18th c.)
193 **Gemünden/Main** (D-8780)
Ruine Scherenburg (13th–14th c.)
194 **Trimberg**
(D-8731 Elfershausen)
Ruine Trimburg (12th–17th c.)
195 **Bad Neustadt/Saale** (D-8740)
Ruine Salzburg (13th c.)
196 **Werneck** (D-8722)
Schloss (18th c.)
197 **Coburg** (D-8630)
Veste Coburg (16th c.)
198 **Kronach** (D-8640)
Feste Rosenberg
(12th, 16th–17th c.)
199 **Kulmbach** (D-8650)
Plassenburg (16th c.)
200 **Bayreuth** (D-8580)
Altes Schloss (17th c.)
201 **Bayreuth** (D-8580)
Neues Schloss (18th c.)
202 **Falkenberg**
(D-8591 Falkenberg/Oberpfalz)
Burg
203 **Saarburg** (D-5510)
Burgruine (12th c.)
204 **Kirn** (D-6570)
Ruine Kyrburg (14th–15th c.)
205 **Dhaun** (D-6571)
Schlossruine (12th–16th c.)
206 **Darmstadt** (D-6100)
Jagdschloss Kranichstein (17th c.)
207 **Bensheim** (D-6140)
Schloss Auerbach
(ruined: destroyed 1674)
208 **Heppenheim** (D-6148)
Ruine Starkenburg (11th c.)
209 **Neustadt/Odenwald** (D-6127 Breuberg)
Burg Breuberg (11th, 13th–17th c.)
210 **Steinbach** (D-6120 Michelstadt)
Wasserschloss Fürstenau (14th–16th c.)
211 **Erbach/Odenwald** (D-6120)
Schloss (16th–18th c.)
212 **Mespelbrunn** (D-8751)
Wasserschloss (15th c.)
213 **Miltenberg** (D-8760)
Mildenburg (13th–16th c.)
214 **Wertheim/Main** (D-6980)
Burg (12th–16th c.)
215 **Veitshöchheim** (D-8702)
Schloss (17th c.)
216 **Würzburg** (D-8700)
Residenz (18th c.)
217 **Würzburg** (D-8700)
Festung Marienberg (13th c.)

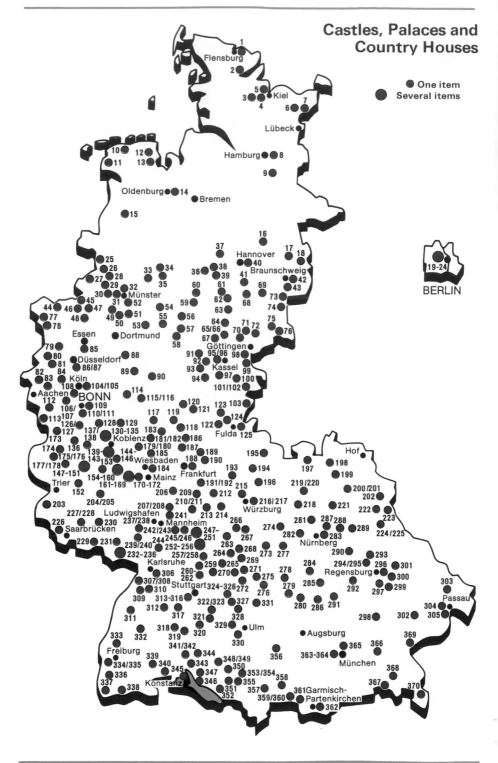

Castles, Palaces and Country Houses

● One item
● Several items

Castles, Palaces and Country Houses

In the picture which tourists from other countries have of Germany its castles, palaces and country houses loom large. Most of them were originally built in prominent situations for strategic reasons, and thus form striking features of the landscape. In more modern times great palaces began to be built for the purposes of display, without any military function, but designed with their magnificence of scale and their beautiful parks and gardens to give expression to the power and splendour of the absolutist rulers of the day.

218 **Pommersfelden** (D-8602)
Schloss Weissenstein (18th c.)
219 **Bamberg** (D-8600)
Ahe Hofhaltung (16th c.)
220 **Bamberg** (D-8600)
Neue Residenz (17th–18th c.)
221 **Pottenstein** (D-8573)
Burg
222 **Neustadt an der Waldnaab** (D-8482)
Schloss (17th c.)
223 **Flossenbürg** (D-8481)
Reichsfeste (ruined: 13th c.)
224 **Leuchtenberg** (D-8481)
Burgruine (14th c.)
225 **Vohenstrauss** (D-8483)
Schloss Friedrichsburg (16th c.)
226 **Siersburg** (D-6639 Rehlingen/Saar)
Burgruine (12th c.)
227 **Kirkel** (D-6654)
Reichsfeste (ruined: 13th c.)
228 **Homburg/Saar** (D-6650)
Schloss Karlsberg (ruined: 18th c.)
229 **Zweibrücken** (D-6660)
Schloss (ruined: 18th c.)
230 **Landstuhl** (D-6790)
Burg Nannstein (ruined: 11th–16th c.)
231 **Gräfenstein** (D-6781 Merzalben)
Burgruine (13th c.)
232 **Dahn** (D-6783)
Burgruine (13th c.)
233 **Vorderweidenthal** (D-6749)
Burg Lindenbrunn (ruined)
234 **Annweiler** (D-6747)
Reichsfeste Trifels
(ruined: 11th–12th c.)
235 **Madenburg** (D-6741 Eschbach/Pfalz)
Burgruine (12th c.)
236 **Klingenmünster** (D-6749)
Burg Landeck (ruined: 13th–15th c.)
237 **Bad Dürkheim** (D-6702)
Ruine Hardenburg 15th–16th c.)
238 **Wachenheim**
(D-6706 Wachenheim a.d. Weinstrasse)
Ruine Wachtenburg
239 **Hambach**
(D-6730 Neustadt a.d. Weinstrasse)
Reichsfeste Maxburg
(ruined: 11th–14th c.)
240 **Edenkoben** (D-6732)
Ruine Rietburg (13th c.)
241 **Weinheim/Bergstrasse** (D-6940)
Burg Windeck (ruined: 12th–13th c.)
242 **Schriesheim** (D-6905)
Ruine Strahlenburg
243 **Heidelberg** (D6900)
Schloss (ruined: 16th–17th c.)
244 **Bruchsal** (D-7520)
Schloss (18th c.)
245 **Neckarsteinach** (D-6901)
Burg Schadeck (ruined: 14th c.)
246 **Hirschhorn** (D-6932)
Burg (13th–16th c.)
247 **Eberbach** (D-6930)
Burg Stolzeneck (ruined: 13th c.)
248 **Zwingenberg** (D-6931)
Burg (15th–16th c.)
249 **Neckargerach** (D-6934)
Ruine Minneburg
250 **Diedesheim** (D-6950 Mosbach/Baden)
Schloss Neuburg
251 **Diedesheim** (D-6950 Mosbach/Baden)
Schloss Hochhausen (18th c.)
252 **Neckarzimmern** (D-6951)
Burg Hornberg (ruined: 11th c.)
253 **Neckarmühlbach** (D-6954 Hassmersheim)
Burg Guttenberg (11th, 14th–15th c.)
254 **Heinsheim** (D-6927 Bad Rappenau)
Burg Ehrenberg
(ruined: 12th, 16th–17th c.)

255 **Bad Wimpfen** (D-7101)
Kaiserpfalz (ruined: 12th c.)
256 **Bad Friedrichshall** (D-7107)
Schloss Lehen (16th c.)
257 **Weinsberg** (D-7102)
Burg Weibertreu (ruined: 11th c.)
258 **Untergruppenbach** (D-7101)
Schloss Stettenfels (17th c.)
259 **Gemmrigheim** (D-7121)
Schloss Liebenstein (14th–16th c.)
260 **Asperg** (D-7144)
Festung Hohenasperg (16th c.)
261 **Ludwigsburg** (D-7140)
Schloss (18th c.)
262 **Ludwigsburg** (D-7140)
Schloss Monrepos (18th c.)
263 **Jagsthausen** (D-7109)
Götzenburg (rebuilt 1876)
264 **Neuenstein**
(D-7113 Neuenstein/Württemberg)
Schloss (13th, 16th–17th c.)
265 **Oppenweiler** (D-7155)
Burg Reichenberg (13th c.)
266 **Bad Mergentheim** (D-6990)
Schloss (16th c.)
267 **Weikersheim** (D-6992)
Schloss (16th–18th c.)
268 **Langenburg** (D-7183)
Schloss (15th, 17th–18th c.)
269 **Schwäbisch Hall** (D-7170)
Stift Comburg (11th, 13th, 18th c.)
270 **Gaildorf** (D-7160)
Wasserschloss (15th c.)
271 **Bühlertann** (D-7167)
Tannenburg
272 **Untergröningen** (D-7081 Abtsgmünd 2)
Schloss (18th c.)
273 **Schillingsfürst** (D-8801)
Schloss (18th c.)
274 **Ipsheim** (D 8531)
Schloss Hoheneck
275 **Ellwangen** (D-7090)
Schloss (17th–18th c.)
276 **Lauchheim** (D-7081)
Kapfenburg (16th c.)
277 **Ansbach** (D-8800)
Markgrafenschloss (18th c.)
278 **Öttingen**
(D-8867 Öttingen/Bayern)
Schloss (16th–17th c.)
279 **Harburg** (D-8856)
Harburg (13th–18th c.)
280 **Leitheim** (D-8850 Donauwörth)
Schloss (17th c.)
281 **Erlangen** (D-8520)
Schloss (18th c.)
282 **Cadolzburg** (D-8501)
Burg (15th–17th c.)
283 **Nuremberg** (D-8500)
Burg (11th–12th, 15th c.)
284 **Weissenburg** (D-8832)
Wülzburg (16th–17th c.)
285 **Eichstätt** (D-8833)
Willibaldsburg
(14th, 16th–17th c.)
286 **Neuburg/Donau** (D-8858)
Schloss (16th–17th c.)
287 **Lauf** (D-8560 Lauf a.d. Pegnitz)
Schloss (15th c.)
288 **Hersbruck** (D-8562)
Pflegerschloss (16th–17th c.)
289 **Sulzbach-Rosenberg** (D-8458)
Schloss Rosenberg
(11th, 16th, 18th c.)
290 **Velburg** (D-8436)
Burgruine (13th c.)
291 **Ingolstadt** (D-8070)
Neues Schloss (14th–15th c.)

292 **Riedenburg** (D-8422)
Rosenburg (13th, 16th c.)
293 **Burglengenfeld** (D-8412)
Burg (10th c.)
294 **Kallmünz** (D-8411)
Burgruine (12th c.)
295 **Wolfsegg**
(D-8411 Wolfsegg/Oberpfalz)
Burg (14th c.)
296 **Donaustauf** (D-8405)
Burgruine (10th c.)
297 **Alteglofsheim** (D-8401)
Schloss (17th c.)
298 **Landshut** (D-8300)
Burg Trausnitz (12th–13th c.)
299 **Sünching** (D-8406)
Wasserschloss (17th–18th c.)
300 **Wörth/Donau** (D-8404)
Schloss (16th c.)
301 **Falkenstein**
(D-8411 Falkenstein/Oberpfalz)
Schlossruine (17th c.)
302 **Arnstorf** (D-8382)
Schloss (15th, 17th–18th c.)
303 **Tittling** (D-8391)
Schloss Saldenburg (13th c.)
304 **Passau** (D-8390)
Veste Oberhaus (13th–16th c.)
305 **Neuburg/Inn** (D-8399)
Schloss Neuburg
(15th–18th, 20th c.)
306 **Ettlingen** (D-7505)
Schloss (18th c.)
307 **Rastatt** (D-7550)
Schloss (17th–18th c.)
308 **Kuppenheim** (D-7554)
Schloss Favorite (18th c.)
309 **Baden-Baden** (D-7570)
Schloss Hohenbaden
(ruined: 12th, 14th–15th c.)
310 **Gernsbach** (D-7562)
Schloss Eberstein (13th, 19th c.)
311 **Oberkirch** (D-7602)
Ruine Schauenburg
312 **Berneck** (D-7272)
Schloss (19th c.)
313 **Stuttgart** (D-7000)
Neues Schloss (18th c.)
314 **Stuttgart** (D-7000)
Altes Schloss (16th c.)
315 **Stuttgart** (D-7000)
Schloss Solitude (18th c.)
316 **Stuttgart-Hohenheim** (D-7000)
Schloss (18th c.)
317 **Tübingen** (D-7400)
Schloss Hohentübingen (16th c.)
318 **Haigerloch** (D-7452)
Schloss (16th–17th c.)
319 **Hechingen** (D-7450)
Burg Hohenzollern (19th c.)
320 **Lichtenstein** (D-7414
Lichtenstein/Württemberg)
Schloss Lichtenstein (19th c.)
321 **Bad Urach** (D-7417)
Burg Hohenurach (ruined: 11th, 16th c.)
322 **Neuffen** (D-7442)
Burg Hohenneuffen (ruined: 16th, 18th c.)
323 **Bissingen** (D-7311)
Burg Teck (ruined: 12th, 14th, 18th c.)
324 **Rechberghausen** (D-7324)
Schloss (18th c.)
325 **Wäschenbeuren** (D-7321)
Wäscherschlösschen
326 **Strassdorf** (D-7070 Schwäbisch Gmünd)
Burg Rechberg (ruined: 12th c.)
327 **Salach** (D-7335)
Burg Staufeneck (ruined)

328 **Geislingen an der Steige** (D-7340)
Burg Helfenstein (ruined: 14th c.)
329 **Blaubeuren** (D-7902)
Rusenschloss (ruined)
330 **Erbach/Donau** (D-7904)
Schloss (16th c.)
331 **Heidenheim** (D-7920)
Schloss Hellenstein (13th, 16th c.)
332 **Wolfach** (D-7620)
Schloss (17th c.)
333 **Emmendingen** (D-7830)
Schloss Hochburg (ruined: 13th, 16th c.)
334 **Freiburg-Zähringen** (D-7800)
Burgruine (13th c.)
335 **Staufen/Breisgau** (D-7813)
Ruine Staufenburg (destroyed in Thirty Years
War)
336 **Badenweiler** (D-7847)
Schloss Bürgeln (18th c.)
Burg (ruined: destroyed in 1678)
337 **Lörrach** (D-7850)
Schloss Rötteln (12th, 14th c.)
338 **Säckingen** (D-7880)
Schloss Schönau (17th–18th c.)
(known as the "Trumpeter's Little Castle")
339 **Donaueschingen** (D-7710)
Schloss (18th–19th c.)
340 **Singen** (D-7700)
Burg Hohentwiel (ruined: 10th, 16th c.)
341 **Hausen im Tal** (D-7792 Beuron)
Burg Werenwag
342 **Beuron** (D-7792)
Burg Wildenstein
343 **Messkirch** (D-7790)
Schloss
344 **Sigmaringen** (D-7480)
Schloss (12th, 15th, 17th, 19th c.)
345 **Insel Mainau** (D-7750)
Schloss (18th c.)
346 **Meersburg** (D-7758)
Schloss (12th, 16th–18th c.)
347 **Heiligenberg** (D-7799)
Schloss (15th–16th c.)
348 **Altshausen** (D-7963)
Deutschordensschloss (16th–18th c.)
349 **Aulendorf** (D-7960)
Schloss (14th, 18th, 19th c.)
350 **Bad Waldsee** (D-7967)
Schloss (16th, 18th c.)
351 **Waldburg** (D-7981)
Schloss (13th, 16th c.)
352 **Tettnang** (D-7992)
Neues Schloss (18th c.)
353 **Bad Wurzach** (D-7954)
Schloss (17th–18th c.)
354 **Unterzeil** (D-7970 Leutkirch)
Schloss Zeil (16th c.)
355 **Kisslegg** (D-7964)
Schloss (16th, 18th c.)
356 **Kirchheim/Mindel** (D-8949)
Fuggerschloss (16th c.)
357 **Kempten** (D-8960)
Residenz (17th c.)
358 **Marktoberdorf** (D-8952)
Jagdschloss (18th c.)
359 **Füssen** (D-8958)
Schloss Neuschwanstein (19th c.)
360 **Füssen** (D-8958)
Schloss Hohenschwangau (19th c.)
361 **Ettal** (D-8107)
Schloss Linderhof (19th c.)
362 **Garmisch-Partenkirchen** (D-8100)
Burg Werdenfels (ruined: 12th c.)
363 **Munich** (D-8000)
Schloss Nymphenburg (17th–18th c.)

364 **Munich** (D-8000)
  Residenz (16th–19th c.)
365 **Oberschleissheim** (D-8042)
  Neues Schloss (18th c.)
366 **Haag** (D-8092 Haag/Oberbayern)
  Burgruine (13th c.)
367 **Aschau** (D-8213 Aschau/Chiemgau)
  Burg Hohenaschau (17th c.)

368 **Herreninsel/Chiemsee** (D-8210 Prien am
  Chiemsee)
  Schloss Herrenchiemsee (19th c.)
369 **Burghausen** (D-8263 Burghausen/Salzach)
  Burg (13th–14th, 16th c.)
370 **Berchtesgaden** (D-8240)
  Schloss (14th, 18th c.)

For the Nature-Lover

Walking

Information about the facilities for walking in the Federal Republic and on the European system of long-distance paths can be obtained from the following bodies:

Verband Deutscher Gebirgs- und Wandervereine e.V.,
Reichsstr. 4,
D-6600 Sarbrücken 3;
tel. (06 81) 39 00 70.

Deutsche Wanderjugend,
Wilhemstr. 39,
D-7263 Bad Liebenzell;
tel. (0 70 52) 31 31,

Europäische Wandervereinigung
Sippelweg 24,
D-7000 Stuttgart 40;
tel. (07 11) 80 11 02.

Useful guidebooks for walkers are the "Kompass-Wanderführer", a comprehensive series published by the Deutscher Wanderverlag Dr. Mair & Schnabel & Co., Stuttgart; as for maps, there are the "Kompass-Wanderkarten" published by the Georgraphischer Verlag Heinz Fleischmann GmbH & Co., Munich. Both the guides and the maps are obtainable through booksellers.

Nature Parks

1 **Hüttener Berge** – **Wittensee**
2 **Westensee**
3 **Aukrug**
4 **Lauenburg Lakes**
5 **Harburger Berge**
6 **Lüneburg Heath**
7 **Südheide**
8 **Elbe** – **Drawehn**
9 **Dümmer**
10 **Steinhuder Meer**
11 **Northern Teutoburg Forest** –
  Wiehengebirge
12 **Weserbergland** – **Schaumburg-Hamelin**
13 **Elm** – **Lappwald**
14 **Hohe Mark**
15 **Eggegebirge** – **Southern Teutoburg Forest**
16 **Solling** – **Vogler**
17 **Harz**
18 **Mass** – **Schwalm** – **Nette** (German-Dutch
  Nature Park)
19 **Bergisches Land**
20 **Ebbegebirge**
21 **Homert**
22 **Arnsberger Wald**
23 **Rothaargebirge**
24 **Diemelsee**
25 **Habichtswald**
26 **Münden**
27 **Meissner** – **Kaufunder Wald**
28 **Northern Eifel** (German-Belgian Nature Park)
29 **Southern Eifel** (German-Luxembourg Nature
  Park)
30 **Kottenforst** – **Ville**
31 **Siebengebirge**
32 **Rhine** – **Westerwald**
33 **Nasau**
34 **Rhine** – **Taunus**
35 **High Taunus**
36 **Hoher Vogelsberg**
37 **Hessian Rhön**
38 **Bavarian Rhön**
39 **Hessian Spessart**
40 **Bavarian Spessart**
41 **Hassberge**
42 **Franconian Forest**
43 **Saar** – **Hunsrück**
44 **Palatinate Forest**
45 **Bergstrasse** – **Odenwald**
46 **Neckartel** – **Odenwald**
47 **Stromberg** – **Heuchelberg**
48 **Swabian** – **Franconian Forest**
49 **Frankenhöhe**
50 **Steigerwald**

In the Südheide Nature Park

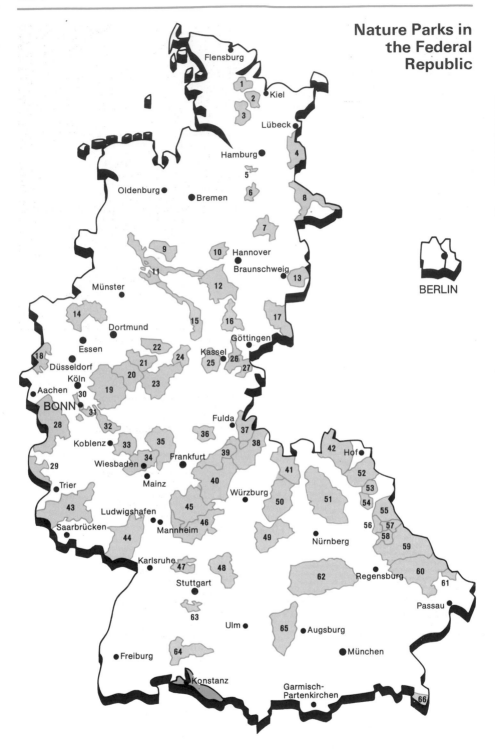

Nature Parks in
the Federal
Republic

BERLIN

Nature Parks

Nature parks are large stretches of country designated as landscape and nature reserves and given statutory protection to preserve them in as unspoiled a condition as possible and make them available for the pleasure and recreation of man. Since 1956 roughly a fifth of the whole territory of the Federal Republic has been protected in this way. Further nature parks are in course of development or are planned.

on the protection of nature and Nature Parks:
Verein Naturschutzpark, e.V.,
Ballindamm 2–3, D-2000 Hamburg 1; tel. (0 40) 33 84 21.
on wild life parks and game parks:
Deutscher Wildgehege-Verband e.V.
Postfach 612,
D-5480 Remagen 6;
tel. (0 22 28) 46 88.

In the Rothaargebirge Wild Life Park

● Zoological Gardens Animal Parks, Bird Parks, Aquariums (selection)

1 **Westerland Aquarium**
   D-2280 Westerland/Sylt
2 **Gettorf Animal Park**
   D-2303 Gettorf bei Keil
3 **Kiel Aquarium**
   D-2300 Kiel
4 **Heligoland Aquarium of the Biological Institute**
   D-2192 Heligoland
5 **Büsum Aquarium**
   ·D-2242 Büsum
6 **Neumünster Animal Park**
   D-2350 Neumünster
7 **Grömitz Children's Zoo "Noah's Ark"**
   D-2433 Grömitz
8 **Timmendorfer Strand Aquarium**
   D-2408 Timmendorfer Strand
9 **Niendorf Bird Park**
   D-2408 Niendorf
10 **Lübeck Animal Park**
   D-2400 Lübeck
11 **Worberg Animal Park**
   Mittelsten Thule
   D-2908 Friesoythe/Krs. Cloppenburg
12 **Jaderberg Animal Park**
   D-2933 Jade
13 **Wilhelmshaven Sea Water Aquarium**
   D-2940 Wilhelmshaven
14 **Westerstede Bird Park**
   D-2910 Westerstede
15 **Sage Heath Animal Park**
   D-2901 Sage/Kreis Oldenburg (Oldb.)
16 **Bremerhaven Zoo and North Sea Aquarium**
   D-2850 Bremerhaven
17 **Wingst Baby Zoo**
   D-2177 Wingst
18 **Petermoor Animal Park**
   D-2830 Bassum

19 **Bremen Bürgerpark**
   (animal enclosure)
   D-2800 Bremen
20 **Overseas Museum Bremen**
   (aquarium planned)
   D-2800 Bremen
21 **Hagenbeck Animal Park**
   D-2000 Hamburg-Stellingen
22 **Walsrode Bird Park**
   D-3030 Walsrode
23 **Nordhorn Animal Park**
   D-4460 Nordhorn
24 **Gronau Bird Park**
   D-4432 Gronau/Westfalen
25 **Metelen Heath Bird Park**
   D-4431 Metelen bei Steinfurt
26 **Rheine Animal Park**
   D-4440 Rheine
27 **Ströhen Nature Park**
   D-2841 Wagenfeld 2 (Ströhen)
28 **Osnabrück Forest Zoo**
   D-4500 Osnabrück
29 **Hanover Zoological Garden**
   D-3000 Hannover
30 **Hanover Aquarium**
   D-3000 Hanover
31 **Springe Bison Enclosure**
   D-3257 Springe
32 **Brunswick Animal Park**
   D-3300 Braunschweig
33 **Kleve Animal Park**
   D-4190 Kleve
34 **Heiden Bird Park**
   D-4284 Heiden/Kreis Borken/Westfalen
35 **Münsterland Bird Park**
   D-4420 Coesfeld
36 **Maria Veen Forest Bird Pak**
   D-4421 Reken
37 **Westphalia Zoological Garden Münster**
   D-4400 Münster
38 **Olderdissen Animal Park**
   D-4800 Bielefeld
39 **Herford Animal Park**
   D-4900 Herford

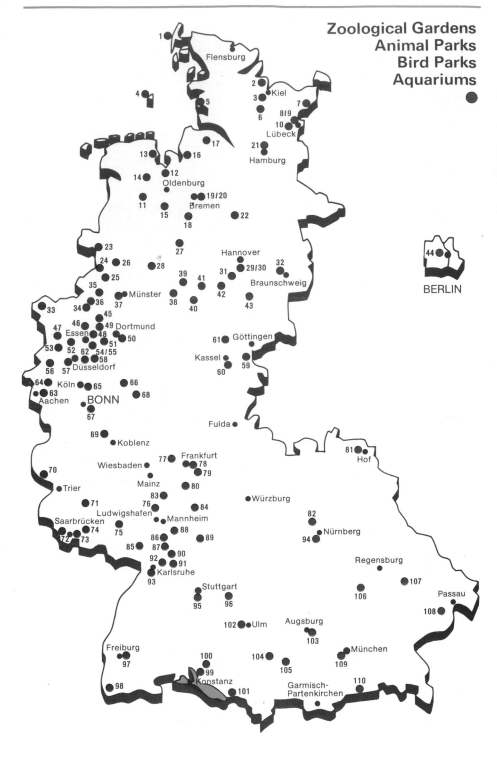

Zoological Gardens
Animal Parks
Bird Parks
Aquariums

Zoological Gardens, Animal Parks, Bird Parks, Aquariums

The object in modern zoos is to house the animals in conditions as close as possible to their natural way of life, and give children in particular an opportunity of coming into contact with animals in a way that would not otherwise be possible in cities. Modern aquariums, too, are now able to provide appropriate conditions for rare and sometimes delicate aquatic species. And bird parks offer many threatened species a chance to survive which they might not otherwise have.

40 Heiligenkirchen Bird Park
D-4930 Detmold
41 Kalletal Animal Park
D-4925 Kalletal-Hohenhausen
42 Hamelin "Zoo am Klut"
D-3250 Hamelin
43 Alfeld Open-Air Zoo
D-3220 Alfeld
44 Berlin Zoological Garden and Aquarium
D-1000 Berlin
45 Recklinghausen Zoo
D-4350 Recklinghausen
46 Gladbeck Bird Island and Aquarium
D-4390 Gladbeck
47 Moers Reptile Zoo
D-4130 Moers
48 Ruhr Zoo
D-4650 Gelsenkirchen
49 Herne Animal Park
D-4690 Herne
50 Dortmund Animal Park
D-4600 Dortmund
51 Bochum Animal Park and Aquarium
D-4630 Bochum
52 Duisburg Animal Park, Aquarium and
Dolphinarium
D-4100 Duisburg
53 Krefeld Animal Park
D-4150 Krefeld
54 Essen Aquarium and Terrarium
D-4300 Essen
55 Essen Bird Park
D-4300 Essen-Rüttenscheid
56 Mönchengladbach Zoo
D-4050 Mönchengladbach
57 Düsseldorf Aquarium
D-4000 Düsseldorf
58 Wuppertal Zoological Garden and
Aquarium
D-5600 Wuppertal
59 Ziegenhagen Zoo and Car Museum
D-3430 Witzenhausen 4
60 Kassel Vivarium
D-3500 Kassel
61 Sababurg Animal Park
D-3520 Hofgeismar Sababurg
62 Solingen Bird Park
D-5650 Solingen-Ohligs
63 Aachen Animal Park
D-5100 Aachen
64 Jülich Animal Park
D-5170 Jülich
65 Cologne Zoological Gardens and
Aquarium
D-500 Köln
66 Reichshof-Eckenhagen Bird Park
D-5226 Reichshof-Eckenhagen
67 Königswinter Reptile Zoo
D-5330 Königswinter
68 Niederfischbach Animal Park
D-5421 Niederfischbach/Sieg
69 Neuwied Zoo
D-5450 Neuwied
70 Bollendorf Falcon Station
D-5521 Bollendorf/Eifel
71 Birkenfeld Animal Park
D-6588 Birkenfeld/Nahe
72 Schwalbach Animal Park
D-6635 Schwalbach/Saar
73 Saarbrücken Zoological Garden
D-6600 Saarbrücken
74 Neunkirchen Zoo
D-6680 Neunkirchen/Saar
75 Siegelbach Animal Park
D-6750 Kaiserlautern 25

76 Worms Animal Park
D-6520 Worms
77 Georg von Opel Zoo
D-6242 Kronberg/Taunus
78 Frankfurt Zoological Garden
D-6000 Frankfurt am Main
79 Kahl Bird Park
D-8756 Kahl/Main
80 Darmstadt Vivarium
D-6100 Darmstadt
81 Hof Miniature Zoo
D-8670 Hof/Saale
82 Erlenbach Mountain Zoo
D-6149 Fürth-Erlenbach
83 Biebesheim Bird Park
D-6081 Biebesheim
84 Eulbach Animal Park and Bison enclosure
D-6120 Michelstadt-Eulbach
85 Landau Animal Park
D-6740 Landau/Pfalz
86 Reilingen Animal Park
D-6831 Reilingen bei Hockenheim
87 Rauenberg Animal Park
D-6909 Rauenberg/Kraichgau
88 Heidelberg Zoo
D-6900 Heidelberg
89 Neckarmühlbach Falcon Observatory
D-6954 Hassmersheim
90 Forst Animal and Bird Park
D-7521 Forst/Baden
91 Bretten Forest Animal Park
D-7518 Bretten
92 Weingarten Bird Park
D-7504 Weingarten bei Karlsruhe
93 Karlsruhe Zoological Garden
D-7500 Karlsruhe
94 Nuremberg Zoological Garden
D-8500 Nürnberg
95 Wilhelma Zoological and Botanical
Garden
D-7000 Stuttgart
96 Göppingen Animal Park
D-7320 Göppingen
97 Mundenhofen Animal Reserve
D-7800 Freiburg im Breisgau
98 Wiesenthal Bird Park
D-7853 Steinen-Hofen
99 Uhldingen Reptile House
D-7772 Uhldingen-Mühlhofen
100 Salem Monkey Hill
D-7777 Salem/Mendlishausen
101 Scheidegg Reptile Zoo
D-8999 Scheidegg/Allgäu
102 Ulm Aquarium
D-7900 Ulm
103 Augsburg Zoo
D-8900 Augsburg
104 Erkheim Animal Park
D-8941 Erkheim/Günz
105 Bad Wörishofen Falconry
D-8939 Bad Wörishofen
106 Abensberg Bird Park
D-8423 Abensberg
107 Straubling Zoo
D-8440 Straubing
108 Irgenöd Bird Park
D-8359 Ortenburg
109 Munich Animal Park
D-8000 München-Hellabrunn
110 Sutten Falcon Observatory
D-8183 Rottach-Egern

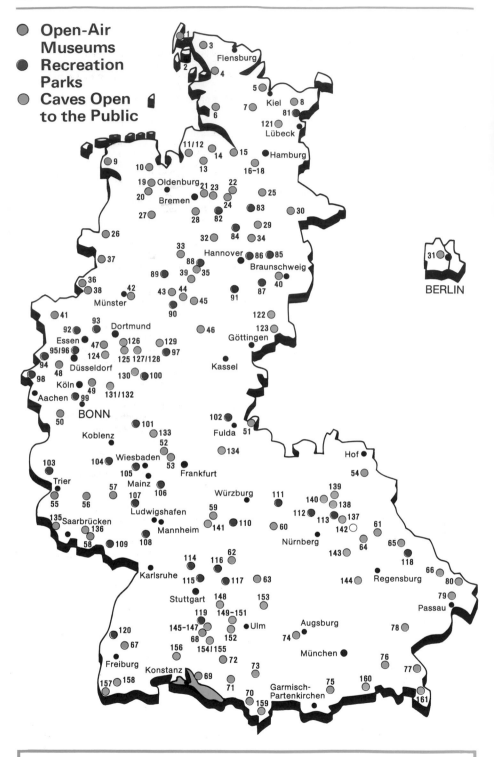

- ⊙ Open-Air Museums
- ● Recreation Parks
- ⊙ Caves Open to the Public

Open-Air Museums, Recreation Parks, Caves Open to the Public

The loss of old buildings, particularly in country areas, has alerted public opinion to the need to save what is worth preserving before it is too late,

and there are now many open-air museums displaying typical local buildings, excellently restored. The recreation parks offer entertainment and leisure occupation for the whole family. For those who want to explore the strange world of stalactites and underground rivers there are numbers of caves with excellent facilities for visitors.

Other Places of Interest

● Open-Air Museums

1 **Old Friesian House**
D-2280 Keitum

2 **Dr. Carl Haeberlin Friesian Museum**
D-2270 Wyk auf Föhr

3 **Friesland Heimatmuseum**
D-2260 Niebüll

4 **Ostenfeld Farmhouse**
D-2250 Husum

5 **Schleswig Holstein Open-Air Museum**
D-2300 Kiel Molfsee

6 **Dithmarsch Farmhouse Museum**
D-2223 Meldorf

7 **"Dat ole Hus" Museum**
D-2356 Aukrug-Bünzen

8 **Old Smoking Hut**
D-2427 Malente-Gremsmühlen

9 **East Friesian Open-Air Museum**
D-2974 Krummhörn 1-Pewsum

10 **Rauchkate Heimatmuseum**
D-2932 Neuenburg

11 **Speckenbüttel Open-Air Museum**
D-2859 Bremerhaven-Speckenbüttel

12 **German Shipping Museum Foundation**
D-2850 Bremerhaven

13 **"Auf dem Brink" Open-Air Museum**
D-2855 Frelsdorf

14 **Bördermuseum**
D-2172 Lamstedt

15 **"Auf der Insel" Open-Air Museum**
D-2160 Stade

16 **Volksdorf Museum vilage**
D-2000 Hamburg-Volksdorf

17 **Open-Air Museum on the Kiekeberg**
(Branch of the Helms Museum)
D-2100 Hamburg 90

18 **Rieck-Haus Vierlände Open-Air Museum**
D-2000 Hamburg-Curslack

19 **Ammerland Farmhouse**
D-2903 Bad Zwischenahn

20 **Tollhus Open-Air Museum**
D-2905 Edewecht-Westerscheps

21 **Bremen Provincial Museum of the History of Art and Culture**
D-2800 Bremen 1

22 **Meyerhof Open-Air Museum**
D-2723 Scheessel

23 **Irmintraut Heimathaus**
D-2802 Ottersberg-Fischerhude

24 **Heimatmuseum**
D-2130 Rotenburg a.d. Wümme

25 **"Dat Ole Huus" Heath Museum**
D-3045 Bispingen-Wilsede

26 **Gross Hesepe Open-Air Museum**
D-4478 Geeste-Gross Hesepe

27 **Cloppenburg Museum Village**
D-4590 Cloppenburg

28 **Regional Museum**
D-2808 Syke

29 **Römstedhaus**
D-3103 Bergen I

30 **Luneburg Heath Agricultural Museum**
D-3110 Ülzen

31 **Düppel Museum Village**
D-1000 Berlin 37

32 **Nienburg Museum**
D-3070 Nienburg

33 **Rahden Museum Village**
D-4993 Rahden

34 **Wietze Oil Museum**
D-3101 Wietze

35 **Minden-Lübbecke Mill Road**
D-4950 Minden

36 **Früchtinghoff Farmhouse Museum**
D-4426 Vreden

37 **Geological Open Air Museum**
D-4444 Bad Bentheim

38 **Gescher Heimatmuseum**
D-4423 Gescher

39 **Museumshof**
D-4970 Bad Oeynhausen

40 **Bortfeld Farmhouse Museum**
(Branch of the Brunswick Provincial Museum)
D-3300 Brunswick

41 **Archaeological Park**
D-4232 Xanten

42 **Mühlenhof Open-Air Museum**
D-4400 Münster

43 **Farmhouse Museum**
D-4800 Bielefeld

44 **Archaeological Open-Air Museum**
D-4811 Oerlinghausen

45 **Westphalian Open-Air Museum Museum of Rural Culture**
D-4930 Detmold

46 **European Sculpture Park**
D-3533 Willebadessen

47 **Westphalian Open-Air Museum Museum of Technical Culture**
D-5800 Hagen

48 **Lower Rhine Open-Air Museum**
D-4155 Grefrath

49 **Farmhouse Museum**
D-5060 Bergisch Gladbach Oberkülheim

50 **Rhenish Open-Air Museum**
D-5353 Kommern

51 **Tann Rhön Museum Village**
D-6413 Tann

52 **Hessenpark Open-Air Museum**
D-6392 Neu-Ansbach

53 **Saalburg**
D-6380 Bad Homburg v.d. Höhe

54 **Kleinlosnitz Upper Franconian Farmhouse Museum**
D-8665 Zell-Kleinlosnitz

55 **Roscheider Hof Open-Air Ethnological Museum**
D-5503 Konz

56 **Geological Open-Air Museum**
D-6581 Sensweiler

57 **Sobernheim Open-Air Museum**
D-6553 Sobernheim/Nahe

58 **Römerhaus Schwarzenacker Open-Air Museum**
D-6650 Homburg-Schwarzenacker

59 **Odenwald Farmhouse Museum Street**
D-6968 Walldürn

60 **Franconian Open-Air Museum of the Middle Franconian District**
D-8532 Bad Windsheim

61 **Neusath-Perschen Upper Palatinate Open-Air Museum**
D-8470 Nabburg-Perschen

62 **Hohenloh Open-Air Museum**
D-7170 Schwäbisch Hall

63 **Open-Air Museum on the Rhaetian Limes**
D-7095 Rainau

64 **East Bavarian Mining and Industrial Museum**
D-8451 Kümmersbruck-Theuern

65 **Upper Palatinate Craft Museum**
D-8463 Rötz-Hillstett

66 **Lindberg Farmhouse Museum**
D-8371 Lindberg b. Zwiesel

67 "Vogtsbauernhof" Black Forest Open-Air Museum
D-7611 Gutach

68 Farmhouse Museum
D-7425 Hohenstein-Ödenwaldstetten

69 Open-Air Museum of German Antiquity
D-7771 Uhldingen-Mühlhofen

70 Farmhouse Museum
D-8974 Oberstaufen-Knechthofen

71 Farmhouse Museum
D-7962 Wolfegg

72 Open-Air Museum
D-7954 Bad Schussenried-Kürnbach

73 Illerbeuren Farmhouse Museum
D-8941 Kronburg-Illerbeuren

74 Oberschönenfeld Museum of Peasant Life
D-8901 Augsburg-Gessertshausen

75 Open-air Museum of the Upper Bavarian Region on the Glentleiten
D-8119 Grossweil

76 East Upper Bavarian Farmhouse Museum
D-8201 Amerang

77 Farmhouse Museum
D-8229 Kirchanschöring

78 Massing in Rottal Lower Bavarian Open-Air Museum
D-8332 Massing/Rottal

79 Bavarian Forest Museum Village
D-8391 Tittling

80 Bavarian Forest Open-Air Museum
D-8391 Finsterau

● Recreation Parks (selection)

81 Hansaland
D-2430 Sierksdorf

82 Verden Recreation Park
D-2810 Verden/Aller

83 Heath Park
D-3040 Soltau

84 Serengeti Big Game Reserve
D-3035 Hodenhagen bei Walsrode

85 Uetze Erse Park
D-3162 Uetze

86 Kirchhorst Recreation Park
D-3004 Isernhagen 5

87 Eulenspiegel Park
D-3201 Holle 5 (Sottrum)

88 Pott's Park
D-4950 Minden

89 Fairytale Forest (Märchenwald)
D-4520 Melle

90 Hollywood Park and Safariland
D-4815 Schloss Holte-Stukenbrock

91 Rastiland
D-3216 Salzhemmendorf

92 Dreamland Park (Traumland-Park)
D-4250 Bottrop 2-Kirchhellen

93 Graf Westerhof Lion Park
D-4660 Gelsenkirchen-Buer

94 Schwalm Valley Nature and Animal Park
D-4057 Brüggen/Niederrhein

95 Minidomm
D-4030 Ratingen 5 (Breitscheid)

96 Fairytale Zoo (Märchenzoo)
D-4030 Ratingen I

97 Sauerland Fort Fun Recreation Park
D-5780 Bestwig-Wasserfall

98 Lion Park
D-5135 Selfkant

99 Phantasialand
D-5040 Brühl

100 Sauerland Panorama Park
D-5942 Kirchhundem

101 Animal and Fairytale Park
D-5438 Westerburg

102 Schlitzerland Animal Park
D-6407 Schlitz

103 Gondorf Eifelpark
D-5521 Gondorf bei Bitburg

104 Hunsrück Recreation Park
D-5449 Leiningen-Lamscheid

105 Taunus Wonderland
(Fairy garden, Western town)
D-6229 Schlangenbad 4

106 Safariland
Wallerstätten bei Gross-Gerau
D-6080 Gross-Gerau

107 Wachenheim Kurpfalz Park
D-6706 Wachenheim
(on the Wine Highway)

108 Holiday Park
D-6733 Hassloch (Pfalz)

109 Tivoli Park
D-6780 Pirmasens

110 Bad Mergentheim Animal Park
D-6990 Bad Mergentheim

111 Leisureland
D-8602 Geiselwind

112 Schloss Thurn Recreation Park
D-8551 Heroldsbach bei Forchheim

113 Franconian Wonderland
D-8571 Plech

114 Altweibermühle, Tripsdrill
D-7121 Cleebronn/Tripsdrill

115 Fairytale Garden (Märchengarten)
D-7140 Ludwigsburg

116 See-Welt Recreation Park
D-7157 Sulzbach/Murr-Bartenback

117 Safari Animal Park, Gmeinweller bei Welzheim
D-7063 Welzheim

118 Loifling Churpfalz Park
D-8490 Cham/Opf.

119 "Bears' Den, Dreamland"
D-7411 Sonnenbühl 2 (Erpfingen)

120 Europapark, Rust bei Ettenheim
D-7631 Rust/Baden

● Caves Open to the Public

121 Kalkberg Cave, Segeberg
(gypsum cave, erosional formations)
D-2390 Bad Segeberg
(22 km W of Lübeck)

122 Iberg Stalactitic Cave
(fossils)
D-3362 Bad Grund/Harz
(40 km NE of Gottingen)

123 Einhornhöhle
(Stone Age finds)
D-3420 Herzberg/Harz
(30 km NE of Göttingen)

124 Klutert Cave
(used for therapeutic purposes)
D-5828 Ennepetal
(10 km NE of Wuppertal)

125 Dechenhöhle
(erosional forms, stalactites)
D-5860 Iserlohn
(32 km NE of Wuppertal)

126 Heinrichshöhle
(skeleton of cave bear)
D-5870 Hemer-Sundwig
(40 km NE of Wuppertal)

In the Attahöhle, Attendorn

127 **Balve Cave**
(Stone Age implements, skeletons of animals)
D-5983 Balve
(46 km E of Wuppertal)
128 **Reckenhöhle**
(bones)
D-5983 Balve-Binden
(46 km E of Wuppertal)
129 **Bilstein Cave**
(stalactites)
D-4788 Warstein
(80 km W of Kassel)
130 **Attahöhle**
(stalactites)
D-5952 Attendorn
(50 km SE of Wuppertal)
131 **Wiehl Stalactitic Cave**
D-5276 Wiehl
(42 km E of Cologne)
132 **Aggertal Cave**
(crystal formations)
D-5250 Ründeroth
(35 km E of Cologne)
133 **Kubach Crystal Cave**
(calcite crystal, pearl sinter)
D-6290 Weilburg-Kuback
(22 km SW of Wetzlar)
134 **"Teufelshöhle" Stalactitic Cave**
D-6497 Steinau
(42 km NE of Frankfurt)
135 **Niederaltdorf Tuff Cave**
(spring tuff, cave sinter)
D-6639 Niederaltdorf-Rehlingen
(32 km NW of Saarbrucken)
136 **Schlossberg Caves**
(artificially constructed sandstone caves)
D-6650 Homburg/Saar
(31 km NE of Saarbrucken)
137 **Maximiliansgrotte**
(stalactites, bones of cave bears)
D-8574 Krottensee/Post Neuhaus
(42 km NE of Nuremberg)
138 **Teufelshöhle**
(stalactites, skeleton of cave bear)
D-8573 Pottenstein
(42 km NE of Nuremberg)
139 **Sophienhöhle**
(stalactites, bones)
D-8581 Kirchahorn/Post Ahorntal
(46 km NE of Nuremberg)
140 **Binghöhle**
(stalactites)
D-8551 Streitberg
(40 km N of Nuremberg)
141 **Eberstadt Stalactitic Cave**
D-6967 Buchen-Eberstadt
(Odenwald)
(25 km SE of Mitenberg)
142 **Osterhöhle**
(sinter basin)
Trondorf

D-8459 Neukirchen bei Sulzbach-Rosenberg
(11 km W of Amberg/Oberpfalz)
143 **König Otto Stalactitic Cave**
(Adventhalle)
D-8436 Velburg
(36 km SE of Nuremberg)
144 **Schulerloch**
(bones)
D-8420 Oberau bei Kelheim/Altmühl
(20 km SW of Regensburg)
145 **Nebelhöhle**
(stalactites)
D-7411 Sonnenbühl-Erpfingen
(16 km SE of Tübingen)
146 **Bärenhöhle**
(stalactites, skeleton of cave bear)
D-7411 Sonnenbühl-Erpfingen
(20 km SE of Tübingen)
147 **Olgahöhle**
(tuff cave)
D-7414 Lichtenstein-Honau
(18 km SE of Tübingen)
148 **Gutenberg Caves**
(stalactites)
D-7318 Lenningen/Württemberg
(15 km SE of Kirchheim/Teck)
149 **Laichingen Cave**
(fossils; Cave Museum)
D-7903 Laichingen
(24 km NW of Ulm)
150 **Schertelshöhle**
(stalactites)
D-7437 Westerheim/Württemberg
(34 km NW of Ulm)
151 **Sontheim Cave**
D-7224 Heroldstatt-Sontheim
(20 km NW of Ulm)
152 **"Hollow Rock" Cave**
(bones)
D-7933 Schelklingen
(12 km W of Ulm)
153 **Charlottenhöhle**
(stalactites)
D-7928 Giengen-Hürben
(26 km NE of Ulm)
154 **Zwiefaltendorf Stalactitic Cave**
D-7940 Riedlingen-Zwiefaltendorf
(50 km SW of Ulm)
155 **Wimsen Cave**
(spring; no stalactites)
D-7942 Zwiefalten
(50 km SW of Ulm)
156 **Kolbing Cave**
(stalactites)
D-7203 Kolbingen
(75 km E of Freiburg)
157 **Tschamber Cave**
D-7888 Rheinfelden 8
(12 km SE of Lörrach)
158 **Erdmannshöhle**
D-7861 Hasel
(20 km E of Lörrach/Baden)
159 **Sturmannshöhle**
(erosional formations; no stalactites)
D-8981 Obermaiselstein
(6 km N of Oberstdorf)
160 **Wendelstein Cave**
(near summit of Wendelstein; no stalactites)
D-8204 Brannenburg
(60 km SE of Munich)
161 **Schellenberg Ice Cave**
D-8246 Marktschellenberg
(15 km E of Bad Reichenhall)

● Specialised Museums (Auswahl)

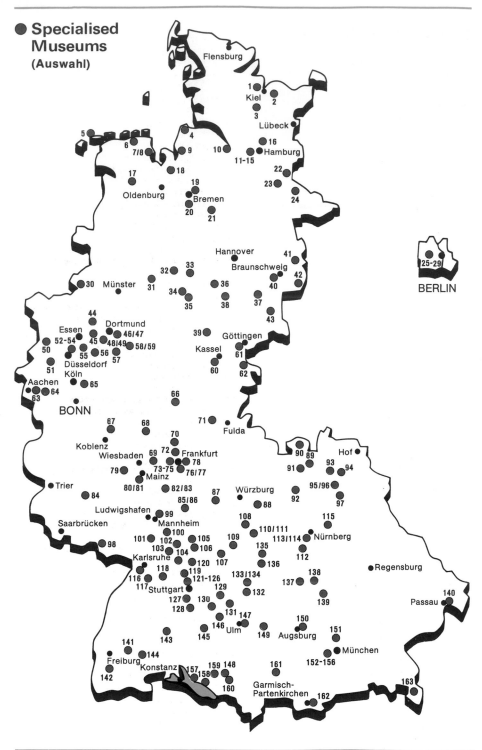

Specialised Museums

Museums are often thought of as rather old-fashioned and antiquated institutions; but any ideas of this kind are given the lie by the many fascinating and entirely up-to-date museums devoted to some particular specialised field. The specialised museums in the Federal Republic cater for every taste: whether you are interested in the development of modern technology, in particular crafts or industries, in toys, in salt-working, in jewellery or in fossils, there is something here for you.

● Specialised Museums

1 **Fire Protection Museum**
D-2300 Kiel-Rammsee
2 **Circus Museum** (by prior arrangement)
D-2308 Preetz/Holstein
3 **Textile Museum**
D-2350 Neumünster
4 **Museum of Wrecks**
D-2190 Cuxhaven
5 **Coast Museum**
D-2983 Nordseeheilbad Juist
6 **Museum of Ships in Bottles**
D-2943 Neuharlingersiel
7 **Coast and Shipping Museum**
D-2940 Wilhelmshaven
8 **Bird Observatory Museum**
(Heinrich-Gätke Halle)
D-2940 Wilhelmshaven
9 **German Shipping Museum**
D-2850 Bremerhaven
10 **Prehistoric Museum**
D-2160 Stade
11 **Model Airport**
D-2000 Hamburg
12 **Milk Museum**
D-2000 Hamburg
13 **"Electrum"**
(Electrical apparatus)
D-2000 Hamburg
14 **History of Tobacco**
(Reemtsma)
D-2000 Hamburg
15 **Museum of Ships in Bottles**
Schulauer Fährhaus
D-2000 Wedel/Holstein
16 **Automobile Museum**
D-2071 Tremsbüttel
17 **Fenland and Shipping Museum**
D-2953 Rhauderfehn
18 **Shipping Museum**
D-2880 Brake
19 **Lower Saxony Coach Museum**
D-2804 Lilienthal-Trupe
20 **Overseas Museum**
D-2800 Bremen
21 **Horse Museum**
D-2810 Verden/Aller
22 **Elbe Shipping Museum**
D-2058 Lauenburg
23 **East Prussian Hunting Museum**
D-2120 Lüneburg
24 **Tin Soldier Collection**
(Heimatmuseum)
D-2128 Dahlenburg
25 **Museum of the Blind**
D-1000 Berlin-Steglitz
26 **German Radio Museum**
D-1000 Berlin-Charlottenburg
27 **Collection of Musical Instruments**
D-1000 Berlin
28 **Gas Lamp Museum**
D-1000 Berlin-Tiergarten
29 **Criminological Museum**
D-1000 Berlin-Schöneberg
30 **Bell Museum**
D-4423 Gescher
31 **Car Museum**
D-4502 Bad Rothenfelde
32 **Museum of Tobacco and Cigars**
D-4980 Bünde
33 **Car and Motorcycle Museum**
D-4970 Bad Oeynhausen
34 **Tile Museum**
D-4937 Lage/Lippe

35 **Bread Museum**
D-4930 Detmold
36 **Pied Piper Collection**
D-3250 Hameln
37 **Car Museum**
D-3205 Bockenem
38 **Münchhausen Museum**
D-3452 Bodenwerder
39 **Organ Museum**
D-3531 Borgentreich
40 **Design Collection**
D-3300 Braunschweig
41 **Volgswagen Works Museum**
D-3180 Wolfsburg
42 **Eulenspiegel Museum**
D-3307 Schöppenstedt
43 **Mining Museum**
D-3392 Clausthal-Zellerfeld
44 **Icon Museum**
D-4350 Recklinghausen
45 **Collection of Stoves** (Heimatmuseum)
D-4690 Herne
46 **Westphalian School Museum**
D-4600 Dortmund
47 **Mining Machinery Hall (Zeche Zollern II)**
D-4600 Dortmund-Bövinghausen
48 **Mining Museum**
D-4630 Bochum
49 **Bochum Geological Garden**
D-4630 Bochum
50 **Textile Collection**
D-4150 Krefeld
51 **Museum of Dolls and Automata**
Lower Rhine Open-Air Museum
Dorenburg
D-4155 Grefrath
52 **Ceramic Museum**
D-4000 Düsseldorf
53 **Regional Museum, "People and Economy"**
D-4000 Düsseldorf
54 **Prehistoric Museum**
D-4020 Mettmann
55 **Lock and Metalwork Museum**
D-5620 Velbert
56 **Historical Watch and Clock Museum**
D-5600 Wuppertal
57 **Blacksmithing Museum**
D-5990 Altena
58 **Cave Museum**
D-5983 Balve
59 **Luisenhütte (Iron Industry)**
Wocklum
D-5983 Balve-Wocklum
60 **German Wallpaper Museum**
D-3500 Kassel
61 **Bread Museum**
D-3403 Friedland/Mollenfelde
62 **Salt Museum**
D-3437 Bad Sooden-Allendorf
63 **International Newspaper Museum**
D-5100 Aachen
64 **Pottery Museum**
D-5163 Langerwehe
65 **KHD Engine Museum**
D-5000 Cologne-Deutz
66 **Museum of Religion**
D-3550 Marburg
67 **Westerwald Ceramics Museum**
D-5410 Höhr-Grenzhausen
68 **Mining Museum**
D-6290 Weilburg
69 **Car Museum**
D-6239 Eppstein/Taunus

70 **Salt Museum**
D-6350 Bad Nauheim
71 **Forestry Museum** (Hohhaus Museum)
D-6420 Lauterbach/Hessen
72 **Hat Museum**
D-6380 Bad Homburg v.d.H.
73 **German Architectural Museum**
D-6000 Frankfurt am Main
74 **Senckenberg Nature Museum**
D-6000 Frankfurt am Main
75 **Federal Postal Museum**
D-6000 Frankfurt am Main
76 **Klingspor Museum**
(Books and writing, graphic art)
D-6050 Offenbach am Main
77 **German Leather and Shoe Museum**
D-6050 Offenbach am Main
78 **Hesse Doll Museum**
D-6450 Hanau-Wilhelmsbad
79 **Wine Museum**
D-6220 Rüdesheim
80 **Gutenberg Museum**
D-6500 Mainz
81 **Kupferberg Collection**
(History of Wine)
D-6500 Mainz
82 **Porcelain Collection**
D-6100 Darmstadt
83 **Schloss Kranichstein Hunting Museum**
D-6100 Darmstadt
84 **Exhibition of Precious Stones**
D-6580 Idar-Oberstein
85 **Ivory Museum**
D-6120 Erbach/Odenwald
86 **Weapon Collection**
D-6120 Erbach/Odenwald
87 **Glass Museum**
D-6980 Wertheim
88 **German Shrovetide Museum**
D-8710 Kitzingen
89 **German Basket-making Museum**
D-8626 Michleau/Oberfranken
90 **Costume and Doll Museum**
D-8632 Neustadt bei Coburg
91 **Collection of Petrifacts**
(Fossils)
D-8621 Banz
92 **Karl May Museum**
D-8600 Bamberg
93 **German Tin Figures Museum**
D-8650 Kulmbach
94 **Steam Locomotive Museum**
D-8651 Neuenmarkt/Oberfranken
95 **Museum of Freemasonry**
D-8580 Bayreuth
96 **Typewriter Museum**
D-8580 Bayreuth
97 **Municipal Museum of Pottery Mugs**
D-8581 Creussen
98 **Shoe Museum**
D-6780 Pirmasens
99 **Railway Museum**
(Narrow-gauge rolling-stock)
D-6806 Viernheim
100 **German Pharmacy Museum**
D-6900 Heidelberg
101 **Wine Museum**
D-6720 Speyer
102 **Museum of Automobiles and Technology**
D-6929 Sinsheim
103 **Museum of Mechanical Musical Instruments**
D-7250 Bruchsal
104 **Faust Museum**
D-7134 Knittlingen

105 **Library of Wood**
Burg Guttenberg
D-6953 Gundelsheim/Württemberg
106 **German Two-Wheel Museum**
D-7107 Neckarsulm
107 **Museum of Seals**
D-7112 Waldenburg
108 **Fire Brigade Museum**
Schloss Waldmannshofen
D-6993 Creglingen
109 **Automobile Museum**
D-7183 Langenburg/Württemberg
110 **Craft Museum**
D-8803 Rothenburg ob der Tauber
111 **Criminal and Torture Museum**
D-8803 Rothenburg ob der Tauber
112 **Bobbin Museum**
D-8541 Abenberg
113 **Transport Museum**
D-8500 Nürnberg
114 **Centre for Industry and Culture**
D-8500 Nuremberg
115 **Shepherds' Museum**
D-8562 Hersbruck
116 **Transport Museum**
D-7500 Karlsruhe
117 **Vehicle Museum**
D-7501 Marxzell
118 **Jewellery Museum**
D-7530 Pforzheim
119 **Watch and Clock Museum**
D-7147 Eberdingen
120 **Museum of Prehistoric Man**
D-7141 Steinheim an der Murr
121 **Porsche Works Museum**
(Cars)
D-7000 Stuttgart
122 **Bible Museum**
D-7000 Stuttgart
123 **Postal History Collection**
D-7000 Stuttgart
124 **Museum of Viticulture**
D-7000 Stuttgart-Uhlbach
125 **Agricultural Museum**
D-7000 Stuttgart-Hohenheim
126 **Daimler Benz Museum**
D-7000 Stuttgart-Untertürkheim
127 **Playing Card Museum**
D-7022 Leinfelden-Echterdingen
128 **Museum of Viticulture**
D-7430 Metzingen
129 **Natural History Museum**
(Fossils, minerals)
D-7320 Göppingen-Jebenhausen
130 **Hauff Museum of the Primeval World**
(Fossils)
D-7311 Holzmaden
131 **Cutlery Museum**
D-7340 Geislingen an der Steige
132 **Optical Museum**
D-7082 Oberkochen
133 **Geological and Palaeontological Museum**
D-7080 Aalen
134 **Limes Museum**
D-7080 Aalen
135 **Craftsmen's Workshops**
D-8805 Feutchtwangen
136 **Craftsmen's Workshops**
D-8804 Dinkelsbühl
137 **Bürgermeister Müller Museum**
(Geology, lithography)
D-8831 Solnhofen
138 **Jurassic Museum**
(Fossils)
Willibaldsburg
D-8833 Eichstätt

139 **German Museum of the History of Medicine**
   D-8070 Ingolstadt
140 **Lower Bavarian Fire Brigade Museum**
   (at present closed)
   D-8390 Passau
141 **Historical Watch and Clock Collection**
   D-7743 Furtwangen
142 **Museum of Bee Keeping**
   D-7816 Münstertal/Schwarzwald
143 **Weighing Machine Museum**
   D-7460 Balingen
144 **Narrenschopf (Museum of Masks)**
   D-7737 Bad Dürrheim
145 **Veteran and Vintage Cars**
   D-7425 Hohenstein-
   Ödenwaldstetten/Württemberg
146 **Cave Museum**
   D-7903 Laichingen
147 **German Bread Museum**
   D-7900 Ulm
148 **Motor Cycle and Car Museum**
   D-7962 Wolfegg
149 **Car and Motor Cycle Museum**
   D-8872 Burgau
150 **MAN Works Museum**
   (Engineering)
   D-8900 Augsburg
151 **Porcelain Collection**
   Schloss Lustheim
   D-8042 Oberschleissheim
152 **BMW Museum**
   (Cars)
   D-8000 München (Munich)
153 **German Hunting and Fishing Museum**
   D-8000 München (Munich)
154 **German Museum**
   (Technology, industry)
   D-8000 München (Munich)
155 **Karl Valentin Museum**
   D-8000 München (Munich)
156 **Theatre Museum**
   D-8000 München (Munich)
157 **Museum of Viticulture**
   D-7758 Meersburg/Bodensee
158 **Zeppelin Museum**
   D-7990 Friedrichshafen
159 **Museum of the Alemanni**
   D-7987 Weingarten
160 **Broom Museum**
   D-7964 Kisslegg
161 **Collection of Crucifixes**
   (Heimatmuseum)
   D-8950 Kaufbeuren
162 **Violin-making Museum**
   D-8102 Mittenwald
163 **Salt Museum**
   D-8240 Berchtesgaden

Steam engine, "Badenia", at Ottenhöfen

● Old-Time Railways

1 **Kappeln – Suderbrarup**
Length: 14·6 km
Gauge: 1435 mm
Steam traction
*Freunde des Schienenverkehrs
Flensburg e.V.*
Postfach 1617, D-2390 Flensburg

2 **Schönberger Strand – Schönberg**
Length: 4 km
Gauge: 1435 mm
Steam and diesel traction
*Verein Vekehrsamateure
und Museumsbahn e.V.*
Dimpfelweg 10, D-2000 Hamburg 26

3 **Spiekeroog**
**Bahnhog Spiekeroog – Sturmeck
(Seepromenade)**
Length: 1·2 km
Gauge: 1000 mm
Horse drawn
Kurverwaltung Spiekeroog
Norderpaad 17, D-2941 Spiekeroog

4 **Bremervörde – Worpswede –
Osterholz-Scharmbeck**
Length: 47·8 km
Gauge: 1435 mm
Diesel traction
*Buxterhude-Harsefelder
Eisenbahnfreunde (BHEF)*
Am Bundesbahnhof 1, D-2165 Harsefeld

5 **Deinste – Lütjenkamp**
Length: 1·2 km
Gauge: 600 mm
Steam and diesel traction
*Deutsches Feld und
Kleinbahnmuseum e.V.*
D-2161 Deinste bei Stade

6 **Buxtehude – Harsefeld**
Length: 14·8 km
Gauge: 1435 mm
Diesel traction
*Buxtehude-Harsefelder
Eisenbahnfreunde (BHEF)*
Am Busbahnhof 1, D-2165 Harsefeld

7 **Bergedorf-Geesthacht**
(irregular service)
Gauge: 1435 mm
Steam traction
*Arbeitsgemeinschaft Geesthachter
Eisenbahn e.V.*
Dösselbuschberg 49,
D-2054 Geesthacht

8 **Heide Express** (to Lüneburg)
Length: between 20 and 80 km
Gauge: 1435 m
Diesel with modern carriages
*Arbeitsgameinschaft
Verkehrsfreunde Lüneburg e.V.*
Th. Haubach Str. 3,
D-2120 Lüneburg

9 **Delmenhorst – Harpstedt**
Length: 22 km
Gauge: 1435 mm
*Delmenhorst-Harpstedter
Eisenbahnfreunde e.V.*
Hoher Weg 12, D-2870 Delmenhorst

10 **Bruchhausen-Vilsen –**
Heiligenberg – Asendorf
Length: 8 km
Gauge: 1000 mm
Steam, diesel and petrol traction
Deutscher Eisenbahn-Verein e.V. (DEV)
Postfach 1106, D-2814 Bruchhausen-Vilsen

11 **Celle – Hermannsburg – Müden/Örtze**
Length: 36 km
Celle – Hankensbüttel –
Wittingen – Parsau
Length: 81 km
Gauge: 1435 mm
Steam and diesel traction
Braunschweigische Landes-
Museums-Eisenbahn
Postfach 5323, D-3300 Braunschweig

12 **Wunstorf – Bokeloh**
Length: 6 km
Gauge: 1435 mm
Electric traction
Interessengemeinschaft
Schienenbus e.V.
Kolbenstrasse 4, D3016 Seelze

13 **Minden-Stadt – Hartum**
Length: 11·2 km
Minden-Stadt – Nammen –
Kleinenbremen
Length: 15 km
Gauge: 1435 mm
Steam and diesel traction
Museums-Eisenbahn Minden e.V. (MEM)
Postfach 2751, D-4950 Minden/Westfalen

14 **Holzhausen-Heddinghausen –**
Preussisch-Oldendorf – Bad Essen –
Bohmte – Schwegermoor
Length: 33 km
Gauge: 1435 mm
Steam and diesel traction
Museums-Eisenbahn Ninden e.V. (MEM)
Postfach 2751, D-4950 Minden/Westfalen

15 **Weserberglandbahn**
Rinteln-Nord – Stadthagen-West
Length: 20 km
Gauge: 1435 mm
Steam traction
Dampfeisenbahn Weserbergland e.V.
Waldstrasse 20, D-3000 Hannover

16 **Barntrup – Bösingfeld – Rinteln**
Length: 23·3 km
Gauge: 1435 mm
Electric traction
Verkehrsbetriebe Extertal GmbH
Am Bahnhof 1, D-4923 Extertal

17 **Emmerthal – Bodenwerder –**
Eschershausen
Journey time: 35 minutes
Gauge: 1435 mm
Steam traction
Verkehrsverein Bodenwerder
Brückenstrasse 7, D-3452 Bodenwerder

18 **Voldagsen – Salzhemmendorf –**
Duingen
Length: 16 km
Gauge: 1435 mm
Steam and diesel traction
Gemeinde Salzhemmendorf
D-3216 Salzhemmendorf

19 **Almetalbahn**
Bodenburg – Sibbesse
Length: 8 km
Gauge: 1435 mm
Steam, diesel and electric traction
Arbeitsgemeinschaft
Historische Eisenbahn e.V. (AHE)
Schwarze Heide 44, D-3201 Barienrode

20 **Berlin:**
Bahnhof Eiswerder – Gartenfeld
Journey time: 50 minutes
Gauge: 1435 mm
Diesel and electric traction
Berliner Eisenbahnfreunde e.V.
Stresemannstr. 30, D-1000 Berlin 61

21 **Gütersloh – Leer –**
Lengerich – Ibbenburen
Length: 66 km
Gauge: 1435 mm
Steam traction
Fremdenverkehrsverband
Tecklenburger Land e.V.
Postfach 1147, D-4542 Tecklenburg

22 **Mühlenstroth**
Circular line
Length 1·8 km
Gauge: 600 mm
Steam and diesel traction
Dampf-Kleinbahn Mühlenstroth (DKBM)
Postdamm 166, D-4830 Gütersloh

23 **Hamm – Vellinghausen – Lippbord**
Length: 18·7 km
Gauge: 1435 mm
Steam and diesel traction
Hammer Eisenbahnfreunde
im Verkehrsverein e.V.
Postfach 750, d-4700 Hamm

24 **Wesel:**
Wesel-Abelstrasse –
Wesel-Fischertorstrasse
Gauge: 1435 mm
Steam traction
Historischer Schienenverkehr
Wesel e.V.
Halterner Str. 2a, D-4230 Wesel

25 **St Tönis – Krefeld –**
Hülser Berg
Length: 13·6 km
Gauge: 1435 mm
Steam and diesel traction
Krefelder Verkehrs-AG
St Töniser Str. 270,
D-4150 Krefeld

26 **Feld und Werksbahn Museum**
Oekoven
Length: 800 m
Gauge: 600 mm
Steam, diesel and electric traction
Feld und Werksbahn Museum e.V.
Postfach 123,
D-4050 Mönchengladbach 2

27 **Hespertalbahn**
Essen-Kupferdreh – Haus Scheppen
Length: 2·8 km
Gauge: 1435 mm
Steam and diesel traction
Ulrich Kroll
Am Hang 13, D-4300 Essen 17
(Burgaltendorf)

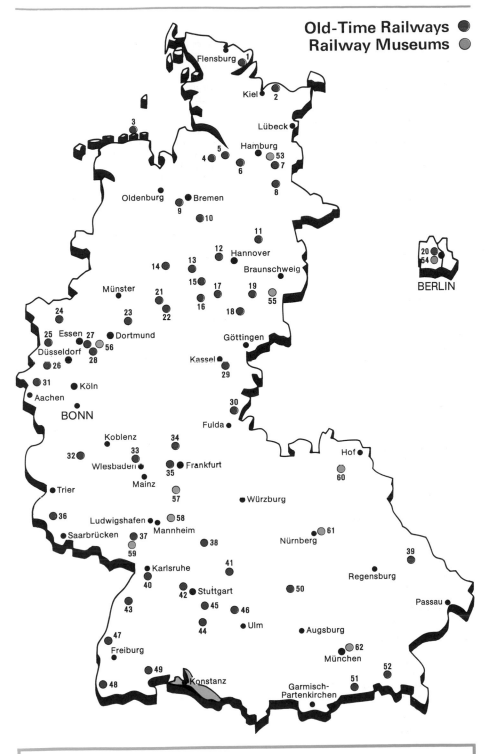

Old-Time Railways ●
Railway Museums ●

Old-Time Railways
Railway Museums

Old-time railways, often with steam engines, are becoming increasingly popular. Most of them are private ventures run by railway enthusiasts, operating only in summer. The times when they operate tend to vary.

The railway museums, apart from the railway sections of the large museums of technology in Munich, Nuremberg and West Berlin, are usually open only on Sundays.

28 Hattingen – Oberwengern
Length: 21 km
Gauge: 1435 mm
Diesel traction
Eisenbahnmuseum
Bochum-Dahlhausen GmbH
Dr.-C.-Otto-Str. 191,
D-4630 Bochum 5

29 Kassel-Wilhelmshöhe –
Elgershausen – Naumburg
Length: 33 km
Gauge: 1435 mm
Steam traction
Arbeitskreis HESSENCURRIER e.v.
Kaulenbergstr 5, D-3500 Kassel

30 Eiterfeld-Arzell
Circular line
Gauge: 600 mm
Diesel traction
Fuldaer Kleinbahn
Schodersstr. 7, D-6419 Eiterfeld

31 Selfkantbahn
Geilenkirchen-Gillrath –
Schierwaldenrath
Length: 5 km
Gauge: 1000 mm
Steam and diesel traction
Touristenbahnen im Rheinland GmbH (TBR)
Postfach 1152, D-5133 Gangelt

32 Brohital-Eisenbahn
Brohl – Oberzissen – Engeln
Length: 17·6 km
Gauge: 1000 mm
Diesel traction
Brohital-Eisenbahn GbmH
D-5474 Brohl-Lützing

33 Bad Schwalbach,
Moorbadehaus – Gerstruthtal
Length: 1·5 km
Gauge: 600 mm
Diesel traction
Dampfbahn Rhein-Main e.V.
Auf dem Schafberg 13,
D-6230 Frankfurt 80

34 Bad Nauheim – Butzbach – Münzenberg
Length: 20·8 km
Gauge: 1435 mm
Diesel traction
Eisenbahnfreunde Wetterau e.V.
Bismarckstr. 18,
D-6360 Friedberg

35 Frankfurt Eiserner Steg –
Griesheim/Mainkur
Length: 5·5 km
Gauge 1435 mm
Steam and diesel traction
Historische Eisenbahn Frankfurt e.V.
Eschborner Landstr. 140,
D-6000 Frankfurt 90

36 Losheim – Merzig –
Wadern-Nunkirchen
Journey time: 105 minutes
Gauge: 1435 mm
Steam traction
Modell-Eisenbahn-Club Losheim
– Eisenbahnfreunde e.V.
Weiherberg 17, D-6646 Losheim

37 Neustadt
Museumszugfahrten
Gauge: 1435 mm
Steam and diesel traction
Deutsche Gesellschaft für
Eisenbahngeschichte e.v. (DGEG)
Hindenburgstr. 12,
D-6730 Neustadt/Weinstr.

38 Jagsttalbahn
Möckmühl – Schöntal – Dörzbach
Length: 39 km
Gauge 750 mm
Steam traction
Deutsche Gesellschaft für
Eisenbahngeschichte e.V. (DGEG)
Postfach 1627, D-7100 Heilbronn

39 Lam – Kötzting
Length: 18 km
Blaibach – Viechtach – Gotteszell
Length: 40 km
Gauge: 1435 mm
Regentalbahn AG
D-8374 Viechtach;
Bayerischer Localbahn Verein e.v.
Postfach 116, D-8180 Tegernsee

40 Albtalbahn
Ettlingen – Busenbach –
Bad Herrenalb
Length: 19 km
Gauge: 1435 mm
Steam traction
Albtal-Verkehrs-Gesellschaft mbH
Tullastr. 71, D-7500 Karlsruhe

41 Bad Friedrichshall-Jagstfeld –
Ohrnberg
Length: 30 km
Gaildorf – Untergröningen
Journey time: 50 minutes
Gauge: 1435 mm
Steam traction
Eisenbahnfreunde Zollernbahn e.V.
Postfach 1168, D-7460 Balingen

42 Korntal – Weissach
Journey time: 60 minutes
Gauge: 1435 mm
Steam traction
Gesellschaft zur Erhaltung von
Schienenfahrzeugen e.V. (GES)
Postfach 71 01 16,
D-7000 Stuttgart 75

43 Achertalbahn
Achern – Ottenhöfen
Length: 11 km
Gauge: 1453 mm
Steam traction
Deutsche Gesellschaft für
Eisenbahngeschichte e.V. (DGEG)
Postfach 1627, D-7100 Heilbronn

44 Kleinengstingen – Gammertingen
Length: 20 km
Gauge: 1435 mm
Steam traction
Eisenbahnfreunde Zollernbahn e.V.
Postfach 1168, D-7460 Balingen

45 Nürtingen – Neuffen
Journey time: 30 minutes
Gauge: 1435 mm
Steam traction

Gesellschaft zur Erhaltung von
Schienenfahrzeugen e.v. (GES)
Postfach 71 01 16,
D-7000 Stuttgart 75

46 Amstetten – Gerstetten
Journey time: 60 minutes
Gauge: 1435 mm
Steam traction
Bürgermeisteramt Amstetten
D-7341 Amsteten/Württemberg

47 Riegel – Endingen – Breisach
Journey time: 22 minutes
Gauge: 1435 mm
Steam traction
Eisenbahnfreunde Breisgau e.v. (MECF)
Eschholzstr. 40, D-7800 Freiburg

48 Kandertalbahn ("Chanderli")
Haltingen – Kandern
Length: 13 km
(not in use)
Gauge: 1435 mm
Steam traction (between Haltingen and Basel/
Badischer Bahnhof
6 km diesel traction)
EOROVAPOR, Zurich
Geschäftsstelle Konstanz
Postfach 2243, D-7750 Konstanz

49 Wutachtalbahn
("Kanonenbahn"; "Sauschwänzlebahn")
Zollhaus-Blumberg – Weizen
Length: 26 km
Gauge: 1435 mm
Steam traction
Stadt Blumberg – Verkehrsamt
D-7712 Blumberg/Baden

50 Fünfstetten – Monheim
Length: 5·6 km
Gauge: 1435 mm steam traction
Eisenbahnclub München e.V.
Oderstrasse 4, D-8000 München 80

51 Tegernseebahn
Tegernsee – Gmund – Schaftlach
Length: 12 km
Gauge: 1435 mm
Steam traction
Bayerischer Localbahn Verein e.V.
Postfach 116, D-8180 Tegernsee

52 Chiemseebahn
Bahnhof Prien – Hafen Prien/Stock
Length: 1·8 km

Gauge: 1000 m
Steam traction
Cheimsee-Schiffahrt Ludwig Fessler
Postfach 21,
D-8210 Prien am Cheimsee

The **Dampfbahnparadies Friedrichsruhe** (D-7111 Zweiflingen: 6 km N of Öhringen/Hohenlohe) has ultra-narrow-gauge trains drawn by steam locomotives modelled on great originals.

● Railway Museums
Map, p. 307

53 Aumühle Transport Local Traffic Collection
(in locomotive shed)
D-2055 Aumühle bei Hamburg

54 Berlin Transport Museum
Railway Section
Urania
an der Urania 15, D-1000 Berlin

55 Linke-Hofmann-Busch-GmbH Works Musem
Railway Carriage Collection
Postfach 41 11 60, D-3320 Salzgitter 41

56 Bochum-Dahlhausen Railway Museum
Dr.-C,-Otto-Str. 191, D-4630 Bochum 5

57 Darmstadt-Kranichstein Railway Museum
Kölner Str. 20 b, D-6100 Darmstadt

58 Rhine-Neckar Railway Museum
D-6806 Viernheim, OEG station

59 Neustadt Railway Museum
Hindenburgstr. 12,
D-6730 Neustadt an der Weinstr.

60 German Steam Locomotive Museum (DDM)
Birkenstr. 5,
D-8651 Neuenmarkt/Oberfranken

61 Transport Museum Nuremberg
Railway Department
Lessingstr. 6, D-8500 Nürnberg

62 German Museum Munich
Railway Department
Museumsinsel 1, D-8000 München 22

In Minden another railway museum is being built.

Winter Sports

Winter sports, and particularly skiing, are now widely popular in the Federal Republic, and there are numerous winter sports areas easily reached either by road or by rail. Skiing is usually possible in the higher upland regions and the Alpine valleys from the end of December to the end of February, in the high Alps and high Black Forest until the end of March or the beginning of April. Really reliable winter weather, bringing good snow even at moderate heights, does not, however, usually begin until mid January, lasting until about the middle of February.

The most popular winter sports areas, from north to south, are the Harz, the Sauerland, the Westerwald, the Eifel, the Hunsrück, the Taunus, the Vogelsberg, the Rhön, the Odenwald, the Franconian Forest, the Fichtelgebirge, the Steinwald, the Upper Palatinate Forest, the Bavarian Forest, the Black Forest, the Swabian Alb, the Allgäu, the Kleinwalsertal and the Bavarian Alps.

Calendar of Events

Karl May Festival in Elspe open-air theatre

January
Munich — Schäfflertanz

Shrovetide
Cologne, Düsseldorf, Aachen — Carnival parades (Rose Monday)
Mainz — Rose Monday parade
Munich — Fasching parade (last Sunday in Lent)
Rottweil — "Fools' Dance" (Rose Monday)
Schramberg — "De Bach 'na-Fahrt" (Rose Monday)
Offenburg — Witches' Revels (Shrove Tuesday)
Villingen-Schwenningen — Fasching parade

March
Burghausen — Jazz Festival
Münster — Frühjahrssend (traditional fair)

March/April
Hamburg — Spring Market

End of April
Harz — Walpurgis Night celebrations

End April/beginning May
Hanover — Spring Fair

May
Mannheim — May Market
Wiesbaden — May Festival

May/June
Weingarten — Historical "Blood Ride" and cavalcade (Friday after Ascension)
Schwetzingen — Musical Festival

Whitsun
Rothenburg ob der Tauber — "The Master Draught" (historical pageant play), with military "campaign" and "camp"
Kötzingen — Cavalcade on Whit Monday

May–August
Lennestadt-Elspe — Karl May Festival

May–September
Oberammergau — Passion Play (every 10 years, 1984 (special) and next in 1990)
Ludwigsburg — Festival in Schloss

June–July
Landshut — "Landshut Wedding" (every 3 years; last time in 1981)
Bamberg — Calderón Festival
Bad Gandersheim — Cathedral Festival (Domfestspiele)
Mindelheim — Frundsberg Festival (every 3 years, next in 1985)

June–August
Hamelin — Pied Piper pageant play (Sundays)
Bad Hersfeld — Festival in ruins of Stiftskirche
Schwäbisch Hall — Open-air performances on steps in front of St Michael's
Jagsthausen — Festival in Götzenburg
Wunsiedel — Festival in Luisenburg

July
Heidelberg — Castle illuminations and firework displays
Kelheim, Weltenburg — "The Danube Aflame" (first Saturday in month)
Ravensburg — Rutenfest, children's procession
Ulm — Schwörmontag ("Oath Monday"), parade of boats on Danube (second-last Monday)
Dinkelsbühl — Kinderzeche (historical festival)

End of July
Konstanz — Lake Night Festival, with gigantic firework display

July–August
Bad Segeberg — Karl May Festival on Kalkberg
Waldmünchen — Historical pageant play, "Trenck der Pandur" (open-air performance)

August
Bayreuth — Wagner Festival
Kassel — "Documenta" (modern art: every 4 years, last time in 1982)
Furth im Wald — Historical pageant play, "The Dragon-Slaying"
Amelinghausen — Heather-Bloom Festival
Koblenz — "The Rhine Aflame", illuminations along river from Braubach to Koblenz (2nd Saturday in month)
Markgröningen — "Shepherds' Race" (St Bartholomew's Day)
Heppenheim — Dramatic Festival
Straubing — Gäuboden Folk Festival

Nuremberg	Hans Sachs Festival	Osnabrück	"Hobby-Horse Parade"
Mainz	Wine Market		(children's festival)
		Fellbach	Fellbacher Herbst (wine
September			festival)
Heidelberg	Castle illuminations and	Frankfurt am Main	International Book Fair
	firework displays		
Bad Dürkheim	Wurstmarkt (Wine	November	
	Festival)	Hamburg	Hamburger Dom (fair)
Frankfurt am Main	International Motor	Several places in Upper	St Leonard's Ride
	Show (every other year)	Bavaria	(cavalcade)
		Soest	Allerheiligenkirmes (All
September/October			Saints Fair)
Munich	Oktoberfest		
Stuttgart	Cannstatt Folk festival	December	
		Nuremberg	Christkindlmarkt (Christ-
October			child Market)
Donaueschingen	Music Days (modern	Many places	Christmas Markets
	music)	Oberammergau	"Star Singers'
Neustadt an der			Procession" (end of
Weinstrasse	Vintage Festival		month)
Bremen	Bremer Freimarkt (folk	Berchtesgaden	Christmas and New Year
	festival)		Shooting Contests

Information

Outside the Federal Republic

Amsterdam
Duits Reis-Informatiebureau,
Spui 24, 1012 XA **Amsterdam**;
tel. 0 20–24 1293.

Brussels
Duitse Dienst voor Toerisme,
23 Luxemburgstraat,
B-1040 **Brussels**;
tel. (02) 5 12 77 66, 5 12 77 44.

Buenos Aires
Oficina Nacional Alemana de Tourismo,
c/o Lufthansa,
Marcelo T. de Alvear 636,
Buenos Aires;
tel. 32 81 71.

Caracas
Oficina Nacional Alemana de Turismo,
c/o Lufthansa,
Av. Francisco de Miranda,
Edif. Bayer. Chacaito,
P.O. Box 62355,
Caracas 106;
tel. 31 35 22.

Chicago
German National Tourist Office,
104 So. Michigan Avenue,
Chicago, Ill. 60603;
tel. (312) 263–2958.

Copenhagen
Tysk Turist-Central,
Vesterbrogade 6 D III,
DK-1620 **København**;
tel. (01) 12 70 95.

Delhi
German National Tourist Office,
c/o Lufthansa,
56 Janpath,
New Delhi;
tel. 32 11 33.

Johannesburg
German National Tourist Office,
Mobil House, 9th Floor,
87 Rissik Street,
Johannesburg 2000;
tel. (011) 8 38 53 34.

Ljubljana
(Representative in Yugoslavia)
TTG Turistična Poslovalnica,
Titova Cesta 40,
61000 **Ljubljana**;
tel. (061) 314–242.

London
German National Tourist Office,
61 Conduit Street,
London W1R 0EN;
tel. 01–734 2600.

Los Angeles
German National Tourist Office,
Broadway Plaza, Suite 1714,
700 So. Flower Street,
Los Angeles, CA 90017;
tel. (213) 688–7332.

Madrid
Oficina Nacional Alemana de Turismo,
c/o Lufthansa,
Paseo de la Reforma 76,
Mexico 6, D.F.;
tel. 5 66 03 11.

Montreal
German National Tourist Office,
P.O. Box 417, 2 Fundy,
Place Bonaventure,
Montreal, Que. H5A 1B8;
tel. (514) 878–9885.

New York
German National Tourist Office,
630 Fifth Avenue,
New York, N.Y. 10020;
tel. (212) 757–8570.

Oslo
Tysk Turistbyrå,
c/o Lufthansa,
P.B. 6840,
St. Olavspl.,
Oslo 1;
tel. (02) 11 30 25.

Paris
Office National Allemand du Tourisme,
4 Place de l'Opéra,
F-75002 **Paris**;
tel. (16) 1–7420438.

Rio de Janeiro
Centro de Turismo Alemão,
Av. Nilo Peçanha 155, Gr/514,
20020 **Rio de Janeiro**;
tel. (021) 242–68 95.

Rome
Ente Nazionale Germanico per il Turismo,
Via Barberini 86,
100187 **Roma**;
tel. (06) 48 39 56.

Stockholm
Tyska Turistbyrån,
Birger Jarlsgatan 11,
Box 7520,
S-10392 **Stockholm** 7;
tel. 08–10 93 90/91.

Sydney
German National Tourist Office,
c/o Lufthansa,
4–6 Bligh Street,
Sydney 2000;
tel. 2 21 10 08.

Tehran
German National Tourist Office,c/o Lufthansa,
311 Avenue Takhte Djamshid,
Tehran;
tel. 82 20 71–8.

Tel Aviv
German National Tourist,
c/o Lufthansa,
Park Hotel,
75 Hayarkon Street,
Tel Aviv;
tel. (03) 5 14 14.

Tokyo
German National Tourist Office,
4–1–13, Toranomon,
Minato-ku,
Tokyo 105;
tel. (03) 437–2385.

Vienna
Deutsche Zentrale für Tourismus,
Brandstätte 1/1, corner of Stephansplatz,
A-1010 **Wien** 1;
tel. 0222–63 14 78/79.

Zürich
Offizielles Deutsches Verkehrsbüro,
Talstrasse 62,
CH-8001 **Zürich**;
tel. (01) 221 13 87.

Within the Federal Republic

Deutsche Zentrale Für Tourismus (German National Tourist Board),
Beethovenstr. 69,
D-6000 **Frankfurt** am Main 1;
tel. (06 11) 7 57 21.

Deutscher Fremdenverkehrsverband,
Beethovenstr. 61, D-6000 **Frankfurt** am Main 1;
tel. (06 11) 75 20 23.

Schleswig-Holstein
Fremdenverkehrsverband Schleswig-Holstein,
Niemannsweg 31,
D-2300 **Kiel** 1;
tel. (04 31) 56 30 27.

Hamburg
Fremdenverkehrszentrale Hamburg,
Hachmannplatz,
D-2000 **Hamburg** 1;
tel. (0 40) 24 87 00.

North Sea – Lower Saxony – Bremen
Fremdenverkehrsverband Nordsee-Niedersachsen-Bremen,
Gottorpstr. 18,
D-2900 **Oldenburg** in Oldenburg;
tel. (04 41) 1 45 35.

Bremen
Verkehrsverein der Freien Hansestadt Bremen,
Bahnhofsplatz 99,
D-2800 **Bremen** 1;
tel. (04 21) 3 63 61.

Lüneburg Heath
Fremdenverkehrsverband Lüneburger Heide,
Rathaus,
D-3140 **Lüneburg**;
tel. (0 41 31) 4 20 06.

Harz
Harzer Verkehrsverband,
Markstr. 45 (Gildehaus),
D-3380 **Goslar** 1;
tel. (0 53 21) 2 00 31.

Weserbergland
Fremdenverkehrsverband Weserbergland-Mittelweser,
Falkestr. 2,
D-3250 **Hameln**;
tel. (0 51 51) 2 45 66.

Teutoburg Forest
Fremdenverkehrsverband Teutoburger Wald,
August-Weweler St. 5,
D-4930 **Detmold**;
tel. (0 52 31) 6 25 38.

Westphalia
Landesverkehrsverband Westfalen,
Balkenstr. 40,
D-4600 **Dortmund**;
tel. (02 31) 57 17 15.

Hesse
Hessischer Fremdenverkehrsverband,
Abraham-Lincoln-Str. 38–42,
D-6200 **Wiesbaden**;
tel. (0 61 21) 7 37 25.
Fremdenverkehrsverband Rhön,
Wörtstr. 15,
D-6400 **Fulda**;
tel. (0 66 10) 10 63 05.

Northern Rhineland
Landesverkehrsverband Rheinland,
Rheinallee 69,
D-5300 **Bonn** 2 (Bad Godesberg);
tel. (02 28) 36 29 21.

Rhineland-Palatinate
Fremdenverkehrsverband Rheinland-Pfalz,
Löhrstr. 103–105,
D-5400 **Koblenz**;
tel. (02 61) 3 10 79.

Saar
Fremdenverkehrsverband Saarland,
Am Stiefel 2,
D-6600 **Saarbrücken** 3:
tel. (06 81) 3 53 76.

Black Forest
Fremdenverkehrsverband Schwarzwald,
Bertoldstr. 45,
D-7800 **Freiburg** im Breisgau;
tel. (07 61) 3 13 17.

Baden-Württemberg
Landesfremdenverkehrsverband Baden-
Württemberg,
Bussenstr. 23,
D-7000 **Stuttgart** 1;
tel. (07 11) 48 10 45.

Neckarland and Swabia
Fremdenverkehrsverband Neckarland-Schwaben,
Wollhausstr. 14,
S-7100 **Heilbronn**;
tel. (0 71 31) 6 90 61.

Lake Constance and Upper Swabia
Fremdenverkehrsverband Bodensee-Oberschwaben,
Schützenstr. 8,
D-7750 **Konstanz**;
tel. (0 75 31) 2 22 32.

Franconia
Fremdenverkehrsverband Franken,
Am Plärrer 4,
D-8500 **Nürnberg** 81,
tel. (09 11) 26 42 02.

East Bavaria
Fremdenverkehrsverband Ostbayern,
Landshuter Str. 13,
D-8400 **Regensburg**;
tel. (09 41) 5 71 86.

Swabia and the Allgäu
Fremdenverkehrsverband Allgäu/Bayerisch
Schwaben,
Fuggerstr. 9,
D-8900 **Augsburg**;
tel. (08 21) 3 33 35.

Munich and Upper Bavaria
Fremdenverkehrsverband München-Oberschwaben,
Sonnenstr. 10,
D-8000 **München** 2;
tel. (0 89) 59 73 47.

Berlin
Verkehrsamt Berlin,
Europa-Center,
Breitscheidplatz,
D-1000 **Berlin** 30;
tel. (0 30) 21 23/4

Information can also be obtained at local tourist offices. The tourist office (*Verkehrsamt*) is usually situated at or near the railway station or near the town hall.

There are Tourist Information Offices at certain frontier crossings and motorway service areas.

Some Frontier Crossings

Wasserslebener Bucht, near Flensburg (on E 3 from Denmark).
Elten, near Emmerich (on motorway from Holland).
Aachen-Vetschau (on motorway from Holland).
Aachen-Lichtenbusch (on motorway from Belgium).
Goldene Bremm, near Saarbrücken (on motorway from France).
Kiefersfelden (on motorway from Austria).
Schwarzbach (on motorway from Austria).

Motorway Service Areas

Hamburg-Stillhorn.
Dammer Berge, near Osnabrück.
Tecklenburger Land, near Münster.
Münsterland, near Münster.
Spessart, near Aschaffenburg.
Frankenwald, near Hof.
Kassel.
Grossenmoor, near Fulda.
Munich (several offices on various approach roads).
Siegburg, near Bonn.
Berlin-Grunewald.
Steigerwald, near Erlangen.

German Motoring and Touring Clubs

Allgemeiner Deutscher Automobil-Club (ADAC),
Am Westpark 8,
D-8000 **München** 70;
tel. (0 89) 76 76–0; tourism and frontier traffic 76 76–62 62.

Automobil-Club von Deutschland (AvD),
Lyoner Str. 16,
D-6000 **Frankfurt** am Main 71;
tel. (06 11) 66 06–1.

Deutscher Touring Automobil club (DTC),
Amalienburgstr. 23,
D-8000 **München** 60;
tel. (0 89) 8 11 10 48.

Auto Club Europa (ACE),
Schmidener Str. 233,
D-7000 **Stuttgart** 50;
tel. (07 11) 5 06 71.

Emergency telephone numbers: see p. 279
see p. 279